The Hungarians

PAUL LENDVAI

The Hungarians

A Thousand Years of Victory in Defeat

TRANSLATED BY ANN MAJOR

Princeton University Press
Princeton, New Jersey

Published in North America, South America, and the Philippine Islands by
Princeton University Press, 41 William Street, Princeton, New Jersey 08540

English translation first published in the United Kingdom by
C. Hurst & Co. (Publishers) Ltd, London

Originally published as *Die Ungarn. Ein Jahrtausend Sieger in Niederlagen* by
C. Bertelsmann Verlag, Munich, 1999

Library of Congress Control Number 2002110218

ISBN 0-691-11406-4

This book has been composed in Bembo by Word Pro, Pondicherry, India

www.pupress.princeton.edu

Printed in Scotland

1 3 5 7 9 10 8 6 4 2

Contents

Illustrations

Maps

Foreword to the English Edition

Hungary is a country with a fascinating and complex, often chilling and sometimes inspiring history. I was born and brought up in Budapest, and my early life as a child and as a young man was directly and indirectly shaped by the demons of nationalism and ethnic hatred which have presented themselves in Central and Eastern Europe in many different guises—Fascism, Nazism, Communism and post-Communist ferment. But even in this volatile corner of Europe, Hungary has repeatedly stunned the world beyond all expectations and lived up to its time-honoured reputation of being a country of extraordinary contradictions.

After my flight to Vienna, after the crushing of the 1956 October Revolution I have worked as a foreign correspondent (with twenty-two years on the *Financial Times*), and as a political writer and television commentator I have been able to observe both the political earthquakes in this region and the corresponding shifts in attitudes to national history. My main intention in this book, which was first published in German in 1999, was to avoid sweeping generalisations and to provide a truthful and dispassionate account, even of policies and actions which I deplore.

As a Hungarian-born Austrian author with Jewish parents and an English wife, now living in Vienna, but travelling and lecturing frequently around the world, I have always tried to avoid excessive partisanship for any nation or cause. The insights offered here into the often turbulent 1,100 years of Hungarian history, the elements of myth-making, the astonishing and enduring intellectual achievements and the beliefs about some divinely-ordered mission to discharge in the Danube basin have been formulated neither with cynical indifference nor with partiality for any particular group but in an effort to present a balanced picture. The fact that *The Hungarians* has also been published recently in Hungarian, Czech and

Romanian convinces me that my effort to contribute, however modestly, to the study of Central Europe has been worthwhile.

I wish to record my gratitude to the Raiffeisen Zentralbank in Vienna and to the Government of Austria for their generous assistance in funding the translation costs of this book from German to English. I am grateful to the Hungarian Ministry of Cultural Heritage for its considerable financial contribution to the production costs of my study. Last but not least, I must thank Ann Major for her excellent translation and Christopher Hurst, the London publisher, for his personal engagement and expert editing of this book.

Vienna, July 2002   PAUL LENDVAI

Introduction

The existence, the very survival, of the Hungarian people and their nation state in the Carpathian basin is a miracle of European history. There are few, if any, nations whose image has been shaped by so many and such contradictory clichés, spun during the course of centuries and epochs, as that of the Magyars. How did "child-devouring cannibals" and "bloodthirsty Huns" become the defenders of the Christian West and heroic freedom fighters against the Mongols, Turks and Russians? Who were these "Asiatic barbarians" who had spread dread and alarm during their forays from Switzerland to France and from Germany to Italy, yet did not sink into oblivion with the last migratory wave from Asia?

Their ancient homeland, their origins, the roots of their language, and the reason for their migration and settlement are still subjects of controversy. However, it can hardly be doubted that, except for the Albanians, the Magyars are the most lonely people of Europe with their unique language and history. Arthur Koestler, who dreamed in Hungarian but wrote his books in German and later in English, once said: "The peculiar intensity of their existence can perhaps be explained by this exceptional loneliness. To be a Hungarian is a collective neurosis." This many-faceted loneliness has remained the decisive factor in Hungarian history ever since the Conquest around 896. The fear of the slow death of a small nation, of the Hungarians' extinction and of the consequences of the forced amputation of entire communities due to lost wars (every third person of Hungarian origin lives abroad) forms the background of the prevalence of death images in poetry and prose.

Myths, legends and folk traditions concealed or distorted reality, but at the same time these myths shaped history in this region, moulding the concept of the nation. A varied relationship, at times crowned by brilliant successes and at others shaped by tragic

1

conflicts, was set in motion between locals and conquerors, new-
comers and the excluded under the crown of St Stephen as the
symbol of the so-called "political nation". The interaction between
open borders and isolation, between cosmopolitanism and nationalism, between the feeling of aloneness and sense of mission,
between fear of death and rebellion against stronger adversaries,
was impressively mirrored in the changing times and culture of
Hungary's history. A long chain of crucial defeats strengthened the
sense of defencelessness ("We are the most forsaken of all peoples
on this earth," said Petöfi, the national poet) that has imbued almost
every generation of Magyars with deep-rooted pessimism. The
devastation of the country after being repeatedly left in the lurch by
the West during the Mongol invasion of 1241, the catastrophe of
Mohács in 1526 with the consequent Ottoman occupation lasting a
century and a half, the crushing of the War of Independence in
1848–9 by the united forces of Austria and Russia, the destruction
of historical Hungary through the harsh terms of the Treaty of
Trianon in 1920, more than four decades of Soviet rule and Communism after the Second World War, together with the bloody
suppression of the October revolution of 1956—all were catastrophes, which time and again intensified the feeling of abandonment.
Yet who could dispute this people's endurance and mastery of the
art of survival?

Despite the threefold carving up of the country during centuries
of foreign occupation, the Hungarians managed to preserve their
national identity. It was passionate love of their country that gave
them the strength to survive when surrounded by Germans and
Slavs, without relatives and isolated by the "Chinese Wall" of their
language, and to weather these catastrophes. One of the keys to
understanding the rise and fall of Hungary from the Conquest till
the end of the First World War, but also the rapidly alternating radical changes between 1920 and 1990, is the exhortation (drawn up
around 1030, probably by a German monk) addressed by the first
Christian king from the Árpád dynasty, St Stephen, to his son:

The Roman Empire has won significance, and its rulers became famous
and mighty, because numerous nobles and sages from various countries
congregated there. [...] As settlers come from various countries and provinces, they bring with them various languages and customs, various

instructive concepts and weapons, which decorate and glorify the royal court, but intimidate foreign powers. A country which has only one language and one kind of custom is weak and fragile. Therefore, my son, I instruct you to face [the settlers] and treat them decently, so that they will prefer to stay with you rather than elsewhere, because if you were to destroy all that I have built and squander what I have collected, then your empire would doubtless suffer considerable loss.

Thus as early as the eleventh century Germans arrived in upper northern Hungary and Transylvania at the invitation of the dynasty. Over the centuries not only the defeated nomad peoples such as the Pechenegs and Cumans, but also Germans and Slovaks, Romanians and Croats, Serbs and Jews were, in a sense, absorbed by the Hungarians. One of the most astounding traits of Hungarian history, subsequently suppressed or flatly denied by nationalistic chroniclers, is that the makers of the national myths, the widely acclaimed heroes of the Ottoman wars, the political and military leaders of the War of Independence against the Habsburgs, the outstanding figures of literature and science, were totally or partly of German, Croat, Slovak, Romanian or Serb origin. Considering that at the time of Emperor Joseph II Magyars formed merely one-third of Hungary's population, but that this had increased by 1910 to 54.5 per cent, the dynamic of linguistic and political assimilation by old Hungary was extraordinary. According to statistical estimates the number of Germans regarding themselves as Hungarian exceeded 600,000, of assimilated Slovaks more than half a million, and of Jews who had become Magyars some 700,000. It has been estimated that already before the First World War the proportion of assimilated Germans, Slavs and Jews made up more than a quarter of statistically established Magyardom.

The Hungarian idea of the state, based on a totally unrealistic vision of the role of a great empire under the Crown of St Stephen in the Danube region, and including the suppression of the nationalities, was not racist but had an exclusively cultural motivation. Everyone who professed to be Hungarian had an equal chance of upward mobility. That included, of course, those Jews who, as Hungarians of Jewish faith, already identified with the Hungarian language and culture at the time of the national movement of 1848 and the subsequent decades. Moreover, Hungary needed loyal subjects to improve the Hungarian proportion within the lands of the

Crown of St Stephen, who would be willing at the same time (together with the Germans and Greeks) to engage in commerce and finance as well as the professions—fields consistently rejected by the Hungarian middle and lower nobility. The unique relationship between Jews and Magyars shaped the radical change in commerce and culture after the *Ausgleich* (Compromise) with Austria in 1867.

The fate of assimilation-keen Jewry belongs to the most dazzling and later, in the inter-war period and particularly after the German occupation of 1944–5, the darkest chapters of Hungarian history. An absurd yet logical consequence of officially promoted anti-Jewish legislation was that many of the greatest talents, among them eight Nobel Prizewinners, achieved their pioneering successes in science and art, finance and industry, not in their homeland but mainly in Britain or the United States.

The relationship between Hungarians and Germans became, and remained, close after the marriage in 996 of St Stephen to the Bavarian princess Gisela, sister of the later Emperor Henry II. German priests, knights and nobles who arrived in Gisela's retinue played a leading role at the court of the first Hungarian king, who looked upon Germanic institutions as models. So too did his successors of the Árpád dynasty by systematically encouraging the formation of larger German colonies; in the words of a Hungarian historian of the nineteenth century, "The Hungarians created the state, the Germans the towns." The attitude towards the Germans of the Magyar upper crust fluctuated between unconditional admiration and deeply-rooted mistrust.

As for the Germans, the royal free cities dominated by German citizenry were spared by the Ottoman wars. While their first large groups were brought by the Hungarian kings into the northern parts of the country and the Saxons into Transylvania, the Habsburgs in the eighteenth century settled them principally in the southern Hungarian regions of Bácska and Bánát. It was the privileges granted to the German burghers which in part aroused jealousy in the disadvantaged Hungarians. However, the movement led by nationally minded nobles and literary figures at the beginning of the nineteenth century aimed at the preservation and renewal of the Hungarian language endangered by Germanization, was politically far more significant. At the time it was thought by many Hungarian families to be bad form to converse in their mother tongue or to mention Hungarian poems or novels. The poet Károly Kisfaludy, who at first corresponded in German even with his own brother, and who had almost to relearn his mother tongue, warned: "People who do not possess a mother tongue do not have a fatherland either." In a fiery speech at the Academy of Sciences in Budapest on the eve of the Revolution in 1848 the writer József Bajza said:

"The German language and culture are a threat to our nation. We should at last come to our senses and realise that this fashion leads us to ruin, and that the penetration of the German language in particular means the end. [...] We should not hate the Germans, but we should be on guard against them. [...] I am not a barbarian, nor do I want to inveigh against education. [...] Nonetheless I regard it as a sin if a nation pays for its education with its own existence."

When the Austro-Hungarian Monarchy came into being after the *Ausgleich* in 1867, and Hungary attained considerable independence within the framework of existing possibilities, the country went the way of an accelerated, indiscriminate and increasingly unbridled Magyarisation. This prompted Franz von Löher, in an aggressive polemic, to accuse the Hungarians of being "a nation without culture" because "the entire thousand years' history of the Magyars is nothing but a yawning void. Help can come only from the diligence and culture of the Germans in Hungary."

It was this dichotomy between cooperation and conflict, alliance and collapse, community of interests and the aspiration for a distinct direction that henceforth moulded the mutual relationship. The more than half-million-strong German minority of rump-Hungary became during the Third Reich at first an obviously privileged tool of the National Socialist regime, and then, with their mother country's final catastrophe, a casualty when half of their number were expelled. For the next decade the remaining minority suffered unjust discrimination.

It is therefore no wonder that during the 1,000-year history of the Magyars the eternal question "Who is a Hungarian?" or "What is a Hungarian?" continues to arise. The answers have never been unambiguous. It also happened that, depending on the prevailing political climate, the same literary historian Julius von Farkas, who was much quoted especially in the German-speaking areas, extolled great Hungarian writers and scientists, only to ostracise them a few years later for their "outlandish race" and "harmful influence" on the nation. That these ostracised literary figures, much maligned as "anti-Hungarians", often wrote Hungarian much better than their tendentious critics belongs just as much among the ludicrous aspects of Hungarian history as the fact that in Hungary ethnic exclusivity in literature and politics was almost always expressed by representatives of totally or partly "foreign races". This was already pointed out by Antal Szerb, author of the still unsurpassed *History of Hungarian Literature*. He gave as an example the famous general and poet Count Miklós (Nicholas) Zrinyi. A Croat by birth, Zrinyi declared himself (in contrast to his younger brother Péter, who translated his great poems into Croatian) to be Hungarian. Szerb emphasised that one of the greatest heroes of Hungarian history had thus proved that nationality was the result of an attitude, a matter of choice. Szerb himself fell victim to the Holocaust.

Who is aware that the Hungarian pioneers of modern times played a considerable part in the invention of the atom bomb, the computer and Hollywood; that the Hungarian genius, of whatever ethnic or religious background, has helped to mould—often decisively—science and art, economies and industries all over the world? The contradiction between brilliant individual achievements and repeated collective national failure remains one of the most fascinating traits of this formerly nomadic people. Is it therefore impossible for the Hungarians as eternal losers to hope for a peaceful union of the mother nation with the dispersed third of its people under foreign rule? Or do they turn out time after time to be at once victors in defeat, victims and masters of *savoir-vivre*, romantics and realists? The writer Tibor Déry remarked after the defeated Revolution of 1956: "What is Hungarianness? A joke dancing over catastrophes."

This book is a personal attempt to acquaint the non-Hungarian reader with the Hungarians and their varied fortune by way of a mixture of historical overview, biographical sketches and vignettes. As a native Hungarian of Jewish origin, transformed into an Austrian after forty years in Vienna, the author feels that he is immune to taboos, and can describe the Magyars with friendly eyes but at the same time from a critical distance.

1. "Heathen Barbarians" overrun Europe: Evidence from St Gallen

During a little more than half a century, between 898 and 955, the Magyars were regarded as the scourge of Europe. In about fifty raids and forays they overran all that stood in their way, plundering, burning and killing. The mounted hordes invaded not only the German lands, but also northern Italy and large tracts of France. Among the cities they pillaged were Bremen and Basel, Orléans and Otranto. These incursions, undertaken largely in the service of various European princes fighting each other, led them as far as the Baltic and the Atlantic coasts. They fought in turn for and then against the Italian King Berengar, then for and against Arnulf of Bavaria, and for and against the interests of Byzantium.

The Old French *Chanson de Roland* describes the Magyars as "breeds of Satan" along with the Huns and Saracens, who left a trail of blood in their wake wherever they appeared. The chroniclers recount unimaginable atrocities, often confusing the Magyars—or Hungarians, as they were then called—with the Huns. Most of these scribes had never seen a Hungarian, but rehashed oral accounts which became more lurid as the distance in time and space increased. This established the image of a "horrifying, cruel tribe" and "bloodthirsty, man-eating monsters from Scythia", spreading fear and panic.

On the other hand, a well-substantiated foray in 926 is of particular interest to the descendants of the intruders because of its detail. Three chroniclers report different versions, written between 970 and 1075, of an attack on the monastery of St Gallen and its surroundings (today in Switzerland). "The heathen barbarians" advanced like lightning through Bavaria and Swabia along Lake Constance, and inflicted heavy damage on the monastery, killing in the process Wiborada, an Aleman noblewoman, who had had herself immured in a cell there ten years earlier. The anchoress was axed to death, and in 1047 Pope Clement II canonised her. Already that spring she had warned the abbot of the exact time of the hostile hordes' incursion from the East, urging him to move the monks, the treasury and the priceless library to safety in time. "Rumours about the onslaught by the enemy increased from day to day," recounts the *Vita Sanctae Wiboradae*; "nonetheless, they were taken seriously only when the barbarians with drawn swords pushed the neighbourhood of Lake Constance to the brink of disaster, killing countless people and burning all the villages and houses."[1] Only then was the seer heeded. Many people and irreplaceable books could still be saved, but Wiborada was unwilling to escape.

The life and death of St Wiborada (also honoured as the patron saint of libraries), as well as the chronicles of the monks Ekkehart I, Ekkehart IV and Herimannus, continually fascinated later generations, inspiring writers, including poets, until the very recent past. The Swiss writer Doris Schifferli published a novel about Wiborada as late as 1998, and in 1992 a Hungarian doctor who had fled to Switzerland and settled in St Gallen after the Revolution of 1956 published a bilingual volume about the Hungarian incursion in the tenth century, which deals with the "very old, initially belligerent but today peaceful-amicable relationship between Hungary and St Gallen". The anniversary of Wiborada's death is still commemorated by the Church. Thus the visit of Cardinal József Mindszenty in 1972 to the St Gallen library on this anniversary, and his signing the golden guest book as Primate of Hungary, was profoundly symbolic.

The interest of Hungarians in general and historians in particular is, of course, directed not so much at the monastery's patron saint and the present-day diocese of St Gallen, but rather at the fact that important sources for the early history of the Hungarian people— the annals and narratives of the chronicler Ekkehart IV—are preserved in its library. The Alemannian Annals, written in the ninth and tenth centuries by various scribes, mention the Hungarians nine times, while the larger St Gallen Annals of the tenth century do so fifteen times. Furthermore, Ekkehart's chronicle, the only contemporary account of the Magyars which does not portray them solely as ogres, contains details of the events of 1 and 2 May 926, which to this day are compulsory reading for Hungarian schoolchildren. It was the first comprehensive, true-to-life account by an eyewitness of the customs and habits of the Hungarians. The source for it was a "half-witted friar named Heribald, whose sayings and pranks were often smiled at". The other monks told him to escape with them, but he refused: "Who wants to flee? I shall never flee, because the chamberlain has not yet given me my yearly allowance of shoe-leather."

Heribald afterwards admitted that the enemy, bursting into the unfortified monastery armed with javelins and bows and arrows, looked extremely menacing, but despite their ferocity not a single hair of his head was harmed. The Hungarians had an interpreter with them, a priest they had taken prisoner, who translated Heribald's utterances, and when they became aware that the person they were dealing with was simple-minded, they spared him and even allowed him to take part in a feast in the inner courtyard of the monastery. As he recounted afterwards, the Magyars consumed the half-raw pieces of meat, tearing at them with their teeth. They also drank deep of the monastery's wine. For entertainment the Magyars tossed the gnawed bones at each other, and are also said to have listened to the two prisoners singing.

Two of the young Magyar warriors climbed up the belfry in the belief that that the rooster at the top was made of gold. One of them, trying to force it off with his lance, lost his footing and fell to his death. Meanwhile the other climbed to the top of the eastern façade, and while preparing to defecate tumbled backwards and was also killed. As Heribald related later, their companions burnt the bodies between the doorposts. Two full wine-casks were left behind on Heribald's entreaty, but much more was probably already stacked on the carts laden with loot. "God protected the imbecile in the midst of enemy swords and spears." remarked the chronicler. When the returning friars questioned Heribald, the eye-witness, about what he had witnessed, he gave the unexpected answer: "They were wonderful! I have never seen such cheerful people in our monastery. They distributed plenty of food and drink."

As a result of the confusion connected with legends about the martyrdom of St Wiborada. Swiss folklore concentrates almost exclusively on the atrocities of the "Hun invasions" that abruptly ended the abbey of St Gallen's golden age, Hungarian writers and scientists regard Friar Heribald's story, written up in the eleventh century, as proving the continuity of the "Magyar national character".

For instance, in the 24-volume collection *The Austrian-Hungarian Monarchy in words and pictures*—sponsored by Crown Prince Rudolf (1858–89), its last volume published in 1902—the historian Karl Szabó referred expressly to the "true-to-life description of a Hungarian horseman": "It is impossible not to recognise in these interesting portrayals… of sturdy, unbridled, lively, unspoiled Magyar youths, intemperate but also easily pacified, the salient traits of the present-day Magyar national character."[2] Decades later, in the five-volume *History of Hungary* by the semi-official historian and long-serving Minister of Education of the inter-war period, Bálint Hóman, and Gyula Szekfü, Friar Heribald is presented as the prime witness for the tradition of the merry, hard-drinking, lustily singing, open-hearted, jovial Hungarian. In these stories one is supposed to recognise the ancestors of the Hungarian peasant.

Modern Hungarian historians refer rather to the unprecedentedly extensive description of the warrior horsemen's strict discipline. The accounts of Friar Heribald indicate highly trained troops, who could take up battle formation within a short time, withdrawing for rest or for the night within a well-guarded encampment, and protecting themselves during march-offs by outposts and rearguards. The units communicated with each other by couriers, as well as signalling with the bugle and fire beacons. When danger threatened, they all swung themselves into their saddles at a command, responding with lightning speed. The astonishing accomplishments of these horsemen, making forays more than 1,000 kilometres from their homeland, were only possible because of this iron discipline.

The technical secret of the devastating military effectiveness of the Hungarian mounted archers was the stirrup. With its help they could twist like corkscrews in their saddles, loosing off in all directions at full gallop—hence the speed of their units of 100 men, and the overwhelmingly superior accuracy of their five-power. The notorious mobility of their fighting tactic of feigned flight confused the cumbersome enemy armies, and it was then easy to pick off the disoriented fleeing knights with arrows and scimitars. The shrill, fearsome, howling battle-cries of the wild, shaven-headed warriors made the blood of those attacked by them run cold.

As with the St Gallen episode, Hungarian historians and authors—particularly of school textbooks—did not dwell on the ravages wrought by the bold nomad horsemen in their raids. The Hungarian chroniclers euphemistically called the time of these forays "the years of roaming". Generations of young Magyars were brought up to be proud of the Hungarian successes. They learned that in the German, Italian, French and Spanish monasteries prayers were offered: "*De sagittis Hungarorum libera nos, Domine*" (Save us, O Lord, from the arrows of the Hungarians).

The diametrically opposed assessments in Western and Hungarian historiography of the St Gallen episode and the behaviour of Hungarian warriors contain small but revealing clues to the way stereotypes develop, which in the course of time solidify into widely accepted national characteristics. There are several reasons why the image of the enemy in the West and the self-image of the Hungarians were learned anew by successive generations, and above all culturally transmitted as unconscious characterisations. At the same time these are frequently preserved and transmitted as consciously nurtured prejudices. Uncritically accepted and sharply conflicting myths of origin are significant components of emotionally charged xenophobia and the rapid flaring-up of disastrous ethnic conflicts. Especially in the case of Hungary, stereotypes of the "other" ethnic groups but also of the "self" were instrumental in shaping the relationship with the neighbouring nationalities, as well as with the ethnic minorities in the former Greater Hungary.[3]

As we shall see, it is almost impossible today in Central Europe to draw lines between historiography, historic stereotypes and national myths. Some picturesque concepts go back to the early Middle Ages. The French historian Fernand Braudel cautioned against sweeping statements: "Until the Renaissance all states claimed to be rapacious beasts... Europe's map has never shown so many and such extensive white patches as before the year 1000."[4] In a later work Georges Duby reached a similar conclusion: that in medieval Europe traces can at best be rated as "bases of vague conjectures". "Thus the interpretation of the Europe of the year 1000 must be left more or less to our imagination."[5] That is valid especially for the Carpathian region.

2. Land Acquisition or Conquest?
The Question of Hungarian Identity

Historians have often referred to the natural unity of the Danube basin, encircled by the protective barrier of the Carpathians. While the western part—called by the Hungarians Dunántúl, land beyond the Danube—had formed an administrative unit under the Romans for four centuries, together with the eastern part of Lower Austria (Pannonia and Noricum), the large plain, the Alföld, between the left bank of the Danube and the Transylvanian foothills, was the actual pivot of the great migration period. Scythians, Sarmatians, Huns (under Attila), Goths and Langobards, Gepids and finally the Avars attempted to settle here for two centuries. Towards the end of the ninth century Pannonia was a border province belonging to the East Frankish empire. Greater Moravia under Prince Svatopluk controlled the area north of the Danube, while the great plains east of the great river and Transylvania were within the sphere of influence of Bulgarian princes. Greater Moravia and the eastern Frankish empire had been bitter enemies during the course of their empire-building attempts.

The native population consisted overwhelmingly of Slav peasantry, including the partly Slavicized Avar clans. They certainly spoke various Slavic languages. On the other hand, the ethnic connections of the inhabitants of Transylvania is a bone of contention between Hungarian and Romanian historians. Hungarian pre- and early historians vehemently deny the no less tenaciously held Romanian assertion that a Romanised Dacian indigenous population had survived in the upper valleys and forests. All areas of the Danube basin were, in either case, sparsely populated when at the end of the ninth century shepherds of a Hungarian tribal alliance arrived with their horses from the steppes of today's southern Russia at the entrance to the Carpathians. Whereas German and

Austrian historians label this the Magyar invasion, the Hungarians themselves regard it as land acquisition (*honfoglalás*). What seemed at first yet another wave of the great migration soon took up a new historical dimension with decisive consequences for Germans and Slavs in the Danube basin.

To their victims and opponents, the intruders represented "the Mongolian nightmare of an Asiatic nomad people". As early as 863 the Alemannian Annals report that "a Hun tribe" had attacked Christendom; the chronicler identified the Hungarians as Huns, as the Hungarians' own national tradition did later. Besides the Scythians, everything that was blamed on the Huns was also imputed to the Hungarians. Byzantine and Arab travellers spoke of a "Turkic people"—a theory still echoed in the nineteenth century in the famous travelogues reports of the orientalist Ármin Vámbéry.

Today all authoritative Hungarian and foreign historians, anthropologists and ethnologists agree that this theory is mistaken. In the absence of written and archaeological sources, the language remains the only scientifically reliable evidence for the origin of the Hungarians—a language from the Finno-Ugrian linguistic family unique in Europe. Their predecessors belonged to the Ugrian people, and there is still disagreement over whether the ancient Hungarians lived on the western or eastern slopes of the Urals (i.e. in Europe or Asia). The nearest linguistic kin of the Hungarians are the Ostiaks and Voguls, now counting a mere 30,000, who remained hunters and gatherers well into modern times.

In the first millennium BCE the Hungarians broke away from the Ugrian people, proceeding with other clans in a south-westerly direction. Later, influenced by Turkic and Iranian tribes, they exchanged their former way of life for that of nomadic herdsmen. The people, who had originally occupied themselves purely in fishing and hunting, switched to agriculture and animal breeding within the framework of nomadic nations that suddenly appear and disappear just as fast. When their later wanderings began, how long they lasted, what directions they took, and with what peoples they had closer contact are unknown. The only sources available on the earliest history of the Hungarians, and even of the Conquest, are myths and legends which originated as much as two or three centuries after the events.

Most researchers acknowledge that the Hungarians' rich treasury of legend contains a kernel of historical truth, or at least regard the mythical accounts as a helpful source for deciphering what really happened. In addition they later served, together with epic songs and legends, as a basis for a new legitimation, for the affirmation of a "historic right": not to an occupied Pannonia, but to the rightful reconquest of their old homeland.

Thus, according to an orally transmitted legend, the brothers Hunor and Magor, sons of the Scythian Kings Gog and Magog, pursuing a miraculous white stag during a hunt, arrived in the region north of the Sea of Azov. Having lost the trail of the animal, they caught sight during a subsequent excursion of the two exquisitely beautiful daughters of Dula, King of the Alans. The brothers carried off and married the two maidens, and the offspring of these marriages are said to be the ancestors of the Huns and Magyars, namely "the famous all-powerful King Attila and later Duke Álmos, from whom the Hungarian kings and dukes originated".

Today linguists and others concede that this cherished legend contains a grain of historical truth: the close link between the Magyars and a Bulgarian-Turkic people, as well as the Alans. While the term "Magyar", used by the Hungarians themselves, harks back to Ugrian times, the appellation "Hungarian", "Ungar", "Hungarus", "Hongrois", is traceable to the tribal organisation of the Onogurs, to which the Hungarians had belonged for a long period; Onogur means "ten arrows", signifying ten tribes. It is also possible that the expression, accepted in the West since the early ninth century, refers to the amalgamation of the original seven loosely linked ancient Hungarian tribes with the three dissident Khazar tribes, the Kabars.

However, it is certain that the Hungarians had for some time been members of the Turkic Khazar empire between the middle Volga and the lower Danube. The ancient Hungarians were never a "Mongol people", as has often been claimed. Since 830 the Magyars had lived, together with various nomadic Turkic peoples, the Alans and the Slavs, in the Etelköz, "the area between two rivers"—an extensive region between the Don, the Danube and the Black Sea. About 200 words of Bulgar-Turkic origin testify to a significant Turkic component in the ancient Hungarian tribal alliance. Despite the mixture of peoples in the settlement area, the Ugrian (i.e. the

Hungarian language) prevailed and the name "Magyar" gained the upper hand in the entire community. This is the more remarkable because—according to the account of the Byzantine Emperor Constantine VII, the first and almost the only reliable source—only two of the seven old Hungarian tribes had Ugrian names (Megyer and Nyék), the names of the remaining five being Turkic. The Emperor also reported that in the tenth century, after the absorption of the Kabar tribes, the Hungarians were still bilingual.

It must be pointed out, particularly because of the historically and politically explosive effects of national-romantic legend-creation in Hungarian historiography and literature, that before and during the Conquest the Hungarian tribal alliance was anything but ethnically homogeneous. As for origins and nation-forming, according to the nationally unprejudiced analysis by the German-Hungarian ancient historian Thomas von Bogyay, all the anthropological and archaeological evidence makes it certain that the Hungarian national entity evolved in the melting pot of the southern Russian steppes.

The Hungarian historian Jenö Szücs has also emphasised that the Finno-Ugrian groups and various tribes of Turkic origin probably left the Khazar Kaganate as early as the eighth century, led by a Khazar dignitary, and that the key element of the Hungarian system of rulership in the ninth century was an ethnically heterogeneous following. According to Szücs, masses of newly-discovered material prove the symbiosis of pagan Hungarians and the Christian-Slavic sections of the inhabitants to have already been consummated during the tenth century. The land-acquiring Hungarian society was therefore not by any means a stratum of homogeneous nomadic warriors. However, later Hungarian tradition disavowed the close relationship with the Khazars, whose leaders adopted Judaism in the eighth century, as well as the real causes for the migration which took the tribes, together with their allies of Khazar or Turkic origin, as far as the slopes of the Carpathians.[1]

According to the account of Constantine VII cited above, the tribal chiefs raised the son of old Álmos, Árpád, on a shield as the leader of the strongest tribe, "in line with Khazar custom and law", sealing their agreement by a "covenant of blood"—the ritual drinking of the blood of the parties mingled together. However, later tradition presented Álmos and Árpád as the first divinely appointed leaders of the people. Egon Friedell wrote in his cultural history of modern times: "The legend is not just one of the forms by which we can imagine, conceive of and experience history but the sole form. All of history is legend and myth, and as such the product of our intellectual ability: our sense of interpretation, creative capacity, our conception of the world."[2]

Two gifted Hungarian chroniclers—"Anonymus", the nameless scribe of King Béla III (1172–96), and Simon Kézai, preacher at the court of King László IV (1272–90)—ensured by their imaginative approach and yarn-spinning propensity that the Hungarians' early history should appear "in the glitter and redolence of a magical event", and that so many generations would mistake fiction for history. The Hungarians and, incidentally, their vanquished neighbours established their own historical image by—consciously or unconsciously—re-evaluating and re-fashioning it as time passed to suit current requirements.

The striving for the historical legitimation of the birth of the nation and the Conquest plays a key role to this day in the life of all the peoples of the Danubian region. And this applies specifically to the Hungarians, who have always suffered from a deep-rooted sense of being alone in the world. That is why myths, and accounts of how they developed into intellectual-political power in the portrayal of the dramatic destinies of peoples and individuals, are often more important than dry data and the family trees of royal dynasties.

According to "Anonymus", the crucial Conquest was predicted in a dream. The charisma of the prince and tribal chief is based on a celestial gift bestowed on him through divine providence by a sacred totem animal. Princess Emese, consort of a Scythian king, dreamed that a *turul*—according to different versions, a hawk or an eagle—impregnated her by divine command, and the bird announced to her the historic mission of her unborn son, who would be like a thunderbolt and rule over distant lands. That is why he was named Álmos (*álom* = dream). Álmos then made preparations with all his people to conquer the new fatherland, bequeathed to him by his ancestors from the House of Attila, king of the Huns. The *turul* showed them the way, until they reached their goal, the Carpathians. Álmos died during their migration, and disappeared from world history.

The tribal chiefs raised his son Árpád on a shield, and pronounced him chief of the tribal alliance, offering a solemn oath of loyalty by making cuts on their arms and letting their blood flow into a sacrificial chalice. They swore to elect their princes in perpetuity from the tribe of Árpád. The nation placed Árpád under the obligation to distribute the land to be conquered fairly between the 108 clans, and grant the descendants of the tribal chiefs the right of free discussion before the prince. If one is to believe Hungarian historiography, this laid "the basis of the first constitution".

The fairy tale of a contemporary constitution, fabricated by "Anonymus", and other legends connected with it were supposed to present the settlement of the Hungarian tribes as a conscious historical act. In a stimulating essay for the catalogue of an exhibition in Berlin (1998) about "Myths of Nations", the writer György Dalos compiled typical quotations from old Hungarian school textbooks,[3] which made clear how the ancient legends had evolved into "historical truth".

The following, one of many examples, propounds the historical legitimation of the Conquest, and can be found in an essay, in a Hungarian history textbook for grammar schools, entitled "Hungary's History" with a particular "Glimpse at the Development of Education and the Life of the Common People of 1864":

In contrast to the scorn and slander of foreign scholars who portray our ancestors as blood-suckers or a barbarian mob, and who, through prejudice, ignorance or national antipathy make it their aim to denigrate our nation, every Hungarian can point with proud self-esteem to a natural constitution—dictated by sober common sense, what is more—as early as the ninth century, when better educated and happier peoples in Europe could not boast of a similar unity as a civil constitution. [...] The Hungarian nation cannot be accused of harming some viable ethnic group or existing national law. Nor can it be reproached for destroying or even diminishing the culture of the lands conquered by it. [...] Our ancestors found no social order or historic law in the conquered territories. And if these circumstances had not sufficed to justify the instinct to search for a homeland, then their 1,000-year history would have proved that the Hungarians had been guided to their home by God himself at the right time.

The word "God" here requires closer definition, particularly since it was the Bavarian King Arnulf who in 892 invited the Hungarian tribes to participate in a punitive expedition against his rebellious vassal Svatopluk, Prince of Moravia. In view of the later devastation wrought by the Hungarians in all of Pannonia, the Eastern Franks and Moravians accused each other in letters to the Pope of having admitted this dangerous enemy to the Carpathian basin as an ally. The destruction must have been on a large scale because the Bavarians and Moravians made peace two years later, and later still proceeded jointly against the "bloodthirsty, heathen Huns". The "civilized" Westerners behaved in certain situations in as barbaric a fashion as the Hungarians were supposed to do, as an assassination in 902 (or 904) testifies. The Bavarians invited the Hungarians' chief prince, the "*kündü*", sacral leader of their tribal alliance, to a banquet at the Fischa east of Vienna. As they took their places at the table, the incumbent *kündü*, Prince Kurszán, and his entire retinue were ambushed and treacherously murdered. This paradoxically strengthened the position of the vice-ruler (*gyula*) and actual military leader, Prince Árpád, and unintentionally paved the way for Árpád's absolute rule; his descendants in the male line ruled Hungary as a pagan-sacral dynasty until 1301. In the course of fighting Svatopluk the Hungarians had realized how weak this land of Pannonia actually was, and consequently in 894 they launched their own expedition of conquest in the Danube basin, inflicting tremendous devastation.

The early Hungarians crossed the Carpathians as allies first of the Moravians and then of the Eastern Franks. The great plains, the last ridges of the Eurasian steppes, appeared to them, as it had already to the Huns or the Avars, as the Promised Land. The significance of the Hungarians in the subsequent destiny of the Germans and Austrians in this region began to show as early as 881—first when they clashed with Frankish troops near Vienna, and then in a battle at Pöchlarn with the Hungarians' Kabar allies. This account in the Salzburg Annals not only (after a hiatus of several centuries) names Vienna for the first time, but is also the earliest mention of the Hungarians from a Bavarian source—thus indicating even at this date interest in the region and in the Hungarians. Herwig Wolfram, the specialist of early Austrian history, rightly emphasises the symbolic significance of the joint entry into history of Vienna and the Hungarians, an association which survived all the whirlwinds of their shared history.[4]

However, the beginning of the 1,000-year swing of the pendulum between hostility and alliance was anything but amicable, as a tragic incident in the year 1000 near Stockerau in Lower Austria demonstrates. The paranoid attitude of the locals towards all foreigners was shown in a virulent form when an Irish pilgrim named Coloman, son of a minor Celtic prince, was mistaken for a Hungarian spy and killed. When—too late—his innocence was established, his body was taken to Melk, where something like a cult of Coloman evolved.

The decisive impetus for the acquisition of land and for a conclusive crossing of the Carpathians came neither from the search for grazing land, nor from increasing population, nor from the mere prospect of plunder, but—in contrast to epic tradition—from a massive defeat by the nomadic Pechenegs, a people of Turkic origin. The disaster began when the Hungarians turned against the Bulgarians to fulfill a military compact with Byzantium. The latter not only made peace with Byzantium but beat the Hungarian army led by the son of Árpád, against which it used the Pechenegs. As most of the Hungarian warriors were fighting in the south or in Moravia, the Pechenegs could easily attack and devastate the virtually undefended Hungarian settlements. The defeated troops and the many ravaged non-combatants escaped across the Carpathians into the, by then, familiar Pannonia. It was therefore "a flight forwards".

Most historians agree that the Hungarian tribes were in severe straits when they set out in the autumn of 895 on their march into the Danube basin. They advanced from the northeast across the Verecke pass, from the east and southeast across the Transylvanian Carpathians, and along the Danube. The pre-history and the sequence of events of this westward progress were portrayed differently in historiography, above all in the records of the chroniclers and in the literature of each of the affected peoples and their later national states. Even if the land, as already mentioned, was far from being uninhabited or deserted at that time, there was clearly no comprehensive political organisation, but rather a political vacuum, and the local residents, who spoke a mixture of Slavic languages, seem to have been more or less defenceless and at the mercy of the invading Hungarians.

Czech, Romanian and Russian historians have estimated the number of invading Magyars at between 200,000 and 500,000, although some of them regard even the lower limit as exaggerated… According to the balanced judgement of modern Hungarian historians, the total number would have been around half a million, and of the local Slavic-speaking population about 100,000; they seem convinced that the latter were far out numbered by the Hungarians. Otherwise the language of the conquerors could not have gained the upper hand so easily, nor would the mingling with the inhabitants have been so trouble-free. At any rate the Hungarians, together with their Kabar and other allies, were strong enough to bring all the habitable parts of the new homeland under their control within five to ten years. Waste land and marshes with natural obstacles were deliberately left untouched, forming a unique frontier protection system known as *"gyepü"*.[5]

The Hungarian tribes were the first steppe peoples who managed to develop into a strong nation with the capacity to adapt, and possessing self-awareness as well as historical self-confidence. How, in detail, the land came to be occupied is as little known as the fate of the inhabitants. In *Nation and History* Jenö Szücs opines that the local ruling class was probably annihilated, while the masses were assimilated and within two to three centuries fused with compatible social strata: warriors with warriors, slaves with slaves and so on. Of prime importance were common lifestyle and interests.

Historians essentially agree that, independent of its national and ideological perspective, the Hungarians' conquest of the Carpathian basin was a decisive factor in the development of medieval Europe. Nonetheless, what Hungarians hail as the heroic deeds of their victorious ancestors remains to this day—in the eyes of Germans, Slavs and Romanians—a "tragedy", a "disaster" and a "great misfortune". Thus Georg Stadtmüller describes the Magyar invasion as a catastrophe: "The Magyars conclusively annihilated the supremacy of the German Empire in the Danube Basin, destroyed German colonisation in western Hungary, and made the continuation of the splendid Bavarian south-east colonisation impossible for more than a century and a half."[6] Some Hungarian historians, e.g. Szabolcs de Vajay in his controversial work *Entry of the Hungarian Tribal Alliance into European History*, claim that the early Hungarians fulfilled a double function: on the one hand as a bulwark in the Carpathian basin against the early "drive towards the east of the German empire", and on the other as having contributed greatly, through the conclusion in 926 of a nine-year armistice, to the unity of the

Germans, who were able to come to an understanding among themselves only in the face of a common danger.

The split in the Slavic world due to the Conquest proved even more significant for European history. By their settlement of the Danube basin the Hungarians drove a permanent wedge between the northern and southern Slavs. At the end of the nineteenth century the eminent Czech historian František Palacký concluded bitterly: "The invasion and settlement of the Hungarian nation in Hungary belong to the most important facts of history as a whole: in all the course of centuries the Slav world has never been struck a more disastrous blow." In Palacký's eyes the Hungarians appear to have inflicted as much misery on the Czechs as the Germans have. In any case, as far as Czech, Slovak and Polish historians and the schoolbooks written by them or under their supervision are concerned, the enduring fissure of the Slav people is by far the most serious outcome of the Conquest and the evolution of the Hungarian state.[7]

The deep-seated resentments between Hungarians on one side and Czechs and, above all, Slovaks on the other are therefore rooted in early history, and have been implanted into the consciousness of succeeding generations on both sides through their legends and attitudes. Thus the Czechs and Slovaks contend that the occupying Hungarians were actually overwhelmingly Slavs, and that even the founders of the state, Árpád and St Stephen, belonged to the Slav people. As for the rumours still rife at the time of the Chief-Prince Géza about "two Hungarys", one "white" and the other "black", the inhabitants of the so-called "white" part (western and central Hungary) are claimed by Slovaks to have been Slavs; however, the Kabars and Pechenegs—Turkic tribes who followed the migration of the Magyars—are said to have lived in "black" Hungary as well as the tribe of the Székelys, whose origin has never been clarified.[8]

The Hungarians, for their part, have given the impression in some legends and in the resulting epics and works of art that the inhabitants of the Carpathian basin received the conquerors under Prince Árpád with undiluted enthusiasm. This image is conveyed above all by the monumental painting by Mihály Munkácsy, "Hungarian Conquest" (Illus. 2), which adorns the great hall of the Budapest Parliament used mainly for receiving foreign dignitaries.

The canvas shows Árpád mounted regally on his white charger with his mounted retinue at the moment of his triumphal arrival in the new homeland. The inhabitants, mostly on foot, cheer their new ruler and offer him gifts. The white horse is an important element in Hungarian legend. Prince Árpád defeats Svatopluk in battle, but before it happens he commands the Prince of Moravia to surrender: Árpád sends him a white horse as a gift, demanding in return earth, grass and water—a symbol for the ancient Scythians of voluntary surrender. The legend tells us that after Árpád's demands had been satisfied, he took all the land into his possession with confidence and an easy conscience. These rites were an established part of agreements and contracts between nomadic tribes.

We learn from a letter written to the Pope by Bishop Theotmar of Salzburg in the year 900 about mutual recriminations between Bavarians and Moravians for having concluded a treaty with the Hungarians according to pagan customs, swearing on a wolf and a dog as totems. Theotmar was killed on 4 July 907 in a large-scale battle fought by the Bavarians, who had hoped thereby to reconquer Pannonia. This attack ended with a shattering defeat at Pozsony (Bratislava) and the death of the Margrave Luitpold and a large number of the Bavarian nobility. The legend of the white horse was further embellished by a fabricated account of the death of Svatopluk, who is supposed to have drowned in the Danube during his flight from the victorious Magyars. In fact Svatopluk had entered into a pact with the Hungarians in accordance with nomadic custom to seal a joint action against the Bavarians (894), and not in an agreement to relinquish his land; the annihilation of the short-lived state occurred only after his death.

The white horse as the symbol of the victorious Hungarians under Prince Árpád was—together with other emblems such as the alleged "blood covenant" of Pusztaszer and the baptism of St Stephen—the theme of grandiose nineteenth-century canvases, above all those produced in connection with the millennium of the Conquest in 1896. Similarly, when Admiral Miklós Horthy (later Regent) entered Budapest, the "sinful city", in November 1919 after the collapse of the Hungarian Soviet Republic, on his white horse at the head of the counter-revolutionary troops, this well-thought-out gesture was easily understood—as the visible signal for a sharp turn to the right towards extreme nationalism. More than two decades later the now elderly statesman once again rode a white horse at the head of Hungarian troops marching into the cities of Kassa (Košice) and Kolozsvár (Cluj) in Transylvania, which had been temporarily regained with the help of the Axis powers through the Vienna Awards. This was seen as symbolic by the Hungarian inhabitants, who received him with delirious acclaim.

Thus a straight line leads from tradition to politically questionable heroic deeds of modern times, which have later boomeranged. The myth of the white horse should be seen as a perpetual resource to fulfill clear-cut national functions in certain situations. To this day national myths clash in the relationship between Hungary and Romania, particularly regarding the historic right to Transylvania claimed by both. The dispute over which of the two peoples was the first after the Conquest to settle as a closed, or at least a numerically significant group and therefore the determining political force in Transylvania, has divided generations of historians, by no means only on the Budapest-Bucarest axis. Thus before the First World War the British historian R.W. Seton-Watson vociferously supported the historical and political interests of the Romanians (and of all Slavs) against the Austro-Hungarian hegemony, while his colleague A.C. Macartney represented a far more balanced approach to the explosive question of the minorities in Greater Hungary.[9]

Such historical and political controversies between several generations of Romanian and Hungarian scholars and writers have outlasted all systems of government—and the prospect of toning down existing textbooks or of a basic consensus between historians, even in the era of a united Europe, is virtually nil. That is why the effect of the legends about the enigmatic origins of the Transylvanian Székelys, handed down in folksong and custom as well as in poems and juvenile literature, is still of consequence today. They belong to the epic cycle that includes Attila and Árpád, the *turul* bird and the white horse, and the alleged common origin in ancient times of Huns and Magyars.

The mythical Csaba, youngest son of Attila, king of the Huns, is the central figure of this cycle. When he saw that his nation was heading for ruin, he shot a magic arrow from his quiver to summon his mother, the sorceress. Where the point of the arrow entered the ground he found a miraculous herb with juice that could heal any wound, and with this magic essence he woke his fallen warriors, lined them up in battle formation, and led them against the enemy. The Gepids were so horrified at the sight of this spectral host that they let the remnants of Csaba's people withdraw in peace. Csaba then escorted the remainder of the Huns with his, by now, mounted army of the dead as far as the border of Transylvania, where he ordered them to settle in today's Székely country. He then led his dead warriors back to their old fatherland, the land of Attila, promising the clans left behind in Székely country that whenever they were threatened by a great peril he and his warriors would rise from their graves and come to rescue them—hence the Magyar-Székely folk legend 'Waiting for Csaba'. The small Székely nation often faced dangers, and each time it was saved, according to the legend, not by self-sacrificing bravery alone but by miracles. Csaba and his Hun warriors hurried forth from the sky with a great roar and scattered the enemy, and to this day Hungarians know the glittering path in the heavens generally called the Milky Way as the "Road of the Armies", brought into being by their horses' hooves.

In the previously mentioned collection published by Crown Prince Rudolf, the popular and prolific novelist Mór Jókai concluded that legends and history are interwoven to such an extent that one either had to swallow the lot, following public opinion, or reject the lot. He was probably right. Only with his thesis of identifying Huns with Magyars did Jókai go too far. However much be would have wished it to be so, the Székelys, originally a Bulgarian-Turkic tribe, are not related to the Huns—although their origins and development remain conjectural. It has been suggested recently that they migrated into the Carpathian basin together with the Kabars, or at least before the Magyars, and fought on the latter's side before the Conquest. Be that as it may, the Székelys used a variant of the Turkic script well into early modern times, and although they spoke Hungarian at an early stage, they preserved for centuries their distinctive social culture and their special position. As early as the thirteenth century the kings assigned them to guard the Transylvania borders, and their area of settlement is still called "Székely country".[10]

What Jókai wrote in 1884 of the belief in the historical unity of the Huns and the Hungarians was an unfortunate psycho-literary phenomenon; the perpetuation of the myth regarding this link was harmful for Hungary's reputation. As already mentioned, it was the devastating raids and marauding after the Conquest which established the Hungarians' unenviable reputation. When a collection of essays entitled *What is a Hungarian?* was published in 1939, prominent Hungarian intellectuals were once again seen—as so often before and since—to be preoccupied with the question of national identity. This prompted the historian Sándor Eckhardt to bring out his still very useful study *The Hungarian Image in Europe*.[11] He ascertained with astonishment that the negative and sometimes gruesome and terrifying images of the Hungarians as portrayed by Western chroniclers (e.g. their supposed cannibalism) were promoted by the early chroniclers "Anonymus" and Kézai as wholly positive traits. Regino, the abbot of Prüm in the tenth century, was the first to record that the Hungarians were rumoured to eat human flesh, drink human blood and tear their enemies' hearts out of their bosoms, which they ate to augment their own bravery. This tale harked back to an ancient stereotype found in Herodotus.

The Magyars were claimed to be descendants of the hideous Asiatic Scythians of legend, half men and half apes, a witches' brood begotten by devils. The sources—chronicles and annals—were all copied from one another, not on the basis of eyewitness accounts but following the characterisation of older chroniclers. Soon the "new barbarians" became identified with the Huns, who are remembered only too well in Europe. Attila had, after all, become in Western eyes the embodiment of barbarism, the anti-Christ, and at the time of the Renaissance he already appeared in Italian legends as the king of the Hungarians, constantly hatching plots, and depicted with dog ears, the bestial offspring of a greyhound and a princess locked up in a tower.[12]

None of this, then or in later centuries, enhanced the reputation of Hungarians in the world. Nonetheless the equivalence of Scythians and Huns, originating from the West, managed to filter into Hungarian historiography. The first chroniclers already presented the Árpád dynasty as originating from the bogeyman Attila the Hun, and as transplants these legends became profoundly and indelibly imprinted into Hungarian consciousness, and developed into a national creed. Not only in the Middle Ages but also in the nineteenth century and partly in the twentieth, the Hungarians were proud to profess this heritage in order to be able to identify their own "creation legend" with the epic of the world-conquering Scourge of God. The first chroniclers' historical fantasies provided a legal justification for the Conquest—an important factor in the Hungarians' historical consciousness. Many more of the Hungarians' forays after the Conquest could be related, together with the collective perception and memory associated with them and their reception by chroniclers and historians. However, what is essential in our context is that the alleged kinship between the Huns and the Hungarians, in conjunction with the "Mongol nomad appearance" of the latter, has, right up till the present, moulded the dialectic between the Western image from outside and the self-image of Hungarians.

3. From Magyar Mayhem to the Christian Kingdom of the Árpáds

Vajay's thesis that the raids during the Conquest were not mere wanton destruction but "premeditated strategic ventures, frequently of European significance and with enormous consequences", is controversial to say the least. However, the successful plundering forays also sowed the seeds of future defeats. The opponents of the Magyars, particularly the Bavarians, soon understood that there was a prospect of successfully overpowering the fatigued homeward-trekking mounted troops, laden with booty and escorting prisoners. Furthermore, the discipline and the agility of the old nomad rider tactics had noticeably flagged as the Hungarians became more prosperous.

Hungarian army commanders were always prepared to spare a region if it offered gold and silver, or to undertake punitive expeditions against others. Italy was the first country to pay the Magyars regular tribute. In 899 a corps of 5,000 Hungarian riders, encircled at the Brenta, beat the Italian army of King Berengar I which outnumbered it three-to-one. After repeated Hungarian raids, the king decided to pay ransom in return for his own and his people's freedom. The Hungarian historian György Györffy ascertained that the sum in question would have amounted to about 30 kilos of gold.

Only the Germans were able to inflict serious defeats on the Hungarians—in 917 and 933—by deploying a well disciplined and heavily armed mounted force in close formation, and by exploiting their opponent's weaknesses. On 10 August 955 they finally won a decisive victory at the Lechfeld near Augsburg, and Horka Bulcsú, the third-ranking dignitary of the tribal alliance, and Prince Lél (Lehel) were sent to the gallows in Regensburg as common criminals. The success of Otto I, later given the sobriquet "the Great", was hailed by German historians as "a turning-point in world history", when Christian culture was delivered from the Asiatic

27

barbarians. According to legend, only seven men out of the entire Hungarian army were left alive—dishonoured for the rest of their years as *gyászmagyarok* (pariahs), they had to become vagrant beggars in their own homeland. According to legend, Lél, condemned to death after the lost battle, sounded his beloved bugle one last time and killed the victorious king with it, exclaiming "You will die before me and be my slave in the hereafter!" The ivory horn was still on show 900 years later in the small town of Jászberény.

In the Hungarian chronicles Bulcsú was said to a powerful and efficient leader, who proclaimed himself and his people, *vis-à-vis* the Emperor, as the "Vengeance and Scourge of God". Still, opinions differ over what were the real consequences of the Lechfeld victory. Modern historians maintain that the defeat was no more serious than the two earlier ones, and that the story of 26,000 Germans overpowering 100,000 or even 128,000 Hungarians was a fabrication; it is thought today that the Hungarian army at Augsburg numbered less than 20,000 men. However, the execution of the powerful leader Bulcsú and the psychological effects of the reverses were decisive. Western Christianity now had the opportunity to win over the souls of the pagan Hungarians.

The fateful battle on the Lechfeld opened the way to a momentous event. We do not know how the people coped with the consequences of the defeat, but the Hungarians did not disappear from the world stage like other defeated bands of horsemen. Instead, situated between Rome and Byzantium, they adopted Western culture and opted for Roman Catholicism. Under Chief Prince Géza, great-grandson of Árpád, a tribal alliance of mounted robbers became, within a generation, settled peasants and herdsmen and did not lose their language or political identity. According to the German historian Zernack, "the Magyars were the first steppe peoples shaped by the established economic and settlement environment and the social-cultural conditions of the period of breakthrough towards Christian rulership." Yet the key to the radical change in Hungary itself lay in the political decision of Géza and his son, the future St Stephen, to follow the path from tribal alliance to its logical conclusion, the establishment of a Christian state. The fact that, as Thietmar of Merseburg reported, Géza considered himself rich and strong enough to sacrifice to more than one god does not lessen the importance of this transformation. During his reign of a quarter of a century (972–97) the nation conclusively renounced its nomadic way of life and within a few decades of the battle of Lechfeld, became—even if not without upheavals—a Christian kingdom.

The territorial unity of the Christian kingdom of Hungary was enforced first during a series of bloody clashes. Following the death of Géza two members of the Árpád dynasty claimed the succession: Koppány, Prince of Somogy, who ruled in the region south of Lake Balaton, stood on his rights under the principle of seniority in accordance with the family's rules which granted inheritance to the oldest member of the clan. The antagonist of this pagan tribal chieftain was Vajk, the still very young son of Géza, who by then bore a Christian name: Stephen (István). The year of his birth is variously given as 967, 969 and 975, and the date of his baptism is also unknown. However, it is certain that Stephen based his claim on the inextricable connection between Christianity and the state, invoking the right of the ruler to determine his successor on the principle of primogeniture.

Although Géza remained essentially a pagan even after his baptism in 973, he ensured that his son Stephen would be brought up a Christian. When ill and about to die, he successfully sought the hand of Gisela, sister of the young Bavarian Duke, later Emperor Henry II, for his son. The marriage took place in 996, and when Géza died the next year, Stephen—under the influence of Bishop Adalbert of Prague—had become deeply pious; in contrast to his father, he was Christian not for tactical reasons but by conviction. Numerous German missionaries and priests, as well as knights and officials, came to Hungary in the retinue of the Bavarian princess. Géza himself had already relied in part on a personal bodyguard of Bavarian knights to enforce his rule, and this now became a regular practice.

Jenö Szücs has pointed out that the sword smoothed the way for the Word and the Cross, but much depended on who wielded the sword and what concept he represented. The crucial battle for the country's future was fought in 998 near the town of Veszprém in Western Hungary. The German knights played a decisive part in defeating the tribal chief Koppány, Stephen's kinsman, who wanted

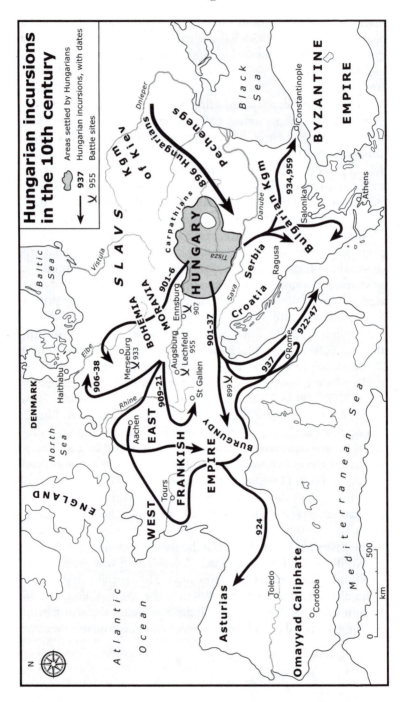

Hungarian incursions in the 10th century

Areas settled by Hungarians
937 Hungarian incursions, with dates
955 Battle sites

to marry Géza's widow Savolta in order to legitimize his claim to the succession in accordance with tribal custom. Legends and chronicles relate that in a scene full of symbolism the young Stephen called together his retinue and the German knights before the battle and, kneeling in their midst, invoked the help of St Martin, patron saint of Pannonia. Then, in accordance with German custom, he had himself armed by the knights with the sword, first blessed by the Church, which he would resolutely wield to further the spread of Christianity.[1]

Two Swabian knights and the famous Wezellin from Wasserburg in Bavaria served as commanders of Stephen's army. The enemy, unambiguously defined as a heathen-barbarian tribal chief representing traditionalism, lost the battle, and Koppány died at the hands of Stephen's knights.

Stephen's real aim was to break the power of the tribal chiefs and their pagan entourages enriched by plundering raids, and re-establish the authority of Árpád's successors over all the tribes. Even though the encounter near Veszprém has gone down in national tradition as a "battle between Teutons and Hungarians", the victory gained with ruthless savagery over Koppány and his followers was the starting-point for the welding together of a firmly structured Christian Hungarian state from a loose, semi-nomadic alliance based on personalities. However, the defeat of the challenger was also the prelude to Stephen's future campaigns against the virtually independent princes of Transylvania (such as his uncle Gyula) and in the south Ajtony, who was said to have allied himself with the "Greeks". The military destruction of unruly clan chiefs was carried out in parallel with the fight against the so-called "black Hungarians", who between 1004 and 1006 were converted "by force and love", as Bruno of Querfurt termed it. The expression "black Hungarians" referred to the Székelys and Turkic people, such as the Kavars and Pechenegs, living in Transylvania and southern Hungary as auxiliary troops allied to the Hungarians.

Stephen's image in Hungarian history is contradictory. Was he kind-hearted and "the most pious", as his German court-chroniclers characterise him? Or was he merciless and cruel? Did he not merely kill his relative Koppány but have his body quartered? The traditional belief that Stephen had three parts of the chieftain nailed to the gates of Győr, Székesfehérvár and the nearby cathedral town of Veszprém, while the fourth was dispatched to his recalcitrant uncle Gyula in Gyulafehérvár, would seem to confirm the second version—that of his harshness and inflexibility. The dates and sequence of events of the individual conflicts are as uncertain as many others in the Hungarian state's early history, but it is certain that, as king and even in his old age, Stephen acted swiftly and ruthlessly against his real or presumed adversaries.

Stephen was canonized in 1083 (being the first of eight saints from the House of Árpád), and is regarded by historians, both foreign and Hungarian, as the "most successful and conscientious worker for Hungary's statehood" (Gyula Szekfű), a truly significant personality and consequently high in popular esteem. The keenness with which he converted his people to Christianity has been compared to Charlemagne's. Undoubtedly Stephen I was deeply religious and hence determined to free himself and his people from their barbaric and pagan past. His crowning as Hungary's first Christian king, probably on the first day of the year 1001 (in some sources the date is Christmas Day 1000), became a turning point in Hungary's history, although the exact prehistory and the international connections of this event remain obscure. The only contemporary source generally accepted by Hungarian historiography is the account by Bishop Thietmar of Merseburg, according to which Stephen, brother-in-law of the Bavarian Duke Henry, received the crown and the blessing of Pope Sylvester II "thanks to the grace and urging" of Emperor Otto III. Even in the mid-twentieth century "constitutional" debates still raged between German and Hungarian scholars over whether Stephen's crown had been bestowed by the Pope or by the Emperor; the consensus is now that he received it from the Pope with the agreement of Otto III.

Accordingly the Hungarian kingdom, unlike Bohemia, Moravia and Poland, did not become a vassal of the Holy Roman Empire but remained *de facto* independent. Furthermore, Stephen transformed his country and his power according to the Christian-monarchic principle in complete independence. It was a sovereign political act, with a significance that cannot be over-emphasized. As the British specialist on Hungary, C.A. Macartney, puts it: "The act of conversion changed the Hungarian people from an outlaw horde against whom a Christian Prince was not only free, but bound by duty, to take up arms, into a member of the Christian family of nations, and their king into one of those rulers by the Grace of God whose legitimate rights his fellow-princes could not infringe without sin."[2] And he points out that, although the King of Hungary was not equal to the Emperor in status, he also was not subject to his overlordship. The apostolic insignia (the holy lance and the apostolic cross) proclaimed that the Hungarian church was free from any authority save that of Rome, and this, Macartney writes, was "an enormous reinforcement of the country's real independence".

Thus a people who till recently had been half-nomadic and pagan became an integral part of Christian Europe without losing their political and ethnic existence. Not only Stephen's ruthless showdown with followers of paganism, but also his radical transformation of the state suggest that his aim was not so much to take over the polity inherited from his father but to repudiate it completely (Gyula Kristó).[3]

Stephen always intended to be a sovereign ruler, and not a vassal, and since his coronation the crown of Stephen has always been the symbol of Hungarian independence and freedom. (We return later to its chequered history and constitutional-political significance.) However Stephen could never have worn the crown, which has been venerated for centuries (it was first exhibited in the Budapest National Museum, but moved later to the Parliament building), since its lower, so-called "Greek" part was made in 1074, almost four decades after his death, while the "Latin" top section probably dates from the thirteenth century. Hungarian historians persistently gloss over the fact that after his victory over insurgents in 1044 near Györ, Emperor Henry III captured the crown and sent it back to Rome. If in its present form it is a myth, why then is it still called the crown of St Stephen? In their work on the subject Professors Kálmán Benda and Erik Fügedi offer a candid reply: "This belief has proved indestructible over the centuries. Historians therefore have no choice but to confess that what is essential in this case is not whether the crown, as an object, was actually Stephen's, but the unshakeable belief in it."[4]

In contrast to the questionable origins of the crown, the truth and the efficacy of the reforms Stephen carried out cannot be doubted. They affected not only the administration, but also the structure of the Church in the entire country. With his coronation Stephen had become king by the grace of God and absolute ruler, and could therefore exercise at his own discretion, as it were, all the prerogatives of medieval kingship. These included, among others, the conduct of international relations and the right to appoint anyone of his choice, regardless of birth, to public office as the representative of the royal will; appoint and dismiss officials; and enact laws. His autocracy was further characterized by immense landholdings and absolute supremacy over the Church's organization.

In his foreign policy the king succeeded by taking a firm but moderate stance to safeguard his creation of the country's Christian organization under the rule of law. After successfully fending off the Bulgarians in the south and the Poles in the north. Stephen managed by 1018 to regain Hungarian control over the entire Carpathian basin. During his reign of more than forty years he was involved in only one serious conflict, when Emperor Conrad II attacked Hungary in 1030 with a strong force. Stephen repelled the attack without great losses and with tactical superiority, even occupying Vienna in the course of his counter-stroke.

In domestic politics the authority of the crown remained undiminished after the victories over the tribal chieftains. The strong centralization of the early Hungarian kingdom prevented the development of feudal relationships. Stephen systematically appropriated the holdings of the clans which were compelled to hand over the bulk of their property, leaving only a third of it in the hands of submissive clan chiefs. He was thus able to extend the crown's property right over the entire area inhabited by Hungarians. The power of the tribal alliances was turned into politico-military and constabulary-administrative units. Along with the suppression of the traditional social alliances the king created about forty counties, headed by bailiffs whom he personally appointed.

The royal counties, i.e. the territorial organizations with a royal castle as the centre of local administration, were identical in most cases to the former settlement areas of the clans. Royal castle domains were created, each headed by a member of the King's closest circle. Although the King used German institutions as models and received suggestions from the Holy Roman Empire, everything in practice was adapted to specific Hungarian conditions. "It was not the feudal hierarchy, but the close personal relationship with the king that became the principle within the society of Christian Hungary," argues Thomas von Bogyay.[5] However, this did not involve ruthless suppression of the old social structure. The body of "freemen"—i.e. descendants in the male line of the tribal chieftains and clan heads who had not forfeited their status due to rebellion or individual crimes, together with immigrant knights from the West and the neighbouring Slavic countries—retained their special prerogatives, and indeed were the sole active political element in the entire population. Only they could participate in political consultations and hold public office and have access to the king's justice. Furthermore, they paid no taxes apart from tithes to the Church. It was their duty and prerogative to perform military duty.

Conversion to Roman Christianity did more than provide a new basis for the ruling dynasty's authority. Along with the adoption of the Latin language and script, it led, beyond the destruction of the old pagan customs, to the integration of Hungary into a network of linguistic, cultural and political dependence. There is a highly important direct source for Stephen's conception: *The Book of Exhortations of St Stephen* to his son. This work was written around 1015 in Stephen's name and on his instructions by an anonymous (according to some sources a south German) priest at the Hungarian court. The main function of the Christian ruler, it says, is the protection of the Church by overcoming paganism. "By preserving the shield of faith, you also don the helmet of salvation. With these weapons you can overcome your invisible and visible foes by legitimate means."[6] Jenö Szücs has emphasized that the territorial unity of the Hungarian kingdom was welded together by the sword in the sign of an idea. The concept of the "foe" has no ethnic-national character, but its essential meaning is "pagan". In the quoted writing Stephen speaks of the Faith as the most important prop of the royal power, the Church being the second and the priesthood the third. The conscious subordination to Christian universalism was part of his state concept. Stephen always based his authority more on the ecclesiastical than on the secular branch. At first, in order to replace pagan priests with Christian clergy, the king invited foreign priests and monks, at least until enough young Hungarians had acquired the requisite theological and administrative knowledge. The conscious imitation of German institutions found expression in the Latin terminology of the law and administration, also in the coinage. Thus it was from Regensburg that Stephen obtained samples, as well as mint-workers, for the first Hungarian coins. In an oft-quoted maxim, the anonymous author of the *Exhortations* author justified the increasing influence of a foreign clergy and high nobility: "A nation consisting of a single language and a single culture is weak and fragile." Stephen emphasizes that "settlers from various countries and provinces bring with them various languages and customs, various instructive concepts and weapons, which decorate and glorify the royal court but intimidate foreign powers. Therefore, my son, I instruct you to face them and treat them decently, so that they will prefer to stay with you rather than elsewhere, because, if you destroy all that I have built, squander what I have collected, then your Empire will with doubtless suffer."

In building a completely new ecclesiastical organization Stephen was assisted not only by the disciples of St Adalbert of Prague but also by a large number of high clergy and missionaries from Germany, Italy, France and the surrounding Slav countries. The training of Hungarian-born priests followed so speedily that already by 1040 some had become bishops. Southern Slavs from Croatia and Slovenia living in Hungary strongly influenced the church idiom, which became interspersed with many loan-words of Slav origin. England, Kiev and Byzantium were also represented in the king's entourage. Thus the title of the commander of his personal guard was *Dux Ruizorum*, in which the expression "Rus" (Hung. *orosz*), signifies an ethnically colourful element in his retinue.

When Stephen died on 15 August 1038 there were two archbishoprics in Hungary—Györ and Kalocsa—and eight bishoprics. On his order ten villages were each obliged to build a church and support a priest. The diocese of Veszprém is said to have been established already before the coronation by Chief-Prince Géza. Outstanding among the monasteries was doubtless the Benedictine abbey of Pannonhalma; among its considerable privileges was the freedom to elect its abbot, his status being second only to that of the Archbishop of Esztergom. Stephen endowed it with the tithe from the former estates of Koppány. The sees and some of the many monasteries founded in his reign were among the largest landowners in the country. Stephen had established a "state-ecclesiastical" system on the Carolingian model, a powerfully centralist and autocratic kingdom, which could claim sovereignty in internal and external affairs, even *vis-à-vis* the Emperor himself. He was canonized in 1083, together with his son Imre who died young, and the martyr of the pagan uprising of 1046, Bishop Gerard (Gellért) of Csanád.

St Stephen as founder of the state and Grand-Prince Árpád as conqueror have always personified a dualism in Hungarian historical consciousness. The quartered Koppány remained the prototype of the rebel, the *turul* bird being the pagan counterpart of the holy crown of Stephen. During various periods of Hungarian history the conflict between the Catholic universalism of a Christian kingdom embedded in Western culture and the self-reliant pagan princehood, legitimized by the conquest of the country and moulded by Eastern roots, was termed "Stephen versus Árpád". On the one hand was Christian universalism, linked with Stephen's testamentary declaration of his belief in the Hungarian kingdom's multinational and multicultural character, and on the other the myth of the nation's homogeneity without consideration for minorities, with Árpád representing national independence and the continuity of traditions since Attila.[7]

4. The Struggle for Continuity and Freedom

The breath was hardly out of King Stephen's body when the young kingdom was plunged into a serious crisis, already latent in his lifetime. The succession had not been settled. Stephen's son had died after a hunting accident in 1031, and this was immediately followed by a desperate struggle between Stephen and his nephew Vászoly, who claimed the throne on the basis of pagan legitimacy. Stephen had him blinded and molten lead poured into his ears, and banished his three sons.

The king designated the Venetian Peter Orseolo, son of his sister and the exiled Doge, as his successor. However, Peter was soon ousted in a palace revolution, and replaced by one of Stephen's ambitious brothers-in-law. Emperor Henry III intervened, and Peter returned to the throne, this time only as Henry's vassal. An uprising finally swept away the stranger, who had favoured his foreign entourage—"blabbering Italians and shrieking Germans"—at the expense of the Hungarian nobility.

The earliest chronicles, already written at the court of the blinded Vászoly's sons, held Stephen's German consort Gisela responsible for the gruesome revenge on Vászoly, and accused Peter of letting the whole country fall into German hands. Other sources maintain that Peter had mistreated Gisela, who was living in Veszprém.

At any rate, Stephen's widow left Hungary in 1045, proceeding with Henry III to Passau, and eventually became abbess of the Niedernburg convent there. It was long assumed that she was buried in the cathedral of Veszprém which she had founded, and only on the eve of the First World War a Munich archaeologist discovered her grave in the church of the Niedernburg convent—which has since become a place of pilgrimage for the Hungarian faithful.[1]

On her marriage Gisela had received the surroundings of Pressburg, Sopron and Szombathely from her husband as a wedding gift, and historians specializing in German-Hungarian relations are certain that numerous German knights, together with ecclesiastics and artisans, settled there. The ancestors of several distinguished noble families introduced the etiquette of the German high nobility to the Hungarian court. At that time and later, German knights commanded the royal armies against attackers from the east, such as the Pechenegs, and habitually interfered in Hungarian disturbances under the protection of German kings and margraves. However, the decisive element in the increasing German influence was the fact that the rulers all favoured it. Future Hungarian kings were also keen to settle Germans in the country's uninhabited territories in order to gain a further undepinning of their power.

Béla von Pulánszky, writing in his *History of German Literature in Hungary* of the reaction to the massive German immigration from the eleventh to the thirteenth centuries, states that in contrast to the Germanophile part of Hungary there was another, larger part of the nation which felt no more than reluctant faith in the new spirit and even at first attempted some resistance. In his basic work published in 1931, the author adds an observation remarkably appropriate to the Second World War: "This dichotomy marks the attitude of Hungarians to German influence throughout their history." In the course of bloody and often obscure affrays between contenders for the throne and in family disputes, the threatened, expelled or victorious rulers frequently turned for help to their mighty German neighbour.

On his return from Kiev, Andrew, son of the blinded Vászoly, was raised to the kingship, and by this act the branch of an outlawed prince secured for the first but by no means the last time the continuity of the House of Árpád and probably also the future of Hungary. The deposed, blinded and emasculated Peter died soon after. Yet the process of consolidation initiated by Andrew I was interrupted and threatened by conflicts of succession many times. Gyula Pauler, one of the greatest authorities on the Árpád period, drew in 1899 the following balance of the time of troubles: "In thirty-nine years the country changed its ruler six times. Three kings—if we include Andrew I—died a violent death, and Béla I was saved from death by being ousted like Solomon, who had to flee his throne three times. The royal family's feuds brought foreign armies—Germans, Czechs, Poles—into the country nine times; it became a German dependency for three years, and five kings pleaded and humbled themselves before the German kings. Law and order within the country was completely destroyed."² There were two pagan uprisings, and within thirty years the kingdom was partitioned.

Only under Ladislaus (László) I, who reigned from 1077 to 1095, did Hungary begin to flourish again. The King became the heroic defender of the country against incursions by the Pecheneg, Uz and Cuman, who penetrated the barely inhabited Carpathians across the mountain passes and could only be halted and repulsed when they had penetrated the interior of the country. Ladislaus was canonized after his death as the protector of his people and of the faith, and as a father to the poor and defenceless.

External political factors in the eleventh and twelfth centuries had a salutary effect on Hungary's development; the country was also linked with the smaller nations through dynastic marriages. After the death of his brother-in-law the Croat King Zvonimir, husband of his sister Ilona, Ladislaus I seized the opportunity to occupy Slavonia, the core of Croatia, dividing it into counties on the Hungarian model. The diocese of Zagreb was founded, and a further push south was planned. However, it was left to his equally notable successor Coloman (Kálmán), nicknamed "the Bookish" (Könyves) for his erudition, to conquer Dalmatia. Coloman's coronation as king of Croatia initiated a union of Hungary with Croatia which lasted, despite interruptions and conflicts, for 800 years. To this day historians of both countries argue, in true Central European fashion, about the true character of these relations.

Coloman managed to secure these new acquisitions by a shrewd diplomatic move: the marriage of Ladislaus' daughter Piroska to John Comnenus, heir to the Byzantine throne. She became Empress of Byzantium with the name Irene, and after her death a saint of the Eastern Church for her selflessness and charity. By intruding into the immediate spheres of interest of Byzantium and Venice, Hungary emerged as a rival of both powers. Emperor Manuel Comnenus, Piroska's son, tried to use his half-Hungarian parentage as a weapon for conquering Hungary, which he invaded no less than ten times in twenty-two years, but the country's independence was never seriously threatened.

The King's Council, established by King Stephen, consisting of the palatine (the King's deputy), the *ban* (governor) of Croatia, the *vajda* (prince) of Transylvania, the bishops and bailiffs—in short, the nobles—began to adopt a political role in times of crisis during the reigns of Ladislaus and Coloman in order to avert civil wars. Nevertheless, the King's authority remained absolute well into the twelfth century. Bishop Otto of Freising, brother-in-law of Conrad III, travelling through Hungary in 1147, reported—presumably not without envy—that if any magnate committed or was even suspected of an offence against the King's authority, the King could send from his court any servant, however humble, empowered to put the offender in chains before his own adherents and carry him off for torture and questioning. However, the Bishop also mentioned that the Hungarians attended long discussions before reaching resolutions, whatever the matter in question. Grandees—barons, tribal chiefs and the offspring of immigrant knights—repaired to the royal court to confer with the king as moderator. They even took their own chairs with them. Sadly quoted time and again, especially in the context of the German image of Hungary, is the Bishop's derisive statement that he did not know whether to accuse fate or admire God's benevolence for giving such a magnificent country to such horrible barbarians.[3]

Hungarian historians have rightly pointed out that the bloody marauding raids and fear of the "Asiatic hordes" stuck much more firmly in the memory of Westerners than the Hungarians' positive achievements—for example, the establishment of a Christian kingdom by St Stephen with his German wife and the help of German knights and monks, or the fact that Stephen's successors invited German settlers into Hungary as colonists and that this distant, peculiar country developed increasingly into a bulwark of Christianity against the flood of invading Pechenegs, Kuns (Cumans) and Mongolian Turks.

For his time Coloman was an intelligent and enlightened ruler. He enacted the famous law against witch trials, "since there are no witches [*quia non sunt*]". He also fought the continuing influence over the people of the pagan *táltos* (shamans). In oral tradition and legend this appellation was also given to a mighty horse with magical properties, even though it was still applied to humans. Despite his law-making achievements and the mitigation of St Ladislaus' draconian punishments for theft (death for stealing a chicken), he was a man of his age. Like others members of the House of Árpád, he was embroiled in a fateful fraternal feud, and had his brother and small nephew blinded in order to secure the succession for his own son. However, this son died without issue and thus, like a century earlier, the branch of the outlawed pretender became once again the guarantor of the Árpáds' continued existence.

Despite the periodic and often bloody struggles for the succession within the dynasty, the most important heritage of St Stephen was secured: the political unity of the country's territory and its Christian allegiance. It has been estimated that since the Conquest Hungary's national territory, excluding Croatia, had doubled and the total population risen by around 1,200,000 to 2 million, a considerable figure for the time.

One cannot overestimate the role that the country's conscious turning to the West played in its move towards a position of significant power in southern Europe. As for German settlers, these were certainly not only noblemen, knights and monks: even about 1150 King Géza II invited peasants from the region around Aachen and the Moselle to settle necer Nagyszeben (Sibiu)—a group later known as Saxons. A royal charter of 1224 enumerated their privileges.[4]

The systematic German colonization in Hungary was carried out in two separate phases: under the Árpáds' settlement policy in the north and Transylvania, mainly to protect the Carpathian borders, and by the Habsburgs after the end of the Ottoman wars mainly in the south. Already at the beginning of the thirteenth century the Zipsers (the name is probably a transposition from Germany into the new homeland) formed a closed political entity. Around the middle of the thirteenth century numerous hill towns were established in Upper Hungary, whose inhabitants were almost exclusively German. Chroniclers mention Swabian inhabitants around Buda and Pest as early as 1217.

In later years the royal free towns were among the most important results of the Árpáds' settlement policy. "In Hungary it was the Hungarians who created the state and the Germans who established the towns," wrote the nineteenth-century linguist Paul Hunfalvy. "Just as the former were the principal factor in conquering the country, so the latter were in the development of society and trade."[5] This view is certainly not irrefutable, particularly because quite different economic and social factors influenced urban development and, especially in the early stages, Italians contributed to the creation and cultural growth of the city centres. However, the role of the Germans in the "century of the cities" was undoubtedly decisive.

In Transylvania too the Germans could claim special national and ecclesiastical rights, and the "Saxons" enjoyed political privileges there up till our own times. In conflicts between the Hungarian high nobility and the ruler of the day, the German knights and settlers always took the side of the ruler. The favour they enjoyed in consequence triggered off bloody skirmishes in Buda as early as 1439, and during the reform and revolutionary era of the first half of the nineteenth century mutual resentments between German and Hungarian townspeople were also vented in pogroms against the Jews, and thus run through the history of the Hungarian multiethnic state as a recurring *leitmotiv.*

The tolerant—one could almost call it "liberal"—attitude of the young Hungarian state towards the non-Hungarian ethnic groups accelerated not only the fusion of the Slavs with the Hungarians, but opened up the country to refugees from the steppes of southern Russia, who served as soldiers or were settled as frontier defenders. In the eleventh and twelfths centuries the Árpád dynasty offered refuge even to their former enemies, the infamous Pechenegs, soon followed by the Jazyges (Hung. Jász), also of Turkic origin. Mounted archers from the steppes were always welcome as auxiliary troops in the royal army. The immigration of the Cumans which had contradictory repercussions—of which more later—formed the completion of the massive influx of warlike horsemen from the East. Over the centuries their groups dissolved, and the warriors were absorbed through the Hungarians' extraordinary ability to assimilate. From that time onwards the Turkic people settled mostly in the Hungarian lowland plains between the Danube and the Tisza.

In regard to the Nazi race theories and the periodic flare-up of controversy over who are "pure" Hungarians, and the chasm between socalled "deep" and "superficial" Hungarians,[6] the German-Hungarian historian Denis Silagi emphasizes that "the Magyars' national character, as far as race-biology is concerned, cannot easily be proved to derive from their Eurasian ancestors. Hereditary factors may play an important role, but it is no less significant that there have always been innumerable typical Hungarians whose ancestors were Slavs, Germans, Romanians or Jews, and definitely not horsemen of the eastern world of the steppes."[7] The development before and after the Conquest, the massive waves of immigration and settlement, especially in the wake of the great national catastrophes of the thirteenth and seventeenth centuries, took place in the open plains of the Carpathian basin, its interior, which became the "melting pot" of nations.

At intervals over the years one encounters the phenomenon that the Hungarians were less united by blood relationships than by language—the belief in the cultural identification of the people with their mother tongue. Or, as the great poet Mihály Babits put it on the eve of the Second World War, "Hungary is a historical phenomenon, and how it developed is not a physical phenomenon but a spiritual one. [...] After all, the Hungarians are a mixed and constantly intermingling people."[8]

Béla III (1172–96), who had been brought up at the Byzantine court, was one of the outstanding and at the same time most cosmopolitan kings of the House of Árpád. In his reign Hungary experienced an unprecedented flowering both in the political sphere, domestic and foreign, and in ecclesiastical and cultural life. His first wife was Anne de Châtillon, a half-sister of the Byzantine Empress; his second was Margaret, daughter of the French King Louis VII, an important link between Hungary and the West. From a document found in a Paris archive it is known that Béla's remittances to his prospective father-in-law for the purpose of drawing up the marriage contract were equal to those of his English and French contemporaries and inferior only to those of the two Emperors. It merely typified the splendour of Béla's reign that in contrast to his predecessors, most of whom married daughters of Polish or Russian princes, he was able to enter into a dynastic relationship with the French royal house. The magnificent palace at Esztergom,* which Béla re-established as his main residence to signify the close link

---

* This town on the Danube was the seat of the prince-primate of the church, and thus had from the beginning a special significance which has lasted to the present.

between Church and state, was the work of French master-builders, yet another token of the absolute ruler's growing self-assurance. The king also kept in close contact with Byzantium. The Byzantine double-cross, later a component of the Hungarian coat of arms, made its first appearance as a Hungarian symbol on his coinage. However, despite the Orthodox influence, Hungary became increasingly anchored in the culture of the Latin West. The king established Cistercian monasteries, with monks brought from France. A significant part of the spiritual élite were educated in Paris. The Chronology mentions, for instance, that in 1192 Béla III sent the Hungarian student Elvin to study music in Paris and, two years later, Nicolaus Hungaricus (Miklós of Hungary) to Oxford.

In external affairs the king managed again to subject Dalmatia and Croatia to Hungarian overlordship, resulting in a fierce 200-year rivalry with Venice. Béla and his successor András II (his younger son), were also embroiled in the conflicts of the Russian princes, which led to Hungary temporarily having control over the principality of Halich, later Galicia. More important than these adventures, however, were the steps taken by the King to introduce the institution of the chancellery, written documents, and reform of the fiscal system.

Hungary's decline began in the reign of Béla's son. András II, a Western-style courtly king fond of extravagance and glory; wars were almost annual events, *inter alia* for the control of Galicia, and as costly as his lavish household, where a German, French and Italian queen in turn called the tune, and where murder and assassination were rife. His first queen, Gertrud, of the Bavarian Andechs-Meranian family, aroused the xenophobic anger of the high nobility because of her preferential treatment of her brothers and their large retinues. On 28 September 1213, during one of the King's numerous campaigns in the East, she fell victim to a bloody conspiracy; Bánk, the king's palatine, was its central figure. Six centuries later József Katona (1791–1830) became the author of the national drama *Bánk bán*, in which the palatine, as defender of his nation, accuses the "foreign" Queen and her family of oppressing the poor people, and kills her with a dagger during a dramatic confrontation. Ten years after Katona, Franz Grillparzer (1791–1872) also took up the subject, but adapted it in a diametrically opposite sense. In his play *Ein treuer Diener seines Herrn* (His master's loyal servant) the Queen is also murdered, but "Bancbanus", a loyal old man, remains unconditionally in the service of his ruler. "Bánk bán is a self-confident, proud oligarch; Bancbanus a reliable, worthy court official", is how a Hungarian literary critic characterizes the differing portrayals of Bánk from the Hungarian and Austrian viewpoints.[9]

On the other hand, the daughter of András and Gertrud, Elizabeth Margravine of Thuringia, brought great honour to Hungary and is revered to this day as a German saint. The medieval poet who tells how Klingsor, the sorcerer from Hungary, predicted the marriage and life of Elizabeth at the court of Eisenach describes a chivalrous Hungarian world under a pious king—a fruitful subject for myth and legend. In his profound essay on the Hungarian image in Europe Eckhardt observes: "It is possible that the explicitly sympathetic portrayal of Attila/Etzel and his Huns in the *Niebelungenlied* mirrors the German minstrels' relationship to the Hungarian court. Although Kriemhild's Huns are brave, they defeat the Germans only thanks to their superior numbers."[10] However, an Austrian scholar has conjectured that Gisela, the wife of St Stephen described in later tradition as gruesome and wicked, could have been the model for Kriemhild's negative traits in the *Niebelungenlied*. One can still agree today with Pukánszky's opinion that the question of how far German-Hungarian relationships influenced the development of the Niebelungen legend cannot be regarded as finally settled. As early as the time of Béla III, probably because of temporary alliances and dynastic links, Hungarians were no longer regarded by Byzantium as "barbaric and deceitful", as is demonstrated by the approving comments of a Byzantine chronicler on the Hungarian people who "have good horses and good weapons, wear iron and chainmail…, cannot be counted like the sand by the ocean, and are unsurpassed in boldness. Independent and freedom-loving, with heads held high, they are their own masters."[11]

In spite of such flattering remarks, emphasized with relief as "valuable contributions" in Hungarian historiography, aversion mixed with fear remained the dominant attitude throughout the world of learning in the West as well as public opinion. No one was disturbed by the fact that it merely echoed ancient portrayals of the Barbarians. Duke Albert of Austria, a future German king, wrote in

1291 after his unsuccessful venture into Hungary that Hungarians could be likened to the hydra: "Cut off one head, and thirty will grow in its place. They are evil, cunning and slip through one's fingers like eels: after a lost battle they will counter-attack with double the power, they emerge from the swamps like frogs."[12] And so on. Others beside the Babenbergs and Habsburgs had occasion to cross swords with the Hungarians of the House of Árpád: András II attained one of his few victories against the Teutonic Order, which tried in 1211 to detach the Burzenland, one of the three main Saxon territories in Transylvania, as well as the adjacent Cuman territory (in today's Romania), as an independent state for itself. This had the support of the papacy, which had put the land at their disposal for settlement, but András defeated this move in 1225.

In 1222 part of the high nobility and, especially, the propertied freemen, the king's servants (*servientes regis*) and others performing military service in the royal castles pushed through a highly significant document setting the agenda for the country's future. The rebellion was directed against the excessive giving away of estates and sources of income to a small circle of—partly foreign—favourites, but it was also a protest movement against the oligarchs' mismanagement and transgressions. András was made to enact the so-called Golden Bull (so-called for its golden seal) in which the King guaranteed the freedom of the royal military against the oligarchs and hence their release from the obligation to take part in wars beyond the country's borders, for the first time granting high dignitaries and nobles the right of armed resistance (*ius resistendi*) if he ruled unlawfully—a right which remained in force until 1687 as the Hungarian nation's special privilege. The King also promised not to devalue the currency and to make his economic reforms retrospective, such as the lease of customs, minting and salt rights to Jewish and Muslim finance officers, and not to give away offices or estates to foreigners without the council's consent. The motto of the happy-go-lucky and easygoing András II—"The measure of royal largesse is its immeasurability"—was to be for ever a thing of the past.

The Golden Bull was enacted only seven years after the English Magna Carta, and became over the centuries one of the pillars of national pride as the harbinger of freedom and civil liberties—"We and the English" became a common idiomatic catch-phrase. The main difference between the two documents was that in England the barons had once and for all done away with royal absolutism, while in Hungary the breakthrough was achieved by the free commoners against the barons. The Golden Bull affirmed the same political rights for all free inhabitants of the country, a collectivity which later usage knew as the "Hungarian nation", meaning the totality of all free men, i.e. the nobles. Although the supremacy of the oligarchy was not broken, the year 1222 was the origin of that broad, legally uniform noble middle stratum, which was to remain the foundation of the so-called political nation well into the nineteenth century.

The weakening of the royal power was the result of the development of large landholdings independent of the king. The political significance of the document, the *Gesta Hungarorum*, drafted by King Béla III's notary known only as Anonymus, should also be seen against this background. The mythical reconquest of Attila's heritage which it fabricated served as an alibi for later generations. By reverting to the Conquest, this chronicle was meant to underpin the rights of the great landholders and high nobility as descendants of the clan chiefs, and to secure for all time their claim to offices and seats on the royal council. The retrospective projection of the reciprocal contractual oaths on to earlier and no longer precisely ascertainable events was therefore no more than a tried and tested means to an end.

In contrast to András II, who in his immoderation and love of luxury had bestowed entire counties and royal estates on greedy aristocrats, his son and successor Béla IV (1235–70) endeavoured to re-establish royal authority. Earnest and pious, he began immediately after his accession to revoke a number of recent donations, even from the Church, yet his actions and probably also his severe demeanour aroused dislike and even anger, particularly among the disgruntled upper and middle landowner strata who were so important for defending the country. The King's unapproachability led to the custom whereby only written petitions were accepted. It was disastrous that domestic tensions rose precisely at a time when the Christian kingdom in the Carpathian basin was threatened by the heaviest calamity of its brief but glorious history: the invasion of Mongol nomad horsemen aiming for world domination.

5. The Mongol Invasion of 1241 and its Consequences

"In this year, after existing for 350 years, the kingdom of Hungary was annihilated by the Tatars." This terse statement by the Bavarian monk Hermann of Niederaltaich appears in the annals of his monastery for the year 1241. At almost the same time, the Emperor Frederick II wrote to the English King: "That entire precious kingdom was depopulated, devastated and turned into a barren wasteland." Contemporary witnesses and chroniclers still called the Asiatic attackers "Tatars", although these already identified themselves as Mongols.[1]

The "Mongol storm" had been in progress in Asia and Eastern Europe for half a generation, buffeting Russians, Cumans and Poles, yet Hungary was the first to be hit with full force by Genghis Khan's successors. On 11 April 1241 at Mohi by the confluence of the Sajó and Hernád rivers, the Mongol horsemen led by Batu Khan annihilated the numerically superior but ill-led and barricaded Hungarian forces. Amid indescribable chaos the majority of the country's religious and lay dignitaries were slaughtered, and it was as if by a miracle that the king and some of his young knights escaped. The Mongols followed in Béla's tracks as far as Klosterneuburg, near Vienna, and finally even besieged the Dalmatian island city of Trogir, where he had taken refuge: in the Mongols' eyes a country was not definitively vanquished while its rightful ruler still lived. For months the siege of Trogir continued, and the king and with him Hungary—indeed probably the West itself—were only saved by the sudden death of the Great Khan in far-away Karakorum. When this news reached Batu Khan in the spring of 1242, he promptly turned his Mongols around to be present at the contest for the succession. They pulled out of Hungary, laden with plunder and numerous prisoners: even thirteen years later, the missionaries Carpini and Rubruquis, travelling through the region of Karakorum, met Hungarian slaves still in bondage.

The Mongol storm resulted in a deep disruption for the Magyar population from which, according to medievalists such as György Györffy, Hungary never completely recovered. Györffy calculated that some 60 per cent of the lowland settlements were destroyed. The inhabitants who survived the massacres and abductions were threatened by starvation and disease. Failed harvests caused by destruction of the fields and the impossibility of tilling them added to the catastrophe. The situation was somewhat less severe in the regions west of the Danube, as these were only plundered and torched during the Mongols' advance and never occupied; here the population loss amounted to about 20 per cent. The Slavs of Upper Hungary as well as the Székelys and Romanians of the Transylvanian mountains had come off fairly lightly. In all, according to older estimates, about half of Hungary's 2 million inhabitants in 1240 became direct or indirect victims of the Mongol invasion.[2]

The attack did not take Béla IV by surprise since he, alone in Hungary and perhaps in all the West, had recognized the deadly danger posed by the Mongols' obsessive expansionist dreams of world domination. Owing to its still existing relationships with the Russian principalities, Hungary was quickly informed of events in the East, including the ruinous defeat of the Russians and Cumans by the nomad horsemen in 1223. Moreover, while still crown prince Béla had despatched a group of Dominican monks to the East in order to convert to Christianity the Hungarian tribes who, according to tradition, had remained in the old homeland; in his search for Magna Hungaria, the land of the early Magyars, Friar Julian actually came across people beyond the Volga with whom he could communicate in Hungarian, and it was from these "relatives" that he heard of the Mongols' unstoppable westerly advance. After their return in 1237 one of the friars wrote an account of his travels and sent it to Rome. When Julian set out a second time on his adventurous journey to the East to scout out the Mongols' intentions, he could no longer reach the ruined homeland of the distant tribesmen, who had by then been overwhelmed. Julian hurried back to Hungary with the terrible news and accurate information about the Mongols' military preparations. Furthermore, he brought a threatening letter from Batu Khan to King Béla, calling upon him to surrender and hand over the "Cuman slaves" who had taken refuge in Hungary. Béla did not reply to the ultimatum. However, unlike the Pope and the Emperor, who had for years been entangled in a controversy over the primacy of Rome, the King took the Mongol threat seriously, being fully aware that if the charges and demands were ignored by those threatened, a devastating campaign would always follow.

Béla IV therefore suspected what was in store for his country, and prepared for battle. He personally inspected the borderlands, had defence installations prepared on the mountain passes, and tried to assemble a strong army. It was not his fault that, despite these precautions and warnings to the Hungarian nobles, and appeals to the Pope, Emperor Frederick II and the kings of Western Europe, the Mongols descended upon Hungary and wrought devastation following their victory at Mohi. Though intelligent and brave. Béla was not a general and did not have a powerful professional army at his disposal. Even before his father's Golden Bull the nation's warriors, formerly ever ready for battle, had become "comfortable landowners"[3] and were no longer a match for the Mongol hordes operating with remarkable precision and planning.

Another factor was present, with consequences hardly ever considered by Western historians with no knowledge of the Hungarian language although it had decisive consequences already in the earliest days of the Hungarian state, and contributed to other great disruptions in the nation's history—defeat by the Ottomans and Habsburgs. This factor was an ambivalence towards everything foreign. Oscillation between openness and isolation, between generous tolerance and apprehensive mistrust was probably the main cause of the essentially tragic conflict with the ethnic group which would eventually form the backbone of the Hungarian army: the Cumans. Although this Turkic people had repeatedly attacked Hungary in the past, they later sought refuge and support from the Magyars, especially in view of the unstoppable advance of the Mongols. While still crown prince, Béla endorsed the Cumans' conversion by the Dominicans and accepted the oath of allegiance of one of their princes who converted together with 15,000 of his people—a bishopric was established for these so-called "western"

Cumans. Ten years later the "eastern" Cumans also fled from the Mongols across the Carpathians, giving Béla the support of another 40,000 mounted warriors against the impending invasion from Asia. Before admitting them he had them baptized, yet the integration of this nomad people into the by then Christianized and westernized Hungarian society led to tensions and rioting. When the Mongol offensive was already approaching, the distrustful Hungarian nobles attacked and murdered the Cuman Prince Kötöny, whereupon his soldiers, swearing vengeance, took off to Bulgaria leaving in their wake a trail of carnage and destruction. Thus four weeks before the crucial battle at Mohi the King lost his strongest allies.

The same groups of nobles who had aggravated existing tensions in the early phase of the Cumans' assimilation then complied only hesitantly and reluctantly with the king's appeals to be in readiness with their contingents. In their accounts the two important witnesses of the Mongol onslaught, Master Rogerius and Thomas of Spalato, revealed clearly the profound differences between the king and a section of the magnates. According to a contemporary French chronicler, Batu Khan heartened his soldiers before the battle of Muhi with the following derogatory slogan: "The Hungarians, confused by their own discords and arrogance, will not defeat you." The barons, as already mentioned, were incensed mainly by the fact that Béla sought to withdraw his father's prodigal donations, and that he overrode their opposition in bringing the Cumans into the country and then giving them preferential treatment. They even spread the rumour that the Cumans had come to Hungary, as the Mongols' allies, to stab the Hungarians in the back at the first opportunity.

The Italian cleric and chronicler Rogerius, who lived through the Mongol invasion, saw this differently. He praised Béla IV as one of the most notable of Hungary's rulers, who had done a great service to the Church by his missionary work among the pagan people: he had tried—as they deserved—to subdue the "audacious insolence" and insubordination of his barons, who did not balk even at committing high treason. Rogerius defended Béla against the accusation of not having taken steps in time to avert the danger from the Mongols. On the contrary, the nobles had been urged early and repeatedly to gather their regiments and rally to the King.

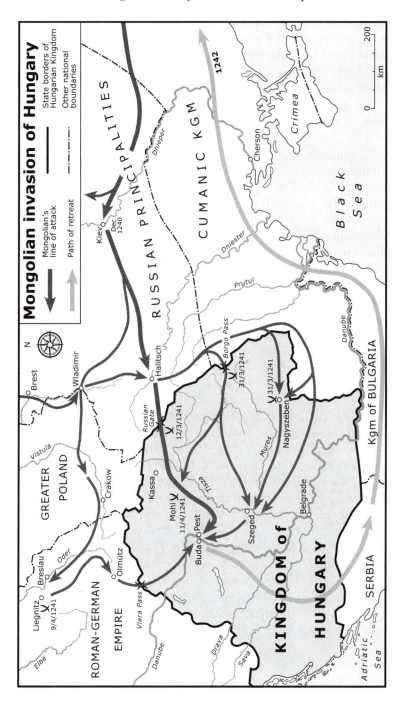

Despite Béla's obvious inability to impose order on the army, Rogerius blamed the nobles whose antagonism to the King not only denied him vital support in the battle, but virtually willed his downfall—"because they thought that the defeat would only affect some of them and not all."

Added to the mistrust of foreigners and the discord within their own ranks was the indifference of a silent Western world. The priestly chronicler accuses the European princes of failure to answer the Hungarian King's calls for help; none of Hungary's friends had come to its aid in its misfortune. Rogerius does not exclude even the Pope or the Emperor from blame; all had miserably failed. In a letter to Pope Vincent IV Béla wrote in 1253: "We have received from all sides…merely words. […] We have received no support in our great affliction from any Christian ruler or nation in Europe." The Mongol nightmare determined, consciously or unconsciously, not only the King's exchange of letters with the various popes and potentates, but also his foreign policy. By far the most important and lasting psychological consequence of the Mongol invasion was the inference "We Hungarians are alone". The sense of isolation, so characteristic of Hungarians, hardened from then on into a "loneliness complex" and became a determining component of the Hungarian historical image. The calamities of the sixteenth, nineteenth and twentieth centuries set this reaction into concrete.

Fear of a second Mongol invasion was bizarrely echoed even in King Béla's dynastic policy. He wrote in a letter to the Pope: "In the interests of Christianity, we let our royal dignity suffer humiliation by betrothing two of our daughters to Ruthenian princes and the third to a Pole, in order to receive through them and other foreigners in the East news about the secretive Tatars." Clearly an even greater sacrifice, mentioned in the same letter, was the marriage of his firstborn son to a Cuman girl; this was supposed to bind the warlike nomad horsemen, called back a few years after the Mongol attack to the depopulated areas of the Danube-Tisza plains, even closer to the House of Árpád, and hasten their absorption into the Western Christian community.

The aversion to foreigners, even when they were urgently needed as allies; the friction within their own ranks, even in times of extreme danger; and finally the justified sense of aloneness and being at the mercy of others, formed the background to the first catastrophe in the history of the Christian Hungarian kingdom. That the Hungarians felt misjudged, betrayed and besieged by enemies was probably also, or perhaps primarily, the result of what is unanimously criticized in international historiography as "brazen blackmail". The Austrian Babenberg Duke, Frederick II, set a trap for the fleeing King of Hungary (his cousin and neighbour, not to be confused with the Hohenstaufen Emperor) robbed and imprisoned him. The Austrian was already nicknamed "the Quarrelsome" because he had fallen out with most of his neighbours, even having been temporarily outlawed and divested of his fief in 1236 by the Emperor.

Rogerius, who—as mentioned above—had lived through the Mongol invasion as an eye-witness and was himself imprisoned for a year, described this deed in the thirty-second chapter of his account:

After his flight from the hordes the King rode day and night until he reached the Polish border region: from there he hurried, as fast as he could, by the direct route to the Queen, who stayed on the border with Austria. On hearing this the Duke of Austria came to meet him with wicked intentions in his heart, but feigning friendship. The King had just laid down his weapons and, while breakfast was being prepared, lain down to sleep on the bank of a stretch of water, having by an act of divine providence made his long escape alone from many horrible arrows and swords, when he was awakened. As soon as he beheld the Duke he was very happy. Meanwhile the Duke, after saying other comforting words, asked the King to cross the Danube, to have a more secure rest on the opposite bank, and the King, suspecting no evil, consented because the Duke had said that he owned a castle on the other side where he could offer more befitting hospitality—he intended not to entertain the King but to destroy him. While the King still believed he could get away from Scylla, he fell victim to Charybdis, and like the fish that tries to escape from the frying pan and jumps into the fire, believing that it has escaped misfortune, he found himself in an even more difficult situation because the Duke of Austria seized hold of him by cunning, and dealt with him according to his whim. He demanded from him a sum of money which he claimed the King had once extorted from him. What then? The King could not get away until he had counted out part of that money in coin and another part in gold and silver vessels, finally pledging three adjacent counties of his kingdom.[4]

According to Rogerius, Duke Frederick robbed the Hungarian refugees and invaded the defenceless country with his army. He even
attempted to capture Pressburg (now Bratislava) and Győr, which
however managed to defend themselves. The chronicler did not
realize that Duke Frederick II and Béla IV had old scores to settle.
Frederick had attacked Hungary several times since 1233, and had
supported an uprising by Hungarian magnates against their King.
When András II and his sons. Béla and Coloman, resisted and
chased him back to Vienna, the duke could obtain a peace agreement only in return for a costly fine. He had never forgotten this
humiliation, and now, against the admonitions of Pope Gregory IX,
exploited the Hungarians' desperate situation.

The historian Günther Stökl referred to the "understandably very
negative impression" which "the treachery of its western neighbour
left in Hungarian historical consciousness".[5] As is well-known,
none of the Central and East European states have school textbooks
that treat in a particularly balanced way their own and their region's
history. Still, the chasm is rarely as wide as in the depiction of the
episode described by Rogerius. Thus the Hungarian historian
Bálint Hóman (1935): "Frederick… capped the disgraceful offence
against the right of hospitality to the greater glory of Christian solidarity with an attack on the country suffering under the Tatars."
The Austrian historian Hugo Hantsch (1947) saw the role of the
Babenberg Duke differently: "Frederick… stops the Tatars' advance
to Germany… Austria once again proves its worth as the bulwark
of the Occident, as the shield of the Empire."

It was an irony of fate indeed that the moribund kingdom was
successful against the expansionist attempts of Duke Frederick of
Austria in particular. After Frederick's death in the battle at the
Leitha in June 1246 Béla even got involved in the succession struggle of the Babenbergs and brought Styria temporarily under his
control, his son and successor becoming its prince for some years.
However, after a serious defeat by Ottokar II of Bohemia at Marchegg
in Austria, the Hungarians were no longer able to assert themselves.
The "annihilation of the kingdom of Hungary"—the laconic diagnosis of the Bavarian monk quote at the beginning of this chapter—
never actually came to pass. On the contrary, Béla IV steeled himself
after his return for the enormous task of rebuilding the ravaged

country, especially the depopulated lowland and eastern areas, which he did with considerable energy, resolve and courage.

Béla, not unjustly dubbed in his country as its second founder after St Stephen for his statesmanship and achievements, still had twenty-eight years ahead of him after the departure of the Mongols. Like Stephen, he was a ruler who practised openness, and the prime mover in an extensive policy of colonization. His realm extended over the entire Carpathian basin and embraced Croatia-Slavonia, Dalmatia and part of Bosnia. The reason why he so quickly regained his political power is partly that the most densely populated western areas of the country were those least affected by the Mongol depredations. Still, his entire domestic and external politics were always haunted by the nightmare of a renewed Mongol incursion, which led to the organizing of a completely new defensive system. The fact that only some castles had withstood the Mongol attacks showed that only well-built forts offered genuine security. That is why the King wanted to see so many cities and smaller places encircled by stone walls. He created a new powerful army, replacing the light archers with a force of heavy cavalry.

Béla managed to resettle the Cumans on the Great Plains, and this foreign tribe came to play an outstanding role in the new army. In his previously cited letter to Pope Innocent IV he wrote: "Unfortunately we now defend our country with pagans, and with their help we bring the enemies of the Church under control." The Alan Jazyges, originally also steppe horsemen from the East, settled in the country with the Cumans. A royal document of 1267 states that the King had called peasants and soldiers from all parts of the world into the country to repopulate it. German colonists as well as Slovaks, Poles and Ruthenes thus came into Upper Hungary (today's Slovakia); Germans and Romanians, but also many Hungarians, moved to Transylvania. Soon French, Walloon, Italian and Greek migrants moved to the cities. The Jewish communities of Buda (newly fortified as a royal seat), Esztergom and Pressburg were under the King's personal protection. Already by 1050, according to the *Historical Chronology of Hungary* by Kálmán Benda, Esztergom was a centre for Jewish traders who maintained the business connection between Russia and Regensburg and are said to have built a synagogue. Minting was assigned to the archbishopric of Esztergom, which in turn entrusted the task to a Jew from Vienna named Herschel.

King Béla finally had to pay a high political price to the predominantly narrow-minded, selfish oligarchs for the surprisingly fast reconstruction, the promotion of urban development and—his priority—the establishment of a new army. The disastrous concentration of power in the hands of the great magnates remained in force, and in stark contrast to Béla's radical measures and the reforms passed before the Mongol attack, they were able to assert their old privileges and, even more serious, they were not after all required to return the royal estates and castles, but even received further endowments. This soon created chaotic conditions.

During the last decade of his reign Béla was already embroiled in a serious conflict with his son, the later Stephen V, who was strong in military virtues but power-hungry. Stephen's rule as sole king lasted only two years; he could not control the mounting tensions between the power of the oligarchs—who by now were feuding among themselves, as were some of the senior clergy—and the lower nobility, who had been supported by Béla as their counterbalance through the granting of privileges. But it was the particularly explosive and unresolved issue of the absorption of the Cuman horsemen into the Hungarian environment which once again impinged disastrously on the royal house itself. Although the Cumans were a mainstay of the new army, especially in campaigns outside Hungary's borders, the complete socio-religious and linguistic assimilation of the tens of thousands of former nomad horsemen took another two to three centuries.

The marriage of Béla's son Stephen to Elizabeth, daughter of the treacherously assassinated Cuman prince Kötöny, was meant to seal a lasting reconciliation with this ethnic group. The plan was to give the Cumans parity of treatment with the nobility, but Stephen's untimely death brought an abrupt end to these endeavours.

Stephen's son Ladislaus IV (1272–90) was still a child, and the Queen Mother Elizabeth, who called herself "Queen of Hungary, daughter of the Cuman Emperor", proved to be a puppet in the hands of the power-hungry oligarchs and blatant favourites, and thus totally unfitted for the task of regency. She and her son trusted only Cumans, hindering rather than fostering the precarious process of integration by their exaggerated and demonstrative partiality towards the steppe warriors.

Only once did the young King Ladislaus IV show his mettle—by a historic action at a decisive moment for Austria's future. It happened on the battlefield of Dürnkrut, where the army of Hungarians and Cumans, estimated at 15,000 men, resolved the conflict between Rudolf of Habsburg and Ottokar II of Bohemia. In the words of the Hungarian historian Péter Hanák, "In the battle of the Marchfeld [Dürnkrut] Hungarian arms helped establish the power-base and imperial authority of the Habsburgs." Apart from this, the life of the young King, already known in his lifetime as "Ladislaus the Cuman" (Kún László), was an uninterrupted series of scandals, intrigues and bloody settling of scores. The passionate, spirited and, according to tradition, continuously love-struck King for some reason refused to produce a successor with his wife, the Angevin Princess Isabella of Naples, and had her locked up in a convent. When his pagan following and numerous mistresses resulted in a papal interdict, the psychopathic monarch threatened (as the Archbishop expressed it in a letter to the Pope) "to have the Archbishop of Esztergom, his bishops and the whole bunch in Rome decapitated with a Tatar sabre". Incidentally, Ladislaus IV is supposed to have performed the sex act with his Cuman mistress during a Council meeting in the presence of the dignitaries and high clergy. He was excommunicated, and finally killed at the age of twenty-eight by two Cumans hired by the Hungarian magnates.

Ladislaus died without issue and anarchy followed. Groups of oligarchs ruled their spheres of interest as if they were family estates, and considered the entire country theirs for the taking, dividing it up between themselves. The last Árpád king, András III, was unable to re-establish central authority or prevent the country's disintegration. He died in 1301, leaving only an infant daughter, and with him the male line of the Árpáds died out. Years of struggle for the coveted throne of Hungary, by now recognized as a member of the European community of states, resulted in 1308 in the victory of the Angevin Charles Robert, grandson of Mary of Naples, sister of Ladislaus IV.

In the long run the politically and, above all, psychologically most significant heritage of the time of "Ladislaus the Cuman" was the "new historical image" of the Hungarians, invented from A to Z by his court preacher Simon Kézai. In his famous letter to the Pope, King Béla still compared the Mongols with Attila and his murderous and fire-raising Huns. Barely a generation later, between 1281 and 1285, the grandson's court scribe saw the Huns in a quite different light. Kézai, a gifted storyteller, perceived Attila as a worthy ancestor of the Christian kings. From sources he found "all around Italy, France and Germany" this court cleric, a man of simple background, calling himself in his preface an enthusiastic adherent of King Ladislas IV, concocted the evidently desired historical image. He produced the surprising theory of a "Dual Conquest": the original 108 clans had in the distant past already made up the same people—who at that time were the Huns, and were now the Hungarians. Coming from Scythia, they had already occupied Pannonia once before, around the year 700, and under Attila conquered half the world. They then retreated to Scythia, finally settling permanently in Pannonia. The 108 clans of 1280 were thus, according to Simon Kézai, the descendants of the original community—without any mingling. Thus was born a historical continuity which had never existed.

This "inventive dreamer", noted Jenö Szücs, supplied a historical, legal and even "moral" basis for the Magyars' "historical right" to the Carpathian basin and for the resolute self-assertion of the lower nobility in their fight for existence in spite of the oligarchs. The ambitious petty nobility were akin to the will of the community of free warriors as the source of princely power. In his essay *Nation and History* Szücs[6] destroyed the royalist cleric's new national concept, which presented the nation of nobles as the buttress of legitimate royal power, threatened by the magnates. In contrast to Western interpretations, Kézai rehabilitated Attila and indeed the entire Hun era. One could easily shrug off these flights of fancy had they not determined the historical self-image of the Hungarian nobility and national historiography well into modern times. Ladislaus Rosdy, the Austro-Hungarian publicist, stressed in an essay on Hungary the alarming long-term effect of this historical fiction, which had virtually become common property:

In all this time there have not been any Hungarians—apart perhaps from a critically-minded minority well educated in history—who have not been convinced by Master Kézai's obviously falsified Hun saga; and even among the otherwise sensitive Hungarian poets of the twentieth century there are many who proudly keep up this tradition, which in reality is no more than the expression, by the "last of the Nomads", of superiority mixed with resignation.[7]

The theory of the "Dual Conquest" was the spring from which historians, scientists and national politicians have drawn at their convenience. The romantic and heroic character of the Hun saga as told by Anonymus and especially by Kézai held an almost irresistible attraction for generations of politicians and writers, the intensity of which is to this day admitted only in secret. Even Count István Széchenyi, the statesman criticized for his qualified royalist sentiments, wrote in his diary on 21 November 1814:

It is proof enough of the fact that I come from the truest race of the Huns that I can never feel as emotional, expansive and enthusiastic in the most beautiful Alps of Switzerland, or fertile valleys and areas of Italy as in the empty plains of my fatherland. […] I have a quite unusual passion for those cataclysmic, devastating wars. […] One of Attila's innumerable horsemen, with whom he laid waste every country, seems according to my own mood, if I dissociate myself completely from all culture and logic, to have been a very happy man.[8]

These words, published only decades after the suicide of Széchenyi, whose career and role are discussed in detail later, give a most revealing picture of the Hungarian psyche. They show the extent to which freedom, courage and soldierly virtues are valued as Hungarian attributes, while others, such as tolerance and political wisdom, demonstrably qualities of most of the Árpád kings, are often overlooked. Be that as it may, it is no exaggeration that there are few nations (perhaps the Serbs come to mind) to which Ernest Renan's words "No nation [exists] without falsification of its own history" are more pertinent than Hungary.

6. Hungary's Rise to Great Power Status under Foreign Kings

With the extinction of the Árpád dynasty in 1301 Hungary entered upon a period of rule by foreign kings, some from far away: among them four Neapolitans of the House of Anjou, a Luxemburger, two Habsburgs and three Jagiellos from Poland and Bohemia. In the 225 years up to the catastrophe of Mohács there was only one locally-born Hungarian king: Mátyás Hunyadi, called Mathias Corvinus. And even he, traditionally the most admired of Hungarians, was of Romanian origin on his father's side.

The nearly eight decades of the French-Italian Angevins' rule blossomed into an economic and political golden age. From the hopeless chaos of the oligarchs' conflicts a centralized, well-managed state emerged, with an economic and fiscal policy that laid the foundations of the country's rise to the status of a great power in medieval Europe. Charles I (the name Charles Robert took as king), was able to isolate the mightiest oligarchs and crush the most important clans in a decisive battle (1312) with the help of the lower nobility and German burghers from the mining towns, as well as determined support from the papal legate Cardinal Gentile. Nonetheless the King waited more than ten years until he dared to transfer his capital from the city of Temesvár in southeastern Hungary to the centrally situated Visegrád. However, the temporarily peripheral royal seat did not hinder Charles I from preparing a radical fiscal reform, and promoting the foundation of new townships by carefully distributed privileges. The place of the disempowered oligarchs was taken by fifty to 100 noble families, on whose royalist loyalties the King could completely rely.

In addition to trade, the rising prosperity of medieval Hungary was based above all on the rich reserves of precious metals. It has been estimated that of all the gold produced in the then known world one-third came from Hungary and two-thirds from Africa. While almost all the African gold remained in the Muslim orient, four-fifths of the European demand was met by Hungary. The country's production of silver also increased, and is said to have made up about a quarter of all the silver mined in Europe. Gold production was effectively stimulated by the establishment of new towns in the mountain regions, as well as by liberalization of mining leases. Furthermore, the King's power-base was consolidated by tax and customs revenues, as well as by precious-metal and coinage monopolies which he introduced. Charles I decreed the minting of gold coins (forint) on the Florentine model, which became a generally accepted and sought-after currency all over Europe.

The King paid most attention to boosting colonization. Slovaks, Czechs, Ruthenes, Poles, Romanians and, last but not least, German mountain-dwellers were invited into the country. Although demographic estimates for the fourteenth and fifteenth centuries still fluctuate, it can be assumed that the during the time of Charles I the population again attained the level of the period before the Mongol invasions, i.e. approximately 2 million.

The cities at the crossroads of great international trade routes were particularly promoted. Esztergom and Székesfehérvár, the most important cities of the Árpád period, had to yield precedence to Buda, the trade centre at the site where the Danube issued from the low mountain ranges and entered the plains, which thus developed into the capital.

In 1335 a historic meeting took place at the invitation of Charles I at Visegrád, 60 km. north of Buda at the Danube bend, with Kings John of Bohemia and Casimir of Poland and attended also by Henry of Wittelsbach, Duke of Lower Bavaria. Polish-Bohemian differences were settled at this conference, and the three kings agreed that in future their western commerce would be diverted to the Prague-Brno route and for Eastern Hungary via Cracow, by-passing Vienna which had insisted on the lucrative role as intermediary. It was therefore of profound symbolic significance when almost 660 years later the heads of state and government of the then Czechoslovakia and Poland met in Visegrád—where only ruins of the former royal castle remain—at the invitation of the Hungarian government to set the agenda for their co-operation after the collapse of Communism. The term "Visegrád states", used in the international conference jargon, originates from this meeting, though with few of the commentators realizing the historical connections.

It was not only through the promotion of economic ties and his peace diplomacy that Charles I secured Hungary its position in the concert of European powers. His dynastic policy served the same purpose: his first wife was a Russian princess from Galicia, the second came from Bohemia from the House of Luxemburg, the third was the sister of King John of Bohemia, and the fourth, Elisabeth, was the daughter of the Polish King Vladislav Lokietek, thus ensuring the House of Anjou's claim to the Polish throne. The marriage of Charles's sons Lajos (Louis) and Endre were to serve further dynastic ambitions in the North and South. Charles could not foresee that his successful and peace-oriented foreign and dynastic policy would sow the seeds of future conflicts. At any rate, the King was able during his long reign to consolidate the borders in the north and west, and recover Pressburg from the Austrian Habsburgs.

A mysterious incident concerning this ruler, who was concerned more about mediation than confrontation, still created waves hundreds of years later. The great Hungarian poet János Arany wrote a famous ballad (*ca.* 1860) centred on Klára Zách, the Polish Queen's exquisitely beautiful lady-in-waiting, who was allegedly seduced or even raped by the Queen's brother Casimir, the future king of Poland. Consequently her father Felicián Zách, a rich magnate, burst with drawn sword into the dining hall of the castle at Visegrád, where the mid-day repast was being served to the royal family, and hacked off four of Queen Elisabeth's fingers before he himself was killed by guards. The poet described the repercussions:

> Your fingers are bleeding.
> But not bleeding in vain:
> What is your wish, royal lady
> What your deserved claim?
>
> For my index finger
> His beautiful young daughter,
> For my lost thumb his
> Grown-up son's slaughter:

For my other two fingers
Whose blood in rivulets ran.
I desire for ever after
The lives of his whole clan.

(transl. by Ann Major)

If this is what happened, the true motives, as so often, are unknown. Possibly this was a political conflict between the King and the most notorious oligarch of the time, in which the oligarch's daughter served merely as a pretext, or was made into one. Be that as it may, the crime of the brother of a foreign queen (as in the case of the German Queen Gertrud a century earlier) must have been regarded as a national disgrace, and the justified revenge would have lived on in the minds of the people and as a literary topic.

Louis I, eldest son and successor of Charles I born in Visegrád in 1326, is the only wearer of the Hungarian crown to whom the sobriquet "the Great" (Nagy Lajos) has been given by tradition and in historiography. Up till the mid-twentieth century the four decades of Louis the Great's era were considered the most glorious epoch in Hungarian history. He was said to have accomplished the "foreign-political dream of the Árpáds—the medieval Hungarian Great Power" as asserted by, among others, Bálint Hóman, the leading historian of the Horthy era. Today one is more sceptical regarding such ambitions ("Anjou power astride the Adria") and in particular the frequent and costly campaigns in the Balkans and northern Europe. Contemporaries and court chroniclers saw only the successes in battle and temporary territorial expansion of Hungary, the Great Power. Today historical scholarship stresses rather the unrealistic character of his concepts and their fateful consequences— especially in the context of the later Ottoman domination.

After the elimination of the oligarchs, peace generally reigned in the interior of the country—then about 300,000 square km. with roughly 3 million inhabitants. Also "no enemy trod on Hungarian soil" during the reign of Louis, according to a late-nineteenth-century treatise. In a spectacular series of adventures Louis even managed temporarily to create a gigantic bloc of territories reaching from the Baltic to the Adriatic. Hardly a year passed without campaigns, and Louis succeeded too in establishing a *cordon sanitaire* of vassal states from Bosnia to Wallachia. Even the rulers of Serbia, northern Bulgaria and Venice acknowledged him as their suzerain for a few years, if only as a formality. His greatest military victory was without doubt the conquest of Dalmatia. Despite Venetian resistance, he retained the upper hand and brought the coastline from Ragusa (Dubrovnik) as far north as Fiume (Rijeka), together with the offshore islands, under Hungarian control: this lasted for several decades.

Louis I waged his most costly wars in southern Italy with the Neapolitan crown as the prize. To attain it for Hungary, Charles I had arranged the betrothal of his younger son András to Johanna, heiress to the kingdom, with the proviso that the Hungarian prince would succeed her father, Robert, on his throne, when the latter died. Paying out enormous sums in bribes, András's widowed mother obtained papal dispensation for the two of them to marry. However, when the time came for András to ascend the throne, neither Johanna nor the Pope, let alone the people, would accept a stranger as ruler of Naples. In 1345, with Johanna's active connivance, one of her numerous lovers murdered András, the first of her four husbands. King Louis I regarded himself as his brother's rightful heir, and to secure the throne for his small child and take revenge, undertook two great campaigns in 1347 and 1350 against Naples, one by land, the other by sea. Although he won both of them, the Pope refused to have Johanna deposed, and as soon as Louis left, the phony regime secured by Hungarian and German mercenaries collapsed. After suffering heavy losses and costs he finally gave up the idea of a lasting foothold in Naples. It was at the time when two or three rival Popes reigned simultaneously that Louis' kinsman Charles of Durazzo was able in 1382 finally to occupy Naples with the help of another Pope and Hungarian troops. The news that the faithless Johanna had been strangled reached Louis the Great on his deathbed.

Louis I also moved against the North. When Casimir III "the Great" of Poland died without male issue in 1370, Louis was elected as his brother-in-law's successor by virtue of a dynastic compact concluded three decades earlier. The fact that his mother was Polish and that he had assisted his uncle in three of his wars against the Lithuanians smoothed his way. However, this was not incorporation of Poland into the Hungarian state, as nationalistic Hungarian historiography has sometimes implied. Considering the Turkish menace, as well as Poland's daunting domestic and foreign problems, the personal union was actually more of a burden than a success for the ailing ruler. Twelve years later, after the death of Louis I, the personal union of Poland and Hungary rapidly broke up although special links were maintained. Hedvig, the younger daughter of Louis, had married Jagiello, Grand Prince of Lithuania, who had converted to Christianity and become King Vladislav II of Poland. Poland's rise to the status of a major power began under the newly established Jagiello dynasty, with Queen Hedvig as progenitrix.

Hungary's significant role under Louis I—in Poland, Naples, Dalmatia, Wallachia and, from time to time, Bosnia—was due to family relationships and a marriage contract. The widowed King had married Elizabeth Kotromanovic, daughter of the *ban* of Bosnia who was related to the Árpáds, and thereafter, being fervently religious, he sought to combat the Bosnian Gnostic sect of Bogomils, which regarded the world as a creation of the devil. As an expression of his unconditional loyalty to the "true religion" and as a gesture towards the Holy Roman Empire, Louis had a Hungarian chapel added to the imperial cathedral at Aachen, which was to receive the relics of Christ, hitherto housed in the treasury. Europe acknowledged the Hungarian King as truly "Great" and a saintly man. More important for his people, however, was the founding of the first (short-lived) Hungarian university in Pécs in 1367.

Louis the Great also lived on in the memory of his subjects and foreign contemporaries as a universally loved, true paladin distinguished not least for his extraordinary physical courage in battle. However, one can also look at it from another angle: next to hunting, Louis regarded war as his favourite pastime. The historian Georges Duby's words, describing the medieval ideal and spirit, seem exactly to apply to this knightly king: "... the intoxication of slaughter, pleasure in bloodshed and destruction—in the evening a battlefield littered with bodies. [...] The overpowering figure of the knight steps into the limelight... a system of values based entirely on the enjoyment of pillage and largesse, and of attack."[1] Occasions for these were plentiful, particularly as Louis, contrary to the supposed

Hungary under King Louis I (the Great) of Anjou, 1342-82

temporary rule

Hungarian influence

Baltic Sea

Lands of the Teutonic Order

Poznán

Warsaw

Bug

Kalisch

Kgm of POLAND

Oder

Elbe

Grand Duchy of LITHUANIA

HOLY ROMAN

Vistula

Crakow

Lemberg

Principality of Halic (later Galicia)

EMPIRE

Trenczén

Halitsch

Danube

Pozsony (Pressburg)

Kgm of

Esztergom

Tisza

Principality of Moldavia

Buda Pest

Nagyvárad

Jassy

Drava

HUNGARY

Kolozsvár

Dniester

Zagreb

Pécs

Kalocsa

Transylvania

Siret

Prutul

Sava

Slavonia

Szeben

Brassó

1308-87 Anjou
1387-1437 Luxemburg

Croatia

Belgrade

Principality of Wallachia
intermittently Hungarian vassal

Danube

Spalato

BOSNIA

Bánság

BULGARIA

Black Sea

Ragusa

Kosovo Polje
1389
(Field of Blackbirds)

Adriatic Sea

Kgm of SERBIA

OTTOMAN

Constantinople

Naples
(Under Hungarian rule 1348-51)

Kgm of NAPLES

EMPIRE

Kgm of SICILY

0   200
km

gentleness persistently attributed to him, had a fiery temperament. For example, he flew into a rage in 1361 because the Emperor Charles IV had made a disparaging comment about his mother, Queen Elisabeth, and immediately ordered a general mobilization and invaded Moravia at the head of his troops. On the other hand, some contemporary observers admired him as a man of peace. The Venetian envoy wrote: "I call God to witness that I never saw a monarch more majestic or more powerful, or one who desires peace and calm as much as he." Another contemporary, quoted by Macartney, noted: "There was no other so kind and noble, so virtuous and magnanimous, so friendly and straightforward."[2]

The brilliance of his court, its culture moulded by Italian and French influence, the generous gifts to his loyal barons and, last but by no means least, the possibilities offered to the minor nobility by the numerous campaigns to distinguish and perhaps enrich themselves, enabled the Angevin kings to rule the country as they saw fit without convoking the Diet for sixty years. However, Louis confirmed the Golden Bull of 1222 granting "the very same liberty" to all nobles, and confirmed the traditional law of inheritance whereby all land was entailed in the male line of the owner's family. This commitment (known as *aviticitas*), which remained in force until 1848, proved harmful in the long run because the cementing of noble land ownership within a family impeded the development of agriculture, and created an insurmountable barrier between free and bond.

At the end of Louis' reign about fifty families owned one-third of the Hungarian land area. Their status was further enhanced by the system of military service introduced by the Angevins, whereby the nobility, who did not have to pay taxes, had to bear arms. The magnates were permitted to command troops under their own banners with their own followers (*familiares*). If a force numbered as many as fifty men, it served under its lord's banner and was known as his *banderium*; many minor nobles took service in these units. As a result of these innovations a considerable part of the lower nobility, among them in particular followers performing military service, became directly dependent on the oligarchs.

After the death of King Louis history appears to have repeated itself. He left no sons, and a power vacuum came about similar to that after the extinction of the Árpáds, which the mighty oligarchs exploited for their own purposes. Louis I had destined his elder daughter Maria—who at eleven years old was betrothed to Margrave Sigismund of Luxemburg, son of Emperor Charles IV—to succeed him on both his thrones, but when the Poles terminated their personal union with Hungary, crowning the younger daughter Hedvig as their queen, bitter conflict broke out among the rival magnates. Thus Maria was crowned "King" and the violent, autocratic and reckless Dowager Queen Elisabeth took over the regency from her base in Bosnia. On the question of female succession the Hungarian nobles were divided, and the guardianship of the widely hated Queen Mother was strongly resisted. A Hungarian group enforced the crowning of the girl's cousin Charles of Durazzo, known as "the Little", and this started a series of bloody vendettas and assassinations among the power-hungry and greedy magnates, whose intrigues and feuds were as abstruse as the plot of a Verdi opera.

At the first meeting of the "little" King Charles with Maria and her mother, the Dowager Queen, in the royal castle of Visegrád, the latter handed Charles a document, and while he was studying it a magnate from the Queens' entourage attacked him with a battle-axe. He died, fatally wounded, a few days later, having reigned for thirty-nine days—the stuff of numerous ballads. Charles's retinue fled to the group of oligarchs resident in the south who, after seemingly conciliatory negotiations, managed to lure both Queens and their followers to their territory, where terrible vengeance was meted out. After the Queens' escort had been dragged from the coach and butchered, the attackers abducted Maria and the Queen Mother to the castle of the clan chief, the *ban* of Croatia, who is said to have strangled the Queen Mother with his own hands in the presence of her daughter, who was held hostage for a year in Dalmatia.

Finally Sigismund managed to enforce his marriage to Maria, and in 1387, after a formal agreement with the most powerful oligarchs and prelates, was elected King. Despite a promise to spare them, he had Charles's closest followers executed, and the alleged murderer of the Queen Mother was tortured and killed. Maria died while pregnant as a result of a riding accident at the age of twenty-four.

Sigismund (Zsigmond) reigned for fifty years, from 1387 to 1437, but not only in Hungary where he appeared only infrequently. He was an astute and shrewd tactician, ambitious and craving admiration, a master of active and passive bribery and at the same time talented and imbued with European projects. By education and background he was a European *par excellence*: his mother tongue was French, but he also spoke excellent Latin, German, Czech, Hungarian and Italian. Of his linguistic ability he is said to have remarked that he spoke Latin with the Pope, Italian with poets and painters, Hungarian or Czech with the political magnates, German with his horses, and French to himself.

His image in history has suffered mainly because he broke his word over the Czech religious rebel Jan Hus whom, as King of the Romans (between election and accession the title of a prospective Emperor), he had promised safe-conduct to the Council of Constance. Nevertheless Hus and his companions were condemned and burnt at the stake as heretics. Sigismund's reign was overshadowed by the fight against the spread of the Hussite doctrine in Bohemia and other parts of Central Europe but especially in Transylvania. Hungary was regarded by Sigismund as a springboard for the achievement of his ambitious plans: the attainment of the Czech royal crown, as well as the Imperial one. But it could only fulfil this role as a centrally administered state. In Hungary itself he was extremely unpopular, being considered an intruder and a foreigner because of his frequent absences abroad, his obligations in the Empire as King of the Romans since 1410, and his actions in and for Bohemia. Notwithstanding the construction of a magnificent residence in the castle of Buda and his testamentary stipulation that he should be buried not in the Empire but in the cathedral of Nagyvárad "at the feet of St Ladislas", many Hungarians complained that he neglected the country's affairs. In the end he wore five crowns, yet in Hungary as well as Bohemia he reigned for years on end only in name. One of his victims flung in his teeth: "By God, I am no servant of yours, Czech swine."

From a Hungarian viewpoint Sigismund's foreign policy was disastrous, and triggered tensions inside the country. He suffered a serious defeat at Nicopolis (1396) in the Crusade he himself led against the Turks and their recurrent incursions in the south,

Dalmatia was conclusively lost to Venice and there were assaults by the Hussites in Upper Hungary.[3] One of the most bizarre events of the reign occurred in 1401 when a group of nobles held the King as a prisoner for several weeks. A council of barons and prelates administered the realm in the name of the "holy crown", but their lust for power and money split them, and the various groups fought or supported each other at the whim of the moment. This rivalry determined the country's internal political instability well beyond Sigismund's reign; he finally obtained his release and the support of the nobles by political and financial concessions. He consolidated his position in particular through his second marriage to Barbara Cilli, the beautiful, rich and frivolous daughter of the powerful head of a family of counts originating from Styria who had acquired large estates in Hungary and close kinship ties with the no less powerful clan of the former palatine Garai.

Despite some useful economic and administrative reforms Sigismund was never really master in his own country, which was more and more ruthlessly exploited by a few dozen power-hungry oligarchs at the expense of the peasantry, who were completely deprived of rights. The first serious peasant revolt in Hungary broke out in Transylvania during the last month of Sigismund's reign, when some of the Székely petty nobility supported its leader Antal Budai Nagy. The uprising could only be suppressed through the panic-driven organization of a "Union of the Three Nations", these being Hungarian nobles, Székelys (free peasant commoners treated as equals of the nobility) and Saxon settlers.

In the elective kingdom of Hungary the so-called "Will of the Nation" was represented solely by some sixty magnate families, now owners of two-fifths of the land. Church property, controlled by prelates co-operating closely with the barons, amounted to one-eighth, whereas the royal castles and estates comprised only a twentieth.

After the death of Sigismund in 1437 his son-in-law Albrecht von Habsburg was duly elected King of Hungary, but died only two years later, causing another dynastic crisis. In spite of the urgency of the Turkish peril, which overshadowed all other problems, the country was again plunged into serious domestic conflict over the succession, into which this time the Habsburg and Jagellonian dynasties were also drawn.

The holy crown of St Stephen became the focus of the crisis. Royal authority was after all conferred on the rightful heir to the throne only by way of ecclesiastical anointing and coronation with this crown, as well as by acclamation of the people assembled at a religious ceremony. Ever since the fifteenth century, the King also had to swear before being crowned an oath to rule according to the stipulations formulated by the noble assembly, and solemnly set this down in a document. There could therefore be no legitimate King of Hungary without the crown.

Elisabeth, the daughter of Sigismund and widow of Albrecht, was five months pregnant at his death and claimed the regency to secure the throne for the posthumous child. Two days before the birth of her son, later Ladislaus V, her lady-in-waiting Ilona Kottaner with some helpers acting on the Queen's orders removed the crown from the castle of Visegrád and smuggled it to Austria. Having gained the acquiescence of Dénes Szécsi, Cardinal Archbishop of Esztergom, Elisabeth succeeded in having the three-months-old child crowned King at Székesfehérvár with the stolen crown, thus confirming the consecration, a crucial condition of legitimacy since the extinction of the Árpáds.

Meanwhile the Hungarian Estates had elected the sixteen-year-old Polish King Vladislav VI Jagiello as King of Hungary under the name Ulászló I. However, the holy crown was under lock and key together with the well-guarded Ladislaus at the court of the future Emperor Frederick III in Wiener Neustadt, and it was almost a quarter of a century before it was returned after Hungary paid a large sum in ransom for it. However, in view of the Turkish peril the *Realpolitik* endorsed by the majority of nobles proved stronger than the sacrosanct principle of legitimacy. The same Cardinal Szécsi, who had administered the rites of royal dignity to the infant Ladislaus in mid-May, was willing to crown Ulászló I King of Hungary in the same coronation church at Székesfehérvár three months later. The Estates then ceremonially declared the coronation of Ladislaus null and void.

But how was Ulászló to become the legitimate king without the crown of St. Stephen? A crown adorning a reliquiary in the church was called into service, and the prelates, barons and nobles present at the ceremony simply transferred "the efficacy and power" of the holy crown which Queen Elisabeth had appropriated, and "which actually depends on the assent of the country's inhabitants", to the substitute one. This precipitated almost two years of civil war between the parties of the Queen and the new King, without regard for the increasing Turkish threat.

Although the young Jagiello King turned energetically against this danger from the south, he lost both the flower of his army and his own life at Varna in November 1444 because of a courageous but rash assault. The Hungarian Estates now united after all behind King Ladislaus, but he was still detained by Frederick III at his court. This signalled the hour of the brilliant general János (John) Hunyadi, whom the Estates nominated as Regent (*gubernator*) in 1446 for the duration of the interregnum.

7. The Heroic Age of the Hunyadis and the Turkish Danger

During the critical time of the twofold danger of feudal anarchy and the resulting unconstrained Turkish incursions, Hungary—according to general consensus—was saved, and its breakdown as an independent state postponed by seventy years, primarily through the genius and courage of a single man, János Hunyadi, one of the most enigmatic and at the same time attractive and popular figures of Magyar history.

One of the many contradictions of our history is that at moments of crisis generals, statesmen and poets have emerged, whose "family trees" and careers have in no way conformed to nationalistic, let alone racial assumptions. Hunyadi came from a Romanian (according to some sources, Slav) family, which had migrated from Wallachia to Transylvania. The Hungarian name stems from the castle of Vajdahunyad (today Hunedoara in Romania), which János's father Vajk, a minor Romanian noble, had received from Sigismund. Hunyadi began his career as a professional soldier, and soon showed such military talent that Sigismund took him on all his campaigns as his favourite officer, and invited him to his court in Prague as a "knight of the household". In fact Hunyadi's rise to international renown as a general and the richest landowner in Hungary was such as to give rise to the persistent rumour that he was Sigismund's natural son.

It was not least due to Hunyadi's heroic deeds against the Turks that the people who had once been seen through Western eyes as "wild Hungarians" became the noble defenders of Christendom, and that their military prowess, formerly synonymous with barbarism, now changed to virtue. Suddenly the "bloodthirsty Scythians" became soldiers of Christ. Hungary's role was extolled all over Europe as "stronghold, citadel, protective wall, protective barrier, rock face, pillar and shield". A single national trait forged this image: courage. Sultan Bajazet himself is said to have described the Hungarians as, next to the French, "the bravest nation among the peoples of the earth".[1]

Calling the Hungarians a citadel has elicited occasional scorn. Thus Friedrich Hebbel remarked that they protected themselves and not Europe: "The person who, having fallen into the water, saves himself by swimming does not deserve any reward because by saving himself he has preserved a citizen for the state." Of course there can be no doubt that by resisting the Turks the Magyars fought above all for themselves, their country and freedom. Yet Hunyadi was not an almost mythical hero only for the Hungarians; other threatened people also pinned their hopes on him. Still, as Hunyadi himself once bitterly complained to the Pope, Hungary had been carrying on the fight against superior Turkish fighting power for sixty years virtually on its own. And in this fight Hunyadi was the general—a man of remarkable courage and perseverance, able to accept setbacks and defeats, but a tactician and strategist of genius and supreme confidence. He grasped early that long-term military victories could not be achieved with noble knights signed up for military duty or not according to their whims; well-trained and regularly paid mercenaries were needed, as well as enthusiastic volunteers. With the help of the Franciscan friar Giovanni Capistrano, who with passionate eloquence whipped up the enthusiasm of the soldiers, Hunyadi inflicted in 1456 such a thorough defeat on the Turks at Belgrade, despite their overwhelming superiority in numbers, that the Turkish menace was averted for seventy years, not only for Hungary but for the entire continent. Here was the measure of Hunyadi's historical significance.

A deed of gift by King Ladislaus V dated 30 January 1453 stated that "what others accomplish with foreign help and with the legal title of their forebears". Hunyadi had achieved through "his own sweat, virtue, talent and labour". King Albrecht granted him "the dignity of imperial baron". As *voivode* of Transylvania, Count of Temes and Captain-General of Belgrade, Hunyadi had won "marvellous victories". However, the "outsider" and "upstart", as he appeared to the higher nobility of ancient lineage, also showed genius where his own enrichment was concerned. After each victory he received royal gifts, and at the peak of his career he could call himself master of 2.3 million hectares of land, twenty-eight castles, fifty-seven towns and about 1,000 villages.

However, like many a great general before and after him, the hero of the Turkish wars was less gifted as a statesman. During six and a half years as governor he failed to carry out any important reforms or to buttress the central power by consolidating the influence of the lesser nobility and checking the might of the barons. In the event his career was cut short when he died soon after his victory at Belgrade (as did Capistrano) of a fever contracted in the camp, probably the plague. Having given the West hope for the future in the month of the fall of Constantinople, he was mourned all over Europe.

Hunyadi's death opened up a new bloody phase in the magnates' smouldering power-struggle. His enemies wanted to get rid of his family, especially his sons László and Mátyás (Mathias), and divide up the Hunyadi estates among themselves. The anti-Hunyadi party received support above all from the young King Ladislas, now thirteen, who had been released from tutelage by Emperor Frederick III a few months before the fall of Constantinople as a result of joint pressure by the Czech and Hungarian Estates, and Ladislaus was recognized as King of Hungary in 1453 without a new coronation, and crowned King of Bohemia in Prague somewhat later. Under the influence of one of his uncles Ulrich Cilli, whom he named as the new Captain-General, the young King pronounced himself against the sons of Hunyadi.

The hated Cilli was the first victim of the bloody conflict that followed: László, Hunyadi's older son, and his supporters killed him during a quarrel in Belgrade. The King, now seventeen, confirmed László Hunyadi as Captain-General with apparent composure, swearing that he would not punish him for Cilli's murder, yet only a few weeks later he had the two Hunyadis, the influential Bishop János Vitéz and their entourage arrested László Hunyadi and had him beheaded in the main square of Buda before the entire court. The other death sentences were not carried out.

Meanwhile a civil war raged between the King and the party of Hunyadi led by his widow and her brother Mihály Szilágyi. His younger son Mátyás, now aged fifteen, was taken as the King's personal prisoner first to Vienna and then to Prague, but the young King soon died of the plague and a new situation arose: the two magnate parties joined in a temporary compromise alliance, opening the way to the throne for the young Hunyadi. Most reference works mention only the bare facts of the matter, without enumerating the bloody events of the two years between Hunyadi's death and his younger son's accession, yet this period before and after the election of the young King constitutes one of the most dramatised topics in Hungarian history. Poems, epics, dramas and operas have described the turbulent and, from the Hungarian viewpoint, glorious life of King Mathias I (1458–1490); how he became king and, as a youthful ruler, withstood the intrigues of mighty enemies still fired the literary imagination as late as the nineteenth century. The name Hunyadi had a ring to it that spelt magic for the lesser nobles and the people. The fifteen-year-old Mathias, released from captivity in Prague, soon proved that he was not only cast in the same mould as his father, but far surpassed him as a politician, diplomat and statesman. He became a typical Renaissance prince who could be merciless or forgiving, vengeful or chivalrous as the fancy took him—and the most cosmopolitan ruler in Hungarian history. Above all he became the personification of the national tradition in the spirit of the "fabrication of history".

The mere fact that he survived the bloody settling of accounts between his family and the oligarchs supporting King Ladislas seemed a miracle. His release, the pact with the anti-Hunyadi faction and finally his accession were all due to the unwavering resolve and ingenuity of his uncle Mihály Szilágyi and the negotiating skills of his mentor, his father's friend Bishop János Vitéz. The latter had made a secret pact with the Czech regent and later King, George Podiebrad, for Mathias's release and betrothal to Podiebrad's daughter Katalin. At about the same time Mathias's mother and uncle arrived at a peace agreement with the hostile palatine Garai, who had enforced the death penalty against László Hunyadi only a few months earlier. The Garai clan were now willing to accept the younger son's accession, provided that he married the daughter of the palatine and did not wreak vengeance on his brother's murderers. The magnates and prelates agreed to his election, and on 24 January 1458 the representatives of the lesser nobles (according to tradition, some 40,000 armed men), assembled on the ice of the frozen Danube, proclaimed the fifteen-year-old Mathias King. The Diet appointed his uncle Szilágyi Regent for five years.

Removed from the custody of his future father-in-law, the young Mathias was brought to Buda and enthroned amid scenes of national rejoicing. However, the coronation did not take place until the crown had been returned by Emperor Frederick III six years later. The first "national" king since the Árpáds proved his mettle, already demonstrating leadership qualities within a few months by freeing himself from the tutelage of the oligarchs who had placed him on the throne. Barely five months after his election the oligarchs, supported by the Regent Szilágyi, conspired against the over-ambitious young King, but Mathias reacted swiftly, dismissing the principal plotters, the palatine and the Transylvanian *voivode* from their offices; his uncle Szilágyi was forced to resign as Regent in the summer of 1458 and arrested a few weeks later for his subversive activities. Thereupon twenty-five magnates, led by the dismissed Garai, elected Emperor Frederick III King of Hungary at Németujvár in February 1459; after all, the Habsburg Emperor had had the holy crown in his possession since 1440, giving the conspirators a pretext: "He who has the crown owns the country." The Emperor graciously accepted the offer, and even referred to the "low birth" of Mathias. The uprising soon collapsed.

The conflict between Frederick III and Mathias I lasted another five years until the peace of Wiener Neustadt on 19 July 1462; five days later the Emperor was at last persuaded to hand over the crown of St Stephen. However, the price Frederick demanded was in every way so high that Hungarian historians present him as the actual victor; Mathias had to pay 80,000 gold florins (two-fifths of the royal revenues in 1454) for the crown and for the town of Sopron, mortgaged twenty-two years earlier by Queen Elisabeth. Furthermore, he kept the title of King of Hungary and obtained the right to inherit the throne should Mathias die without issue. Since the King was twenty-seven years the Emperor's junior this clause gave the contract an air of unreality, but in fact Frederick was to outlive his young challenger by three years. It was small consolation that the Emperor adopted Mathias as his son.

In the following spring "Mathias I Corvinus" was at last ceremonially crowned. He received the name Corvinus after the raven in his crest, for which his court historian Antonio Bonfini later invented a pedigree, tracing the Hunyadis' ancestry back to a Valerius Corvinus, a Roman knight, said to have defeated a Gallic giant, the "descendant of Jupiter", with the help of a raven. In short, it was a matter of legitimising a parvenu, who was not considered to rate with the Habsburgs and Jagiellos. The imperial ambitions of the King's foreign policy were thereby brought into line with his personal need for self-assertion.

During the coronation ceremony, while the Diet at Székesfehérvár was sitting, Mathias rode to the top of a hillock where, with his hands held high to heaven, and swinging his sword to the four points of the compass, he swore to uphold the country's constitution incorporating András II's Golden Bull of 1222 and the law of Louis the Great of 1351, i.e. the combined privileges of the nobility, proclaiming that he would defend the country against enemies from any quarter.

During the first five years of his reign before the coronation, Mathias I had already established the preconditions of his kingship's absolute power and for the curtailment of the great feudal landowners' privileges. In these five years he rid himself of any supervision by his uncle (Szilágyi fell into Turkish captivity at the end of 1460 and was beheaded on the orders of the Sultan); he crushed the opposition of the old aristocracy, won victories over the Turks, subdued the notorious Jan Giskra, ringleader of the mercenaries who had long been plundering the northern borderlands, and, as his crowning success, recaptured the fortress of Jajce in Bosnia from the Turks, thus ensuring peace along the southern borders. He was not only successful but also extremely popular, a veritable "soldier-king", who went into battle with his soldiers, and at nightfall slept among them wearing his greatcoat.

But did Mathias underestimate the looming Turkish menace for Hungary and for Europe? Or were the burdensome wars and conflicts that flared up at intervals with Bohemia, Poland and Austria a part of his imperial ambitions? Was his ultimate ambition to attain the crown of the Holy Roman Empire? Either way, his primary interest was in establishing supremacy in Central Europe. His administrative, political and fiscal reforms were designed to secure domestic accord for his daring foreign policy, which was disputed

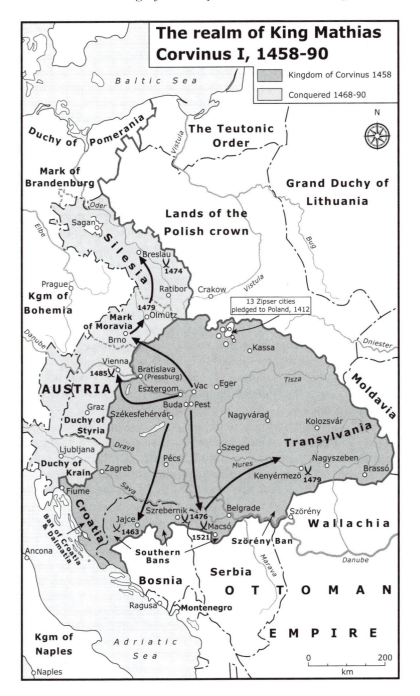

The realm of King Mathias Corvinus I, 1458-90

Kingdom of Corvinus 1458

Conquered 1468-90

N

Baltic Sea

The Teutonic Order

Duchy of Pomerania

Mark of Brandenburg

Grand Duchy of Lithuania

Oder

Sagan

Elbe

Lands of the Polish crown

Silesia

Breslau
1474

Prague

Kgm of Bohemia

Ratibor

Crakow

Vistula

1479

Olmütz

Mark of Moravia

Brno

13 Zipser cities pledged to Poland, 1412

Danube

Vienna

Bug

Dniester

Kassa

1485

Bratislava (Pressburg)

Esztergom

Vac   Eger

Tisza

Moldavia

AUSTRIA

Graz

Duchy of Styria

Buda Pest

Székesfehérvár

Nagyvárad

Kolozsvár

Ljubljana

Drava

Pécs

Szeged

Transylvania

Duchy of Krain

Zagreb

Mures

Nagyszeben

Brassó

Sava

Kenyérmező 1479

Fiume

Croatia

Szrebernik 1476

Belgrade

Szörény

Jajce
1463

Macsó

1521

Szörény Ban

Wallachia

Ancona

Ban of Croatia & Dalmatia

Southern Bans

Bosnia

Serbia

Marava

Danube

O T T O M A N

Ragusa **Montenegro**

Kgm of Naples

Adriatic Sea

E M P I R E

0   200

Naples

km

even by his former mentor and closest adviser János Vitéz, by now Archbishop and Chancellor, as well as Vitéz's nephew Janus Pannonius (János Csezmicei), the renowned poet and Bishop of Pécs. In 1471 both plotted with other nobles and prelates to topple the King and replace him with the Polish King Casimir IV, but Mathias was able to quell this rebellion at its outset, like many others.

By restructuring the entire tax system and promoting the so-called county nobility, whose representatives were elected in some eighty bailiwicks, the King established for himself a political power-base, and laid the groundwork for the creation and upkeep of the famous "Black Army", supposedly named for their black shields and helmets. This troop of mercenaries, answerable only to the King, freed Mathias from dependence on the magnates' private armies, and by means of constant inspection of its discipline and equipment and appointment of good commanders, he turned it into a powerful army. Apart from his securing of the Bohemian crown Mathias could ascribe the conquest of Moravia, Silesia, Styria, Carinthia and Lower Austria with Vienna (1485), and two years later the residence of Frederick III in Wiener Neustadt, to his military and diplomatic superiority.

Macartney wrote of him: "Exceedingly talented in every respect, he was a brilliant natural soldier, a first-class administrator, an outstanding linguist—speaking with equal fluency half a dozen languages—a learned astrologer, an enlightened patron of the arts and himself a refined connoisseur of their delights."[2] When in 1476 he married his second wife Beatrice, daughter of King Ferdinand of Naples, Hungary was opened to the Renaissance. Never before and probably never since has the cultural and artistic influence of Italy been greater than in the last fifteen years of this true Renaissance prince's reign.

The contemporary Italian historian Antonio Bonfini wrote in his opus on Hungary that this event completely altered the King's lifestyle:

After the arrival of Queen Beatrice the King introduced arts to Hungary that had hitherto been unknown here, and at great cost invited notable artists to his court. He engaged painters, sculptors, engravers, carpenters, goldsmiths, masons and builders from Italy at good salaries. Singers from Germany and France enhanced the services in the royal chapel. He even called to his court ornamental gardeners, fruit-growers and expert agricultural workers who made cheeses in the Italian, French and Sicilian manner. To these were added jesters and actors for whom the Queen had a particular fondness, also players of wind instruments, zither-players and other musicians. His gifts attracted poets, orators and linguists. Mathias loved and supported all these arts with admirable munificence; he strove to make Hungary into a second Italy. The Hungarians, however, condemned his great extravagance and daily accused the sovereign of playing thoughtlessly with money, of squandering on useless things taxes intended for other purposes, straying from the old kings' frugality, and neglecting the strict old mores and customs which he replaced with Italian and Spanish pleasures and depraved practices. However, like any patron of the arts and supporter of talent, the divine King endeavoured gradually to introduce culture to the country. He encouraged the higher and lower nobility to live in a cultivated manner, obliging them to build splendidly according to their wealth, to live like burghers, and to behave better towards strangers, whom they outrageously despised. He spurred everyone on by his own example.[3]

The royal court swarmed with foreigners, and the King did indeed spend vast sums on his lavish court, not least for manuscripts illuminated by Italian scribes, a total of 2,500 volumes which now constitute the renowned Bibliotheca Corviniana. In Mathias's collections were pictures, sculptures, jewels, products of the goldsmith's art and other *objets*. Twenty architects, the best of their time, laid out gardens and lakes in the residences at Visegrád and Buda, and in Vienna after its conquest built splendid colonnades, towers, reception and dining halls and fountains of red marble with silver-plated roofs. Bonfini also mentions a large monument in the courtyard of the palace in Buda: the central figure was Mathias, helmeted and leaning on his shield and lance, deep in thought; on his right was his father and on the left his brother László. "For pomp", wrote Bonfini, "his palaces were not far behind the luxury of the Romans."

In his reign Hungary's second university was founded in Pressburg (Pozsony), but this was as short-lived as the first one in Pécs. The Italian historians and Hungarian humanists wrote in Latin; few books were printed, although the first press of András Hess was already working at the time. However, although the language of culture was Latin, the first Hungarian translations of parts of the Old Testament and other religious texts were already being drawn up.

The ancient Roman "lineage", symbolized by the cognomen "Corvinus", was only one part of the flourishing Mathias cult. Since no enemy seemed to be a match for the King, sobriquets such as "Attila secundus" or "the Scythian Mars" were coined to gratify Mathias's need for admiration and love of his country. The glorification of Attila and his Huns, then held to be the Hungarians' ancestors (considered by Macartney an "absurd side-effect"), expressed the political faith of the nobles and people, long moulded by literary tradition.

On the one hand, Mathias used taxes to supply the royal revenues—five times those of Ladislas V—for the expenses of his court and the 30,000 predominantly foreign "Black Army" mercenaries; on the other, he was called "the Just" for his severity towards the magnates and his military successes. He is said to have often donned disguise in order to mingle incognito with the people and redress the wrongs done to them by the prompt settling of scores for abuses. The King is said to have given the following explanation to the Italian humanist Aurelius Brandolini:

"No one is allowed here to be too sure of his power, nor should anyone lose confidence altogether because he is defenceless; everyone can insist on his rights—if need be, even against us... Here governors do not dare to repress the people into some kind of bondage, because they know they are merely servants at my pleasure. It is not the laws that are the source and guarantee of this just system of law, but the King, who is not the servant or tool of the law but stands above it and determines it."[4]

What his contemporaries held against him—and was not without repercussions for the country—was the fact that neither of his marriages produced children. He therefore tried to promote his illegitimate son John Corvinus as his successor, but this plan for a new native dynasty came to nothing when Mathias died in 1490.

Despite his military successes and attempts at domestic reform, his real significance for Hungarian history lies primarily in the splendid and long-lasting intellectual charisma of his personality and epoch. He was the King with the most opulent lifestyle, yet he had the common touch in a way that was not remembered of any other monarch. Hence the saying "King Mathias is dead, and justice has gone too!"

Mathias the "King of the People" embodied the splendour of the Hungarian nation and the acme of Hungarian power. Thus it is understandable that several generations of Hungarian historians delivered panegyrics on his era. Through the centuries of division, foreign control and decline, poets as well as the common people lamented the vanished grandeur. Jenö Szücs soberly summarised the reason for this nostalgia: "Since the campaigns of Mathias, Hungary has seen many victorious battles, but not a single victorious war. Since 1485 we have had only losses—apart from a liberating campaign at the end of the seventeenth century against the Turks, which was largely fought by a non-Hungarian army. The successes of Bocskai, Bethlen and Rákóczi were, when all is said and done, victorious battles in the course of a permanent war, lost in 1711...."

It is significant that two representative surveys in the 1990s, half a millennium after his death, showed King Mathias to be the most liked personality in Hungarian history, ahead even of St Stephen and the heroes of the 1848 revolution, Széchenyi and Kossuth.

8. The Long Road to the Catastrophe of Mohács

After the death of King Mathias an orgy of vainglory, power-hunger and rivalry descended on Hungary, and conflicts between the high and lesser nobility brought the country close to disaster.

In the intrigues and battles between various interests over the succession, the political, military and social system established by Mathias was completely upset. His illegitimate son János Corvinus was too weak and pacific by nature to press his claim, and the Habsburg King (later Emperor) Maximilian was too strong for the magnates, who wanted a king they could dominate. Such a man was to hand in Vladislav Jagiello (Ulászló II, 1490–1516), who fulfilled the feudal aristocracy's expectations so completely as to earn from them the sobriquet "Dobže László", meaning something like "OK László". The successor to the great Mathias went down in history as a king who assented without objection to every proposal laid before him.

As a counter-balance to the so-called "court party" of the barons, who manipulated the indolent and weak King as they pleased, a "national party" arose supported by the middle and lesser nobility. Its tone was set by the ambitious János Zápolyai, later *voivode* of Transylvania, and his family. The key figure in the drama that unfolded was Tamás Bakócz, a bishop who had been Secretary under Mathias and was later promoted Archbishop of Esztergom. As Chancellor to the new King he was all-powerful; unscrupulous and cunning, he allied himself with the Habsburgs, and as head of the "court" faction sought to circumvent the resolution of the Diet of 1505 whereby "no foreign king, of whatever nation or tongue" could ever again be elected. In fact the dynastic contract of Pressburg drawn up in a 1491 between Jagiellos and Habsburgs had already assured King Maximilian I the succession as King of Hungary if

Ulászló remained childless, but this was never submitted for approval to the Hungarian Estates.

The birth of an heir to the throne, Louis, in 1506 brought about a new situation. The next year a so-called double betrothal was arranged between the family of Ulászló and Maximilian's grandchildren, sealed by a formal marriage ceremony in July 1515 at the Stephansdom in Vienna, in which the nine-year-old Louis married Maria, sister of Archduke Ferdinand, who in his turn married Anna, the Hungarian King's older sister. On the death of King Ulászló in 1516 Louis was a mere ten years old, and although he ascended the throne without any particular resistance, a regency held power until he came of age. Tamás Bakócz, promoted meanwhile to Cardinal, had the final say in this body as well. This hugely ambitious man of simple background had even aspired to the Papacy but was narrowly defeated in the election of 1513 by Giovanni de' Medici (Leo X). After his return home the versatile Cardinal was entrusted by the new Pope, probably as a consolation prize, with the task of making propaganda for a large-scale Crusade against the growing Turkish menace. This was to prove the beginning of the end of united Hungary.

Peasants were recruited for this purpose by the Franciscan friars and, armed and aware of their numerical strength, used the opportunity for their own ends, turning against the large landowners. The Archbishop and the King ordered them to disband, but instead they elected a courageous officer, György Dózsa, as their leader, and were joined by several priests and frars, who placed themselves at the head of the rebellious masses. After months of savage fighting, particularly in eastern Hungary and Transylvania, the peasant uprising of 1514 was put down with almost inconceivable vindictiveness by János Zápolyai, *voivode* of Transylvania. The magnates also took fearful revenge: Dózsa was enthroned on a flaming stake and a red-hot crown was placed on his head. The other ringleaders, after being starved for two weeks, were forced to bite into his burning flesh and eat it while Dózsa was still alive. Reprisals such as this and the torture and execution of the Franciscan monk Lörinc were meant to demonstrate to the people the hopelessness of any future rebellion. The nobility now punished the entire class of peasants for their "faithlessness" with "perpetual servitude". They were denied any ownership of land; henceforth no law or law-court protected them against the lords. In time Dózsa became transfigured, first in oral tradition and later in song, poetry and drama, into a symbol of rebellion against the ruthless and sybaritic landlords.

The same Diet that decreed the peasants' "perpetual" servitude in retaliation for their uprising was coincidentally presented with a codification of Hungarian customary law drawn up by the jurist István Werböczy, leader of the petty nobility. Known as the *Triparti-tum*, this split Hungarian society into two: an all-powerful "political nation" and a completely disfranchized populace. Werböczy's ingenious thesis was simply to make the lesser nobility (by no means only the magnates and high clergy) into the personification of the "mystical body" and "limb of the holy crown". The fiction of *"una et eadem libertas"* (one and the same liberty) of all the privileged classes, as well as the definition of the crown as the essence of the noble nation and the wellspring of authority, became the basis of the Hungarian nation's constitutional identity. Every noble, even the poorest, was to be a component of the holy crown. The peasantry and townspeople were thereby denied the right to regard themselves as elements of the country or of the crown.

Hungarian historians rightly maintain that Werböczy's doctrine drove a wedge between Hungarian society and the development of Europe. Although the *Tripartitum* was not signed by the King and was therefore never formally promulgated, it became and remained the basis of legal practice till 1848. Indeed the political, social and psychological division between the nobility and the rest of the people remained entrenched until the radical social changes that followed the Second World War.

In his work *The Three Historical Regions of Europe* Jenö Szücs,[1] referring to the eminent Hungarian scholar István Bibó, stresses that during the whole first half of the second Christian millennium Hungary was "structurally", i.e. in its social construction, part of the West or at least moving towards it, but that historical catastrophes led to the country then being "blown off course" for the next 400 years towards a structurally East European form. Another important factor was the numerical strength of the nobility. At the end of the Middle Ages one in between twenty and twenty-five inhabitants of Hungary was a nobleman, while in France the proportion was no more than one in 100. By contrast, in Hungary only one person in forty-five was a free citizen, as against one in ten in France. Thus in Hungary the Middle Ages bequeathed to modern times an exceptionally large titled stratum, consisting of 4–5 per cent of the population. This included that raw and uneducated but privileged petty nobility judged by Bibó and Szücs as "that most pernicious phenomenon of modern Hungarian social development". It is little wonder then that the *Tripartitum* became the nobility's bible, being re-issued fourteen times in the sixteenth century alone and more than seventy times in later centuries.

It is instructive to read in the *Chronology of Hungarian History* what the middle and lower nobility were discussing in the Diets at the exact moment when Sultan Suleiman II ("the Magnificent") was preparing his decisive blow against the divided country: they were engrossed in trying to improve their finances by a moratorium on debts and tax concessions on their town-houses. A permanent state of war was ablaze over the rights and power of the executive between the magnates and the lesser nobility who had risen to high positions under the able leadership of Werböczy. He and the petty nobility were the main instigators of anti-foreign edicts; the privileges of the German cities, with their own laws and jurisdiction, were their main targets. For many decades the Hungarians—and the Slovaks—did not have equal rights in the towns inhabited predominantly by Germans. In the capital, Buda, "only a German man with four German grandparents" could be elected city judge, while the tax judge, the notary and the majority of jurors were elected from among the German burghers. A Hungarian's testimony against a German was valid only if it was supported by Germans. In Besztercebánya and Pest, for example, the purchase of land was permitted only to full German citizens. Already in 1439 apprehension over excessive German influence had led to conflict between Hungarians and Germans in Buda.[2]

Of course, the fact that in the sixteenth century, shortly before the disastrous battle of Mohács and the Ottoman capture of Buda, the Diet was still so intensely preoccupied with German influence testifies to the virulence of national tensions in the cities and their surroundings, due not to linguistic nationalism but to economic and social conflicts. Strangers meant unwanted and even dangerous competition for the German "original inhabitants" of the cities.

Hence a direct thread runs between these defensive actions by the isolated Saxon and German bourgeoisie against the influx of Hungarians, Slavs and later Romanians, and the bloody pogroms by German traders and artisans against Jews in Pressburg and Pest during the radical revolutionary changes of 1848.

The young Louis II's preparations against the Turkish onslaught—which was aimed not at Hungary itself but primarily at Vienna and Austria—must be seen against the background of these political, social and in part national-religious tensions (German Hungarians were the main movers in Protestantism before 1526). Louis, married to Maria von Habsburg, had neither the vigour nor the means, let alone sufficient international backing, to arm in time against the looming assault from the south. Moreover, the rivalry between the magnates and the lesser nobility had reached a new climax. As leader of the (temporarily) victorious group Werbőczy had himself elected palatine, and one of his first measures was to terminate the leases for the copper and silver mines of Besztercebánya in Upper Hungary held by the Fugger banking family, who represented Habsburg interests. This provoked an uprising by the 4,000 miners who were put out of work in consequence. The unrest was ruthlessly suppressed, but Hungary irrevocably lost the Fuggers' credit just when the Turkish danger was most acute.

Hungary tried desperately to muster help through diplomatic letters and the personal entreaty of envoys sent to Rome, Venice, Vienna and London. However, in the view of Pope Clement VII the Turks poised on the Danube were not the greatest enemy of faith; that was Martin Luther. The Spanish-Habsburg Emperor Charles V became the focus of a French-Italian coalition inspired by the Pope. The Turkish attack on Hungary was probably also encouraged by the alliance between the Most Christian King in Paris (the Kings of France had received this honorific from Pope Paul II in the fifteenth century) and the Muslim challenger of the Christian West. Be that as it may, Archduke Ferdinand in Vienna was neither able nor willing to come to the aid of his desperate brother-in-law.

Already at that stage there was hostility in Hungary because of this, a feeling experienced even more intensely later when it was perceived that the Austrian Habsburgs concentrated their strength primarily on furthering their position in the West and above all in

Hungary, neglecting the fight against the Turks. In short, the Hungarians were welcomed everywhere, encouraged to fight against Suleiman and even blessed in Rome, but in each case they were dismissed empty-handed.

Without waiting for the 10,000-strong detachment of *voivode* Zápolyai from Transylvania, Louis II went into action at Mohács, a small town near the Danube, on 29 August 1526, leading a hastily assembled, poorly trained and amateurishly led army of barely 25,000 against an Ottoman force three to five times its superior in numbers. The Hungarians had almost no artillery or foot soldiers at their disposal, the ecclesiastical and lay dignitaries being more afraid of their own disfranchised and repressed peasants than of Suleiman's warriors. Technically and tactically the Turks far surpassed the Hungarians, especially in their artillery.

Sultan Suleiman achieved an easy victory at Mohács within an hour and a half. After a brief and heroic fight almost all of Hungary's dignitaries, including seven bishops, and some 15,000 soldiers (mainly German, Polish and Czech mercenaries) died. The King fled in full armour, but his horse fell during a cloudburst and he was drowned with it in a swollen stream; it was widely rumoured afterwards that the fleeing King had been killed by nobles, who wanted to offer the throne to Ferdinand, but no evidence has ever been adduced to support this. The circumstances surrounding the young King's death have never been totally clarified, nor has the contemporary supposition that Zápolyai deliberately sat tight with his force at a safe distance awaiting the outcome of the battle. The fact that in his struggle against Ferdinand for the succession he swore allegiance to the Sultan barely three years later on the very same battlefield of Mohács retrospectively fed suspicion concerning his conduct in the battle itself.

Looting, discord and complete disarray afflicted the Hungarians— signs of their inexorable loss of strength. Queen Maria, escorted by fifty horsemen, fled Buda with the most precious royal treasures, first to Pressburg and then to her brother in Vienna. She was escaping not only the Turks but also the Hungarians, who had never liked the Habsburgs and their German courtiers. The Queen and her household had lived in isolation, and when she did appear in the capital, hatred of the Germans was said to have increased.

After his timely flight from Mohács, the palatine István Báthory—not related to the later Prince of Transylvania of that name—spent his time with his friend Count Batthyány plundering the fleeing ecclesiastics; ancient treasures in the bishop's palace at Pécs fell into their hands. Other Hungarian nobles and officers looted the treasury of the archbishopric at Esztergom, raided the Queen's ship and raped her ladies-in-waiting. The historian Szekfü wrote: "While wounds were still bleeding, burning towns smoking and the thousands of Hungarian prisoners not yet on their way to distant lands, only a single passion fired the dispersed nobles: jubilation over the fall of the German court and the flight of the German Queen." He added that it was primarily the agitation of the lesser nobility that unleashed so much hatred for "the German woman". German traders, artisans and medical men were temporarily forced into hiding.[3]

Thus there is no reason to doubt the veracity of an account by the Polish envoy who wrote two months after Mohács that the Hungarians were like people reborn. Wide circles of the nobility were rejoicing that foreign rule had now ended. Perhaps these were the same as those who had boasted before the battle: "We shall smite the entire Turkish army with our signet rings alone." But, as so often in Hungary's history, the atmosphere of "joy instead of grief" was due to self-deception. In the century and a half that followed, the lesser nobility, as well as all others, were to find out what a foreign yoke really meant.

The victorious Ottoman army captured and plundered the royal residence, town and castle of Buda, and ravaged Transdanubia and the Danube-Tisza plains before withdrawing for the time being with tens of thousands of prisoners. However, the domestic and external situation of the country—three times the size of today's Hungarian state—was totally and irrevocably changed by the catastrophe of Mohács. The gravity and the political, geographic and demographic consequences of the debacle have only been realised by later generations.

For these later generations "Mohács" became the synonym for national cataclysm, with Hungary disappearing as an independent political power from the political map of Europe for almost four centuries. The Hungarians appeared to have been obliterated. Even the Magyars' temperament—the "characteristic mixture of the sanguine, the phlegmatic and the melancholic" (Jókai)—can be explained by this deep-seated and historically determined feeling of being endangered. The preoccupation with "Magyar national death", pessimism as a basic attitude, the nation's solitariness, hope when all seems hopeless, the individual living under constant threat—these became the great themes of the national literature. Numerous poems have been written about the national destiny.

In his masterpiece *School at the Border* (1950), barely known outside Hungary, Géza Ottlik memorably sketched this unique relationship between the Hungarians and their defeats by the example of a class:

The 400th anniversary of the battle of Mohács was approaching. It seems a remarkable thing to celebrate a defeat, yet the mighty Ottoman Empire, which could have celebrated its victory, no longer exists. All traces of the Mongols have also vanished, as indeed—almost in front of our very eyes—have those of the tenacious Habsburg empire. We have therefore got used to celebrating on our own our great lost battles which we survived. Perhaps we also got used to regarding defeat as something exciting, made of more solid material, and more important, than victory—at any rate we regard it as our (true) possession.[4]

9. The Disaster of Ottoman Rule

The national catastrophe of Mohács marked a break not only in the history of Hungary but also in that of Eastern and Central Europe. Pope Pius II described Hungary as "the bulwark and shield of Christianity". Now, however, this Central European great power, for almost 150 years a brake on Turkish expansion and the spearhead in the Balkans of resistance to Ottoman rule, became a no-man's-land before the gates of Vienna, as well as a battlefield for the constant struggle between Habsburgs and Ottomans and its alternating fortunes. Although the Turkish army, heavily laden with booty, had already moved on from Hungary at the beginning of October 1526, the two large rival groups of nobles had learnt nothing from the defeat. On the contrary, amid the wreckage of the country they persisted in their mindless contest for the empty throne. After the unexpected (albeit only temporary) withdrawal of the Turks, the squabblers, believing that the danger was over, embroiled themselves in a fateful civil war which eventually led to the complete destruction of the idea of a Hungarian state, unparalleled bloodletting and the division of the Carpathian basin into three.

Instead of putting up a united front to fight the external danger, a life-or-death struggle now erupted: between János Zápolyai, Hungary's richest landowner and the cruel avenger of the 1514 peasant uprising, who presented himself as the dominant national figure supported by the lesser nobility, and his opponent Ferdinand von Habsburg, who insisted on his rights according to the succession contracts signed with the House of Jagiello. Scenes from 1440 were repeated: the two rivals were again crowned in the same church in Székesfehérvár, Zápolyai first and a year later Ferdinand, and again the same church dignitary crowned the two kings. Many of the same high nobles were present at Ferdinand's coronation who had attended that of the other king a year earlier. Neither king was strong enough for the other to agree to permanent capitulation, let alone to defy the Sultan. Of the two János was the weaker; he returned from brief exile in Poland to continue the fight against Ferdinand only with the help of the Sublime Porte and France. Because he had already recognized and paid homage to the Sultan as his sovereign at Mohács, his opponents regarded him as a vassal of the Turks and capable of anything.

That a historic chance for a settlement between the two kings nonetheless took place, thus avoiding a total rift, was only thanks to the endeavours of one of the ablest, most enigmatic and also most tragic figures of these turbulent times: Georgius Utješenić-Martinuzzi, known to history as Frater György. His significance and role are explained by the fact that for a century and a half the Magyars had fought on two fronts—against both the Turks and the Habsburgs. In this confused and sometimes rapidly changing war both sides had their heroes, traitors and martyrs.[1]

György, born about 1480, came from a Croatian family of lesser nobles, and in 1522/3, after years as a soldier, entered a Pauline monastery. Ordained a priest, he held important offices at the court of King János, eventually becoming his treasurer. Not only did György prove an indispensable counsellor and of absolute moral integrity; he was also a convinced champion of Hungarian unity (according to Szekfü he "came to love the Hungarians and hate the Germans"), and it was thanks to him that the two kings reached an agreement in 1538 at Nagyvárad (Oradea Mare), which secured peace and contained a secret succession treaty in favour of the Habsburgs. György was rewarded with the important diocese of Nagyvárad, and later became Cardinal Archbishop of Esztergom.

Although his aim was to unite Hungary under Ferdinand, he was also determined to let the Habsburgs have Transylvania only if he actually took measures to defend Eastern Hungary and the heartland of Transylvania against the Turks. The role of Frater György became decisive when, shortly before the death of King János in 1540, a son János Zsigmond was born to his consort, the Polish Jagiello Princess Isabella, the dying king entrusted the infant to his care. György immediately proclaimed the child king, proceeding with him and the Queen Mother to Buda. While the two rival kings squabbled amid the nation's ruins, the Turks gradually occupied the fertile Danube-Tisza plains and its fringe territory. After twice seizing the capital Buda briefly, Suleiman managed by an act of double-dealing to occupy it permanently without firing a single shot or a single blow stroke of the sword. He claimed to have done so to protect the rights of the year-old János Zsigmond and his mother. Hungary was now split into three parts, with the kingdom of Hungary proper consisting only of a few western counties and Upper Hungary (today's Slovakia), ruled from Vienna as an Austrian province.

Transylvania continued to exist as an independent principality, albeit under the Sultan's aegis, due above all to the efforts of Frater György, who for ten years tried to maintain this triangle of the Turks, Ferdinand von Habsburg and the Queen Mother, a policy acceptable to all, but basically serving Hungary's interests and aimed at achieving its unity. The Queen Mother, surprisingly, turned out to be his enemy; because of her dislike, later uncontrollable hatred, she would reject any advice that originated from the over-powerful Frater and so jeopardise the interests of her son and family. Yet it was precisely his diplomatic ability, numerous contacts and sophisticated way of dealing with Ottoman commanders of South Slav background which, despite his essential loyalty to the indecisive King Ferdinand, made him in the end appear to all sides ambiguous and devious. In the summer of 1551 (by this time he had been named *voivode* of Transylvania by Ferdinand) György concluded yet another agreement between the Habsburgs and Isabella, whereby she left the country and her son János Zsigmond was to receive the principality of Oppeln in Silesia in return for relinquishing the throne. Ferdinand was recognized as king by the Transylvanian Estates, and the holy crown, which had been in the Zápolyai family's possession since 1532, was brought back amid much rejoicing to Pressburg (Pozsony), the new capital of Royal Hungary (the rump Hungarian kingdom's official designation under the Habsburgs). Meanwhile Giovanni Castaldo, Ferdinand's mercenary general, entered Transylvania with a small German-Spanish force. The Turks at first took no notice of this, but a little later the Sultan sent a punitive expedition. György, who in the mean time had been made a Cardinal at Ferdinand's suggestion, once again tried to ward off the imminent Turkish assault with the accustomed mixture of gold, personal contacts and psychological empathy, naturally combined with cunning and secret diplomacy. His enemies suspected that his real design was to get rid of the Zápolyai family with Habsburg help, and then to outmanoeuvre Ferdinand with Turkish backing in order finally to obtain undivided rule over Transylvania for himself. The bewildered General Castaldo is said to have been alerted by the Cardinal's secretary in a midnight audience of an impending trap, whereupon Castaldo in a dramatic letter requested King Ferdinand to authorize him to get rid of the Cardinal if the need should arise.

On 17 December 1551 György was set upon in his castle during morning prayers by Sforza Pallavicini and eight Spanish and Italian officers, and stabbed fifty times, the body remaining in the plundered castle, unburied, for seventy days. It is entirely possible that persistent rumours concerning the Cardinal's wealth and the gold and silver treasures in his possession were the real cause of his murder. Because of his high ecclesiastical rank, the trial of his assailants took place in the Vatican and lasted three years. No evidence of György's alleged treason came to light, but Ferdinand, Castaldo and the other participants were eventually exculpated through the Emperor's intervention.

The dagger struck not only the body of György but also that of Hungary, as Szekfü wrote of the bitter aftermath. György alone could have achieved the union of Eastern Hungary with Royal Hungary under the Habsburgs. The subsequent Turkish offensive and the ensuing clashes between the Habsburg and the newly-installed Prince of Transylvania, János Zsigmond Zápolyai, allow only one conclusion concerning György's murder, endorsed by most Hungarian historians and summed up in Talleyrand's aphorism after the shooting of the Duc d'Enghien: that it was worse than a crime—it was a mistake.

The conflicts which now flared up again over the redrawing of borders between Royal and Habsburg Hungary and the extensive territories occupied by the Turks did not improve the chances of Hungary's reunification in the following years. On the contrary, they resulted in the final loss of Transylvania. János Zsigmond, proclaimed Prince of Transylvania by the Sublime Porte, conducted government business after his mother's death in 1559, while continuing the fight against Emperor Maximilian II (1564–76).

Meanwhile Sultan Suleiman made his final attempt to capture Vienna. A strong Turkish force crossed the Danube from Eszék on its way to Szigetvár, which it took it after a month-long siege. Miklós Zrinyi, *ban* of Croatia and legendary hero of the Turkish wars for both Hungarians and Croats, defended the fortress with a few hundred soldiers until the end, and died during a last sortie against the Ottomans' superior force. Suleiman also succumbed shortly before the fort was taken, but news of his death was at first kept secret. Emperor Maximilian, commanding an army of 80,000, meanwhile stood idly by in the vicinity of Győr; he neither launched an attack against Esztergom to take the pressure off Szigetvár, nor took advantage of the confusion caused by Suleiman's death to terminate Ottoman rule in Hungary, but instead merely accepted Hungary's division in the 1586 Peace of Adrianople (Edirne), recognizing Suleiman's conquests as integral to the Ottoman empire. János Zsigmond renounced the title of King of Hungary, calling himself henceforth "Prince of Transylvania and Ruler of Parts of Hungary", i.e. of the counties east of the river Tisza. The principality had to pay tribute to the Sultan. The peace treaties thus formally sealed the division of the Carpathian basin into three separate parts for more than a century and a half.

It is pointless to speculate today whether it was the defeat at Mohács or the fall of Buda that denoted the lowest point for historic Hungary. However, all Hungarian historians agree that the 170 years of Ottoman rule represented the greatest catastrophe of Hungarian history, with fateful demographic, ethnic, economic and social consequences. One can say without exaggeration that the amputation of historic Hungary through the coercive peace treaty of Trianon in 1920 had its origins 400 years earlier in Turkish times.

It was particularly tragic for Hungary's future that the almost exclusively Magyar-inhabited regions—the Great Plains and the hilly country of Transdanubia—suffered the greatest losses, while the German-inhabited towns and the settlements of the Slovaks, Romanians and Ruthenes in northern Hungary and Transylvania got off relatively lightly. What had once been the richest territory in southern Hungary, and the central middle plains, suffered the worst devastatation during the first phase of the fighting, and its inhabitants were wiped out already in the mid-sixteenth century. Before

Mohács Magyars had represented 75-80 per cent of the total population, which was estimated at 3.5-4 million, but by 1600 it was assessed at only about 2.5 million. Around 1720, after the withdrawal of the Turks, it was about 4 million, i.e. little more than in the late Middle Ages.[2]

There are two important factors to consider with regard to these figures. According to Thomas von Bogyay, the population should have increased at least threefold over 200 years under normal circumstances, and by this calculation the natural increase of 8–10 million was completely lost—almost entirely to the detriment of the Magyars. Szekfü even went so far as to say that without the Turkish intervention the population could have risen to 15–20 million by the end of the seventeenth century, the proportion of Magyars being 80–90 per cent. More critical was the radical shift in the ethnic mix to the disadvantage of the Hungarians. They had borne the brunt of the fighting, and Hungarian slaves were considered especially desirable in the Ottoman Empire, commanding high prices. Having no inaccessible mountain regions in which to hide, Hungarians suffered more than the inhabitants of the Balkans, and in further contrast to the Balkans, the number of converts to Islam was small.

The steady flight of Serbs northwards and of Slovaks southwards, as well as the massive influx of Romanians from Wallachia, diminished the Hungarian share of the total population to approximately half. In 1690/1 alone, on Emperor Leopold's command, about 200,000 Serbs fleeing a Turkish counter-offensive had to be taken in by Hungary. If we consider the deliberate large-scale settlement of Germans and Slavs in the eighteenth century, it is not surprising that the census of 1787 showed only a 39 per cent Hungarian share of the 8.5 million inhabitants. These bare figures mask a tragic national development.

The Great Plains south of the Györ-Buda-Debrecen line were changed over the decades into a treeless steppe-like *puszta* by destruction, depopulation and deforestation. Once flourishing villages became uninhabited after the flight of the peasants. In 1605 a traveller met a handful of peasants in Vác, not far from Buda, who knew only from hearsay that there had once been a rich town where their humble village now stood. Edward Brown, a traveller from England,

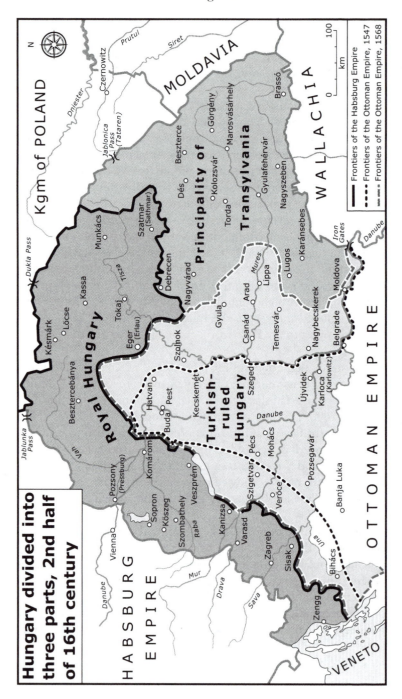

Hungary divided into three parts, 2nd half of 16th century

N

Kgm of POLAND

MOLDAVIA

WALLACHIA

HABSBURG EMPIRE

OTTOMAN EMPIRE

VENETO

Principality of Transylvania

Royal Hungary

Turkish-ruled Hungary

Frontiers of the Habsburg Empire
Frontiers of the Ottoman Empire, 1547
Frontiers of the Ottoman Empire, 1568

0   100
km

Prutul
Siret
Czernowitz
Dniester
Jablonica Pass (Tataren)
Dukla Pass
Jablunka Pass

Brassó
Görgény
Marosvásárhely
Beszterce
Dés
Kolozsvár
Gyulafehérvár
Torda
Nagyszeben
Karánsebes
Iron Gates
Danube
Lugos
Moldova
Nagybecskerek
Belgrade

Munkács
Szatmár (Sathmar)
Késmárk
Lőcse
Kassa
Tisza
Tokaj
Eger (Erlau)
Debrecen
Nagyvárad
Besztercebánya
Szolnok
Gyula
Arad
Csanád
Mures
Lippa
Temesvár

Hatvan
Buda Pest
Kecskemét
Szeged
Újvidék
Karlóca (Karlowitz)

Váh
Pozsony (Pressburg)
Komárom
Veszprém
Pécs
Mohács
Pozsegavár
Banja Luka
Danube

Vienna
Sopron
Kőszeg
Szombathely
Kanizsa
Szigetvár
Verőce
Raba

Varasd
Zagreb
Sisak
Bihács
Zengg
Mur
Drava
Sava
Una
Danube

reported in 1669–70 that on his journey from Vienna to Belgrade he passed through a seemingly endless dark green grass steppe that impressed him as like an immense ocean.

On 16 January 1717 Lady Mary Wortley Montagu, on her way to Constantinople with her husband, the new English ambassador to the Sublime Porte, wrote to her friend in Vienna:

Prince Eugene was good enough to tell me all this, in order to talk me into awaiting the thawing of the Danube, and to travel in comfort by water. He assured me that the houses in Hungary did not even give shelter against the weather, and that I would have to travel from Buda to Eszék without encountering a single house for three or four days through barren, snow-covered plains, where the cold is so severe that it has already killed several people. I confess that these horrors have left a deep impression on my mind....[3]

The effect of Ottoman rule in central Hungary and Transdanubia was the complete devastation of entire areas. In the mid-seventeenth century the damage in the Turkish-occupied areas extended over 90 per cent of the plains and two-thirds of the arable land, and affected half the livestock. That was not all; after the occupation of southern and central Hungary the Sultan's armies devastated everything that stood in their way, including entire villages, not only in the "great" wars but also during incessant skirmishes in times of so-called peace. Especially dreaded were the Crimean Tatar auxiliary troops, who marched through Hungary and Transylvania leaving a bloodstained trail in their wake.

Even in Buda, the administrative centre, Turkish officials registered a drop in the taxpaying households from 58,742 in 1577/8 to only 12,527 in 1661/3. Armed clashes, famines, endemic disease, slave-raids and, last but not least, the killing of numerous fugitives depopulated once flourishing regions. Now Romanians and Serbs who had infiltrated or already settled there mostly lived in primitive wooden huts, half sunk into the ground, which they abandoned when land became fallow, or at the first sign of danger from border clashes. Nothing illustrates the devastation better than the fact that even a generation after the Turks had left Debrecen, the largest town in eastern Hungary, it had only 8,000 inhabitants and Szeged in the south as few as 5,000. Within a radius of 40 km. outside these towns barely a single settlement remained. Transdanubia was also badly affected. At the end of the Middle Ages, in the 1490s, this region was settled almost exclusively by Hungarians, and the number of inhabitants was 900,000. Under Turkish rule the population fell to a third, and as late as 1720 only half a million people were counted, the share of Hungarians in the total having fallen to about half.[4]

The Turkish conquerors divided the country into five administrative areas or *pashaliks* under the control of Beglerbeg, Pasha of Buda. All the land passed into the absolute ownership of the state, which kept one-fifth of it for the so-called "Khas" lands "for Allah", administering it directly. While the state lands offered a certain legal security and stability of administration, and the peasants often bore lighter burdens than under the former landlords, the Turkish professional soldiers (*spahis*) and officials wanted to make the maximum profit from their revocable fiefs. The result was wanton exploitation and the peasants' consequent flight from the land. The famous *puszta* in eastern Hungary with its extensive cattle- and horse-breeding is primarily the inheritance of these times.

The administration of the Turkish-occupied third of Hungarian territory remained virtually a foreign entity. The conquerors' only aim was to safeguard their suzerainty in the territories they occupied. The frequent changes of officials and handing over (enfeoffments) of feudal benefices served this purpose. The higher the rank of an official, the shorter the time he stayed in Hungary—Constantinople used this rule of thumb to prevent the growth of personal links. During the 145 years of Turkish occupation of Buda there were ninety-nine pashas in that high position.

The relative national and religious freedom was the result of an administration which ignored local institutions, cementing its own existence by just that fact. As long as obligations to the occupiers were adhered to, the Turks did not interfere in the domestic affairs of their Christian subjects. There was no attempt to blend or assimilate the Hungarian population, whose number under direct Turkish rule, according to various estimates, was between 1 and 1.5 million. Furthermore the Turks did not differentiate between nobles and commoners. A simple soldier on the battlefield and a loyal peasant could with relative ease receive a patent of nobility. At first this was meaningless, which probably explains why it was so easy to attain, and why there was a steady increase in the number of poor petty nobles, not only in Royal Hungary and the principality of Transylvania but in the Turkish territories. The Turks tolerated the peasants and the communities paying dues to the Hungarian state or their absentee landlords, and even submitted communal projects and lawsuits to the county authorities in the Royal Habsburg part of the country. The absence of closed frontiers and the freedom of traders and clerics to travel freely from one territory to another gave the national will to survive an immensely important long-term stimulus.

The political jokes of communist-ruled Hungary 400 years later assume a special relevance against this background:

Q. Why did Nikolai Podgorny [the Russian head of state] go on an official visit recently to Turkey?
A. To find out how the Turkish army managed to stay in Hungary for 150 years...

A variant concerned the regular celebrations in Hungary of the anniversary of its "liberation" by the Red Army, considered by most Hungarians as slavery.

An envoy from Moscow travelled to Ankara and interviewed a high official to get some information from the appropriate authorities:

Q. How did the Turks manage to rule these recalcitrant Hungarians for 150 years?
A. We never forced them to celebrate the anniversary of the Battle of Mohács.

The Turkish system at its best was barren and unconstructive and at its most frequent worst savagely destructive. So concludes Macartney, who adds that the Turks brought nothing to Hungary except fortresses and a few bath houses, and what they found there they destroyed or allowed to fall into ruin. However, Turkish motives are repeatedly looked for in the poems of the greatest Hungarian poet Bálint Balassi, who died a hero's death in the siege of Esztergom in 1594, and whose poetry, according to the literary historian György Mihály Vajda, reflects "true religiosity" as much as "sensual unrestraint". Originating from a family of medieval robber barons and

Renaissance adventurers, Balassi wrote and spoke a new language. Sometimes he complained of "the ruin of the Hungarian nation", then he sings the praises of the Viennese girls Susanna and Anna-Maria who live in "Tiefengraben". He acquired fame for his love-affairs but even more so as a soldier on the battlefield. His most beautiful love poems were, incidentally, found and published as late as 1879.

Balassi was not the only lyricist to die a hero's death, but until the death of Sándor Petőfi in 1848 he was the most inspired. Then, as well as later, the skirmishes for frontier forts along the borderlands of Royal Hungary and Transylvania, the daring sallies from besieged bastions, and the legendary duels between renowned warriors provided subjects for poets and composers. Heroic commanders of castles and frontier forts such as Miklós Jurisich at Kőszeg, György Szondi at Drégely, István Dobó at Eger and, especially, Miklós Zrinyi at Szigetvár repeatedly held up Turkish attacks against Vienna with great daring and so entered the annals of Hungarian and German-language literature. Thus almost a century later the famous general Count Miklós Zrinyi wrote the epic poem *The Peril of Sziget* about the heroic death in battle of his great-grandfather with the same name. A century and a half later the poet Theodor Körner used the same topic in his play *Zrinyi*, first performed in Vienna in 1812, in which one of the characters exclaims: "A free Hungarian bows only to his God or his king!" The hymn about the courage of the Hungarians and their loyalty to their ruler is said to have been thunderously acclaimed by the Viennese with their fight for freedom against Napoleon in mind.[5] (We return later to the totally different relationship between the Zrinyi family and the Habsburgs.)

Hungarian bravery was already famous throughout Europe at the time of the Turkish confrontations. Aeneas Sylvius Piccolomini, later Pope Pius II, wrote in a private letter that if the Hungarians had not shed their blood, the other European nations would have had to do so. Contemporary German, French and Italian observers also extolled the Hungarians' fighting qualities. The Croat Georgievitz, who called himself "Peregrinus Hungaricus" (a traveller in Hungary), exclaimed in 1554: "Which nation is more courageous than the Hungarian?"

In a profound essay on the Hungarian image in Europe. Sándor Eckhardt remarks that this approbation is sometimes combined with compassion, as for example in Voltaire: "Among all the peoples who in the course of history have passed before our eyes there were none as unlucky as the Hungarians... Nature brought forth their strong, handsome, clever men in vain...." Eckhardt also quotes Jean Bodin, who believed that the key to the Magyars' military aptitude was to be found in atmospheric conditions' according to ancient climatic studies: "Hungary is a windy country; that is why its inhabitants are more spirited and warlike." The Frenchman, on the other hand, is polite and of pleasant habits because he lives in a temperate latitude....[6]

10. Transylvania—the Stronghold of Hungarian Sovereignty

There is no doubt that the autonomy of Transylvania, achieved by that tireless champion of Hungary's unity Frater György, became an important locus of Hungarian statehood in the midst of German and Ottoman domination and a haven of Hungarian culture and identity that was significant for the nation's future.

The trisection of Hungary resulted in the nation being split into two camps above and beyond the explosive religious division. The principality of Transylvania, being ruled by Hungarian princes nominated or approved by the Sultan, was an obvious stepping-stone for the Ottoman Empire's expansionism. Because the isolation and weakening of the Habsburgs served Turkish interests, princes of European stature such as István Báthory (who was elected king of Poland), István Bocskai and Gábor Bethlen could develop Transylvania into a bastion of twofold resistance against the Habsburgs and the Counter-Reformation which they so strongly promoted.

At the end of the sixteenth century Transylvania was larger in area than the Hungary of today: 100,000 as against 93,000 square km. The principality comprised the so-called "*Partium*" as well, i.e. those northern and south-eastern counties that had been separated from the Hungarian rump kingdom by a Turkish-controlled wedge. The fertile and densely populated borderlands added considerably to Hungarian predominance. Estimates suggest that about 955,000 people lived at this time in the principality of Transylvania: about half a million Hungarians including 250,000 Székelys, 280,000 Romanians, 90,000 Saxons and about 86,000 "others", mainly Serbs and Ukrainians. However, the core of Transylvania, i.e. without the counties and towns belonging to the "*Partium*", was only 60,000 square km. and had a mere 650,000 inhabitants. This clarification is important because in the seventeenth century during domestic turmoil and external attacks the rich region of the "*Partium*" was temporarily occupied by the Turks.[1] The significance of this relatively small principality can only be understood against this multiethnic and multicultural background. Just at the time when Hungarian spiritual and cultural life was almost extinguished in the parts of the country ruled by the Habsburgs and the Turks, Transylvania proved to be the bastion of tolerance and national culture.

From the sixteenth to the eighteenth century the matter of religious freedom and the battle between Reformation and Counter-Reformation could not be divorced from the political right of self-determination and the political aspects of the Turkish system of vassalage. The Ottoman Empire was uninterested in this religious conflict, yet the positions of the protagonists involved cross-border relations. However, the desire for reunification with Royal Hungary, especially in the sixteenth century, played an important role in the principality's foreign policy. The Sublime Porte identified the Catholic position with the Habsburgs, their most formidable enemy, and the Protestant position with the Transylvanian protectorate. At a later stage alliances were made against the Habsburgs by rebellious Transylvanian princes and French kings, with the Sultan's benevolent support—the result simply of the Turks regarding the enemies of their arch-enemy as their friends.

For almost two centuries, between the tragedy of Mohács and the forced peace of Szatmár following the failed fight for freedom by Ferenc Rákóczi II in 1711 (see Chapters 14 and 15), the greatest and most courageous princes, magnates, soldiers, clerics, thinkers, poets and students endeavoured to salvage Hungary's national existence from the clutches of the two greatest potentates, the Emperor and the Sultan. It was a constant conflict, a confusing tug-of-war between realism and illusion, between recognizing the situation and maintaining the claims of ancient greatness. During the era of foreign rule and domestic anarchy, concepts such as loyalty and treachery, freedom and suppression conformed to no clear-cut pattern with, on the one side, Christendom and, on the other, infidel Islam. Particularly during the period of Reformation and Counter-Reformation the sense of Christian unity was not always stronger than the aversion from "the Germans", i.e. "the Habsburgs", even amounting to hatred. In times of necessity the Defenders of

Christendom joined even with the Turkish arch-enemy against Vienna and the excesses of the Counter-Reformation, to which was added the cruelty of foreign mercenaries.[2]

Hungarian nationality and religious freedom were inseparable, particularly in the fight against the Catholic-Germanizing trend in the sixteenth and seventeenth centuries. The choice between temporary agreement with the Turks, or uncompromising struggle against the infidel was a question which, in different circumstances and to different degrees, split Hungary's political and intellectual élite more than once. When the nation's survival, culture and statehood were being considered, the great national task was reunification of a country arbitrarily divided into three parts. The option of independent or less independent action, of bad or not so bad solutions, of the greater or lesser evil, called for some dramatic changes of course and infinite flexibility. The Ottomans and Habsburgs were enemies, and at the same time allies of divided Hungary. Hungarians, fighting in both camps, took part in bloody confrontations against one or the other on several occasions. Contemporaries interpreted the concepts of friend and foe very differently. In both camps there were champions of "the true cause of the beloved country", who regarded those in the other camp as traitors. Especially during the Reformation and Counter-Reformation, the heroes and apostles of religious freedom from and in Transylvania were branded "guilty of high treason", "power-hungry adventurers", "Turkish mercenaries" and "enemies of Christianity" not only in Royal Hungary but also in the German literature of the time.

After the battle of Mohács the Reformation swept like wildfire over Hungary. A year before the fateful defeat, the Diet had still demanded that the followers of the Lutheran confession (at that time still almost exclusively Germans) be burned at the stake. The agents of Protestantism were Hungarian and German students from Hungary. For instance, in 1616 the University of Wittenberg alone counted 340 Hungarian students. Others studied in Basel, Geneva, Leiden, Utrecht and even Oxford. Up to the end of the sixteenth century 2,850 students from Hungary were registered at foreign universities (their ethnic origin was not recorded).[3]

However, Lutheranism prevailed in the districts and towns of northern Hungary inhabited partly by Germans and Slovaks, and in

Transdanubia, while the Hungarians, particularly in Transylvania, turned to Calvinism. The Nationality and religious denomination over-lapped, creating a bulwark against Islam (the Turks), Catholicism (the Habsburgs) and Orthodoxy (Romanians and Serbs). The Reformation thus embodied a national character; men of the cloth became the vanguard and mainstay of the national idea, and students returning from Switzerland and the Netherlands became creators of a national literature that arose from religious writings and Bible translations.

In his work *The Three Historical Regions of Europe*, quoted earlier, Jenö Szücs referred to the reasons for the delay in the change from Latin to Hungarian: "The lack of feudal courts and a chivalrous milieu delayed Hungarian becoming the written language by three centuries." The earliest coherent literary relic in Hungarian—a funeral oration—was found in a Latin codex from the end of the twelfth century. The ancient Hungarian *Mary Lament*, one of the most beautiful poems in the language, originates from around 1300; the *Legend of Princess* (Saint) *Margaret* and the *Legend of St Francis* were written around 1310 and 1370 respectively; both survive only in later copies. They were probably the earliest Hungarian translations. The authors of religious texts and poems began to write in Hungarian only as late as the end of the fifteenth century. The first Hungarian-language books were printed in Cracow in 1527 and Vienna in 1536, and the first press in Hungary itself that printed in the native language was established in 1537. The most important book to be produced was arguably Gáspár Károlyi's first complete translation of the Bible, which appeared in 1590.

A surprising aspect of the birth and upsurge of Hungarian culture was that so many of the greatest intellects between the sixteenth and nineteenth centuries belonged to men of Croat, German, Slovak and Jewish origin. Their Hungarianness was the result of choice, not of accidents of birth. This was true, for example, of the Lutheran pastor Caspar Helth, who was active in the largely Hungarian-inhabited city of Kolozsvár. The Saxon cleric learned Hungarian only as an adult, and because of his love of the language he became its first great stylist and at the same time printer and publisher of Hungarian Bible translations and other works (1552–66). He is known in Hungarian literary history by the name Gáspár

Heltai. The first bishop of the Hungarian Calvinists in Kolozsvár, originally called Franz Hertel, later become known as the Protestant philosopher and preacher, Ferenc Dávid.

There was never religious persecution in Transylvania, and the principality even became the bulwark of religious tolerance, a rarity in the Europe of the day. The first Prince, János Zsigmond, changed his religion four times. His great successors provided for a peaceful coexistence of the various faiths; several Diets (1550, 1564, 1572) declared the right to religious freedom, first for Catholics and Protestants and later, after the split within Protestantism into Lutherans, Calvinists and Unitarians, for all creeds. During the "golden age" of Gábor Bethlen (1613–29) Transylvania served as a unique example of tolerance. Thus Bethlen recalled the Jesuits, expelled earlier from the principality, and even gave financial support to the Bible translation of the Jesuit György Káldor. For his own reformed Church the Prince founded a Calvinist academy, printing press and library, but at the same time he assented to a vicar-general for the Catholics and a bishop for the Greek Orthodox Romanians, and freed the Romanian clergy from their "bondage obligations" and the Jews from wearing the yellow Star of David. Romanian Orthodoxy counted as a "tolerated" religion because the Romanians did not constitute a nation of Estates (like the Hungarians, Székelys and Saxons since 1437); thus although Orthodoxy could be freely practised, its followers were denied political equality.[4] Bethlen settled in Transylvania a group of Anabaptists, persecuted elsewhere in Europe.

In the mean time the Habsburg Counter-Reformation was proceeding with full force in the kingdom of Hungary. The central figure and architect of the successful re-Catholization was the Jesuit Péter Pázmány, Cardinal-Archbishop of Esztergom (1570–1637). He crossed swords with the Protestant preachers in Latin and Hungarian in his persuasive style, winning back thirty magnate families to the Catholic fold; in most cases everyone living on the magnates' estates had to follow suit according to the principle of *cuius regio eius religio* that operated after the 1555 Religious Peace of Augsburg. Pázmány also founded a university in 1635 at Nagyszombat (Trnava), which still exists today in Budapest.

Re-Catholization exacerbated the confessional split between Hungarians in the west and east as well as the attitude towards the

Turks. Hungarian poets, philosophers and politicians called the seventeenth century the century of "Hungarian decay". Even though Turkish domination was the decisive factor in Hungary's decline, the consequences of the intolerant and at times cruel rule of the Habsburg representatives in Royal Hungary and Transylvania counted too. For Protestants harried by the agents of the Counter-Reformation in Royal Hungary their persecutors were "worse than the Turks". The so-called Fifteen Years' War that broke out between the Habsburgs and the Ottomans in 1591 also plunged Transylvania into turmoil and misery.

The alliance of Emperor Rudolf and the young Prince Zsigmond Báthory (1581–97), nephew of the first elected Prince and later great King of Poland István Báthory, at first achieved significant successes against the Turks. This young, athletic prince at first appeared brave and attractive, but soon turned out to be a sinister and aberrant figure, like a Shakespearean villain. His decline into an unpredictable and bloodthirsty psychopath was hastened by his unhappy and unconsummated marriage to the Habsburg Princess Maria Christina. Zsigmond was impotent, and to keep this a secret—and compensate for it—he was constantly on the run from his wife and his country, which he plunged into chaos with his bizarre escapades. He announced his abdication no less than five times, only to return soon afterwards. Zsigmond left Transylvania first to the mercy of the imperial commander Giorgio Basta, then to the equally cruel intervention of Michael the Brave, *voivode* of Wallachia, and finally to the Turks, eager for revenge.[5]

In the mean time Emperor Rudolf II strove by coercion to re-Catholicize predominantly Protestant Transylvania, mainly by forced conversions and confiscation of estates on trumped-up charges of high treason. His general Basta unleashed a reign of terror against the Hungarians of Transylvania with his mostly Walloon. Italian and Spanish mercenary troops. Although the inhabitants of the German towns in Upper Hungary looked up to the Princes Bocskai, Bethlen and Rákoczi as the champions of religious freedom, the conduct of the mercenary armies and their generals fuelled the dislike and later sheer hatred of Germans in general, and by extension the Habsburgs.

These punishments and atrocities inflicted by the imperial authorities provoked a revolt led by one of Zsigmond's generals (and his uncle), István Bocskai, previously one of the Emperor's most loyal supporters. In the midst of bloody chaos, this Calvinist landowner and gifted soldier raised an army of daring warriors, the Hajduks. Of Slavic background, they had originally been wild herdsmen of the plains, but later consisted mainly of Magyar refugees driven from their homes by the long war against the Turks and Germans and living on the fringes of society. Even though the expansion of Lutheranism aroused the Hungarians' dislike of German influence, the Habsburgs' unrelenting Counter-Reformation hit the German-speakers in the towns of Upper Hungary with particular force. Bocskai's fight for political and religious freedom therefore gained the support not only of Hungarians, but also of German burghers and the lesser nobility.

Bocskai had been known as one of the Habsburgs' most loyal followers and a Turcophobe, and his volte face and fervent calls also to the nobles in Transdanubia proved the most convincing argument that a patriot could make common cause even with the Turks in the interests of the country, the Hungarians and religious freedom. An attack by the new imperial commander Barbiano on Bocskai's estates was crucial in this *volte face*. The Hungarian Hajduks changed sides from the Emperor to Bocskai who, with the help of Turkish and Tatar units, soon scored overwhelming victories. Elected Prince of Transylvania in 1605 as well as of Hungary—he refused the kingship that was offered to him—Bocskai concluded a peace treaty with the Emperor. This recognized his life tenure in Transylvania, which was enlarged by four counties. The Imperial powers also had to guarantee wide-ranging religious freedom for all ranks of the nobility, the free cities and the market-towns, extension of the nobles' political rights, and restoration of the office of palatine. In November 1606 Bocksai mediated the Peace of Zsitvatorok between the Emperor and the Sublime Porte on the basis of the *status quo*. Soon after this he died, probably poisoned by his over-ambitious Chancellor, who in turn was hacked to pieces a few days later by the Hajduks.

Bocskai's victories and diplomatic successes ushered in a new phase of Hungarian history. In an impressive testament, unpublished till about two centuries later, the Prince urged "the Transylvanians... never to separate from Hungary, even if they have a different Prince;

and the Hungarians that they should never toss away the Transylvanians from themselves, but should regard them as their brothers, their own blood, their own limbs". He considered the equilibrium between the Germans and the Ottoman Empire vital for Hungary, and he therefore unequivocally declared himself in favour of a strong Transylvanian principality under the aegis of the Sultan: "So long as the Hungarian crown is in the hands of a stronger nation, the Germans, and so long as the Hungarian kingdom is dependent on the Germans, it is necessary and useful to maintain a Hungarian prince in Transylvania, since he will protect the Hungarians as well." Transylvania as the stronghold of Hungarian sovereignty until the re-emergence of a Hungarian kingdom, followed by a confederation between it and Hungary—this was the political credo of Bocskai. His statue can be seen next to Calvin's on the monument of the Reformation in Geneva.[6]

Although the Habsburgs succeeded in re-Catholicizing Royal Hungary, east of the Tisza the Reformation remained almost intact in the spirit of peaceful coexistence between the three recognized nations and respect for their diverse creeds. Referring to the Habsburgs' destruction of Bohemian independence during the Thirty Years' War, an anonymous late-seventeenth-century pamphlet entitled *The Moaning and Wailing* declared that the Habsburgs did not succeed in dressing the Hungarians "in Czech trousers".[7]

11. Gábor Bethlen—Vassal, Patriot and European

"If only he had not been born at all, or else had lived forever!" With these words János Kemény, loyal follower, biographer and successor of Gábor (Gabriel) Bethlen (1613–29), lamented the passing of this Prince of Transylvania. Bethlen, called by some the "Hungarian Machiavelli", was one of the most significant and at the same time unfathomable and unpredictable of all Hungarian statesmen, as well as the most successful and internationally noted ruler of the Principality of Transylvania.

In his *Wallenstein*[1] Golo Mann sketched a dismal and in parts superficial portrait of the man regarded as creator and symbol of the relatively brief "golden age" of autonomous Transylvania. According to him Bethlen was "a vassal almost in bondage of the Turks", "a Magyar and firm Calvinist... but fickle in worldly matters, for ever turning over new political projects in his mind", "unreliable", "chasing daydreams... before existing systems" with "a fevered fantasy born of rambling ambition and fear"; a man who "appeared in a place suddenly with his barbarians, raising hopes, posing riddles, only to disappear again". Golo Mann also made fun of the books describing Bethlen as "a barbarian and stranger to European ways", "a circumcised and clandestine Muslim", even "a Tatar and many other things", but conceded that the Prince came from an "old Magyar noble family" and that his second marriage was to Catherine of Brandenburg. The latter is correct, but the assertion that Bethlen wanted to establish a "Magyar-Slav empire", a "half Protestant, half Orthodox kingdom of Dacia, including Moldavia and Wallachia" is fiction; no evidence of such aims can be found either in his 1,500 surviving letters or in the numerous studies of his times.

Two decisions the Prince made alone, which have been much discussed in Hungarian and international historiography, demonstrate rather that he was always guided by a cautious sense of the reality of power. One occurred in November 1619 when, faced with what was thought to be an imminent attack by Vienna, he ordered his troops to retreat to Pressburg, and the other a year later when he declined coronation as King of Hungary, which was not only offered to him but had been approved by his Ottoman patrons. That the ruler of a small state "in Europe's deepest South-east" (thus Golo Mann) could have had influence well beyond his tiny principality, and shuffled the cards against the Habsburgs by three attacks, each carried out with a different ally, during the first phase of the Thirty Years' War, was clear evidence of his prestige as an undefeated general and his accomplished diplomacy. Bethlen was essentially a cynical tactician, who kept his country in an iron grip even while on campaigns.

One reason for the apparent unpredictability of Hungarian history is the intermittent emergence of charismatic personalities— sparks who lit a fuse or managed to master a seemingly hopeless situation by the art of small steps. Gábor Bethlen was unpopular and distrusted, but on one aspect his followers, admirers, critics and enemies agreed, even if reluctantly: his distinction as a statesman and politician.[2]

The circumstances surrounding Bethlen's seizure of power were unusual. Born in 1580, he first served three princes as diplomatic adviser, fought in thirty-four battles, and was wounded several times. Only after emigrating twice did the thirty-three-year-old seasoned veteran of palace intrigue and power struggles take the decisive leap for the top. The reigning Prince Báthory, after several escapades, had wanted to come to some arrangement with the Habsburgs, whereas Bethlen steadfastly followed the line of preserving Transylvania's independence under Turkish protection. Although he had once helped Báthory to power, mutual alienation and an alleged murder plot by the Prince against his pro-Turkish adviser had followed, whereupon Bethlen fled with fifty followers into the Ottoman domain. This afforded him the opportunity to consult and scheme with the influential Turkish pashas in Temesvár, Buda, Belgrade and Edirne against the ever more unreliable Báthory, and above all to gain the trust of the Grand Vizier and the Sultan.

Everything went according to plan. Bethlen, as the Porte's representative, was entrusted to relieve the luckless Báthory, and he was accompanied by Turkish-Tatar-Romanian troops sent from all directions. For the first time in Transylvania's history a Turkish commander, Pasha Skender of Kanizsa, convoked the principality's assembly to Kolozsvár—in order to "elect" as their prince the candidate of the Sublime Porte, namely Bethlen. About 80,000 foreign soldiers were on hand to support Bethlen's claim to power, and it was said that so many Turks and Tatars had never been in the principality as in that fateful year, 1613. Despite intimidation by the Pasha, the election was carried out in an orderly fashion to keep up the appearance of legitimacy. Already during the election Bethlen gave eloquent proof of his diplomatic acumen by asking the Estates, assembled on Pasha Skender's orders, to lift the ostracism pronounced against him after his flight in 1612; he then left the chamber. It was a polite obeisance before the Transylvanian nobility at the moment of their unprecedented humiliation.

The stocky, bearded man, lacking anything more than basic education, had to look on while the troops who had helped him to power left a trail of destruction and abductions in their wake. Even the Pasha lost control over their orgiastic killing spree. The Prince expressed no remorse for the infamous deeds of his patron's troops, just as he never bothered to establish an aristocratic group or party before the "election", or ascertain whether he had the support of the King or the magnates in Royal Hungary. Public opinion seems not to have interested him. The challenger of the reigning Prince based everything on support from Constantinople, knowing that Transylvania's fate would be decided there and only there.

Four days after his election, in broad daylight, Hajduk soldiers assassinated the dismissed Báthory. Although persistent rumours that Bethlen had instigated the murder could never be substantiated, the Spanish nobleman Don Diego de Estrada, dancing master at Bethlen's court, maintained in his memoirs, printed 300 years later in Madrid, that Bethlen confided to him that Báthory had to pay for having raped Bethlen's first wife during his absence.

Despite Bethlen's loyalty, his ability quickly to find a way to appease his Saxon and Hungarian opponents, and his courageous compromises, he could not enforce his power undisturbed; his patrons wanted additional tangible and, for the vassal's prestige, particularly embarrassing confirmation of his dependence. The Porte sent high-ranking envoys to try and force the surrender of two forts which Hungarian fighters had held for several years. After lengthy negotiations Bethlen got the demand reduced, so that the Turks only took the castle of Lippa in the southeastern border region. Its garrison put up a stiff resistance, and Bethlen was reluctantly obliged to take the fortress himself and hand it over to the Turks after thirteen days of bloody fighting. No Hungarian ruler had ever before voluntarily surrendered a castle to the Ottoman power, and the case probably marked the nadir of the Prince's career, as the three-volume *History of Transylvania*, published by the Hungarian Academy of Sciences in 1986, makes clear:

Had Gábor Bethlen died at the time, he would be counted among the most disastrous figures of Hungarian history. But that did not happen, and he reigned for another thirteen years, rising to rank among the greatest historical personages.

But how did Bethlen accomplish this political miracle, caught between the mistrustful nobility and people of Transylvania, the ever-watchful Sublime Porte, and—frequently in the midst of complicated negotiations—the fickle Hungarian magnates in Royal Hungary? Ágnes Hankiss[3] points out in a fascinating study that Bethlen attempted to reduce national dependence by relying on one foreign power while covertly fighting against another. It was a tightrope act carried out partly with a historical target and partly with inevitable opportunism: for Bethlen the end justified the means, which may have made him a Hungarian Machiavelli of Calvinist persuasion. Florentine fatalism and Calvinist predestination did not seem to him contradictory notions. But what of the aim? This was the gradual achievement of a concept that was boldly pan-European. Its most important aspects were securing the independence of Transylvania with Turkish help against the political expansion and religious intolerance of the Habsburgs; alliance with the Protestant Estates of Bohemia and Moravia and, after their defeat in 1620, with Sweden, the Netherlands and England to open the way to a re-established united Hungary; enthronement of a national king; and establishment of a pan-European anti-Habsburg coalition, which would also provide an extended band of security against total subordination to the Ottomans.

Thus Bethlen's vision was a re-birth of King Mathias's empire, with the help of that selfsame Turkish power which it had annihilated barely a century earlier. To condemn him outright, as some historians (Golo Mann among them) have done, is surely mistaken. Bethlen's bold pan-European plans were based partly on miscalculation, not least regarding the balance of power between the Great Powers and Hungary's potential; he was also deluded over the attitude of the magnates and the nobility in Royal Hungary. However, it is facile to dismiss an experiment with hindsight and full knowledge of subsequent history. From the viewpoint of his own time it was not implausible—and at least worth the attempt. According to Szekfü, Bethlen's tragedy was that he came too soon, when the Hungarians in the West still believed that their wishes could prevail in Vienna without resort to arms. Half a century later it would have been easier, but then the ruler was the much weaker Prince Mihály Apafi, a true vassal who nonetheless succeeded by clever manoeuvring to give his subjects a long period of peace.

Bethlen's foreign policy was a veritable cavalcade of ideas, intrigues and darting actions, which frequently confused contemporaries and therefore provoked retrograde reactions. This brilliant power-politician was in no way a tool of the Sublime Porte, and he did not act only in the Ottoman interest. He was a "tightrope-walker and a master of small steps" (Hankiss); if he revealed his true intentions he would be faced sooner or later with a Turkish reaction, while if he concealed them too cunningly he could hardly expect to gain, let alone keep, the confidence of the people and his allies. In the judgement of an unnamed Turkish dignitary, "This infidel never helped the armies of Islam; he always thought only of his own country." Sir Thomas Roe, English ambassador to the Sublime Porte, did not see it in such clear terms: he admired the crafty prince but never understood his character, and concluded his reports to London with the words "but all this is dissimulation".[4]

Bethlen's extensive correspondence, as well as the memoirs and evidence of contemporaries, leave no doubt as to his true convictions: he did not believe that the House of Habsburg could have ejected the Turks from all of Hungary or even wanted to do so. According to his concept, only a re-established national kingdom of Hungary could open the path to independence, at first under the aegis of the Porte but eventually, after a change in power relations, against the "protecting power". In contrast to his most significant opponents on the Imperial-Catholic side—most notably the head of the Church, Péter Pázmány, spokesman of the Counter-Reformation, and Miklós Eszterházy, the powerful governor—Bethlen subordinated his entire policy to the immediate goal of repelling Habsburg expansion to the east. In the final analysis, the Turkish system of vassal states left enough scope not only for Bethlen but also for his successor György Rákoczi I to pursue their own concepts—so much so that the two of them could even forge an alliance with Sweden and Brandenburg against the Emperor.

Bethlen immediately recognized the significance of the Prague uprising against the Habsburgs and did not want to remain neutral under any circumstances. With the acquiescence of his Turkish patrons he made contact with Protestant Hungarian aristocrats and Czech insurrectionists, and in the late summer of 1619 offered help to Bohemia and, after an extraordinarily swift advance over long distances, became embroiled in the Thirty Years' War. With a crafty feint followed by a large-scale attack, his troops took the town of Kassa in north-eastern Upper Hungary and Pressburg, then capital of Hungary, where the palatine handed over to him the crown of St Stephen which had been kept there in the citadel. In a short time Bethlen captured almost all of Royal Hungary, and appeared before Vienna at the head of an army consisting of some 50,000 Bohemian, Moravian and Hungarian troops.

There were presumably several reasons for the Prince's decision to move on Pressburg. Officially his motive in discontinuing the siege of Vienna was the appearance in Eastern Hungary of Polish mercenaries who had advanced across the Carpathians, making common cause with his arch-enemy, the Catholic magnate Homonnai, and threatening his rule in Transylvania. However, it is more likely that he had recognized the hopelessness of besieging Vienna. Bethlen preferred a moral to a military defeat, which still did not lessen his popularity in Hungary.

Only a year later Bethlen with his light cavalry was again in Royal Hungary. Faced with a reinforced Habsburg central power, the majority of the Hungarian magnates supported him, this time as candidate for the Hungarian throne, although this would have deprived him of almost all power and transformed the new state into a playground for the nobility's unlimited privileges. In fact, the royal election took place on 25 August 1620 in Besztercebánya (Banská Bystrica), but Bethlen decided to postpone the coronation, awaiting the outcome of the war or an agreement with Emperor Ferdinand II.

In the mean time he had to cope with all kinds of adversities, particularly a serious humiliation by the Pasha of Buda who, instead of supporting the Prince's fighting army, besieged and captured the castle of Vác. On 8 November 1620 the Bohemian Estates suffered a crucial defeat at the battle of the White Mountain near Prague, and in view of this debacle and the terrible retaliation that followed, the Estates in Royal Hungary refused to take any more risks with Bethlen. However, he fought on alone without capitulating and took in many Protestant refugees in the territories under his control. Leopold von Ranke remarked of this period that Prince Bethlen had become a powerful leader of the worldwide Protestant movement.

Meanwhile Bethlen bombarded the Sublime Porte with letters, presenting precise plans for military actions against Vienna. For instance, he wrote on 10 February 1621 that he could capture even Prague and Cracow with 11,000 Tatars and 4,500 infantrymen as reinforcements for his own troops. The Hungarian Estates capitulated and obtained a full amnesty, as well as considerable tax relief from Emperor Ferdinand II. At the end of December Bethlen finally agreed in the Peace of Nikolsburg (Mikulov) to renounce his royal title and return the crown of St Stephen. In a *quid pro quo* he gained control over seven counties in Upper Hungary and secured self-government for the Estates in Hungary, as well as religious freedom for Protestants. In 1623 he again involved himself in the war on the side of the German Protestants, resulting in a renewed peace agreement mediated by the Hungarian palatine.

In 1626, in alliance with the English-Dutch-Danish coalition, Bethlen again attacked the Habsburgs. However, the planned large-scale pincer movement which—with troops from Brandenburg and France, supplemented by a Turkish-Russian coalition against Poland—would have secured the rear of the Swedish King Gustavus Adolphus, did not materialize. Some of Bethlen's other projects were dropped;

by this time he already had the mark of serious illness on him. These last bold projects only became possible through his marriage to Catherine, sister of the Elector of Brandenburg, which connected him to the King of Sweden. In a letter to the Elector, Bethlen argued that the Habsburgs would never stop hatching plots; and therefore had to be annihilated, or at least completely humbled.

Few were aware at the time that just two years earlier, Bethlen had sought a quite different dynastic association. He had asked for the hand of Ferdinand II's daughter Catherine, planning to turn against the Turks as Regent in Hungary supported by the Emperor; he believed that they could be driven out of Hungary completely within four to five years. The unexpected offer elicited bafflement, and was eventually rejected as implausible. It was only after this failed attempt at shifting alliances that the Prince asked for the hand of Catherine.

It is because Gábor Bethlen was one of Hungary's great correspondents, who as Prince wrote at least one letter every day, often in his own hand, that so much is known today of his devious tactics, mendacious arguments and hypocrisy. Bethlen did not want more land or more power in the conventional sense, but the re-establishment of the kingdom of Hungary split into three, naturally under his overall control, and he attempted to exploit all sides to attain his goals. Even though at the time it was relatively easy for diplomatic arrangements and manoeuvres to be kept secret, a number of Bethlen's intrigues and his promises given simultaneously to various conflicting sides were known. His many secret emissaries, constantly criss-crossing Europe over great distances to deliver his messages, were sometimes intercepted or simply bribed.

The self-revealing letters[5] which found their way into print harmed Bethlen's reputation in a narrow but politically influential circle, but this did not alter the fact that while he lived he secured a strong and significant position for the small principality of Transylvania. His army was never vanquished; even Wallenstein refused to fight a decisive battle against him. During the sixteen years of his reign—as he declared in his testament—no enemy set foot in Transylvania.

Moreover, as already mentioned, Bethlen was not only a dedicated champion of religious tolerance but also a patron of culture

and science. Of the thirty-three students from Transylvania studying at Heidelberg in 1617 six were on stipends from the Prince. In a
letter to his posthumous biographer Gáspár Bojti he offered to
finance his studies for four years, advising him to study in Padua
and Paris as well—theology in addition to philosophy so that Bojti
would later be able to serve him and his country in religious as well
as secular matters. He established a university at Gyulafehérvár with
a library attached to it and invited German poets and musicians,
Viennese goldsmiths and artists from Venice.

Hungarian historians therefore judge Bethlen to have been the
most successful ruler since King Mathias, developing his power
according to the tenets of a modern, mercantilist absolutism. The
principality remained immune from any ill effects of his wars, and
indeed Transylvania enjoyed a "golden age". Bethlen's bountiful
sponsorship of trade, industry, mining and exports bore fruit quickly.
Living standards rose and state revenues doubled, creating the basis
for his ambitious foreign policy and later for princely pomp and
display.

Bethlen read copiously, and took his books with him on his campaigns, having them set up on a desk in his tent. As early as 1620 the
pomp at his court amazed the Duc d'Angoulême, who remarked
that during his visit he had found *"rien de barbare"*. Especially after
marrying Catherine of Brandenburg the Prince increased the
expenses of his court—in the last years of his life from one-tenth to
half of his income. Although hardly anything is left of the palace's
furnishings, we know from inventories and contemporary memoirs
that he matched contemporary monarchs in the splendour of his
court. Thus in 1624 alone the Prince bought 1,000 rugs and in
1625 thirty-one precious rings.

Three decades after Bethlen's death the keeper of the Transylvanian
archives, János Szalárdi, wrote in *The Praise of Prince G. Bethlen*:

He introduced freedoms in the country and with it the service and free
exercise of the holy Lutheran religion, so that his renown and prestige
increased in all of Christendom; the Porte and the Turkish nation trusted
and respected him during his whole life. The result of this was that the
country lived in agreeable peace during his entire reign, and was spared by
external enemies. Each estate appreciated not only in numbers but in
wealth, and the population of the country multiplied. He protected his

people in many wars, carrying out the arduous distant campaigns with mercenaries since he did not want to pit his luck and his people against the Emperor's large army—he saw this as neither desirable nor useful, and thus kept out of violent battles.

Sparing no expense, he introduced from abroad good craftsmen, learned inventors, masons… In other words, he began to build his house, and had his life lasted only a little longer, he would have bequeathed to posterity lasting, glorious works to the benefit and diffusion of religion and the welfare of the nation….[6]

Bethlen's personality and his concepts, political ambitions and achievements are still subjects of controversy in historiography and in the judgement of posterity. In his letters he never ceased criticizing the Hungarian Estates' cowardice and even perfidy in the matter of national liberation. For the magnates and nobility in Royal Hungary the main issue was the preservation and, if possible, augmentation of their privileges. They had no wish for the re-establishment of Hungary's political unity under Bethlen's leadership. The re-Catholicized Estates committed themselves to the Habsburgs. In short, the nobility were split and remained so, and his campaigns and diplomatic machinations made him appear an agent of polarization rather than of harmony. A determined champion of Hungarian independence, he did all in his power to thwart political unity under the Habsburgs, and as the fervent champion of religious tolerance he embroiled Hungary, hitherto spared religious conflict, in armed hostilities between Reformation and Counter-Reformation lasting for decades.

Many personages on the Catholic-Habsburg side such as the Primate Péter Pázmány and the royal governor Miklós Eszterházy were in their way, and in spite of Emperor Ferdinand's guarantee of substantial favours, Hungarian patriots, even if their concepts were fulfilled by the Habsburgs only two generations later and in a quite different way from that envisioned by them. The general situation, as the Hungarian historian Domokos Kosáry argued in his study *The Dangers of History*,[7] was multifaceted: on the one hand, the Habsburgs did not want to commit too much of their military capability to Hungary, and as a result they lacked the resolution to regard more of Hungary as theirs than a mere strip of land necessary for Austria's defence. On the other hand, it was an illusion for

Hungary to believe that it could operate on the side of the Ottomans unscathed and more or less independently as an entity; the
Turks wanted direct conquest or—a more favoured variant—a vassal state.

The question "With whom against whom?" remained ever topical for Hungarians despite radical changes up to the late twentieth
century, as the choice between revolution and reform, conflict and
compliance continually presented itself, and it is therefore a yard-
stick for measuring those figures who played a key role in their
time. Thus during the late phase of the regime of János Kádár in the
1980s, after the commemoration of the 400th anniversary of Gábor
Bethlen's birth, comparisons were made between the Transylvanian
prince and the Communist General Secretary. The evocation by
Ágnes Hankiss, mentioned earlier, of Bethlen's "tightrope walking"
and "art of small steps" triggered off clandestine comparisons, particularly because Kádár too was designated as a vassal in the service
of the conquerors (after the crushing of the October 1956 Revolution by the direct and undisguised military might of the Soviets).
The fact that later, during the 1960s, he managed to follow a course
of conciliation and small reforms without endangering Soviet supremacy merely added to the resemblance. Actually neither Hankiss's
essay of 1983 nor the filmscript *Affectionate Leave from the Prince*,
written two years later and more erotic than political in character,
was written (so the author assured me) as an allegory of Kádár and
his era. That it was interpreted in this way in some intellectual circles was demonstrated by the spontaneous effect of the actual or
putative similarities in some of the details of the practice and preservation of power in the shadow of the "great despotism" (Golo
Mann).

In fact Kádár too came to power in a seemingly hopeless situation, and he managed the tightrope walk between the perpetually
vigilant oppressor and the oppressed—at first disappointed by lack
of Western support and later resigned to their fate—by a mixture of
brutal coercion and clever peripheral concessions. He too was able
to boost the economy, and after a time of bloody turmoil to offer
the people modest affluence and a kind of synthetic stability. However, the differences between Bethlen and Kádár were far greater in
reality than appear at first glance from the striking similarities.

Compared to Communism and Soviet colonial rule, the Ottoman Empire was, apart from periodic assaults, a system of tolerance and multicultural diversity. The scope Bethlen enjoyed in foreign policy, with his offers and contacts in all directions, would have been unimaginable for a Communist Party boss within the Soviet Union's direct sphere of influence. The difference between the control mechanism of the Ottomans and the Russians was like that between an abacus and a computer; and the two personalities, Bethlen and Kádár, represented different worlds, leaving aside the eras in which they lived.

Bethlen led a full life in every way, never losing his zest for diplomatic activity and even war. He was a Baroque prince, whose jewels were worth a fortune, who dressed day and night in gaudy colours, and who was surrounded by musicians, singers and actors. He was a gourmet, who relished saltwater fish, oysters and tropical fruit. The little we know about János Kádár suggests the opposite: even during his time of relative popularity, he was colourless and introverted, interested only in chess, fishing and shooting. There is more murderous sarcasm, keen irony, flashing anger, hearty affection and sympathetic solidarity in a single letter by Bethlen than in all the stereotyped speeches, statements, letters and interviews of the one-time Hungarian party boss, all carefully vetted before publication, and purged of any uncouth language.

12. Zrinyi or Zrinski? One Hero for Two Nations

When the Croats in Tito's Yugoslavia began to defend themselves against the creeping "Serbianization" of their theatre, radio, higher education and economy, young protesters first undertook sporadic leafleting campaigns. Then during one of my early trips to Zagreb—that was still in the 1960s—the public's passionate applause after a performance of the Croat national opera *Nikola Šubic Zrinski* turned into a demonstration with incalculable consequences. "What on earth", I asked myself and then later the professor of German Studies, Zdenko Skreb, "does a Hungarian national hero have to do with the conflict between pan-Serb ambitions of hegemony and Croat national consciousness?" The scholar was amused by my ignorance. Patiently and with concrete examples he spelt out the concurrent but conflicting trends of the Serbs' so-called "Yugoslavism" and the Croats' drive for national self-determination.

Miklós Zrinyi, who had heroically defended the small fortress of Szigetvár in southwest Hungary, and died during an attempted sortie against the Turks, has always been for me, as well as for generations of Hungarian schoolchildren, one of our authentic patriots. Numerous historians have portrayed both Zrinyis, the hero of 1556 (see above, p. 98) and his great-grandson with the same name, as Hungarian freedom fighters. Few of us in Hungary ever discovered that just as many generations of Croat schoolchildren were taught to regard the two Zrinyis as perhaps the greatest heroes of their national history.

In fact both sides were right. The Zrinskis—their original name was Šubic—belonged to those ancient Croat families with which the Hungarian King Coloman had concluded the so-called contract of union at the beginning of the twelfth century. They adopted the name Zrinski in the mid-sixteenth century on being given the large estate in the Muraköz with the fortress Csáktornya (Cakovec) by Emperor Ferdinand I. Zrinyi (Zrinski) was also *ban* of Croatia, and there is no doubt that his mother-tongue was Croat. On the other hand, Croatia at that time had already been an integral part of Hungary for 400 years, albeit under a special administration. As a member of the high nobility, Zrinyi therefore belonged to the *natio Hungarica*, the political nation of Hungary which, however, was not an ethnic but a juridico-political category. Zrinyi/Zrinski fell as a Croat nobleman in the fight against the Turks for Emperor Ferdinand, who was at the same time crowned King of Royal Hungary. He died as a Croat for Hungary. At that time his ethnic affiliation had nothing to do with language, as it would in modern Hungary.

Nonetheless, the so-called ethnic affiliation of the hero of Szigetvár remains a controversial issue in historical debates, particularly where the contention between "patriotism" and "national nihilism" is concerned. As a result of the Estate-based notion of nationality, every nobleman living within the borders of the country was considered a member of the *natio Hungarica*, irrespective of his mother tongue, the *lingua franca* anyway being Latin. Later, in the nineteenth century, this concept was extended also to bourgeois society, and then to every citizen of the state. Thus the Law of 1868 confirmed that all citizens of Hungary were equal members of a single, indivisible, unitary Hungarian nation. In German political literature, on the other hand, and later in other European languages, a distinction was made between "Hungarian" (*Hungarus*) and "Magyar"—the Hungarian language knows only the latter appellation. We shall deal later in detail with the explosive problem of the assimilation process, "Magyarizing". The term "Hungarian" has been in use ever since the end of the eighteenth century in its narrower sense, i.e. for those citizens who speak the Hungarian language and belong ethnically to the Hungarian nation.

Thus the intricate and still topical problem of national affiliation did not arise in the era of the Zrinyis/Zrinskis but, anachronistically, in retrospect. Although Zrinyi/Zrinski was of Croatian origin, he spoke Hungarian too, and therefore in the view of Jenő Szücs—who has also drawn attention to the dangers of arbitrary "adjustment" of historical personages and events—he could not be classified either as a Croat or as a Hungarian. For Hugo Badalic and Ivan

Zajc, the librettist and composer of the opera *Nikola Šubić Zrinski*, first performed in 1876, the hero was of course a Croat. Theodor Körner, as already mentioned, saw him as a free and royalist Hungarian—which is naturally what Hungarian poets and dramatists believed. Even the historian of the inter-war years, Gyula Szekfü, emphasized: "In spite of Croatian paternal and maternal extraction, he regarded himself as a Hungarian. *Dulcis patria* [beloved fatherland] meant for him not Croatia but Hungary."

The history of the Zrinyi/Zrinski family followed a tortuous path and was fraught with drama: military victories and political defeats, love and suffering, frivolity and intolerance, treachery and death were inseparably linked here with the unhappy fate of a miserable, ravaged Hungary, bleeding from innumerable wounds and split into three parts. Whether they bore witness to being Croats or Hungarians was ultimately of no importance for the rise and fall of the members of this noble family.

Count Miklós Zrinyi, soldier, poet, statesman and thinker, and great-grandson of the hero of Szigetvár, remains an enigmatic and fascinating figure. He attained European fame for his victories against the Turks, and a book was published in London during his lifetime about the heroic deeds of Count "Serini", as his name was known in the West. He was indeed proud of his military fame, but in reality he grasped the sword with only one hand, while the other held the pen. As a twenty-six-year-old general he wrote an epic poem about the defence of Szigetvár and a polemic entitled *The True Remedy against the Turkish Poison*, but these could not influence his contemporaries since most of his writings remained unpublished until four decades after his death, and it was only at the beginning of the nineteenth century that they were re-discovered and made available to a wider readership. Then, in the words of the critic Antal Szerb, the life and works of this man who embodied a mixture of two human types, "the mystical visionary poet and the Machiavellian realpolitician in the mould of Wallenstein or Gábor Bethlen", kept generations of Hungarian intellectuals and politicians in their spell.

What then was this second Miklós Zrinyi: Croat or Hungarian? Born in 1620, son of George Zrinski (for the Hungarians György Zrinyi), *ban* of Croatia, he was educated by the Jesuits in Graz and Vienna, studying for a further two years in Italy. At the age of

eighteen he took part in military expeditions against Turkish border forts. His brilliant successes led to recognition by Emperor
Leopold, who made him a general at the age of twenty-six and a
year later rewarded him with the position of *ban* of Croatia. There
is no doubt that all his forebears were Croatian, just as he was by
birth, yet even Croatian reference books mention that he wrote his
epic about his great-grandfather and the siege of Szigetvár in Hungarian. The fact is that the soldier-poet was completely bilingual.
The only volume of poetry published in his lifetime was translated
into Croatian by his brother Péter. There are Croatian motifs in
Zrinyi's epic, but also southern-Hungarian (so-called Göcsej) idi-
oms, and both Turkish and Latin expressions.

Zrinyi's poems and prose were certainly less elegant and artistic
than, say, the works of his admired models Tasso and Machiavelli,
but their appeal was regarded as political, ethical and national. What
is more, they are still readable today because the author was himself
an epic hero who had personally experienced the battle scenes and
clashes with the Turks that he describes. As Antal Szerb pointed out,
Zrinyi wrote plainly and simply in Hungarian, because Hungarian
was what he professed to be:

Even his Hungarianness is the result of his volition. There is no need to
conjure away the fact that Zrinyi was Croat by birth. His younger brother
was a Croat patriot and a Croat poet... But Zrinyi's nationality was determined by what nationality he wanted to be—and that is how he became
the most Hungarian of Hungarians. His example demonstrates that a person's nationality is determined not by blood but by resolve.[1]

Zrinyi wrote his poetry in Hungarian, and did more than any of his
contemporaries to unite Hungary. Yet his background was deeply
cosmopolitan: this humanist and warrior spoke six languages flu-
ently: Hungarian, Croatian, German, Italian, Latin and French.
Hungarian writers have called him "a European in the true sense"
and "a European Hungarian to his bootstraps". In contrast to the
poet Balassi and his guardian, the eloquent prelate Péter Pázmány,
Zrinyi looked to Italy and not to Latin and German literature as his
model. In political literature he was fascinated by Machiavelli and
among the poets by Tasso and Marino.

Zrinyi was a man of contrasts on many levels: a dare-devil soldier,
but one who shunned the carousing of his peers and stood apart

from the petty nobility because of his aristocratic manners. Between forays against the Turks, he read his Italian books imported from Venice in his picture gallery and library in the citadel of Csáktornya, or wrote letters and essays about the ways and means of Hungary's liberation in Hungarian, Latin or French. Despite his loyalty to the royal house in Vienna, he found himself embarrassed because the court disapproved of his attacks on the Turks. The Habsburgs strove instead for quiet coexistence and eventual peace with the Sublime Porte, at first because of the Thirty Years' War and later in the interests of its power struggle against the French. Although re-Catholization, so successfully promoted by Pázmány, cemented the bond of the magnates with the dynasty, the military—especially such independent figures as the *ban* of Croatia—were distrusted. The famous imperial general Raimondo Montecuccoli, who considered that treasure alone was necessary to wage war successfully, hated the Hungarians, whether Catholics or Calvinists:

It is impossible to keep these ungrateful, unbending and rebellious people within bounds by reasoning with them, nor can they be won over by tolerance or ruled by law. One must fear a nation that knows no fear. That is why its will must be broken with a rod of iron and the people sternly kept in their place…. After all, the ferocity of a restive steed cannot be controlled by a silken thread, but only with an iron snaffle.[2]

The imperial commander's view of the country he was supposed to defend against the Turks—as inhabited by "rebels, robbers and dastardly people"—was shared by other influential figures in the imperial war council and at the centre of power. It was only to be expected therefore that, despite public opinion in Hungary, the court blocked Zrinyi's election as palatine of Hungary; at the last moment the King himself struck him off the list of candidates.

Strictly the life of this extraordinary man was a series of failures. The *ban* of Croatia, like so many other Hungarians, pinned his hopes on the reigning Prince of Transylvania, György Rákóczi II, as the possible King of a liberated Hungary. That was the deeper meaning of Zrinyi's book on King Mathias (1656), in which he implied that only a new hero—Prince Rákóczi, or perhaps he himself—could free Hungary from the Turkish yoke. But this dream too was shattered when the Prince, driven by excessive ambition, marched into Poland at the head of his army with an eye on the Polish throne, only to lose both his life and his empire. The victorious Turks captured the most important fortresses, laid Transylvania waste, detached the bulk of the rich outlying western territories, and installed their obedient vassal Mihály Apafi to head the rump principality. Transylvania as an autonomous factor was thus ruled out of Zrinyi's daring schemes.

Meanwhile Zrinyi achieved further victories in the south, and his winter campaign aroused a mood of expectation throughout Europe. His success in destroying the long bridge at Eszék across the river Dráva, vital for the Turkish army, elicited special admiration. However, he was forced every time by the order of the war council to withdraw at the last moment, give up his own fortress and, through the intrigues of his arch-enemy Montecuccoli, refrain from delivering decisive blows against the Turks.

After repeated calls for help from Transylvania and occupied Hungary, but also pressed by appeals from the West, Emperor Leopold reluctantly intervened in the conflict. At the head of an international army. Montecuccoli achieved a resounding victory over the Turks at Szentgotthárd close to the Styrian border. However, instead of the expected great offensive for the liberation of at least part of Hungary, the Emperor made peace. The resulting treaty of Vasvár was supposed to be valid for twenty years; it recognized all Turkish acquisitions, and even granted generous reparation payments to the vanquished. News of these incomprehensible concessions caused consternation not only in Hungary but throughout Europe, but Viennese court circles and above all Leopold's closest adviser Prince Lobkowitz were delighted: they had killed two birds with one stone. The Emperor gained a free hand towards the West and a certain security in the south-east: any possibility that the Hungarian Estates would launch an attack on Vienna with Turkish backing could now at least be ruled out.

Bitterness against the court because of its sell-out of Hungarian interests was so great that even hitherto loyal Catholic magnates, Zrinyi among them, turned away from the House of Habsburg. French officers and envoys of Louis XIV sought contacts with Zrinyi, who in a memorandum to the Emperor vented his anger over the false strategy. In a letter discovered centuries later Louis wrote in 1664: "I was in secret contact with Count Serin [Zrinyi], in order to stir up trouble in Hungary in case I started a war against the Emperor."[3]

V.-L. Tapié, the French authority on Central Europe, who quoted this letter in his book *The People under the Double Eagle*, sees in it "undisguised evidence of France's mischief-making policy, which subordinated the Hungarian question to friendship or hostility towards the House of Austria". In fact the freedom of the Hungarian Estates was a matter of indifference to Louis XIV. During the ensuing decades he fanned the flames of antagonism against the Austrian Habsburgs through contacts with conspirators and insurgents, but apart from a little money and many expressions of sympathy nothing was forthcoming to the Hungarians. Although Zrinyi recognized the bleak reality, he was still confident that the Hungarians could one day liberate themselves without outside help. This belief, born of the utter hopelessness of Hungary's future, this "sudden veering from rational hopelessness to irrational confidence" in the future (Szerb), has remained a characteristic trait of Hungarian poetry ever since Zrinyi. It is expressed, for example, in the astonishing and for many readers incomprehensibly optimistic conclusion at the end of the profoundly pessimistic poem *Thoughts in the Library* (*c.* 1850) by Mihály Vörösmarty, and Imre Madách's drama *Tragedy of Man* (*c.* 1860). These passages are among the finest ever written in Hungarian.

The sharp castigation of the Estates' moral depravity, camouflaged as an introduction in Zrinyi's last great work *The True Remedy against the Turkish Poison*, should be viewed in this context. The fiery manifesto of his belief in Hungary stands at the beginning and the end of his challenge for the establishment of a national army and the mobilization of the entire country:

Hands off the Magyars! Poor Hungarian nation, are you in such straits that no one cries out for you in your extreme danger?—that no one's heart rails against your distress?—that no one utters even a single word of encouragement in your decisive battle? Am I your only guardian, who proclaims the danger in which you find yourself? Although I find this task arduous, but the Lord gave me the gift of love for my Fatherland, and behold, I cry out: "Hearken, you living Hungarians, yonder is the danger, yonder is the all-consuming fire! I swear to you Almighty God, I call out all that I know so that you do not hold me to account for the blood of my people because I was passive.[4]

Having portrayed the Hungarian people's sufferings as the result of the latest campaign of extermination by the "horrible monster, the Turk" in Transylvania, Zrinyi concludes that no help could be expected from Christendom. What the Hungarians needed were "weapons, weapons and more weapons, and fearless resolution". He recalls their ancestors' heroic deeds, only to add bitterly that today's Hungarians have nothing in common with them apart from their language. Why?

Because we did not keep up the discipline of fighting, because we are lazy drunkards who hate each other... There is no nation which boasts so much about its titles of nobility as the Hungarian and who, as God is my witness, does so little to preserve and prove this nobility.

Yet after a catalogue of lapses, deficiencies and transgressions by Hungary's nobles Zrinyi suddenly exclaims:

If you ask me which people I desire and to which nation I want to entrust myself, the answer is: the Hungarian! And why? Because it is the one best adapted to its situation, the strongest, the swiftest and, if need be, the bravest. Two centuries have gone by now since the Hungarians were fighting the Turks. How often did the Turkish Sultans come personally to our country with hundreds of thousands of men? Suleiman alone, the bravest of the Ottoman Sultans, made five expeditions against us, and still God did not allow all of us to perish. What was corrupted because so for the most part in peacetime when we had entered into sham alliances, and not through war. And that is why I choose Hungary as my protector, not Indians or Teutons, not Italians, Germans or Spaniards.

He concludes with the warning:

If we Hungarians do not reconquer Nagyvárad and if we lose Transylvania, then we are not Hungarians: we fled the country in shame. There is enough land in Brazil. Let us ask the Spanish [*sic*] king for a province, let us establish a colony, let us become citizens there! [...] But those of you who trust in God love your fatherland and still have a drop of Hungarian blood left within you, do not give up but take up your weapons!

His last sentence is written in this spirit: "*Volenti nihil difficile* [Nothing is difficult for him who has the will]."

This great leader and poet, and at the same time Hungary's most original thinker of the seventeenth century, had tried in vain to find a third way, an individual solution "between Turkish opiate and German bait", as he put it. His time had run out: on 18 November 1664 he was killed by a wounded boar at a hunt. The death of "the master of the small war" (thus Krone's *Handbook of Austrian History*[5]) seemed the crowning misfortune of the national tragedy, and Hungarians were unable to regard it as a tragic misadventure. Even for a literary historian of Antal Szerb's standing Zrinyi's hunting accident has remained "an eternal enigma". After hinting at the murder plot against Wallenstein, he recounts in his *Literary History* that a rifle is allegedly kept in Vienna, labelled "This is the boar that killed Miklós Zrinyi".

The incomprehensible Peace of Vasvár was traumatic for the anti-court magnates even after Zrinyi's death. The highest dignitaries of the land, the palatine Ferenc Wesselényi and Archbishop György Lippay of Esztergom, were the most important instigators of a conspiracy, which was based on false expectations of material support from France, reinforced by contact with the French ambassador in Venice. In a letter to Louis XIV, the ailing Wesselényi asked for financial support, while other Hungarian and Croat magnates contacted the French ambassador Gremonville in Vienna, revealing to him far-fetched plans, including the creation of an alliance between Hungary, Croatia, Transylvania and Wallachia. For instance, Péter Zrinyi (Petar Zrinski), brother of Miklós and by then also *ban* of Croatia, proposed in a letter of September 1666 the landing of 2,000 armed Frenchmen and technical experts on the Adriatic coast. If that were done, according to Peter Zrinyi, "all of Hungary would rise against Vienna". He even offered one of his sons as hostage in confirmation of his promise. More and more nobles from Hungary and Croatia became involved in this operetta-like cabal, only to head for disaster. Letters were exchanged and negotiations entered into until not only Paris but Constantinople, Venice, Warsaw and finally Vienna knew that a conspiracy was afoot.

While Péter's wife, Anne Catherine Frangepan, conferred with the French envoy in Venice, his colleague in Vienna Gremonville, disguised as a trader, held several meetings in a village inn near the city with Count Ferenc Nádasdy, Chief Justice of Hungary, and

Péter Zrinyi. After the death of Wesselényi and Lippay, Nádasdy (who wanted to become palatine) and Zrinyi took over the group's effective leadership. The former urged an armed uprising, while the latter made foolhardy plans: to capture the Emperor during a hunt and keep him incarcerated until he agreed to meet their demands. Envoys were sent to Adrianople and Warsaw appealing for support. The Grand Vizier wanted to uphold the peace with Vienna, and the interpreter—in the pay of Vienna—had advised the court of the contacts even before his Hungarian-Croat masters. The Emperor was well informed of every development, not only through informers but also by the Sublime Porte.

Moreover Nádasdy and Zrinyi had, independently of each other, revealed their plans and betrayed their co-conspirators to gain pardon, only to carry on with their scheme and finally, far too late, beg Emperor Leopold for mercy. In fact, nothing much had happened apart from confused and ill-concealed machinations and intrigues. Nádasdy had personally told the Emperor everything. The conspirators were arrested, found guilty of high treason, and executed: Nádasdy in Vienna and the others—Péter Zrinyi, Franjo Kesto Frangepan and the Styrian Count von Tattenbach—in Wiener Neustadt. Zrinyi's wife Anne Catherine was interned in the Dominican convent in Graz, where she died mentally deranged.

Zrinyi's son-in-law, Prince Ferenc Rákoczi, became head of the insurrection attempt in Upper Hungary, which also soon collapsed. His mother Zsófia Báthory, closely connected with Jesuit circles at the court, obtained her son's pardon in return for a substantial payment. The possessions of those executed and condemned to long prison sentences were confiscated; Nádasdy's assets alone gained the court 200,000 guilders. After many years of contact with the dilettante magnates Louis XIV with consummate cynicism heartily congratulated Emperor Leopold on the "detection of this dangerous conspiracy" in order to extricate Gremonville.

The kingdom of Hungary was henceforth treated as a conquered enemy province. The fact that, contrary to the constitution, the conspirators were dealt with not by a Hungarian court but by an Austrian one was already a foretaste of the, in every way, counterproductive "forfeiture theory" whereby the Hungarians had forfeited their self-administration and civil rights by their recalcitrance and rebellion. Leopold I suspended the constitution and took Hungary on a tighter rein. Administration was placed under a directorate established in Pressburg, headed by the Grand Master of the Teutonic Order, who was also in charge of the forcible re-Catholization of Upper Hungary. He organized a witch-hunt for "unreliable elements"; hundreds of Protestant clerics were subjected to bloody retaliation, and either had to convert or to serve as galley slaves. Hungarians had to pay for 40 per cent of the costs of the imperial forces stationed in Hungary. Of the 11,000 "untrustworthy" Hungarian soldiers manning the border fortresses about 8,000 were discharged.

The forcible policy of *Gleichschaltung* gave the permanent tension between the absolute monarchy and the Estates-based state a powerful added twist. At the same time it prepared the ground for a new insurrection by the mainly Protestant rebels, petty nobles and peasants, who called themselves the "Kuruc". The insurgents soon achieved great results under the leadership of the young, handsome and daring Count Imre Thököly with whom Ilona, daughter of the executed Péter Zrinyi and widow of Prince Ferenc Rákóczi I, fell in love (he was fourteen years her junior). She brought not only a large fortune to the marriage, which took place several years later, but also her small son, Ferenc Rákóczi II. This completed the circle of the Zrinyis/Zrinskis, Báthorys and Rákóczis. The infamous "forfeiture theory" soon turned out to be an extremely unfortunate idea for its inventors, as well as its victims.

13. The Rebel Leader Thököly: Adventurer or Traitor?

Towards the end of seventeenth century Hungary was hopelessly divided. In the west of the country the élite of the nobility—by now overwhelmingly Catholic—such as the Pálffy, Batthyány, Széchenyi and, above all, Esterházy families, who had increased their fortunes thanks to the Habsburgs, felt an obligation to the Emperor and the tradition which regarded Hungary as a bulwark and shield of Western Christendom. They expected the liberation of the entire country from the court, and were therefore prepared to co-operate, provided that their old privileges were guaranteed. However, this was synonymous at the time with the defence of Hungarian national self-determination and the sovereignty of their nation. Gyula Szekfü saw the tragedy of later Hungarian history in the fact that this national side of the Hungarian Estates was not recognized, let alone taken into consideration, by the Habsburgs. Thus not a single Hungarian could be found in the bureaucracy of the Viennese exchequer or the Imperial council of war.

Apart from individual shifts of emphasis in the policy of the various Habsburgs towards Hungary, the conflicts between Viennese-type absolutism and the Hungarian Estates' sovereignty claims, even after the successful re-Catholization in the west, could not be overcome. This involved not only principles but tangible interests concerning the upkeep of border forts and mercenaries, distribution of resources and allocation of estates in areas devastated and eventually abandoned by the Turks—as could be observed repeatedly during the decades following their expulsion. Jenö Szücs in his *The Three Historical Regions of Europe* showed both sides of the hypocrisy:

The dynasty avowed that it wanted to do the best by the Hungarian "people", and only the rebellions had prevented them from doing this. That

137

was a lie. The nobility spoke of the incessant suffering of the "Hungarian nation", which in time turned into a double lie because the nobility, when speaking of the nation, meant exclusively themselves (although such an equation in the Europe of the time counted already as an outright lie), and they suffered little.[1]

Transylvania, though decreased in size and obliged to pay an increased tribute to the Porte, enjoyed relative stability under the vassal Prince Apafi. In the 1670s numerous nobles, fleeing from reprisals, found sanctuary in Transylvania. Meanwhile Louis XIV tried time and again to support the anti-Habsburg forces in the south-east. In May 1677 an alliance was even formalized in Warsaw between France, Poland and Transylvania, and in the autumn about 2,000 French soldiers and military experts arrived in Transylvania from Poland.

The draconian measures against the Protestant nobles and clerics, as well as the ruthless severity of the military regime set up by Leopold, nourished a new rebellion in Upper Hungary, supported by Poland and France, and especially in Transylvania. Under the leadership of the young Imre Thököly, it had temporarily achieved some spectacular but only temporary successes. The name by which the rebels referred to themselves—"Kuruc"—was not, as often maintained, derived from the Latin *crux* (cross) as borne by Dózsa's insurgent peasants in 1514, but from the Turkish word *kurudsch* (rebel or insurgent).

The Kuruc were at first small, undisciplined bands of horsemen, which the barely twenty-year-old Thököly formed into powerful units. He was from an ennobled family of merchants who had fled to Transylvania after the death of his father, one of the Wesselényi-Zrinyi conspirators, and the capture of his castle on the Árva in Upper Hungary. His military successes, the rapid occupation of the mining towns in Upper Hungary and the bold raids of his mounted bands in Moravia made Thököly's name known throughout Europe, finally forcing the Emperor to change his policy towards Hungary. In 1681, after an interval of nineteen years, Leopold I re-convoked the Diet at Sopron, abolished the oppressive punitive taxes, and restored limited religious freedom for Protestants. At the same time the Diet was permitted to restore the office of palatine by electing Pál Esterházy (Thököly's brother-in-law). However, the Kuruc did not make an appearance at Sopron or reply to the Emperor's offer of amnesty. Thököly continued the fight with Turkish support.

In considering why so many Hungarians, at least temporarily, joined Thököly's party instead of the cause of Christianity, one recalls an observation in Macartney's *Hungary*: that it was an open secret that "three Hungarians out of four had now reached the stage of regarding the Habsburgs and 'Austria' as their mortal enemies".[2] After the aborted aristocratic conspiracy a French traveller recorded: "This peculiar and eccentric nation harbours an unbelievable hatred of the German government and wants to elect a king of its own. Its privileges allegedly entitle it to do so."[3] Historians also point out that during clashes with the Turks, and even more after Hungary's liberation, the Imperial armies behaved as if in conquered enemy territory. Hungarians often had cause to complain that the Emperor's soldiers committed just as many atrocities as the Turks, which was all the worse because they called themselves Christians.

The actions of the Kuruc, especially the horsemen, usually seemed like virtuoso performances, though lacking in discipline. They attacked courageously and remained agile and imaginative during sudden retreats. Thököly led his men with determination and gained their devotion because he lived with them in their tents during forays. Numerous skirmishes took place in the beautiful wine-growing areas of Upper Hungary, and both sides, the Imperial troops and the Kuruc, sometimes suffered defeats there simply because the soldiers were drunk. Surprise attacks became a national sport—thus there were times when Thököly had literally to jump out of bed and run off in headlong flight without his effects or his war correspondence.

The dashing Kuruc captain was also a good organizer, who used his reputation in the areas under his control to introduce fiscal administration. Through his marriage with Ilona Zrinyi, who had the vast Rákóczi family estates at her disposal, Thököly, now aged twenty-six, was assured of the necessary financial basis for extending the Kuruc rebellion. The Sublime Porte was clearly disappointed by the Transylvanian Prince Apafi's cautious, hesitant stance regarding the proposed attacks against the Habsburgs, and supported more and more the seemingly successful Thököly. As a reward for the occupation of Kassa and the fortress of Fülek the Sultan had him enthroned as Prince of Upper Hungary, which resulted in the kingdom now being divided into four parts: besides Royal Hungary,

Transylvania and the Turkish *pashaliks* there was now Upper Hungary controlled by Thököly.

Thököly's politics have been the subject of wide-ranging controversy in Hungarian historiography. Would it not have been wiser to accept the compromise solution offered by the government in Vienna, rather than pursuing an alliance with Turkey? For Vienna the fight against French expansion and the crisis over the Spanish succession loomed larger than the activities of the young Ottoman-backed Kuruc leader. While Szekfü regarded the Turkish alliance as a disastrous move by Thököly, followers of the Kuruc movement saw in it the continuation of the path that led from Zápolyai and Bocskai through Bethlen to Rákóczi. The same reasoning would have traced the 1848 War of Independence back to it.

The fact that Thököly had the title of King conferred on him by the Pasha of Buda did not mean that he was exclusively a hanger-on of the Ottoman Empire. As a diary entry of November 1681s recorded by his wife Ilona Zrinyi reveals, the young Kuruc leader dreamed that with his own strength alone he would "liberate our Fatherland from the Turks" after the expulsion of the Habsburgs. Thököly wanted immediate action, but he completely misjudged the prevailing balance of power in the fast-changing European scene, becoming its quarry and then its victim. His biographer Dávid Angyal wrote that he was a master only of the "small war", both in politics and on the battlefield. He had at his disposal no diplomatic apparatus or sources of information, and was driven purely by ambition.

His most fateful mistake, which of course proved a blessing for Western Christendom, was his encouragement to the Sublime Porte to go for an all-out attack on Vienna. He had overestimated the strength of the Ottoman armies and did not consider the international shock caused by his co-operation with the Turks. However, during his northward progress, other Hungarian magnates besides Thököly paid homage to the Grand Vizier Kara Mustafa, who commanded an Ottoman army numbering 150,000. This persuaded the Prince of Transylvania Mihály Apafi I, as the Sultan's vassal, to wait upon the Grand Vizier with his own army. The Sublime Porte's master of ceremonies described the scene that took place in Kara Mustafa's camp on 22 August 1683 as follows:

The King [i.e. Prince Apafi]… proceeded with a number of his closest followers to the three-masted tent, where he sat down on a chair near the wall. The interpreter stayed at his side for a while, to advise him about the main points of the ceremony. In the mean time the state chancellor and the marshal appeared, wearing court turban and state fur, and behind them the illustrious, all-powerful, victorious commander in his vizier's turban and ermine-trimmed outer garment of camelhair. He entered with infinite dignity, offering the *Salaam*, and seating himself on his sofa.[…] Then the honour of kissing the hem of the gracious Grand Vizier's robe was bestowed upon the King, whereupon he was offered a seat; he did not sit down immediately, but once again stepped before the Grand Vizier and laid his face against the hem of the robe. When the Grand Vizier once again offered him a seat, he bowed and finally sat down. And during the various questions and answers he once again approached and kissed the hem of the gracious Grand Vizier's robe, thus performing all the rites of paying homage. Coffee, sherbet and tobacco pipes were handed round...[4]

While Prince Apafi was devotedly kissing the hem of the Grand Vizier's robe, presenting him afterwards with a coach and six, half a dozen silver goblets covered with gold leaf, a saddle horse and four team horses, the siege of Vienna was under way. The Transylvanian Prince went at the head of his 5,000-strong army to Kara Mustafa's camp, because he feared, not unreasonably, that his patrons might hand over Transylvania to Thököly, who was operating so successfully in Upper Hungary, while he, the faithful vassal of twenty years' standing, would be disposed of. For his part, Thököly, with his 20,000 Kuruc, kept clear of the siege, and instead undertook forays into Transdanubia and southern Hungary. In his efforts to enlarge his "empire" he even conquered Pressburg at the end of 1683, but this victory was only temporary.

Neither Thököly nor Apafi could guess that barely three weeks after the humiliating acts of homage in the Grand Vizier's tent the "victorious commander" would suffer an annihilating defeat. In the battle on the Kahlenberg on 12 September 1683 Duke Charles of Lorraine and the King of Poland Jan Sobieski sent the Ottoman army into a headlong retreat, thus inaugurating a new chapter in European history. To this the Hungarian troops who fought with Charles of Lorraine under the leadership of the palatine Pál Esterházy made a modest contribution.

With the unexpected historic turning point at Vienna and the international counter-offensive in Hungary, financed by Pope

Innocent XI, Thököly became a pathetic figure. Ilona Zrinyi's heroic defence of the fortress of Munkács in north-eastern Hungary eclipsed her husband's role. It was an unbelievable affair. This Catholic countess from one of the oldest noble Croat families, brought up in an anti-Turkish tradition, fought for three years in league with the Turks against the Imperial troops, i.e. against that army which on 2 September 1686 had also liberated the Hungarian capital Buda from Turkish occupation after 145 years. We cannot tell whether she did it out of hatred for those Habsburgs who had executed her father and uncle, or because of love for Thököly, who still continued the fight. Ilona gave up the fight only in January 1688. The court forbade her any contact with her husband, and her son, who had lived through the three years of siege, and her daughter were taken from her.

However, the adventurous saga of the Thököly-Zrinyi couple was not yet at an end. Thököly often had to retreat hastily and give up one castle after another before the imperial troops, which now comprised quite a number of former Kuruc fighters. Numerous magnates, towns and counties accepted the amnesty offered by the Emperor. The Turks had come to regard Thököly as a nuisance and made him into a scapegoat, using him as a negotiating counter to obtain better peace terms. On 15 October 1685 the Pasha of Nagyvárad invited Thököly to a feast, but had him put in fetters and conveyed to Belgrade.

News of the fall of the Kuruc leader, who still inspired fear but was widely regarded in Europe as a traitor to Christendom, came as a great shock. There were gloating reports of "disloyalty punished" and the "rightful punishment" of the rebel. However, the Turks soon realized that they had blundered; Thököly was released at the beginning of 1686 and "rehabilitated", but in the mean time many of his Kuruc had changed sides, relinquishing the town of Kassa. Most of the 15,000 Hungarian soldiers who had fought at the siege and liberation of Buda had originally been Thököly's Kuruc.

Although Thököly remained a high-ranking officer in the Turkish army, he wrote in 1687 to Louis XIV: "I live wretchedly and miserably in the Ottoman hell." In 1690 the "King of the Kuruc" had his last chance when, after Apafi's death, the Porte appointed him Prince of Transylvania. The Diet too elected him Prince after he had crushed the imperial troops at Zernyest (Zärnest) with an army of 20,000. Most of the Hungarians and Székelys, outraged by the plundering and bullying of the Imperial forces, switched to Thököly's side, but only two months later Margrave Ludwig Wilhelm of Baden drove the "Turkish Louis" for ever out of Transylvania.

In the course of their victory at Zernyest the Turks captured the Imperial general Donat Heister, which gave Thököly a chance in 1690 to exchange the prisoner for his wife Ilona. After the Peace of Karlóca (Karlowitz) on 26 January 1699, which sealed Hungary's conquest by the Habsburgs, Thököly was interned in Nikodemia in Asia Minor. Ilona Zrinyi stayed with him until her death in 1703. He died in 1705 aged forty-eight.

La Mortraye, an envoy in the service of England, described in a French-language travel account his visit to the sick, gout-afflicted Thököly, whom he found embittered at not having been permitted in 1701 to hand a memorandum to the Sultan in Adrianople, and being ordered instead to reside in Nikodemia. Only the Princess's courage had given him strength. Nevertheless, Thököly asked the envoy several times to intercede on his behalf to end his exile, which he believed to be due to the machinations of the French court.

Another traveller, the French antiquarian Paul Lucas, visited Thököly shortly before his death in June 1705. The ailing Prince invited him to dine: "The food was excellent, wine flowed. In this the Hungarians resemble the Germans: it is the only thing in which they do not want to be different from them. The following day the Prince received me yet again for an hour-long audience. He was interested in everything, inquiring and witty..."[5]

The Sultan refused Thököly's last wish to be buried in Transylvania or Hungary, and only two centuries years later was the "tragic hero" who had lacked true statesmanlike acumen laid to rest in the town of his birth, Késmárk (Kežmarok) in Upper Hungary.

His help to the Turks in 1688 to suppress a popular revolt in Bulgaria belongs to the darker side of Thököly. His stepson, freedom-fighter Ferenc Rákóczi II, called him "a snake which slithered into my mother's bed". Yet today on the Pest side of the Danube the boulevard named after Lajos Kossuth that runs from the Elisabeth

Bridge leads directly to Rákóczi and thence to Thököly street.
Thus the Kuruc leader joined the pantheon of failed freedom-
fighters: the man in whom human greatness and moral turpitude
were so thoroughly mixed that a fair judgement about him still has
not been reached.

14. Ferenc Rákóczi's Fight for Freedom from the Habsburgs

Having withdrawn from Hungary and Transylvania, the Sublime Porte also had to move out of the greater part of Slavonia after Prince Eugen's decisive victory over the Turkish army on 11 September 1697 at Zenta. Only the Bánát, the environs of Temesvár, remained under Turkish control. The Peace Treaty of Karlóca signed on 26 January 1699 thus signalled the end of more than 150 years of Turkish rule over Hungary, and at the same time Austria's emergence as a European great power. The House of Habsburg "now ruled a well-rounded, enclosed territory which included the Eastern Alps, the Sudetenland and the Carpathian countries, with the Danube as its axis."[1]

In contrast to the positive result for Austria, and because—even after Thököly's adventures—Hungarian soldiers functioned only in an auxiliary capacity, the outcome of the liberation did not appear so promising for Hungary, which remained under foreign control. As Bogyay put it with admirable clarity, "The expulsion of the Turks brought Hungary neither true liberation nor satisfaction."[2]

Shortly after the reconquest of Buda in 1686 (this date, not 1699, is still regarded in Hungary as marking the end of Turkish rule), the legislature in Pressburg, "as proof of gratitude", recognized the hereditary right of the male line of the House of Habsburg and relinquished the nobility's right of resistance which it received in the Golden Bull of 1222. This renunciation of free royal elections and of the *ius resistendi* was a significant step towards absolute monarchy. The following saving clause was added to the King's pledge under oath and in writing to observe the country's laws and privileges: "… as the King and the assembled Estates shall agree on the interpretation and application thereof". After this, however, Leopold did not convene the Diet. His rule "was, in fact, a malevolent dictatorship exercised by the *Hofkriegsrat*, the *camera* (staffed largely by Germans) and the Primate of Hungary, Kollonics."[3]

On 4 December 1691 the Emperor issued the so-called *Diploma Leopoldinum*, declaring Transylvania a crown land independent of Hungary. Due to direct Imperial administration and increased re-Catholization, religious and national friction broke out, and it was under pressure from these complex conflicts that a "Transylvanian mentality" evolved: consciousness of a certain political independence and a special religious position. It manifested a temporary weakening of the overall Hungarian feeling of solidarity.

Cardinal Leopold Kollonics, by birth a Croat nobleman, worked out a large-scale plan for the reconstruction of a devastated and in parts totally depopulated Hungary, the *"Einrichtungswerk"* (a blueprint for drastic reorganisation). There is no firm evidence for the oft-quoted saying of Kollonics: "First I am going to pauperize the Hungarians, then Catholicize them, and finally Germanize them." However, what counted in politico-psychological terms was that the Cardinal's attitude and his actual measures lent such sayings credibility. The Viennese special commission, the so-called *Neoacquistica Commissio* (setup to check title deeds) carried out a ruthless colonization procedure by allocating huge estates to the imperial (non-Hungarian) military and royalist magnates. German and Serb peasants were settled in newly-established villages. The *Hofkriegsrat* established the so-called Military Frontier, a wide zone inhabited mainly by newly-settled Serbs and administered by the army. There was therefore a compact mass of non-Hungarians along the southern border of historical Hungary: worse still, there were divided ethnic groups whose "other half" lived on the other side of the border under a different regime. Even the rather pro-Habsburg Szekfü declared in his *History of Hungary*:

Hungarians thus found themselves in a position where Hungary's enemies, who could be stirred up at any time against it over the centuries, were installed on its territory in a protected and privileged position. One cannot imagine a greater debasement of Hungarian independence; none of the people of Western and Central Europe had to suffer anything similar.[4]

The special commission invented a clever method to demand—on the pretext of "reimbursement of liberation costs"—large sums of money from the old and hence legal landowners in formerly

Turkish-occupied central Hungary—very few of whom could pay up. The price Hungarians had to pay during the sixteen years of the War of Independence and after was disproportionate: on top of the loss of life and devastation caused by the Turks during their advance and retreat, there was now plunder by the "liberating armies". It was not only that rump-Hungary, already bled dry, had to cover 70 per cent in 1685 and 51 per cent in 1686 of the expenses of the troops fighting the Turks. On top of that, 40,000–50,000 foreign soldiers were now garrisoned in Hungary, but they did not live in barracks: most were billeted with peasants, and some too with townspeople and nobles. In 150 years, wrote the palatine Pál Esterházy, Hungary had not paid so much to the Turks as it had to pay now in two years to the Imperial armies.

By no means only the soldiers but also generals and officers behaved abominably towards the civilian population whom they had "liberated". A particularly evil figure was General Antonio Caraffa, scion of a distinguished Neapolitan family. In 1685–6, as "General Commissioner of War", he first extorted huge amounts of money and food from the citizens of the eastern Hungarian town of Debrecen by barbaric methods of torture. A year later this rapacious robber even invented a wide-ranging "conspiracy", and after torturing numerous nobles and burghers, Germans as well as Hungarians, had twenty of them executed in the town of Eperjes (Prešov) in Upper Hungary. Caraffa promptly confiscated the entire fortunes of these completely innocent men.

The incompetence, corruption and despotism of the military administration extending all over Hungary had a disastrous effect on the future attitude of the Hungarians towards Habsburg rule. Caraffa's "kangaroo-court" at Eperjes and the special courts established by Kollonics, which condemned hundreds of Calvinist ministers, caused many "liberated" Hungarians to long for the return of the Turks. Towards the end of the seventeenth century, suffering under the rigid, absolutist and at the same corrupt regime, Hungarians fulminated more than ever against their German masters. The fact that the most bloodthirsty generals and officers were Belgians, Italians and Spaniards did not mitigate the growing bitterness and antagonism towards the Germans.

However, the smouldering hatred flared only under pressure from the absolutist political figures and princes of the Church.

Disbanded soldiers from the former frontier forts and roving persecuted Protestant Hajduks and nobles, harmed or even dispossessed
by the *Neoacquistica*, repeatedly launched smaller rebellions just
before the turn of the century. Sheer indigence caused peasant uprisings to erupt spontaneously in north-east Hungary. Tension
mounted, and an explosion was inevitable.

That the sporadic outbursts of unrest, all easily subdued, developed into a dangerous conflagration of European significance was
due to the appearance of a unique individual in a unique situation.
The involvement of the Habsburg Empire in the War of the Spanish Succession created the framework for a renewed countrywide
Kuruc uprising. This far exceeded anything engineered by Thököly,
and soon brought all of Hungary and Transylvania under Hungarian control. None of this would have been imaginable without the
charismatic leader Prince Ferenc Rákóczi II.

Jacob Burckhardt had this to say about "Historical Greatness" in
his *Reflections on History*:

History tends at times to become suddenly concentrated in one man, who
is then obeyed by the world. These great individuals represent the coincidence of the general and the particular, of the static and the dynamic, in
one personality. [...] Their nature is one of the true mysteries of world history. Their relationship to their time is a *hieros gamos* (sacred marriage).
Such a union can only be consummated in terrible times, which provide
the one supreme standard of greatness and are also unique in their need of
great men.[5]

Burckhardt then deals with the criteria of "relative", "momentary"
and "historic" greatness, only to remark in a subsequent reflection:

The rarest thing of all in men who have made history is greatness of soul. It
resides in the power to forgo benefits in the name of morality, in voluntary
self-denial, not merely from motives of prudence but from goodness of
heart, while political great man *must* be an egoist, out to exploit every
advantage.

If "greatness of soul" is indeed the real "morality", this explains
why Ferenc Rákóczi II, a most reluctant and later most unusual
rebel, remains to this day a romantically transfigured personality.
Sudden and extraordinary changes and contrasts moulded the life
of this arguably most pure and noble figure of Hungarian history:

heroism and vacillation, love and a passion for gambling, naïve gullibility and iron resolve, immense wealth and desolate exile. He was a cosmopolitan and European, but with an unshakable loyalty to his country and the underprivileged. Of his fifty-nine years he spent only twelve as an adult in his own county, almost four in Poland, more than four in France and eighteen in Turkey. Zoltán Szabó (who also died in exile two centuries later) wrote in an essay that Rákóczi was as much a European inside Hungary as he was outside it, and that outside he was as much a Hungarian as in Hungary. The fate of his family mirrors the highs and lows of Hungarian history. Among the paternal ancestors of Ferenc Rákóczi II, born in March 1676, were four princes of Transylvania, and in his mother's family were four princes, among them Stephen Báthory, one of Poland's greatest kings. Ferenc was the grandson of the executed Péter Zrinyi and son of Ilona Zrinyi, the heroine of Munkács who, as an exile, was separated from her children. As a child Rákóczi lived through the forays of his stepfather Imre Thököly, followed by three years in the beleaguered fortress of Munkács.

On the orders of Emperor Leopold, the young Rákóczi was educated as a foster-son under the direct guardianship of Cardinal Kollonics in the Jesuit college at Neuhaus, and later by Jesuit professors at Prague University. Besides Latin and French, his main interests were mathematics and the natural sciences. In the Viennese palace of his brother-in-law, Field-Marshal Count Aspremont, the precocious and attractive young man soon became accustomed to the lifestyle of a magnate, part and parcel of which were extensive travels in Italy, glittering receptions, horse riding, hunting and passionate gambling. All this was possible only because the Emperor had not confiscated his family's huge estates.

Appointed chief *ispán* (equivalent to Lord Lieutenant) of Sáros county and Prince of the Holy Roman Empire, the eighteen-year-old Rákóczi took possession of his estates, amounting to almost 700,000 hectares. Some time earlier the young man had married Charlotte Amalia, the beautiful fifteen-year-old daughter of the reigning Prince Karl of Hesse-Rheinfels and a direct descendant of the Thuringian Margrave Ludwig IV and of St Elisabeth, daughter of King András II (1205–35) of the House of Árpád. The wealthiest and at the same time first man of Upper Hungary spoke barely any

Hungarian at the time, and wanted to avoid any involvement in politics. When a rebellion broke out in the vicinity of Tokaj and the rebels tried to make him their leader, he fled to Vienna, even requesting the Emperor to exchange his estates in Upper Hungary for ones of similar value elsewhere in the Empire—which the Emperor refused. However, the expectation that the immensely rich young man would remain loyal to the court and disregard the woes of his people was illusory. Influenced by their increasing privations and the arrogance of the imperial military administration, Rákóczi entered into a close and lifelong friendship with his insurgent neighbour, the highly educated, eloquent Count Miklós Bercsényi, who was preparing a renewed insurrection against Vienna with the aid of Polish friends and French contacts. The relationship with Bercsényi helped the young Prince to relearn his mother-tongue, although he was to write his *Memoirs* in exile in French and his *Confessions* in Latin.

In 1700 Rákóczi himself finally took the initiative to take up direct contact with the French King Louis XIV and his minister Barbesieux, sending his confidant Captain Longueval to Paris, bearing a letter. The King did not react and Barbesieux's answer was reticent. The disappointed messenger denounced Rákóczi at the Imperial court immediately after his return; the Prince was arrested in April 1701 and thrown into the same prison from which his grandfather had gone to the scaffold. Under interrogation Longueval repeatedly incriminated his erstwhile master—the first of a number of agents, confidence tricksters and swindlers who at various times, and particularly during his exile, insinuated themselves into the Prince's confidence.

That Rákóczi managed to escape from his prison on 7 November 1701 was the doing of his blithe and resolute wife, whose Rhenish aristocratic family had French sympathies. Charlotte used her charm and powers of persuasion on the Prussian commandant of the fort, Captain Gottfried Lehmann, helped by a letter from the King of Prussia, and Lehmann declared himself willing to help with the escape. Rákóczi contrived to cut through the bars and left the prison disguised as a guard. In his excitement he took the wrong direction but, realizing his mistake, impersonated a drunken soldier, proceeded through the gate singing, and casually entered the coach waiting for him outside. Lehmann was executed, Jesuit confessors at court were incriminated for aiding and abetting the escape, and Charlotte and her children were held hostage in Vienna.

Five days later Rákóczi crossed the Polish border and met Bercsényi, who had escaped to Poland with some of his loyal followers to avoid arrest—and soon made the acquaintance of Princess Sieniawska, whose castle was close to the border, and who became the great love of his life. When almost two years later Rákóczi left the Princess' castle on the rainy night of 16 June 1703 and stepped on to Hungarian soil accompanied only by two servants, the freedom fight against the Habsburgs, which was to last almost eight years, began in earnest.

The beginning was anything but auspicious. Rákóczi himself described in his *Memoirs* how, instead of the promised 5,000 foot-soldiers and 500 horsemen, he was met at the border by only a ragged band of 250 and fifty respectively, armed with swords, and Hungarian, Slovak and Ruthenian peasants with pitchforks and scythes. Yet this small group grew within a few days to 3,000 men and over the next three years expanded into an army of 75,000. It was a unique and fateful encounter between the country's greatest landowner and noblest of aristocrats with the poorest, most debilitated and most fiercely determined peasants.

What had started as the dilettante conspiracy of a handful of magnates was able to evolve into a national mass movement because for the first time in Hungary's history a magnate, in the person of Rákóczi, regarded taxpaying drudges as his allies in the fight to defend its freedom. Ferenc Rákóczi was the only noble commander during the entire rebellion who cared about and tried to alleviate the misery and suffering of the serfs. The anguish he felt for them and his natural modesty and altruism lent a peculiar magic to his character. He was a brilliant public speaker who could extemporize in Hungarian, Latin and French (he also spoke and read German, Italian and Czech), yet he was not a general and his Memoirs are essentially the story of lost battles. That the Kuruc, despite their numerical advantage at least up to 1708 and their fighting spirit, could not win a decisive battle was due to the incompetence of their generals and officers, and the lack of tactical ability, discipline and co-operation between the various units. In his Memoirs the

Prince himself sharply criticized the state of affairs in his army as well as the national attitude towards the conduct of war inherited from Thököly:

Pitch camp a long distance away from the enemy, do not set up guard-posts, eat and drink plentifully, and when the men and horses have recovered, catch up with the enemy in two- or three-day forced marches, attacking him with wild frenzy; if he flees pursue him, if not beat a fast retreat … I do not deny that I caused much damage during the fighting because of my ignorance; but looking at it with commonsense, it was lack of money and general ignorance of how to conduct a war that brought this war, which had begun bravely and well, to an end…[6]

On the other hand, it was due to his organizational talent and total self-sacrifice that Rákóczi succeeded for the first time since King Mathias in creating a national army, arming it, kitting it out and equipping it from nothing: between 1704 and 1710, for example, he managed to supply his troops with 51,000 pairs of boots and 46,000 greatcoats.

That the Kuruc soldiers were able so quickly to gain control of the greater part of the country—especially the Danube-Tisza plains and Eastern Hungary, Upper Hungary (till 1708) and alternately Transdanubia or Transylvania—was not due only to popular support. Because of its involvement in the War of the Spanish Succession the Habsburg empire was forced to withdraw most of the imperial regiments from Hungary. The timing of the Kuruc's fight for freedom was therefore propitious. From the very beginning Rákóczi staked everything on an alliance with Louis XIV and the Bavarian Elector Max Emanuel II, to whom the Diet of Ónod even offered the Hungarian crown in 1707 in the event of a Habsburg defeat.

Although fighting lasted several more years and international efforts to mediate led to many meetings with Rákóczi, the die was cast as early as August 1704 when Prince Eugen and the Duke of Marlborough won a resounding victory over the French-Bavarian army at Höchstadt. Rákóczi, who since 1704 had borne the title of Prince of Transylvania and since 1705 that of a "Reigning Prince of Hungary", suffered a heavy defeat in the battle of Trencsén (Trenčín) in 1708. The Kuruc suffered the loss of 2,500 killed and 400 taken prisoner while the Imperial losses were a mere 160 men. Trencsén was a turning-point because, with the Habsburg victories on the western front, more and more soldiers deserted the Kuruc cause.

The legendary commander László Ocskay defected with his entire regiment a few weeks after Trencsén—a grievous loss, although the traitor was captured and executed by a Kuruc unit in 1710.

The will to resist also waned because, in spite of orders from the Prince, many nobles forbade their serfs to join the army. The poor peasants, for their part, could see no improvement in their situation and in the last years of fighting were less and less willing to take up arms. An epidemic of the plague since 1708 also reduced the manpower of the fighting units: according to official estimates it claimed 410,000 victims, whereas the armed conflict took 80,000 lives.

The military situation became hopeless. Nonetheless the Prince declined the Emperor's peace offers conveyed by his wife and sister, as well as various English and Dutch efforts at mediation. Together with Bercsényi he doubted the genuineness of the promises made by Vienna and held out till the last for the independence of the Transylvanian principality. Above all, right up to the end Rákóczi counted on Russian help. Tsar Peter I had not only met Rákóczi several times, but had offered him the Polish crown. Although from time to time France supported the Kuruc with money, as well as by sending officers, this never covered more than the pay of 4,000 soldiers, and at the height of co-operation there were only eighty-six French officers in Hungary. Moreover, Louis XIV was against Rákóczi's desperate attempts at a Russian alliance, counselling instead pacts with Sweden and Turkey. France's diplomatic support was therefore barely worth mentioning, but it was still more than that contributed by other countries.

Louis XIV's policy towards his allies was depicted in a contemporary skit as consisting of the King sitting on the river-bank and casting his fishing rod, while in the water before him several heads are visible and Rákóczi is taking the bait, but this impression was false: Hungarian and French historians agree today that the initiative came from the Hungarian side, i.e. from Rákóczi. In the event, amid the web of intrigue and negotiations for supremacy in Spain and northern Europe, all his efforts to find for active and reliable allies were doomed.

He himself described in his *Confessions of a Sinner* the last days of his increasingly hopeless struggle against a powerful enemy:

I was under increasing pressure from day to day. Although the few counties that stood behind us sufficed for provisioning of the mounted troops, the fleeing magnates, nobles and the great number of soldiers' families who had remained loyal to us and who voluntarily left the counties occupied by the enemy to follow us, extremely aggravated the situation of the distressed people. Winter raged, and enormous masses of snow covered the ground, so that even horsemen could only use the roads: the fleeing masses with their loaded peasant carts wandered from village to village, searching partly for sustenance and partly for security in the mountains and hiding places in the swamps. Soldiers deserted the flag in order to save and feed their families, and the sorrowful lament of the people and the refugees constantly sounded in my ears. Forced by the cold, the almost barefoot soldiers abandoned their posts, some took their weapons, others their horses, and all of them their pay. They made their justified complaints to me: they had not given up soldiering because of disloyalty or ill-will, but because the situation had become intolerable... I was worried and saddened by the miserable fate of those who, in the course of my life, have remained true to me, and not by my own state of mind. I was distressed not at having to leave the country or by exile from my homeland, but because I had not safeguarded the lives of any of them...[7]

Armistice and peace negotiations began, with the Prince's consent, against this dismal background. Actually the commander of the Imperial troops, the Hungarian-born Count János Pálffy, had already taken the initiative in the late autumn of 1710 in a personal letter to the Kuruc general, Sándor Károlyi. The final destruction of the decimated Kuruc army, driven back and encircled near Munkács and Kassa in north-eastern Hungary, was by now only a matter of time. The terms of the peace treaty, negotiated between Pálffy and Károlyi and signed at Szatmár on 30 April 1711, were of course less favourable than those offered by Emperor Joseph I five years earlier. At the last minute Rákóczi rejected them, relieved Károlyi of his command, and made a proclamation calling on the Kuruc to fight on, but the Diet authorized Károlyi to sign the peace treaty and capitulate. On 1 May 1711 the Kuruc relinquished 149 flags and 12,000 soldiers, and with Károlyi took the oath of loyalty to Emperor Joseph I. They did not know that the Emperor had already been dead for two weeks, his demise having been kept secret. Rákóczi, Bercsényi and others who remained faithful to the cause declined the offer of amnesty and went into voluntary exile.

15. Myth and Historiography: an Idol through the Ages

Did Károlyi betray the cause of the Kuruc when he concluded peace against the wishes of the Prince while the latter was absent in Poland negotiating with Tsar Peter I? Or was it a last chance to prevent a still worse fate, and by compromising to obtain breathing-space for the despoiled country and its unfortunate people? Generations of Hungarian historians, politicians and intellectuals have pondered these questions.

In *Reconstruction and Embourgeoisement, 1711–1867*, the doyen of historians in today's Hungary, Domokos Kosáry, views Károlyi's "treachery" as one of those legends used by nineteenth-century nationalistic romantics to explain the dilemma which faced him. In the prevailing conditions there was simply no alternative to that compromise which, inspite of everything, finally gave the country's peace, stability and the prospect of reconstruction.[1] Emperor Charles VI, who had himself crowned as King Charles III of Hungary, harboured none of his father's antagonism towards the Hungarians. He saw Hungary's liberation as extremely important, and acknowledged that "the Hungarians must be relieved of the belief that they are under German domination."[2]

The persistence of the memory of Rákóczi's War of Independence in every stratum of society, as well as in literature and journalism, was connected with the traditional image of the young, noble and selfless Prince's distinctive personality. His tragic fate, the decades of exile and the pathos of his political downfall fired the imagination of Hungarians far more than the negotiator of the Compromise of Szatmár, who gained at best cool recognition. As a journalist put it at the beginning of the twentieth century when discussing the first great Rákóczi biography, "Successful voyages are often less appreciated than shipwrecks."

155

Rákóczi's magic had its effect even at the court of the Sun King, Louis XIV, at Versailles. In his famous *Memoirs* even the sarcastic Duc de Saint-Simon expressed appreciation of the personality of the Hungarian: he was wise, modest and thoughtful, if not very witty—with a rare dignity but not haughty, principled, loyal, courageous.[3]

In the year of Louis' death the Prince took up residence in a house near the monastery of the Camaldulian brothers at Gros-Bois, where he spent his time in religious contemplation and writing his Memoirs. When in 1717 the Sublime Porte promised him armed support and money for a further war against the Habsburgs, he saw an unexpected chance and, ignoring warnings by the French Regent, the Russian Tsar and others, he sailed for Turkey aboard a French ship. In the mean time, however, the Turkish army suffered devastating defeats at the hands of Prince Eugen. During the war about 1,000 exiled Kuruc invaded Transylvania several times from the Bánát and Wallachia, but achieved no lasting effect. At the same time General Pálffy's hussars fought in the Austrian army before Belgrade against the Turks. However, the role played by the Hungarian units on both sides was no more than marginal.

At the peace conference the Emperor's negotiators demanded that Rákóczi be put in chains and handed over to them, but although this was sharply rejected, clause 15 of the 1718 Treaty of Passarowitz (Požarevac) stipulated that the Prince and his generals be exiled far from the Hungarian border. At first they were lodged in the small village of Jenikö on the European side of the Bosphorus, but after 1720 they were billeted in twenty-two houses at Rodosto (Tekirdag) on the Asiatic shore of the Sea of Marmara, two days' journey from Constantinople. The Prince spent his days there in religious meditation, writing his *Confessions* modelled on those of St Augustine, and pursuing his hobby of carpentry, with occasional diplomatic activity. Almost all his foreign secretaries and aides were informers and swindlers, most in Imperial pay but also selling their information to the Russians and the Dutch.

An indelible mark was left in French history by the founding by the son of Count Bercsényi of a Hussar regiment in which many Hungarian refugees enlisted. László Bercsényi had been in the service of the French since 1712 and later became a Marshal of France.

His regiment formed the nucleus of the "Berchenyi Hussars", who were deployed as paratroopers in Bosnia in the 1990s.

One of the Prince's barely noticed court squires became a significant figure for future generations of Hungarians and for the development of Hungarian literature. This was a young Transylvanian, Kelemen Mikes, who spent forty-four years in exile, and sent over 200 letters during that time to a make-believe aunt living in Constantinople. These letters talk of the apparently uneventful life in Rodosto, the exiles' hopes and disappointments, the activities and finally the death of the lonely, unapproachable Prince immersed in meditation, the Prince's feelings when Empress Maria Theresa brusquely refused a petition for amnesty, and the profound hopelessness of exile. They represent a unique literary work, not only in the Hungarian literature of the eighteenth century. The work was published only forty years after the author's death, and took even longer to become available to the reading public.

"Is it irony, or perhaps a symbol of Hungarian fate, that this, the first of our social authors, was also the loneliest of them all: an outcast, exiled, unread author, playing the charming role of a literary man of the world in daydream surroundings?" This question was asked by Antal Szerb in his essay on the Székely petty nobleman, who in the "pipedream of an imaginary literary world" not only immortalized the tragedy of Rákóczi's emigration but also translated thousands of pages of his French writings.

It was only in 1906 that the Hungarian parliament declared the law of Rákóczi's exile as traitor null and void, and passed a resolution—in accordance with an Imperial order of 1904—to bring back from Turkey the mortal remains of the Prince and his followers. According to press reports, peasants, Hungarians, "Saxons", Romanians, "Swabians", Serbs and Slovaks knelt at the railway embankments along the route as the special train passed. On 28 October 1906 tens of thousands paid their respects at the lying in state of Rákóczi, his mother and son, and members of the Bercsényi family in Budapest's St Stephen Basilica before the coffins were finally laid to rest in Kassa. Only one of the exiles, Kelemen Mikes, was missing because the delegation had been unable to locate the grave of the "truest of the true".

When in 1976 a group of Hungarian émigrés travelled from Germany to Rodosto on the bicentenary of Rákóczi's birth, hardly

any trace of the one-time exile was discovered.[4] His banishment
had long since been turned into a saga that had its place at the heart
of national romanticism, thus a careful exposé of the hero's human
weaknesses published two centuries after his death, albeit shortly
after the ceremonial repatriation of his remains, provoked one of
the great scandals of Hungarian historiography. It was caused by the
work of the then (1913) almost unknown Hungarian historian
Gyula Szekfü, who was employed (from 1908 to 1925) in the
archives of the Imperial family, the Imperial household and the
Austrian state in Vienna. *Rákóczi in Exile* was a blunt, sometimes
ironic but well researched portrayal of the Prince's love affairs, passion for gambling and political naiveté. What triggered off a storm
of indignation was the revelation that the Prince, chronically plagued
by lack of funds, commissioned his close associate, the Abbé Brenner,
to set up a gambling den at the Hôtel de Transylvanie in Paris. This
establishment at 15 Quai Malaquais yielded profits for years, from
which Rákóczi allegedly drew an annual income of 40,000 livres.
The revelation that the Prince had left the country even at important moments during the War of Independence in order to "satisfy
his appetite for life"; that with Bercsényi he danced all night and
went on sleigh-rides in the company of beautiful Polish women;
and that he left his pregnant wife to visit one of his mistresses in a
neighbouring chateau was the final straw. Szekfü was accused of
disparaging the hero and discrediting the political emigration and
its mission of independence at the instigation of Viennese court circles. Rabid nationalists publicly burned the book. Szekfü defended
himself, proving in a new book that his data and sources were
watertight, and stating that Rákóczi authorized the casino (which
incidentally is mentioned in Puccini's *Manon Lescaut*) to prevent
the "starvation of his countrymen". As for his womanizing, he himself
had made no secret of it in his *Confessions of a Sinner*. Szekfü's apo-
logia, published in 1916, was supported by numerous historians.

    The shock of this scandal probably helped, directly or indirectly,
consciously or subconsciously, to shape the future direction of the
life of this most respected of inter-war historians. After the Revolution of 1918 the Communist government offered him a professorship in Budapest, which he neither declined nor took up. While in
Vienna he married a widowed Jewish coffee-house owner, who

accompanied him to Budapest when he finally accepted a chair at the University in 1925. Meanwhile, in 1920, his best-known and most influential book, *Three Generations*, was published—a devastating settling of accounts with the nobility and assimilated Jewry, on whom he laid most of the blame for the decline of historical Hungary. Szekfű became the ideologue of the "subtle" anti-Semitism of the middle classes, which eventually paved the way for its murderous version. He subsequently wrote a five-volume *History of Hungary*, together with Bálint Hóman (for many years Minister of Education, condemned in 1945 to life imprisonment). In contrast to his co-author, he had already turned against the pro-Hitler, rightwing direction of the government by 1941.[5]

After 1945 Szekfű wholeheartedly sided with the new regime and during the crucial period of the Communist take-over between January 1946 and September 1948, he even held the post of Hungarian ambassador to the Soviet Union. In 1947 he published an anthology entitled *After the Revolution*, in which, after censuring the Horthy regime and the persecution of the Jews, he sang the praises of the Soviet system with special emphasis on Stalin, whom he called "the object of highest esteem and love". The Soviet people loved Stalin, he wrote, because they knew that in his simple way of life, almost like a "hermit yesterday, today and tomorrow", he worked for their welfare.[6]

After his return from Moscow in 1953 the Communist Party appointed him a parliamentary representative, and a year later he was promoted a member of the State Presidential Council. Hóman died in prison, Szekfű as a member of the collective headship of state. From Rákóczi to Stalin the controversial changes in the life of a great historian testify to the repeated oscillations of the Hungarian intellectual élite amid the chaos of history's turning-points.

16. Hungary in the Habsburg Shadow

Hungarian historians have continually debated whether the 1711 Peace of Szatmár, passionately denounced by Prince Rákóczi, started Hungary's descent to the status of an Austrian province, perhaps even of a colony, resulting in its people ceasing to be a nation in the multinational land of the crown of St Stephen. On the other hand, the historian Domokos Kosáry argues that expressions such as "woeful destruction" and "national disaster" are not justified. He also rejects the idea that, compared to the seventeenth century, the eighteenth was a time of decline and denationalisation. In the introduction to his extensive analysis of the period 1711–1867, he stresses that the eighteenth century saw instead the gradual regeneration and inner recuperation of a devastated country. The Estates had tried to defend their privileges, and national self-determination was one of them. In short, it was a "relatively successful emergence from a grim situation".[1]

What was the nature of this compromise, which for two generations greatly lessened—even if they did not remove entirely—the tensions between the Estate-based state and absolute monarchy? At his coronation Charles promised to respect the laws of Hungary and rule the country in co-operation with the Diet. Apart from the *ius resistendi*, already cancelled in 1687, the King recognized all the political, social and economic prerogatives of the nobility, including the right not to be arrested without valid legal title, to be subject only to him, and to enjoy total exemption from taxes. Because tax-exemption had been justified by the nobles' duty of military service since the Middle Ages, this obligation to obey the ruler's call for a general levy was successfully retained by the Estates, but because as early as the sixteenth century the army of the nobles had already ceased to be capable of defending the country against the Turks, it had become completely obsolete. Hungary's liberation, as we have

160

seen, was due not to the nobles but to mercenaries and the Habsburgs. However, they agreed to an Imperial-royal standing army, for which the expenses (i.e. war taxes) at any given time had to be approved by the Diet—they were of course paid by the disfranchised and the peasants, exploited as ever by both secular and clerical landowners.

Unlimited power over the serfs and the administrative autonomy of the Estates-controlled counties remained permanently pledged to the nobility. The general amnesty guaranteed at the peace treaty of Szatmár was strictly adhered to by the Court. Even the principle of *aviticitas*, raised to law by Louis the Great—whereby land belonged not to the individual noble owner but to his family, and could therefore only be inherited and not sold—was not tampered with. The Austrian historian Moritz Csáky (himself the scion of an old Hungarian aristocratic family) is of the opinion[2] that by in effect guaranteeing the continued existence of feudalism in the peace of Szatmár the Habsburgs wasted the last chance to abolish political and social structures that were already anachronistic.

During this period 108 members of the high nobility belonged to the so-called Magnate Table (Upper House) in the Diet, without whose agreement no resolutions could be passed: two princes, eighty-two counts and twenty-four barons, who owned one-third of the country. The separation of the Diet into the Upper Table of magnates and bishops and the Lower Table, comprising the middle-ranking and lesser nobility, representatives of the counties and boroughs and the lower clergy, had been institutionalized by Ferdinand in 1608. The high nobility—great landowners—had always played a decisive role, especially since the successfully concluded Counter-Reformation. Most of them changed their religion twice during the course of 120 years, and by the end of the seventeenth century were firmly re-Catholicized.

The middle-ranking and lesser nobility, who had remained preponderantly Protestant, made up only 5 per cent of the population. Of the 9.3 to 9.5 million inhabitants of Greater Hungary, i.e. including Transylvania, Croatia and the Military Border, about 400,000 belonged to the nobility. This collective term was misleading in so far as there was an unbridgeable gulf between the high nobility and the so-called "sandalled nobility" (the poor *bocskoros nemes* immortalized in literature). The approximately 200 intermarried magnate families (only half of them actually Hungarian), including the bishops and archbishops from their ranks, owned enormous latifundia.[3] Visiting the then uninhabited castle at Kismarton (Eisenstadt) in 1839, the travel-writer John Paget reported the following about the Esterházy family:

Great as is the splendour of some of our English peers, I almost fear the suspicion of using a traveller's licence, when I tell of Esterhazy's magnificence. Within a few miles from this same spot, he has three palaces of equal size. [...] England is famous for her noble castles, and her rich mansions: yet we can have little idea of a splendour such as Esterházy must formerly have presented. Crowded as it was by the most beautiful women of four countries,—its three hundred and sixty strangers' rooms filled with guests,— its concerts directed by a Haydn,—its opera supplied by Italian artists,—its gardens ornamented by a gay throng of visiters.—hosts of richly clothed attendants thronging its antechambers,—and its gates guarded by the grenadiers of its princely masters—its magnificence must have exceeded that of half the royal courts of Europe! I know of nothing but Versailles, which gives one so high a notion of the costly splendour of a past age as Esterház. [...]

The winter flock of Merinos is maintained at 250,000, to every hundred of which one shepherd is allowed, thus making the number of shepherds 2,500! But as a *spirituelle* of the neighbourhood observed when we were discussing these matters: "*Les Esterházys font tout en grand: le feu prince a doté deux cent mâitresses, et pensionné cent enfans illégitimes.*"[4]

Under the Habsburgs many magnates received hereditary titles, soon forming a separate closed class. Between 1670 and 1780, 160 families were elevated to the standing of count and baron—added to whom were the 249 foreign families of the high nobility, who were accepted into the list of Hungarian nobles. As the Viennese court got into debt during the incessant wars, officers and purveyors to the Court received first lands and then titles of nobility. For example, an exceptionally resourceful baker in Linz named Franz Harruckern first looked after victualling, then became head of the commissariat, and later managed large estates in the counties of Békés and Csongrád. The King finally made him a baron and appointed him chief *ispán* of Békés county, and the formerly modest family from Linz married into, among others, the House of Károlyi.[5] The latter, in turn, profited from the timely desertion of Field-Marshal Sándor Károlyi who, against the wish of Rákóczi, had negotiated and signed the peace of Szatmár with his compatriot on the other side, Count János Pálffy. The following year the Baron became Count Károlyi—and generations of Hungarian schoolchildren were taught that he had been a traitor. However, the historian Kálmán Benda observed that the agreement concluded by Károlyi had been appropriate under the prevailing circumstances; no better outcome would have been possible at the time, and had he not availed himself of the chance, the participants in the War of Independence would have suffered.[6]

The loyalist officers and soldiers were called "*Labanc*" (foot-soldiers), and when the huge estates of Rákóczi and Bercsényi were shared out, the old or newer Labanc aristocracy were appropriately rewarded. But the foremost beneficiaries were foreign nobles, such as Prince Trautsohn and, in the vicinity of Munkács, Count Schönborn, Archbishop of Mainz; these foreigners received right of domicile, and soon moved up into the ranks of the Magnate Table. One of these was Antal Grassalkovics, who had risen from lesser noble to count and acquired a huge fortune in the process, and who built the famous palace at Gödöllö where Maria Theresa was entertained, and where Empress Elisabeth (wife of Franz Joseph I) was to stay on many occasions. Nor were such well-known families as the Andrássy, Festetich and Podmanitzky of ancient lineage, having received their titles in recognition of loyal service.[7] In this period of conspicuous display, Prince Esterházy could boast of a magnificent book, ordered by the palatine Pál Esterházy in the mid-seventeenth century and made in Nuremberg by Tobias Seidler, in which the members of the Esterházy family were presented as descendants of Adam, with kinship relations to such tribal chiefs as Örs, Attila and Hunor.

Between the very rich magnates and the poor petty nobles there were 25,000–30,000 propertied families, the "*bene possessionati*", many owning a few thousand hectares of land, and the "*possessionati*" whose holdings were smaller. Many of the smaller nobles were in the service of the magnates, while the living standards of the "sandalled nobility" were often lower than those of Austrian peasants.

This Estates-based society, deeply divided in its social status, formed the "political nation". The national-ethnic differences within the nobility broke out with full frenzy only during the fight against the reforming line of Emperor Joseph II towards the end of the eighteenth century. However, there was already a deep breach earlier during the Kuruc conflicts between the predominantly re-Catholicized nobility in the west and the mainly Calvinist east, particularly over attitudes towards the House of Habsburg. The split, reduced to the simple formula of Labanc (loyalist) against Kuruc (rebel), dominated the superficial polemics of day-to-day politics, journalism and historiography—usually far removed from the country's real affairs. As Macartney pointed out, the most difficult parties during the peace negotiations of Szatmár were the Hungarian Labanc nobles, because the amnesty deprived them of the hope of further enriching themselves at the expense of their fellow-countrymen.

The Pragmatic Sanction—the agreement concerning the succession in the female line—adopted by the Diet in 1722–3 was a far-reaching step on the way to Hungary's incorporation into the Habsburg Monarchy. Furthermore, the Upper House accepted the principle that the theoretically independent kingdom of Hungary should regard itself as united with the hereditary Habsburg lands *"indivisibiliter"* and *"inseparabiliter"*. Consequently Hungary ceased to be a politically independent factor. The eminent American authority on the history of the Dual Monarchy, Robert A. Kann, believed that the compromise was useful to both sides, but in the long run more so for Hungary's cause. Throughout the reigns of King Charles III (Emperor Charles VI) and Maria Theresa—i.e. for two generations—Hungarian national rights within the modest framework of the Peace of Szatmár were not tampered with.[8] What mattered above all to Karl was to secure undivided control over his lands by the recognition of his daughter's succession.

During the ensuing decades a contradictory development took place. On the one hand, the country of the Magyars was eliminated as a factor in European power politics, with foreign affairs, defence policy, finance and education subordinated to the King or to a central authority. The territorial autonomy of the lands of the Crown of St Stephen was never reinstated: the principality of Transylvania, the Bánát, Slavonia and the Military Border districts remained under the control of different Viennese central authorities. Finally in 1723 the King created a new chief administrative authority at Pressburg—a gubernatorial council subordinated directly to the ruler and headed by the Palatine or a royal *ispán*—responsible for the country's entire internal administration until 1848. National independence was evidently not on the agenda.

On the other hand, in practice the executive power was vested in the fifty-two counties, i.e. not in the central authorities or the Hungarian Diet, which was convoked at Pressburg not, as should have been the case, every three years, but only at ever-longer intervals. The *ispán* appointed by the King often had to be satisfied with being a mere figurehead, while the officials elected by the middle and lesser nobility exercised power. They controlled the direct administration that affected everyday life, from ensuring public safety to the delicate tasks of collecting taxes and provisioning the army.

The complacent and narrow-minded local patriotism of the Estates, their effect on the day-to-day politics and activity in the counties and the lifestyle of the pipe-smoking "petty potentates" (François Fejtö), have been brilliantly portrayed in the short stories and novels of nineteenth-century Hungarian writers such as József Eötvös and Kálmán Mikszáth. But even an explicitly Hungarophile English traveller such as Julia Pardoe was not sparing in criticism:

The besetting sin of the Magyar is vanity. He is proud of his nation, of his liberty, of his antiquity, and above all, of his privileges. In short, he admits no superior, and scarcely an equal, when he has high blood, a long pedigree and an apparent rent-roll. I say apparent, for perhaps Europe cannot present collectively so pauperized a nobility as that of Hungary.... There are not twenty nobles in the country who are not de facto bankrupt.

This is a startling assertion, but one which can be easily borne out.... The Hungarian noble sacrifices everything to show, and luxury, and ostentation: and thus his necessities ever outrun his income, and he is compelled to dispose of the productions of his extensive estates to a swarm of Jews and traders, who profit by his inconsiderate prodigality.

"The idea of a commercial treaty with England is at best a bubble for the present," said one of the most intelligent of the Magnates.... "We still have much to do ere it can be brought to bear. The Magyars have not yet learnt to be traders: and as to the nobles—we one and all prefer sitting quietly upon our sofas, and disposing of our produce for a given number of years to an accommodating individual who will pay down the price in *argent comptant*, even though it be at a loss of fifty per cent, to having the trouble of speculating, calculating and waiting...."[9]

In a different context John Paget sketches a portrait of the young
liberal nobility:

Lacking any knowledge of the political or commercial circumstances of
their fatherland or the neighbouring countries, they are all completely
convinced that Austria is the source of all the ills they are suffering from,
and they therefore regard this power with fear and resentment. No radical
in England grumbles more about taxation than the liberals in Hungary;
but they mix the privileges of the nobility so peculiarly into their
vituperations that it would be difficult to discover something of the principle in their opposition. In fact they do not clearly differentiate between
right and prerogative. [...]

Some Hungarians speak with silly vanity of their *subjects* and their *vassals,* forgetting that, instead of impressing a foreigner with an admiration
for their greatness, such remarks only fill him with disgust at their injustice.
What renders it still worse is, that this language is sometimes used by men
who talk loudly of the oppressions they suffer from Austria,—of attacks on
their rights and privileges: they may talk long enough before they excite
the sympathy of an Englishman, when they utter in the same breath complaints of the disobedience and insubordination of their own *vassals*!

The nobility's exemption from taxes had... serious consequences, as all
public expenses were carried by the serfs, subject to statute-labour. The
lesser nobility preferred until recently to live in relative poverty rather than
like the burghers, to be subject to payment of taxes, tolls and duties which
were associated with the pursuance of a profession. They interpreted their
liberty as their privileges.[10]

In spite of all these complaints, the nobility were of course thoroughly satisfied with the rules of Charles and Maria Theresa—and
sufficiently satisfied with themselves to invent the adage "*Extra
Hungariam non est vita. Si est vita, non est ita*" (There is no life outside
Hungary. And if there is, it is not really life).

It is against this background that the mentality of the Hungarian
nobility—who to the very last considered engaging in commerce
or industry to be beneath their dignity—should be seen. The country's modernization was delayed by more than a century—not,
observes Csáky, because of Turkish domination, but because of the
legal entrenchment of the nobility's privileges. The continued existence of long obsolete Estates-based structures were the decisive
factor in the decline of Hungary's economy and culture, and the
country's subsequent backwardness.

The advantages of the compromise concluded by the House of Habsburg with the Estates of Hungary manifested themselves sooner than expected. After two unlucky wars on the side of Russia, Charles III left his daughter Maria Theresa (1740–80) a militarily, financially and morally shaken empire. When in April 1741 the Austrian army suffered a devastating defeat by the Prussians at Mollwitz near Breslau, France, Spain and Bavaria also fell upon the Habsburg Hereditary Lands. In the face of this military catastrophe, as Sir Thomas Robinson, the English ambassador in Vienna, noted, the twenty-three-year old Maria Theresa, "lacking money, lacking credit, lacking an army, lacking experience and knowledge, and lacking advice", demonstrated perhaps the most important attribute of a ruler, namely courage in misfortune. Robinson depicts the reaction in the Council of State when the bad tidings of the Prussians' and the united Bavarian-French army's advance into Upper Austria reached Vienna: "The deathly pale ministers fell back in their chairs; only one heart remained steadfast: that of the Queen."[11]

Four months after her coronation as King of Hungary (the masculine form was used by design since she herself was the ruler and not the wife of a king) Maria Theresa decided, with her infallible sense for the feasible, to mobilize the Magyars—the last unused resource in her dramatically shrunken empire—by a personal call to arms; this in the teeth of advice from her father's high officials, who warned her not to ask for money or soldiers since no one could foresee what the Hungarians would do with the weapons. An adviser is supposed to have said: "Your Majesty would do better to rely on the devil."[12]

Despite all the warnings and after thorough preparations by her Hungarian confidant palatine Count János Pálffy, who had fought as a general in the Turkish and Kuruc wars, and by Cardinal Imre Esterházy, Archbishop of Esztergom, Maria Theresa appeared on 11 September 1741 at eleven in the morning before the Diet in the castle of Pressburg. Several anecdotally embellished versions exist of how the ruler, dressed from top to toe in mourning, with a sword at her side, slowly passed along the rows of members of the two Houses, mounted the throne, and in a dramatic Latin speech, interrupted by weeping, appealed to "Hungarian courage and loyalty". She was very beautiful and spoke with a firm voice—but she did not have the heir to the throne, her six-months-old son Joseph, in her arms, as has been conveyed to posterity in painted and poetic portraits; this scene was enacted ten days later when the ceremonial oath on the Hungarian constitution was taken by her co-regent Francis.

The speech given in a truly emotional fashion "by the poor Queen abandoned by all the world" was a great political and theatrical achievement:

"The very existence of the Kingdom of Hungary, of our own person, of our children and of our crown are now at stake. Now that we are forsaken by all, our sole resource is the fidelity, arms and long-tried valour of the Hungarians; exhorting you, the Estates and Orders to deliberate without delay in this extreme danger on the most efficacious measures for the security of our person, our children and our crown, and to carry them into immediate execution. In regard to ourself, the faithful Estates and Orders of Hungary will enjoy our hearty co-operation in all things which may promote the pristine happiness of this ancient kingdom and the honours of the people."[13]

The success of the appeal was overwhelming. The Hungarian nobles thundered with swords drawn: "*Vitam et sanguinem pro rege nostro Maria Theresia!*" (Blood and life for our King Maria Theresa!) However, there was one blemish on this superb scene, which most of the reference works fail to mention: it is said that a loud and clear voice was heard from the back rows, where the representatives of the Protestant counties of eastern Hungary stood, adding "*sed non avenam!*" (but no oats!)—in other words, no material obligations.[14]

The Estates' emotional response was no empty gesture: the Hungarians at first wanted to provide altogether 100,000 men from the lands of St Stephen, but eventually an army of 60,000, consisting of over half of the nobility's general levée and a force of conscripted peasants, took to the field in great haste.[15] Directly and indirectly the Hungarians saved Maria Theresa and Austria in their time of greatest need—it was barely thirty years since they had been humbled by that same dynasty whose highest representative now appealed to them for their assistance, devotion and loyalty. Not only was the size of the military contingent important, but also the fact that an armed uprising, comparable to the one forty years earlier during the War of the Spanish Succession, would certainly have dethroned

Maria Theresa. Furthermore, it would have been impossible to liberate Linz and Prague and even to occupy Munich without the
psychologically vital military aid from Hungary. The success in
Hungary and the intervention of the nobles' mounted force and
the infantry regiments set up by them surprised and bewildered
Austria's enemies and helped to turn the fortunes of war even
before England's intervention.

Maria Theresa had won this difficult game in Pressburg with
charm, chivalry and skill, but also by means of explicit concessions
strengthening and expanding the nobility's privileges. Among other
things she promised to maintain their tax exemption as part of the
nobility's "fundamental rights and freedoms", non-intervention in
local jurisdiction, and the organization of serfdom. "I have come
not only to take but to give," she declared, thus guaranteeing the
majority of rights demanded by the Diet.

Henceforth, in writing as well as by word of mouth, Maria Theresa
repeatedly declared her gratitude to the "Hungarian nation" whom
she regarded as "fundamentally good people, with whom one can
do anything if one takes them the right way". During disturbances
twenty years later she came out in favour of the serfs against their
inhuman treatment by the aristocracy. "I am a good Hungarian,"
she wrote to her brother-in-law, then governor of Hungary. "My
heart is full of gratitude to this nation."

During the Seven Years War (1756–63) two gifted Hungarian
army commanders ensured that the bravery of the Hungarian regiments would make a great impression on Europe and arouse the
Queen's profound admiration. When on 17–18 June 1757 General
Ferenc Nádasdy won a decisive victory in three successive cavalry
charges against Frederick the Great of Prussia at the battle of Kolin,
the Empress was overjoyed, calling it "the birthday of the Monarchy", and established the Order of Maria Theresa for outstanding
military achievement. Nádasdy was one of the first recipients of the
Grand Cross. This most talented of Maria Theresa's generals next to
Laudon was the grandson of the Count Nádasdy executed in
Vienna on the order of Leopold I for his participation in the
Zrinyi-Wesselényi conspiracy in 1671.

However, the most daring manoeuvre was accomplished some
months later by General András Hadik (born in 1711 at Esztergom),

who had already won spectacular successes during the Silesian wars. By a brilliantly executed stratagem Hadik took the war right into the enemy's heartland, advancing directly on Berlin behind the back of the Prussian army as it marched westwards against the French. His raiding party consisted of a mere 3,500 cavalry and infantry, the artillery being represented by four cannons. On 16 October 1757, after a short and bloody clash, he forced an entry through the Köpenick gate and blew up a bridge, penetrating the city with 1,700 of his men; another party took the Cottbus gate. The frightened and confused Berliners estimated the strength of the attackers at 15,000 men, and in the belief that this force was merely the vanguard of a large Austrian army, the city council was willing to pay 125,000 silver thalers as tribute, giving Hadik a promissory note for a similar amount and an additional 25,000 thalers as a gift to the soldiers. The threat of bombardment had served its purpose. The following day Hadik disappeared without interference from the city with his men and the six banners and 400 prisoners they had captured. The infantry marched 50 km. a day and the cavalry rode at least 80 km. A unit of 300 hussars commanded by Colonel Ujházy held up the pincer movement of the pursuing Prussian troops. During one skirmish Magyars once again fought Magyars since the vanguard of the Prussian infantry included hussars under Colonel Mihály Székely. The frightened Court returned to Berlin on 18 October, following the Prussian troops who had re-entered the capital only the night before. King Frederick himself set out with his army in pursuit of Hadik—his order of the day was "These men must be ours, dead or alive!" However, he did not succeed in catching up with Hadik's little unit.

According to the Habsburg historian Adam Wandruszka, Hadik's exploit filled Maria Theresa with special pride, since she hated the Prussian King, whom she called the "thief of Silesia". In a handwritten letter she told Hadik of her "most gracious satisfaction at the cleverly and successfully carried out enterprise against Berlin", awarding him 3,000 ducats and the Grand Cross of the Military Order of Maria Theresa. Needless to say, Hadik's bold venture furnished rich and colourful material for stories. According to one, he sent the Queen from Berlin a box of gloves of the finest leather— but because of the hurry it contained twenty-four for the left hand only.

Hadik was given the status of hereditary count, promoted Field-Marshal, appointed military governor of Transylvania and later of Galicia, and in 1774 chairman of the Supreme Military Council (*Hofkriegsrat*), a position he held until his death in 1790. The significance of this appointment, which marked the peak of his career, can be gauged by the fact that no Hungarian had ever before been permitted to appear even as an adviser to this authority. As the historian Julius Miskolczy put it: "Over the centuries not a single Hungarian statesman was honoured by participation in the government.[...] Even the country's highest dignitaries, the palatine and the Chancellor, were kept away from the government of the Habsburg Monarchy. The reason for this was lack of trust."[16]

Maria Theresa was without doubt the outstanding figure in the history of the House of Austria. Frederick II himself paid homage to her in his Testament as "the wisest and politically most gifted" princess: "This woman, who could be regarded as a great man, has consolidated her father's unstable monarchy."[17]

"Despite the fourteen years of war", wrote Wandruszka, "despite the birth of sixteen children, despite the nobility's and the clergy's resistance, Maria Theresa was a great reformer blessed with benevolence, feminine charm and the talent of a virtuoso for choosing and treating her advisers." He concludes:

No ruler before or after her in the long line of the old Habsburg and Habsburg-Lorraine dynasties, which had become merged within her person, knew how to place the right man at the right time in the right place: no one but she carried out, in the midst of critical wars, so many fundamental and revolutionary innovations which also stood the test of time. Whatever sphere of Austria's modern history one deals with, be it administration, fiscal and trade policy, education, the armed forces, justice and health, one reaches the conclusion that the decisive reforms and beneficial institutions can be traced back to the reign of the great Empress.[18]

With unfailing political instinct Maria Theresa tried always to take into consideration factors relating to tradition in her dealings with the Monarchy's most difficult country, and from time to time at least partly to win over the suspicious and eccentric nobility to the central reforms. Distribution of offices, decorations and personal marks of favour were of great help in these efforts. The Hungarian policy of the court was doubtless moulded by the Queen's humane disposition. A few weeks before her death she summoned the Chancellor of Hungary, Count József Esterházy, to an audience and said to him: "Tell the Hungarians again and again that I shall think of them with gratitude until my very last moment."[19]

This attitude and her various educational, scientific and religious initiatives had far-reaching and sometimes unforeseen consequences for Hungary's future, and indirectly for the Monarchy. Maria Theresa succeeded first and foremost in enticing the high and well-to-do section of the middle-ranking nobility into Vienna's sphere of interest. In 1746 she established the Theresianum, the élite academy for training young nobles, which up to 1772 already attracted 117 sons of Hungarian aristocratic families. Numerous Hungarians also graduated from the Military Academy in Wiener Neustadt, and officers who attracted attention for their bravery were decorated with the newly-established Order of St Stephen. While Protestants were restricted in practising their religion and Jews were mercilessly persecuted and even occasionally expelled from Bohemia and Moravia, the pious Empress strongly supported the Catholic Church, partly in the interest of the Empire's standardization. The victorious Counter-Reformation created a pro-dynastic but also explicitly Hungarian patriotism of a Baroque-Catholic flavour, culminating in the notion of the *Regnum Marianum*, deliberately linking it with the medieval national kingdom's cult of Mary.

Two gestures in particular impressed the national-religious feelings of the Hungarians. After 1757 Maria Theresa again bore the title "Apostolic King of Hungary", a new-old privilege, conferred by Pope Clement XIII in recognition of the Hungarian people's sacrifice in the fight against the Turks. It harked back to the time of St Stephen, whose right hand was ceremonially repatriated from Ragusa (Dubrovnik) to the royal palace of Buda, to even greater effect.[20]

As for national interests, although Transylvania continued to be separated from the mother country, Maria Theresa re-incorporated into Hungary the thirteen Zipser towns mortgaged to Poland 300 years earlier by King Sigismund, the port of Fiume and the Military Border districts of the Tisza-Maros region.

By far the most significant gesture for the future of the Hungarian language, literature and national identity—even if at the time it was not fully recognized—was the establishment in 1760 of a Hungarian noble regiment of the Queen's Guards in Vienna. Two young nobles were sent to Vienna by each county to serve in it for five years, and to these were added twenty delegates from Transylvania. The Queen later raised the number of her Life Guard to 500. It is a paradox of Hungarian history that the renewal of the Hungarian language was not initiated in Hungary proper but in the capital of a foreign country, making Vienna the centre of the Hungarian literary movement.[21]

It was an eighteen-year-old guardsman György Bessenyei (1747–1811) who, having mastered French and then German (he wrote poems in these languages), concluded that the ideas of the Enlightenment could only be spread through the mother tongue. That, however, required renewal of the language itself in order to adapt it to the higher intellectual demands. The second task was to motivate people to read, and the third was the creation of a literature to rouse their interest and lead them in the direction of reforms. It is not an exaggeration to regard Bessenyei the forerunner of the modern Hungarian language even though the style of his works, published from 1772 onwards, make them almost unreadable today. Nonetheless he and his friends gave the first impetus to language reform and the introduction of the language movement. The essayist Paul Ignotus, who wrote an English-language *History of Hungary* in emigration, may be correct in a deeper sense when saying that through his literary renaissance Bessenyei "had invented the Hungarian nation".[22] Previously only a handful of Hungarian writings, mostly religious, had been published. The first Hungarian newspaper, *Magyar Hirmondó*, printed in Pressburg, appeared first in Latin, then in German, and only from 1780 in Hungarian.

Through the philosophy and literature of the Enlightenment France exerted a strong cultural-linguistic influence on the Hungarian magnates, both directly and indirectly. Thousands of French books were housed in the libraries of the 200 castles built during Maria Theresa's reign. One brilliant figure of the Hungarian Enlightenment was Count János Fekete, a general of half-French, half-Turkish background, who carried on a lively correspondence with Voltaire; he sent numerous French poems to the sage of Ferney, which the latter conscientiously corrected and praised, even asking his admirer to send new works. His interest in the versifying general may not have been purely literary, since Fekete always sent 100 bottles of Tokai with his poems.[23]

Very few precursors of Romanticism took up the cudgels for Hungarian. Latin was the nobility's second language—how else can one explain that the most revolutionary work of the period, Rousseau's *Le contrat social*, was published in Hungary (and only there!) in Latin? John Paget wrote even years later: "Only the magnates. I suspect, have a better reason than mere courtesy for not speaking Hungarian—simply because they cannot do so. A large part of the higher nobility is denationalized to such an extent that they understand every European language better than their own national language."[24]

Maria Theresa was extraordinarily popular in Hungary, although the massive settlement (*impopulatio*) of foreigners decreed by her altered the ethnic composition to the Hungarians' disadvantage. While the primary aim was to reconstruct the devastated and depopulated swamplands, the loyalty of the new settlers was not unimportant, in the words of Bishop Kollonics, "in order to tame the Hungarian blood, which is inclined to revolution and turmoil".[25] Since the end of the seventeenth century the Imperial Court regularly sent agents from Buda to Austria and Bavaria to recruit colonists with the promise of tax exemption for three to five years or immunity from the dreaded billeting. The mainstream of willing immigrants came from south-western Germany, particularly the neighbourhood of Lake Constance, central Rhenish villages and the Moselle region. Germans as such were preferred because of their diligence and loyalty to the Court. At first Catholics were favoured as settlers, but later Protestants were also accepted. Under Maria Theresa the Bánát and Bácska in southern Hungary were settled in this way; between 1763 and 1773 alone, the authorities dealt with 50,000 German families, and it is estimated that the number of settlers of German origin in 1787 was 900,000, i.e. a tenth of Hungary's 9.2 million population.[26]

Along with the creation of "loyal islets" of diligent Germans there was also an inconspicuous immigration of Slovaks and Ruthenes from the north, Romanians from the east and southeast (they were already in an absolute majority in Transylvania) and Croats and

Serbs from the south. As a result of the catastrophes at the end of the Middle Ages and the Turkish occupation, Magyars in 1787 amounted to only 35–39 per cent of the population.[27]

These statistics explain the shock which the partly organized and partly illegal influx caused to the distrustful middle-ranking and lesser nobility. Although Maria Theresa was masterly at manipulating the Hungarian aristocracy's need for admiration and pride to her own advantage, she kept a watchful eye on a possible flare-up of rebellious ideas or nostalgia for Kuruc leaders:

One day Count Aspremont drove to his estate at Onod. The heavy coach sank into the mud, and the horses could not pull it out. While this was happening, peasants were dashing by in their light vehicles on their way from holy mass at Onod. None of them stopped. They only laughed at the predicament of the loudly cursing Germans stuck in the mud. Finally the Count climbed on to the coach-box, angrily shouting at the laughing peasants: "So you let Rákóczi's grandson roll in the mud?" When they heard the name, they immediately hastened to the coach, pulled it out and, cheering, accompanied the Count to Onod. News of this adventure soon reached Vienna, and when the Count appeared at Court, Maria Theresa shouted at him, red with anger: "Listen, Aspremont! We don't expect you to remain stuck in the slime, but you'd better forget about this Rákóczi farce, or we'll have you but in prison!"[28]

The massive settlement programme supported by the ruler was less a deliberate striving at Germanization than part of an attempt to centralize Hungary's and the Habsburg Empire's absolutist administration. In this context the Diet of 1764, the last during the Queen's lifetime, signalled a momentous turning point. The Estates stubbornly and in the event successfully resisted the Queen's determination to raise war taxes, tax the nobles' private property and reduce the burdens of the peasantry. Maria Theresa nonetheless enacted by royal decree the "Urbarial Patent" rejected by the Diet, fixing the normative legal size for a peasant holding and the maximum services which the landlord could exact (in the Middle Ages the *urbarium* was the land and mortgage register). Although the Queen did not act overtly against the constitution and the nobility's selfish and shortsighted opposition, from that time onwards she allowed a discriminatory economic policy to take its course against Hungary.

The underdevelopment resulting from the country's colonial status enforced by Austria, as expounded by many Hungarian historians in the past, is seen differently and in a more sophisticated way today. Thus Kosáry points out that it was not the Austrian customs and trade regulations that made Hungary into a backward agrarian country and a buyer of Western industrial products; it merely exploited this situation.[29] The Diet was never again called into session after 1764, and Hungary sank increasingly to the position of supplier of food and commodities to other crown lands. Although slow economic development did take place, the nobility's insistence on tax exemption gave the Viennese bureaucracy welcome excuses for separating Hungary from Austria by an internal customs barrier and deliberately making Hungary's already adverse position worse, with detrimental long-term effects on the other Habsburg lands as well. This continued till 1848.

In spite of her immigration and economic policies, Maria Theresa was and remained a generally admired and beloved ruler. On the other hand, the drastic reforms decreed by her son Joseph without any knowledge of human nature and a disregard for Hungarian sensibilities had far-reaching consequences, including loss of the old mutual trust. On the contrary, the imperial innovations dictated totally in the spirit of the Enlightenment gave an enormous stimulus to Hungarian nationalism, which in 1848 was to change the political map of Central Europe dramatically.

17. The Fight against the "Hatted King"

No other Habsburg is the object of such divergent opinions as Joseph II (1780–90). Was he a great reformer or the leading bureaucrat of his state?—a people's Emperor and liberator of peasants, or a "purifier of the faith" and "doctrinaire"?—an "imperial revolutionary" or a tragic heir to the imperial throne whose failure still dominates the style and way of thinking of the Austrian ruling classes? Joseph was certainly motivated by true humanism, but was far ahead of his time. His intensely tradition-bound people, especially Catholics who had been infused with devout piety by the Counter-Reformation, could not follow this free-thinker. When he enforced relief for the Protestants, the Orthodox and, last but not least, the Jews with his Patent of Toleration, he was simply met with lack of understanding. He decreed the abolition of serfdom, the extension of personal liberties including choice of profession, promotion of a new type of official, and the extension of education and health care to the entire empire. It has been estimated that during his reign of barely ten years Joseph enacted 6,000 decrees and 11,000 new laws.[1]

He went down in Hungarian history as the "hatted king" (*kalapos király*) because, uniquely, he refused coronation with the crown of St Stephen in order not to have swear an oath on the Estate-based constitution, the object of his "campaign of liquidation". Instead, with lack of both realism and sensitivity, he had the crown of St Stephen and the Bohemian crown of Wenceslas brought to the Vienna Hofburg to be displayed in the jewel room as mere museum-pieces. In order to have a free hand he did not convene the Diet, and replaced the counties and their elected officials with a strictly centralized administration consisting of ten districts, headed by imperial-royal officials.

The ruler's ideal was a strictly conformist state with a standardized administration, army and political organization. In his "fanaticism for the welfare of the state", as he himself called it. Joseph tried to convert the multi-faceted monarchy into "a single province, equal in all its institutions and responsibilities... a single mass of people all equally subject to impartial guidance".[2] The most important instrument of this autocratic reform-driven unity was the introduction of German as the sole language of administration on 18 June 1784. Officials had three years to master it.

These measures decreed without consideration for historic idiosyncrasies and entrenched mentalities, together with the census and land surveys to prepare the assessment of taxes on noble landholdings, aroused widespread indignation among the Hungarian nobility. Joseph's intention was not Germanization but a hierarchically structured, reliable and, of course, German-speaking bureaucracy, a massive enforced coordination of the Monarchy with the help of the predominant German element. Apart from that, it was irrelevant to him what language the Hungarians, Croats, Slovaks or Romanians used for their private affairs. With this goal in mind, he admonished the Hungarian Court Chancellor Count Esterházy in the following cut-and-dried royal memorandum of 26 April 1784:

The use of a dead language such as Latin is surely a disgrace to a nation for its enlightenment, as it *tacite* [tacitly] proves that either that nation does not have a proper mother tongue, or that no one can speak or write it. [...] If Hungarian were prevalent in all of Hungary, then it could serve on its own. [...] Therefore no other language besides German can be chosen as that of the Monarchy from both the military and political viewpoints.[3]

The Emperor's ill-advised foreign policy, the Turkish war embarked on in alliance with Russia in which Hungary had to bear the main burden, the successful uprising in the Austrian Netherlands and the machinations of Prussian agents, aroused extraordinary resistance from every stratum of the Hungarian nobility. Above all the intended introduction in 1789 of a tax of 12.22 per cent for noble landowners sent the Estates into violent uproar, with the counties even refusing to supply the army. The Josephist system of enlightened absolutism suffered shipwreck in Hungary. On his deathbed the Emperor revoked all his controversial reforms with the exception of the Toleration Patent, the Peasant Patent and the Pastoral Patent, promised to convoke a Diet, and ordered the holy crown to be returned to Hungary.

Convoying the crown from Vienna to Budapest took four days, and throughout country, but especially in the counties along the route, people were carried away by enthusiasm. The Calvinist minister József Keresztesi described in his diary the triumphal progress through Kittsee, Györ and Esztergom to Buda.[4] He also noted that "untold masses of people assembled in Vienna to see the crown's departure, because here even the Germans believed that the great rise in prices was God's punishment for having kept the crown."

When the procession, including an escort of hundreds of horsemen and foot-soldiers, mounted nobles and guardsmen, representatives of the counties and the city council, reached the royal palace, six selected nobles carried the chest with the crown into the great hall, placing it upon a three-tiered dais covered in red velvet:

Károly Zichy, the chief judge, delivered a short speech and wanted to open the chest, but the lock did not yield. He asked for another key in German, whereupon Zsigmond Nemes, a Hungarian gentleman standing nearby, said: "Gracious Sir, this is not a German crown, it does not understand German: should Your Excellency try to address it in Hungarian, not German, it will soon open up!" Everyone had to smile, and the Chief Judge spoke in Hungarian, the chest was opened and the crown taken out and shown to the assembled crowd in the palace hall. The chest was then dusted and re-locked, and when a German lackey wanted to sweep up, a Hungarian youth addressed him: "Away with you, you German, how dare you do that with your German hands?" Then he did the sweeping.

When Joseph II died on 20 February 1790, he bequeathed to his brother and successor Leopold II (1790–2) a reign threatened from several quarters, an almost pre-Revolutionary situation, but the new king succeeded with great tactical skill in improving the relationship between the dynasty and Hungary. At the Diet of 1790–1 the Estate-based national constitution was confirmed and embodied in Law X. Leopold pledged to rule Hungary "in accordance with its own laws and customs and not those of other countries". While the alarm bells of the French Revolution were already ringing, the Estates believed that they could continue to enjoy their privileges and isolate their country from the new political and social developments by restoring the old administrative system. It was due not only to Leopold's concessions, but above all to the collective fear of an insurrection, that neither the coalition wars against the Revolution nor Napoleon's appeal from Schönbrunn in 1809 resulted in a noble opposition movement endangering the Viennese central government. A delegation from the county of Szabolcs expressed a widespread view: "Just as the King's power is weak if there is no nobility, so the nobility cannot exist without the ruler." At the same time the Hungarian nobility could bring arguments to bear that were not available to the French nobility: the defence of privileges was synonymous with protecting the interests of the country, whose king resided abroad.

In Hungary the ideas of the Enlightenment fell on fertile soil, and this was linked with the slow but sure development of an intellectual stratum. It is estimated that between 1700 and 1790, 3,000 young men from Hungary studied at universities abroad—primarily in Germany, but also in Switzerland, the Netherlands and even England. According to the census of 1787, the first to enter into such great detail, the number of intellectuals amounted to less than 5,000 (there were 18,487 priests!), but Hungarian historians estimate today that the figure would actually have been nearer 15,000–20,000, albeit from a total population of 9.1 million.[5]

Freemasonry played an important role, enabling intellectuals to forge close contacts with enlightened aristocrats (Joseph II was a Lodge brother). In 1780 there were something like thirty lodges in Hungary with 800–900 members. The increasing number of subscribers to Hungarian-language newspapers, as well as the presence of 1,500 physicians, lawyers, civil servants and progressive noblemen in Pest-Buda the administrative centre (the two were united only in 1872), formed fertile soil for the growth of anti-feudal ideas.[6]

At the same time the campaign for the national language, which Bessenyei and his friends had placed on the agenda during Maria Theresa's reign, had a mighty upsurge because of resistance to Joseph II's regulations, which were regarded as attempts at Germanization. What began as a defence of Latin as an official language soon turned into passionate endeavours to promote the use of Hungarian as the language of state. The Magyars' growing national consciousness led in turn to tensions with Serbs and Romanians, and later with Slovaks and Croats also. However, in the resulting "nation of nobles" Hungarians still formed a strong absolute majority in contrast to the general population, and their fight for the introduction of Hungarian as the administrative, scientific and educational language overshadowed the conflicts with the Viennese court and its allies. Béla Grünwald, historian of the "old Hungary", characterized the state of affairs almost a century later (1910) as follows:

A foreign enemy kingdom, an intolerant, repressive clergy, a denationalized high nobility, an uneducated lesser nobility overwhelmingly indifferent to the national interest, a shrunken German bourgeoisie, an oppressed, poor peasantry, an imperialized army, an alienated Protestantism, ethnic masses—Romanians, Ruthenes, Serbs, Germans, Slovaks—lured by other centres, these elements determined the character of public life in Hungary.[7]

Hatred of Germans was rampant, because at the time Hungarians considered only two types of strangers as "Germans": the Court and government representatives, with whom the average Hungarian had little personal contact, and as ever the army with its foreign soldiers. The latter could be Walloons, Italians or Spaniards, but as Imperial mercenaries they bore in Hungarian eyes the indelible mark of Germanness. All historians point out that for centuries the Imperial mercenary caused cruel destruction on Hungarian soil, and many reports to Vienna confirmed that "the mercenary wrought worse havoc among the unhappy population than the Turk."[8] The Germans in turn regarded the Magyars as "abominable heretics" (because of their Calvinism) and "disloyal rebels" (because of memories of the Kuruc uprisings).[9] "All the hatred, underestimation and resentment that had been imputed to the Hungarians since the Conquest, suddenly erupted with terrible new vigour," writes Domokos Kosáry in his monograph on Hungary in the Baroque period.

Leopold Alois Hoffmann, transferred from Vienna to the University library at Budapest where he spied for Leopold II, fought with his pen against the revolutionary spirit of the Hungarian Association of Reformers. He wrote: "A Hungarian village noble knows scarcely as much as a porter in Paris."[10] Another German author, J. Reimann, said: "It has always been the a nature of the Hungarians to prefer a nimble horse and a naked sword to a rare book."[11] We shall return later to the theory of "cultural difference" and the changeable relationship between Germans and Hungarians. The significant fact is that already in the Enlightenment the literary representatives of Josephism used Hungary's historical catastrophes, the two-century-long retardation in development, the failure or belated making up of lost time to forge an indictment against the Hungarians. There was no understanding, let alone sympathy for Hungary's specific circumstances.

On the other hand, the greatest representatives of Hungarian culture were deeply troubled by the dramatic drop in the Hungarian population in both absolute and proportional terms. The poet Sándor Kisfaludy wrote of a journey he took as a young soldier in 1792 when he had encountered so many more Slovaks, Swabians, Romanians and Germans than pure Hungarians that he feared for "the end of the Hungarian nation".[12]

It was in that same year, and probably not by accident, that the father of romantic folk nationalism, Johann Gottfried Herder, made his gloomy prophecy about the future of the Magyars in his book *Ideen zur Philosophie der Geschichte der Menschheit*: "Here they are now, the minority of inhabitants among Slavs, Germans, Vlachs and other peoples, and after centuries perhaps even their language will have disappeared."[13] In the next two centuries probably no other foreign observer was cited as frequently as Herder because of the warning of impending disaster, and also as a beacon for the national War of Independence, by which such a small nation as the Hungarians ("a mere Asiatic fragment"), attempted to assert itself in a strange and hostile environment.

However, there was much sympathy at this time among intellectual circles in Hungary too for the philosophy of the Enlightenment and the French Revolution—clearly demonstrated by the Jacobin plot (described in the next chapter), a mighty shock in the first years of the long reign of Emperor Francis II (1792–1835), making its mark on the ruler's mistrustful attitude towards Hungary. In contrast to his gifted and flexible father, Francis was a "narrow, dry, reserved and generally untalented man, whose political achievements consisted chiefly in keeping his head above water in troubled times."[14]

18. Abbot Martinovics and the Jacobin Plot: a Secret Agent as Revolutionary Martyr

In the early hours of Wednesday 20 May 1795 five wooden carts, each drawn by four horses, rumbled along towards the great meadow below the royal castle in Buda. They carried the leaders (called "directors") and the founder of the Jacobin movement to the gallows. The carts were placed in such a way that the condemned men could not see the beheading of their comrades. The principal accused was Abbot Ignác Martinovics, and only he was compelled to watch the execution of his accomplices, scheduled for half past six.

Count Jakob Sigray was the first to bend over the block, and the executioner had to strike three times before the young count's head was separated from his body. Another noble, Ferenc Szentmarjay, was next, followed by János Laczkovics, a former captain of the Hussars, who five years earlier, with other officers, had petitioned the Reichstag to introduce Hungarian as the language of command and the assignment of Hungarian officers to Hungarian regiments. Next in line was the jurist József Hajnóczy, a former deputy *ispán*, who for years had published tracts critical of the intolerable situation in Hungary. The forty-year-old Martinovics suffered an epileptic fit while he was being dragged to the scaffold. The drama reached its climax when the executioners ceremoniously burnt Martinovics' writings. Hundreds of curious onlookers watched he gruesome spectacle. The bodies were buried on the spot.

Two weeks later another two young Jacobin organizers were decapitated in the same place. Ever since then the meadow has been called Vérmezö (Field of Blood), at first only in the vernacular, but later officially as well. Only in May 1914, 119 years after the event, were the remains of the seven martyrs finally found, and since

1960 they have rested in a mausoleum at the Kerepesi-cemetery in Budapest.

In the summer of 1794 the conspirators, altogether fifty-three noblemen and burghers, writers and professors, officials and jurists, were arrested and charged with high treason. Only one of them was over fifty; fifteen were under twenty-five. Two committed suicide. Eleven of the eighteen death sentences were commuted to long prison terms, and the condemned men disappeared, in chains, into the infamous dungeons of Kufstein, Brno and Munkács. Ferenc Kazinczy (1759–1831), the greatest reformer of the Hungarian language, and a great translator and admirer of German literature who wrote better in German than in Hungarian, spent 2,387 days behind bars, and the poet Ferenc Verseghy ten years because he had dared to translate *La Marseillaise* into Hungarian.

From beginning to end the diabolical and in some ways brilliant Martinovics stood at the centre of the movement. His turbulent life seems like a mixture between a psychiatric case-study, a detective story and a tale of the French Revolution.[1] Consequently differing opinions were held about the personality and the role of this man who, though virtually ignored in Western historiography, powerfully influenced the Habsburg Court's attitude towards Hungary for several decades.

Martinovics' ancestors, together with tens of thousands of refugee families from Serbia, came to Hungary at the end of the seventeenth century. Whether, as he claimed, his father was an Albanian nobleman serving in the army or a Serbian tavern-keeper is unclear. Enough to say that Ignác Martinovics, born in 1755 to a pious petty-bourgeois German woman in Buda, entered the Franciscan order aged sixteen at his mother's urging. He made his vows as a monk, and completed his theological and scientific studies with excellent results, but as early as 1774, frustrated by the life of the order, he asked to be released from the monastery; at the request of the prior he retracted his application, but further conflicts with his superiors and the friars followed. Finally family connections in the army secured him the chaplaincy of an infantry regiment in Czernowitz.

He immediately proceeded to Bukovina, seeking approval only retrospectively from his abbot, and in Czernovitz he made contact with Count Ignác Potocki, who was to become a government minister during the Polish War of Independence in 1794. The Polish nobleman was so impressed by the well-educated, eloquent and witty priest that he invited Martinovics to accompany him on a study trip to France, England, Switzerland and Germany. A convinced follower of the Enlightenment, Potocki forged links with like-minded people everywhere, and when after almost a year the two of them returned at the end of 1782, Martinovics stayed on in Lemberg (Lvov), where he cultivated close contacts with Freemasons, and was appointed professor of physics and later dean at the University by Joseph II; his scientific discoveries and philosophical books and studies in the spirit of the Enlightenment also made his name known, including abroad. He now openly broke with the Franciscans and became a secular cleric, but towards the end of the 1780s he declared himself an atheist, a follower of materialist philosophy, and a dedicated anti-clerical and enemy of the aristocracy. However, at the same time he still expected reforms from above, i.e. from the enlightened monarch.

Martinovics became involved in all sorts of conflicts; ambition, over-estimation of his own position and contempt for others led him into a blind alley. After relinquishing his position as dean he tried for five years to obtain a chair in Vienna or Pest, but all his efforts failed—partly because of the intrigues of the Jesuits, whose influence was again on the rise. These were his circumstances when a momentous turning-point came in Vienna in July 1790. Martinovics met the former Buda café proprietor Ferenc Gotthardi, whom Joseph II had appointed chief of the secret police in Pest. After the succession of Leopold II, Gotthardi rose to head the entire secret police with direct access to the Emperor, who himself proved a master of the art of sophisticated double-dealing and deception in the ring of informers encompassing the whole Empire. While the Emperor adopted a course of compromise and demonstrative reconciliation with the Hungarian Estates, he himself composed leaflets, which he had circulated, stirring up the peasantry against the landlords. At the same time Leopold was fomenting the Hungarophobia of the ever-loyal Serbs. By this dangerous game he intended to put the Estates under pressure and take the wind out of the sails of their separatist tendencies.

Chief of Police Gotthardi, appointed to the administration of the Court Theatre for clandestine purposes, built up a solid network of informants which consisted of Gyula Gabelhofer, professor and head of the Pest University library, prominent writers such as Count János Majláth and Baron A. Mednyánsky, aristocrats, book dealers and businessmen.[2] However, they failed to deliver any useful information about the Freemasons or the Jesuits, and Gotthardi was therefore delighted when Martinovics offered his co-operation. The scholar's hope that he could attract the ruler's attention and establish a political career for himself with his confidential and at the same time greatly exaggerated reports on the subversive activities of various secret societies was not misplaced. It is said that the Emperor received him three times on the police chief's recommendation.

With his vivid imagination and great ambition Martinovics peppered his reports with all kinds of invented plots, involving variously the Masonic Illuminati, the Jesuits and the patriots. All the authentic, semi-authentic and invented scraps of information served a single goal—to gain the Emperor's confidence[3] and with it political power. Martinovics endeavoured to prove his value, even indispensability, with ever more stories and denunciations. His writings were meant to persuade the Emperor to undertake reforms, but exclusively in the interests of the Monarchy and the ruler, in the spirit of enlightened absolutism, with concurrent sharp rejection of Estate-based and national strivings in Hungary. Leopold commissioned him to write two leaflets against the Hungarian constitution, the Estates and the clergy. The historian Kálmán Benda, believes him to have been a cosmopolitan in the modern sense, who declared himself at one time a Hungarian and at another a Serb. He was, in short, an enlightened reformer with a European perspective but without patriotism.

At the end of 1791 Martinovics was spending much time in Vienna, repeatedly offering his services as secretary of the cabinet, head of foreign policy or adviser to the Court Chancellery through the intermediation of Chief of Police Gotthardi, who was spellbound by him. But Leopold refused, seeing in him only a first-class informer, who was being richly rewarded both financially and with the title he so much coveted, that of Court Chemist. At the beginning of 1792 the Emperor commissioned his principal agent secretly to incite the peasantry against the landlords in order to clamp down on the Hungarian nobles, and to recruit associates for this surreptitious project. To Martinovics the road to the very top now appeared open at last, but Leopold was not able to realize his plans, worked out by a "staff of secret assistants", for the transformation of Hungary. He died unexpectedly on 1 March 1792, which also marked the end of this unusual agent's hoped-for career at Court.

Emperor Francis II was not interested in either Gotthardi or Martinovics; they fell out of favour, and a new police chief terminated their monthly allowances. They tried desperately to regain the goodwill of the Emperor, to whom Gotthardi said: "Although it is true that Martinovics is one of the leaders of the Illuminati, it is also true that he made the others known by name... If he were sent to hell, he would achieve results there too." Martinovics sent Francis II a series of denunciations and memoranda; one such was a sealed envelope containing the names of ten alleged leading Austrian Illuminati. Yet all was in vain. The new Emperor was not interested in Martinovic's reform suggestions and passed the unopened envelopes to the new chief of police.

The reports testify to Martinovics' inner conflict, his true feelings as an enlightened reformer and his craving for recognition. He was constantly ready to sacrifice his convictions to make a career for himself—which is why he repeatedly made contradictory suggestions and denounced his closest associates. Although a legal suit brought against him because of his irregular withdrawal from the Franciscan order was dropped, and although he was named titular abbot of Szászvár and given a pension by the Emperor, it was too late.

In the spring of 1794, spurred on by a combination of wounded vanity and the desire for revenge, the bitterly disappointed Martinovics assumed the leadership of a patriotic revolutionary movement—effectively placing himself in the vanguard of those he had denounced. His élan, his acumen and above all his strong leadership carried along nobles and intellectuals who had hitherto gone no further than theorising—even those who did not like or quite trust him. The former police agent decided to organize two societies, the "Association of Hungary's Reformers" and the "Association of Liberty and Equality", writing for them so-called catechisms. The first organization aimed to win over the lesser nobility and create a republic ruled by them—implying the overthrow of the Monarchy. Although the nobility would retain their prerogatives, the liberated peasants would become free tenants. Martinovics' objective, like that of the reformers of 1848, was to harmonize the interests of the enlightened and pro-reform nobility with those of the radical intelligentsia.

Suddenly Martinovics took on the role of champion of Hungarian patriotism. He had a masterly understanding of how to convert the Hungarian nobility's old resentments against the Habsburgs and their concrete complaints into a devastating indictment of foreign rule. The Hungarians should mount a sacred uprising following the Polish example, strip Emperor Francis of his royal title and proclaim the republic; after all, Hungary could stand on its own! The 9 million people, living in a fertile country, were quite capable of holding their own against the Turks as well as the Germans if only they were well organized.

The Monarchy's historian Julius Miskolczy regarded another of his notions as particularly inspiring. In the reformers' catechism Martinovics suggested that the Hungarian republic of nobles, separated from the Austrian dynasty and its state, be reconstructed into a federal republic ("federated *res publica*"), each nationality being allocated its own territory and individual constitution and having the right to use its own language and practise its religion. The territories should be linked by a close alliance, and show a unified, indissoluble front to the outside world.

Martinovics saw an armed uprising as the way to realize this concept. Yet the task of the second secret Association—Liberty and Equality—was to go beyond the national aim, and guide the bourgeois transformation under its leadership. The noble reformers were, of course, kept ignorant of the existence of the more radical second society, which would use members of the first group as its tools. The second concept was in accordance with the Jacobins' body of thought, i.e. an alliance of intellectuals with the peasantry.

After only a few months the two societies already boasted of of 300 or more members. Martinovics repeatedly indicated to the four directors and other leading members that he was receiving his orders directly from the Jacobins' headquarters in Paris, and that there was a real prospect of financial and armed assistance; thus they were being deliberately misled. In fact the two groups' operations consisted merely of discussions on human rights and reforms, as well as circulating the Association of Reformers' catechism. Members of the society were mainly aristocrats, half of them intellectuals, whose average age was between twenty and thirty.

In spite of strict secrecy, police agents reported the dissemination of inflammatory declarations in Hungary, and the high command in the northern counties feared an armed uprising. Troops were assembled and reinforcements transferred to Hungary. The police swooped in July 1794 and arrested twenty people, among them the erstwhile head of the secret police Gotthardi, the young Emperor's former mathematics professor Baron Andreas von Riedel, and Ignác Martinovics. As was to be expected, it was once again Martinovics who denounced the Hungarian Jacobins, but it was in vain that he protested during interrogations that he had acted only according to the wishes of the deceased Emperor Leopold II.

The Jacobin movement consisted of a handful of highly educated idealists, who were both patriots and humanists, but without a power base or financial means they posed no real danger to the state or the Monarchy. However, Martinovics' implication of almost the whole of official Hungary in aiding and abetting his scheme had wide-ranging consequences. He claimed that the society had existed already for the past three years with thousands of members, hinting at the complicity of such high dignitaries as the Chief Justice Zichy and Bishop Verhovacz of Zagreb. Whether Martinovics hoped to gain leniency by this dramatization and exaggeration of his own dangerous character is not clear, but the consequences were unexpected.

Archduke Alexander Leopold, the palatine of Hungary, who had at first been pro-Hungarian, was shocked and disappointed. He immediately removed all relatively moderate Hungarian dignitaries, and worked out an extremely reactionary programme for his brother, Francis II, which assumed that the Hungarians had already acted in accordance with Martinovics' plan at the Diet of 1790. Although the young Archduke soon died in an accident, this programme left a deep impression on the narrow-minded Emperor, and henceforth the Viennese Court based its actions entirely on censorship and police power to safeguard law and order in the Monarchy.

"Examples had to be set to frighten the country," wrote Ferenc Kazinczy (1759–1831), the great reformer of the Hungarian language who was for many years a political prisoner, and it was for that reason that the martyrdom of the Hungarian Jacobins was never forgotten. And the enigmatic figure of Ignác Martinovics occupied the minds of later generations as well. The revolutionaries of 1848 saw him as a great forerunner of revolutionary thought, and in 1919 the Soviet republic had a postage stamp printed bearing his image and erected a plaque in his honour on the Field of Blood. Conservative historians and journalists on the other hand see him as an unscrupulous and unprincipled adventurer, a secret agent of the Emperor.[4] He was probably both: an informer and denouncer motivated by pathological ambition, and at the same time a daring thinker and a revolutionary organizer before his time.

The fact remains that the basic questions of absolutist despotism so perceptively formulated by Martinovics continued to be relevant throughout the forty-three-year reign of Francis II. During the Nazi and Communist eras people were affected by the problem of the intellectual fighting against a dictatorial or authoritarian regime but at the same time doing business with it and so becoming ensnared in treachery.[5] Did they not have very similar experiences? That is why the remarkable case of the Abbé Martinovics has remained more than just a footnote in Hungarian history.

19. Count István Széchenyi and the "Reform Era": Rise and Fall of the "Greatest Hungarian"

In his *Reflections on History* Jacob Burckhardt differentiates between "victorious" great men and those who "succumb": "In the case of the latter, the feeling of posterity takes vengeance and atonement upon itself and repeats the whole drama, though this is often done for reasons of personal vanity." He then deals with the relationship between those who initiate and those who accomplish "historical movements":

These initiators, therefore, are never the accomplishers, but are devoured because they represented the movement in its first phase and hence could not keep pace with it, while the next phase already has its men ready waiting. In the French Revolution, where the shifts occurred with striking precision, really great men [Mirabeau] could no longer cope with the second stage... Meanwhile the man born to bring the culminating movement to its close, to calm its separate waves and stand astride the abyss, is slowly growing to maturity, threatened by huge dangers and recognized by few.[1]

No great man before or since—a "succumber", an "initiator" and not an "accomplisher"—has played such a decisive role in Hungary's history as Count István Széchenyi during the exciting "reform era": 1825–30 and 1848. His opponent, rival and "accomplisher" of the movement from reform to revolution, Lajos Kossuth, called Széchenyi in 1840 "the greatest Hungarian". Historians and essayists regard him as the most "interesting", the most "romantic" and even the "loneliest" of men of talent and courage who moulded the politics of those decades. In his personality we find (in Burckhardt's sense) the interaction of "the general and the particular, of the static and the dynamic": "the existing and the new [the Revolution] culminate" in his person.

Széchenyi's only official function before the Revolution was as chairman of the Gubernatorial Council's transport commission from August 1845. From March 1848 until his nervous collapse in September he was Minister for Transport in Hungary's first government. Still, Szekfü could write: "No other Hungarian has played his role as successfully in the history of the nation since St Stephen as did Széchenyi."[2] And Denis Sinor, the American historian of Hungarian origin: "Since Turkish times Hungary owes no one as much as to him."[3] Széchenyi was a unique phenomenon, even in an epoch of outstanding, though very varied Hungarian politicians. The "Széchenyi factor" and its enormous significance can only be understood against the whole national and international background, especially in regard to the fight for the Hungarian language.

At the beginning of the nineteenth century, as we have seen, Hungary was little more than a glorified Austrian colony. Hungarians were perhaps never as popular in Vienna as in the times of Maria Theresa and Joseph II, i.e. around the turn of the eighteenth and nineteenth centuries. However it was only the Hungarian magnates and landowners of the middle nobility who give this impression. This is also true of the enthusiastic observation made in Vienna by the Berlin publisher and journalist Friedrich Nicolai:

… Hungarians stand out favourably, so that one can recognize them even if they are not wearing their national costume. This nation is known to be healthy, robust and well-built. A Hungarian walks upright and has a certain way of holding his head up, which in other nations would appear as pride. This, however, is not the case and stems perhaps from the consciousness of belonging to a free nation.[4]

However, only the nobles were free at that time: 540,000 out of the 12.9 million inhabitants of Greater Hungary (11.3 million without Croatia), of whom four-fifths were Hungarians and the rest Croats. Germans and Romanians. They alone were eligible to take part in political life. Latin was the official language and the means of communication between members of the polyglot *natio Hungarica*, the political nation. The highest organ was the Diet, consisting of two chambers, the Table of Magnates (Upper House) and the Table of Estates (Lower House). The elected representatives, the nobles' deputies from the fifty-two counties and the royal free cities, sat in the Lower House. Each noble deputy had one vote. The 576,000 city-dwellers had only one vote in the Diet, hence the totality of burghers represented in the Lower House carried only as much weight as a single nobleman.

The rejection by the Hungarian nation of nobles of the reforms supported by Maria Theresa and Joseph II was a pyrrhic victory, causing Hungary "to be left behind in the Middle Ages from an economic, social and intellectual point of view", as Harold Steinacker, a sharp critic of Hungarian nationalism, wrote in 1963.[5] Although industrial production quadrupled between 1780 and 1840, Hungary, with 55 per cent of the Monarchy's land, still delivered only 7 per cent of its total industrial output. According to official statistics there were only 548 industrial enterprises in Hungary proper, i.e. without Transylvania, Croatia and the Military Frontier (according to the Opposition the number was 412), while the number of factories in the Monarchy as a whole had risen to 10,000. At the beginning of the nineteenth century all the Hungarian towns combined had fewer inhabitants than the city of Vienna. A feudal social structure existed in the towns, combined with an obsolete guild system. Only 1,000 citizens with full rights were registered in Buda in 1839. Except in the rural towns of the plains, the bourgeoisie was predominantly German. Of the total population the proportion engaged in trade or industry[6] was 1 in 14 in Austria, 1 in 9 in Lombardy, and only 1 in 89 in Hungary.

The fundamental evil was, as ever, the nobility's exclusive right of landownership and exemption from all tax burdens, coupled with the system of serfdom, abolished only in 1848. One of the few noble economic reformers, Gergely Berzeviczy, highlighted the hopeless situation of Hungary proper: "The nobility owns four-fifths of the land for which it does not pay taxes, the rest of the 6,628,000 inhabitants have no political rights, own one-fifth of the land and have to bear all the public burdens." Not only did his suggestions go unheeded, but he was accused of treason for his criticism of serfdom.[7]

The Diets of 1790–2 initiated a political turning-point: the inauguration of the fight, never less than passionate, for the introduction of Hungarian as the national language. It was simply a matter of the nation's survival. The aristocracy with few exceptions resided in Vienna, where they had their town residences and spent at least the winter. Patronizing the German theatre and Italian opera, only a fraction were interested in the renewal of the Hungarian language. Thus in the Diet of 1811 several counties resisted the introduction of Hungarian as the official language because, as minuted verbatim, "there would be no one among the nobles who could speak Hungarian". The historian Béla Grünwald referred with bitter derision to the almost unnoticed fact that Hungary did not possess a capital:

It is unique in the history of nations that there is one that does not have a capital where its language is understood. The Hungarian capital was so German that a Hungarian artisan, settled here fifty years ago, forgot his mother tongue within a few decades to the same extent as if he had emigrated to Germany. [...] If the king or a member of the ruling house "dons Hungarian pants" or utters a few words of Hungarian, the assembly where that occurs is moved to tears, forgetting that the Hungarian pants and the few words appear only when the Hungarians are needed.[8]

Pressburg was a purely German city in the centre of a preponderantly Slovak-inhabited county, and the magnates preferred it to Buda, even long after the Turkish peril had ceased, because it was much closer to Vienna where they had their splendid mansions. It was simply far more comfortable, and in Pressburg one was *entre nous*.

It was also typical of Hungary's quasi-colonial status that Francis II did not deem it necessary to convoke a Diet for thirteen years. It was probably Chancellor Metternich who realized that, in view of the growing resistance of the counties to the tax-squeeze and the end of the wartime boom turning into inflation, it was advisable to resume dialogue with the increasingly nationally self-aware Estates; hence a Diet once again came into being in 1825.

Julia Pardoe, the English traveller, conveys the atmosphere of such an assembly:

Outside the Orient I have never in fact seen a more picturesque group than that presented by an assembly of the Hungarian Estates. Bishops in their ample garments of black silk, their golden chains and crosses and crimson-coloured capes; the older country nobility in their lavishly fur-trimmed jerkins and astrakhan busbies; the high-ranking officials in their green or scarlet furs trimmed with gold and their magnificent shakos; the younger and more modern members of the House in their luxuriously lapelled jerkins with flowing satchels of light-coloured cashmere, in their splendidly embroidered headgear, many of them adorned with egret plumes; and at everyone's side golden scabbards, crimson-red sword belts carrying their swords, the scabbards of polished steel or carved ivory or other precious and richly worked materials. I have to add to this description of my general impression of the chamber that it would probably be impossible in any other European country to find a similar number of handsome heads in one gathering.[9]

Even though the Diet of 1825 is often considered to have begun the Reform era, there is no doubt that those Hungarian historians who advance the beginning of this significant phase of Hungarian history to 1830 are also right. Nonetheless, 1825—or, to be more precise, the Diet assembled in that year—marks a turning point inasmuch as it represented the first sensational appearances of Count István Széchenyi.[10] There was a palpable shock when, in the Upper Chamber at Pressburg on 12 October 1825, this thirty-four-year-old cavalry captain made a speech in Hungarian. It was not what he said or how he said it that was significant; it was the fact that a magnate had given a speech even in broken Hungarian—a truly unheard-of, indeed scandalous event in the eyes of courtiers— that made the incident unprecedented. Széchenyi's second thunderbolt followed barely three weeks later; when he offered the entire income of his estates of almost 50,000 hectares for a year to establish an Academy of Sciences. The figure in question was considerable: 60,000 gulden. His action electrified the younger magnates, and at the same time caused him to be placed under constant surveillance by the secret police. However, he cultivated a special contact with Metternich, submitting two memoranda with reform suggestions after his dramatic interventions—which were immediately rejected by the all-powerful Chancellor. Metternich's wife, Countess Melanie Zichy, had been in love as a young girl with the dashing Count, and thus a certain personal relationship existed.

Born in Vienna in 1791, Széchenyi was a professional officer until 1826, and as a scion of one of the oldest noble families led a carefree life, constantly embroiled in peccadilloes. In 1814 the young officer, who—despite repeatedly cooling his heels in the Emperor's ante-room—had not obtained the expected promotion to major, began keeping a diary. He travelled in England (he was an anglophile), France, Italy, Greece and Asia Minor, attended not only by two servants and a chef but by a landscape painter. The multilingual Hungarian danced with the Queen of Naples and the Prince Regent's daughter Princess Charlotte, played whist with royal highnesses and lords, and met Chateaubriand, Lamartine and Wilhelm von Humboldt at social gatherings. During the Congress of Vienna Széchenyi noted how Tsar Alexander I classified the Hungarian beauties as "angelic", "devilish" or "coquettish". He loved horses and women. However, his will directed that his faithful secretary of many years should mercilessly erase or make illegible all references in the close on 5,000 pages to platonic or poetic declarations of love, disappointments, or remarks that could have placed the author posthumously in an unfavourable light.

These diaries do not portray a hero, but rather a man showing genius but constantly teetering on the edge of despair, already in his youth plagued by *ennui* and depression and toying with the idea of suicide. His unhappy love for his sister-in-law, who died early, probably added to this, as did his decades-long love for a married woman, whom he could not marry while her husband lived. The maturing of his patriotism can be traced in his diary from the early 1820s onwards. He was deeply touched by the painful recognition of Hungary's hopeless backwardness. At a later stage Széchenyi did not shy away from upsetting the sensibilities of the petty nobility, "that ignorant crude lot": "To say that there is no life outside Hungary is a pointless dictum eliciting ridicule or pity."

Since there was only a German bourgeoisie in Hungary at this time, farsighted members of the privileged class, with Széchenyi at the forefront, initiated the movement which was to open the way for bourgeois reform, modernization and a liberal nationalism which would secure Hungarian as the official language. His political ascent appeared like a never-to-be-repeated miracle in Hungarian history, not least because the widely-travelled aristocrat could not speak or write fluent Hungarian. Indeed, because of his upbringing he did not really master any language, writing his diaries and some of his political works in German, interspersed with lengthy French paragraphs. He spoke Italian and Latin, although a secret police report alleged that his Latin was very poor, and he therefore could not be employed in the public service. The magnate perfected his knowledge of Hungarian over the years, but he could generally express himself better in his indifferent German—of which his diaries are eloquent proof.[11]

Széchenyi formulated his most intimate reflections and moral pathos in staccato phrases, half-sentences and wild mental leaps. The international environment was certainly favourable for the appearance of this unusual personage, with events such as the French Revolution of 1830, the Polish War of Independence (of special appeal in Poland-loving Hungary), the peasantry's growing dissatisfaction, and a cholera epidemic that claimed more than 250,000 lives. No wonder one of his biographers writes:

> Without Széchenyi progress would probably have begun much later, and would unquestionably have taken a different course. Széchenyi did not come in order to pick a ripe fruit, which he had noticed sooner than all the others: what he accomplished were Herculean feats.[12]

While acknowledging international and intra-Hungarian economic and social developments, one must not underestimate the significance of the policy-shaping individuals, both the "victorious ones" and those who "succumbed", particularly during the Hungarian "*Vormärz*" (the pre-Revolutionary period) and the War of Independence of 1848–9. Their enormous influence on the course of history is undeniable, in contrast to the assertions made during the time of Marxist-Leninist historiography's forced boom. The Era of Reform was moulded first of all by Széchenyi and in its second phase by his greatest opponent Lajos Kossuth.

Széchenyi was not a practical politician in the usual sense. He was much more: he embodied the national movement of renewal, and the moral energy and conscience of the entire nation. Although the forward march of Hungarian literature as the essential means of national self-assertion would not have been possible without the immense labours of the language reformer Ferenc Kazinczy, Széchenyi was in every way its pioneer, as he was also of Hungary's integration into Europe. Seen from his ethical standpoint, what mattered was not only the improvement of existing institutions and the creation of new ones, but a radical cure for what he considered to be his country's diseased psychological condition. "In the development of Hungarian statehood and nationhood he means just as much as Baron von Stein in the line of German development," wrote Szekfü.[13] By organizing horse races and establishing the Casino of Pest (later renamed National Casino) along the lines of an English club, he created a picturesque milieu for a kind of discussion society for young nobles, but this was just the beginning. As early as 1823–6 he jotted down his real ideas:

> But is Hungary a free country? Good Heavens, no! The nobleman is free— the peasant is his servant, a slave!...
>
> Defending this anti-liberal constitution is not a noble endeavour. We see 400,000 souls who want to assert the privileges against 10,000,000, who are not even mentioned in the Diet...
>
> And then we speak of the emancipation of mankind, of freedom, of liberalism, of Christian philosophy! No, we are not born reformers. First we have to reform ourselves. We have to go through the school of humility and self-denial...[14]

Széchenyi's thinking was influenced by Christian humanism but also by the national myth. As a liberal nationalist he was not free from the anti-Semitic prejudices of his time. He is perhaps best described as an "enlightened reformer with romantic elements". His election slogan was "Hungary *has been*; I like to believe *she will be!*" Yet for reasons of *Realpolitik* he saw the Hungary he strove for as being exclusively in coalition with the Habsburg Monarchy. However, he was a man of action, not a theoretician. He had sworn before first appearing in public to regenerate his nation. "The endeavour is worth a man's life," he wrote to his friend, the Transylvanian Baron Miklós Wesselényi, another spokesman of the reform movement who, having lost his sight in prison, and as a hero of the Pest flood disaster of March 1838, later found a place in history.

Széchenyi set to work with extraordinary energy and courage. The man who feverishly confided his thoughts to his diary in German and who had not yet quite mastered Hungarian, took the risk in 1830 of jettisoning the sacrosanct taboos of the noble nation in his Hungarian-language book *Hitel* (Credit). He vehemently supported the cause of the serfs and the abolition of the nobility's tax exemption. In particular he attacked *aviticitas*, which for six centuries had declared the nobles' land inalienable, preventing the owners from borrowing on their security; normal credit relations were necessary to modernize agriculture.

Historians have compared the effect of these heretical ideas written in an unsophisticated and, despite overlong sentences, generally intelligible style to a "flash of lightning" or an "earthquake". In a country where 200 copies was a normal sale, Széchenyi acquired a readership of 2,000 with his first Hungarian book. Four editions were printed within a year and two German translations followed.[15]

In *Hitel* and two follow-up volumes, *Világ* (Light, 1831) and *Stádium* (1833), the aristocratic author called for an end to guilds, monopolies and other restrictions, and improvements in transportation. He urged the introduction of Hungarian as the language of trade and administration with an invocation that became familiar: "The nation lives in its language" (*Nyelvében él a nemzet*). As well as his literary activities, Széchenyi founded the first stockbreeding association, procured ships from England, and created a harbour and a shipyard in Óbuda. Experts from abroad were engaged. This was the beginning, and within two decades the number of steamships had risen to forty-eight—they soon plied on Lake Balaton as well. Other achievements were the regulation of the Tisza river, making the Lower Danube navigable at the Iron Gates, and construction of the famous Chain Bridge, directed by the Scottish engineer Adam Clark. This was the first permanent, year-round connection between Pest and Buda, and *all* users of it, including noblemen, had to pay a toll—the first symbolic undermining of the nobles' tax exemption.

We can only mention here a few of the many other initiatives of this great reformer: the building of a tunnel as a continuation of the Chain Bridge underneath Buda's Castle Hill, a public promenade on the Pest side, the Hungarian National Theatre, a music conservatorium and a trade school—followed by the first steam mill, the first modern engineering works, a foundry, the first sports club and a rowing association. His three major works were celebrated in an ode by an epic poet of the time, János Arany.[16]

Széchenyi's interventions in the "Long Diet", infused with passionate love for his people, decisively influenced the debates on Hungary's future. Typical was his speech of 21 January 1833 about the Babel-like conditions prevailing in legislation:

"Legal questions are first discussed at home in German, debated in the Diet in Hungarian, presented to the Throne in Latin, then translated into

German for the advisers who speak neither Hungarian nor Latin, followed
by the imperial command written in German, forwarded in Latin translation to the Diet, which discusses it in Hungarian, only to pass the law in
Latin."

Almost all reform suggestions foundered on the resistance of the
magnates and the Emperor, or rather his Chancellor Metternich.
Nonetheless, the opposition movement launched by Széchenyi's
initiatives could not ultimately be thwarted. The dynamics of the
swelling nationalist movement, especially regarding the elevation of
Hungarian to the country's official language, were at first misread—
not only by Metternich and his advisers. In Vienna Széchenyi was
nicknamed "Count Stefi" and treated as an eccentric utopian; even
as distinguished a figure as the poet Grillparzer judged Hungary and
its abilities with the same arrogance, as noted in his diary in 1840:

Hungarian has no future. Without links to any other European language
and limited to a few million mainly uncultured people, it will never have a
public, quite apart from the fact that the Hungarian nation has never
shown any talent in science or art. Had Kant written his Critique of Pure
Reason in Hungarian, he would perhaps have sold three copies. […] A
Hungarian who speaks no other language is uneducated and will remain
so, however great his abilities.[17]

In the same vein he wrote after a visit to the Diet in Pressburg some
years later: "One could hardly criticize what the Hungarians want if
they were a nation of thirty million. Under the actual circumstances
most of their aspirations are ridiculous."[18] Of course these and similar remarks of Grillparzer's such as "The foremost failing of Hungarians is that they are slow on the uptake and quick to judge" were
not exceptional. Even progressive Austrians saw the Magyars as an
exotic and chauvinistic people behind the "Chinese Wall" of their
incomprehensible language. Thus Grillparzer prophesied: "The
German provinces of Austria, by their link to educated Germany…
will gain such dominance that all Slav and Hungarian aspirations
will burst like so many bubbles."[19] It was during those years when
Grillparzer wrote with such condescension that some of the greatest Hungarian poets arrived on the scene, such as Sándor Petőfi,
who became known throughout Europe in 1848–9; Mihály Vörösmarty and Mihály Csokonai-Vitéz; and József Katona, the dramatist
who wrote the play *Bánk Bán*.

During the years of Metternich's absolutism the fight for the survival and renewal of the Hungarian language became the most important lever against the previously unstoppable Germanizing drive. The best example of the national inferiority complex *vis-à-vis* the German language and culture during the time of national self-assertion, was the famous case of the poet László Pyrker, Patriarch of Venice and later Archbishop of Eger.[20] In his letter-style autobiography Pyrker wrote that he had first learned German at the age of twenty, but this was quickly followed by a further letter asking that this information should not be published; his reputation would suffer because it would be clear from his late acquisition of the language that he did not come from Hungary's leading stratum.

The reverse of the coin was a vociferous conflict that arose on Pyrker's account between the young writers and their revered master Kazinczy, who had translated his epic *Perlen der heiligen Vorzeit* (Pearls of the sacred days of yore) into Hungarian. The young critic Ferenc Toldy, a pioneer of the literary renewal, attacked him fiercely: why, he asked, had Kazinczy translated the work of a Hungarian who wrote in German? Such a man was a disgrace to the fatherland. It was amusing for those in the know that Toldy (originally Schedel) himself came from a German burgher family in Buda and had written his first work *Handbuch der ungarischen Poesie* in German.

Yet Toldy became the counterpart of Pyrker, developing into the most significant "Hungarian by choice", the founder of Hungarian literary history and a crucial guiding spirit of the upsurge of Hungarian culture. Above all, he fought vehemently to check German influences. Károly Kisfaludy, the popular poet, who corresponded with his brothers in German, also became a "Hungarian by choice", indignantly refusing an offer to write for a German-language journal.[21] It is against this background that one has to understand the inferiority complex of so many educated Hungarians with regard to the German culture, and Széchenyi's exclamation "Hungary is going to drown in German intelligence". The decidedly Germanophile historian Steinacker's retrospective remark on Magyar nationalism refers to this problem: "Like the Czechs, the Hungarians were in danger of being swamped linguistically, spiritually and in education, and they were fully aware and apprehensive of this."[22]

Széchenyi did not shrink from censuring the nation when the truth demanded it. He tried by every means, even biting mockery

and irreverent-seeming criticism, to shake the nobles out of their
self-satisfaction, and narrow-minded placidity. His sharp criticisms
and risky suggestions frequently elicited violent opposition; outraged
petty nobles were even known to have burnt his books. The ever-
spreading liberal opposition admired and respected rather than
loved him.

A young contemporary writer Karl Maria Kertbeny wrote of the
Count in the early 1830s:

The name Széchenyi echoed from every direction. And that was not
the name of an unsubstantial, invisible *deus ex machina*—the person of the
reformer was palpable and visible everywhere, and if one strolled in the
streets still being built along the Danube, in Váci street or the Graben in
Pest, a spirited, hurried, gesticulating figure would come bounding forward, usually talking away with one or two companions, fleetingly greeting people on all sides, sometimes swiftly dashing across the street, accosting
and stopping someone—and all the passers-by greeted him reverently,
many of them stopping and gazing after the strange, quicksilver-like appa-
rition. Then one of the passers-by would say to the other: "That is
Széchenyi!"

Even the good old palatine of Hungary did not command such awed
respect as the noble Count, who talked to everyone in the street, treated
every burgher as his equal, entered every shop loudly laughing and talking,
and yet by his curious courtly behaviour spread a nimbus around himself
that made everyone bow deeply.[23]

Széchenyi's popularity reached its peak around 1840 and he was
deluged with honours. However, this apogee was deceptive. Although
the lawyer and politician Lajos Kossuth, reprieved after spending
three years in jail, named him "the greatest Hungarian", the conflict
between the rising star from the landless petty nobility and the cosmopolitan aristocrat came to overshadow the political scene.
Széchenyi wanted reform and feared revolution. His personal dislike of Kossuth, whose admission to the Pest Casino and the Academy he had once blocked, gave the conflict over Hungary's future
an explosive character. His increasingly passionate public polemics
against Kossuth, whom he reproached for kindling a revolution, lost
him popularity. Meanwhile the fight for Hungarian as the official
language was becoming a centrifugal force where not only Vienna
but also the non-Hungarian inhabitants of historic Hungary were

concerned. National awakening also gripped Slovaks, Romanians, Croats and Serbs, whose literary-intellectual élites were not willing to accept the transformation of the political nation into a Hungarian-language community, i.e. the equation "Hungarian = Magyar".

Striving to make the borders of their own linguistic nation identical to the country's political borders, the patriotic reformers became entrapped in a war on two fronts—against the Habsburgs and against the non-Hungarian majority of the population—which could only end in defeat for them and their country. It was this conflict over the introduction of Hungarian as the official language throughout the country which eventually brought down the kingdom of Hungary. At the time Kossuth too was under the spell of this awakening nationalist idea. He cited "the historical right of 1,000 years" against the Slovaks and Croats who wanted to keep Latin as the language of administration; no man in Hungary could possibly doubt that "the authority of the Hungarian holy crown enveloped this land", and that consequently the language of administration could only be Hungarian.[24]

Széchenyi confessed his misgivings in his diary: "I am afraid they will regard me as too Hungarian in Vienna—and here much too Austrian."[25] Yet he did not hesitate to take a stand against enforced Magyarization in his opening speech at the November 1842 general meeting of the Academy of Sciences, which he himself had founded: "He who changes his language does not thereby change his soul." No one should lose sight of the rule: "Do not do to others what you would not wish done to you."

Our numbers are so small, they constantly moan, that it is almost impossible not to melt into the great surrounding mass of Germans and Slavs. So language and nationality must be expanded. Yes, correct! But *how* to do it is of prime importance because not all methods reach the goal, and the fashionable ones of today actually distance us from it. I was never worried about our *small number*, but our survival has worried me all the more—and this should be clearly stated at last—because the material and spiritual existence of our race is so *lacking in substance*. This is the evil, and let us at last swallow this bitter pill of self-knowledge—because only thus can we regain our strength. The central issue of spiritual power is not quantity but quality, and accordingly our existence is in danger not because there are not enough of us, but because we do not have enough influence.[26]

Most of the nobles underestimated the danger to them of the law passed by the Diet of 1843–4 which finally made Hungarian the official language in a country where people of other awakening language communities also lived. Széchenyi made no secret of his view that every policy which further aroused nationalist passions was dangerous. He had warned in advance that exaggerated liberal and national demands would cause a catastrophe.

The peaceful but victorious revolution in March 1848—the "lawful revolution" (the title of István Deák's book[27])—once again filled the confused and depression-plagued Széchenyi, who had become Minister for Transport in the new government, with hope that Hungary could achieve its rise within the Monarchy by evolutionary means. When he realized that Vienna wanted to rescind the reforms, including the April constitution, with the help of the stirred-up Serbs and Croats, and in the end with the army, he became tormented by nightmares and suffered a nervous collapse during a cabinet meeting on 4 September 1848. He envisioned a conflagration and "blood, blood, blood everywhere".

Delusions, a deep guilt complex and an exaggerated sense of responsibility for everything that happened in and around Hungary drove him to attempt suicide on the way to a private mental hospital in Döbling, a leafy suburb of Vienna. Although he never left it, he was essentially cured by 1856, and began once again to write political tracts. In an anonymous satirical essay published in London and smuggled into Hungary, he poured scorn on the neo-absolutist regime introduced by Vienna after the defeat of the War of Independence in a Hungary now muzzled by censors. The subsequent search of his premises and threats by the Chief of Police brought on renewed anxiety and delusions, and on the night of 7–8 April 1860 he took his life. Although due to police instructions his funeral at Nagycenk took place a day before the announced date, almost 10,000 people attended, and some 80,000 came to the requiem mass held in Buda-Pest at the end of April.[28]

The rivalry between Széchenyi and Kossuth has exercised the minds of Hungarians since 1840. The polarity between them was always seen in politics and historiography as "heart versus head". Who was right? Széchenyi wanted to achieve the country's transformation without conflict; Kossuth claimed national self-determination, although until 1848 he too expected that a solution would be made possible by the House of Habsburg. The prevailing assessment of the two personalities and their diametrically opposed approaches formed an important part of the later misrepresentation of history by the right-conservative establishment of the Horthy era (1920–44) and later still by Communist propaganda.

Széchenyi could never attract strong personal support; that was reserved for the popular Tribune of the Plebs, Kossuth. Yet even in defeat Széchenyi, the peace-loving pioneer of a new era, demonstrated stature: "The greatest Hungarian", as his rival and the "accomplisher" described him, had written in his Diary as early as 4 July 1823 with tragically clear perception: "In this world one has to be either a hammer or an anvil. I am the latter...."

20. Lajos Kossuth and Sándor Petőfi: Symbols of 1848

Twice within half a century—in 1947 after the end of the Second World War and in 1991 after the collapse of Communism—pollsters asked a representative cross-section of the population what they considered the most glorious and the most dismal epochs of Hungarian history. While views regarding the most dismal period turned out to be varied there was remarkably agreement over the most glorious era. On both occasions 24 per cent chose the 1848 War of Independence, and the time of King Mathias was chosen by 20 per cent in 1947 of the respondents and 13 per cent in 1991.[1]

The continuing appeal of the events of 1848 despite enormous changes and the passing of generations is convincing evidence that Hungarians give priority to their striving for national independence. The issues at stake then were not some obscure diplomatic or military entanglements, but a fight dramatized by the country's greatest poets and writers—a fight for independence fought against the House of Habsburg as well as the Croats. Romanians and Serbs allied to Austria, and eventually against Russia which had been called upon to assist the oppressor. The attitude of all the European great powers was negative. Hungary was totally isolated, and from today's vantage-point defeat would have appeared inevitable. But that is precisely why the Hungarians' lawful revolution in that year of revolutions is perceived not only as epoch-making, but also as the source of romantic tradition, which is always invoked in times of crisis. As István Deák so aptly put it, "We still do not know exactly what happened in March–April 1848, but there is a national consensus that it was something magnificent. [...] The Hungarian Spring has become all things to all people in that country."[2]

The revolutionary year of 1848, the War of Independence up to the capitulation in the autumn of 1849, the opposition inside and

outside the country to the new absolutism, and finally the great
controversy over the feasibility of the Austro–Hungarian compromise of 1867—all these have always been linked to no one more
than Lajos Kossuth. No other Hungarian politician was ever the
object of such hero-worship from all strata of the people, and at the
same time so demonized by politicians of the neighbouring countries. His long life (1802–94) is associated with the victories and
defeats of his nation.

Contemporary prejudices and misinformation distort his image
in international historiography, as did attempts by his Hungarian
opponents to discredit him. For Golo Mann "this rousing, far too
self-admiring revolutionary [was] the craziest nationalist who had
emerged till then. He offered the non-Magyar people the choice
between total subjugation without any political existence, or eradi-
cation."[3] The English historian A.J.P. Taylor saw Kossuth's role in a
similar light: "He was the first dictator, who came to power by the
prostitution of idealism in the service of national passions."[4]

In his book *The Fall of the House of Habsburg* the journalist and
historian Edward Crankshaw went to the extreme with an absurd
comparison: "As Hitler wanted to be a German, as Mussolini wanted
to be a Roman, so Kossuth wanted to be a Magyar. He was not a
Magyar at all: he was a Slav, one of the peasant Slovaks… his mother
spoke no Magyar."[5]

In his biography of Emperor Franz Joseph the German historian
Franz Herre repeats the thesis circulated by journalists in the nineteenth century that Kossuth was a Slovak, but felt Hungarian "with
the fervour of a renegade".[6] As might be expected, Hungarian historians, to prove the opposite, have traced his genealogy back to
1263, in the time of Béla IV, producing a flood of investigations into
Kossuth's ancestry.[7] The word "*kosut*" means billy-goat in Slovak,
and it is therefore possible that the Kossuth family with its many
branches could have been partly of Slovak origin, Lajos Kossuth's
mother Karolina Weber came from a Zipser, i.e. German family,
which had settled in Eperjes in Upper Hungary. His native language, however, was undoubtedly Hungarian, although he was fluent in German. Crankshaw's assertions about Kossuth's mother are
demonstrably false; she had corresponded with her son in Hungarian, and multilingualism was a regional, not a family characteristic.

However, the distinctive Hungarian-Slovak-Zipser environment does not alter the fact that Kossuth himself wrote in a note "I was born Hungarian and brought up as a Hungarian." He mastered the other languages as foreign ones. In old age he regarded as a "peculiarity" of Austrian historians their tendency to impute to him a Slovak background, and he once even spoke of his—never previously mentioned—"ancient Hungarian" origin.

Be that as it may, doubts as to whether Kossuth was a Hungarian are unfounded. Since Western historians were more likely to be adept at German and Czech than Hungarian, the fiction of Kossuth the "turncoat" and "renegade", quoted from sources in those languages, has been widely disseminated. The multilingualism of his earlier or distant relatives is in any case irrelevant because in Upper Hungary particularly, there were dozens of noble families of Slav or German descent whose Hungarian national consciousness in the nineteenth century was indisputable. Occasional allusions to Kossuth's "typical Hungarian attributes", or even to his "typical Hungarian facial characteristics", also go off at a tangent. It was and remains of overwhelming importance for Hungarian history that Kossuth regarded himself as wholly Hungarian, and that people remained faithful to him in spite of his defeat.

It happened during the night of 5 May 1837. A violent storm raged above the hills of Buda, as the soldiers surrounded the isolated inn called "God's Eye". It was here, according to confidential reports, that the dangerous journalist Lajos Kossuth had for some time been preparing a revolution; he had taken rooms there several days earlier to finish a major task, while his family remained on the Pest side of the Danube. After months of preparation the authorities struck; Kossuth was arrested and charged with revolt and high treason. The lawyer and journalist, known so far only in the relatively narrow circle of subscribers and readers of his *Parliamentary Reports* (344 editions were delivered between 1832 and 1836, each in seventy-two handwritten copies), refused to be defended because, according to the constitution, he was entitled as a nobleman to be arrested only after a legally valid court case.

That night was to be a turning-point in the life of the thirty-five-year-old lawyer. Scion of a landless petty noble family from the small, predominantly Slovak-inhabited Zemplén county in Upper

Hungary, the bearded young man of pale complexion, dark-brown hair and a talent for writing and rhetoric became known as the victim of despotism. His arrest was perceived as a clear sign of a new hardline in Vienna's policy towards Hungary, but it resulted in a storm of protests throughout the country. Kossuth defended himself with such expertness and persistence that judgment was pronounced only two years after his arrest. He was sentenced to three years in jail, which a higher court increased to four years, thus making Kossuth a martyr. The action against him and Baron Miklós Wesselényi, the leader of the Opposition, turned out to be a failure. Henceforth the ostensibly legal questions of reform became identified with the issue of national freedom.

Confinement was a fruitful time for Kossuth, spiritually and intellectually. Although cut off in the barracks at Buda from the outside world, with which he was permitted no direct contact apart from visits by his mother, he was allowed to write and receive letters, and above all he was regularly given books. In due course he was even allowed to subscribe to the *Augsburger Allgemeine Zeitung* at the government's expense. But he occupied himself mainly with the works of Shakespeare, producing a partial translation of *Macbeth* and mastering English in the process to such an extent that later, when in exile, he could spellbind his English and American audiences as much as his compatriots. He also read the poetry of Byron and Lamartine, and the works of Gibbon, Hume, Béranger, Racine, Voltaire and the German writer Jean Paul (1763–1825).

In the mean time the so-called Secret State Conference, which carried on government business on behalf of the mentally handicapped Emperor Ferdinand I, adopted a more moderate course. As an expression of the new line, Kossuth was given early release, on 10 May 1840. Some months later he received the surprising offer from a printer called Landerer to establish a newspaper and become its editor-in-chief. Landerer, as it turned out, was a police informer and his offer was made with the knowledge and probably the personal connivance of Metternich. The motives for this step have never been resolved, but it is likely that the court reasoned that the brilliant dissident lawyer would now keep away from politics for fear of losing his new lucrative position. It was also hoped that his radicalism would be dampened by censorship. However, the government was under a misapprehension. The twice-weekly *Pesti Hirlap* (Pest Journal) became a popular and respected mouthpiece for the Opposition, and a commercial success for the printer as well as the editor-in-chief. Thanks to Kossuth's journalistic talent and diligence, the print-run rose from 60 to 4,000 within six months and had reached 5,200 by the beginning of 1844. Because of the great interest it aroused, the newspaper is reliably estimated to have reached almost 100,000 readers—in a country where the total of those entitled to vote was a mere 136,000 and there were fewer than a million people who could read and write.[8] Information came from correspondents all over the country, but almost all the editorials—altogether 216 in three and a half years—were written, often unsigned, by Kossuth himself. It was his idea to place the editorial on the front page—not least to shake up the readers. In spite of his continuous tug-of-war with the censors, who incidentally banned only seven of his leading articles, the press at that time—compared to the later practices of the extreme-right and Communist regimes— was almost totally free.[9]

Kossuth's motto was "Nothing about us without us". In other words, he worked towards national self-determination within the Monarchy. The *Pesti Hirlap* spoke up for abolition of the nobles' immunity from taxation, emancipation of the peasantry, humanitarian reforms in prisons and hospitals, union with Transylvania, and the introduction of Hungarian as the official language in the entire country. The fact that by then the majority of Transylvania's inhabitants were Romanian was irrelevant to Kossuth, as to almost all the reformers, radical or conservative. Writing in the *Pesti Hirlap* he spelt out the rights of the Magyar nation:

In Hungary, Magyar must become the language of public administration, whether civil or ecclesiastical, of the legislature and the executive, of the government, of justice, of public security, of the police, of direct and indirect taxation and of the economy. [...] To accept less would be cowardice; to insist on more would be tyranny; both would mean suicide on our part.[10]

The main question at the time was how Hungarian as the state language could be used to advantage in relations with Vienna, and not involve Magyarization of the non-Hungarian nationalities. Kossuth himself had nothing against the use of minority languages in private life, and he spoke up repeatedly against forcible attempts at assimilation. Let the Slavs, Romanians and Germans cultivate their own customs and languages, as long as they accepted that there was only one nation under the holy crown: the Hungarian nation.

The reformers were filled with anxiety by the danger of Panslavism—who would have thought at the time how deep the rupture between Russians, Poles, Czechs, Croats and Serbs would become? Hungary was seen as a country poised between Russian and German influence. In reply to conjectures in the *Augsburger Allgemeine Zeitung* on an impending conflict between Germans and Slavs, Kossuth commented that in such an event Hungary would take the side of the Germans, but as an independent nation, not amalgamated with them. Like most Hungarians, he was willing to make an exception of the Croats, and indeed they were by now demanding from Vienna the same rights as the Hungarians. The Law of 1844 made Hungarian the language of public administration in all of Hungary with the exception of Croatia. The romantics of liberal nationalism dreamt of Hungarian hegemony in the lands of the holy crown, ignoring the fact that similar nationalistic feelings were stirring in other ethnic groups: lacking independent states, those also sought self-assertion through their languages.

Language therefore played a central role as a means of spiritual revival in the diverse Slav pre-revolutionary movements as well. Since the 1830s the Croat writer Ljudevit Gaj had been trying to establish a great Southern Slav-Illyrian state and found a common literary language, but whether or not he was actually a paid agent of the Austrians his "Illyrian" project proved to be a fantasy. Still, his efforts fostered cultural development in Croatia, just as the linguistic initiatives of the great Serb poet Vuk Karadžić, living in Vienna, imparted decisive impulses to Southern Slav literature. In the first half of the nineteenth century Slovaks also produced poets and writers such as Jan Kollár, Pavel J. Safarik and Lúdovit Stúr, who reinforced the Slovak national ideal.

Kossuth was certainly not satisfied with fighting only for Hungarian as the official language. Kossuth's brilliantly written articles and the reports in the *Pesti Hírlap* were also focused on the question of economic independence in general and the problem of tariffs in particular, which were constant bones of contention between the Government and the Opposition. However, demands for economic parity with German-speaking Austria went unheeded in Vienna. The influential banker Georg Sina had this to say:

It is a moot question whether Austria would gain anything if Hungary became a civilized country. Every handful of grain, head of cattle and Hungarian product in general pays a high duty at the Austrian border. On the other hand, Hungary buys anything from Austria, even the poorest industrial product.[11]

The inflexible and arrogant attitude of the central authorities gave the radical wing of the reform movement around Kossuth ever more stimulus. The issue electrifying the Opposition was no longer the abolition of protective tariffs separating Hungary from the rest of the Monarchy, but the idea that these customs barriers—no longer under Austrian but under Hungarian control—should be strengthened. Kossuth not only demanded protective tariffs, but even called for a boycott of Austrian goods. That proved to be the last straw, and Metternich ordered the Pest printer to get rid of his editor-in-chief forthwith. At first Kossuth believed that the proprietor's move was the result of their disputes over his share of the profits, but he was soon made to realize that he was barred from any further access to the press.

Thus it came about in May 1844 that a memorable meeting took place between the mighty Chancellor and the Leader of the Opposition, his junior by thirty years, at the former's Ballhausplatz office. The discussion lasted two-and-a-half hours, and was Metternich's last attempt indirectly but unambiguously to buy Kossuth off in his guise as an "independent writer". Kossuth wrote to Wesselényi in June that Metternich was a "diplomat in the truest sense of the word, who does not believe in the honesty of a man's character, because he has probably not met even ten honest men in his life. I hope he has at least learned from me that not every Hungarian can be bought."[12]

Even without a newspaper Kossuth remained the spokesman of the nobles' reform movement. He now founded a trade association, of which he became managing director, and the Trade Defence League with several branches in the country. He introduced the palpably catchy slogan "Buy Hungarian!" and invented one that was even more popular, "To the sea, Magyar!", with the aim of building a railway from Pest to the Adriatic port of Fiume (today Rijeka). In the process Kossuth was taken in by an eloquent young Hungarian confidence trickster from that city, who disappeared in the autumn of 1846 leaving behind unsecured debts of 150,000 gulden. Kossuth's various associations promptly collapsed, and he lost not only his directorship but also his modest savings to pay off some of the shareholders. Despite its evident failure, even this campaign was effective in arousing national sentiment in ever wider sections of the population.

After his unsuccessful economic experiments Kossuth again turned his energies exclusively to politics, soon taking on the undisputed status of tribune of the people. As one of the most respected and popular politicians of the liberal Opposition, he played an important role in the election campaign for the Diet which had been convoked for the autumn of 1847. The real sensation was that Kossuth, a member of the penniless petty nobility, and therefore a man without the necessary funds for campaign costs, stood for election in the county of Pest, the most important constituency.

Several liberal magnates led by Count Lajos Batthyány, later Prime Minister, supported the campaign of the famous candidate with large contributions. According to all reports, Kossuth was a speaker who could rapidly and instinctively find his way to the hearts of every audience—now with velvety tones and theatrical gestures, now with thundering, heart-rending exaggeration—and his opponents in Vienna and Pest, particularly the conservative aristocrats including Széchenyi, became increasingly worried by his growing influence. Metternich once remarked in a very personal conversation with Széchenyi that the government had committed four mistakes in connection with Kossuth: he was imprisoned and then set free; he was given a newspaper to run, and it was then taken away from him. What should be done now? "Use him or hang him" was Széchenyi's prompt riposte. One day, in a flight of irony, he told Kossuth what he had said to Metternich: the two men were so different in character and temperament that Kossuth could not understand this, and believed that Széchenyi had threatened him. He wrote in his notes:[13] "What does that serpent want from me? And this serpent is called man!"

On election day, 18 June 1847, the time for the public casting of votes lasted from 9 a.m. till 6.30 p.m. Kossuth was supported by the liberal magnates led by Batthyány, improverished nobles, intellectuals and burghers. The result of the election could be foreseen: Kossuth received 2,948 votes and his opponent 1,314. In Pest county, with 600,000 inhabitants, only the 14,000 nobles were entitled to vote. Thus only a fraction of the voters exercised their rights.

Already in the ensuing months, the newly-elected deputy directed most of the reformers' offensive and his wrestling with the wing in the Diet, which was ready to compromise, confirmed the worst fears of the deputy *ispán* of Pest county:

Kossuth is an agitator and not a peaceable and quiet character as had been recommended by His Gracious Majesty in his letter convening [the Diet]. He is of the kind who will cause more trouble on his own than all the rest of the Diet combined.[14]

The storm broke in February 1848 in France, and news of the Paris revolution triggered off explosions in breathtaking succession in various parts of the Habsburg Empire. Reformers and revolutionaries in Vienna, Budapest (still officially Buda-Pest), Pressburg, Zagreb, Milan and Venice influenced one another in a not necessarily lasting atmosphere of solidarity. The transition from a liberal, constitutional and socio-agrarian revolution to a conflict between the eleven ethnic groups in the Monarchy soon confirmed Grillparzer's aphorism from 1849: "The road of the new culture leads from humanity, through nationality, to bestiality."[15]

The Hungarian drama was part of the great European Revolution, which determined the possibilities and the limitations of events in Hungary. These in turn strongly influenced the fate of the Monarchy and the future of the people in this region. Pressburg and Buda-Pest were the principal arenas, and from the beginning Kossuth, with his exceptional appeal, was the crucial personality. However, his decisive role and his charismatic leadership were recognized only in September 1848 after the conclusive breach with Austria, not only by the broad mass of the population but by the political élite of the reform movement.

When news of the Paris Revolution hit the longwinded discussions of the Diet in Pressburg like a bombshell, Kossuth's political genius rose to the occasion. On 3 March 1848 he delivered a rousing speech at an unofficial meeting of the Lower House, which Macartney fittingly dubbed the "inaugural address of the Revolution": "A pestilential air wafts out of the leaden chambers of the Viennese system, which depresses and poisons everything, paralyses our nerves, and drags down our soaring spirit."

Kossuth gave an ultimatum to Vienna, demanding that the Austrian half of the Monarchy receive a constitution similar to the Hungarian half: "The dynasty must choose between its own welfare and the preservation of a rotten system." In addition he announced new elections to the Diet, demanded a responsible Hungarian ministry, the reorganization of the army, a separate Hungarian financial system, taxation of the nobility, abolition of feudal dues, and equal political rights for the urban middle class and the peasantry.[16]

Some historians, such as Edward Crankshaw, perceived behind "this fiery declaration of war on Austria" a desire for destruction "imbued by Cato's *leitmotiv, Austriam (Carthaginem) delendam esse,* this Austria has to be destroyed. The magnates and the masses only disagree about the ways and means of bringing it about."[17] At the time Kossuth was still bent on a modernized, internally independent Hungary *within* the Monarchy.

His speech also fanned the flames of revolutionary fervour in Vienna; the stirring text was immediately translated by friends into German and distributed in the capital, where it was repeatedly read out in the streets, eliciting a tremendous response from students. On 13 March revolution broke out in Vienna, claiming some fifty lives, and that same evening Metternich was summarily dismissed, his fall giving the signal for further riots. Meeting on 14 March, the Diet in Pressburg adopted without a debate Kossuth's proposed Address to the Throne, which had earlier been rejected by the magnates, including Széchenyi. It also accepted his new proposal for a deputation of members of both Houses to bring the Address before the King in Vienna.

However, the die was cast not in Pressburg or Vienna but in Pest, and the leaders of the revolution on 15 March were not professional politicians but young intellectuals with the radical poet Sándor Petőfi foremost among them. What transpired that day in Buda-Pest is the most frequently mentioned event in Hungarian history, whose details schoolchildren still have to know by heart more than a century and a half years later, and which the authorities of the day pay tribute to and exploit according to their political orientations.

In front of Petőfi's statue beside the Danube and on the steps of the Budapest National Museum Hungarians annually commemorate 15 March, the opening of the most important and controversial revolution in their history. Each year on that day students of all ages and patriotic adults sport the red, white and green rosette, the symbol of national pride. Ever since 1848 authoritarian or overtly dictatorial regimes have been terrified of the explosive potential of this anniversary. Thus during the Second World War the largest independence demonstration against the authoritarian Horthy regime's alliance with the Third Reich took place on 15 March 1942 in front of the Petőfi monument. The Communist regime under Kádár decreed particularly strict security precautions surrounding the celebrations, but unauthorized gatherings regularly took place after the official and well-guarded functions were finished. The police made baton charges against the young people singing patriotic songs and marching to the traditional memorials. Of course the issue was no longer the Habsburgs, let alone the Austrians who were then by far the most popular foreign country in Hungary. As always the issue was freedom as such.

What actually happened on that memorable day in the year 1848?[18] The vanguard of the revolutionary movement in Pest, which initiated the historical changes, consisted of about fifty young writers, journalists, clerks, members of the petty bourgeoisie and a handful of nobles. Their spokesman Petőfi was twenty-five, the writer Mór Jókai twenty-three and the historian Pál Vasvári only twenty-one. They belonged to the "Society of Ten", a club founded by Petőfi, who called themselves "Young Hungarians". Already at that time Petőfi's ideas went far beyond Kossuth's reform proposals. He was a radical republican who affirmed his hatred of kings through both the written and the spoken word, an apostle of national freedom and the liberation of the disenfranchised classes. On Kossuth's urging, the young men formulated a twelve-point programme, which was soon transformed into a catalogue of radical demands: First, freedom of the press and abolition of censorship, appointment of a ministry in Buda-Pest responsible to a parliament elected by the people, civic and religious equality for all, formation of a national guard, elected juries, a national bank, creation of a Hungarian national army, removal of foreign (i.e. Austrian) troops from Hungary, the freeing of political prisoners, and union with Transylvania. (The country's non-Magyar inhabitants were not mentioned.)

When news of disturbances and an incipient revolution arrived from Vienna on 14 March, the Young Hungarians decided to proclaim the Twelve Demands at once in public. Added to this was a patriotic poem, written by Petőfi for the occasion:

> Arise Hungarians, your country calls
> You to the Struggle.
> The hour has struck—
> Shall we be slaves or free?
> Choose!
> It is a matter of honour and rights.
> To the God of the Hungarians
> We swear that
> Never again shall we bow down
> Before tyranny![19]

On the morning of 15 March the Young Hungarians gathered at their favourite meeting place, the Café Pilvax in the centre of Pest, where they read out the Twelve Demands and Petőfi recited his rousing National Song. Petőfi, Jókai and Vasvári mobilized the students at the University and marched with a following of 2,000 towards the Landerer-Heckenast printing shop to have the Demands and the poem printed without the censor seeing them. Early that afternoon 10,000 people assembled in front of the National Museum to hear the Demands and the National Song. From there a crowd of almost 20,000 marched through the streets, forcing the municipal authorities and the Viceregal Council to endorse the Demands. The only political prisoner, the socialist agitator Mihály Táncsics, was freed. The members of the Viceregal Council capitulated, "pale and trembling" in fear of the demonstrating multitude, which after all comprised about half of the adult males of Pest—and probably also because they could not rely on the mainly Italian soldiers garrisoned in the town.

What eventually moved the Diet in Pressburg and the Court in Vienna to accept the radical demands was not the "great day" but alarming rumours that over 40,000 armed peasants led by Petőfi were planning to proclaim the republic and a peasant uprising, possibly on the so-called Joseph's Day when the market was due to open in Pest. In reality the market took place only a few days later, and the story about armed peasants was imaginary: the peasants were flooding into Pest to do business, and their only connection with the schemes of the young radicals was that the radicals had originally wanted to use the market as a forum. Nevertheless the rumours proved to be a means to hasten the accomplishment of the Hungarian reformers' political aims. Although historians later rejected Petőfi's claim that the abolition of serfdom in the Diet was entirely due to the young revolutionaries of Pest led by him, the importance of the role played by Petőfi's "Society of Ten", not only during the bloodless revolution in Pest but in the ensuing breakthrough in Vienna and Pressburg has been universally acknowledged.[20]

Numerous experts have dealt with the life and role of Sándor Petőfi, the most popular Hungarian poet (1823–49) at the time of the Revolution and the War of Independence, and we therefore need to do no more here than touch briefly on the person of this national poet, whose name is more closely bound up with the spirit of the Revolution than all the politicians (apart from Kossuth) and generals put together. The powerful and repeated nightmare of a peasant rising led by him arose from this passionate revolutionary's speeches and above all his political poetry. The radical ideas of the French Revolution inspired Petőfi—the plebeian as well as the utopian socialist. He had experienced the people's misery and lack of rights first-hand; aged sixteen he already had to fend for himself, as an errand-boy, a backstage hand in the theatre, and acting as an extra in a touring company. He wandered across the entire country getting to know the land and the problems of the people. His first volume of poetry appeared in 1844, and he promptly became a well-known figure in cultural circles. With courage and spirit if not always with discernment he attacked aristocrats and bureaucrats, feudalism and the enemies of the imminent revolution. No less than 20,000 people listened to his impassioned prediction of the coming revolution in front of the National Museum. With like-minded friends he established a Jewish company of the National Guard and spoke out against the anti-Semitic pogroms in Pressburg and

Buda-Pest, instigated largely by German burghers and traders. When, under pressure from these disturbances, the government backed down over the question of Jewish emancipation, it was Petőfi, Táncsics and other radicals who protested in their paper *Március Tizenötödike* at the "government's cowardice". However, Petőfi's burning republicanism, yearning for the radical revolution (for him March was only the "first act") and hatred of crowned heads isolated him from the political class and from Kossuth.

But the people listened to him. In his literary history Antal Szerb compared Petőfi to Heine and Byron; through him the language spoken by the common people and folksong became an accepted vehicle of artistic expression. Before him it was only Karl Beck, a German-Jewish poet of Hungarian origin, who in his poetic narrative *Janko, der ungarische Rosshirt* (1814) extolled the romance of the Great Hungarian Plains. Petőfi's other great topic was love, and he wrote accomplished love poetry.[21] First and foremost he felt attached to his bitter-sweet Hungarianness:

> I am Hungarian. Solemn is our race,
> Just like our violins when first they play.
> A smile may sometimes flit across my face,
> But sound of laughter rarely comes my way.
> When I am filled with joy, my eyes are sad:
> In high emotion, tears well up in me;
> But in the time of grief, my face is glad,
> For I do not desire your sympathy.
>
> I am Hungarian. And my face is red
> With shame, for shame it is to be Magyar!
> For here at home no dawn is breaking yet,
> Though sunlight streams on other lands afar.
> Yet my country I never would leave,
> Not for fortune or for fame,
> Because I cherish and adore
> My nation even in its deepest shame.

His deep and passionate patriotism reached its climax in his poems written during the War of Independence:

> From wild Carpathians to the Lower Danube
> One howl of rage. One tempest loud makes me moan:
> With bloodstained forehead and hair dishevelled

Amid the storm the Magyar stands alone.
And I would join this nation, I declare it,
If I were not Magyar from my birth,
For they are friendless, and the most deserted
Of all the peoples of this circling earth.

This best-known Hungarian poet, the first to gain international acclaim through translations, came from a family that was originally Serbian but since the time of his great-grandfather had been Slovak. Even his parents, a butcher and a serving maid, could not speak Hungarian without an accent. His name was originally Petrovics, and he used Petöfi only after 1842.

In June 1848 his candidature for parliament was thwarted under scandalous circumstances in a small town of the Plains. The local nobility attacked him not only as a "rabble-rousing fanatic", practically running him out of the neighbourhood; they also spread rumours that he was a "Russian spy" who wanted to return the country to the Slovaks, for whom they used the pejorative slang expression "*tót*".[22]

The poet enlisted in the *honvéd* army,* was promoted to major, and became adjutant to the Polish General Bem, commander of the Transylvanian army. He was killed in the battle of Segesvár (Sighişoara) against superior Russian forces on 31 July 1849. Because his body was not found, the poet's heroic death in battle, barely aged twenty-six, became the subject of oral and written legend, every political orientation enlisting the martyr of the Revolution to its cause. During the First World War, a rumour was spread by returning Hungarian prisoners-of-war about a Petöfi grave in Siberia; there were even photographs of it. After the collapse of Communism in 1989, a well-known businessman sent an expedition to Russia to locate and repatriate the poet's remains. According to a recent legend, Petöfi was supposed to have sought asylum in Russia, married the daughter of a Siberian postal clerk, and written poetry under the Russian name "Alexander Petrovich". The skeleton presented to the Hungarian public as Petöfi's corpse by the businessman (who

---

* The *honvéd* army, established in the summer of 1848, was a militia and subsequently the national army. The term *honvéd* eventually became synonymous with "soldier".

went bankrupt in the process) was identified by anthropologists as that of a pregnant woman.[23]

The mythology surrounding Petőfi's disappearance has not faded to this day: he embodies the grief over the lost War of Independence against superior enemy strength. There is no Hungarian anywhere who can not recite at least a few lines from the most popular poems of this truly national poet.

21. Victories, Defeat and Collapse: The Lost War of Independence, 1849

In the spring of 1848 Vienna and Budapest were still in the grip of the same revolutionary fever. Eyewitnesses describe the enthusiastic reception given by Vienna to the noble gentlemen arriving by steamboat from Pressburg on 15 March. They were resplendent in their Hungarian dress uniforms, with richly decorated swords and egret feathers adorning their caps, and only Kossuth appeared as always in his simple black national dress. The delegation brought along the text of the pre-formulated Address to the Throne. The scene was described by an eyewitness as follows:

> In this hour of jubilation the fiery Hungarians, with Kossuth and Batthyány in the lead, also arrived in Vienna... The jubilation that broke forth is almost indescribable. Endless shouts of "*éljen!*" [hurrah]. The national flag fluttered in the air, and while kerchiefs are waving, garlands and flowers flying from all the windows in the Jägerzeile and the city, the carriages slowly proceed along the streets... The next goal of the procession was the University, where a stirring speech by Kossuth, the brandishing of sabres and a chorus of acclaim celebrated the joyful avowal of friendship, and raised the hope that all barriers between Austria's peoples had fallen and a firm moral alliance would unite them in the future.[1]

On the morning of 17 March the Emperor-King Ferdinand assented to Count Lajos Batthyány forming a Hungarian government, as well as the appointment of Archduke Stefan as his plenipotentiary, and promised to approve every law passed by the Diet under the direction of the palatine. Apart from later complications and still open questions, the Hungarian reformers had achieved this success without bloodshed and, what is more, not through the Monarchy's disintegration but in the spirit of independence already recognized in 1791. The King granted Hungary not only a constitution but also the right of unification with Transylvania, sovereignty over Croatia-Slavonia and the re-incorporation of the Military Border.

Within a few weeks the Hungarians had won a great victory. Even Széchenyi admitted in a confidential letter of 17 March: "Kossuth staked everything on one card, and has already won as much for the nation as my policy could have produced over perhaps twenty years."[2] According to the new constitution, Hungarian became the official language of the unified state; comprehensive liberal reforms were introduced and a constitutional government was appointed, answerable to a representative body that would soon be elected. After the electoral reform 7–9 per cent of the population received the franchise instead of the earlier 1.6–1.7 per cent. Considering that even after the 1832 Reform Bill only 4 per cent of the population of England had voting rights, the Hungarian achievement was remarkable.[3]

Whether out of idealism or, as in Poland, fear of peasant uprisings or for a variety of other possible reasons, the nobility waived their rights of tax exemption, and agreed to the abolition of feudal dues and services. Thirty-one laws were worked out in feverish haste, which were supposed to transform the feudal Estate-based state into a Western-style parliamentary democracy. Hungary was also granted the right to an independent financial administration, a Foreign Ministry and its own Minister of War.

The new Prime Minister, Count Batthyány, one of the country's greatest landowners, was an eminent statesman, even if too moderate for the Pest radicals and too progressive for Viennese court circles. Kossuth became Minister of Finance; Széchenyi Minister for Public Works and Transport ("They will hang me together with Kossuth", he wrote in his diary); Baron József Eötvös, the writer and enlightened humanist, Minister for Culture and Education; Bertalan Szemere Minister of the Interior (later Prime Minister); and the respected liberal politician Ferenc Deák Minister of Justice. Hungary's first constitutional government consisted of four aristocrats and five representatives of the lesser nobility—all of them rich apart from Kossuth. The Foreign Minister, the conservative Prince Esterházy, the richest man in the country, was seen as an extension of the Court; he wanted to neutralize Kossuth, "that deadly poison".

Many questions regarding Hungary's relationship to the Habsburg Monarchy remained open, such as agreement on the functions of the two Foreign Ministries and the military authorities. Nonetheless, Batthyány's government prepared the way for an impressive surge of economic and cultural development, liberated the peasants, and at the same time guaranteed the nobility's economic survival. The insurrectionist tendencies of workers and peasants were subdued, as was anti-Semitic rioting. Despite many and increasing tensions, a new and viable parliament was duly elected, in which the followers of the reform movement gained the majority. Kossuth proved his extraordinary abilities as a resolute and conscientious Minister for Finance: under adverse and confusing conditions he managed to conjure up an independent fiscal administration out of nothing. His political influence went far beyond his nominal position, not least because from July he had his own newspaper and from time to time acted as "leader of the Opposition within the government".

The fateful questions of the Hungarian Revolution were the tense relationships with Austria, Croatia and the most important non-Magyar ethnic groups, such as the Romanians, Serbs and Slovaks. The Hungarians had always fought against the centralizing efforts of the Court and the Austrian government, but their own centralizing steps now elicited similar resistance from the Slavs and Romanians. In contrast to the representatives of national romanticism. Hungarian historians of our time, such as Domokos Kosáry, emphasize that the radicalization of these nationalities was not the result of Vienna's policies, Pan-Slavism or rabble-rousing foreign agents. These ethnic groups, in their own social and political development, had reached a similar level of national feeling and national assertion as the Hungarians, but Kossuth and most of the authoritative Hungarian politicians were unwilling to accept their demands.[4] Their principal aim was to secure the territorial unity of the lands of the crown of St Stephen, not their disintegration; moreover, many Hungarians lived in the territories claimed by the nationalities, and if they relinquished them, they would come under foreign dominance. Even the most progressive and revolutionary Hungarians believed so strongly in the efficacy of social reforms and the attraction of newly-won freedom that they feared no serious complications.

The culpability of the Viennese government lay in its exploitation of the national disagreements to its own advantage, using the Serbs and Croats supported by Belgrade—then still the capital of an autonomous principality within the Ottoman Empire—to provoke an armed conflict with Budapest. The Court wanted from the first to reverse the Hungarian reforms, which they regarded as a threat to the Monarchy's unity. It was totally unimportant to Vienna whether one ethnic group or another achieved what it wanted; all that mattered was to gain allies against the Hungarians.[5] That is why the representatives of the nationalities were so disappointed after the defeat of the Revolution. A Croat allegedly remarked later to a Magyar: "What you are getting as punishment we are getting as a reward."[6]

One of the most conspicuous characteristics of the Revolution and the War of Independence was the confusion in the army, as well as among the aristocracy and lower strata of the nobility. It tends to be forgotten that the Hungary of the time had three times the area of today's republic, and the Magyars were less than 40 per cent of the population. The ethnic groups were already demanding autonomy and self-administration in the spring of 1848, partly—as with the Croats—within Hungary, and partly within the framework of the House of Habsburg.

The Serbs in Southern Hungary, supported by the principality of Serbia, made territorial demands, and unleashed an open revolt against the Buda-Pest government with the help of 10,000 armed "irregulars" in the service of the Belgrade government, who attacked Hungarian, German and Romanian settlements indiscriminately. Two-thirds of the Hungarian infantry regiments were serving abroad, and of the twelve hussar regiments only half were stationed in Hungary. The Batthyány government requested support from Imperial-Royal* regulars to supplement units of the newly-created Hungarian National Guard. It turned out later, however, that the Serb border guards were led by Habsburg officers, flying Imperial-Royal flags. Habsburg units were now fighting each other.[7] In his much-quoted book on the Hungarian Revolution István Deák gave a few graphic examples of the problem of distinguishing between friendly and enemy soldiers and units, and of the moral dilemma

* This clumsy compound is the closest approximation to the German "*Kaiserlich und Königlich*".

facing the Imperial-Royal officers. The following befell Colonel Baron Friedrich von Blomberg:

In the summer of 1848 a Habsburg army colonel named Blomberg—a German national at the head of a regiment of Polish lancers—was stationed in the Banat, a rich territory in southern Hungary inhabited by Germans, Magyars, Orthodox and Catholic Serbs, Romanians and Bulgarians. Confronted by the threat of an attack from Serbian rebels, Blomberg turned to his commanding general for further instructions. The commander, a Habsburg general of Croatian nationality though not very favourably disposed to the Budapest government, instructed the colonel to fight the *Grenzer*, and the foreign volunteers. The local Hungarian government commissioner, who happened to be a Serb, issued an identical order. Blomberg fought successfully, but when the leader of the Serbian rebels, a Habsburg army colonel of German-Austrian nationality, reminded Blomberg of his duty to the Emperor and not to the King (the two, of course were one and the same person), Blomberg ordered his Poles out of the region, leaving his German co-nationals, who happened to be loyal to the Hungarians, to the tender mercies of the Serbs. Totally uncertain, Blomberg now turned to the Austrian Minister of War, writing in a letter: "Have pity on us, Your Excellency, in our predicament; recall us from this place of uncertainty. We can no longer bear this terrible dilemma." But Blomberg was not recalled because his regiment, so the Austrian Minister of War reminded him in his reply, was under Hungarian sovereignty. Blomberg was advised instead to "listen to his conscience". The territory formerly under his protection was occupied by the Serbs, not without violence and plundering, yet it was twice liberated by Hungarians, first under the command of a Habsburg officer of Serb nationality and later by a Polish general.[8]

Deák adds as a typical footnote that both Blomberg and his onetime opponent on the Serb side became generals in the Habsburg army, while the Hungarian government representative and the Polish General József Bem went into exile at the end of the war, and the Hungarian commander of Serb nationality, General János Damjanich, was hanged by the Austrians.

The strongest organized military resistance against the Hungarian Revolution came from the Croats. Their spokesman was Josip Jelačić—who had been promoted shortly before from colonel to general and appointed *ban* of Croatia—a Croat patriot, deeply loyal to the Emperor and a rabid hater of the Hungarians.

Separation from Austria and the deposing of the dynasty was not at all on the agenda until the autumn of 1848. Thus it was in the interest of the so-called "Camarilla", the reactionary Court party and the high military in Vienna, with Jelačić as their most important and determined tool, to create an unholy confusion by their intrigues among the officer corps and the simple soldiers.[9] Immediately after his appointment the new *ban* refused to comply with the orders of the Hungarian Prime Minister and the Minister of War. The latter, Colonel Lázár Mészáros, was not even in Buda-Pest at the time but fighting in Italy under Field-Marshal Radetzky in the Emperor's service, and could not take up his post until May because Radetzky did not want him to leave Italy. In the mean time, with the agreement of the Emperor, the Hungarians declared Jelačić a rebel, and on the urging of the Buda-Pest government relieved him of all his posts. Barely three months later the Croat general was again on top—as the spearhead of the Austrian attack.

The course of that critical summer demonstrates how complex and confusing the Hungarian War of Independence was for the participants on both sides. The resolutions of the newly-elected parliament in Buda-Pest such as creating a separate (*honvéd*) army, a separate national budget and issuing banknotes were a provocation to the Imperial government.

On 11 July 1848 Lajos Kossuth, nominally "only" Minister of Finance, gave the most significant speech in Hungarian history. He was ill with fever and had to be supported as he mounted the dais in the Parliament at Buda-Pest; and when he left it around mid-day all the deputies jumped enthusiastically to their feet. In a voice which was at first a whisper but soon rose to its full strength, he spoke about Croatia, the Serbs, the Russian menace, and relations with Austria, England, France and the new German state. All his arguments were directed at just one end: that Parliament should vote a credit of 42 million gulden for the establishment of a 200,000-man national army. Kossuth pulled out all the stops, and witnesses regarded the speech as a masterpiece of rhetoric.

"Gentlemen! (Calls of 'Sit down!' to which he answered 'Only when I get tired.') As I mount the rostrum to demand that you will save the country, the momentous nature [of this moment] weighs fearfully upon me. I feel as if God had handed me a trumpet to awaken the dead, so that those who are sinners and weaklings sink to eternal death, but those with any vital spark left in them may rise up for eternity! Thus at this moment the fate of the nation is in the balance. With your vote on the motion. I am placing before your God has confided to you the power to decide the life or death of the nation. You will decide. Because this moment is so awe-inspiring I shall not resort to weapons of rhetoric... Gentlemen, our Fatherland is in danger!"[10]

In his oration Kossuth depicted the Serb and Croat danger and the dynasty's underhand attitude (with ironic asides about the "collision" between the Austrian Emperor and Hungarian King combined in the same person), to heighten the impression of Hungary's isolation in the Europe of the day. He spoke of England, which would support the Magyars only if it was in its interest. Kossuth then expressed his "deepest empathy" with the trailblazers of freedom, but he did not wish to see Hungary's fate dependent on protection from France: "Poland too relied on French sympathy and that sympathy was probably real, yet Poland no longer exists!"

Finally Kossuth spoke of relations with the German Confederation. The Hungarians, still harbouring illusions, sent two politicians to the Frankfurt Assembly. They hoped that Austria would join the German Confederation, believing that in that case the Pragmatic Sanction of 1722–3 would become null and void, and Austria-Hungary could then settle its own fate. The King would reside in Buda and an independent Hungarian monarchy could be preserved. According to Hungarian sources, as late as May even the Austrians believed in a German-Austrian-Hungarian alliance against the Slavs. Be that as it may, Kossuth made no bones about the importance he attached to an alliance with Germany:

"I say openly that I feel this is a natural truth: that the Hungarian nation is destined to live in a close and friendly relationship with the free German nation, and the German nation is destined to do the same with the free Hungarian nation, united to watch over the civilization of the East... But because the Frankfurt Assembly was still experiencing birth-pangs, and nobody had yet developed the form in which negotiations could have been brought to a conclusion—and this could happen only with the ministry formed after the election of the Regent—one of our delegates is still there to seize the first moment when somebody is available with whom one can get into official contact to start negotiations about the amicable alliance which should exist between ourselves and Germany—but in a way that does not require us to deviate even by an inch from our independence and our national liberty."

After the frenzied applause at the end of the speech, with which his request for the necessary funds was answered ("We shall give it!" the deputies shouted, rising to their feet), the weary Kossuth, moved to tears, concluded:

"This is my request! You have risen as one man, and I prostrate myself before the nation's greatness. If your energy in execution equals the patriotism with which you have made this offer, I am bold enough to say that even the gates of hell shall not prevail against Hungary!"

Despite Kossuth's pessimistic assessment of the European situation and the ebbing of the revolutionary tide from France to Poland, the radical Left put the government under pressure. It should, first and foremost, refuse the King's request to provide 40,000 recruits from Hungary to suppress the Italian war of independence. The cabinet was split, and the differences between the moderate Batthyány and the energetic and determined Kossuth became increasingly sharp and undisguised. Vacillation over the question of the recruits further fanned the flames of conflict with the dynasty—for which, meanwhile, the situation had vastly improved. In Prague Field-Marshal Windisch-Graetz had defeated a revolt by the Czechs. Hungarian politicians did not recognize—or, if they did, it was too late—the psychological and political significance of the ageing Field-Marshal Radetzky's victory at Custozza over the Piedmontese army and the effect the re-conquest of Lombardy would have on Austrian morale.

The die was cast on 11 September 1848, when 50,000 Croat soldiers, border guards and national guardsmen entered Hungary led by General Jelačić, whom the Emperor had reinstated the previous week. They crossed the river Dráva and advanced towards Buda-Pest flying black and yellow flags, covertly encouraged by members of the court and the Viennese Minister of War. In this war Habsburg generals were leading troops against Habsburg generals, or—as the Hungarian aristocrat Count Majláth aptly described the confused situation in the summer of 1848—"the King of Hungary had declared war on the King of Croatia while the Emperor of Austria remained neutral, and these three monarchs were one and the same person."[11]

In these days Kossuth made a round-trip across the Great Hungarian Plain which had immense political and psychological importance.

He addressed crowds in settlements and villages, and recruited thousands of volunteers for the *honvéd* army. This tour was a unique experience in the lives of the peasants, as is amply reflected in Hungarian literature and art. No one else for a century held such powerful appeal for the dour and suspicious people of the Puszta. Almost every community of any size named a street after Kossuth or erected a monument to him. He lives on in folksong to this day:

> Lajos Kossuth—golden lamb,
> Golden letters on his back;
> Whoever is able to read them,
> Can become his son.
> Lajos Kossuth is a writer
> Who needs no lamplight.
> He can write his letter
> In the soft glow of starlight.[12]

During the September days Kossuth was already playing a leading role in every particular. He managed to obtain the House's consent for the election of a small permanent committee to assist the Prime Minister; this soon became the National Defence Committee, which on 8 October took over the government under the leadership of Kossuth as its newly-elected President.

The court no longer regarded the government as Hungary's legitimate representative, and appointed Field-Marshal Count Ferenc Lamberg, a moderate Hungarian magnate, as royal commissioner and commander-in-chief of all armed forces in Hungary. Simultaneously, a little-known politician was entrusted with forming a new government in place of Batthyány's. Meanwhile the palatine as well as Batthyány resigned. Lamberg's appointment, not endorsed by the acting Prime Minister, caused general indignation, and shortly after his arrival from Vienna, in broad daylight, the "traitor" was dragged from his carriage by an enraged mob and lynched.

King Ferdinand immediately dissolved the National Assembly, declared a state of siege, and appointed General Jelačić royal plenipotentiary and commander-in-chief. However, Jelačić could not assume the absolute powers conferred on him because on 29 September his army was beaten by a Hungarian unit at Pákozd near Pest, and his troops were now marching not towards Pest-Buda but in the opposite direction. Just over a week later the Second Croatian

Army suffered a shattering defeat at Ozora south of Lake Balaton. Both victories, which temporarily saved the capital and the Revolution, were celebrated in poetry and drama.

Several days later, again on Kossuth's recommendation, Parliament declared the royal manifesto null and void. Open war between Hungary and Austria was now inevitable. On that day Kossuth's reign began: between September 1848 and April 1849, as president of the National Defence Committee, he became *de facto* "temporary dictator dependent on parliament", i.e. for the duration of the crisis. Kossuth was not only the political leader, but also the inspiration, the organizer and the chief propagandist of the fight. That the Revolution was carried through into a War of Independence and that the nation chose the road of armed resistance, was doubtless due in the first place to the charismatic aura of this veritable tribune of the people. Much has been written by historians and former associates about his negative traits: his jealousy and vanity, coldness and egotism, his inability to put himself in the place of opponents, and lack of understanding of the concerns of the nationalities. His illusions about foreign politics are perhaps best explained by the fact that until 1849 he had never set foot anywhere west of Vienna. Of his generals he encouraged incompetent ones and persecuted Artúr Görgey, the most gifted; he drove them into battle when all hope of winning the war has gone.

Why then did people forgive Kossuth everything? He was the liberator personified; he was the one who did away with the last vestiges of feudalism, freed the peasants, emancipated the Jews, promoted industry. But above all he embodied—not only for his compatriots—the *concept of independence*.[13]

The Vienna October Revolution was a turning-point in Austrian history, with far-reaching consequences for Hungary's future as well. The rising of workers and students broke out on 6 October. The spark that ignited the tinderbox of accumulated discontent was the mutiny of a Grenadier battalion of the Viennese garrison, which the Minister of War, Latour, wanted to send to the aid of Jelačić in Hungary. Latour himself was attacked and lynched in the Ministry building and his mangled corpse was strung up on a lamppost. The Emperor, the Court and the highest officials fled to Olmütz in Moravia.

The appeal by the revolutionary German poet Ferdinand Freiligrath in his poem "Wien" (Vienna) to the Germans to rise up was just as futile as the hope that the Hungarian revolutionary troops would succeed in relieving Vienna from the besieging Imperial troops. The Austrian-Croatian Imperial Army defeated the somewhat reluctantly advancing small Hungarian force at Schwechat. On 31 October Field-Marshal Windisch-Graetz marched into Vienna, drowned the uprising in a bloodbath, and set up a military dictatorship which lasted till 1853. The Polish revolutionary General József Bem managed to flee, but First Lieutenant Messenhauser who had refused to turn his guns against the people, was executed together with a number of radicals, among them Robert Blum, a deputy of the Frankfurt Assembly.[14]

Both sides now armed for war. Austria had gained a new prime minister in the person of the diplomat and general Prince Felix Schwarzenberg, incidentally brother-in-law of the ambitious Windisch-Graetz: he was, in Robert A. Kann's assessment, "an adventurer and political gambler".[15] Radetzky controlled Northern Italy and Windisch-Graetz became commander-in-chief of the impending campaign against the Hungarian rebels.

Schwarzenberg, together with Archduchess Sophie, succeeded in persuading Emperor Ferdinand to abdicate in favour of Archduke Franz, his eighteen-year-old nephew and the Archduchess's son. The change of rulers took place on 2 December 1848. The arrogant and imperialistic Schwarzenberg (Széchenyi called him a "cold-blooded vampire") was determined once and for all to downgrade Hungary to the level of a province. The new Emperor, who added to his name that of Joseph to signify his recognition of enlightened *"Josephinismus"*, relied on Schwarzenberg as he did on none of his subsequent advisers. The consequences of this reliance were more than questionable: thus, for example, the forcible dissolution of the Austrian Reichstag at Kremsier and the arrest of several deputies in March 1849.

Meanwhile the Magyars refused in mid-December to recognize the new Emperor as their king, because he had not been crowned with the Crown of St Stephen and did not feel bound by the royal oath of his predecessors. Kossuth had not intended this conclusive break, but probably welcomed it.

In December Austrian troops attacked Hungary from all sides. A peace mission to Vienna of moderate Hungarian politicians, among them the former Prime Minister Batthyány and the Minister of Justice Deák, failed; Windisch-Graetz refused even to receive them. The Hungarians were fenced in from all sides. Parts of the Austrian army under General Schlick attacked from Galicia in the north, and in the south-west the Romanians and Saxons joined the offensive. The Serbs advanced from the south, the Croats approached across the Dráva and the Danube, and Windisch-Graetz struck from the west. They occupied Buda-Pest in January 1849, and Kossuth fled with the deputies and officials—altogether about 2,000—to Debrecen, 220 km. to the east. The provisional capital was no more than a giant village, with only a single doctor in private practice, but as a centre of Calvinism it counted not only as the most distant town from the attacking Austrian army, but also as a symbol of resistance to the Catholic Habsburgs.

By the end of 1848 all appeared lost for the Magyars; the Austrians believed they had throttled the Hungarian Revolution "as in the coils of a boa-constrictor", as Friedrich Engels wrote in the *Neue Rheinische Zeitung*.[16] Yet the Hungarians fought on with ever-increasing ferocity, though with varying success. Windisch-Graetz proved a rather ineffective commander, and fell victim to his own vanity as well as to the tactical superiority of the Hungarian revolutionary generals. After a strategically unimportant victory at Kápolna, to the east of Buda-Pest, over troops led by the Polish General Henryk Dembinski, Windisch-Graetz believed that the Hungarians had been finally beaten, and in a report to the Court, which was still at Olmütz, announced his imminent entry into Debrecen. This ill-considered move led to the above-mentioned imposed constitution of 4 March, which gave the resisting Hungarians an enormous psychological boost to their by now victorious military campaign against Austria.

On 14 April 1849 the Hungarians replied to the proclamation of the octroied (granted) constitution, which eliminated Hungary's ancient rights and denied it Croatia-Slavonia, Dalmatia and Transylvania, with a psychologically understandable but politically unwise "Declaration of Independence".[17] In it the parliament in the great Calvinist church at Debrecen proclaimed the dethronement of the

House of Habsburg-Lorraine, Kossuth was unanimously elected provisional Head of State with the title of "Governor-President" and Bertalan Szemere Minister of the Interior.

Hungary was isolated, yet its army fought on with such success that many people spoke of a "springtime miracle". One of the revolutionaries' principal demands was the creation of a national army with Hungarian as the language of command. Commands, however, still had to be drafted and conveyed in German, because many of the key officers did not understand a word of Hungarian. One of Kossuth's most devoted associates was the Englishman General Richard Guyon, who had been a first lieutenant in a Hungarian hussar regiment before the Revolution and who, having a Hungarian wife, had become an ardent Magyar patriot. Another of the numerous foreign professional officers was General Count Karl Leiningen-Westerburg, a member of the Hessian ruling house and related to the Coburgs and hence the English royal house; through marriage and predilection he also became Hungarian.

In the autumn of 1849 close on 50,000 members of the Imperial-Royal army were fighting on the Hungarian side, including about 1,500 professional officers. These regular units were not integrated into the new *honvéd* army; the soldiers kept their uniforms, leading to tragicomic misunderstandings, since it was often impossible to differentiate between friend and foe. The bugle and drum signals, the drill and, as already mentioned, the language of command remained the same. At least 1,000 officers or approximately 10 per cent of the Habsburg officer corps decided in favour of the Hungarian cause. The military historian Gábor Bona estimates that of the *honvéd* army's 830 generals and staff officers 15.5 per cent were Germans, 4.2 per cent Poles and 3.6 per cent Serbs and Croats.[18] The cosmopolitan character of the revolutionary force was maintained from the hopeful beginning to the bitter end of the War of Independence. Hungarians of German origin (excluding the Transylvanian Saxons) generally stood by the Magyars, as did many Slovaks and, without exception, the Jews who hoped for emancipation. About 3,000 Poles, many of them officers, fought for the Magyars.

But it was first and foremost Kossuth who, with his dynamism and incorrigible optimism, supplied the motley army with tens of thousands of recruits, with arms and munitions from abroad, and eventually created a war industry out of nothing. By June 1849 Kossuth succeeded in mustering a *honvéd* army of 170,000.

At a time when the tide of revolution was receding and reaction was being consolidated, the Hungarians' dazzling victories in the spring of 1849, culminating in May in the reconquest of the capital, moved all of Europe. In Germany Karl Marx, Friedrich Engels, Heinrich Heine and Ferdinand Freiligrath, among many others, took a deep interest. The first edition of the *Neue Rheinische Zeitung* for the year opened with Freiligrath's poem "Ungarn", extolling the Hungarians' fighting spirit.[19] The unconditional support of Marx and Engels for the Magyars was connected with their admiration for the last active revolutionary movement. Engels wrote in the *Neue Rheinische Zeitung*: "For the first time in a very long time there is a truly revolutionary personality, a man, who dares to take up the gauntlet of the desperate fight for his people, who is a Danton and a Carnot combined for his nation—Lajos Kossuth."

While the Hungarians were still retreating in the autumn of 1848, Engels wanted to mobilize the public in his newspaper in order to protect "the greatest man of the year 1848". In April 1849 he already praised the Magyars' "well organized and superbly led army", calling Generals Görgey and Bem "the most gifted commanders of our time". At the same time Engels (as well as Marx) expressed his contempt for the Czechs and above all the South Slavs—the Serbs, Croats and Slovenes, who were "nations lacking history". The Austrian South Slavs were nothing more than the "ethnic rubbish" of a complicated "thousand-year evolution". Since the eleventh century they had lost "any semblance" of national independence, and were "torn tatters" dragged along by the Germans and Magyars.[20]

During that spring, despite the splendid victories achieved by the Hungarian troops led by Görgey, Bem, Klapka and other talented officers, and the liberation of all of Transylvania and most of Hungary, the inevitable catastrophe—the intervention of Russia—was fast approaching. By March that intervention had already been agreed upon as the Austrian government proved unable to master the situation on its own. This was the natural consequence of the cooperation between the Habsburgs and the Romanovs, which had become even closer since the defeat of the Polish Revolution of

1830–1. It was thus not Kossuth's Declaration of Independence that had prompted the invasion.

After repeated calls for help Emperor Franz Joseph was finally obliged to appeal to Tsar Nicholas I in an official letter—printed in the *Wiener Zeitung* on 1 May 1849—for armed assistance in "the sacred struggle against anarchy". The Tsar replied by return, advising that he had ordered the Viceroy of Poland, Field-Marshal Prince Ivan Paskevich, to hasten to the aid of their Austrian comrades-in-arms. Austrian humiliation culminated in Franz Joseph's arrival in Warsaw, where on 21 May 1849, with a genuflection, he kissed the hand of the Ruler of all the Russias. The young Emperor enthusiastically reported the event to his mother:

He received me exceptionally graciously and cordially, and at 4 o'clock I dined with him *tête-à-tête*. We travelled very fast, and the Russian railways are especially outstanding for their good organization and smooth ride. Altogether everything is so pleasantly orderly and calm here.[21]

Hungarian and foreign historians, and in particular contemporaries have long debated whether Russia's intervention, so detrimental to Austria's prestige, was really necessary for the defeat of the Revolution. In a report on the campaign Captain Ramming von Riedkirchen, chief of staff to the Austrian commander, Haynau, appointed at the end of May, stated:

The question is often raised whether the Austrian state in that situation, without Russian aid, would have been able to defeat the Hungarian uprising, which, after its unexpected successes in the spring of 1849, grew so rapidly and became so immense.[…] In order to attain a decisive military superiority, which was also assured in all aspects of foreign relations, the Russian armed intervention was indispensable in Hungary and Transylvania. The mighty and imposing aid of a Russian army would inevitably lead to success, and result in the establishment of peace in Austria and the whole of Europe, even if Austria's performance were less energetic and successful.[22]

The Austrian historian Zöllner is also of the opinion that "the victory of the monarchical conservative forces would not have been possible without foreign help."[23] Deák, on the other hand, believes that the Austrians could have achieved victory by themselves, even though it might have taken them longer. A breakdown of war casualties cited by him, appears to confirm his thesis:

The Austrians kept inadequate records, the Hungarians kept almost none. It seems that about 50,000 Hungarians died and about the same number of Austrians. The Russian expeditionary forces lost only 543 killed in battle and 1,670 wounded. On the other hand. Paskevich's army buried 11,028 cholera victims.[24]

In the event Russia's intervention sealed the fate of Hungary. Against 194,000 Russians and 176,000 Austrians with a total of 1,200 artillery pieces, the 152,000 *honvéds* (according to some estimates 170,000) with 450 field-guns did not stand a chance. Yet the fighting lasted until August.

The Hungarians were totally isolated. Kossuth and his Prime Minister Szemere addressed a desperate appeal to the peoples of Europe: "Europe's freedom will be decided on Hungarian soil. With it world freedom loses a great country, with this nation a loyal hero."[25] Even Kossuth's emissaries in London and Paris, Count László Teleki and Ferenc Pulszky, both with excellent social connections, could achieve nothing. As so often before and after in Hungarian history (from 1241 to 1956), no European power lifted a finger in the interests of the Magyars. Lord Palmerston, for example, never wavered from his belief in the necessity of preserving the Monarchy's integrity. Even though in Parliament he publicly declared himself disturbed by the Russian intervention, in a personal conversation with the Russian ambassador in London he expressed the hope that the Tsar's army would act swiftly.[26]

Paskevich, Haynau and Jelačić attacked the Hungarian units from all sides, forcing them back into the far south-eastern corner of the country. Until that time the deputies still held their meetings in the National Assembly in the southern city of Szeged, and on 28 July they crowned their work with two significant and symbolic enactments on the equality of nationalities and the emancipation of the Jews. The Nationalities Law was passed after Kossuth had negotiated in July with the Romanian liberal intellectual Nicolae Balcescu, and Serbian representatives over the possibility of reconciliation and co-operation. Although Law VIII of 1849 reinforced Hungarian as

the official language, it also envisaged the free development of all
ethnic groups: every citizen had the right to use his own language
in his dealings with the authorities; the majority would determine
the language to be used in local administration; and primary schools
would use the local language.

The bill for the emancipation of the Jews provoked no debate.
The government and deputies recognized the community as equal;
it had stood by the nation with 10,000–20,000 volunteers and
numerous officers in the *honvéd* army and made donations for
weapons as loyally as the Christian Hungarians. After the war the
Jews paid a high price for the public avowal of their Hungarianness;
some of their leaders were arrested, and some communities had to
pay colossal fines.[27]

In retrospect the optimism at Szeged is incomprehensible. The
government was in flight; many of the weary and depleted units
were surrounded, and some were actually in retreat. Hundreds of
deputies had already left; mighty armies were inexorably moving
across the country—and yet hope still persisted in this second temporary capital. The Prime Minister, Szemere, spoke optimistically
of the British and French governments' "awakening". Kossuth declared to the assembled peasants: "The freedom of Europe will
radiate out from this city."

Barely a fortnight later the dream was over. After defeats at Szeged
and Temesvár Kossuth abdicated and fled, disguised as the butler of
a Polish nobleman. He shaved off his distinguishing beard, changed
his hairstyle and, armed with two passports, one in the name of a
Hungarian ("Tamás Udvardi") and an English one in the name of
"James Bloomfield", took off for Turkey. On August 11 he had
already transfered full military and civilian authority to Görgey, the
Minister of War, who—as Head of State for a day—surrendered to
the Russians at Világos near Arad with his shrunken army of eleven
generals, 1,426 officers and 32,569 other ranks, with 144 field-guns
and sixty battle flags.[28] Whether Görgey's preference for laying
down his arms before the Russians and not the Austrians goaded
the Austrians to even more appalling retribution against the revolutionaries is a moot question. The surrender at Világos marked the
end of revolution in the Habsburg empire, which had run its course
several weeks earlier when the last German republicans capitulated

to Prussia. Heinrich Heine in Paris saw the collapse of Hungary as the final act in the drama of the Europe-wide Revolution: "Thus fell the last bastion of freedom…." Prince Paskevich reported to the Tsar: "Hungary lies at the feet of Your Majesty." The Tsar exhorted the Austrians to show clemency to the defeated rebels.

The young Emperor celebrated his nineteenth birthday at Bad Ischl. His mother, as always, had arranged everything beautifully: there was a large birthday cake with nineteen candles, a Tyrolean choir sang the Austrian national anthem, and the happy young man bagged six chamois bucks. Afterwards, however, Franz Joseph committed a grave error: as always, he needed the advice of his implacable Prime Minister Schwarzenberg, and on 20 August the Council of Ministers, presided over by the Emperor, determined that all the Hungarian ringleaders, from staff officers upwards, should be court-martialled.[29]

The retribution was entrusted to the infamous German General Baron Ludwig von Haynau, illegitimate son of the Elector Wilhelm I of Hesse-Kassel. He had earned himself the sobriquet "the hyena of Brescia" for his gory deeds in Italy where, after occupying the Lombard city, he ordered the public flogging of local insurgents, among them women, and the arrest and execution of a priest who was dragged from the altar. In the words of the old Field-Marshal Radetzky, "He is my best general, but he is like a razor that should be put back into its case after use." Feldzeugmeister Haynau worked fast, without mercy and delighting in his assignment. "I am the man who will restore order, I shall have hundreds shot with a clear conscience," he wrote to Radetzky. Originally no death penalty was to be carried out without approval from Vienna, but the Emperor and the government finally gave in to Haynau's urging; it would suffice to announce the executions retrospectively.

On 6 October 1849, the anniversary of Minister of War Latour's murder, thirteen generals of the Hungarian revolutionary army were executed in the fortress of Arad. A fourteenth former officer of the Imperial army was also condemned to death as a Hungarian general, but at the last moment his sentence was commuted to life imprisonment. The thirteen heroes of the Revolution, whose anniversary is annually commemorated in Hungary, included a German of Austrian origin, a German-Austrian, two Hungarian-Germans, a

Croat, a Serb from the Bánát and two Hungarians of Armenian origin. Not all the five "pure" Hungarians were familiar with the Hungarian language. Six civilians were executed in Pest, among them the moderate former Prime Minister of Hungary, Count Lajos Batthyány. He had stabbed himself in the neck with a dagger smuggled into the military prison by his sister-in-law and, although army doctors saved his life, it was impossible to hang him and he had to be shot despite the terms of the original sentence.

On Haynau's orders 2,000 officers and civilian patriots were imprisoned, and 500 former Habsburg officers, including 24 Imperial-Royal generals, were court-martialled, and about forty officers (though no more generals) were executed, while most of the others were condemned to years of imprisonment in chains. The total number of executions has been estimated at 120.

In his *History of the Habsburg Empire, 1526–1918* the American historian of Austrian origin, Robert A. Kann, assessed the reprisals thus:

To the enduring shame of the Schwarzenberg government even the intervention of the czar for the brave Hungarian commanders was rejected… The action of the Schwarzenberg government and its henchmen stands in contrast to Grant's generous attitude toward the officers of the South after the surrender at Appomatox in the American Civil War. Schwarzenberg managed to unite English, French, German, and even Russian feelings in common revulsion against him and Haynau, who was publicly insulted during his subsequent "goodwill" visits to Brussels and London.[30]

Haynau soon became intolerable to the Court as well, and was pensioned off in 1850. Strangely he bought an estate in Hungary and was even outraged that the "New Landowner" (as he was caricatured in one of Jókai's novels) was shunned by the other landowners. He died, supposedly insane, in 1853.

The other principal character on the Imperial side, *Ban* Jelačić, lived on for a few more years, but also mentally deranged. As a disappointed Croat patriot he had given up on his cause; the Austrian government kept only very few of the promises made to the Croats. Each historical turning-point influenced the Jelačić myth. Thus in 1866, before the settlement between Hungary and Croatia, an equestrian statue was erected to him in the main square of Zagreb, pointing his index finger towards the north in the direction of Hungary. Eighty years later, in 1947, the statue was dismantled and the place renamed "Square of the Republic". After the rebirth of Croatia in 1990, the government restored the statue, this time with the index finger pointing south, i.e. towards neither the long-forgotten Hungarian enemy nor the new arch-enemy Serbia. The place is once again called "Ban Josipa Jelačić square".

22. Kossuth the Hero versus "Judas" Görgey: "Good" and "Bad" in Sacrificial Mythology

The corpse of defeat was not yet cold when opposing yet inextricably linked trends of glorification and demonization began to emerge. The cult of heroes and of the dead has always played a significant role in Hungarian historiography and literature, and Hungarians habitually seek and find scapegoats for their shattered illusions and for national nostalgia. At the same time there was an inclination, especially in critical situations, to stereotype the political opponents of the day as traitors to the nation. This way of dealing with problems runs like a thread through the whole of Hungary's modern history from the Kuruc uprisings of the seventeenth and eighteenth centuries to the 1956 Revolution.

The most famous and tragic victim of this deplorable myth-making after 1849 was Artúr Görgey, and the architect of the myth of treason attached to him was Lajos Kossuth himself. For a century and a half not only politicians and historians but also poets, novelists playwrights and film-makers vied with each other to compare and contrast the hero Kossuth and the traitor Görgey. Only in 1994 did a 775-page, two-volume work by Domokos Kosáry demolish this myth. The then eighty-year-old president of the Academy of Sciences, who had grasped this nettle already in his dissertation written in 1936, analysed the main problem in his *History of the Görgey Question* without regard for hallowed taboos: "How did and how does historiography and the conception of history, and in a wider sense society's historical consciousness, deal with the realities of the past?"[1]

Just as the reform movement was marked by the rivalry between Széchenyi and Kossuth from 1840 to 1848, the history of the War of Independence was dominated by the incessant contention between Artúr Görgey and Lajos Kossuth. Not only Friedrich Engels but also most officers were enthusiastic about the taciturn, calm and sometimes sarcastic general. Even Kossuth, albeit grudgingly, had to pay tribute many times to the brilliant strategist and courageous commander after his great victories.

On 1 November 1848 Kossuth had promoted the former Hussar lieutenant, sixteen years his junior—who had to quit military service for financial reasons and then graduated with honours in chemistry from Charles University in Prague—after only five months' service in the revolutionary army, to general and supreme commander of the main Hungarian army. In contrast to the emotional, often rash but inspired and brilliant Kossuth, the thirty year-old officer, whose mother—like Kossuth's—came from a Zipser-German burgher family, was cold, puritanical and introverted. His wife, whose mother was French and father English, had learnt German as an orphan in Nuremberg and met and fell in love with Görgey in Prague, where she was engaged as a language teacher and lady's companion. Görgey always lived modestly, refusing the gifts of money and splendid titles offered to him by Kossuth after his victories.

An able organizer, who showed boldness in battle however hopeless the situation, Görgey represented a diametrically opposed view to that of Kossuth on two fundamental questions. First, he wanted a regular, efficient professional army, however small, in order not to rely on volunteers, national guards and auxiliaries, and secondly, in spite of being a fervent patriot, he adhered to the constitution sanctioned by King Ferdinand, and strove for an improvement in Hungary's situation within the Monarchy. Görgey was suspected of treason when on 5 January 1849, after several of his officers had gone over to the Imperial side, he publicly declared his loyalty to the principle of constitutional monarchy. He did so to save his officer corps from disintegration, but aroused the mistrust of Kossuth as president of the National Defense Committee, which led to his temporary replacement by General Henryk Dembinski. Admittedly Kossuth repeatedly interfered in military matters and caused confusion by issuing contradictory orders; these were often ignored by Görgey, but Görgey too caused perplexity and discord in the army in grave situations by independent decisions, uncoordinated with various superiors appointed by Kossuth.[2] Misunderstandings, lack of communication and, last but not least, intrigues in Kossuth's intimate circle aggravated the rivalry. The defeat of Hungary was doubtless accelerated, if by no means sealed, by this antagonism. On 11 August 1849 Kossuth resigned, vesting full powers in Görgey. But already the next day he wrote to Görgey as follows:

I should consider it treason if you were not to exploit every reasonable opportunity to save the nation. I should consider it treason if you begin negotiations, not in the name of the nation but in the name and interest of the army.[3]

Historians, not blinded by the trappings of romantic nationalism, see in this letter a calculated prelude to Kossuth's famous-infamous open letter of 12 September from his Ottoman asylum in Vidin (today in Bulgaria) to his envoys and political representatives in England, France and the United States. In this letter Görgey is publicly branded "Hungary's Judas", who had betrayed the War of Independence out of lust for power or cold egotism. Not even the united forces of Austria and Russia, he asserted, could have beaten Hungary if Görgey had not been a traitor. Continuation of the fight would have brought results: internal subversion activity and not external superiority had caused the defeat. In short, Kossuth, who had meanwhile withdrawn his resignation, needed a scapegoat, a traitor who would restore his own shattered self-confidence and lay the basis for his leading role in exile. His aim was perfect: Görgey was never able to free himself from Kossuth's reproaches. In his *History of the Habsburg Empire* Robert A. Kann comments: "Magyar nationalism has always and rightly approved of Kossuth's action to escape the Austrian gallows, while it has unjustly denounced Görgey for his justified decision to end useless slaughter."[4]

The legend of treachery did not, of course, arise solely from Kossuth's personal sentiments *vis-à-vis* Görgey. He did not need the traitor exclusively as a means to salvage his reputation and popularity, as the Socialist historian of the 1848 Revolution, Ervin Szabó, pointed out before the First World War. The issue was rather that by claiming that the nation could only have been defeated by subterfuge, it would be possible to keep hope for the future alive and gain support for the preparation of a renewed War of Independence.

But what happened to Görgey? Thanks to Tsar Nicholas's personal intervention he escaped retribution after the war. Field-Marshal Prince Paskevich and the Tsar personally tried to secure an amnesty for all the Hungarians, but only Görgey benefited from this plea; he was obviously convinced by the word of honour given in good faith that officers who laid down their arms would not be extradited. The fact that he wrote to every field commander and fortress commander, urging them to follow his example because the Fatherland needed peace, and his acceptance of a purse of 1,100 gold coins from the Russian commander-in-chief as a token of the latter's respect, instead of refusing the gift—such things served to show the Hungarian general in a bad light. In fact Görgey distributed most of the money, and saved the lives of thousands of soldiers and civilians. Neither the Russians nor he had tried to lure the officers and soldiers into a trap by the surrender. The real tragedy was that possibly many officers could have evaded execution or prison if they had fled the country instead of succumbing to the charisma of their supreme commander. The fact that Görgey was treated with relative generosity made the accusation of treachery credible to some extent in the eyes of embittered contemporaries and uninformed posterity.

He had to pay a high price for his ten months of fame as modern Hungary's only great general. For seventeen years from September 1849 he lived under house arrest in Klagenfurt. In 1852 he published his memoirs entitled *My Life and Work in Hungary during the Years 1848–49*, which appeared first in German and later in English, Italian and Swedish; it was banned in Austria and its publication in Hungary was only permitted in 1911. Engels described the book as "mean" because in it the author distanced himself from contemporary revolutionary tendencies. One of the most distinguished literary critics of the time, Jenö Péterfy, wrote: "It appeared to the aroused hearts that the accused was cold-bloodedly dissecting the corpse, that is the Revolution, at whose bier the entire nation, fearful for its future, was grieving. The greatest obstacle to establishing the truth is that public opinion is convinced that the more darkly Görgey is painted, the brighter Kossuth shines."[5]

Görgey's brother, a lawyer, tried all his life to combat this unjust ostracism. He revealed the truth about the general's work in three thick volumes from numerous documents. When, after his return to Budapest, Görgey was given a modest post as inspector of the tolls collected on the Chain Bridge, a storm of public indignation broke out. He also had to be dismissed as manager of a coal and brick works because of protests from his colleagues. When he was about to take on the supervision of several hundred workers at a railway construction project in Transylvania, the other office workers refused to accept the "traitor" as their colleague. Görgey was the "victim of national vanity and nationalistic romanticism", wrote the well-known critic Pál Gyulai, adding: "We are a nation of enthusiasts and of antipathy for irrefutable evidence."

Görgey remained the victim of national mythology, a figure still being exploited in the twentieth century in accordance with the prevailing political atmosphere. In 1935 the Horthy regime erected an equestrian statue to him in Buda; it was damaged during the Second World War and not repaired by the Communists, who melted it down to use for the statue of Stalin which was toppled and smashed by the crowd on 23 October 1956. Almost forty years later the post-Communist government set up a two-and-a-half-ton equestrian statue of Görgey in front of the castle in Buda—the ultimate irony of this saga being that the red marble of the new statue's plinth had previously been used for a monument to Lenin.

In spite of the best efforts of historians, the General was still depicted in a schoolbook published in 1958 as a wily capitulator—just as he had been during the present author's school years. Extreme nationalists and Communists tirelessly rallied to their common cause of demonizing Görgey. The cult of Kossuth, together with the apotheosis of the martyr Petöfi, determined the traditional image, and Görgey's "treason" fitted well into it.

The historian Kosáry concluded in his pioneering work that Görgey was an exceptional person: not a traitor but an excellent and, until the last, genuinely patriotic commander. He may have taken a few wrong steps or misjudged situations, but he never wanted to seize political leadership. In short, he was not a political animal but a gifted soldier. Kosáry warned against distorting the complexities and overlooking the international factors of the Revolution and the War of Independence by a primitive mythology of the Hungarian leaders fighting against each other as personifications of Good and Evil. Admitting that Görgey was an excellent soldier and a patriot does not diminish Kossuth's historical significance.

The myth of a stab in the back in the Hungarian War of Independence and of Görgey the "traitor" persisted as stubbornly as Rákóczi's accusation against General Károlyi in 1711. The parallels between the capitulations at Majtény and Világos formed the framework for the identical reproaches against the two traitors, Károlyi and Görgey. When in 1869 Görgey appeared at the funeral of Bertalan Szemere he was abused in parliament, and it was only after 269 officers demanded his rehabilitation in 1884 that he finally received a pension from the government. This tragic protagonist of Hungarian history died at the age of ninety-eight in May 1916. His body lay in state in the great hall of the National Museum, and thousands of his countrymen filed past the bier.

Kossuth did not live quite as long. He survived the War of Independence by forty-five years, exerting an influence on Hungarians from his exile until his death on 20 March 1894. The human weaknesses of this great man—his boundless ambition, his often wounding arrogance, his tendency to gamble in international questions—created a favourable breeding-ground for settling old scores in exile, as well as at home. The writer Zsigmond Kemény described Kossuth as a passion-driven fanatic, who plunged his country into catastrophe; the liberal politician Pál Nyári called him a "damned comedian"; and Szemere, once Minister of the Interior and later Prime Minister, bitterly attacked him from Paris: in a book, pamphlets and letters to *The Times* of London he condemned Kossuth's policies as Governor-President and his machinations in foreign affairs from exile.[6]

However, needling by intellectuals and his affectations in exile did not affect his enormous prestige with the masses in Hungary, in the Anglo-Saxon world and in most European countries. Nothing enhanced the myth-creation around Kossuth and the dead Petőfi more than the neo-absolutist regime which followed the time of repression. For the third time after the failed attempts by Leopold I and Joseph II, the notorious "forfeiture theory" was put into effect. It meant nothing less than that the Hungarians had "forfeited" all their claims; in practice they were completely subordinated and had lost their constitutional rights. Transylvania, Croatia, the Voivodina and the Bánát, as well as the Military Frontier, were once again taken from Hungary. The system established and named after the Austrian Minister of the Interior, Alexander Bach, relied on the presence of sixteen gendarme battalions, secret police and innumerable Austrian and Czech civil servants transferred to the Hungarian crown lands. The hated civil servants were popularly known as "Bach hussars". However, the system of neo-absolutism did not succeed in Germanizing the school system and administration; rather, antagonism toward Germanization led to hatred of anything German.

Memories of the War of Independence and the heroes of the revolution were transfigured by the attempted subordination. Neither suppression nor economic measures could break the people's passive resistance or bring the rich Hungarian nobility to heel. Hungary had lost the War of Independence, but in the long run it had achieved peace. The most significant consequence of the lost war was that because of the sacrifices of 1848–9 no Austrian government could resist Hungary's bid for equality in the Monarchy or the national hegemony of the Magyars in historical Hungary. Of course, the tireless efforts of Kossuth and the Hungarian émigrés had a direct and indirect effect on this development.

The growth of Kossuth's stature in exile was linked in part to the charismatic effect he had on audiences all over the world, and in part to the belated but lasting admiration for the Hungarians' lonely fight against two great powers, Austria and Russia, whose brutal reprisals only added sympathy. Kossuth, Szemere, Bem and altogether 5,000 Hungarians, mainly officers and other ranks in the army, fled from certain execution—first to Vidin. Prime Minister Szemere and some associates had buried the Crown of St Stephen near the border town of Orsova, and when Austrian police found the hiding place in 1853 some émigrés suspected Szemere, then living in Paris, of having betrayed the site. In fact the Viennese police authorities found it as the result of large-scale infiltration of émigrés and by bribing an officer of the revolutionary army who had helped Szemere bury the crown. The actual informer, István Vargha, enjoyed widespread respect after his return to Hungary from English exile, becoming chief notary of the city of Nagyvárad and member of the Academy of Sciences. When he died in 1876, his funeral was one that befitted a fighter and upright patriot. Only after the opening of the secret imperial archives did it come to light that he had been a well-paid Austrian agent.[7]

Right from the start Bach, the Minister of the Interior, devoted great attention to creating a secret service, also operating abroad. With the Emperor's agreement he and his men concocted hare-brained schemes to abduct or even kill Kossuth; no less than sixteen police agents spied on the émigrés. Austria and Russia demanded the immediate extradition of the refugees, but under English and French pressure the Sultan rejected those demands, although he declared his willingness to transfer Kossuth and some other émigrés to Kütahya in Asia Minor and intern them there. After some weeks most of the soldiers and refugees availed themselves of the Austrian offer of amnesty, and returned home; only a few hundred remained on Ottoman territory in the town of Šumla, now in Bulgaria. In the mean time the Austrian government decided to try the émigrés. In September Kossuth, Szemere, the last Foreign Minister Count Kázmér Batthyány, the future Foreign Minister of the Monarchy Count Gyula Andrássy, and other prominent revolutionaries were sentenced to death *in absentia*, and a military executioner posted their names on the gallows.[8]

By then Kossuth was already on board the American frigate *Mississippi* with fifty-eight loyal followers on his way to London. On the very day when he was hanged in effigy in the prison at Pest, an enormous multitude was waiting to acclaim him in the port of Marseille. However, the authorities there did not allow the danger-ous visitor to come ashore, whereupon a bootmaker named Jean-Baptiste Jonquil, in his eagerness to convey the salutations of the French people, jumped into the water, swam to the frigate anchored outside the harbour, climbed on deck and, almost naked and shiver-ing from cold, threw himself on his knees in front of Kossuth exclaiming: "Now that I have set eyes on the saviour of humankind, I am ready to die!"[9]

Kossuth completed his triumphal journey in England and then, from December 1851 to July 1852, in the United States as Gover-nor-President. After his arrival at Vidin Kossuth had lost no time in revoking his resignation on 11 August 1849 at Arad, explaining that it had been extorted from him by Görgey under threat of death, and that he wanted henceforth to be addressed again as "Governor" and treated as a head of state. In short, from the very beginning of his exile he made no bones about his position as spokesman of the Hungarian émigrés. He conquered the hearts of Englishmen in London, Manchester and Birmingham within the span of barely a month in October 1851 with his speeches in poetic English, embellished with quotations from Shakespeare. There followed a seven-month round trip in the United States, where he was received with unbounded enthusiasm everywhere. Banners raised in his honour compared him to Jesus, Moses and George Washington. He was the first foreigner since General Lafayette to speak to the combined Houses of Congress: he was received by President Millard Fillmore who, like most of American officialdom, knew almost nothing about Hungary. He delivered more than 500 speeches, most of them in English.

His journey was as futile politically as were his later negotiations with Napoleon III and Cavour about French and Italian aid for an uprising against the Habsburgs. The various military successes in Italy of Generals István Türr and György Klapka—the renowned commander of the fort at Komárom, who surrendered only at the beginning of October 1849—and the spectacular careers of the hundred or so Hungarian officers who made their name in the American Civil War as brigadier-generals and colonels, added to the Magyars' international standing. Yet none of this, including the manifestos and secret missions, brought the fatherland's liberation any closer. In short, the political result of the innumerable covert and overt, and often bizarre missions and amateurishly organized conspiracies in Hungary proper was precisely nil.[10]

Despite the sober retrospective judgement of historians, it remains true that, with his personal charisma, his impressive speeches in English, his mastery of several languages, his energy and erudition. Kossuth was the most interesting and, from the viewpoint of the absolutist regime, most dangerous figure among the émigrés. From Vidin to London and Turin he became a magnet and at the same time as a target for the intrigues of other émigrés and Austrian secret agents. Marx and Engels were among the many émigrés then living in democratic England, as were the Russian patriot Alexander Herzen and the Italian revolutionary Giuseppe Mazzini. Herzen made the following observations in *My Past and Thoughts*:

> [Kossuth] is far better-looking than all his portraits and busts; in his youth he must have been a handsome fellow and the romantically pensive character of his face must have been fearfully attractive to women. His features have not the classical severity of Mazzini's, Saffi's or Orsini's; but—and perhaps because of this very fact—he was more akin to us northerners. Not only a powerful intellect but a deeply sensitive heart could be discerned through his gentle, melancholy expression; his musing smile and his somewhat enthusiastic manner of speech put the finishing touches to his charm. He speaks extremely well, though with a distinct accent, which is equally persistent in his French, his German and his English. He does not try to carry things off with fine phrases, nor rely on commonplaces; he thinks with you, listens and develops his thought almost always originally, because he is much freer than others from pedantry and the spirit of party. Perhaps a legal training may be detected in his manner of advancing arguments and objections but what he says is earnest and well thought out.[11]

All the same, he had many critics and enemies. The fact that he had shouted "*Vive la République!*" in Marseilles but "God Save the Queen!" in Southampton was taken amiss by his former admirers Marx and Engels, who denounced him in their private correspondence when he tried to gain support for Hungary from Napoleon III, Garibaldi and even Bismarck. Marx was not unduly bothered by Kossuth conspiring with the French Emperor, but extremely so that he let himself be deceived in the process: "It is permissible in politics to ally oneself with the devil in order to reach a certain goal—but one has to be certain that the devil is the one who is deceived, and not the other way around."[12]

The two revolutionaries followed with growing distrust the hectic activities of the man whose praises they had sung so loudly only a little earlier. Kossuth, said Marx, was showing "symptoms of shaky weakness, entangled contradictions and deceitfulness. He possesses every attractive virtue, but also all the effeminate failings of the 'artistic character'."[13]

Marx was kept informed by his friend Joseph Weydemeyer of the enthusiastic reception given to Kossuth who, as Marx informed Engels, had travelled from Southampton to New York in the company of the famous dancer Lola Montez. This voyage was also

reported by one of Kossuth's intimates, the then state secretary
Ferenc Pulszky, who mentioned in his memoirs that the dancer was
very brazen and had said to Kossuth in his presence, "General, if you
will once again wage war against Austria, present me with a Hussar
regiment." To this Pulszky claims that he himself replied: "Made-
moiselle, I am convinced that nothing less would gratify you."[14]

Not until almost a century after the public altercations between
Marx, Kossuth and the former Prime Minister Szemere did a Hungarian historian discover in the course of researches in Austrian,
Hungarian, Russian and English archives and correspondence that
two top Hungarian agents of the Austrian secret service not only
reported on the prominent émigrés, but also sowed the seeds of discord between them, particularly in regard to Kossuth.[15] In fact the
Austrians were already being kept well informed concerning the
émigrés during their time in the Ottoman empire. Thus Interior
Minister Bach, who had already warned of the incalculable danger
from the "subversives", read out details from the reports during a
cabinet meeting to support his thesis. Once in a while Prince
Schwarzenberg backed him up—almost farcically—with quotations from letters by Szemere. After Schwarzenberg's death Baron
Kempen-Fichtenstamm as Police Minister took over the direct
supervision of the network of agents.

The most enigmatic, stylistically gifted and, perhaps, ambitious
agent of the Austrians was the journalist and active revolutionary
Gusztáv Zerffi, born in 1820. He had been engaged as an informer
immediately after his flight to Ottoman territory in the autumn of
1849, and by the end of May 1851 he had dispatched a total of 260
reports to Vienna from Belgrade under the codename "Dr Piali"
and from Constantinople as "Gustav Dumont". He even succeeded
in winning the confidence of the Sardinian consul in Belgrade, a
loyal Kossuth follower. Zerffi also lived for months in the consul's
house, which served as the nerve-centre of the émigrés' correspondence from Turkey, especially for Kossuth himself. Zerffi spied for
Austria until 1865, delivering no less than 1,897 reports during
those fifteen years, usually under a codename, and from "Poste res-
tante Wien". Each report was 3–5 pages long, clearly laid out with
subtitles in the margin. Most originated from London (some from
Paris) with documents and handwritten copies of letters attached.

Zerffi himself engaged informants, among them one of the best-known Hungarian actors of his time, Gábor Egressy, who had been a National Guard officer in the War of Independence. In 1923 a historian discovered the actor's name in the Vienna archives on a list of individuals drawing pensions and allowances from the Austrian secret police. When he wanted to publish it in a journal of the Historical Society, its president, the later Minister for Education Count Kuno Klebelsberg, forbade it on the grounds that the Hungarian people should not be robbed of all their illusions. The authorities were so satisfied with Zerffi's work that by 1851 he earned more than all the six other agents working in the East put together. The principal subject of his reports was Kossuth, in which the gifted writer mingled fact, fancy and critical observation so skillfully that his reports were discussed at the highest level, i.e. between Schwarzenberg and Kempen, and sometimes even passed on to the Russians.

Another top agent from Hungary—János Bangya de Illosfalva, a former editor of the *Pressburger Zeitung*—was active mainly in Paris. He and Zerffi had met already in the spring of 1848 during the Revolution. Bangya was even promoted colonel during the War of Independence, and his last appointment was as police chief in the fortress of Komárom. After the surrender of the city in 1849 he was placed on the wanted list, like most of the émigrés, and went to Hamburg where, the evidence shows, he became an Austrian agent in the spring of 1850. He soon moved to Paris and reported from there on the Hungarian and German émigré circles, first only to Vienna but later also allegedly to the Prussians and the Paris police. He gathered additional information by becoming a member of a Masonic lodge. In contrast to Zerffi, however, Bangya was not circumspect. He earned 400 forint a month, about three times the salary of a university professor, and his lavish lifestyle eventually aroused suspicion among the émigrés. The two Hungarian informants worked together for a year and a half, first and foremost trying to isolate and preferably discredit Kossuth by spreading false information. Szemere's pathological jealousy and bitterness played into the hands of the two spies. Szemere and the former Foreign Minister Kázmér Batthyány published open letters in the London *Times*. With the help of a colleague Bangya translated Szemere's memoirs, a malicious attack on Kossuth and Görgey, into German. Karl Marx himself checked the German version.

The two agents also caused a manuscript by Engels about the Hungarian Revolution to disappear, and stirred up the animosity of Szemere and Marx against Kossuth. The results of this clever policy of disinformation are evident in various demonstrably spurious assertions in the articles of Marx and his friends about Kossuth's political actions, particularly regarding France and Italy. Although Marx and the other German and Hungarian revolutionaries in London and Paris eventually came to realize that Bangya was an informer and a fraud, some of the damage he did was irreparable. In 1854 Bangya decamped to Turkey and entered the Ottoman army under the name of Mehmed Bey. According to Marx he married for the third time, became leader of the Circassian tribes fighting the Russians, and was found guilty of treason, court-martialled and sentenced to death; however, he managed to wriggle out of this predicament by making a confession, shifting the entire blame to Kossuth. Nothing further is known of Bangya's activities.

Although Zerffi was not found out, his role as an agent came to an abrupt end in the mid-1860s when he was unmasked, not by his victims but by his employer, the Ministry of Police, which dismissed him for discrepancies in his reports. But at the age of forty-five Dr G.G. Zerffi, now a British subject, appeared in a new role: he made his name as the author of several books, the London College of Arts, and taught art history at the National Art Training School in London, and lectured on history and philosophy. His career reached its highpoint at the end of 1880 with his election as President of the Royal Historical Society. On his death in 1892 *The Times* published an obituary acknowledging his academic career and with only a brief mention of his role as a captain during the Hungarian Revolution. However, an article that appeared in the *Wiener Lexicon* during his lifetime described him exclusively as a notorious conspirator and spy against Austria and made no reference to his career in England. He was undoubtedly a highly gifted man, but he wore many masks and played a destructive role during the era of the failed revolutions.

The name of Bangya was so repugnant to the German Socialist leader Eduard Bernstein, who was the first to publish the correspondence between Marx and Engels, that he deleted every reference to his name. Zerffi's infamous role was discovered only much later; the correspondence between Marx and Szemere as well as Zerffi's letters to Marx came partly to light only after the Second World War. Extensive studies on Zerffi and Marx-Kossuth-Szemere appeared respectively in 1978 and 1985 in Vienna and Budapest.

Probably no one caused as much damage to the international reputation of the Hungarian revolutionary émigrés from within as Bertalan Szemere, the former Minister of the Interior and last Prime Minister. Although his hostile journalistic activities and his sway over Marx by means of his letters and writings were influenced by Bangya and Zerffi's gossip factory, the initiative in fact came from Szemere himself, who was constantly jealous of Kossuth. It was less well known that Szemere wanted to establish business contacts with Marx and particularly Engels because he had lost the whole of his wife's capital of 150,000 francs through failed speculations by a trusted friend in Paris. In this situation Szemere tried to keep afloat by importing wine from Tokay, Eger and the Lake Balaton region and selling it in England and France. He sent two dozen bottles to Engels in Manchester, but Engels considered it too sweet. This venture turned out a failure, and when the estate of Szemere's wife was auctioned in 1865 in Paris, 250 bottles of "Hungarian wines, red and white, of good quality" were offered for sale. The series of fiascos hastened the advance of mental derangement and forced Szemere to return to Budapest, where he spent his last years in a mental institution and died in 1869 aged fifty-seven. One of the avenues near the Parliament bears his name. His lasting achievements are the laws for the emancipation of Jews and for the equality of the nationalities from the last days of the Revolution.

Lajos Kossuth, whose personality and manifold activities captivated not only his own people but statesmen all over the world, was also not spared tragedies. The Austro-Hungarian *Ausgleich* (Compromise), with its far-reaching consequences, isolated him in exile and caused him increasingly to give up the struggle. He spent another twenty-seven years in Turin and its surroundings, making his presence known only by two political initiatives.[16] The first was manifested when his closest and most loyal associate, the Jewish journalist and later Hungarian deputy Ignác Helfy, published in a

Milan journal Kossuth's suggestions for the creation of a Danubian confederation consisting of Hungary, Croatia, Serbia and the Romanian principalities. This alliance with a population of 30 million was to have a common council for foreign, defence and fiscal policys, sitting alternately in Budapest. Zagreb, Belgrade and Bucharest. Each village and locality in Hungary would determine its official language. The inhabitants of Transylvania would also decide for themselves whether to become constitutionally united with Hungary or be joined only by a personal union. The article stated: "With the motto 'all for one—one for all' we shall let bygones be bygones on the Swiss pattern." However, no one in Hungary was willing to discuss a possible special status for Transylvania, and everyone, even the pro-Kossuth Independence Party, maintained a stony silence over the plans for a federation. Kossuth himself eventually toned down the basic idea, and others blamed Helfy for its premature publication.

The second initiative, which created a far greater sensation, was his impassioned "Cassandra Letter" written in May 1867 to Ferenc Deák, his erstwhile comrade-in-arms and later initiator of the idea of a reconciliation with Austria, in which Kossuth warned him of future disaster. He maintained that Austria could not protect Hungary against either internal or external dangers, against centrifugal nationalistic forces or against Tsarist imperialism. His warning went unheeded without any practical political effects, but remained an important part of the discussions that flared up repeatedly over the advantages and disadvantages of the historic Compromise between Vienna and Budapest.

Kossuth remained personally active. Even in his eighties he went on long excursions, collected plants and studied works of military science; but most of all he busied himself with replying to thousands of letters, and received numerous official delegations and private visitors from the Fatherland. The "hermit of Turin", as the nation and the Hungarian press called him, outlived most of his opponents and his companions, and also his only daughter. His sons lived in Italy, where Lajos was appointed President of the State Railways; Ferenc later returned to Hungary and because leader of the Independence Party, but he turned out to be a weak character and incompetent politician.

Kossuth lived a secluded life under increasingly difficult circumstances. In 1881 he lost almost all his assets for the third time as the result of an Italian bank crisis, and only thanks to several contracts for the publication of his memoirs and the indirect relief provided by his followers, such as the premature purchase of his library, could the old man make ends meet. Almost blind, he worked on energetically and incessantly to fulfill his obligations.

The appearance in Kossuth's life of a young girl in the spring of 1884 suddenly brought a ray of sunshine into this dreary atmosphere; this was Sarolta, the seventeen-year-old niece of József Zerk, an émigré Hungarian and honorary American consul in Turin.[17] The famous old man and the pretty girl from Transylvania were a strange couple, yet a seven-year-long, if only occasional, correspondence evolved between them after Sarolta's departure, in which Kossuth revealed the innermost thoughts and worries of his last years in Turin. "I have lived over twenty years in this city of 300,000 inhabitants, yet I have not made contact with a single soul apart from my tailor and shoemaker. No ray of sunshine pierces the fog of ceaseless solitude through which I struggle."

Although Kossuth was elected to parliament time after time, and given the freedom of thirty-three towns, including Budapest, he remained in Turin. His homelessness, he wrote to his young beloved, was a "living protest against the Hungarian kingdom of the Habsburgs". Even forty years later Kossuth alerted Sarolta to the fact that his correspondence was being opened by the "Imperial and Royal" secret police and that he was still on the "Wanted" list. Sarolta should therefore destroy his letters immediately and be generally very careful:

Anyone who wants to make a career for himself in Hungary today must avoid me like the plague. It is as if they were still frightened of me. Not because my old bones are so dangerous, but the Hungarian people still think of me with total devotion, and they are afraid that this willingness to make sacrifices may one day call forth from the grave of the past the ideas linked to my name.

In Hungary itself the two irreconcilable arch-enemies, Kossuth and Franz Joseph, were enmeshed over the years in inextricable bonds, and at the same time far removed from petty political squabbles. This symbolic reconciliation gained expression in a declaration by the citizens of Vác—condemned by Szekfü in an essay on the old Kossuth as an "unconscious and natural lie". In 1894 Vác granted the freedom of the city to the former Governor, who had never resigned or concluded a peace with the King, honouring him as the creator of constitutional life after the dark days, whose work was being continued by His Apostolic Majesty King Franz Joseph!

However, this remarkable joint acclaim for the two could not bridge the gulf between the rebel leader and the now ageing monarch. When Kossuth died on 20 March 1894 aged ninety-two, Franz Joseph refused to declare his funeral a state occasion despite violent protest demonstrations; government and Parliament were not permitted to be present in an official capacity.[18] With great pomp and ceremony the city of Turin handed the body over to a delegation of Budapest city fathers, which organized a special train to Budapest and declared official mourning: the capital was shrouded in black for three days. Tens of thousands of peasants from the country spent the night in the streets to pay a last tribute to their hero. The coffin lay in state in the great hall of the National Museum and was carried to its last resting place on 1 April amid a crowd of half a million people.

This was Kossuth's last written message before his death:

The hand of the clock does not regulate the course of time, it only shows it. My name too is like the hand of a clock, showing the time which will come, which has to come, if fate does not hold back the future for the Hungarian nation. This future connotes a free Fatherland for Hungarian citizens! This future connotes the country's independence.[19]

Kossuth was a man of the century in the truest sense; the history of 1848–9 is concentrated in his actions and in his person. He bequeathed the inspiring but also dangerous notion that the Hungarians were destined for exceptional tragedy and exceptional glory. In spite of all human weaknesses he had no blood on his hands, or any traces of the cynicism, hypocrisy and cruelty which marked so many of his successors of different political hues.

In 1952 when Stalinism, with its contempt for mankind, was at its height the dictator Mátyás Rákosi commissioned a two-volume collection of essays on the 150th anniversary of Kossuth's birth in the name of the ruling Communist Party. The chief ideologue of the regime, József Révai, even used Kossuth's name to confer legitimacy on the forced removal of unreliable bourgeois elements from Budapest and other cities to remote areas of the country, which was being initiated at that time. The Communist Party, he claimed, was rightly regarded as fulfilling his work. One of the contributors even committed the blasphemy of invoking the "trinity" of Stalin, Rákosi and Kossuth.

However, the Communists had an almost insurmountable problem, which had already caused them worries at the centenary celebration: Russia's role in the suppression of the War of Independence. Here neither glorification nor demonization could help them but only fantasy. Thus a talented Hungarian writer found the way from Kossuth and Petőfi not only to Stalin and his "best Hungarian pupil", Rákosi, but also to a heroic Russian freedom fighter named Captain Alexei Gusev.

23. Who was Captain Gusev?
Russian "Freedom Fighters" between Minsk and Budapest

Among the officers and men of the *honvéd* army and the National
Guard who died during the Hungarian War of Independence were
Poles, Germans, Austrians, Englishmen, Croats, Slovaks and even
some Serbs. Until 1945, however, no one knew that there were also
Russian officers of the Tsarist army who had rebelled against the
intervention in 1849 and were court-martialled and condemned to
death or banishment for life. The first information about this to find
a place in Hungarian historiography was contained in a 55-page
pamphlet entitled *Hungarian-Russian Historical Connections*, published
in 1945 by the recently-formed Hungarian-Soviet Cultural Society
in Budapest in the series "Library of Good Neighbourliness".[1]

Two intellectuals, the philosopher Béla Fogarasi and the writer
Béla Illés, both just returned from Soviet emigration, dealt in eight
brief essays with several pieces of evidence, hitherto insufficiently
known in Hungary, of the amicable sentiments of Russians for the
Hungarian people. In a chapter entitled "Russian officers for Lajos
Kossuth"[2] Illés described the fate of artillery Captain Alexei Gusev
and his comrades. He claimed that in 1936, while arranging the
archives of the Tsarist administration, the academic staff of the historical section of the Academy of Sciences in Minsk had come
across a yellowed bundle of files with the title "Criminal case—
Alexei Gusev, captain of artillery, and his gang, May-August 1849".
It contained two documents, the indictment against Gusev and his
fifteen companions, and the verdict. The confessions of the accused
were not in the files, but the available papers presented the most
important facts: Gusev and the fifteen other officers were arrested in
May 1849 because they had spoken in favour of the independence

movement and spread anti-interventionist propaganda within the Russian army sent to suppress the Hungarian uprising. According to the indictment, Gusev and his comrades had extolled Kossuth and the "other rebels", and been in contact with the enemies of His Majesty the Tsar, and they were thus guilty of high treason. In the verdict there was no mention of contacts with Kossuth; evidently the prisoners had merely been on their way from their garrison to Hungary. However, the verdict cites a few sentences from Gusev's interrogation, which must have been regarded by the judges as a confession:

Should we fight against the Hungarians, because they are enemies of the Habsburg Emperor? That is no reason for spilling Russian blood. The Russian people have no grounds to harbour friendly feelings towards the Habsburg Emperor; indeed they have every reason to regard the Habsburgs, who oppress the small Slav peoples, as enemies. Or should we fight against the Hungarians (as we are constantly being told), because the Hungarians oppress the Slav people living there? If we defeated the Hungarians, we would not liberate the Slavs living in the Habsburg Empire; all we would achieve would be that not only the Slavs but also the Hungarians would become slaves of the Germans. We should fight not for that but against it. If the Hungarian liberation movement triumphs, the Hungarians will need the friendship of their Slav neighbours to protect their freedom attained by bloody sacrifices. And thus the victory of the Hungarians' cause would achieve the result (the liberation of the Slavs living in the Habsburg Empire) which we, so they say, want to accomplish by drowning the Hungarian movement in blood.

The indictment also asserts that Gusev had been diligently reading the writers and orators of the French Revolution.

Illés reports that the trial before the court-martial in Minsk lasted two days, beginning on 29 July and concluding with the announcement of the verdict already on the 30th. Seven of the sixteen defendants were demoted, cashiered and hanged, and seven were banished to Siberia. The mildest sentence was fifteen years. Captain Gusev was made to watch while his six comrades were hanged before suffering the same penalty himself. The sentence was carried out on 16 August in the courtyard of the Preobrazhenskii barracks in Minsk with Prince Galitsin, the Governor, present. Because the Tsarist authorities were determined to surround the arrest, trial, verdict and execution with strict secrecy, Prince Galitsin decreed that the next-of-kin of the condemned should not be notified of their fate. Concluding his report, Béla Illés remarked that he did not know whether the historic documents of the Minsk trial had been destroyed "as victims of the German bandits who had set fire to Minsk", but he was certain that copies of extracts from them were to be found in the archives of the Leningrad Museum of Military History.

Four years after the appearance of the long-forgotten pamphlet mentioned above, the central organ of the by now totalitarian Communist dictatorship, *Szabad Nép* (The Free People), with a circulation of almost 800,000 copies, published a full-page article by Béla Illés on 16 August 1949 entitled "On the hundredth anniversary of the Gusev trial". In it the author repeated verbatim the details of his chapter in the pamphlet, expanded by some new revelations—for example, that in 1927 the Soviet Commissar for Education, Lunacharski, drew the attention of historians to the fact that in the neighbourhood of Minsk they still talked about the Russian officers who were hanged for "converting to the Hungarian religion". This legend survived into recent times, persuading researchers to get to the bottom of it.

Illés added that after the Second World War further "fragmentary files" concerning the traitorous group of officers had turned up. Even the available fragments indicated that the pro-Hungarian officer movement was far more extensive than the verdict in the Gusev trial suggested, especially since two newly-discovered files contained cross-references to the trial. According to local hearsay, wrote Illés, an enormous blaze broke out in the building of the Minsk military administration on the day of Gusev's execution, and although it rained all day the fire could not be put out and the building was burnt to the ground. Illés concedes that the historians of the township of Minsk had never heard of this fire, but the legend had a metaphorical justification inasmuch as the fire lit by Gusev and his Russian freedom fighters reduced all the fortresses of Tsarist tyranny to ashes. The newspaper added in an editorial note that the People's Army would solemnly commemorate the Russian officer friends of the Hungarian War of Independence. "Lieutenant-General László Sólyom will unveil a memorial plaque at eleven o'clock on the building of the Ministry for Heavy Industry. The street will be named after Gusev, and two days later a Gusev commemoration will take place in the House of the People's Army, where Lieutenant-General-Sólyom will give a commemorative speech about the heroic Russian Captain Gusev."

Barely a year later Chief of the General Staff Sólyom was executed after a secret trial in the course of a purge of army leaders. The memorial plaque remained in place, and a relief sculpture was affixed on the opposite side of the street depicting Gusev and three 1848 *honvéds*. Over the years, when various revolutionary ceremonies were taking place, other generals and party functionaries would deliver speeches and lay wreaths and red carnations. When the Soviet President Mikoyan came to Hungary, he did not miss the opportunity of honouring the legacy of Gusev and his heroic comrades in a long speech in Parliament.

Meanwhile stubborn rumours were afloat that Gusev, the hero after whom streets were named in a number of towns, had never actually existed. He was said to be a figment of Illés's vivid imagination, born by order of the Party. Béla Illés was known as perhaps the last of a line of story-tellers. Born in Kassa in 1895, he played a role in the Hungarian Soviet Republic of 1919 and emigrated to the Soviet Union in 1923. Author of a number of novels with social-revolutionary political themes, he was for many years general secretary of the International Federation of Proletarian Writers. As secretary to Béla Kun, leader of the Hungarian Communist Party in exile, who was later executed, he too fell out of favour, was briefly under arrest, and got expelled from the Party. At the outbreak of the Second World War, he volunteered and performed such courageous and inventive subversive propaganda at the front line that both the Party and the army reinstated him. As a lieutenant-colonel in the Red Army Illés was editor-in-chief of the Hungarian-language army and later occupation newspapers, and between 1950 and 1956, when Stalinism was at its height, was editor-in-chief of the weekly *Irodalmi Ujság* (Literary Review), which became highly important during the Thaw.

Is it possible that a respected, long-serving Communist would have made a fool not only of the Hungarian people but also of the Soviet comrades over such a politically delicate question as the story of a pro-Hungarian Russian hero? Almost twenty years after Illés' death and on the centenary of his birth, a principal witness came out into the open, years after the collapse of Communism. This was Gábor Goda, a writer and essayist, who had been city councillor for culture in 1949[3] and had to make a speech on the occasion of the renaming of Sas-utca (Eagle street) as "Gusev Street". Goda had never heard of Gusev, and his secretary could only ascertain that Illés had written something about him. The city councillor was not particularly worried, being an old hand at unveiling memorial plaques and street signs, and as a rule only a few dozen relations, colleagues and inquisitive passers-by were present on such occasions. Goda recounted the following in his memorial article:

It was an astonishing sight in the quiet street in the textile quarter. I have never seen so many officers, generals and marshals together at one time. The street was aglow with the red stripes on the generals' trousers, and a military band, a guard of honour and a long red carpet lent the function an even more festive note. I had no idea what to say about Gusev, because I did not know who he was, I asked my friend, the historian and army bishop, and he did not know either. I then lifted the veil off the plaque and caught sight of the inscription: "Captain Gusev…who changed sides in the War of Independence of 1848–9". That sufficed for my speech. Illés was in hospital, as always during precarious times, and did not lift the receiver. I went to the hospital after the ceremony and, taking no notice of the "Strictly no visitors" sign on the door, asked Illés about Gusev…

Illés then gave the city councillor the same facts as were contained in the original story. Later some young Hungarian historians even travelled to Minsk to research the events—Illés was not worried, since he knew that the archives had been reduced to rubble. When the young researchers had given up all hope, they discovered a treatise on the Gusev case in the semi-official Soviet monthly *Voproszi Istori* (Historical Questions), but the very first footnote read "Béla Illés, 'Delo Guszeva'". They then went to Uncle Béla to get the story from the horse's mouth, but he replied with the eternal pipe in his mouth: "Go to Minsk, the files were there. Or don't go—after all, everything was burnt to ashes."[4]

Goda and the other writers of recollections of Illés started from the assumption that the Communist Party, which had organized a series of large-scale functions to celebrate the centenary of the

Revolution, needed "Captain Gusev" to distract attention from the Russians' shameful suppression of the War of Independence. I first came across the correct date and the original story of the Gusev trial in a footnote in Domokos Kosáry's monumental Görgey study: here it was stated that Illés had already invented Gusev in 1945, and all he had to do in 1949 was renew the old "facts" and fabricate additional ones for this occasion.

Rumour has it that at the time the Communist poet Antal Hidas, the son-in-law of Béla Kun who still lived in Moscow, took Illés to task: "Tell me, Béla, why are you trying to make a fool of the world? Gusev never really existed." To which Illés retorted: "Gusev did exist, and if he didn't then there were other Russians."[5]

That is how the legendary and widely celebrated Russian hero Gusev became a phantom and a taboo subject in Communist times, at least as long as Illés was still alive. Gyula Háy, a former Moscow émigré who later lived in Switzerland and was imprisoned for several years after the Revolution of 1956, wrote in his Memoirs: "Illés was a man of whom I can only speak with sympathy despite his many human weaknesses. [...] The bravest man in war and the greatest coward in civilian life. A liar, but one who lied passionately with imagination and flair."[6]

When the dreaded dictator Mátyás Rákosi was toppled in the summer of 1956, Illés sat in his office as editor-in-chief. Tears streamed down his furrowed face as he called out to his young colleagues in a faltering voice: "You don't know, boys, how frightened we were and how many lies we told for thirty years—out there!"[7]

After Rákosi's fall the street, the memorial plaque and the sculpture with Gusev's name remained untouched for decades. Only in the early 1990s was the little street, together with many others, given back its old name, "Sas utca". And Gusev's inventor? He died in 1974. A satirist coined this inscription for his grave-stone: "Here lies Béla Illés, if it's really true."

24. Elisabeth, Andrássy and Bismarck: Austria and Hungary on the Road to Reconciliation

It was the day of the coronation, 8 June 1867, and all Budapest (until 1872 still officially divided into Pest, Buda and Óbuda) was on its feet at 5 a.m.[1] Already at that early hour people in festive attire were streaming in from the countryside to line the streets on both sides of the Danube embankment. At seven the coronation procession set off from the Castle. First a unit of hussars rode out through the Castle gate, trumpets blaring, followed by pages, guardsmen and then the country's most eminent personages. Eleven standard-bearers, chosen from the high nobility, preceded Gyula Andrássy, who wore the large cross of the Order of St Stephen and carried the holy crown of Hungary. He was followed by the bearers of the state insignia, and finally came Franz Joseph in the uniform of a Hungarian general. All were on horseback. However, the cynosure of all eyes in the procession from the Castle to the Mathias Church in Buda was the Queen, in a closed carriage drawn by eight white horses. The *Pester Lloyd*, the German-language liberal paper, reported:

On her head was the diamond crown, the glittering symbol of sovereignty, but the expression of humility in her bowed bearing and traces of the deepest emotion on her noble features—so she stepped, or rather floated, along as if one of the paintings that adorn the sacred chambers had left its frame and come to life. The appearance of the Queen here at the holy site produced a deep and lasting impression.

The coronation ceremony in the church took less than an hour. The choir sang psalms to traditional settings and the coronation mass specially composed for the occasion by Franz Liszt, the most noted "Hungarian by choice". Franz Joseph was anointed by Prince-Primate János Simor: then the two highest dignitaries placed the crown on the head of the kneeling King, the Primate on the right and Prime Minister Andrássy—representing the palatine—on the left. Elisabeth was also anointed and, following an old custom, Andrássy held the crown over her right shoulder. He then stepped into the sanctuary before the altar and pronounced the traditional sacred words: "Long live the crowned King!" The cry '*éljen!*' (hurrah) rang out three times, echoing first in the church and then magnified a thousandfold in the city.

After the coronation the men proceeded across the Chain Bridge to the platform erected on the Pest side for taking the solemn constitutional oath. All the participants, even the bishops, were mounted, and the King, on his coronation white horse, wore the Crown of St Stephen and a resplendent cloak. The eyewitness Ludwig von Przibram reported:

What was offered here in splendour of national costumes, opulence of harness and saddles, value of gems in clasps, sword-belts and pins, antique weapons, swords studded with turquoise, rubies and pearls, and so forth corresponded more to the image of an oriental display of magnificence than to the descriptions of the impoverishment and exhaustion of the country which enliven debates [in the Hungarian Parliament]. The overall impression was of a feudal-aristocratic military review. One truly believed oneself transported to the Middle Ages at the sight of these national barons and standard-bearers laden with splendid accoutrements and followed in silent submission by the armed vassals and men in their service; and most particularly the *banderium* [groups of horsemen] of the Jazyges and Cumans, variously clad in hauberks and bearskins, their most striking adornment being animal heads or buffalo horns, recalling the time when Christian Europe was forced to defend itself against incursions from the pagan East. There were no traces of the bourgeois elements, of guilds or trades.

The magnates displayed all the pomp of the high nobility. Count László Batthyány had a massive silver harness made for the occasion—his horse blanket alone weighed twenty-four pounds—and his brother Elemér's costume was reconstructed by a painter from medieval drawings; it consisted of a silver coat of mail made of 18,000 links assembled by hand. Count Elemér Zichy wore his famous family emeralds, some the size of hens' eggs.

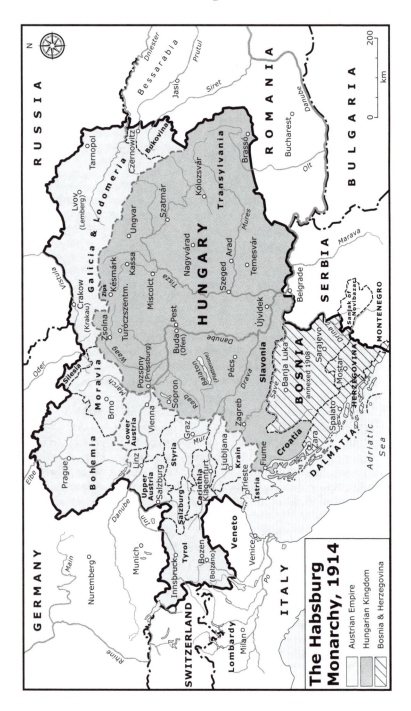

The Habsburg Monarchy, 1914

Austrian Empire
Hungarian Kingdom
Bosnia & Herzegovina

The historic Hungarian coronation ceremony was replicated down to the smallest detail. Members of both Houses of Parliament were positioned on both sides of the dais, which was itself bedecked with precious carpets. Here, under the open sky, Franz Joseph repeated after the Prince Primate the words of the sacred oath: "We shall uphold intact the rights, the constitution, the lawful independence and the territorial integrity of Hungary and her attendant lands." He then rode to the Coronation Hill opposite the Chain Bridge on the Pest embankment, made of soil from every county in Hungary on the pattern of the one in Pressburg. Here the so-called "royal stroke" was performed: after the traditional gallop up the hill, the King swung his sword to the four points of the compass as a sign that he would defend the country against its enemies, from whichever direction they might come.

The public festival took place that evening in the Pest town park. Oxen were roasted, and the meat, and wine, were free for all. The religious and constitutional coronation festivities were followed the next day, Whit Monday, by the capital's own celebration, the royal pair watching from the balcony of the Castle as Hungarians in their national costumes paraded bearing the peoples' gifts. The most famous Hungarian writer of the time, Mór Jókai, erstwhile revolutionary turned loyal Habsburg monarchist, concluded his description of the coronation with the following words in an album published on its twenty-fifth anniversary: "Such a splendid stage-play is to be seen only once in a lifetime, never to be forgotten!"

Of course, the pageantry of the coronation was in glaring contrast to the poverty of the peasants and many town-dwellers. Some foreign observers were less lyrical than the newspapers of the capital. The Swiss envoy wrote: "The entire procession, despite its splendour and genuine grandeur, nevertheless affected the detached observer somewhat like a carnival masquerade. [...] This re-creation of the Middle Ages simply does not suit our times." The wife of the Belgian envoy also viewed the scene with mixed feelings: "In everything there was a relic of barbarism."

The coronation set the seal on a breathtaking political sea-change, full of drama and surprises. Personal factors, the hatred and love of the protagonists, were just as important as the great shift in European politics brought about by the inexorable rise of Prussia. The

Monarchy's failures in Italy had led to a gradual relaxation of police and administrative oppression in Hungary, and in the early 1860s also to constitutional concessions—which, however, were unanimously rejected by the Hungarian Diet. From his exile Kossuth insisted on Hungary's complete independence in the spirit of his April 1849 manifesto on the dethronement of the Habsburg dynasty. During the difficult years of passive resistance the erstwhile Minister of Justice in the Batthyány government, Ferenc Deák, was the key figure in the Opposition Party. This self-effacing, imperturbable and at the same time highly intelligent politician became the "Sage of the Nation" in a seemingly hopeless situation. The people were devoted to Kossuth, who cast a spell over them even from abroad, but some of the more sophisticated regarded him as symbolising the Hungarian sickness of "passing fancies". By contrast, Deák's tactics of passive resistance were grounded in the continuance of the laws of 1848. He represented sober realism. In "What is a Hungarian?", a collection of essays by various hands, the poet Mihály Babits called him the "characteristic Hungarian politician". This corpulent and unusually clever landed nobleman from Zala in the southwest of Transdanubia never aimed at fame or power, and even as a leading politician of the Liberal Party lived in a small apartment at the Queen of England Hotel in Budapest.

Notwithstanding the achievements of Deák, Franz Joseph's coming to terms with dualism was due first and foremost to Bismarck.[2] Austria's defeat at Königgrätz in 1866 and its final ousting from Germany offered Hungary a unique chance, which Deák did not allow to pass. Hungary's importance in the Monarchy grew considerably as the Habsburg empire's political centre of gravity shifted to the south and south-east. Whether the Monarchy could survive in the long term as a "Great Power" between Germany and Russia would depend essentially on the level of understanding and, ultimately, of lasting reconciliation it reached with the strongest "historic nation" of the Monarchy. Franz Joseph had to recognize after Austria's defeats in 1859 and 1866 that the course of absolutist subordination of Hungary was no longer feasible. In this situation Deák, with his unrivalled sense of the attainable, offered a solution that would be acceptable and face-saving for both parties.

His famous "Easter article", published on 16 April 1865 in the daily *Pesti Napló* (Pest Diary), was the prelude to the struggle for the

Compromise (*Ausgleich*) between Vienna and Budapest on the basis of recognition of the 1848 constitution granted by the Court. Deák presented the Hungarian standpoint firmly but level-headedly, and at the same time in an impressively considerate way. Even a historian as critical of the Hungarians as Steinacker recognized Deák's statesmanship:

The unique authority with which he carried through this solution is thanks to a characteristic seldom found in his people: he possessed moderation. He held on imperturbably to his line notwithstanding the changeable balance of power and public sentiment. He had an infallible compass in his unwavering sense of right, which amounted not only to his perhaps somewhat formalistic but mostly cogent juristic logic, but was based also on a strongly moral personality, which did not let itself be clouded by interests and ambitions. Deák did not adapt to unfavourable situations, but waited until they changed. A simple nature but a great man, unique in his own way, as was Széchenyi.[3]

The Emperor was accommodating, and the Court agreed to give up the notorious "forfeiture theory" which had declared the Hungarians forfeit of all their constitutional privileges after the Revolution of 1848–9. The unofficial and at first sluggish negotiations entered a decisive phase after the defeat at Königgrätz. It was in this sense that by his victory over the House of Habsburg Bismarck had indeed paved the way to the Compromise. "What does Hungary demand?", the Emperor asked during the first audience he granted to Deák at Schönbrunn after the debacle. "The Hungarian nation asks no more, but no less, from Vienna now than before Königgrätz," Deák replied in his unruffled way.

A change at the top of the Austrian government took place at the beginning of 1867. The Prime Minister Count Richard Belcredi, who had opposed the looming dualism in favour of a confederation of states consisting of five political entities, was replaced by the former Prime Minister Ferdinand von Beust, a Saxon. The latter was on good terms with Count Gyula Andrássy, the spirited and eloquent politician, second in importance only to Deák, who had returned to Hungary from exile in 1858. This is how in 1867 Andrássy, sentenced to death and hanged in effigy a decade and a half earlier, was appointed Prime Minister of Hungary by the Emperor at Deák's suggestion.[4] The situation was almost a paradoxical one.

The fact that, despite his famous "Cassandra Letter" of May 1867 addressed to Deák with dire warnings of impending dangers, Kossuth's influence could be largely eliminated, and that Archduchess Sophie's protests against an agreement with the hated "band of rebels" remained ineffective, was due to the role of Empress Elisabeth. Robert A. Kann says in his analysis of the Compromise negotiations:

In Hungary neither Deák's integrity, Andrássy's dexterity, the popularity of both men, nor the good will of Franz Joseph might have sufficed, had it not been for the mediation of the Queen-Empress Elisabeth, who struck a chord in the chivalrous hearts of the Magyar gentry.[5]

Elisabeth's role was clear to the newspapers as well. At the time of the coronation the *Pester Lloyd* wrote:

And who would underestimate that the nation's love is totally and collectively devoted to the Queen? This gracious lady is regarded as a true daughter of Hungary. Everyone is convinced that the sentiments of patriotism dwell in her noble heart, that she has acquired the Hungarian mentality along with the Hungarian language, and that she has always been a warm advocate of the Hungarians' needs.[6]

In his report of the coronation the Swiss envoy noted that Elisabeth was "currently the most popular figure in all of Hungary". Two acts of mercy have transported "all Hungary into an almost frenetic enthusiasm". The first was a general amnesty for all political crimes since 1848, and the other was the traditional coronation gift, a sum of 100,000 gulden, which on Andrássy's request was granted to the widows and orphans of the fallen and the disabled veterans of the *honvéd* army—the survivors of that same army which had fought the Imperial forces.

The indignant outburst of Adjutant-General Count Crenneville in a letter to his wife illustrates the ill-feeling these gestures aroused in the western half of the empire: "It is a despicable act. I would rather be dead than live to see such dishonour! Where is this leading us? To follow the suggestions of such a scoundrel is not governing. Andrássy deserves the gallows today even more than he did in 1849." In another letter the anti-Hungarian courtier complained from Budapest that Elisabeth wanted to attend a ball given by Andrássy, "who may perhaps no longer be a traitor, but is still a deceitful scoundrel influenced by women". On a previous visit by the Imperial pair a year earlier this same watchful aristocrat had already noted in a letter to his wife that during a court ball the Empress had spoken for a quarter of an hour in Hungarian with Andrássy, so that "the ladies-in-waiting understood none of it". He followed this piece of news with three exclamation marks.

The focus of gossip of the time, and of the literary kitsch of subsequent decades, was the relationship of Sissi, as she was popularly called (she herself signed her letters "Sisi"), and Andrássy. The historian Brigitte Hamann, who used every possible scrap of newly available evidence in her seminal biography *The Reluctant Empress*, comments:

In spite of the immense curiosity and almost criminal inquisitiveness of a great many court appointees in an effort to establish an "indiscretion" on the part of the Empress with Andrássy, such attempts always failed. Both the Empress and Andrássy were under constant sharp surveillance by innumerable members of the court. There can be no doubt that the two loved each other; but that their feelings led even once to a definite "lapse" is, according to the sources, quite unthinkable—quite apart from the fact that Elisabeth was not a woman who found anything in physical love that seemed worth the effort, and that in any and every situation Andrássy never lapsed from being the carefully calculating politician.[7]

This, however, does not alter the fact that Elisabeth was truly a passionate advocate of the Hungarian cause, and played a key role in expediting the historic political decision of the Court. Brigitte Hamann ascribes her sympathy for Hungary to her opposition to the Viennese Court, especially her powerful mother-in-law Archduchess Sophie. Instead of Czech, the preferred language of the Archduchess, Sisi insisted on studying Hungarian and realised her wish in February 1863. The objection by the Emperor and his mother that Hungarian was too difficult and she would never be able to master it made the Empress all the more determined. Her close friendship with Ida Ferenczy, a daughter of the landed gentry four years younger than herself, born in the country town of Kecskemét, became extremely significant. Because of her lowly origin she could not become a lady-in-waiting, but only "reader to Her Majesty", yet she remained Elisabeth's closest friend for thirty-four years until the Empress was assassinated in Geneva. Her entry into the Viennese Hofburg marked the beginning of Elisabeth's enthusiasm for the Hungarian reconciliation. Ida is said to have been the confidante of Deák and Andrássy, which enabled the Hungarian liberals to exploit the isolation of the young Empress for their own purposes. Through Ida's good offices Elisabeth was given a portrait of Deák dedicated to her in his own hand in 1866; it hung above her bed in the Hofburg till the last. It is noteworthy in this context that the Emperor had a painting of the one-time Hungarian Prime Minister Batthyány's execution hung in the Burg apartments. The writer István Lázár remarked that it was a question for psychologists why Franz Joseph kept this painting in a place where he would see it every day. "Was he so imbued with hatred towards him? Or was this his peculiar way of repenting?"[8]

Be that as is may, the fact remains that at the age of fifteen Elisabeth had already received history lessons from the Hungarian-born Count János Mailáth—*inter alia* about the Hungarians' special historic privileges and the constitution (abolished in 1849). Her trips to Hungary in 1857, 1865 and above all 1866 reinforced her empathy with the country and its inhabitants, and the Hungarians attributed the gradual relaxation of political tension to her direct or indirect influence.

It was in January 1866 that the paths of the twenty-eight-year-old Sisi and the forty-two-year old Andrássy first crossed when a delegation of the Hungarian Parliament travelled from Hungary to Vienna to convey birthday wishes to the Empress and officially invite her to visit Hungary. The Hungarians were thrilled when Elisabeth, wearing Hungarian national costume, expressed her gratitude for the Prince-Primate's good wishes in faultless Hungarian. Andrássy was a tall, dark-bearded, smouldering-eyed fairy-tale prince in his gold-embroidered and fur-trimmed ceremonial dress of the Hungarian aristocracy: a medieval Magyar straight out of a picture-book. The first conversation between the Empress and this attractive guest took place that evening at the after-dinner reception—in Hungarian.

Andrássy who had spent the years until his pardon mainly in Paris knew how to make an impression. In the salons of the French capital the ladies called him the "handsome hanged man" (*le beau pendu*) because, as already mentioned, he together with Kossuth and other rebels had been sentenced to death *in absentia* and hanged in effigy in September 1851. Thanks to his mother's support the linguistically proficient Andrássy, in contrast to most of the Hungarian exiles, never had money problems and managed to strike up excellent connections with diplomats and the press. The sophistication he developed during this time would be of great benefit to him later. After his rehabilitation by the Emperor in 1858 he returned home and soon became Deák's closest associate. During the Imperial couple's visit to Hungary in February 1866, the man reputed to be "irresistable" became Elisabeth's favoured conversational partner. Hamann writes: "Ida's passion for Andrássy confirmed Sisi in her very obvious infatuation, and she now put all these feelings at the service of Hungary's cause."

In the summer of 1866, during that critical time for Austria after Königgrätz, and a decisive one for the Compromise, Elisabeth spent almost two months in Hungary with only short interruptions. Both in letters and orally, directly and indirectly, she supported the Hungarian side and ingeniously influenced the Emperor. The exhausted Prime Minister Belcredi noted that she was exploiting the Emperor's dejection to promote the Hungarian cause more emphatically than ever, having previously done so without success. When Franz Joseph was hesitant about meeting Deák and Andrássy, she even wrote from Budapest to the Hungarian Court Chancellor György Mailáth in Vienna entreating him to persuade the Emperor to appoint Andrássy foreign minister or "at least" Hungary's minister. The last lines of her letter indicate the depth of her personal involvement: "If you can accomplish what I could not achieve, millions will bless you, and my son will pray for you daily as his greatest benefactor." Sisi turned even more passionately to the Emperor in a long, effusive letter of 15 July 1866 after a meeting with Andrássy:

He expressed his views clearly and precisely. I understood them and gained the conviction that if you trust him, but entirely, we—not Hungary alone but the Monarchy—can still be saved. But you must *at least* speak to him yourself, and I mean at once, for each day can shape events in such a way that in the end he would no longer assume it. [...] But like any man of honour he is also prepared, at the moment when the state is facing ruin, to contribute everything in his power to salvage it: whatever he has, his reason, his influence in the country, he will place at your feet. [...] For the last time I beg you, in the name of Rudolf, not to let this last opportunity slip by. [...] If you say "no", if you are unwilling at the final hour even to listen to disinterested advice any longer... then I have nothing to fall back on but to reassure myself with the knowledge that, whatever happens, I will one day be able honestly to tell Rudolf, "I did all in my power. Your misfortune does not weigh on my conscience."[9]

Franz Joseph yielded to his wife and in separate audiences received first Deák and, the next day, Andrássy. However, the Emperor remained suspicious: "They covet everything in the widest sense and offer no guarantees of success..." The lonely and depressed ruler appealed to Sisi's understanding of his situation—"that it would go counter to my duty for me to adopt your exclusively Hungarian point of view and to discriminate against those lands which, in unswerving loyalty, have endured unspeakable suffering and which now more than ever require special consideration and care."

However, Sisi went through fire for Andrássy, using all the wiles of a beautiful wife to force concessions from the Emperor: "Hope to be able to hear from you soon that the Hungarian matter has finally been settled and that we can soon find ourselves in Ös-Budavára. When you write that we can go there, my heart will be calmed, because I shall know that the yearned-for goal has been reached." In his biography Hamann sees the Empress as "a willing, even fanatical tool" of Andrássy's person and his politics. "He was extremely clever at making her feel that she was the saviour of Austria (and Hungary)."

In addition to the direct and secret line between Elisabeth and Andrássy, with Ida Ferenczy as the intermediary, there was another important one in the autumn of 1866 through the journalist Miksa Falk, who gave the Empress Hungarian lessons at her request; in fact they were lessons in Hungarian history and literature, rather than in language. Falk, a close friend of Andrássy who at the time was employed by a bank in Vienna, also mediated a link with the liberal politician and writer Baron József Eötvös, who had been Minister for Education in 1848 and was to fill this post after the Compromise, from 1867 to 1871. Correspondence between Falk and Eötvös—actually meant for Elisabeth's eyes—was now added to that between Elisabeth and Andrássy, which was addressed through Ida Ferenczy. Miksa Falk, whose Jewish background was widely known, had had close contact with Count Széchenyi in the latter's last years,[10] and hence came to the notice of the secret police in 1860. During a house search they confiscated his entire correspondence. Falk also spent some time in jail for offences against the press laws. The importance of such direct and partly covert contacts between Elisabeth and these great men of Hungary cannot be overestimated. According to Hamann, Elisabeth was "entirely under Hungarian influence", a view that is surely no exaggeration. She worked "with unparalleled fanaticism and energy for one goal and one goal only: conciliation of the sort envisaged by Deák and Andrássy".

Falk himself was a prominent Hungarian publicist, and his editorials and reports on foreign affairs appeared in the leading Hungarian papers. His well-known signature "Fk" was a mark of quality and originality. After the coronation he was made editor-in-chief of the respected *Pester Lloyd*, which soon boasted 10,000 subscribers—a great journalistic and publishing achievement for that time. He also became an influential parliamentary deputy. After his death a street was named after him in the inner city of Budapest, but in 1943 he no longer appeared acceptable because of his origins, and so the street was renamed. After the war he was "rehabilitated" insofar as his street got back its old name, but not for long; in 1953 it was given the name Nephadsereg utca (Street of the People's Army). Only after the collapse of Communism did Miksa Falk once again come into his own, and the street was given his name for the third time.[11]

Then and later Elisabeth kept up contact with the great spirits of Hungary—Deák, Andrássy, Eötvös and Falk—and made no effort to conceal her admiration for them. She thus wrote to the Emperor in 1869: "Deák is coming to dine today, a great honour for me." The fact that the Queen wept at his bier is commemorated in a painting by Mihály Zichy, commissioned by the Hungarian government for the National Museum. In it Elisabeth places a wreath on Deák's catafalque, while the nation's guardian spirit holds a garland of stars above her head.

After 1867 astonishing attempts were made to prove the ruler's Hungarian origins. Festivities in connection with the "descent of Franz Joseph from the House of Árpád" were held, which were supposed to turn the Emperor into a Hungarian. Genealogists had already let it be known at the time of his coronation that he was a descendant of Béla III (of the House of Árpád) and Anna of Antioch, and Franz Joseph had his "royal ancestors" interred at his own expense in a separate chapel in the castle at Buda, and a marble tablet with the genealogy from Árpád to Franz Joseph was set up next to the tomb. During the much-publicized millennium celebrations in 1896 the Emperor appeared as the "new Árpád".[12]

While these imaginative efforts could not make the Emperor any more popular, the cult of his wife struck a chord in the Hungarian psyche. It was announced at the time of her marriage that the new Empress was fifteenth in line of descent from the Hungarian Princess Elisabeth (Erzsébet), who was canonized after her death in 1321. In the festive rhetoric of the turn of the century the (already murdered) Queen was represented as the second Saint Elisabeth.

Another manifest sign of the Hungarians' affection was the decision to present the castle at Gödöllö, near Budapest, built in the 1830s with about 100 rooms for Count Grassalkovich, as a coronation gift to the royal couple. Already, at a time when the imperial finances were strained, Sisi had asked the Emperor to buy it—the 10,000-hectare forest was ideally suited for hunting—but because of shortage of funds he had refused. Thus the gift of the Hungarian nation was received by the Queen as more than a symbolic recognition of her exertions on behalf of the Hungarians' cause.

Sisi had spent only 114 days in Hungary before the compromise. Hungarian historians calculate that after her coronation as the Queen of Hungary she passed 1,549 days there, mostly at Gödöllö but also in Buda. In a letter to Jókai she wrote that in Hungary she always felt free,[13] and her attitude towards the Hungarians never changed—either during the difficult negotiations over the Compromise or later when she suffered increasingly from depression and had retired from involvement in politics. She remained till the end of her days closely involved with the Hungarians' cause in particular and with liberalism in general. Her many poems written in secret under the influence of Heinrich Heine may be amateurish, but these more than 500 pages contain Elisabeth's "most intimate and personal statements about herself, her environment and her time" (Brigitte Hamann). One of these poems—"O könnt ich euch auch den König geben!" (Could I but give you the King as well)—has a particular political explosiveness. In 1868, three months before the expected birth of her child, the pregnant Queen settled in Budapest, and the Swiss envoy reported to Bern the "universally expressed wish that the child she expected might be a girl, for there was no denying that, in spite of the Pragmatic Sanction and all the pacts concluded subsequently, a boy born to the Queen of Hungary in the castle of Buda would be destined to become King of Hungary, and in time this would bring about a separation of the Hungarian crown lands from Austria."[14] What today seems merely a bizarre idea was taken seriously at the time, and there was general relief in Vienna when Sisi's youngest child turned out to be not a son but a daughter, Marie Valerie. Archduchess Sophie noted in her diary the joy of pro-Imperial Hungarians, because the birth of a boy in Buda "could have been a pretext for detaching Hungary from the Monarchy".

Elisabeth made no secret of her profound condemnation of the reprisals against the victors in the revolutionary years of 1848–9, and once remarked with unbelievable candour to Bishop Mihály Horváth: "Believe me, if it were in our power my husband and I would be the first to bring Lajos Batthyány and the martyrs of Arad back to life." Her son Crown Prince Rudolf was brought up in this spirit, and his very first political memorandum was a declaration of belief in Andrássy's politics and his fascinating personality.[15] Andrássy himself noted in his diary on 30 July 1866: "It is certain that, if any success is achieved, Hungary will have to be thankful to the Beautiful Providence which guards it, more than can be imagined." The "Beautiful Providence" did much for Hungary and later especially for Andrássy.

The Austrian historian Friedrich Engel-Janosi wrote of the reorganization of the Monarchy: "Hungary can be envied for having available in these decisive years two personages of significance, Deák and Andrássy."[16] Yet without Austria's enforced separation from Germany at the behest of Bismarck and the good fortune of an Empress falling completely under the spell of Hungary, the *Ausgleich* could not have proceeded so smoothly.

The Romanian-French philosopher E.M. Cioran believes he has discovered yet another interesting motive for Sisi's love of Hungary:

There is a specific Hungarian sadness. Everything Hungarian had an uncanny fascination for Sisi, and perhaps it was the only thing that really gripped her. From a political viewpoint her predilection for Hungary was suicidal, because Hungarian politics and Hungarian chauvinism was the main reason for the collapse of the Monarchy. She always favoured the Hungarians at the expense of the other ethnic groups, whose revolts were directed not so much against Vienna as against Budapest. Seen from a political viewpoint, Sisi's stance was a grave mistake. She was enthralled by everything that is so seductive in Hungarians... The main reason, understandably, was the mentality, the language, the people that gripped her so. It is no coincidence, of course, that a particular tree at Gödöllö attracted her particularly—in other words, her best friend was a Hungarian tree! The fantasies, moods, idiosyncrasies of a Sisi... formed, as it were, the background to the impending tragedy, of which everyone was more or less conscious. That is why this figure is so significant and superb![17]

Cioran believes that Brahms and Elisabeth represent the acme of nineteenth-century melancholy, and both of them had a blind love of Hungary. The great Hungarian poet Mihály Babits wrote that it is not cynical bitterness that is characteristic of Hungarians but shoulder-shrugging, somewhat melancholy resignation. It is no coincidence that a Hungarian adage says "*Sirva vigad a magyar*" (Magyars take their pleasures mournfully).

25. Victory in Defeat: The Compromise and the Consequences of Dualism

On 19 December 1867, some months after the coronation and the adoption of the historic agreement which became known as the Compromise between Vienna and Budapest, Ferenc Deák, the "Sage of the Nation" and most influential Hungarian politician, gave a speech outlining the basic principles. The spokesman of the Liberals drew up an extremely positive balance-sheet before a delegation of citizens in the capital:

It can be said that never since the defeat at Mohács have the lands of the crown of St Stephen been so united. It can be said that never since the Austrian dynasty began to rule has the relationship between ruler and nation been so trusting. It can be said that never has there been so little disagreement and bitterness between us and Austria as now. It can be said that foreign capital, which has so far not even risked getting to our borders, is flowing now to a greater extent and more freely into the country, and our people are capable and clever enough to take advantage of this for our fatherland. If we want to upset all this, then we are attacking the basis of the compromise, and the entire edifice will most likely be toppled.[1]

Without mentioning Kossuth, viewing these events rancorously from his exile, the architect of the pioneering agreement hinted in this speech at the criticism of the national opposition, in whose eyes the country had not attained true independence:

Most European powers are so great and have at their disposal so much power that Hungary could not exist in their midst as a single, independent entity without an alliance offering secure support. Fate has placed our country in the midst of Great Powers, each of which could undoubtedly sweep us away with its superior armed force if it believed that we stood in the way of its wishes and plans.

281

Was the Compromise, accepted on 29 May 1867 by the Hungarian parliament with 209 deputies voting for it and 89 against, and ratified by the "Emperor of Austria and Apostolic King of Hungary" on 12 June, a "victory in defeat"? Or was it a fatal capitulation to Austria—even "the death of the nation", as Kossuth claimed in an open letter from Paris, printed three days before the vote?

Generations of politicians, historians and intellectuals in Budapest and Vienna have argued over the character and consequences of the transformation of the "Austrian Empire" into the "Austro-Hungarian Monarchy". Most of them—with different motives—had hardly a good thing to say about the dualistically structured Monarchy. Austrian and German supporters of the idea of a united Monarchy, as well as the majority of non-Hungarian historians, agree that it was basically a case of a Hungarian victory. As late as 1963 Georg Stadtmüller wrote: "By this retreat the Germans renounced the leadership and command of the central Danube region."[2] In his biography of Franz Joseph, Franz Herre phrased this in a less pan-German but still more unequivocal way: "The rush for accommodation in the panic after Königgrätz" was a serious political error, "nothing less than an acceptance of Hungarian conditions".[3]

Many notable personalities in the Cisleithanian part of the Monarchy reveal in their diaries and notes their indignation at these events. Thus the diplomat Alexander von Hübner complained that "Hungary, vanquished with Russia's help, is now being handed back to the defeated revolutionaries of 1849"; Franz Joseph had left himself at the mercy of the Hungarians.[4] Some of the contemporaries quipped that the Dual Monarchy of "the kingdoms and realms represented in the Vienna parliament, the Reichsrat" (Cisleithania) and the "Lands under the Holy Hungarian Crown" (Transleithania) was a "monarchy subject to notice". The French historian Louis Eisenmann coined the pithy but scientifically disputed formula in 1904 that where "common affairs" were concerned, the Compromise meant "parity of rights: Austria carrying two-thirds of the costs, and Hungary wielding three-quarters of the influence". The impression of Hungary's predominance and its disastrous role in the collapse of the Monarchy was echoed in the works of outstanding Austrian writers of the turn of the century and the first half of the twentieth, such as Rilke, Kafka, Franz Werfel and above all Joseph Roth.

The Dual Monarchy was in fact an extremely complex structure, with elaborately built-in traps, snares and failings. The acronyms alone required esoteric erudition. The joint institutions were named "imperial and royal" (*kaiserlich und königlich* or *k.u.k.*), the Hungarians having insisted on the "and" as a mark of their equality. The purely Austrian offices were called "imperial-royal" (*kaiserlich und königlich* or *k.u.k.*); the purely Hungarian ones "royal" (*königlich* or *k.*), and in Hungary the expression "*magyar királyi*" (Hungarian Royal), shortened to "*magy.kir.*", was in general use.

Robert Musil wrote about this unholy muddle and the painful disappearance of the expression "Austrian" in his novel *Der Mann ohne Eigenschaften* (The Man without Qualities):

... It did not consist of an Austrian part and a Hungarian part that, as one might expect, complemented each other, but of a whole and a part; that is, of a Hungarian and an Austro-Hungarian sense of statehood, the latter to be found in Austria, which in a sense left the Austrian sense of statehood with no country of its own. The Austrian existed only in Hungary, and there as an object of dislike; at home he called himself a national of the kingdoms and lands of the Austro-Hungarian Monarchy as represented in the Imperial Council, meaning that he was an Austrian plus a Hungarian minus that Hungarian; and he did this not with enthusiasm but only for the sake of a concept that was repugnant to him, because he could bear the Hungarians as little as they could bear him, which added still another complication to the whole combination.

... the Hungarians were, first and last, simply Hungarians and were regarded only incidentally, by foreigners who did not know their language, as Austro-Hungarians too; the Austrians, however, were, to begin with and primarily, nothing at all, and yet they were supposed by their leaders to feel Austro-Hungarians and be Austrian-Hungarians—they didn't even have a proper word for it. Nor was there an Austria. Its two components, Hungary and Austria, made a match like a red-white-and-green jacket and black-and-yellow trousers. The jacket was a jacket, but the trousers were the relic of an extinct black-and-yellow outfit that had been ripped apart in the year 1867.[5]

These quotations (and some of Musil's other reflections) about "Kakania" and its political and national conflicts give us an idea, which is still vivid to this day, why so many Austrians heartily loathed the Compromise, both in form *and* in substance. Even such a balanced chronicler of the Habsburg Empire's history as Robert

A. Kann stressed that "Austria became the political prisoner of the Hungarians' interpretation of the Compromise".[6] Understandably the Slavs living in the Monarchy, who made up 47 per cent of the total population, and the Romanians (with 6.4 per cent) rejected out-of-hand the distribution of power among the Germans (24 per cent) and the Magyars (20 per cent), which turned them into second-class nations. Far more complicated, and much-debated, is the question why public opinion, notable historians and many politicians in the land of putative "victories", i.e. the Hungarian half of the Monarchy, complained so vigorously about the subordinate position, political and economic dependence and even the alleged "colonial position" of the Hungarians.

In order to understand future developments, above all the evident and politically explosive discrepancy in Hungary between fact and perception, between objective conditions and subjective impressions, we have to examine closely the essential mechanism of the Compromise. It was more than a personal union, i.e. a coalition of two states with a single ruler; it was a real union (a *Realunion*), strictly a treaty between two separate and, in important ways, sovereign states—but by no means in all. The French historian Victor-Lucien Tapié described the agreement as one of the "most peculiar constitutional documents of the nineteenth century, as far as content and form are concerned".[7] Many constitutional experts racked their brains over what "dualism"—the Dual Monarchy—meant in legal terms. The Compromise created neither a federation nor a confederation; there was no state above the two member-states as in a federation, nor were they fully sovereign as in a confederation. Nor were the Austrian and Hungarian versions of the Compromise embedded in the constitutional law of both states with complete equality, which of course made for additional complications.

It was indeed a unique political structure. Each half of the Monarchy had its bicameral parliament, its own government with a prime minister and ministers with individual portfolios; each had, to a limited extent, its own territorial armed forces (*Honvéd/Landwehr*) and autonomous financial administrations. Further, there were three "imperial and royal" (*k.u.k.*) ministries: foreign affairs, defence and *common* finance (those pertaining primarily to foreign affairs and defence matters). The joint "*k.u.k. imperial ministries*"

So ich nun auff die zeytt Otto des kayſers pm ko
men ſo wil ich von den dingen ſagen die zů ſti
nen zeytten zů auſſpurg geſchechen ſend Do ſieb d'
kayſer otto berayttet wider berengarium den künig bo
lomparden als wider ain wieterich vnd geitigen on
der alle gerechtikait vmb gelt gůb Doch ſo forcht
in der ſelb wieterich wan er die machtikait des kay
ſers wol wiſſet. vnd durch ratt des hertzogen bo luth
tringen. Kam er zů dem kayſer vnd begeret frid Do

1. On 10 August 955, on the Lechfeld near Augsburg, the Germans defeated the Hungarians, who had been terrorizing Western and Southern Europe for almost half a century. However, the Hungarians did not
disappear like other mounted hordes, but adopted Western culture and
Roman rather than Byzantine Christianity.

2. The triumphal arrival of Hungary's founder, Árpád, at the moment of
"Conquest", as depicted by Mihály Munkácsy (1893, detail). The white
horse is a significant element in Hungarian legend.

3. János Hunyadi
   (1407–56),
   Hungary's greatest
   soldier; governor of
   Hungary 1446–52.

4. King Mathias (Mátyás)
   I Corvinus (1440–90),
   son of Hunyadi, com-
   mander, patron of the
   arts, and conqueror of
   Moravia, Silesia and
   Lower Austria includ-
   ing Vienna and
   Wiener Neustadt.
   A Renaissance prince
   and the most admired
   of Hungarian rulers.

5. Torture and execution of the rebel peasant leader György Dózsa, 1514.

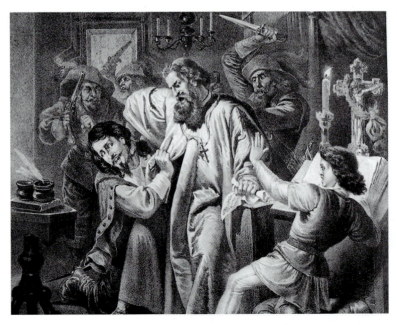

6. The Pauline monk George Martinuzzi, champion of Hungarian unity, murdered by Italian mercenaries, 1551.

7. István Bocskai, magnate and Haiduk leader, Prince of Transylvania 1605–6.

8. Gábor Bethlen, statesman and Prince of Transylvania 1613–29.

9. Count Miklós Zrinyi (1620–64), general and poet; *ban* of Croatia 1647–64.

10. Kuruc leader Imre Thököly (1657–1705), Prince of Upper Hungary and Transylvania 1682–5.

11. Ferenc Rákóczi II
    (1676–1735), freedom
    fighter, Prince of
    Transylvania (and of the
    Confederation from 1705).

12. Count István Széchenyi
    (1791–1860), "the greatest
    Hungarian", reforming
    politician and statesman.

13. Execution of Ignác Martinovics, leader of the Hungarian Jacobin
    conspiracy, and his accomplices on the Field of Blood, Buda, 20 May
    1795.

14. Sándor Petőfi (1823–49),
    poet and revolutionary,
    killed fighting the Russian
    army.

15. Lajos Kossuth (1802–94),
    driving force of the
    Revolution; Governor
    1848–9.

16. Lajos Kossuth and Palatine Stephen enthusiastically received in Vienna,
    15 March 1848.

17. Execution of Count Lajos Batthyány (1807–49), Prime Minister 1849.

18. General Artúr Görgey (1818–1916), commander of the Honvéd army 1848–9.

19. Ferenc Deák (1803–76),
Minister of Justice 1848,
architect of the Compromise
(*Ausgleich*) of 1867.

20. Count Gyula Andrássy
(1823–90), Prime Minister
of Hungary and Foreign
Minister of the Dual
Monarchy.

21. Queen Elisabeth at the
bier of Ferenc Deák
(painting by Count
Mihály Zichy, 1906).

22. Emperor Franz Joseph crowned King of Hungary 1867.

23. Photomontage of Franz Joseph and Elisabeth approaching the railway
    station in Budapest, 1897. This was Elisabeth's last visit to the city.

24. Procession on the Margaret Bridge from Buda to Pest during the millennium celebrations, 8 July 1896.

25. A suspect being handcuffed, 1896. Gendarmes were dreaded symbols
of authority up to 1945.

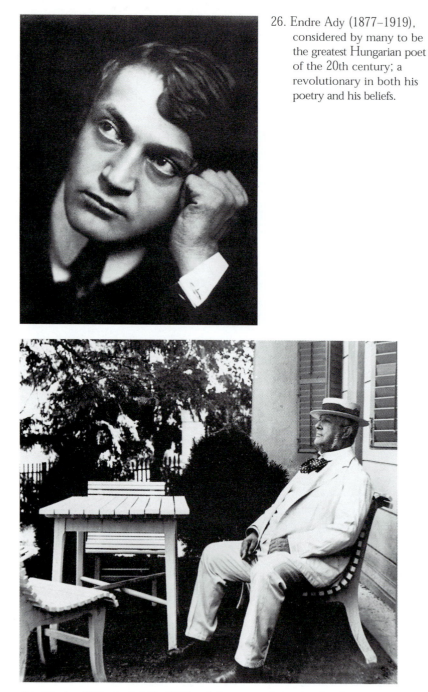

26. Endre Ady (1877–1919), considered by many to be the greatest Hungarian poet of the 20th century; a revolutionary in both his poetry and his beliefs.

27. Sándor Wekerle (1848–1921), of German origin, the first bourgeois Prime Minister in Hungary's history. Minister of Finance (1889–95) and several times head of government.

28. Baron Zsigmond Kornfeld
(1852–1909), one of the
most influential ennobled
Jewish bankers, seen in
dress uniform 1905. He
more than once saved
Hungary from bankruptcy.

29. A group of Hungarian generals 1913. *Front right* Baron Sámuel Hazai,
Minister of Defence 1910–17—this son of a Jewish manufacturer of
spirits was the highest-ranking officer in the Monarchy next to the
Chief of the General Staff.

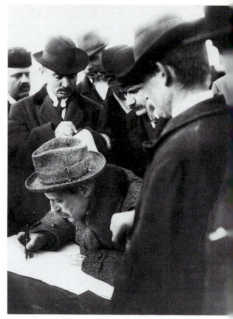

30. Count István Tisza, Prime Minister 1903–5 and 1913–17; killed by an unknown assassin, October 1918.

31. Count Mihály Károlyi, President of the first Hungarian republic, signs a document distributing his landed estates, 23 February 1919.

32. The Communist leader and commissar Béla Kun addressing workers at the Csepel engineering works after nationalization, April 1919.

33. Admiral Miklós Horthy entering Budapest at the head of the National Army, 16 November 1919.

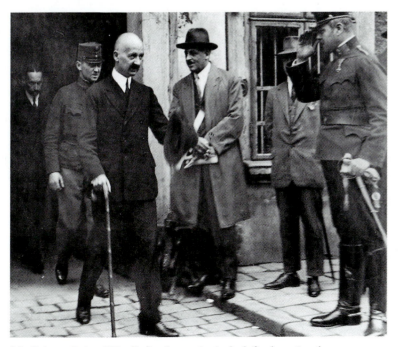

34. Prince Lajos Windischgrätz, principal defendant in the money-forging scandal, leaving court in 1926.

35. Prime Minister Count
    István Bethlen (*left*) arriving
    in London, June 1930.

36. The Austrian Chancellor
    Engelbert Dolfuss and the
    Hungarian Prime Minister
    Gyula Gömbös with Benito
    Mussolini in Rome, 17
    March 1934.

37. The composer Béla Bartók (1881–1945), a dedicated democrat and anti-Nazi, who left Hungary in 1940 and settled in the United States.

38. Miklós Radnóti (1909–44), a Catholic of Jewish origin who wrote his memorable poems during a Nazi death march.

39. Attila József, poet of the inter-war years, who committed suicide at the age of thirty-two.

40–43. Ignaz Trebitsch-Lincoln (1879–1943), arguably the twentieth century's most successful international confidence man. Born into an orthodox Jewish family in southern Hungary, he was in turn a Presbyterian missionary in Montreal (*above left*), a British Member of Parliament, a bankrupt businessman, a spy in Berlin (*above right*) and the Buddhist abbot Chao Kung during the early 1930s in Peking and Shanghai (*below*).

44. After the first Vienna Award on 2 November 1938: *from left* the Czech Foreign Minister Frantisek Chvalkovsky, the Axis Foreign Ministers Count Galeazzo Ciano and Joachim von Ribbentrop, and the Hungarian Foreign Minister Kálmán Kánya.

5. Viscount Rothermere, the British newspaper magnate, receiving an accolade in front of the Parliament in Budapest for his pro-Hungarian stance.

46. Rothermere with Admiral Horthy during the Hungarians' triumphant entry into Kassa (Kosice), 11 November 1938.

47. Admiral Horthy on a state visit to Germany, August 1938, seen here in Kiel with Hitler.

48. The Arrow Cross leader Ferenc Szálasi arriving at the Prime Minister's residence, 15 October 1944, after his putsch assisted by the Germans.

49. Jewish deportees from the Western Hungarian township Köszeg, summer 1944. Between 15 May and 7 July 427, 402 Jews were deported to Auschwitz, of whom only a minority survived.

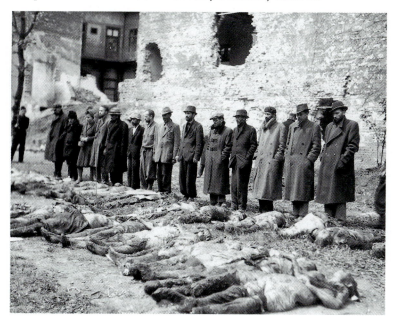

50. Exhumation of victims massacred in January 1945 at a Jewish hospital in Budapest. Facing the corpses are the arrested murderers, 22 April 1945.

51. Party chief Mátyás Rákosi (*centre*) at a congress of outstanding workers, 1951. Behind him is his own portrait, flanked by images of Stalin
and Lenin.

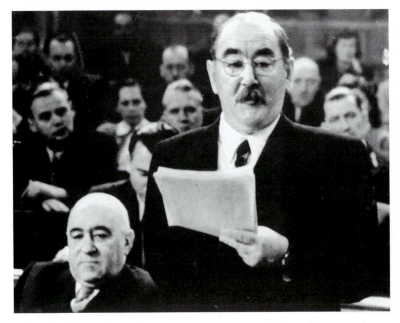

52. The new Prime Minister Imre Nagy announces the reform party line
after Stalin's death, July 1953. *On the left* Party chief Mátyás Rákosi.

53. The toppling and dismantling of the massive Stalin monument in Budapest, a hated symbol of foreign rule and Communism, was the first manifestation of the spontaneous popular rising which broke out on 23 October 1956.

54. A damaged Soviet tank commandeered by freedom fighters after fierce fighting, end of October 1956, Joseph Boulevard, Budapest.

55. Hungarian Party chief János Kádár bidding farewell to Leonid Brezhnev, First Secretary of the Soviet Communist Party, at the end the latter's goodwill visit to Hungary in 1979.

were responsible to so-called "delegations": two executive committees, each consisting of sixty members, elected by the Austrian
Reichsrat and the Hungarian Parliament. All joint matters had to be
discussed by the three *k.u.k.* ministers with the delegations, which
met once a year alternately in Vienna and Budapest. The committees communicated with each other in writing, and sat jointly only
when a vote was necessary on contentious issues. The Magyars
requested this cumbrous method to stress that no superior parliamentary body existed. For example, the foreign minister had to
submit his report to the two delegations separately and account for
it twice before a unanimous decision could be reached. The resolution of the delegations became law by means of the Emperor's
confirmation.

Concerning defence, the determination of the number of recruits
from each state, implementation of general conscription, and the
organization of national militias were left to the two states. In contrast to 1848, however, the unity of the *k.u.k.* army was preserved.
The language of command in the armed forces was to be German—a regulation which, as the Magyars saw it, impaired their status of equality, and which was to be abolished forty years later during
the ultimately failed campaign for absolute military sovereignty.
Approval of the armed forces budget and the quota of recruits were
determined at the Compromise negotiations held every ten years
and often used as a means of exerting political pressure.

The determination of the bilateral share in the common expenditure, the contest for the so-called "quota", was the central problem. During the negotiations in 1867 the agreed Hungarian share
was 30 per cent, but by 1907 Hungary's contribution to the common expenditure had reached 36.4 per cent. While Austrian historians detected a bias in favour of the Hungarians in this area. Péter
Hanák, a Hungarian scholar who took a particularly moderate
stand in matters of the Monarchy, considered this increase of 6.4 per
cent "a realistic measure of the economic level's progression towards
that of developed Austria".[8] Despite an impressive economic upturn,
the Austrian half still produced twice as much in goods and services
as the Hungarian half. Customs, the monetary system and a common railway system were also on the agenda of the Compromise
negotiations.

The ten-yearly regular disagreements over the "quota" tested the coherence and indeed the viability of the Monarchy. Karl Lueger, the controversial Viennese politician, probably spoke for many Austrians when he asserted in the Lower House in 1895: "I regard Dualism as a misfortune, the greatest misfortune my country has ever had to suffer, a greater misfortune even than the lost war."[9] Despite this bleak statement, difficulties were always ironed out— for the last time in May 1917 during the Great War.

The highest administrative and executive organs of the Dual Monarchy were made up not only of the Hungarian and Austrian governments respectively, but they also comprised a third joint force. The three "common ministers" and the prime ministers of both halves of the Monarchy formed a Common Council of Ministers chaired by the foreign minister. This at least gave the two governments indirectly a share in the conduct of foreign and other joint affairs.

The Compromise recognized the constitutional demands of the Magyars, above all the integrity and political unity of the historical territory of the "Lands under the Holy Hungarian Crown", together with Transylvania, today's Slovakia, the Carpatho-Ukraine, the Bácska and Bánát, and the kingdom of Croatia and Slavonia, including the Military Border. Approximately 15 million "Transleithanians" inhabited a total territory of 325,411 square km. Of these about 40 per cent were Magyar (at the official census of 1850–1 only 36.5 per cent), 14 per cent South Slavs (Croats and Serbs), 14 per cent Romanians, 9.8 per cent Germans, 9.4 per cent Slovaks and 2.3 per cent Ruthenes. Without Croatia-Slovenia, which possessed full internal autonomy, Hungary's territory amounted to 282,870 square km., and the proportion of Magyars rose to 41.6 per cent. When calculating the Magyar share of the total population. Croatia was almost always omitted. That is how their percentage could be increased by 1890 to 48.6 and even, at the last census in 1910, to 54.5 per cent. Taking the official realm of the crown of St Stephen as the point of departure, the applicable figures were merely 42.8 (1890) and 48.1 per cent (1910) respectively. It meant, in words, that the other nationalities still made up the absolute majority of the population which in the meantime had grown to 20,886,487. All in all, the rapid increase of Magyars during these years is conspicuous:

their proportional growth reached 106 per cent as against only 60 per cent in the Monarchy as a whole. As a result of the greater natural population increase and massive Magyarization, the percentage of Hungarians within the Dual Monarchy rose from 15.5 to 20.6 per cent.

Hungary's religious structure (without Croatia) in 1910 was: Roman Catholics almost 50, Orthodox 12.8, Uniate 11, Calvinist 14.2, Lutheran 7.2 and Jewish 5 per cent. The picture was different for the Magyars themselves (i.e. without the other nationalities): Roman Catholic 59, Calvinist 26 and Jewish 7 per cent.[10] Calvinism was regarded as "the Magyar religion", and the role of the Calvinists (as also of the Jews) in the nation's cultural and political life was far above their numerical proportion.

While in the western half of the Monarchy German hegemony weakened where its ratio of the total population was concerned (there was a drop from 36.2 to 35.6 per cent), as well as from a political and economic point of view, the Hungarian half showed an opposing trend: a steady consolidation of Magyar political, economic and cultural hegemony.

As for the Magyars' role in the Dual Monarchy, it was significant, sometimes even decisive, in common foreign affairs and in finance. It suffices to point to the activities of the first Hungarian (also the most successful) foreign minister of the Dual Monarchy, Count Gyula Andrássy (1871–9). Incidentally, it was a particular irony of fate that his son, also Gyula Andrássy, was the Monarchy's penultimate foreign minister for ten days: from 24 October to 2 November 1918. It was he who, unsuccessfully, sought a separate peace from the Entente.

Three of the ten foreign ministers who held office between 1867 and 1918 and five of the eleven ministers of finance were Hungarian. In 1914 the number of Hungarians serving in the Foreign Ministry and the diplomatic corps had reached 27.5 per cent. A Hungarian lesser noble, Benjamin Kállay, was the longest-serving common Minister of Finance (1882–1903); he was also responsible for the administration of Bosnia-Herzegovina, which was occupied in 1878.

If the political, economic and financial facts are viewed objectively, it has to be admitted that the Hungarians were less victims than beneficiaries during this period of their history. For the first time since the catastrophe of Mohács they were masters of their own destiny. Much—though not everything—depended on the policies carried out by the Hungarian ruling classes, especially in the realm of the nationalities and social questions within the framework of mutual dependence. This has been repeatedly stressed by Domokos Kosáry, while C.A. Macartney regretted that the real and substantial benefits which the Compromise conferred on Hungary remained half-hidden from the eye of the nation "by the mists of suspicion engendered by the centuries in which the Austrian connection had brought it so much disadvantage".[11]

The army and the role of the Emperor/King were the "Achilles heel of Dualism". In view of the complicated, precarious and at the same time cumbersome institutions "by which the independence of Hungary as well as the conditions of security and the survival of the Empire intact are guaranteed" (preamble to Article XII of 1867), the joint ruler played a decisive role as the final arbiter in all disputed matters—a fact overlooked by many observers and contemporaries. The Hungarian government submitted the most important motions not directly to Parliament but first to the monarch, for the so-called "preliminary sanction". Franz Joseph discussed the two governments' proposals with members of the royal family and with his aristocratic and, last but not least, his military advisers, and used the same method for disputed questions on which the "delegations" of the two parliaments could not reach a joint decision. The Hungarian historian László Péter had this to say:

The sovereign's control of the army—which was chiefly outside the constitutional-legal sphere—normally gave Franz Joseph a free hand in all matters decisive for the Monarchy as a great power: in foreign affairs, defence and imperial finances. In the highest sphere of state politics Franz Joseph remained an autocrat even after 1867. He made decisions, having consulted the Ministerial Council for Common Matters (sometimes called the Crown Council), which was more a consultative than an executive body with imprecisely defined membership and no formal constitutional status.[12]

In his outstanding work *The Dissolution of the Habsburg Monarchy*, written while he was an émigré in America, the social scientist Oszkár Jászi stressed that, by comparison with other states of the Monarchy, no single ideal or sentiment existed which could have united the Hungarian people in some sort of political solidarity. That the ruler often reached his decisions to the satisfaction of the Hungarians was due first and foremost, during the Deák-Andrássy era, to the two statesmen's persuasive power and moderation, as well as to the enduring pro-Hungarian stance of Queen Elisabeth. She herself once told Andrássy: "You see, when the Emperor's affairs in Italy go badly it gives me pain; but when the same thing happens with Hungary, that is death to me."[13]

The Austrian historian Hugo Hantsch voiced a widely held opinion when he noted: "The great existential questions of the Monarchy always meant less to the Hungarian politicians than the interests of their own state." While the constantly squabbling Austrian parties suffered the frustration of observing the increasing influence of the Hungarian half of the Monarchy and Hungary's slackening ties with the Imperial unity, the future Socialist State Chancellor and theoretician of the national question, Karl Renner, devised the formula "organic community without a communal will". If the monarch tended in so many questions to incline rather towards the Hungarian view, people in Vienna spoke in undertones "of the Hungarian King's absolutism against the Emperor of Austria".

Only in the key area of "military matters" did the Emperor and his advisers retain a virtually exclusive control, almost as in "the good old times" before the Compromise. Franz Joseph was the commander-in-chief and exercised unlimited authority over the army, whose language of command was German; he alone had the right to declare war or make peace. The *k.u.k.* army, this "imperial army without an empire", represented "the last cohesive element in the divided monarchy". The Austrian military historian Johann Christoph Allmayer-Beck saw the *k.u.k.* army's principal merit in the fact that "even after the Compromise it remained an Imperial institution, a unique and indispensable school of all-Austrian national consciousness, and this in an army where out of every 100 soldiers 24 were German, 20 Magyar, 13 Czech, 11 Serbo-Croat, 9 Polish, 9 Ruthene, 6 Romanian, 4 Slovak, 2 Slovene and 2 Italian."[14]

It was precisely this "all-Austrian" character which was an emotive word for Hungarians, and by no means only for nationalists. Examining the social psychology of nationalism more closely, Hanák's view that the army was the "Achilles heel" of the Monarchy is indeed fitting.[15] In the period between 1867 and 1918 not a single defence minister was Hungarian. Hungarians were represented by only 6.8 per cent among the ministry staff, and this proportion never rose above 10 per cent. According to official army statistics, four out of five professional officers were German and only 8–9 per cent Hungarian, although the American historian István Deák contends in his book *Beyond Nationalism* that this percentage is excessive, and the German share was actually no more than 55 per cent.[16] Be that as it may, this army was regarded in Hungary as an autonomous, anti-Hungarian state within the state, even as an army of occupation. The Hungarian government had no influence over the conduct and politics of the Ministry of Defence. In this sensitive sphere Hungary remained dependent on the ruling circles of the Court and of the Austrian half of the Empire.

Not wanting to endanger the great accomplishment of political parity, Andrássy as Prime Minister carried through the military agreements in Parliament. However, he had to promise that the government would endeavour to gain greater military autonomy by all possible means. Hungary produced each year 40,000 recruits out of a total of 100,000. The *k.u.k.* army rose from its peacetime level of 250,000 men to 500,000 in 1914 and during the war to 1.5 million. After a tug-of-war in the Ministry of Defence, Andrássy succeeded in obtaining Franz Joseph's consent to the creation of a militia in Austria and Hungary (together with Croatia). This force, called the *Honvédség*, was to have its own insignia and flags; even, more important, Hungarian was to be the language of command. The *Honvédség* was envisaged as the core of a national army, but for that very reason the monarch did not grant it even its own artillery. This territorial armed force never had more than 10,000–12,000 soldiers; in 1912, on the outbreak of the first Balkan War, its strength rose to 25,000 men and only then did it obtain artillery.[17]

The passionate arguments every ten years about army legislation proved to be an explosive device embedded under the precarious structure of the Dual Monarchy. The constitutional relationship with Austria in general, and the question of a separate army under Hungarian command in particular, were regarded as the most vital matters affecting the nation. Andrássy, with the mark of death already on him, made his last great speech in the Upper House on

5 April 1889 against the creation of a national army. The former *honvéd* colonel, who had fought the imperial army at Schwechat, told his countrymen: "It is the Great Powers exclusively who decide the great international questions, the questions of European balance, on which every country's security depends today, and they make their decisions not from a legal point of view but as military Great Powers." It was therefore necessary "that each member of the army, officers as well as soldiers, should regard the army as a bulwark of all that that he has learned to love at home, all that is fair in the Monarchy. The common army cannot be something foreign, some third state within the state, but the joint protector and joint possession of both halves of the Monarchy."[18]

It was, incidentally, seen as a great achievement that the army was renamed *k.u.k.*, i.e. "imperial-and-royal", and no longer called simply "imperial-royal". Franz Joseph's famous Order of the Day issued from the manoeuvres in Chlopy, Galicia, on September 1903 was an open and emphatic warning against "unilateral efforts" to loosen the "solid structure" of the army; he reiterated in clear terms his intention that the army should remain a "common and uniform" force. It is pointless to speculate today whether the whole conflict over the army could have been avoided with a little flexibility. In the Great War, Hungarian troops fought bravely in the *k.u.k.* army as well as in the *Honvédség*. At the same time the ironic fact, stressed by István Deák, was that "the majority of the last fighting troops of the Habsburg Monarchy were Slavs, Romanians and Italians, and therefore theoretically allies of the Entente armies."

With the passing years the increasingly acute clashes over the incompatible concepts of the army were not only the driving force behind the two leading nations' contest for hegemony, but also resulted from it. This was exacerbated by the fact that the struggle of the by no means united nationalities against the supremacy of the Germans and Magyars hindered the introduction of comprehensive reforms, and thereby entrenched the nationalities question. Musil pointed out this problem:

… the national movements…were so violent that they jammed the machinery of government and brought it to a dead stop several times a year, but in the intervals and during the deadlocks people got along perfectly well and acted as if nothing had happened. […] In this country one

acted—sometimes indeed to the highest degree of passion and its consequences—differently from the way one thought. [...] Kakania [was], un-
beknownst to the world, the most progressive state of all; a state just barely
able to go along with itself. One enjoyed a negative freedom there,...[19]

A glance at the ethnic diversity and the relevant figures shows how
the Compromise prevented a national federative solution, as well as
national autonomy of a personal and territorial nature. There are, at
the same time, strong arguments favouring the view of the Hungarian historian Gyula Miskolczy, taking stock at the time when the
centenary of the Compromise was being celebrated: "The Compromise of 1867 was not the best solution for the Habsburg dynasty
and monarchy, but it was the only one whereby it could possibly
preserve its great power status."[20]

The ethnic diversity of the Monarchy demonstrates that comparisons between it and the United States or the Switzerland of
today are fundamentally inappropriate. According to the statistics of
1910, only six of the eleven greater nationalities represented in the
Monarchy—the Germans (23.9 per cent), Magyars (20.2), Czechs
(12.6), Croats (5.3), Poles (10), Italians (2), Serbs (3.8), Slovaks (3.8),
Slovenes (2.6), Ruthenes (7.9) and Romanians (6.4)—were represented in both halves of the empire. These were the Germans,
Croats, Italians, Serbs, Ruthenes and Romanians. In the words of
Kann, any attempt to federalize the western half would have resulted
in "an unfortunate torso".

In contrast to the stormy national struggle against the traditional
leading position of German-Austrians, the history of national movements in uniformly Magyar-dominated Hungary proceeded seemingly far more smoothly. In reality, however, the "peace and quiet"
in Hungary spelt far more danger than the noisy parliamentary
upheavals in Vienna. Of the 413 deputies in the Hungarian parliament only eight represented the nationalities whereas, according to
the population figures, there should have been 215 Hungarians and
198 representatives of the nationalities. The almost complete denial
of legal representation to the Romanians, Serbs and Slovaks, as well
as the very limited concessions to the Croats (mainly confined to
questions of autonomy) led the national Opposition at an early
stage into anti-monarchical, subversive, irredentist channels where
the aim was not national reform but the disintegration of the
Austro-Hungarian Monarchy.[21]

As for the development of the eastern half of the empire, one should not automatically extrapolate from the collapse at the end of the Great War to a desperate situation back in 1867. Andrássy's cabinet set about translating his ideas of equality in the spirit of liberalism into action with élan and energy. The Prime Minister, a man of big concepts, tactical flexibility and great flair for the art of the possible in foreign affairs, could rely on the enormous esteem enjoyed by Ferenc Deák although he was not a member of the cabinet. He had been offered the office of prime minister and the special honour of standing next to the throne with the Prince-Primate during the coronation in place of the palatine. When the King asked him if he had any particular wish, the answer was: "All I wish for is that after my death Your Majesty should be able to say 'Ferenc Deák was a decent man'."

Intellectually the most significant member of the government, and at the same time author of the most important laws, was Baron József Eötvös, the Minister of Religious Affairs and Education, who had held the same post in 1848 in the Batthyány government. Because of the German-speaking milieu from which he came, he had only learnt Hungarian at about the age of adolescence. As a constitutional philosopher and writer he corresponded with Montalembert and de Tocqueville in Paris, and acted as deputy to Andrássy in the latter's absence. His friend Miksa Falk characterized Eötvös as "a statesman who loved his country with the intellect of a German philosopher and the warm-heartedness of a poet".[22]

Eötvös, Deák and Andrássy were true liberals not only in name, and their influence was manifested in the laws for the emancipation of Jews, the nationalities question and the Croatian-Hungarian Compromise (*Nagodba*)—even if not in all the ways in which those laws were later implemented. From Deák and Eötvös to Kossuth in exile, all Hungarian politicians at the time pronounced themselves in favour of at last according full civil rights to the 540,000 Jews, something that had already been done in 1849 in the last days of the revolutionary government. "No nationality has stood by us more loyally than the Jews, and we have treated none more unfairly," said Mor Jókai, the writer and friend of Petőfi. Eötvös and Deák were enthusiastic when the first elected Jewish deputies entered parliament.

The Nationalities Law of 1868 was meant to be a promising start in coping with the bitter experiences of 1848–9, when the other nationalities (apart from most of the Danube Swabians and Slovaks) joined in suppressing the revolution; at the same time it was intended to translate into action the promises of the nationality law, with its emancipation of the Jews, passed at Szeged. Its authors, particularly Deák and Eötvös, were the best representatives of the liberal high and middle nobility, and stressed that the authority of the state must not be the instrument of Magyarization and of Magyar nationalism directed against the non-Magyar peoples. During the Reform era Széchenyi had already warned against antagonizing Hungary's other nationals by over-zealous attempts at Magyarization, because if the "Hungarian earthenware" were to knock against the German and Slav "iron pot", it would soon be shattered.

As has already been mentioned, the exiled Kossuth had submitted a plan for a Danubian confederation as an alternative to the Habsburg Monarchy. His former envoy in Paris, Count László Teleki, went even further and spoke out in favour of a compromise of interests between the smaller nations of Central Europe, with a simultaneous renunciation by the Hungarians of their "historic rights". In 1861, after his forced return from emigration (Austrian agents abducted him from Dresden) and the Emperor's amnesty, he committed suicide apparently in despair at the situation.

By reverting to the Estate-based, supranational notion of the *natio hungarica*, the Nationalities Law laid down that "all citizens of Hungary form one nation in the political sense, which is the indivisible uniform Hungarian nation, every citizen of the Fatherland being its member with equal rights, to whichever nationality he belongs".[23] Still, the preamble also stated that this equality of rights related in particular to the official use of languages within the country, and could be the subject of a special regulation only insofar as it was demanded by the unity of the country, the government's practical requirements and the fair administration of justice. These formal comments later acquired great importance because the law was used by future governments, especially after 1875, as the instrument of Magyarization.

Hungarian was proclaimed to be the official language of government, Parliament, administration, justice, the counties, and secondary education, thus conferring more far-reaching linguistic, cultural and religious-political rights on the individual citizen than were to be found almost anywhere outside the Monarchy. The Primary School Law of 1868, which made education compulsory for all children between the ages of six and twelve, required teaching to be in the language of the local inhabitants. The Nationalities Law secured the use of non-Magyar languages in the administration and justice at the lower levels, education in the mother-tongue, the right to establish non-political cultural institutions and organizations, and autonomy for the national (e.g. Serbian and Romanian Orthodox) churches. Teaching of the official state language as a subject was not stipulated even in the primary and secondary schools, and the churches were free to use non-Magyar languages. Another feature of the liberal nationalities policy was that any minority forming at least 20 per cent of the local population could apply for the use of a second or third language in the community in question.

Although the law opened up a broad field of activity where freedom of assembly and association was concerned, and the protection of minorities defined in it would have redounded to the honour of many a government in the inter-war years and after the Second World War (e.g. in Czechoslovakia, Romania and Yugoslavia), it was rejected outright even by the moderate representatives of the nationalities. Even liberal Hungarian statesmen considered collective rights or territorial-administrative autonomy for the nationalities incompatible with the "Hungarian national concept of the state" and the historical integrity of the kingdom. Instead of recognizing the national equality demanded by the Serbs, Slovaks, Romanians and Ruthenes, they were willing to offer the non-Magyar nationalities only theoretical equality in cultural matters and on a personal-individual basis within the unity of the "political nation".

The constitutional compromise with Croatia-Slavonia, passed Parliament on 17 November 1868, proved an unsatisfactory solution for most Croats, who wanted from Budapest basically the same rights as those granted by Vienna to Hungary. They had to give up their hoped-for status as an independent political unit within the Monarchy. The country remained linked to Hungary, and although the *ban* was responsible to the *Sabor* (the Croatian parliament), the appointment of the *ban* by the King was still made on the recommendation of the Hungarian prime minister. The fact that the port of Fiume (today Rijeka) and the region of the Muraköz remained in Hungarian hands was a further grievance for the Croats. On the other hand, in local matters such as administration, justice, religion and education they were totally autonomous. Croatian became the exclusive official language of the country. In their contacts with the central authorities, as well as in Parliament where forty deputies, delegated by the *Sabor*, represented Croat interests, they could use their own language. Nonetheless, they considered the "Small Compromise" just as unfair as the Hungarians did their own Compromise with Vienna.*

Yet, despite all the later acknowledgement of Croatia-Slavonia's constitutionally far-reaching autonomy (in comparison with the great-Serb hegemony of the 1918–41 period), the relationship between Budapest and Zagreb became gradually more strained because of the mistakes of increasingly intolerant Hungarian government policies. Over the nationalities question the liberalism of Eötvös and Deák came into serious conflict with the nationalism of the majority in the ruling classes. Liberal thinking was increasingly disregarded and forced into the background. Even Ferenc Deák with all his authority had to experience this in a seemingly minor but in fact symbolic matter—over the issue of a budget subsidy for the Hungarian National Theatre. The representatives of the Serb ethnic minority promptly demanded a similar contribution for a theatre in the Voivodina. Deák had approved both subsidies, and steadfastly refused to cast a vote only for the Hungarian theatre, but he was voted down by the majority, although the liberals, called the Deák Party, held a two-thirds majority in Parliament.

With the death of Eötvös and Andrássy's appointment as Austro-Hungarian Foreign Minister, followed by Deák's retirement from day-to-day politics, those politicians whose supreme aim was Magyarization, and who detected only tendencies of latent separatism or outright treason in the nationalities' demands for the use of their own languages, gained the upper hand.

---

* While on a visit to the then Yugoslav Republic of Croatia in the 1960s, I found the frequent references of nationally-minded Croat Communists to the autonomous rights bestowed on them by Hungary a century earlier revealing and amusing. Their conflict with the Serbs and with the centralizing forces already evident in the Tito era was an unmistakable indicator of the lozoming collapse of the second Yugoslavia.

Under the leadership of Kálmán Tisza, the longest-serving Prime Minister in Hungarian history (1875–90), the Liberal Party, which resulted from the merger of the old Deák Party and the so-called "Left Centre", adopted a course in which consolidation of the "Hungarian national state" was the aim. This corrupt and cleverly manoeuvring government and its shorter-lived successors became slaves for two generations to a state idea which can only be described as "megalomania" (Oszkár Jászi). The distinctive features of this disastrous policy were underestimation of the role of Austria and particularly that of the Slavs, overestimation of the Magyars' significance, disregard of Hungary's nationalities, striving for the full Magyarization of public life, and limitation of the political and cultural development of the non-Magyar nations.

It was only with Croatia that the Hungarian nobility were willing, initially at least, to negotiate as equal partners—"from nation to nation", as Deák put it in 1861. In his declaration of principles on the occasion of the parliamentary scrutiny of the Nationalities Law on 24 November 1868 Deák stressed, to general approval, that this law did not apply to Croatia-Slavonia, which was a "political nation" possessing its own territory; and that in addition the Hungarian-Croatian Compromise was valid and binding in regard to language use. Deák regarded the Hungarian-Croatian relationship as one between states, not nationalities. As early as 1861 he said with statesmanlike wisdom and moderation: "Croatia possesses its own territory. It is in a special position: it was never incorporated into Hungary, but was our associate, sharing our rights, our duties, our good times and our hardships."[24]

The fact that the Austro-Hungarian Compromise awarded Dalmatia to Cisleithania and Fiume as well as the Military Frontier to Hungary caused constant ill-feeling. However, it was the blunders of the Budapest ministry concerning "common matters"—the extension of Magyarizing measures to Croatia, the abolition of bilingual place-names and railway signs, and the appointment of officials who could not speak Croatian—which aroused indignation. Efforts to play off the seemingly loyal Serbs against the powerful Croat opposition proved to be political boomerangs. In the end the *bans* appointed by Hungary usually had to rule in an absolutist style without the *Sabor.*

Particularly hated was the corrupt regime under Count K. Khuen-Héderváry (1883–1903), described sarcastically by the Austrian Social Democrat Otto Bauer as the "Hungarian Pashalik" (after the Ottoman province where the pasha oppressed the Christians). The Magyarization of the Croat state railways during the ministry of Ferenc Kossuth, the incompetent son of the freedom hero, triggered off passionate protests, as did the embarrassing show-trial of Croat and Serb politicians (1909), whose subversive connections with Serbia were supposed to be proved by forged documents. Due to shortsighted Hungarian policies, the occupation (1878) and subsequent annexation (1908) of Bosnia-Herzegovina did not achieve the actual aim of creating a strong Croat-Bosnian counterweight to Serb expansion. On the contrary, the tripartition of the Croatian people (Dalmatia, Slavonia and Bosnia) provided the Serbs with additional room for manoeuvre. Gusztáv Gratz, historian and former Hungarian Foreign Minister, expressed this view in *The Era of Dualism* (1934). Gratz, himself an ethnic German, wrote of a "tragic development", since "Croatia could rightly be [described] as Hungary's Achilles heel."[25]

26. Total Blindness: The Hungarian Sense of Mission and the Nationalities

The situation of the "others", the non-Magyar half of the population, did not develop at all in line with the liberal–humanist foundations of the Nationalities Law. The transformation of a multinational state into a purely Magyar national and centralist one was a highly dynamic process, driven by a growing Hungarian sense of mission. The Prime Minister, Kálmán Tisza, sensing that he had been released from legal obligations, did not beat about the bush, and declared in 1875: "There can be only one viable nation within the frontiers of Hungary: that political nation is the Hungarian one. Hungary cannot become an eastern Switzerland because it would then cease to exist."[1]

What this meant to the "others"—the Slovaks, Ruthenes, Romanians, Serbs, Croats and Germans—is no longer shrouded in silence even by Hungarian historians as it was in the period of romantic nationalism. Széchenyi's adage "The nation lives in its mother-tongue" denoted the unity of the national community and linguistic community within the historic borders of the country. The "others", namely the nationalities, were left out of this definition of nation and state, borrowed from French constitutional law. The hallmark of the "nation" was the centrally forged national language. Nation and state formed a unity.

In his penetrating study of the nationalities question in Hungary Lajos Gogolák observes that the country's reorganization towards a "general monopoly of the Magyar state and educational language" had already been pursued as early as 1790–1.[2] The downside of the modern Hungarian nation's blossoming, which bequeathed significant linguistic and poetic landmarks, was the final alienation of the educated, nationally-minded élite of the population's "other" half, who increasingly followed the tendencies of Pan-Slavism,

Czechoslovakism, Dacoromanism, Serb irredentism and the "Illyrian idea".

The impressive rebirth of Hungarianness in terms of the mother-tongue became a visible symbol of a triumphal super-elevation of the national identity, but the tragic and inevitable consequence was the standing provocation to the other half of the population, most of all in everyday life. The state patriotism of the past had foundered on the idea of Magyarization being a universally applicable state and existential notion. Now the mother-tongue was to become, in every area of life, the essence and epitome of the ethnic-national identity, and at the same time of political existence. The catastrophe of 1918–19—Hungary's break-up—was thus essentially programmed over a century earlier.

The Education Laws of 1879, 1833 and 1891 made the teaching of Hungarian compulsory in kindergartens and primary and secondary schools. Soon there were no Slovak secondary and higher elementary schools in Slovakian Upper Hungary, and between 1880 and 1890 the number of church schools fell from 1,700 to 500. Between 1869 and 1891/2 the proportion of purely Magyar primary schools in Hungary increased from 42 to 56 per cent, while that of the non-Magyar ones fell to 14 per cent; the others were mixed-language ones. The reason why this trend was not more accelerated was that four out of five primary schools were denominational and there the material means for the complete nationalization of all non-Magyar-language schools were lacking.

The strongest measures for implementing Magyarization and sanctions against incompetent or unwilling primary schoolteachers were ordered by Count Albert Apponyi, Minister of Education from 1906 to 1910, who was a polyglot humanist and a Catholic. On the basis of the notorious "*Lex Apponyi*" the number of ethnic schools fell by half between 1899 and 1914; only in 20 per cent of all primary schools was there teaching in non-Magyar languages.[3] Béla Grünwald, historian and spokesman of hard-line, forced assimilation, illustrated the situation in Upper Hungary by the metaphor of the meat-grinder: ethnic peasant boys were forced in at one end and Magyar gentlemen, alienated from their ethnic group, emerged at the other. Grünwald, scion of an old Carpathian German family, even suggested the abolition of the Nationalities Law. He was of the opinion that non-Magyars were "not capable of independent advancement"; that it was "the destiny of Magyardom to assimilate them, to absorb them into a superior people", thus fulfilling the Magyar "duty to humanity, to elevate them as if we were the champions of civilization."[4]

The predominance of the Magyars was reflected also in the fact that 84 per cent of secondary school graduates and 89 per cent of students were Magyar. At the turn of the century Magyars constituted 48.1 per cent of Transleithania's population and 54.5 per cent of Hungary's (without Croatia). Even more explosive politically were the data for the composition of the public service. In 1910, 96 per cent of civil servants, 91.2 per cent of all public employees, 96.8 of judges and public prosecutors, 91.5 of secondary school teachers and 89 per cent of medical doctors had Hungarian as their mother-tongue. Similar percentages were found in the staffs of libraries, publishing houses and newspapers.[5]

During the 1890s Prime Minister Bánffy raised the illusion of a unified national state almost to government policy, but meanwhile public opinion became less and less able to understand the significance and nature of the nationalities problem. Oszkár Jászi has pointed out that most of the bourgeoisie and intellectuals were convinced that not only was there no suppression of nationalities, but that on the contrary the Magyar nation granted so many freedoms and privileges to the "inferior" ethnic groups that its liberalism was unprecedented in history. It must have seemed outrageously ungrateful that second-class people should respond to this magnanimity with dissatisfaction and try to incite public opinion in foreign countries against the Magyars with false accusations and slander. According to Jászi, the public were genuinely convinced of this opinion, both by upbringing and by press reports. Educated and politically interested circles had no contact with the intelligentsia of the other nationalities, and knew nothing of their opinions, even if they lived in the same town.

Jászi describes an experience of his own in the "better" social circles in a predominantly Slovak area. Returning from a rail trip, a distinguished Magyar says indignantly: "The brash and impertinent way that these Pan-Slavs have begun to behave is unbearable. Today, for instance, I was compelled to travel in a first-class compartment with five Pan-Slavs, who didn't even hide what they were." Asking for details of this terrifying experience, Jászi was informed that the men had had the nerve to converse in Slovak, which to the Magyar gentleman had reeked of Pan-Slavism. In Jászi's view, the chasm between the so-called "historic classes" and the nationalities became so wide during the decades of this policy of assimilation that even the idea of the oppression of the nationalities seemed absurd to them. At this time of national euphoria, which reached its climax with the Millennium celebrations in 1896, even the brother-in-law and successor of József Eötvös as Minister for Religious Affairs and Education, Ágoston Trefort, who held that post for sixteen years, declared: "I do not want to enforce Magyarization on anybody. However, I must assert that in Hungary the state can survive only as a Magyar one. The aspirations towards a polyglot status are politically crude, and short work has to be made of them."[6]

Despite "Magyar linguistic chauvinism" (Moritz Csáky), despite official prohibitions and press trials, despite sporadic bloody infringements,* it has to be said that for the Hungarians the suppression of the other nationalities was cultural and never racial: the distinctive mark of being a Hungarian was solely language! Everyone professing to be Hungarian had the same chances, irrespective of background, and at this time the decisions were generally political and national, and not personally motivated, thus affecting the private sphere. They cannot therefore be compared to the collective and terrorist measures in the successor states during the inter-war and post-1945 years.

Nonetheless, the belief that the individual national groups' political élites that were slowly becoming organized and their new, albeit still weak middle classes would accept a purely Magyar state as a common Fatherland was a disastrous illusion. The vision of new national states built on the ruins of historic Hungary was gaining ascendancy. Even such a man as Crown Prince Rudolf, brought up from childhood in a pro-Hungarian spirit, sharply criticized Hungary's nationalities policy in his private correspondence and in the political writings he published under various pseudonyms:

The sad thing for Hungary is the Magyars' lack of consideration and inability to understand that nothing can be achieved by bad treatment and

---

* When the nationalist village priest and Slovak leader, Andrej Hlinka, sentenced to two years' imprisonment in 1907, wished to consecrate a new church in his local parish of Cernova despite his suspension from office, the gendarmerie intervened causing the death of fifteen people.

contempt and momentary vehement regulations with the nationalities, who are numerically superior, and of whom one has absolute need in order to preserve the Hungarian state in the same size, which today it still possesses… In many, in fact most parts of the territories of the Crown of St Stephen only the nobility, the officials and the Jews are Hungarian—the people belong to other tribes.

In their boundless blindness even the influential Hungarian circles forget that in 1849 Serbia and Romania still belonged to Turkey, that they were then quite uncivilized and politically immature countries, whereas today the kingdoms of Serbia and Romania, as well as nearby Bulgaria, have entered the line of European states, and education, culture and prosperity have grown by leaps and bounds. The Romanians and Slavs of Hungary, who have also developed, are in constant contact with these countries, and this is a great problem for Hungary today. Old Hungary had no idea of this, and could therefore handle the subjugated people quite differently.[7]

Rudolf, a relentless critic of anti-Semitism and friend to many Austrian and Hungarian Jews, went even further in reaction to the anti-Semitic turmoil of the 1880s in Hungary. In an anonymous article in the *Neue Wiener Tagblatt*, he warned: "An abyss is opening up in Hungary, and much that still appears viable today can easily fall into it."[8]

Immense damage was caused to Hungary's international standing by the government's over-reaction and lack of understanding of the wishes not only of individuals but of the national groups for an identity and for territorial or personal autonomy; by the restriction of the franchise from 6.7 to 5.9 per cent (1870–4) of the total population; and by the corrupt practices of the political classes. In his book *The Lost Prestige* (1986) the later Foreign Minister Géza Jeszenszky described the deteriorating perception of Hungary in Britain between 1896 and 1918, as reflected in the press and diplomatic reports. The main instruments of this were the newspaper articles and books of Wickham Steed and R.W. Seton-Watson (who also published under the pseudonym "Scotus Viator"), which aroused a strongly negative response. The "massacre" of Cernova in today's Slovakia was the turning-point, writes the author, quoting from a leading article in the London *Times*: "Liberal Hungary adopts the policy of Russian despotism."[9]

Still, it would be wrong to attribute only chauvinism and arrogance to this unrestrained intensification of a Hungarian national state. It was not only blind advocates of Magyar superiority who aggravated the national conflicts, but noble idealists labouring under delusions played an unwitting and tragic part too. As a result of the historical strokes of fate described in earlier chapters, anxiety complexes always existed which, in both literature and politics, influenced national attitudes to Vienna and the nationalities. Széchenyi wrote: "Many people think that if they see an animal with two horns in Vienna it is the devil, though it is only an ox." In other words, it was not always ill-will, but also stupidity and inefficiency, which in the pre-revolutionary period of 1848 shaped the policies of the Court towards Hungary.

The double anxiety about Vienna and the numerically superior but culturally inferior nationalities was the reverse side of a power psychosis nurtured by romantic nationalism. Politicians dabbling in poetry and poets involved in politics have helped to mould the difficult process of becoming a nation. The issue was more than ever the prevailing "primacy" of an ethnic group: for the Hungarians it was the prerogative of the Conquest, for the Slovaks and Romanians the principle of original habitation before the Conquest. The historical-political and later ethnic-racist sense of superiority of the self was inextricably linked to hatred and contempt for the "other". The utterly unrealistic romantic belief in the mission and indivisibility of the national state was akin to a "national secular religion" (Gogolák); however, the dismemberment of historic Hungary had already been in the offing in 1848, and probably even earlier. The political-spiritual nationalism of the smaller ethnic groups directed against Hungarian national rebirth became the explosive device which, in conjunction with the Great War of 1914–18, brought about catastrophe.[10]

The Compromise or the reconciliation between the ruler and the high and middle nobility on the backs of the South Slavs, Slovaks and Romanians made Hungary's political class yet more short-sighted, bearing in mind that the basic idea of a unitary state had already been enunciated by Kossuth in 1848 and Deák in 1867: "There are several nationalities in Hungary but only one nation." Only one deputy, Lajos Mocsáry, warned with admirable steadfastness of the consequences of Magyarization: many times, in his far-seeing pronouncements, he demanded equality, toleration and the implementation of the requirements laid down in the Nationalities Law. This Hungarian nobleman, incorruptible and unafraid as a man and as a politician, was expelled from his own party and hounded out of political life.[11]

The spokesmen of romantic nationalism found plenty of emulators, and their spiritual following, unwaveringly representing the historical-heroic tradition of greater Hungary, persists to this day. The fact that even the most liberal Hungarians did not comprehend the power of the nationalities—or, as Gusztáv Gratz put it, "were completely at a loss regarding the nationalities question"—was connected with a literature imbued by romantic nationalism and, above all, by the Hungarian historiography of the nineteenth century. After the Compromise the tragic spirit of defeat and endangerment, characteristic of Hungarian poetry, was eclipsed by a naive optimism.

"History is the realm of the true lie,"[12] wrote Antal Szerb. The special trap of the poetically immortalized beginnings of Hungarian history was already the topic of Friedrich Schlegel's Viennese lectures of 1812. Referring to the old heroic sagas, heroic songs and the literary works of Anonymus and Kézai, the legends about Attila and King Mathias "who all of a sudden wanted to turn his Hungarians into Latins and Italians", but also to examples from the chronicles and the national sagas of the contemporary author Sándor Kisfaludy, Szerb warned against "drawing constitutional conclusions [from all these] or linking them to quarrels".[13] We do not know whether Schlegel had heard of, or indeed met, the "highly gifted-maniacal" contemporary historian István Horvát (1784–1846), but Horvát's historical myth-making far surpassed even the fantasies of medieval chroniclers. His books and lectures at the University on Hungary's early history inspired an entire generation. On the basis of a few words of similar sound he sought the Magyars' ancestors in Persia, Greece and Italy. He claimed that Adam and Eve had spoken Hungarian in Eden, and it went without saying that Homer and Hercules were actually Hungarians. The ancient Hungarians had been of such massive stature that they were called "giants" and "titans". That this man was a university professor in Pest from 1823 to 1845 and found willing listeners for these absurdities showed, said Szerb, "the entrenched optimistic national self-perception". This optimism prepared the way for "the many shocking political mistakes of the succeeding generation". It was testimony to Horvát's influence that on his death no less a person than Eötvös wrote a glowing obituary.[14]

Even though Horvát remained a bizarre exception in Hungarian historiography, such conjurations of the glorious past and the continuous assertions of Magyar superiority over the other ethnic groups produced an alarming excess of their national consciousness. That was the true measure of the "Magyars' lack of consideration and comprehension" of which Crown Prince Rudolf so disapproved. Reading the speeches of influential politicians and the editorials and historical works of this post-Compromise period, some of the phrases evoke Paul Valéry's warning of the seduction of history.

History is the most dangerous product contrived by the human brain. [...] It transports the nations into a dream-world, into raptures, leads them to believe in a specious past, exaggerates their reflexes, causes their sores to fester, disturbs their peace, drives them to megalomania or paranoia, and embitters the nations, causing them to be full of themselves, insufferable and conceited. [...] History justifies whatever one wants it to. It clarifies virtually nothing because there is nothing that cannot be proved by it.[15]

If some of the absurd statements about Hungarian history had been no more than polemics between historians or constitutional lawyers, then the books produced by the wave of romantic nationalism could be disregarded. But they were important elements in political ideas and actions, and formed the ideological basis of Hungarian hegemony in Transleithanian Greater Hungary at a time (1880) when the Magyar share of the total population amounted to only 41.6 per cent. The question of historical continuity since the Conquest and of the constitution (there was no written one either before or during the Dual Monarchy) became an explosive subject. Thus Count Albert Apponyi commented to his colleagues at a meeting of the Interparliamentary Union in St Louis, Missouri, that Hungary had the oldest representative government in all of Europe. The Hungarian constitution was as old as the Magyars themselves; he stressed that, though never written down, it had grown organically and succeeded in solving the problem of strengthening the Monarchy without sacrificing freedom better than any other.

Another politician, the younger Count Gyula Andrássy, wrote the following in a three-volume history of his country:

.... Hungary's present constitution can be traced back in an unbroken sequence to the freedom of the nomad era... Of the peoples, who established states in Europe up to the ninth century, only we have succeeded in... maintaining the unity of the state from the first moment in an unbroken continuity by preserving ... the hegemony of the nation until this day.[16]

In 1911 the Hungarian Academy of Sciences awarded its highest prize to Andrássy's book. The author was even more frank in newspaper articles: "The Hungarian people far surpass all their allied nations in political talent and the ability to maintain a state."[17]

In a manual on constitutional law, of which five editions were issued within eight years, the writer Ernö Nagy claimed "a victory of the Hungarian constitution... because civilized states by and large have adopted that organization which, in the whole continent, rests on historical foundations only in Hungary."[18] Other Hungarian constitutional experts pointed out that the "compact sealed with blood" at Pusztaszer in 896 made the Hungarians the first European nation to have smoothed the way towards parliamentary control of the executive organs. A late-nineteenth-century *Legal History of Hungary* tells us that "Hungary has preserved the nations' concept of freedom and hindered the development of universal-monarchical absolutism. Without Hungary either the Germans or the Slavs would today be masters in Europe." The Austrian historian Harold Steinacker criticised these and numerous similar writings in some bitingly ironic studies. "The Magyars", he wrote, "regard themselves as the chosen people of constitutional history." He reproached his Hungarian colleagues for "not daring to quell the fires of chauvinism, and even adding fuel to the fire. In this they were surpassed only by history-writing politicians."

The professors' theories formed the basis of populist utopian scenarios. The famous editor-in-chief of the influential daily *Budapesti Hírlap* (Budapest Journal), Jenö Rákosi, exclaimed in an oft-quoted article in 1899: "What we need is a nation of thirty million Magyars! Then we would possess the East of Europe... That is why every Hungarian, politician or not, must tack on to his flag '30 million Magyars'; then all our problems would be solved in one stroke… The Hungarian nation must rise to the higher realms of a sovereign nation, and she can achieve that when she becomes, in all her members and institutions, totally Magyar, when every man in Hungary feels in his innermost soul that he has become a Magyar chauvinist."[19] This leading publicist, who constantly sermonized about the Hungarian character and was considered the spokesman of nationalism, was himself of German descent (his name had originally been Kremsner), and broke with Germany only in his eighteenth year—a fact he did not like mentioned in his later years. As well as Béla Grünwald, mentioned earlier, the most influential conservative writer, Ferenc Herczeg (1863–1954), and the author of the most popular patriotic novels for young readers Géza Gárdonyi, (1864–1922), also had German roots.[20]

Two other nationalist politicians besides Jenö Rákosi distinguished themselves through authorship. Gusztáv Beksics wrote many books on the great future he envisioned, prophesying that with its higher birthrate and power of (forced) assimilation Hungary's population would rise by about 1950 to 24 million, of whom 17 million would be pure Magyars. According to Rákosi, Hungary only needed numerical superiority to take the lead over Austria, the Czechs, Romania, Serbia, Bosnia and Dalmatia.

Of the vision of a "Greater Hungary" Pál Hotsy wrote in 1920 that Hungary could never be dismembered; it would always remain Hungary—"after all, it could not be otherwise." Within a short time this Hungarian state would integrate the southern and eastern neighbours into its sphere of interest. The nation would impose its will on Serbia, even if it did not actually occupy it. It would depend on the Serbs whether they would wait until force was used, or give in voluntarily, since they did not possess the qualities necessary for an independent national existence. Bulgaria too would eventually have to recognize Hungarian supremacy. "Our descendants will perhaps live to see the Hungarian language spoken in Sofia as well, and Hungary bringing her influence to bear directly. Romania's relationship with us will develop similarly."[21]

In view of this and other similar flights of imagination Gratz rightly observed that realism was never the strong side of Hungary's political perceptions. The "unhealthy mixture of politics, law and history" diagnosed by Steinacker in Apponyi's speech unfortunately remained a constantly recurring motif not only in the euphoria following the deceptive victory of 1867 but also after the collapse of 1918–19. The cancer of nationalism and its ramifications in the Hungarian politics of the nineteenth and twentieth centuries were analysed and demonstrated, in a way that looked also to the future, only after 1945 by such major historians and intellectuals as István Bibó, Jenö Szücs, Domokos Kosáry and Péter Hanák. This is also true of the roots and consequences of the success story of this half-century between 1867 and 1918, and the breakthrough and assimilation of Germans and Jews and their role in the blossoming of the economy, the sciences and culture in Hungary.

27. The "Golden Age" of the Millennium: Modernization with Drawbacks

The church bells tolled all over Hungary at midnight on New Year's Eve of 1895, and again in Budapest five hours later to announce that the first day of Hungary's second millennium had dawned: 1,000 years earlier, in 896, the Magyar tribes led by Árpád had ridden into Hungary to conquer and settle it. For at least fifteen years the government, the opposition, historians, artists, architects and businessmen had been preparing these celebrations. Yet at the outset even the date of the Conquest was highly controversial.

The historians consulted by Education Minister Trefort in 1882 would agree only that the Conquest had probably taken place "sometime" between 888 and 900. They finally compromised on 1895, but as early as 1893 the government "shifted" the year of the Conquest to 896 because of the sluggish progress of several projects. Thus 1896 became the jubilee year and 896 the official date of the Carpathian crossing.[1] Only at the last minute did Gábor Baross, in charge of economic policy, who had refurbished the entire transport and railway system, manage to thwart the idea of a world fair suggested by a megalomaniac magnate and, instead of the nightmare of a full year's programme of events, stage a national exhibition and construct some public buildings.

This year of commemoration demonstrated impetuous national self-confidence, confirmation on a large scale of the Hungarian idea of state standing up against Vienna and against the increasingly troublesome nationalities. The millennium monument was declared the most important artwork, and its construction on Heroes' Square, though begun in the jubilee year, was completed only in 1929 after several necessary alterations. The central core, still unchanged to this day, consists of the equestrian group of the seven conquering tribal chieftains with Prince Árpád in the centre. To the left and right several statues are arranged in a semicircle, and of these only Árpád and St Stephen have remained in their original places. The Habsburgs were replaced after the Second World War by great personages of Hungarian history (for example, Franz Joseph gave way to his irreconcilable enemy Lajos Kossuth). The site where the monument stands today formed the grand entrance to the Exhibition of 1896. In greater Hungary, from Dévény (today Devin in Slovakia) to Brassó (Brasov in Romania) and Zimony (Zemun in Serbia), seven national columns of remembrance—symbols of the Hungarian national idea—were erected in various townships.

Continental Europe's first underground railway,[*] the Gallery of Fine Arts and the last section of the Pest boulevard were finished in time for the Exhibition. The representative central part of the Parliament building with the great hall was also completed—the construction work on this, the largest parliament building in the world (in a country which till 1990 never had genuinely free elections), was actually only finished in 1902. During 1896 the famous "Iron Gate" on the lower Danube, a Danube bridge in Budapest and another in Pressburg, and the Supreme Court building were opened and a new wing of the Castle was begun. Numerous conferences and international congresses were held—among others, of dentists, stenographers, geologists, art historians and tailors. There were press, mining and peace congresses. Most of the events took place in the capital, but festivities were also organized in many towns and villages, above all for the official opening of 400 new primary schools, but also for the unveiling of monuments and memorial tablets.

But all this was overshadowed by the Millennium Exhibition in the City Park, with 234 pavilions. On an area totalling 4,850 square meters approximately 14,000 exhibits made available by 832 Hungarian and 48 foreign collectors, were shown. The exhibition consisted of two main parts, historical and modern; Vajdahunyad castle, built in an eclectic style, is still in use today—as the Museum of Agriculture. The Exhibition was opened on 2 May by Franz Joseph

---

[*] This line Deák Ferenc tér/Hősök tere is still in operation. The particularly low, rattling carriages of the "M 1" are worth a ride, to say nothing of the Art Nouveau stations.

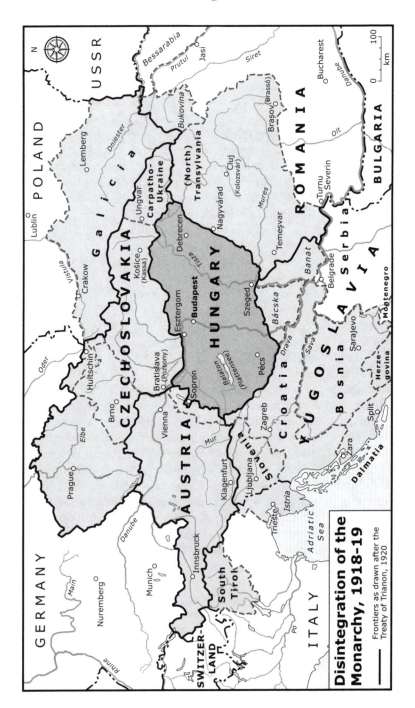

Disintegration of the Monarchy, 1918-19

Frontiers as drawn after the
Treaty of Trianon, 1920

and Elisabeth. Archdukes and archduchesses, and many dignitaries led by Prime Minister Miklós Bánffy, escorted the royal couple. Only one prominent person was missing: the wife of the Prime Minister, and the liberal daily *Pesti Napló* "revealed" in an unsigned leading article that she was on a lengthy Italian journey. However, the real reason for her absence was that she was a trained school-teacher who had actually worked before her marriage, and the aristocrats considered it "unacceptable" that such a person should play the part of Hungary's "first lady" on such an important occasion. The newspaper article concluded: "The bluebloods are said to have given the Prime Minister the alternative in anonymous letters that either she went—or the whole Millennium would go."[2]

The monarch began his tour at 11.35 a.m. and, according to newspaper reports, spent exactly two and a quarter hours at the exhibition. Some reconstructed straw huts and farms were set up near the historical pavilion. A young upstanding peasant stood in front of one of them. Franz Joseph pointed at the house and asked "Do you live here?" "Thank God, Your Majesty", said the peasant, "only for the Millennium, then I can go home."

There were balls, receptions and celebrations all over the country. On the morning of 9 May the Court and all the dignitaries took part in a ceremonial *Te Deum* in the recently renovated Coronation Church, celebrated by the Archbishop of Esztergom, Kolos Vaszary. His sermon, printed in all the papers, was a rhetorical masterpiece on the topic of the alliance between the monarch and Hungary. The Jewish community also celebrated the Millennium with a service in what was then the world's largest synagogue and the newspaper of the religious community proudly reported that 8,000 men and women had been present, dressed in tail-coats and elegant dresses. The first rows were filled with government representatives, ennobled magnates, well-known bankers and industrialists; most wore full-dress, uniforms with dolmans thrown over their shoulders, jewelled trimmings, egret plumes, sabres and boots with gold or silver spurs.

The second series of events took place on 8 June, the anniversary of Franz Joseph's coronation. It began with a gloriously colourful mounted procession of delegations of high dignitaries from the counties and towns parading before the royal couple. Franz Joseph, in the white uniform of a Hungarian hussar general, then rode from the Castle to Pest in a Baroque coach dating from Maria Theresa's time. St Stephen's crown and the coronation insignia were borne to the still unfinished Parliament building. During a solemn sitting the Law of the Millennium was pronounced. The two Houses paid homage to the King, and after his reply cannons fired a salute. As during the transfer of the crown after the death of Joseph II a century earlier, there was a hitch on this occasion: the aristocratic guardians of the crown could not open the badly rusted hasp and lock of the old iron chest. Other dignitaries also tried their hand, then their adjutants and servants, but in vain, and a locksmith had to be found who broke the chest open. The meticulously worked-out order of events, published in all the papers, got into an unholy mess. Opening the chest took an hour, and during that time rumours spread among the crowd of tens of thousands that something untoward had happened to the crown or to the King. Eventually all the festivities passed off successfully even if with some delay. Like almost thirty years earlier, masses of people assembled in the evening on the great open field under the Castle (Vérmező), where the wine ran in streams and oxen were roasted on giant spits.

Behind the brilliant façade of the Millennium festivities, however, the ancient sparks of conflict between the tradition of pagan tribal chiefs and the sacred function of the King crowned in the name of God—the conflict between Árpád and St Stephen—continued to smoulder. This came to the fore even more acutely—despite old Jókai's effusively loyalist stance and writings—two years later to the day on the occasion of the two "round" jubilees; "here" fifty years since the Revolution and War of Independence, "there" fifty years of Franz Joseph's reign. The fundamental conflict between the cult of the ruler—half-heartedly directed from above and, because of familiarity built up over decades, accepted from below— versus the national hero-worship embodied by Kossuth, to which the mass of the people clung, was insoluble.

The real feelings of the Prime Minister and ministers towards the monarch, whom they outwardly served so loyally and obsequiously, mostly remained hidden. What the writer Géza Gárdonyi confided to his diary on the day of the jubilee is all the more revealing:

Haven't donned tails. I looked on in disgust as the German family accepted the homage of "my Hungarians". The King like a bald vulture... I felt sick at the sight, had to lie down after lunch. In the evening at Bánffy's. We chatted about how the King had humiliated the Hungarian nation on this day. He suddenly paused, tears in his eyes. The same happened to me. Then I took the handkerchief from my eyes, and exclaimed "An Austrian scoundrel!" I felt that it didn't matter if they hanged me for it. But Bánffy had already risen and was looking out of the window, as if he hadn't heard my remark… I bowed and left.[3]

It speaks volumes that on such a day such a conversation could take place in the Hungarian Prime Minister's study, and that Bánffy, a disciplinarian from Transylvania who did not care what means he used to suppress protests and opposition to the government, passed over this passionate outburst against the King in silence. It testifies to the wounds reaching to the deepest levels of consciousness and festering in the souls of so many Magyars.

But to the very end the relationship with Queen Elisabeth was different. Although for many years she had been in flight from the Court (and from herself), and completely removed from politics, during the *Te Deum* she fought back tears under her black veil when listening to the Prince-Primate's thanks on behalf of the nation for "having with her maternal, delicate hand once woven the golden band by which the Magyar people and their dearly beloved King were now inseparably bound together."

When two years later, in the critical year 1898, an Italian anarchist stabbed Elisabeth in Geneva, the entire Hungarian nation grieved. In Hungary Sisi was such a popular and legendary figure that, with the King's agreement, a small museum was established for her in the Castle. Even during the decades of Communism her memory was never eradicated. And it was a widely noted sign of easing of the Habsburg question, and a growing political relaxation, when her statue was re-erected in the 1970s near the bridge in Budapest that bears her name.

The Millennium Exhibition was not only a declaration of continuity and of the Hungarian nation's independence; it also advertised the meteoric rise of the Hungarian economy, technology and culture. Only economic historians and economists of our day, without nationalist blinkers, could assess and describe the true dimensions of this general upswing. According to contemporary newspaper reports and books, 3.3 million people perceived the Exhibition as some sort of revelation. To large sections of the population it showed that, barely thirty years after the Compromise and half a century after the lost War of Independence, Hungary and in particular its recently united capital were riding on the crest of the wave. For decades it had been a truism that Hungary was something like a "glorified colony". Even an open-minded liberal such as Oszkár Jászi described Vienna in his work on the Monarchy as "an economic tyranny, which had hindered the progress of the Hungarian, Slav and Romanian territories of the Monarchy... and stood in the way of the people's welfare". Other Hungarian writers have also claimed that Hungary was being plundered by Austria through the uneven exchange of goods. Today most economic historians, Hungarians included, reject this thesis and assert that both Austria and Hungary profited from the Compromise.

Estimates of the tempo of economic development differ widely.[4] Thus the first comprehensive study (by Iván Berend and György Ránki) established that the annual growth-rate of the national income between 1867 and 1914 was 3.2 per cent, representing a fourfold increase during that period. Other surveys (László Katus) took the gross national product (GNP) as a basis according to which, at an annual growth rate of 2.4 per cent, the GNP tripled during the same period. The annual growth rate per person of 1.7 per cent was higher than the European average, and only surpassed by Germany, Denmark and Sweden. Of course, in international terms Hungary still lagged far behind Western and Central European countries. *Per capita* income before the Great War was half that of Germany and France and amounted to only 85 per cent of the Austrian level. Calculations from 1920 (after the loss of two-thirds of the country's territory and almost three-quarters of its population), revealed a per capita GNP (*ca.* US$ 372) 31 per cent below the European average and 52 per cent below that of Germany.

As a result of its fast growth, Hungary was on the way from being a purely agrarian country to a semi-industrial one. The ratio of purely agricultural goods fell from 80 to 56 per cent of GNP, while mining, industry and crafts rose from 18.4 to 30.4 per cent and trade and transportation almost doubled from 7.2 to 13.2 per cent. All this naturally involved considerable shifts in the employment pattern: between 1869 and 1910 the proportion of people active in agriculture fell from 75 to 60 per cent, while that of people employed in industry and mining rose from 10 to 18.3 per cent, in trade and transportation from 1.9 to 6 per cent and in other services from 13 to 15.6 per cent.

Hungary's economy achieved significant results not only in absolute terms, but also relative to Austria. In 1841 Hungary produced 41.9 per cent of the Monarchy's agricultural output and in 1911 47.8 per cent. Its share of the total Austro-Hungarian industrial production had grown steadily from 21.5 per cent in 1841, 23.5 per cent in 1858 and 28.2 per cent in 1913. Although Hungary lagged considerably behind Austria on the eve of the Great War, the long-term trend was towards a reduced disparity between the development levels. Of Hungary's total foreign trade 75–80 per cent was with the western half of the Monarchy.

Foreign capital's interest in Hungary, hinted at in Deák's speech already quoted, played a major role in industrialization and modernization. About half of the foreign capital—8 billion crowns—invested in the Hungarian economy between 1867 and 1914 originated from Cisleithania. The major targets of investment were the railways and industrial plants, but also large estates and banks.

Railway building was one of the driving forces of modernization, and in 1867–1913 the network grew from 2,200 to 22,000 km. The dynamic Minister of Transport, Gábor Baross, reformed the entire transport system; fares were cleverly re-graded and travelling times decreased, resulting in a large growth in passenger and goods traffic. At the beginning of the twentieth century the Vienna to Budapest leg of the journey in the famed Orient Express took only forty minutes longer than an international express in the 1980s. Their present sad state notwithstanding, the two great Budapest rail terminals, the West and East stations (completed in 1878 and 1883 respectively), were in their time among the largest and most modern in Europe.

The influx of foreign capital was also reflected in the dramatic rise in banking. The number of banks and savings and credit bodies increased from 107 in 1867 to 2,700 at the turn of the century and had almost doubled again by 1913. While capital investment had amounted to no more than 17 million crowns at the time of the Compromise, by 1900 it had reached 2.5 billion and by 1913

6.6 billion crowns. Banks such as the Hungarian Commercial and the Hungarian Credit Bank enjoyed a Europe-wide reputation, and their general managers were in the same league as international bankers. Five big banks held 58 per cent of the banking sector's total capital, and after the Second World War their palatial buildings served among others as the British embassy, the temporary headquarters of the Communist Party, and (still today) the seat of the once-feared Ministry of the Interior. At the outset of vigorous industrialization foreign investors controlled two-thirds of Hungarian industry—by 1900 this had dropped to 50 per cent and before the outbreak of the Great War to one-third. The concentration of heavy industry was significant even in the early stages; less than 1 per cent of enterprises employed 44 per cent of industrial workers and delivered almost two-thirds of total production.

However, the infrastructure was less favourable than in Austria and the value of Austrian industrial production was still almost three times that of the Hungarian. The *per capita* net national product in 1913 totalled 435 crowns in Hungary and 516 in Cisleithania: in the territory of today's Austria it was 790 crowns. After 1920 Hungary could only show 521.[5] Clearly there was a trend towards the Austrian economic level, but in spite of everything a manifest backwardness as well. Hungary, though not exploited by the western half of the empire, had to adjust to the advantages and disadvantages of the Monarchy in its efforts at modernization, and that in turn meant cementing the precedence of agriculture and an unhealthy social structure, especially on the land.

Despite the dynamic development of industry, finance and transport, the upswing was confined mainly to Budapest, which became *par excellence* the workshop of embourgeoisement. The combination of three towns—still separate in 1848—to became the capital of Hungary happened with astonishing speed. At the beginning of the 19th century it had less than 60,000 inhabitants (Vienna then had more than a 250,000) but by 1914 it had emerged as the seventh-largest European metropolis with a population of over a million. But this could not hide the fact of the country's feudal social structure and agrarian-peasant character. As Jászi made clear,[6] in no other country apart from Poland before its partition in 1793–5 and Russia did the feudal church and nobility so dominate economic and political life or possess such power. Between 1867 and 1914 over one-third of the country was still in the hands of ecclesiastical and lay landowners. According to Count Mihály Károlyi, President of the First Republic, in 1818–19 324 landowners owned 20 per cent of the arable land with an average of 20,000 to 25,000 hectares each. The Catholic Church owned about one million hectares of land, and the Archbishops of Esztergom and Kalocsa and the Bishop of Nagyvárad had over 10,000 day-labourers at their disposal.[7]

The richest magnates lived in a luxurious world of their own which is almost unimaginable today, secluded even from the middle nobility. Quite a number of the few hundred aristocrats were not of Hungarian stock, prompting Szekfü to write: "There was scarcely a privy councillor, general or courtier of German and Italian extraction who did not succeed in becoming lord of a large estate in Hungary with thousands of hectares. We know of 250 such foreign families before 1715." The Counts Schönborn, the Prince of Coburg-Gotha and Austrian archdukes organized their immense estates as *fideicommissa*—indivisible family possessions to be bequeathed to descendants in the male line.

The wealth of many of these 2,000 big landowners, 800 of them aristocrats, was so great that they did not even know what they actually owned, or where it was. Most of them spent more time in Vienna and Paris, at the Ascot horse races in England, or at the Court in Schönbrunn than in Hungary. Prince Esterházy owned more than 300,000 hectares of land from Lake Fertö to the Great Hungarian Plain: at the height of their power the Esterházys possessed more than 700 villages and 21 palaces.[8]

Károlyi too came from one of the greatest aristocratic families, who were the only Hungarian family with the right to have eleven points in their coronets instead of the nine that were customary for counts. He himself owned 13,000 hectares of forest and 17,000 hectares of meadow and arable land, several hunting grounds, a mansion with seventy-five rooms in the inner city of Budapest, a coal mine and the estate of Parád which was turned into a spa because of its health-giving waters. According to his own estimates, his holdings had a value of about 100 million gold forints.[9] Mihály Károlyi once asked his friend Prince Sándor Esterházy for his opinion of one of Gerhard Hauptmann's recent novels. The magnate, who later became Queen Zita's court chamberlain, replied without hesitation: "I somehow cannot get interested in the private lives and love entanglements of people whom I have never met. Hauptmann mostly writes about professors, architects, doctors and that kind of person." To him "that kind of person" represented a big grey mass, as Károlyi wrote in his memoirs. When the Prince of Wales came to Hungary to shoot and stayed at the house of a well-known Jewish banker, the brother of Károlyi's stepmother, Count Miklós Pálffy declined an invitation to a reception there for the Prince with the remark that he would not set foot inside a Jewish house. In a conversation with the German consul-general in Budapest at the beginning of the twentieth century, another Count Károlyi (not the "black sheep" of the family to whom we shall return later) aptly expressed the mentality of the high nobility. At the end of his visit to the family château, the German guest asked him why the members of the Károlyi family who lived there played no musical instruments. The Count promptly answered that that was the job of the Gypsies. "Just as we keep gypsies to play music, because we are too lazy to do it ourselves, we also keep Jews to do our work for us."[10]

The nobility's claim to their leading role goes back, as already mentioned, to the jurist Werbőczy. They drew political-power themselves: they alone, as laid down in the so-called *Tripartitum* of 1514, constituted the "*populus*", who controlled the peasantry, the "*misera plebs contribuens*", without restriction. This traditional aristocratic system of values, which remained largely unaltered despite the great reform generation of Széchenyi, Eötvös, Deák and Kossuth and the Revolution of 1848, was in many ways incompatible with the development of a middle class and modernization. Thus Baron Zsigmond Kemény, writer and politician during and after the 1848 Revolution (incidentally one of those originally responsible for Kossuth's "demonizing"), stressed that although in the modern economy everyone was motivated by his own interests, "the egotism of the upper bourgeoisie is often tinged with cosmopolitanism, while the egotism of the landowner is often cloaked in higher patriotism." The notable liberal Károly Eötvös (the defending advocate in the notorious ritual murder trial of Tiszaeszlár,* who exposed the

---

* This was the most notorious blood libel case in Hungarian history. The suicide of a fourteen-year-old girl in the village of Tiszaeszlar in April 1882 was taken as a pretext for a ritual murder trial on trumped-up charges. It set off waves of violent anti-Jewish incidents even after the acquittal of all the accused in August 1883.

manipulations behind the prosecution and secured the release of the accused) shared this opinion: the German and Jewish merchant or banker strives for capital, while the Hungarian nobleman strives for landholdings.[11]

And Péter Hanák emphasized in his book *Der Garten und die Werkstatt* (The garden and the workshop):

The Hungarian national consciousness and national character were determined by the leading figures of the nobility. At the acme of the traditional system of values was the ownership and cultivation of land, giving power over a legion of subjects, farm-hands, servants and livestock, which went with horse-breeding and racing, the breeding of dogs and hunting. Beyond these the only occupations appropriate to their rank were national or county politics, the military, the diplomatic service, and the Church. Commerce, trade, speculation with money and goods, banking and generally any "business activity" had no place in the noble scheme of things. [...] The "Hungarian" left it to the Greeks, Serbs, Germans and Jews to trade, but then he looked askance on them and despised them if they enriched themselves in the process.[12]

This way of life and thinking was characteristic not only of the apex of the aristocratic hierarchy. One has to start from the fact that about 6 per cent of the total population in Hungary and Transylvania and 12–13 per cent of Magyars were members of the nobility. The majority of these were poor peasant- or "sandalled" nobles, artisans or intelligentsia without land. Most of the petty nobles, who had no servants and tilled their smallholdings on a peasant level, fell victim to modernization after the Compromise. Among the 30,000 noble families there were, apart from the 2,000 or so great landowners, about 7,000 "middle" landowners with 100–500 hectares of land (4–5,000 belonged to the nobility); in 1910 they owned a total of more than 7 million hectares. These families, especially the so-called "1,000-*hold* gentlemen", who owned at least 575 hectares (1 "hold" = 0.5754 hectare), regarded themselves as the nation's only truly qualified representatives.[13]

During the entire Dualist period the high nobility dominated politics. Of the fifteen prime ministers nine were aristocrats and four noble landowners, and only two came from bourgeois stock. Sándor Wekerle, of German origin, was Hungary's first non-noble politician to reach the highest office. Aristocrats and landholding middle and petty nobility comprised 44 per cent of government ministers between 1867 and 1914. The "1,000-*hold* gentlemen" were the connecting link between the high nobility and the landed middle and petty nobility (since 1875 called the "gentry", a term borrowed from England), who were frequently debt-ridden and impoverished. A third of the leading county officials also came from that class. Members of the gentry played a dominant role in parliament (48 per cent) and among the chief officials of the counties (58–77 per cent), as well as in the magistracy and the officer corps.[14]

The so-called "gentlemen", the "historic", later "Christian gentlemanly middle class", consisted not, as in other countries, of self-assured burghers but at first almost exclusively, and even later as the majority of the 500,000 or so members of the gentry. The impoverished middle and lesser nobility who had wholly or partly lost their estates found a comfortable haven in the expanding national, metropolitan and county bureaucracy.

Hungary differed fundamentally from other European countries where the situation of the nobility was concerned. Whereas in the mid-nineteenth century in Bohemia the ratio of nobles to commoners was 828:1, in the Alpine regions (today's Austria) 350:1 and in Lombardy and Venice 300:1, in Hungary this figure was 16:1 and among the Magyars an astonishing 8:1. No wonder then that members of this large section of the population, with their nationalism and historically conditioned haughtiness and arrogance, became the objects of literary preoccupation. Their prejudices, superiority complex, snobbery, frivolity and addiction to gambling—"the amplitude of their pretensions and the emptyness of their purses"—provided fertile material even for great writers of the epoch such as Kálmán Mikszáth and Zsigmond Móricz. The lavish hospitality of noble families, their tendency to cheerful-melancholy *mulatság* (boisterous partying where the smashing of crockery was something of a ritual), garnished with Gypsy music, and their modest quota of work in public service—as a rule four to five hours a day—were satirized in cabarets, revues, operettas and, later, films.[15]

The fact that the Hungarian and *k.u.k.* civil service was divided into twelve grades, with aristocrats at the top levels and the gentry between levels 4 and 9–10, was complicated enough. But the forms of address for the various ranks from above to below and *vice versa* were elaborate in the extreme. In the civil service the proper appellation for an official of the highest rank was *kegyelmes* (Gracious Sir or Madam); the next grade was *nagyméltóságu* (Excellency); for grades 3–5 *méltóságos* (Dignified); further down the scale *nagyságos* (Great); and for grades 10–11 *tekintetes* (Respectable). There were other graded titles for the clergy, for young and old landowners, and even for simple peasants (*kend*). Moreover, the Hungarian language has three forms of address (*Te, Maga, Ön*—the last a polite, even lofty form allegedly invented, or at least disseminated, by Széchenyi). The proper form of address and choice of language to use *vis-à-vis* members of various social strata has remained a sensitive matter to this day.[16]

The concepts of chivalry, bravery and honour, originating in knightly traditions, belonged to the image of the gentry and the general codex of Hungarian norms of conduct, and provided the basis for the social evil of duelling which was spreading even during the epoch of embourgeoisement. Kálmán Mikszáth (1847–1910), the leading novelist of the late nineteenth century, once wrote: "A Member of Parliament is easily identifiable: he is occupied with a duelling affair, involving either himself or an important friend." The first question to be answered was always whether the opponent's rank or station was compatible with one's own, i.e. whether he was "capable of giving satisfaction". Then came the question of seconds and the choice of weapons (sabres or pistols), and the time and place of the confrontation. Although duelling had been prohibited by law since 1878, duellers were treated as having committed mere peccadillos, and prison warders in charge of them functioned more as servants of their exalted prisoners. In his monumental history of the Jews in Hungary, the Hungarian–American professor of Judaic Studies, Raphael Patai, reported with grudging pride that in 1888 nine out of the seventy-one individuals convicted of duelling (13 per cent) were Jews, i.e. three times as many as the percentage of Jews in the population.[17]

Despite the economic decline of the majority of noble families, the gentry left their mark on the manners and lifestyle of the rising upper and middle bourgeoisie. According to various estimates, alongside the aristocrats and noble landowners, an upper middle class of about 800 to 1,000 families was quickly developing. Its core consisted of the often intermarried and, since the Compromise, ennobled 100–150 families who controlled the banks and the most important branches of industry. During the period of Dualism Franz Joseph and his successor Charles raised to noble rank about 2,000 families, quite a number of them Germans, Greeks, Swiss and Serbs living in Hungary who had made names for themselves in commerce or the army.

Before 1918, 346 Jewish patrician families acquired titles of nobility (including twenty-eight baronies), and most of them bought landholdings. Before the Great War a fifth of the land was in Jewish ownership, and a considerable part of the great landed estates had Jewish leaseholders. The financial bourgeoisie consisted in the first place of Jews, who at the turn of the century held about 55 per cent of the key positions in banks, the stock exchange and industry. However, an unwritten pact with the high nobility ensured that their socio-political influence remained insignificant. At the same time, representatives of the aristocracy took on key positions in the fast developing capitalist economy. The symbiosis of the feudal Estates and the "financial aristocracy" is best illustrated by the families of Counts Zichy and Széchenyi and of Margrave Pallavicini, whose members held lucrative positions in thirty-four, twenty-nine and twenty-seven banks and industrial concerns respectively. The Hungarian nobleman accepted embourgeoisement, yet he clung to the traditional system of values and would never have dreamed of adopting the capitalistic principle of hard work and ruthless money-making.[18]

Lajos Hatvany hit out at the flight of the gentry into the world of make-believe with the help of its many-tiered links to the higher administration:

The Hungarian gentry are blamed for being helpless. Unjustly so! Is there a greater achievement than to get by without working, to find daily sustenance everywhere? And if not everywhere, then in Vienna, where the modern Kuruc receives his necessary elixir. This was the strength of Prime Minister Tisza: he governed with Austrian help the feeble class of Hungarians, whom he mistook for the whole population...[19]

Hatvany himself was the scion of a wealthy Jewish flour- and sugar-milling and eventually banking dynasty, which was ennobled at an early stage and later raised to the rank of baron. However, Lajos was not a businessman but a highly gifted writer: besides founding an influential literary magazine *Nyugat* (The West), he also played an important role in Hungarian culture and literature as the generous sponsor of the two outstanding twentieth-century poets, Endre Ady and Attila József. The fact that after his courageous return from emigration in 1928 (he had been a comrade-in-arms of Károlyi before the 1918 bourgeois revolution, but had no part in the subsequent Communist regime) Baron Hatvany was condemned to seven years' imprisonment for "defaming" the nation adds a symbolic footnote to the history of the inter-war years.

The Viennese view of the gentry's image was similar to Hatvany's sarcastic sketch, as shown by the colloquial but apt remarks about the Hungarians by the Austrian writer Otto Friedländer:

A real Hungarian will only become an innkeeper, politician or soldier. Never a writer, manual worker or merchant. The Swabians and Jews are the officials, industrialists and traders. The real Hungarian is a gentleman or a peasant, and nothing else. It is certainly an achievement that these few real Hungarians have managed to turn the culturally superior Germans and Jews into chauvinistic Magyars. However, one has to bear in mind that Hungarian gentlemen could not live for a single day without the labour of the German officials, the Jewish merchants and the Slav manual workers— but they are after all gentlemen. Yes, they are gentlemen—but in quite a different way. They rule over their estates, in their rural counties. They are great, great, powerful gentlemen, the Hungarian magnates, mighty orators, fearless fighters—perhaps the last gentlemen existing in this world... who have received their greatness, strength and the magnificence of their might by the Grace of God—bestowed on them without a struggle, without the sweat of their brows, as a distinction and as a duty.[20]

As a result of the Estate-based structure and the inherited feudal self-image, two big dividing lines evolved between the "historic" (read "Christian") and assimilated bourgeois (read "Jewish") social classes on the one hand, and the so-called "gentlemanly middle class" and the lower orders, i.e. the people, on the other. "In Hungary the spirit of the caste system is still in full bloom as far as the gentleman and the peasant are concerned. The gentleman sees the peasant not as a person, but in line with the old caste conception as half a head of cattle." These words were spoken not by a radical agitator but by a Catholic bishop of Slovak origin, Ottokár Prohászka, in 1899. He subsequently became a leading Hungarian nationalist and spokesman for the "Christian awakening" movement. This concept served "modern" anti-Semitism as a standard catchword.[21]

Nonetheless, Prohászka's words reflected the miserable reality on the land. Although the regulation of rivers (the "second Conquest") increased arable land by 3.9 million hectares, peasant landholdings in 1914 did not even amount to half of the country's total area. A third of the peasants were semi-proletarians with mini-holdings of less than three hectares. The large size of the agrarian proletariat was a special characteristic of Hungarian society. In 1910 there were 3 million poor peasants and, with the addition of the semi-proletarians, this rose to almost 4 million. The majority of these were seasonal workers and day labourers. Destitution increased around 1890 when the large-scale excavations for the regulation of rivers and railway building ceased, while at the same time the spread of threshing machines and modern ploughs cut back the need for agricultural labourers. The impoverishment of this sector forced many of them to migrate, and the critical state of those remaining on the land led to the great agrarian-socialist movements in the region between the Tisza and Maros rivers in south-eastern Hungary. Embourgeoisement of peasants occurred only in western Transdanubia and the agrarian towns of the Great Plains.

In the nineteenth century certain agrarian communities (market towns) developed in the Plains such as were to be seen nowhere else in Western and Central Europe: giant villages with 20–30,000 inhabitants; Debrecen, Kecskemét or Hódmezővásárhely were prototypes of this kind of settlement. A third if not half of the inhabitants of these "towns" lived outside the urban core on individual farms.[22]

Another characteristic form of settlement of agrarian labourers was the so-called "puszta" or leasehold farm, on which tens of thousands of labourers lived completely cut off from the rest of the world. One of the great Hungarian poets and dramatists of the twentieth century, Gyula Illyés, described in *People of the Puszta* the life and thinking of these people:

Almost half of Hungary's total arable land was tilled by the farmhands of the puszta. This class of people differed sharply from all others in their customs and habits, in their view of the world, even in their gait and the way they moved their arms. They lived as if concealed in total isolation, even if this was in the vicinity of a village. Because they were busy all day, even on Sundays, they almost never left the puszta; on the other hand, because of the great distances, bad roads, the specific Hungarian circumstances and their ingrained suspicions, it was harder to approach them than to research a Central African native tribe. The public at large began to devote its attention to them only after the Great War.[23]

At the beginning of the twentieth century approximately 15 per cent of Magyars lived on individual farms and on the puszta of the great landed estates, 30–35 per cent in cities and towns or market towns and 50–55 per cent in villages.

While the traditional order of village life, and above all the totally disproportionate property distribution passed on from feudal times, remained basically unchanged until 1918 (and was only marginally corrected between then and 1945), Budapest, as already briefly mentioned, became a dynamically growing industrial centre with 880,000 inhabitants (or, if one includes the suburbs, more than 1.1 million). Perhaps in no other European country was the unfolding of modern industry and finance capitalism so strongly concentrated in the capital as in Hungary. In 1910 Greater Budapest represented only 5.1 per cent of the total population, but housed 28 per cent of factory workers and two-thirds of major enterprises; 62 per cent of the country's banking assets were to be found in the safes of its financial institutions. Budapest was the city not only of 600 coffee houses, forty brothels and the largest number of flourmills in the world, but also of slums inhabited by casual and unskilled workers and day labourers, mostly Slovaks and Germans. At the turn of the century a quarter of the population lived in miserable and over-crowded conditions.[24] Even during the elation of the Millennium festivities the deputy Károly Váradi reminded the plenary meeting of Parliament of the petition of the Budapest bakers:

Although apprentices who are younger than fourteen are only allowed by law to work ten hours and under the age of sixteen twelve hours, there are many bakeries where five or six apprentices are forced to work sixteen to eighteen hours a day. The adult workers also complain that nine persons have to share three beds and that the masters distribute only two towels a week for eight workers.[25]

From the viewpoint of Hungarian supremacy it was important that in 1910 86 per cent of the inhabitants of Budapest officially used

Hungarian as their mother tongue. In 1880 the figure had been 58.6 and in 1850 a mere one-third. With twenty-two daily newspapers, five of them German, Budapest was also the newspaper metropolis of the time. In the number of students its University was the second largest in the Monarchy and the fifth largest in Europe—bearing in mind that in 1850 there had only been 810 Magyar secondary school students in the Dual Monarchy; by 1914 the figure had risen to 16,300.[26]

Budapest was a double symbol of Magyarization and embourgeoisement in the spirit of modernization. In addition to the assimilation of locally-born or long-resident German burghers, the settlement and assimilation of Jews contributed greatly to this development. The population proportion of Magyars in 252 localities with over 5,000 inhabitants reached 63.5 per cent by 1880 while the countrywide average was only 46.6 per cent; this was due to the unforced and even enthusiastic assimilation of the Jews, who in 1910 accounted for 12.4 per cent of town dwellers and in Budapest even for 23 per cent, although the Jewish share of the total population was only 4.5 per cent.

Magyarization was a sweeping success. Between 1880 and 1910, according to statistics, approximately 700,000 Jews, 600,000 Germans, 400,000 Slovaks, 100,000 Romanians, 100,000 South Slavs and 100,000 persons of other origins declared themselves to be Hungarians.[27] Without this "demographic revolution" the rapid rise of the capital and blossoming of commerce, culture, the media and science would hardly have been possible. The Hungarian-Jewish symbiosis was in every way the essential cement for Hungary's national, political, economic and cultural position within the Monarchy. This was not merely a matter of statistics. This emotion-tinged relationship can be compared only to the German-Jewish one. The predominant part of Hungarian Jews were virtually "infatuated" with Hungary, just as the German Jews were with Germany (Sebastian Haffner).[28] But of course in both cases the "relationship" contained a fatal flaw: it was one-sided.

28. "Magyar Jew or Jewish Magyar?" A Unique Symbiosis

"There is no other example in all of the eastern part of Central Europe of such complete, rapid and, to all appearances, successful assimilation and equality as that of the Hungarian Jews."[1] Robert A. Kann wrote this in 1945, *after* the destruction of European Jewry. Of course, this phenomenon was also noted by those with an opposite standpoint. Thus the anti-Semitic mayor of Vienna, Karl Lueger, had invented the expressions "Judaeo-Magyars" and "Judapest" as early as the turn of the century. "I coined the word Judaeo-Magyarism and I am still proud today that I thought of something so clever at the time," he said later of "the connection between the two evils of the Empire".[2] The well-known crude attacks on the "gravediggers" of the Monarchy had an accurate core, insofar as they pointed to the quantitative and not qualitative aspects of the Magyar-Jewish relationship. Although similar processes of assimilation took place in Germany to those in Austria, Austrian anti-Semites would never have thought of talking of "Judaeo-Germans".

Rolf Fischer,[3] who for many years has investigated Hungarian anti-Semitism, correctly pointed out that the concept of "Judaeo-Magyar" emphasized a feature of the Magyar-Jewish symbiosis which before the Great War had no counterpart elsewhere in Central, Eastern and Southeastern Europe. The objective of the Jews who settled in Greater Hungary was clear from the outset: to be Hungarian citizens of the Jewish faith. Since, however, due to existing conditions the acknowledgment of Hungarianness was the politically decisive option, the question was "Hungarian Jew or Jewish Hungarian?"—as formulated a century and a half earlier by the Jewish schoolteacher at Pécs, Lipót Hartmann, in the title of his book. After the lost War of Independence and as a result of the Emancipation Act passed in 1867, an increasingly large section of the numerically fast-growing Jewry declared themselves "Magyars of Mosaic faith" or "Hungarians of the Israelite confession". Denomination was the determining factor of affiliation: the Jews were not a separate ethnic group or national minority but an integral part of the political nation—only their religion happened to be Mosaic.

This concept was legally sealed, though only in 1895, by the so-called *recepció* (the Magyarized form of Latin *receptio*), i.e. admission of Judaism among the legally recognized religions of Hungary. The consequence of this politico-legal solution was that the Jews no longer had to be identified in national statistics as a separate ethnic group. The "demographic revolution" in favour of the Magyars (mentioned earlier) would have been impossible without the mass of Jewish assimilants.

The great aim of Hungarian liberalism and of the liberal nobility who governed till 1918 was the complete civic and political equality of Jews with the Christian population, as proclaimed in Paragraph I of the Emancipation Law. Many experts in Jewish and Hungarian history stressed the uniqueness of the "Hungarian way". The issue was neither the nobility's charitable attitude nor a conspiracy by the Jews to usurp economic and financial power, as was argued later, and has continued to be to this day, by anti-Semitic ideologues. The singular relationship between Hungarians and Jews came about partly because already during the Revolution the Jews had identified themselves with the Magyar national cause, the Hungarian language and, to a great extent, Hungarian culture. And partly, too, Hungary needed people who were politically loyal and who tipped the balance statistically in favour of Magyardom within the lands of the crown of St Stephen. The following figures show what this meant for the consolidation of Hungarian national hegemony and the transformation of a relative statistical majority into an absolute one. Although Jews had lived in the Carpathian basin almost without interruption for 1,000 years, no massive immigration began till the eighteenth and nineteenth centuries. From 80,000 in 1787 their number had tripled by 1840 to 238,000. After the doubling of the Jewish congregation to about half a million during the years after the Compromise, it reached 911,000 in 1910—thus 5 per cent of Hungary's population (without Croatia-Slavonia) were Jews. More important yet, 705,000 or over 75 per cent of them declared

Hungarian to be their mother tongue, and no less than 7 per cent of Magyars belonged to the Jewish faith.[4]

Together with the Germans and Slovaks, the Jews formed the spearhead of Magyarization, and as such were consciously targeted by the noble political élite. The increase in the Jewish population was by no means the result of immigration alone. Especially in the last decades of the nineteenth century, their higher birthrate and stricter hygiene, which largely protected them from the consequences of the last great cholera epidemic in 1872–4, played important roles.

The upsurge of Budapest attracted Jewish merchants and traders, and later also skilled workers and intellectuals, to the metropolis, and they in turn contributed to it. Statistics demonstrate that due to their influx the proportion of Jews in the population rose from 13.8 per cent at the time of the 1848 Revolution to 23 per cent in 1910, or in absolute terms from 18,000 to 203,000; thus every fifth Jew in Hungary lived in the capital. In a private letter Crown Prince Rudolf called Hungary "the England of the East: a similarly free haven of enlightenment and progress". In Budapest there was "vitality, revival, self-assurance and confidence in the future, features which every liberal era can produce, and which can be observed here with pleasure and contentment, but which unfortunately are almost totally lacking on the other side of the black-and-yellow frontier posts".[5]

Not even the meteoric rise of the Jewish population can convey the true significance of Hungarian Jewry as the pioneers and mediators of economic and cultural change. Jews formed the major section of the middle class between, on the one hand, the landed aristocracy, the impoverished "gentry" and the state bureaucracy ruled by the latter, and, on the other, the millions of farm workers and smallholders. The free burgeoning of the cultural, scientific, financial and professional influence of the Jews was in no small measure responsible for Budapest becoming the greatest financial and media centre of Europe east of Vienna. Already in 1906 thirty-nine daily newspapers were being published there compared with twenty-four in Vienna, twenty-five in London and thirty-six in Berlin.

The linguistically and culturally Magyarized Jewish immigrants made a decisive contribution to the creation of a new bourgeoisie, acting as energizers of that process of modernization which brought about radical social change in the country's long-petrified structure, and which in the end inevitably affected everyone. The characteristics of such a rapidly rising urban middle-class society—such as a striving for change, success and achievement, and the questioning of existing values and deeply-rooted traditions—were frequently interpreted in overt and covert anti-Semitic writings and fictional characters as "typical Jewish attributes". No other "foreign" group had assimilated as rapidly as the Hungarian Jews, yet social discrimination against them lasted longest. Among researchers of this complex network of relationships, Viktor Karády has traced the contradictory threads of the process of assimilation, pointing out that even during the "successful" phases of assimilation only bilateral hypocrisy could deny or cover up the existing tensions.[6]

There can be no doubt that the starting point for the impressive social and cultural ascent of the Jews was their better-than-average education. In 1910, according to official statistics, 72 per cent of the population as a whole where literate; in the case of the Jews the proportion was 90 per cent. More than half of the students in secondary business schools and 23 per cent in high schools and other secondary schools were Jews, and before the Great War they accounted for 46 per cent of medical students, 27 per cent of law students and 33 per cent of students in technical colleges.

Jewish assimilation was far more rapid in Hungary than in the other states of Central and Eastern Europe. The Jews were simultaneously upholders of embourgeoisement and of the Magyarization which was so important politically. Their representation was particularly strong in the independent professions as a kind of surrogate middle class. In 1910 they provided almost half the lawyers and medical practitioners, over 40 per cent of journalists, a third of engineers and a quarter of artists and writers. It is true that the great Jewish banking and industrialist families largely controlled the financial system and industry, and that more than half the owners of commercial enterprises and 85 per cent of the directors and proprietors of financial institutions were Jews. These statistics were blown out of all proportion by the anti-Semites, who deliberately glossed over the fact that the capitalists, landowners and leaseholders represented as insignificant a portion of the Jewish community as the big landowners did among the non-Jewish Magyars. At the same time over 70 per cent of the gainfully employed Jews belonged to the lower middle class (38.3 per cent) and working class (34.4 per cent, of whom 16.4 per cent were industrial workers), while 20 per cent belonged to the professions and civil service. Yet the social structure of Jews was essentially different from that of the non-Jewish population—not only in regard to agriculture, which at the beginning of the twentieth century employed two-thirds of the total population but less than 5 per cent of Jews.[7] Moreover, Jewish participation in the political and administrative, central and local bureaucracy long remained minimal: in 1883 there were only ten Jews in the government apparatus, none in local administration and five in both Houses of Parliament.[8] Although the situation changed for the better in later decades, the "division of labour" between the political power of the aristocracy and gentry on the one side and the financial-industrial supremacy of the Jews on the other remained substantially the same. It was easier for a gifted man of Jewish origin, after converting to Christianity, to become a university professor, a nobleman or even (like the historian Vilmos Fraknói) a Catholic bishop than to attain a hierarchically insignificant but, in the eyes of the gentry, desirable position as a small-town magistrate or a member of one of the gentry's clubs.

Historians and sociologists have stressed the special conditions of the Jewish breakthrough in society and the economy:

From humble beginnings as moneylenders, grocers and retailers of livestock and agricultural produce, they used the generously offered opportunities for earning money which the gentry had ignored, demonstrated their willingness to be integrated, and consequently underwent linguistic assimilation from Yiddish to Magyar via German. Zionist ideas were relatively uncommon. The desire to advance socially by joining the emergent middle class, their gratitude for the law's protection and the wide scope for activity available to them turned them into convinced supporters of the idea of a Hungarian nation-state. Since most of the impoverished gentry and members of the nobility who were now forced to earn a living viewed the civil service as the only respectable form of employment, the Jews, now concentrated in the rapidly growing cities, did not represent competition for their positions and livelihood... The spread of a pro-Magyar nationalism among Jews in no way arose from opportunism, as in the case of other assimilated groups, but was fostered by a doubtless genuine sense

of allegiance to their adopted country which they often expressed with
enthusiasm.[9]

The anti-Semitic agitation between 1919 and 1945 (its roots were
clearly recognizable much earlier) sought to belittle the degree of
the Jews' assimilation and their profound emotional loyalty to the
Hungarian Fatherland by vague and manipulative concepts such as
the "deep Magyar race", the "Magyar soul" the "Magyar nation"
and the "Magyar genius", and to discredit the loyalty of outstanding
figures of cultural and scientific life as "mimicry". In his study of
anti-Semitism quoted earlier, Rolf Fischer rightly pointed out that
among those who were apt to apostrophize about the "Magyar
soul" there were typically many whose families had been denizens
of the German Black Forest or thereabouts only a few decades earlier.[10] Thus the literary historian (still quoted today) Julius von
Farkas (Gyula Farkas) made an abrupt about-turn when director of
the Hungarian Institute in Berlin and professor at the University of
Berlin during the Third Reich. In his book *During the Time of
Assimilation* he claimed that "the Magyars of good race have always
loathed the Jews, who have deserved this loathing". In a devastating
review of the book in 1940 the critic Aladár Komlós called this a
pitiful attempt by a "German assimilant", with the help of forged
quotations and by withholding facts, to prove retrospectively the
pernicious influence of Jewish writers and scientists since 1848—
and this in blatant contrast to Farkas's own history of Hungarian
literature published in Budapest only a few years previously. Farkas
also adopted an anti-Semitic tone in the Institute's Hungarian Year-
books, which he edited; in this way Sándor Eckhardt's essay, mentioned earlier, on the Hungarian image in Europe was carefully
"purged" in the German translation of quotations from Heine and
critical references to German influence.[11]

Because of these and similar examples of anti-Semitic propaganda it is necessary to recall how fruitful in many spheres the coexistence with Hungarian Jewry was for Hungarians as well. In his last
years Count Gyula Andrássy remarked, at the height of the anti-
Semitic agitation in connection with the notorious ritual blood
libel of Tiszaeszlár (1882), that he wished there were more Jews in
Hungary, not fewer. Prime Minister Kálmán Tisza described the
Jews at the time as "the most diligent and constructive part of the

Hungarian population". This unique double function of the Jews as the driving force of both modernization and Magyarization was the rationale behind the pact, which lasted till the collapse of the Monarchy, between the political élite of the liberal nobility and the successful Jews, who were loyal to the Hungarian state idea.

In the border areas of Hungary, where the nationalities were the majority, the Jewish Hungarians functioned virtually as outposts of Hungarian culture. In the Romanian and Slovak villages Jewish shopkeepers and country doctors were often the only people who spoke the Magyar language, and thus tended to become for better or worse the natural allies of the civil servants, gendarmes and other officials representing the government in Budapest.

The fate of these people, who belonged to the Hungarian cultural group and mostly spoke German as well, was to be particularly tragic in the subsequent period. They were, as before, targets of traditional social and religious anti-Semitism, and were doubly hated because they remained proud Hungarians even in the successor states of Romania (in its new enlarged form that included Transylvania), Czechoslovakia and Yugoslavia, and were, as a rule, not prepared to profess to being members of the majority among whom they then found themselves. Thus they had to pay a further price for being "Jewish Hungarians" when, some years later after the Vienna Award by the Axis powers and the re-annexation of the territories lost at Trianon, they were the first to be deported to Auschwitz in the spring of 1944.[12]

During the "golden era" of liberalism in Hungary the immigration and embourgeoisement of Jews was welcomed by the political and social élite for reasons of long-term interest. Even Szekfü, whose work *Three Generations*, written after the collapse of the Dual Monarchy, was by no means free of anti-Semitic prejudice, conceded that "without the establishment of factories by the Jews, Hungary would either have become a colony of Austrian capital or stagnated at the agrarian level of the 1860s."

It was entirely a pact of mutual interests. The first well-known Jewish poet and founder of the most important literary journal before the turn of the century, József Kiss, wrote a poem about "the blessed land of Hungary". The Jewish, German, Greek and other assimilants established the lucrative fields of finance, trade and

industry—at the conscious and express wish of the state and its supporting political class. This was naturally a sophisticated barter. The
political apparatus needed the modern economy for reasons of
power, status and prestige, and the individual members of the political élite asserted themselves through lucrative directorships and
membership of supervisory boards. For example, in 1896, according to official data, fifty-five Liberal deputies filled seventy-seven
positions in the railways and other transport enterprises, while a
further eighty-six Liberal politicians held 193 positions in banks
and various industries. However, the issue was not primarily one of
financial gain. The national factor was, as already mentioned, almost
a matter of life and death, because without the 5 per cent weight on
their side the Magyars would have entered the twentieth century as
a minority in their own country. In addition there was the matter
of political loyalty. In Budapest almost every second voter was a
Jew, and Liberal deputies were elected with impressive majorities
even when the voters in other constituencies took a stand against
the government.[13]

The governments of the day not only safeguarded conditions
favourable for the profitable development of Jewish firms, but made
philo-Semitism the hallmark of the liberal era. This was not just an
empty phrase; when in the 1880s a great anti-Semitic wave swept
the countries of Central Europe, Kálmán Tisza not only denounced
it as "shameful, barbaric and injurious to the national honour", but
also proceeded to use his party machine to undercut the electoral
support of the rising anti-Semitic party of the renegade deputy
Győző Istóczy. Moreover, it was at this very time that the finishing
touches were put to emancipation of the Jews by recognizing their
congregations as being on a basis of equality with the Catholic and
Protestant denominations. This was sealed by granting the Jewish
communities representation in the Upper House.

Independently of the early split of Hungarian Jewry into so-called
progressive and orthodox (the latter mostly but not exclusively in
Carpatho-Ruthenia and the northern borders of Transylvania),
Zionism remained a very small movement, static and almost imper-
ceptible. Nothing better illustrates the Jews' special relationship at
the time to the Hungarian state than the fact that in the native
country of Theodor Herzl and Max Nordau the ideas of these most

significant exponents of Zionism produced barely an echo. To the Hungarian Jews, a Jewish state in Palestine appeared neither necessary nor desirable. It is relevant in this context that in 1897 the number of Jewish reserve officers in the *k.u.k.* army, was 1,993, equal to almost a fifth of the entire reserve officer corps. While in Prussia no Jewish officer candidate was promoted to the reserve, the Austro-Hungarian army was willing to commission one-year volunteers as officers. It was a different story in the professional officers corps: also in 1897 there were only 178 Jewish professional officers, 1.2 per cent of the total. Documents cited by István Deák in his work on the *k.u.k.* army demonstrate[14] that the highest-ranking Jewish officer in the *k.u.k.* army, the Hungarian-born Field Marshal Eduard von Schweitzer, had never converted to Christianity. According to contemporary sources, old Schweitzer regularly attended the synagogue in Budapest, kept the rules of kosher food and, when dining with the Emperor, applied for permission from the religious authorities to be allowed to eat forbidden dishes.

The most successful officer of Jewish background served in the Hungarian *Honvédség*. Baron Samu Hazai (originally Kohn) was born in 1851, the son of a prosperous spirit merchant. He and his two brothers joined the *Honvéd* army as private soldiers. Hazai became a lieutenant in 1867, converting soon after to Christianity. He was promoted colonel on the general staff in 1900, becoming a general in 1907 and Hungarian Minister of Defence in 1910, in which capacity he served till 1917 when Emperor-King Charles promoted him to senior general and chief of the reserve troops for the entire armed forces. In this capacity Hazai was the officer next in importance to the Chief of the General Staff.

The Hungarian Jews proved their loyalty in the Great War, with 10,000 being killed in battle. Tens of thousands were wounded and many received high decorations for bravery. Besides Hazai there were a further twenty-four generals who were Jews or converts, and of these General Márton Zöld was one of the most decorated officers in the Army. Deák wrote: "The most gruesome paradox in the history of Central European Jewry is reflected in the medals and photographs of the front left behind by Jewish veterans of the Great War on the walls of their Aryanized apartments when they had to set out to the Third Reich on the way to the gas chambers."[15]

The bitter and, in hindsight, indisputable fact is that the more the Jews underwent Magyarization and westernization, the more they were confronted by envy, dislike and finally hatred. This reactive anti-Semitism was directed not, as has so often been claimed, against the "*Galizianer*", the eastern Jews—approximately 160,000 Yiddish-speaking orthodox Jews living mainly in the border regions of northern Hungary and Transylvania—but primarily against assimilated, successful and linguistically proficient Jews, and especially the Jewish middle class in the capital. The historian Ignác Acsády wrote: "Apart from the envious and prejudiced German petit bourgeoisie, the anti-Semitic movement found its strongest echo in the ranks of the economically distressed middle landowners. Unfortunately the enrichment of the Jews coincided with the impoverishment of the nobility."[16]

Unlike in most other European countries. Jewish entrepreneurs acquired more and more landed estates. Already before the Great War one-fifth of substantial holdings were owned by Jews, and—even more important—73 per cent of all big tenants were Jewish. A conservative deputy stated with remarkable bluntness in parliament: "The truth is, gentlemen, that if you have a gentile for a tenant he will come at the end of the year and appeal to your Christian brotherhood and mercy. On the other hand, you can be sure that your Jewish tenant will pay the rent even if his wife and children have to freeze or go without food."[17]

Theodor Herzl, who as a child wrote Hungarian letters to his father in Budapest, repeatedly quarrelled with patriotic Jews in his former hometown and regarded the disproportionately high share of Jewish agricultural landholdings and real estate as a great mistake. He went on to prophesy that virulent anti-Semitism would break out if the Liberal government, kept in power with the aid of Jewish capital, were to collapse.[18] The problem was made into the central theme of the anti-Semitic press, above all by spiteful caricatures in precursors of *Der Stürmer.* The Hungarian clerical comic paper *Herkó Pater* demonstrated in 1894 the change in the Jewish image and deep-seated paranoia as the cause of anti-Semitism. The Jewish peddler of the mid-nineteenth century was still a modest and diligent mendicant, treated contemptuously by the owner of the manor house, but by the end of the century the situation had been reversed:

the peddler had become a great landowner and the new master of the auctioned-off manor house, and was already wearing the braided coat and trousers of the impoverished gentry, smoking his pipe, and treating the erstwhile nobles arrogantly and disparagingly.[19]

After the turn of the century the sons and grandsons of successful entrepreneurs began to enter on the same course as the scions of the established German bourgeoisie. Within a decade the number of Jews in the administration rose from zero to 5.2 per cent, not including converts. In 1910 István Tisza's Parliament had eighty-four deputies, or 22 per cent of the total, of Jewish parentage. Conversion to Christianity represented a "ticket of admission". Besides General Hazai the number of ministers and secretaries of state of Jewish origin in the government reached five before the Great War. The Chief Burgomaster of Budapest from 1913, Ferenc Heltai, was incidentally Herzl's nephew.[20]

The consequences of assimilation, and above all of the fact that 346 converted Jewish families received titles of nobility—200 of these during the four years of the second Tisza government—opened the way to mixed marriages between prominent aristocratic families and Jewish high finance. Above and beyond figures and mere names, individual careers are what tell the true story of the vertiginously rapid change in the social position of the founders and descendants of famous families.[21]

When, after finishing his studies at the Yeshiva (Talmudic school), the young Moravian-born rabbi Aaron Chorin left Mattersburg in 1789 to settle in Arad, Transylvania, he would probably never have dreamed that his grandson Ferenc, who was two years old at Aaron's death, would become a key figure of Hungarian capitalism. Born in 1842 in Arad, Ferenc studied law in Budapest and abroad, and practised law in his home town, where he launched an anti-Habsburg daily, *Alföld* (The Plains). In 1867, at the young age of twenty-five, he was elected to Parliament as a representative of the left-centre, and as a fervent Hungarian patriot, for a while critical of the Compromise. Because Prime Minister Kálmán Tisza no longer insisted on the establishment of an independent Hungarian national bank, Chorin, by then a Liberal deputy, broke with the government party in 1875 and helped to organize the parliamentary opposition. Meanwhile he was also actively engaged as an industrialist and became involved in coal mining, and as president of the Salgótarján Mining Corporation eventually controlled 40 per cent of the country's total coal output. When he founded the National Association of Industries in 1901 the new conflict of interest law forced him to resign from the House.

After a quarter of a century in Parliament and attaining a leading position in the industrial world he decided, close to the age of sixty, to convert to Catholicism. This—to many—surprising step demonstrated the irresistible lure of the aristocracy: a baptismal certificate was equivalent to a passport to the sought-after clubs of the magnates and gentry. Two years later he was appointed a member of the Upper House, and the sons and daughters of the Chorin family married members of other rich and in part ennobled Jewish families. The great-grandson of the Arad rabbi played an outstanding role in Hungarian economic life, and between the World Wars belonged to the intimate circle of Regent Miklós Horthy, whose regime was jointly responsible for the downfall and eventual destruction of the greater part of Hungarian Jewry. Together with some other Jewish captains of industry, he stood by Horthy until the German occupation.

One of the most colourful and influential figures on the Hungarian economic scene was Zsigmond Kornfeld, born in 1852 in the Bohemian Golcuv Jenikov. As the son of a destitute family he had to support himself from the age of eleven as a clerk in a Prague bank, but by the age of twenty the gifted boy was already director in Vienna of the Böhmischer Bankverein and had close contacts with the Rothschild family, who in 1878 rescued the Hungarian General Credit Bank from insolvency and appointed Kornfeld as its general manager. That same year the young banker, with the Rothschilds' help, organized a loan of 150 million crowns for the all but bankrupt Hungarian state. On three later occasions—in 1881, 1888 and 1892—he arranged the extremely favourable conversion of the state debt for Hungary, with the result that the Credit Bank became the *de facto* Hungarian state bank. Under his aegis it became involved in railway, shipping and flour- and sugar-milling enterprises, as well as in the development of the port of Fiume and the expansion of the important Ganz Iron and Machinery Works.

In 1891 Kornfeld, who first came to Budapest at the age of twenty-six, became a member of the Budapest Stock Exchange and, having by now mastered the Hungarian language, came forward with a plan to Magyarize that institution. Such a patriotic attitude was deeply characteristic of the Jews of Hungary, including those of foreign birth—"an acquired but all the more cherished trait", as Raphael Patai put it in his chronicle of Hungarian Jewry. In 1899 Kornfeld was elected president of the Exchange, in 1902 he was appointed a member of the Upper House, and shortly before his death he was created a baron.

However, despite his manifold activities, Kornfeld remained a practising Jew; he was vice-president of the Neologs, the reformist Israelite congregation, and an active philanthropist. On the eve of the Russo-Japanese war of 1904–5 he negotiated a sizeable loan for the Russians on behalf of the Austro-Hungarian government, but refused the decoration which the Russians offered him, informing the Tsar's ambassador that he had conducted the negotiations as a banker at the request of his government, but that as a Jew he could not accept any mark of favour from a country in which Jews were persecuted and even massacred, as in the recent pogroms of 1903; he also refused remuneration for his part in the transaction. Having been deprived in his youth of the advantages of higher education, he sought the company of the greatest Jewish scholars of his time. That Zsigmond Kornfeld was a man of extraordinary talent cannot be denied; whether he could have had a similar career and achieved such nationwide importance in any country other than Hungary (and perhaps England) is an open question.

His son Baron Móric Kornfeld was likewise an industrialist: he made his name as general manager of the Ganz-Danubius machine factory and president of the National Association of Hungarian Ironworks and Machine Factories. He was also an art collector, a major donor to the Hungarian Academy of Sciences and, after conversion to Christianity, a member of the Upper House as well as the author of conservative-nationalist sociological studies.

The family Csepeli Weiss occupied a special place in the trio of the greatest Jewish capitalists. The first Weiss was in the 1820s a modest maker of pipes in an outlying district of Pest. His son Adolf worked as a travelling salesman trading in grain and spirits, and although he managed to send his youngest son Manfréd to a German university, he was neither prominent nor particularly prosperous.

The family became significant only after 1882, when Adolf's eldest son Berchtold founded Hungary's first meat-canning works in the vicinity of Budapest. After 1885 Berchtold and Manfréd acquired the family's first government contract, to fulfill the Hungarian share of provisioning the *k.u.k.* army with cans of goulash—soon the brothers manufactured other canned goods as well. In 1892 they established a munitions factory on the Danube island of Csepel, south of Budapest, which became so successful that Berchtold and Manfréd had to split their interests in it: Berthold dealt in textiles (his factory supplied the army with tents) and on the Corn Exchange, incidentally acquiring a seat in Parliament, and Manfréd founded a metal works with a view to gaining independence from foreign metal producers. He was ennobled by Franz Joseph in 1896, and King Charles conferred on him the title of baron. In the mean time had become a powerful armaments manufacturer. Manfréd's sons and daughters inter-married with members of the Kornfeld and Chorin families.

With these three families in the lead, ten originally Jewish but mostly converted family dynasties, closely related to each other and to some of the oldest noble houses, also dominated about half of Hungary's industry during the inter-war years. An anti-Semitic German writer had already identified between 1900 and 1918 twenty-six aristocrats with ancient lineages, whose wives stemmed from Jewish industrialist families. Thus, for example the wife of Prime Minister Baron Géza Fejérváry came from a Jewish family; the daughter of László Lukács married into the well-known Hatvani-Deutsch sugar dynasty; and so on.[22]

Their multifarious links with the aristocracy and above all their immense wealth enabled forty-seven members of the Weiss, Chorin, Kornfeld and Mauthner families to reach Portugal and Switzerland via Vienna and Stuttgart in the midst of the Nazis' extermination programme when it was running at full speed in Hungary during the spring of 1944. It was a complicated agreement, negotiated between the SS and the families without the knowledge of the Hungarian authorities or the German foreign ministry. With the concurrence of Heinrich Himmler, head of the SS, Standarten-führer Kurt Becher guaranteed them safe-conduct in exchange for 51 per cent of the shares held by the "Aryan" members of the families in the newly-founded "Property Management Company Ltd", whose core was the enormous Manfréd Weiss Works in Csepel, a heavy industrial armaments complex with 40,000 workers. The SS would act as trustees for a period of twenty-five years, receiving 5 per cent of the gross income as a fee. In accordance with the contract, signed on 17 May 1944, members of the families would receive from the SS US$ 600,000 and 250,000 Reichsmark. All the members of these families got away unscathed because of the prevailing "circumstances", but in the event the SS was unable to remit the greater part of the payment in US dollars.

The tug-of-war between the SS and the German Foreign Ministry, and the correspondence between the Hungarian government of the time—in a country already occupied and controlled by the Wehrmacht—the various German officials about the duration of the trusteeship and the appointment of Hungarian personnel—all this reads today like the scenario for a piece of "theatre of the absurd". Yet at the time the issue was the total handing-over of Hungary's industrial and, above all, munitions capacity to the Third Reich under the direction and control of the SS. While 437,401 Jews were being deported from Hungary to Auschwitz with seventy deportees packed into each cattle truck, members of the "family groups", as Chorin called them, strolled along the Bahnhofstrasse in Zurich and the avenues of Lisbon with Swiss and Portuguese visas forged by the SS in their passports. On 30 July 1944, just before the end of the deportations, the SS allowed 1,684 wealthy and prominent Jews to leave the country in an overcrowded train in the direction of Switzerland in exchange for $1,000 per person. Even during the darkest period of the history of Hungarian Jewry the Orwellian dictum held good: all were equal, yet some were more equal than the others. The deep divisions and the controversy—still alive today—over the role of the Jewish Council and its leading personalities (such as the Zionist leader Rezsö Kasztner, murdered in Israel in 1957) can be traced back to this period and the rescue of the rich.[23]

Of course, the role of the Jews was far from being confined to the economy and finance and the sometimes tragicomic attempts by the ennobled grandchildren of former innkeepers or rabbis to conform. From the very first, that is as early as the War of Independence of 1848–9, Jewish Hungarians had already found a new field of endeavour in the sciences, arts and literature. György Lukács, the son of an ennobled Jewish banker, made his name as a controversial Marxist philosopher, and Ferenc Molnár, an internationally popular playwright, feature prominently in German- and English-language studies of Central Europe or Hungary. Less well-known or almost forgotten are those who belonged to the "generation of giants" (to quote Aladár Komlós) in scholarship towards the end of the nineteenth century and the beginning of the twentieth.

No Hungarian Jew encountered so many humiliations or received so many honours as Ármin Vámbéry, the great orientalist. The congenitally lame scholar, born in 1832 at Dunaszerdahely in what is today Slovakia, described in his memoirs, first published in English, how he supported himself as a tailor's apprentice from the age of twelve. While working as a tutor he managed to put himself through his studies privately and pass the high school exam, mastering seven languages in the process (Latin, Hungarian, German, Slovak, Hebrew, French and Italian,[24] to which he later added Spanish, Danish and Swedish). He had a phenomenal memory and concentrated on Turkic, Arabic and Persian dialects because of his special interest in the origins of the Hungarians.

Vámbéry must have had a remarkably attractive personality, because when he was barely twenty-two the Minister of Education, Baron József Eötvös, provided him with a bursary to go to Constantinople where, soon after his arrival, the Foreign Minister of Turkey, Mehmet Fuad Pasha, employed him as his private secretary. He also won the sympathy of Sultan Abdülhamid II. In order to become fully accepted, he converted to Islam. During the six years he spent in Turkey he published a German-Turkish dictionary, and wrote several scholarly works. He became a member of the Hungarian Academy in 1860.

In 1861 Vámbéry set out disguised as a dervish on a seven-and-a-half-month voyage to Armenia, Persia, Afghanistan, Khiva, Bokhara and Turkestan, and in 1864 published, in English, *Travels and Adventures in Central Asia* about the languages, dialects, religions, folk customs and political systems he had encountered. While in Persia he established contacts with the British legation, and his reports on India and other countries were forwarded directly to the Prime

Minister Lord Palmerston. It was a slight to him that after his return he could only obtain funding from the Academy for a trip to England after personal intervention by Eötvös and in return for the deposit of his most valuable manuscripts. However, in England he was fêted and lionized; a frequent guest at Windsor Castle, he became personally acquainted with the Prince of Wales, the future King Edward VII. Allegiance to a religion was not one of his conspicuous attributes: in the East he was a Muslim and in the West he became a Christian in order to qualify himself for the professorship of oriental languages at the University of Budapest, which he held from 1864 to 1905. All the Hungarian scholars in this field were his students.

Despite his popularity abroad, whether in England or in Turkey, he always returned to Hungary. In one of the two autobiographies he wrote in English (published in 1885 and 1904) he tells us that when, on his return from Constantinople in 1862, he once again stepped on to Hungarian soil at Mohács he fell on his knees and with tears in his eyes kissed the ground of his homeland. But the cosmopolitan freethinker, who had regarded himself as a Hungarian patriot ever since childhood, soon came to realize that he was rated higher as a dervish than a loyal Hungarian. At home he saw himself surrounded by religious fanaticism, anti-Semitic prejudice and malicious insinuations, although he was world-renowned in academic and diplomatic circles. He willingly introduced Theodor Herzl to Sultan Abdülhamid at the former's request. When the Prince of Wales on a visit to Budapest asked after him, Vámbéry was immediately offered membership of the most exclusive clubs and casinos. When the Prince noticed that his friend was not treated by the Hungarian aristocracy with the respect extended to him in England, he gave a reception and entered the hall arm-in-arm with "his friend", Ármin Vámbéry.

"A Jew cannot be a Hungarian in Hungary, although I have long been an agnostic and researched the origins of the Hungarian language at the risk of my life," Vámbéry wrote in his autobiography. Once, when he was a guest of Queen Victoria, the heir to the throne brought him a jug of water. "Not bad, I thought to myself: a prince waits upon a former Jewish pauper." And in Paris too, where Napoleon III granted him a long audience, his experiences contrasted diametrically with his often insulting treatment in his homeland. Nonetheless, the most famous Hungarian author of his time, Mór Jókai, replied when asked what was his favourite reading matter: "The Bible, Shakespeare and Vámbéry". In the eyes of the literary historian Komlós, the fate of Vámbéry, despite all his successes, symbolized the failure rather than the success of assimilation.

Heine's adage "The certificate of baptism is the admission ticket to European culture" held good in Hungary throughout the nineteenth century, as is demonstrated by the all but incredible fate of the child-prodigy Ignáz Goldziher, born at Székesfehérvár in 1850. At the age of twelve he published a study of the origins and composition of the Hebrew sermons (the printing costs were paid by his father), and four years later was admitted by Vámbéry as his student. After earning his doctorate in Leipzig and further studies at Oxford and Cambridge, Goldziher became a *privatdozent* (honorary lecturer) at the University of Budapest. With a bursary granted by Minister Eötvös, he set out on a journey to Damascus and Cairo where, in contrast to Vámbéry, he openly identified himself as a Jew, and was still admitted to the highest institute of religious studies in the Muslim world. Goldziher's mastery of Arabic and knowledge of Islamic religious philosophy and jurisprudence astounded his Egyptian colleagues. Meanwhile he learned not only Turkic and Persian dialects but also Sanskrit and Russian.

Still, after his return Goldziher could not, as a Jew, secure a professorship at the University of Budapest (a *privatdozent* could give lectures but received no salary), and was forced to work for thirty years as secretary to the Israelite Congregation of Pest, until in 1905 he was finally given a chair. During his interminable service at the Israelite Congregation he came to regard his employers as vulgar, ignorant and contemptible. Yet he rejected all the invitations he received—from Vienna, Prague, Leiden, Berlin, Oxford and Cambridge—preferring to continue his "slavery" in Budapest. One wonders whether this will-power had anything to do with his Hungarian patriotism. Be that as it may, Goldziher wrote his great works, almost all in German, during these years of having to work for eight to ten hours a day for "idiotic" employers. He was elected to all the scientific academies in Europe, including that of Hungary. Such was the size of his literary output that one of his students, compiling a bibliography in Paris, listed 580 books and major studies. Nonetheless his diaries, "purged" by his wife and published only fifty years after his death, reveal a pathologically jealous, almost paranoid man, who fell in love with his own daughter-in-law and had only venomous things to say of his no less gifted colleagues, not least his former mentor Vámbéry whom he called a "*Schwindelderwisch*" (fake dervish).

Two other eminent but less renowned scholars and former students of Vámbéry, Ignác Kúnos and Bernát Munkácsi, published pioneering works on the Turkic languages and the Ural-Altaic connections of the Hungarians, the Ostyaks, Chuvash and Vogul people, in Hungarian, and co-founded an important international orientalist journal. Yet these two talented scholars also failed to receive their due. Kúnos was fifty-eight when, in 1918, he was finally appointed professor in Budapest, and retired a mere two years later, possibly because of the rampantly anti-Semitic atmosphere of the time. His colleague Munkácsi was elected a member of the Academy, but never received a chair at the University. Today these two are considered almost of equal status with Vámbéry and Goldziher. The Finno-Ugrian roots of the Hungarian language are nevertheless questioned and even denied by nationalistic and narrow-minded pseudo-scholars and charlatans—not least, concludes Károly Rédei, Professor of Finno-Ugrian studies at the University of Vienna, because most of the greatest linguists in that field were of Jewish or German origin.[25] In this company Sándor Kőrösi Csoma (1784–1842), the great Tibetologist from Transylvania, should not be overlooked.

29. "Will Hungary become German or Magyar?" The Germans' Peculiar Role

No other foreign author has ever provoked so much indignation in Hungary with a single book as the Munich University professor Franz von Löher with his *The Magyars and other Hungarians*, published in 1874.[1] Only direct quotes can do justice to his outrageous insolence, which characterized the whole anti-Hungarian campaign of the 1870s and '80s, and which had long-term effects on the Hungarian image in German-speaking countries:

There is not a single cultural idea—whether in the laws, the military and the state, in religion and customs, in art and science, or any other field—nor is there even some odd product of industry or trade—which would have found its way from Hungary to the educated world. It is a curious trait of the Magyars that they do not leave any traces...

It is really true: the Magyar people are still about on the same commercial level as they were 1,000 ago, when their tents were still shining over the wide Asiatic steppes... If the whole of Hungarian literature suddenly disappeared, would the world really be any poorer?

After looking back at the "rapine greedy for blood and fire", which "filled even the patient Germans with such revulsion and fury that after the great battle of reckoning they threw dead and living 'Huns' into a hole", and after a summary of the German waves of immigration, Löher arrived at his conclusion in a chapter entitled "Will Hungary become German or Magyar?":[2]

The Magyars never have been and never will be a civilized people. The Magyar character has no inner source of energy for higher education, no individual ambition for it...Others are supposed to adopt a language which will always remain a dialect, and to sacrifice themselves to a people who—in line with their entire history, nature and circumstances—will always lag behind and merely imitate the major peoples.

348

Löher's tone was in part a reaction to the onset of cultural Magyarizing efforts. How dare a backward, primitive people presume to
turn "Germans and Slovaks" into Magyars to enable them to read
Magyar books? This was the essence of the arguments marshalled
against the domineering, profligate and uneducated Hungarians. In
Löher's opinion some of these old-timers were afraid to touch
books, as if the mere act of doing so would burn their fingers.

The popular novels of Adam Müller-Guttenbrunn (1851–1923),
a Swabian from the Bánát, pursued a quite different aim: to
strengthen the anti-Hungarian Germans and weaken the dynamic
behind the assimilation of 1.9 million of them. The industrious
Swabian peasant settles on land devastated by the Turks, while the
pipe-smoking and permanently drunk Hungarian gentleman is
presented as his antagonist. The thesis that Hungary was a "cultural
wasteland without its own civilization" was connected also with the
caricature of Puszta and paprika, Gypsies and *csikós* (horse-herdsmen),
unintentionally disseminated particularly by such romantic "elective Hungarians" as Lenau and Liszt (see below). This cliché has
maintained its hold into our times, lately even reinforced by the
flood of tourist brochures which are read nowadays far beyond
Europe.

Eckhardt's essay on the Hungarian image notes: "We ourselves
have virtually inflicted these Asiatic components on the outside
world." However, the wild, arrogant and extravagant comic figure
portrayed in the Viennese satirical papers was less unattractive than
a depiction from the early eighteenth century, which can be viewed
in the museum of local history at Bad Aussee in Styria: the anonymous artist shows ten figures in their national costumes, classified by
seven typical traits. Among them are Spaniards, Germans, Englishmen, Turks and naturally Hungarians, who are described as "disloyal and treacherous, rebellious, cruel and bloodthirsty, brainless
and idle".

The indisputable creator of the romantic Magyar image in German-language literature was Nikolaus Lenau (1802–50), who spent
most of his childhood and youth in Hungary. Nationalistic-minded
historians and literati blamed him for falsifying the Hungarian
image by his romantic and "exaggerated" Gypsy figures, causing
Gypsies to be identified with Hungarians in the popular German
perception.[3]

In fact Lenau (who took his *nom de plume* from Niembsch von Strehlenau), who is nowadays regarded as the most significant Austrian lyric poet of the nineteenth century, was not at all the forerunner of a "puszta-romanticism" but a poet of revolt against the Metternich system; his heroes were rebels, heretics, revolutionaries, outsiders and opponents of temporal and spiritual authority: Faust, Savonarola, the Albigensians and Rákóczi.[4] Lenau, who became mentally deranged at the age of forty-two, became in the course of time—depending on the prevailing political climate—"a Hungarian to his last breath", then "Hungarian-German", "German-Hungarian" and, from the mid-1830s on, purely German and sometimes even the "poet of folksy south-east Germanness". The Hungarian Germanist Antal Mádl pointed out not only the misinterpretations of this great poet, but also his place alongside Heine and Petöfi "as the most significant pioneer of social progress and the revolutionary spirit in the Central Europe".[5]

Hungarians also blamed Franz (Ferenc) Liszt for being so strongly influenced by Lenau that his famous—in Hungary infamous—book about the Gypsies was copied from the French translation of Lenau's *Three Gypsies*, and that his "Hungarian Rhapsodies" fostered abroad the idea that "gypsy" and "Hungarian" were synonymous.[6] Liszt, a pianist and composer of genius and one of the great artists of the Romantic age was undoubtedly the best known, and at the same time the proudest, Hungarian "by choice". Although he spoke German all his life, he always proclaimed his Hungarian ancestry. The English travel writer, Julia Pardoe, devoted a whole chapter[7] to the enthusiastic reception given to him by the Budapest public in 1839 and how 5,000 Hungarians escorted him after his performance from the stage to his quarters. On that triumphal tour he was presented in the theatre after his concert with a jewel-encrusted sword that had once belonged to István Báthory, the Prince of Transylvania, and declared with tears in his eyes that he looked upon this sword as authorising him to lead his people—who had once distinguished themselves by their martial skills—to world fame in the realm of the arts. Should the Hungarians be forcibly hindered from building their nation, swords would once again have to be unsheathed, and "our blood shed to the last drop for our rights, for king and country". The fact that during the War of Independence in 1848–9 Liszt withdrew to the court of a minor German prince and that his sword remained in its sheath was the subject of Heine's satirical poem "Im Oktober 1849".[8] All the same, he stressed many times, as in a letter dated 7 May 1873, that "notwithstanding my lamentable ignorance of the Hungarian language I am, and shall remain until the end, a Magyar with all my heart and soul". He had started to learn Hungarian in 1829, but after the fifth lesson, encountering the word *tántoríthatatlanság* (unshakability), he gave up disheartened. Nevertheless, he composed the coronation mass in 1867, and took up the position of president of the Hungarian Academy of Music.[9]

Even though Liszt did not succeed in learning the language of his beloved people, Magyarization made unexpected progress among Hungary's dispersed German population, despite the protests of their traditionalist politicians and intellectuals. For a number of reasons the situation of the Germans was essentially different from that of the other nationalities in Hungary.[10] First, they did not form a tight community that had developed over a single period. The earliest German settlers came in the time of the Árpáds to Transylvania (the Saxons) and to Upper Hungary in today's Slovakia (the Zipser Saxons). During the eighteenth and nineteenth centuries, after the end of the Turkish occupation the Swabians and many others from various regions settled the Bánát, the Bácska and the so-called "Swabian Turkey" (the western Hungarian counties of Baranya, Pécs and Tolna). The differences of dialect, economic situation and settlement conditions hampered any cohesion.

Secondly, the Germans—in contrast to the Slovaks, Serbs, Romanians and, of course, Croats—were dispersed all over the country. Except for the Transylvanian Saxons, they lacked a closed settlement area, and common linguistic, cultural and historical traditions. Thirdly, their social structure was lopsided. For instance, there was no contact at all between the burghers of the towns and the peasants in the villages, and the social differentiation was heightened by the special role played by the urban Germans in the embourgeoisement of Hungary. Finally, the linguistic ties with the Austrians in the Habsburg Empire and the inhabitants of Germany itself gave a consciousness of natural alliance with these countries. This factor helped to mould the German national movement in Hungary, and came to play an important and fateful role after the collapse of the Monarchy and the emergence of the Third Reich. Széchenyi's catchy axiom "*egyedül vagyunk!*" (the notion, we are alone!) basically signified dissociation not only from the Turks but also from the Germans—and later from the Slavs as well. The German-Hungarian relationship contained many contradictions.

The proportion of Germans in the total population of Hungary (without Croatia) declined from 13.6 per cent in 1880 to 10.4 in 1910. This was due to a low birth-rate, a larger share in emigration and increasing assimilation. Magyarization had a marked effect on German schooling (except in Transylvania). In 1850 almost two-thirds (in 1848 even three-quarters) of the capital's inhabitants spoke German as their first language, in 1880 the proportion was still over a third, but in 1910 it had dropped to 9 per cent. In that year there were no longer any German primary schools in Budapest, and the last secondary school had closed by 1906–7.[11]

Reasons of state were incomparably more important for German foreign policy than the Hungarian Germans. Bismarck himself reassured the Hungarian leaders that the German government would not interfere in Hungarian domestic matters. It would not concern itself with the German element in Hungary because, it was explained, "the strength and unity of the Hungarian nation is so important" to the German Empire that "emotional needs have to take second place."[12]

Bismarck had not forgotten that in 1871 Andrássy had been for and not against Germany in the Franco-Prussian war, and had prepared the reconciliation between the adversaries at Königgrätz, bringing to realisation the Austro-German or "Dual" alliance of 1879 before his retirement as Foreign Minister. Bismarck wanted a willing ally later too, and took a stand against the national aspirations of the Transylvanian Saxons. On the other hand, the occupation (1878) and subsequent annexation (1908) of Bosnia-Herzegovina suggested by Bismarck and urged by Andrássy turned the Dual Monarchy into the hated enemy of the South Slavs and were therefore fatal errors. Evil tongues have always alleged that Bismarck had manipulated Austria-Hungary's move into the Balkans in order to keep the German Austrians out of the new German empire.

Spokesmen for the German national movement in Hungary tried to influence the circle of close advisers around the heir to the throne, Archduke Franz Ferdinand, to abolish Magyar supremacy and institute reforms within the Monarchy.[13] The Archduke for his part tried through letters and by word of mouth to conscript his friend Kaiser Wilhelm II (who always addressed him in letters as *"Mein lieber Franzi"*) as an ally against the Hungarians. In a long letter, written on 7 August 1909, Franz Ferdinand gave free rein to his feelings:

For the thousandth time this is proof of my repeated assertion that the so-called noble, chivalrous Magyar is the most infamous, anti-dynastic, lying and unreliable fellow, and that all the difficulties we have in the Monarchy have their roots exclusively in the Magyars. [We must] break this preponderance of the Hungarians! Otherwise we shall indisputably become a Slav empire.

However, the Kaiser had long cherished a liking for the Hungarians. He was Colonel-in-Chief of the Kassa Infantry Regiment No. 34 and the Seventh Hussars and used to visit them, even personally commanding them on manoeuvres. Count Ottokar Czernin reported to the Archduke that he had heard directly from Prince Max Egon Fürstenberg that the Kaiser (of whom he was a personal friend) would never intervene against the Hungarians; he feared only the Slav danger, but loved the Hungarians. Austria could therefore never count on his support against Hungary—something widely known in Hungarian political circles.[14]

It was not surprising under these circumstances that, leaving aside the Jews, the German ethnic group should have played such an important role in the process of Hungarian embourgeoisement and modernization. There was a peculiar triangular relationship between Hungarians, Jews and Germans. "The Hungarian gentleman from the country did not particularly like the German burgher; both of them abhorred the Slovak, Romanian or Serb merchant, trader or peasant; and all of them were united in hating the Jew." That was Péter Hanák's probably correct analysis in his study *The Image of the Other.*[15] Between 1850 and 1910 approximately 700,000 Jews and 600,000 Germans had become assimilated Magyars, and in 1910 every fourth Jew was still a German-speaker. We have already seen that from the Middle Ages up till the process of assimilation after the pogroms of 1848–9 and 1883 the towns were also scenes of "competitive anti-Semitism".

Unlike the Jews, however, assimilated Germans and their descendants had no difficulty in gaining positions in the civil service, the officer corps and the Church. The proportion of men of German origin in the four most important ministries between 1890 and 1910 rose from 23.7 to 26.4 per cent. In 1930 it was estimated that 15–20 per cent of the educated middle class were of German background.[16]

Magyarization helped, as with the Jews, to mask one's origin. Apart from the large proportion of German skilled workers, the large breweries, paper and agricultural machine factories, the most successful construction companies, and the best-known patisseries and restaurants, such as Gundel and Kugler, were established by German immigrants. The composer of the Hungarian National Anthem and of several operas, Ferenc Erkel (Franz Erkl); the renowned writer Ferenz Herczeg (Franz Herzog) and his younger colleague Sándor Márai (Alexander Grosschmid); a popular actress Gizi Bajor (Gisela Bayer); and the architects who shaped the cityscape of Budapest—József Hild, Ödön Lechner, Mihály Polláck, Frigyes Schulek, Imre Steindl and Miklós Ybl—were just as certainly of German origin as Mihály Munkácsy, the most renowned Hungarian painter of the nineteenth century.[17]

The financial expert Sándor Wekerle could boast of the most glittering career. After almost twenty-five years in the Ministry of Finance as section head, permanent secretary and, from 1889, department head, he became in 1892 the first prime minister from the middle class. It was under his aegis and against strong opposition from the Church, the aristocracy and the court that new legislation introducing compulsory civil marriages and granting the Jews civic equality with all the other denominations was carried through. Because of it Wekerle had to resign, but he was twice again appointed head of government, the last time in 1917–18 before the collapse. This son of a Swabian family led the government three times for a total of eight years. Having married the daughter of a "1,000-*hold* noble" and chief county official Zemplén, the adroit politician had entered the highest social stratum.

Löher's pathetic question whether Hungary would become "German or Magyar" was partly answered in tragic circumstances. After the Second World War the minority had to pay an enormous and deeply unfair price for the fact that Hitler's Germany tried to mobilize the Hungarian Germans for the Waffen-SS and the Nazi-led Volksbund. Everyone who had declared German nationality in the census of 1941 was summarily expelled to Germany in 1946—over 135,000 to West Germany and 60,000–70,000 to the Soviet Union. Those who remained in Hungary were blatantly and illegally discriminated against *de jure* till 1950 but *de facto* till 1955. At the time of writing 200–220,000 Germans live in Hungary, constituting about 2.5 per cent of the population. Most are fully assimilated, i.e. completely bilingual, and at the same time they receive generous support from Germany for cultural and educational purposes.

30. From the Great War to the "Dictatorship of Despair": the Red Count and Lenin's Agent

The murder of Archduke Franz Ferdinand and his wife in Sarajevo on 28 June 1914 by the Serbian student Gavrilo Princip did not evoke particularly strong feelings of grief among the Hungarian public, since everyone knew that the Archduke had been an unyielding opponent of the Hungarian claim to hegemony. It was the ultimate irony of fate that the champion of the Slavs became a victim of assassination at the behest of the South Slav secret society, the "Black Hand". It was part of that curious curve of conflict which came to light in the collapse of the Danube Monarchy. Who in Hungary could then even have imagined let alone wanted a war to avenge the death of the detested Archduke? The idea of dying for a Habsburg, and in particular a hater of the Hungarians like Franz Ferdinand, was grotesque.

There is a scene in Joseph Roth's *Radetzky March* in which the mere rumour of the Archduke's murder brings to the surface the national tensions between the officers of a border battalion:

Count Batthány, who was drunk, hereupon began speaking Hungarian to his compatriots. The others didn't understand a word. They remained silent, glancing at each speaker in turn and waiting, a bit stunned all the same. But the Hungarians seemed determined to go merrily along for the rest of the evening; perhaps it was a national custom. While the non-Hungarians were far from grasping even a syllable, they could tell by the faces of the Magyars that they were gradually starting to forget that anyone else was present. Sometimes they laughed in unison. Jelačić, a Slovene, hit the ceiling. He hated the Hungarians as much as he despised the Serbs. [...] He went over to the table and slapped it with his flat hand. "Gentlemen", he said, "may we request that you continue the conversation in German." Benkyö, who was speaking, broke off and replied: "I will say it in

German. We are in agreement, my countrymen and I: we can be glad the bastard is gone!"[1]

Nevertheless, the note, the ultimatum and finally the declaration of war on Serbia were received with just as much enthusiasm as in the Austrian half of the Monarchy. What kindled national emotions above all was the fact that at last the "Tsarist barbarians" could be taught a lesson for the defeat of 1849. Hugo von Hofmannstahl's sentiments, expressed in one of his letters, would no doubt have been echoed by most Hungarian intellectuals: "Believe me, and tell it to all our friends, that all of us here, to the last woodcutter, are entering into this matter and everything that it entails with determination, even gladly, to an extent that I have never experienced nor would ever have believed possible."[2]

The interval of a month between the assassination and the declaration of war was due to the disagreement of the Hungarian Prime Minister István Tisza—this only became common knowledge after the Great War. In contrast to the Austrian and German annexation strategists, Tisza considered the time unsuitable and the pretext inadequate. The issue for him was the preservation of the Magyars' leading role in Hungary; an extension of the war or even only a possible increase of the Slav population's share could eventually threaten Dualism, i.e. Hungarian supremacy, in historic Hungary. The statements on foreign policy by the Hungarian leadership were therefore accordingly lukewarm. In the event, however, Tisza had to give in to the united pressure from Vienna and Berlin, and agreed to the ultimatum to Serbia with the proviso that Serbia, once conquered, was not to be annexed to the Monarchy.[3]

Because Tisza was known in domestic politics as an advocate of the firm hand against the Opposition, who had already physically ejected obstructionist deputies from the chamber with the help of the police, he was regarded both at home and abroad as a warmonger. On 31 October 1918, the day of the bourgeois-democratic revolution, he was murdered in his villa by several armed soldiers in circumstances that remain unclear to this day. Only years later did the records of the Council of Joint Ministers prove that Tisza had been the only leading politician to warn the Monarchy of the consequences of a war. However, once he had submitted to the decision he remained to the last, in this regard too, the Court's "whip".

Tisza, writes Robert A. Kann, was incorruptible, a man of resolute abilities but politically blind.[4] Even in the last hours of the
Monarchy he had no comprehension of the nationalities' concerns
(or of their right to vote), and showed this plainly during his legendary visit to Sarajevo in 1918. Wearing the uniform of a Hussar
colonel, he met a delegation of Bosnian politicians who handed
him a memorandum (he had meanwhile been relieved of the prime
ministership by King Charles). He did not invite the Bosnians to be
seated but barked at them: "Perhaps we shall perish, but be assured
that before we perish we shall have enough power to smash the men
who are willing to play into the hands of our enemies at home."
Whether it is true, as reported, that he even flicked his horsewhip at
the memorandum has not been corroborated by other sources.[5]

During the first half of the war, as leader of the parliamentary
majority, Tisza retained firm control of the government, but the
longer the war lasted the more the population felt the worsening of
the economic and food supply situation. The real wages of blue-
and white-collar workers fell respectively by 47 and 67 per cent, 3.4
million men were conscripted into the army from Hungary and
Croatia, 530,000 were killed and 1.4 million were wounded. The
number of prisoners-of-war from Greater Hungary reached 833,000.[6]
There was no ethnic breakdown of these figures, so that one cannot
estimate the losses of the individual nationalities.

Dissatisfaction and bitterness increased. There were hunger protests, demonstrations and later strikes; by 1917 the unions had over
200,000 members. In addition to the Social Democrats, other opposition groups were also demanding fundamental reforms in domestic politics. When the eighty-six-year-old Franz Joseph, who had
served as the symbolic unifier of the Dual Monarchy's people, died
on 21 November 1916, an epoch came to an end. People in the
multinational Danube state talked about a new era of freedom.
After the Russian Revolution and the abdication of the Tsar in
early 1917 and President Wilson's peace proclamations, and in view
of the hopeless stagnation on the southern and eastern front, Hungary too experienced political tensions and the emergence of new
left-oriented groups.

Several libraries could be filled with works dealing with the collapse of the Dual Monarchy and the manifold consequences of the

Great War, Europe's "primeval catastrophe" (George Kennan). Most claim that the stench of decay was already detectable in the Habsburg Monarchy by that time, but some later works have disagreed that the concept "decline and fall" is relevant to its history in the nineteenth and early twentieth centuries; it went under because it had lost a decisive war.[7] Even an expert on the Monarchy of the stature of a Louis Eisenman, could write in 1910 of its viability, and believe that "all Austrian, Hungarian and Austro-Hungarian questions could be settled from within. Therein lies progress, therein lies the great trust in the future."[8]

Nowadays most Hungarian historians share the opinion that the cause of the collapse lay in the dynamics of modern nationalism. At the same time the way the dissolution of the Monarchy of historic Hungary unfolded, and the contours of the new order, were in no way predestined. They depended, rather, on the outcome of the war, the strategic interests of the Great Powers and the internal conditions in the country, gripped by revolutionary fever.[9] In his final reflections on the dissolution process of the Monarchy, Kann stated: "When Austria-Hungary, in condoning the war with Serbia, committed suicide from fear of death the Dual Monarchy lost the only chance it had to survive: namely by the help of time itself."[10]

Rephrasing Churchill's words, one cannot even say that the last cabinets appointed by Emperor-King Charles in Vienna and Budapest completed the dissolution of the empire—they could only stand by and watch it. On 16 October 1918 the spokesman of the Opposition, Count Mihály Károlyi, spelt out the heart of the matter in the Budapest Parliament: "We have lost the war; now it is important not to lose the peace." Twenty-four hours later, to the astonishment of his party, Tisza, still the most influential Hungarian politician, stated in the same place: "I must acknowledge the truth of what Mihály Károlyi said in his speech yesterday. We have lost the war." Károlyi, a principal witness above suspicion, wrote of the effect of these words in his Memoirs:

This sentence fell like a thunderbolt among the stupefied majority. It was clear that, under the pressure of events and the burden of his own terrible responsibility, Tisza had broken down. This was the hardest blow the reactionaries could suffer. Tisza's announcement spread like wildfire through the country, in the trenches and behind the lines. It was only now that many believed the truth simply because Tisza had spoken it.[11]

The revolutions in October 1918 and March 1919 and the coun-ter-revolution of 1919–20 were all the direct outcome of defeat. These were not, or at least not primarily, class-conditioned social revolutions, but the products of tensions caused by national rivalries and by the unfairness of the measures adopted by the victorious Allies. The "crisis of the unforeseen" (Paul Valéry) aptly illustrated what occurred in Hungary within less than fifteen months. When the poet and essayist was asked in 1932 to make conjectures about what could happen in fifty years' time, he referred to the motto of a dissertation topic, "We are going backwards into the future", add-ing: "It becomes ever more dangerous to rely on yesterday and the day before in order to make prognostications; but it is wise to be prepared for anything, or almost anything."[12]

It was not either anonymous forces or great ideologies that dom-inated the political stage but individuals in whom history became personified—even though they lacked political greatness in the sense advanced by Jacob Burckhardt. The forty-three-year-old Mihály Károlyi (1875–1955), the "sphinx" of Hungarian politics, was one of the main protagonists in the transitional period after the collapse of the Monarchy.[13]

The practice of politics in old Hungary was very much like a comic opera with a handful of aristocrats as actors, who changed their political positions on a whim, or as their mutual personal situ-ations determined. István Tisza was by far the strongest political personality and a consistent advocate of alliance with Germany, yet in the eyes of the aristocratic families such as the Károlyis, Apponyis, Esterházys, Zichys and Pallavicinis he was and remained an upstart (Tisza received his title of Count only towards the end of the nine-teenth century) and a representative of narrow-minded gentry. The magnates were against Tisza's hard-line politics and wanted at least a marginal move towards democratization. King Charles pressed for the introduction of universal equal and direct suffrage, as had pre-vailed in the Austrian half of the Empire since 1907, but they were not keen on that in Hungary. The Saxon envoy Baron Alfred von Nostitz was probably not far wrong when he reported: "Anyone at all aware of Hungarian conditions will strongly question whether the Opposition's performance is meant sincerely, because the Andrássys and Apponyis are just as opposed deep down as Tisza to the eman-cipation of the non-Magyar nationalities."[14]

In Parliament the aristocrats held the highest political positions. Count Albert Apponyi, who greeted the declaration of war by loudly exclaiming in the Chamber "At last!", characterized the parliamentary habits of his countrymen as follows: "Whenever three Hungarians talk politics, they form a party: one is President, the other Vice-President, and the third becomes Secretary-General and regards it as his duty 'to make an important statement' every time there is an occasion to do so."[15] The break-up of groups into cliques and factions was a common practice in this peculiar form of parliamentarism, at a time when only 6 per cent of the population (in Transylvania only 3, in Croatia 2) were permitted to vote—naturally not by secret ballot. When the bourgeois revolution led by Count Mihály Károlyi triumphed, it was not by chance that in Hungary even the leader of a revolution was a magnate.[16] Politics before the outbreak of war in 1914 seemed like the "playground of four counts" (Andrássy, Apponyi, Károlyi, Tisza), but during the war Károlyi's politics increasingly became an unpredictable factor.

Nothing in Károlyi's youth pointed to his later career.[17] As scion of one of the oldest and richest aristocratic families, the young count grew up in a way typical of one of his rank, with pocket-money equivalent to the salary of the current prime minister. He spoke fluent English, French and German and understood Italian, but did not master the writing of any of the languages, not even his mother tongue. Until he entered Parliament he spent the winter months at his uncle's villa at Menton on the Côte d'Azur, and lived a life of dissipation between Paris, London, Vienna and Budapest. He was known as a passionate card-player; he lost unbelievably large sums, and before his marriage to Katinka, the stepdaughter of Gyula Andrássy who was almost twenty years younger than himself, his debts reached an astronomical 12 million crowns. But he was by nature a fighter and a gambler and did everything with total commitment. This may have been a compensation for a congenital speech defect, which even an operation on his palate by the renowned Professor Billroth of Vienna could not completely overcome; the more Károlyi tried to conquer the defect in his public utterances, the more difficult it became for him to be understood.

He was already known as an Entente-friendly politician before the outbreak of war, trying during an extensive lecture tour of the

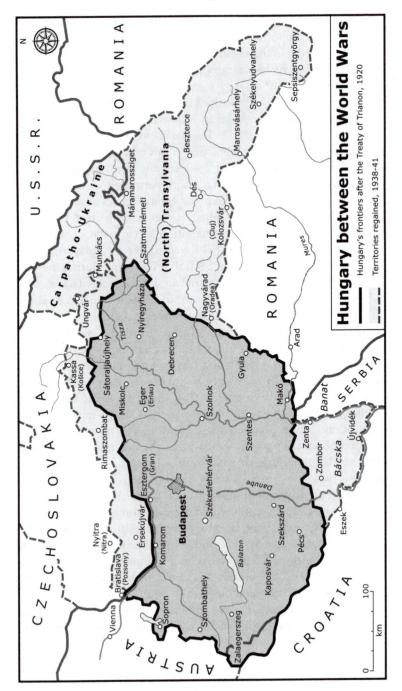

Hungary between the World Wars

Hungary's frontiers after the Treaty of Trianon, 1920

Territories regained, 1938–41

United States in 1914 to promote his concept of a democratic transformation and federalization of Hungary. In the autumn of 1917 he spelled out his ideas in neutral Switzerland, and he was granted a long personal audience by the French President Poincaré. His orientation in foreign policy was in stark contrast to that of his stepfather and the Apponyis. The political turning-point came in July 1916 when, together with twenty-three deputies, Károlyi broke away from the opposition United Independence Party to form the New Independence Party. In June 1917, together with the small Democratic Party of the later Minister of Justice Vilmos Vázsonyi, as well as the Social Democrats and bourgeois radicals (under Oszkár Jászi), who were not represented in Parliament at that time, he founded a "suffrage block".

The memoirs of the protagonists and the later reflections of comrades and contemporaries show the operetta-like aspects of these events, taking place in the midst of a radical political change and a national tragedy. Károlyi himself admitted years later in his Memoirs: "Thinking back on those days—a month or two before the fall of the Habsburg Monarchy—I feel better able to understand the historical blindness of Louis XVI when he heard of the storming of the Bastille." In September 1918, on the eve of the collapse, and in a looming revolutionary atmosphere, the leader of the Opposition went deer-stalking with the Andrássy clan in the Gyalu highlands in Transylvania. In a letter to a friend dated 25 September, he wrote that no essential change could be expected before the spring. Andrássy was hoping for the position of *k.u.k.* Foreign Minister, his dream being to follow in his father's footsteps.

On 26 September Bulgaria capitulated, and the Balkan front collapsed. This opened the way for the French Salonika army to enter the Danubian basin. While Prime Minister Wekerle sent a special train to pick up Andrássy, Károlyi had ridden to the nearest town a day earlier to take the train to Budapest, which he reached on 29 September, to be greeted at the station in the early hours of the morning by a delegation. Károlyi later remarked: "The calendar of revolutions can never be made until afterwards... A friend of mine reproached me: How could I hunt at that time? Well, at that time, 'that time' had not yet become '*that time*'."

The race against time and for the King's favour was played out to some extent within the close Károlyi-Andrássy family. Katinka

Károlyi proved to be her husband's loyal and passionate political partner, while Andrássy, partly because of his ambitions and partly because of his close relationship with King Charles and his entourage, was the greatest opponent of his son-in-law's political plans. The two men argued over the breakfast table, and Katinka reported to her husband what she had heard in her own family about her stepfather's intrigues.

Meanwhile events unfolded in a rush. King Charles sent Andrássy on a senseless reconnaissance trip to Switzerland, while the government still balked at the fundamental reforms demanded by the Károlyi group and the masses. On 25 October Károlyi's party, the bourgeois radicals and the Social Democrats formed a "Hungarian National Council" under his leadership, which was ready to assume responsibility. A twelve-point program drawn up by Jászi demanded the immediate conclusion of a separate peace, independence from Austria, reconciliation with the nationalities without endangering the country's territorial integrity, introduction of universal suffrage, and land reform.

However, the old ruling class with Andrássy at its head wanted to hinder Károlyi's appointment as Prime Minister by every means possible. Andrássy was even willing to become Hungary's Prime Minister; he could then have had his stepdaughter's husband promptly arrested, as he already regarded him as the leader of the revolution.

At any rate Andrássy succeeded in persuading the King to appoint Count János Hadik and not Károlyi as Prime Minister and himself as Foreign Minister. The family row was complete. The exasperated Károlyi sent his wife to the station to persuade Andrássy before his departure to stop blocking his appointment as Prime Minister, but in vain. On the other hand, Andrássy and Hadik had no power-base to speak of. More and more people demonstrated for Károlyi and the implementation of his programme, but Károlyi still procrastinated and did not leave, losing valuable time in the process.

The dissolution of the Dual Monarchy and of the Kingdom of Hungary could no longer be prevented. Even before the change of power in Budapest, the Romanians, Czechs, Croats, Slovaks and Ukrainians announced their secession from the Monarchy. During the night of 30 October the bloodless "Chrysanthemum Revolution" prevailed: military units, which had already sworn allegiance to the National Council, occupied the post office, the telephone and telegraph exchanges, the railway stations and other strategic points. King Charles had no option but to appoint Károlyi Prime Minister on 31 October. The signing of an armistice on 3 November 1918 in Padua marked the end of the Great War for the Austro-Hungarian Monarchy.

Károlyi emerged as the most popular politician mainly because of his pacifist attitude and his effective opposition role. On 11 November Emperor Charles renounced taking "any part in the affairs of government" and the Republic of Austria was been declared the following day. The Károlyi government proclaimed the Republic on 16 November, and on 11 January 1919 the National Council elected him President.

Despite the best intentions and the appointment of some of the most able politicians and experts to the government, all the important reform plans, such as land reform and the new electoral law, fell by the wayside. All the preconditions for the realization of the great political, social, economic and national tasks were lacking. In *The Magyars' Guilt—Hungary's Atonement: Revolution and Counter-Revolution in Hungary*, his deeply embittered and emotional analysis of events, Jászi—the key figure apart from Károlyi—did not mince words: from the first the armistice agreement was breached by Czech, Romanian, Serb and French troops:

The entire public was convinced that the Entente would reward the great and devoted struggle which Mihály Károlyi had carried on during the whole war against the imperialist policy of the Central Powers, and that the nationalities would accept my staunch peace policy with understanding. However, it soon turned out that both assumptions were illusory. The armistice negotiations of 8 November in Belgrade, the crude, malicious, sabre-rattling and uneducated conduct of Franchet d'Esperey [the French commander], the merciless armistice obligations imposed upon us, deeply embittered… the Hungarians. […] Our greatest misfortune was not really that we received wretched terms of capitulation, but that even that bad contract was not adhered to. The shining promises of the Wilsonian League of Nations, the just peace, the right of self-determination, the plebiscite, burst like so many bubbles….[18]

Even in retrospect Jászi's diagnosis appears correct. The military, the students and the workers in the munitions factories were "the actual ferment of revolutionary activity". At first the revolution was military and national, and only much later became "social, socialist, even Communist". After the collapse of the fronts, the demobilized soldiers and those returning from prisoner-of-war camps multiplied the host of refugees from Transylvania, Upper Hungary and other occupied territories. Among the most pressing tasks of the Károlyi government were the restoration of law and order, measures against pillage and the establishment of a republican army out of the remnants of the old army. A colonel of the general staff, Béla Linder, was the Minister for War who uttered the memorable words, often quoted against him and the whole government: "I don't want to see any more soldiers!" This ministerial statement in the face of attacks by foreign troops and threats to the core territories proved a fiasco. A possibly even greater one was Jászi's negotiations to transform Hungary into an "eastern Switzerland" at a time when the nationalities were either in the process of forming their own states or joining their neighbouring co-nationals.

The Károlyi government had a further Achilles heel in the unresolved problem of land reform.[19] The new President Mihály Károlyi set a good personal example and began to redistribute the land on his own great estates at Kálkápolna on 23 February 1919. Whereas the rural proletariat looked upon the proposed legislation as far too cumbersome and lax (only estates above 150 hectares were to be expropriated for compensation), the large landowners of course regarded it as too "radical". In the mean time some of the conservative and right-wing elements began to gather around the President's brother, while radical officers under the leadership of Gyula Gömbös, a general staff captain who later became Prime Minister, founded secret organizations.

However, the greatest direct danger was from the left. When the journalist and insurance clerk Béla Kun, disguised as an army surgeon, returned to Budapest from Russian captivity with eight of his comrades on 16 November 1918, few could have foreseen that barely four months later this tiny group would set the agenda for a fusion of the great Social Democrat Party with the small Communist Party, founded on 24 November, and the establishment of a Soviet Republic.[20]

The Communists, whose number—according to Jászi's estimates—never exceeded 5,000 activists, even at the height of their short-lived rule, exerted growing pressure and benefited from the chaotic conditions. The final spark which ignited this frenzied atmosphere of national humiliation, progressive social deterioration and unrestrained demagoguery struck from the outside: on 20 March 1919 the French Colonel Vyx handed Károlyi the Allies' infamous ultimatum ordering withdrawal to new demarcation lines in the southeast, which would cut off old Magyar territories from Hungary. In reply to a query, Vyx added that this new line was to be considered final, and even though, after a storm of indignation, he later denied this explanatory addition, this political bombshell had an enormous effect. Jászi noted: "We felt not only defeated, dejected and debauched but—far worse—psychologically swindled, betrayed and bamboozled."[21]

In this hopeless situation, confronted by the failure of all the concepts he had espoused in foreign policy on the basis of amicable connections with the Entente, Károlyi decided to resign and transfer power to the revolutionary council formed by the united Social Democrats and the Communists. In fact he had wanted to appoint a purely Social Democrat government ("on behalf of the proletarian class"), but he was not aware that the majority of Social Democrats had concluded a pact behind his back with the Communist functionaries (imprisoned for the past few weeks) with a view to establishing a soviet-type government. Károlyi asserted till his death that he had never signed the proclamation, printed and read out at the meeting of the revolutionary council, by which he was supposed to have voluntarily handed over power. However, he did not publicly distance himself from the Soviet Republic, which the Austrian Social Democrat Otto Bauer called a "dictatorship of despair",[22] and left Hungary for Prague only in July 1919.

Within barely a few months the saviour and fêted hero of the nation, and last hope of a country bleeding from a thousand wounds, had become a traitor and a gambler who had risked everything for his own aggrandizement. Like Görgey in 1849, Károlyi was now the scapegoat for everything that ensued: the atrocities of the red terror and even the later and more lengthy white reign of terror.[23] Today it is clear that Károlyi was the visible symbol of the revolution and not the person who directed it. In his "psychological attempt" written shortly after the collapse Jászi compared Károlyi, "the legendary hero turned hated and despised culprit", to Prince Myshkin in Dostoyevsky's *The Idiot*, because he took principles and characters seriously.

Democracy, socialism, pacifism were for him not political slogans but ethical realities, powerful personalities as it were, with whom he was in almost mystical communion (a fatally dangerous situation for a politician who never had any contact with life's true realities, and who had always observed men and matters from the extraterritoriality of his aristocratic home).[24]

Already during the initial stage of emigration, wrote Jászi, Károlyi told him how he had turned from "an emotional socialist into a Marxist revolutionary". In his exile, first in Prague and then on the Dalmatian coast (he had a Yugoslav passport at his disposal till 1946), in Paris and eventually in London, he was not a crypto-Communist but rather a convinced, if not always uncritical, fellow-traveller. As the "Count of the Comintern" he closely cooperated with the Hungarian Communist Party, particularly during the later 1920s and early '30s. However, his relationship with Béla Kun, the Soviet Republic's people's commissar for external affairs and long-standing head of the CP in exile, who once casually called Károlyi the "Hungarian Kerensky", was never truly amicable.

The Horthy regime confiscated the assets of the aristocrat accused of high treason, and by special legislation transferred part of his estates to the family of his brother (the fact that it was a cousin of the "traitor", Count Gyula Károlyi, who established the first rival government in 1919 and "invented" Vice-Admiral Horthy as Minister for War, and that it was Horthy who in turn appointed the "good" Károlyi prime minister in 1931–2, is a further interesting facet in the history of this strange family).[25] The sincere idealist without statesman-like qualities, the Don Quixote of Central European politics, was rehabilitated only twenty-seven years later, in February 1946, by the first freely-elected Hungarian Parliament, the judgements of earlier times being dismissed as unfair and invalid. The famous Károlyi palace in the heart of the city was returned to him, and as a member of the resistance he was eligible for 150 hectares of land. Although by then over seventy, he was willing to take up the position of ambassador to France. Some of his old friends, among them Jászi, then Professor of History at Oberlin

College in the United States, took it amiss that he did not resign during the show-trial of Cardinal Mindszenty at the beginning of 1949, and only broke with the Budapest regime after the arrest of the Communist Foreign Minister, László Rajk, and his closest Paris colleagues. Károlyi died in French exile in 1955.

After a personal meeting between his wife, the "Red Countess", with the Party leader János Kádár in 1961, the regime, keen to have Western acceptance, gave permission for the bodies of Károlyi and his son, who had died as a student at an air training school in England, to be buried in Hungary. The subsequent erection of a statue of the "aristocratic *enfant terrible*" (Robert A. Kann), with such impressive moral and human qualities but with such a controversial and ultimately unsuccessful political career, in a small park in front of the Parliament House is a reminder of that episode whose repercussions are still felt to this day.

And what of the Soviet Republic, the Communist dictatorship? It lasted all of 133 days, and was in fact a double boon both for the covetous neighbouring states, which could use anti-Bolshevist rhetoric to cover up Hungary's dismemberment, as well as for the no less harsh subsequent regime of the authoritarian Right, which for a quarter of a century identified democracy and liberalism with Bolshevism and terror, and criticism with treachery. The real tragedy was that the short-lived Communist regime was established on the ruins of the bourgeois revolution as if it had been its natural, organic outcome.[26]

The Hungarian Soviet Republic did not come into being through a revolutionary coup, but resulted from a virtually desperate transmission of power to a disparate group of left-wing socialists, centrists and naive Communists, blinded by revolutionary rhetoric. Béla Kun had taken part as a prisoner-of-war in the Russian October Revolution and founded the first exile group within the Bolshevik Party, and in addition was a personal friend of Lenin and his family, and was therefore regarded in Russia as one of the most influential foreign socialists. It was therefore virtually a foregone conclusion that, although Kun was formally responsible only for foreign affairs, he acted in all respects as the strongman of the revolutionary council, but good orator and organizer though he was, he was a total failure as a leader. He constantly promised help from Soviet Russia and the approaching Red Army, but the expected intimidation of the Allies never happened. On the contrary, seen in terms of Hungarian national interests the red dictatorship proved a boomerang. Because Kun was gambling on world revolution, the French, led by Clemenceau, never envisaged a place for Hungary in the makeshift "Little Entente" improvised by them, and agitated against its realisation, depicting Kun as the bogeyman of bolshevism. Wilson and Lloyd George too were won over at the Paris Peace Conference to the notion of strengthening the "Romanian citadel" against "red" Hungary.[27]

Kun could not fulfil the expectations he had aroused—partly in the middle class but mainly in the proletariat. The Communist government made fatal mistakes in every sphere that it touched, but particularly in agrarian policy and in its attitude towards the churches. Instead of putting a radical land reform into effect, land was nationalized; so too were all commercial concerns employing over twenty workers. Some positive steps in the cultural field (under People's Commissar György Lukács) and in social policy, such as combating illiteracy, were soon overshadowed by the continuous and worsening economic crisis and the creation of an apparatus for the ruthless persecution of actual and potential opponents.

The only internationally noted achievement was the unexpectedly tough defence by the Hungarians against the Czech and Romanian armies' invasions. Kun himself, the commander-in-chief Vilmos Böhm, and the chief of staff Aurél Stromfeld, a former colonel on the general staff, managed within a few weeks to raise an army of 200,000.[28] Brilliantly led by Stromfeld and with dozens of young officers, later generals in Horthy's army, in its ranks, the army launched a victorious offensive in the north, driving back the Czechs from occupied territories. On 16 June a Slovak Soviet Republic was even proclaimed at Eperjes (Prešov) with Hungarian help.

Of course, the Hungarian Red Army fought not for world revolution but for the threatened fatherland. An ultimatum by the Entente forces stopped the offensive. Concurrently with the withdrawal of Hungarian troops to the old demarcation line, the Romanians were also supposed to withdraw to their initial positions. To gain international approval and because of the difficult supply situation and growing domestic opposition, Kun pulled back the Red Army—causing Böhm, Stromfeld and many other officers to quit the service in protest. The retreat had demoralized the army. At the same time the Romanians once again did not keep their promises, and stopped by the river Tisza. When Kun tried to repair the damage with a surprise attack, and clear the regions on both sides of the river, the plans fell into the hands of the Romanians, forcing the Red Army into a hasty retreat. Kun and most of the leaders fled to Austria, and on 4 August the Romanians entered Budapest. After a rather unsuccessful career in the Russian Party and the Comintern apparatus, Kun, like so many former commissars and Communist activists, met his death in one of Stalin's jails; he was arrested in June 1937 for anti-party activities and subsequently executed, aged fifty-two. For decades after their seizure of power in 1948 Hungarian Communist leaders withheld information about Kun's real role and his fate. Mátyás Rákosi, by then dictator of Hungary, who at the time of the Soviet Republic of 1919 had still been a second-ranking player, was retrospectively built up as almost the key figure in the events, and Kun was made to sink into oblivion. Only at the beginning of 1956 did the Soviet party paper *Pravda* pay tribute to the non-person Kun on his seventieth birth anniversary as "an outstanding personality of the international workers' movement"—an unmistakable sign for the initiated, especially in Hungary. Kun was later posthumously also awarded various high decorations, including the "Order of the Red Banner" which in April 1964 the Soviet ambassador ceremonially handed to his widow, who had spent many years in Central Asian exile but now lived in Budapest. On the forty-fifth anniversary of the Hungarian Soviet Republic a school and street were named after him in Leningrad.[29]

Despite his high-profile rehabilitation, the dead Kun managed to cause an embarrassing incident as late as 1979. In the first comprehensive and objective account of his life György Borsányi related some unknown episodes. As a young Social Democrat activist in Transylvania, Kun had claimed 110 crowns for a trip he never took, and been obliged to repay the amount to the Party after the matter was exposed. Even more embarrassingly, during a mission in Vienna from Moscow, he inadvertently left in a taxi an attaché-case containing secret documents about the underground activities of Hungarian comrades, and did not advise those affected or the Party of the fact. The taxi-driver promptly delivered the explosive Hungarian-language papers to the Hungarian legation in Vienna. Detectives summoned from Budapest immediately photographed them before they were returned to Kun and his Viennese hosts. The consequences for the illegal Party were catastrophic.[30]

In the course of the factional fights within the Hungarian Party in exile, Kun denounced no less than twenty opponents as "Trotskyist conspirators", arranging for their arrest. At that time, in 1929, it was still possible to prove one's innocence and be released—a few years later these comrades would certainly have been shot out of hand, just as Kun was in November 1939. All of this and other similarly compromising material is in Borsányi's biography.

The whole affair would probably have aroused little interest in Hungary had not Kun's family protested at Party headquarters and allegedly also at the Soviet embassy over this "humiliating and provocative" conduct, especially on the eve of an official visit to Hungary by the Soviet Party leader Leonid Brezhnev. The Central Committee of the Party acted at once: all unsold copies of the biography were collected and pulped overnight, and the book could no longer be found anywhere.*

---

* I received a barely legible photo-copy from my friend, the writer István Eörsi. Thus on the day of Brezhnev's arrival in Budapest, and to the great annoyance of the Agitprop functionaries, I could report in my newspaper: "Brezhnev came— Kun vanished!"

31. The Admiral on a White Horse: Trianon and the Death Knell of St Stephen's Realm

A single word, Trianon, sums up for all Hungarians to this day the most devastating tragedy in their history. In the Trianon palace, in the park of Versailles, the Allies presented the death certificate of the 1,000-year realm of St Stephen, and two representatives of Hungary, whose names have long been forgotten, had to sign the dictated settlement on behalf of the government and Parliament. On that fateful day, 4 June 1920, church bells rang all over the country, black flags flew over buildings, traffic came to a standstill, newspapers appeared with black borders, and funeral services were held in churches.

Trianon meant the vivisection of the Hungarian nation and the end of historical Hungary. The independent "Kingdom of Hungary", which emerged as a result of the Trianon peace treaty, was left with only 93,000 of the 282,000 square km. of the pre-war kingdom (together with Croatia it had covered 325,000 square km.). According to the 1920 census the population now numbered 7.6 million compared with the earlier figure of 18.3 million (20.9 with Croatia). The victors distributed the booty among the three neighbouring states: Romania, whose change of sides was as timely when it joined the Allies in 1916 as it was to be in 1944, received an area of 102,000 square km. with 5.4 million inhabitants, i.e. all of Transylvania including the Székely region, the eastern Bánát, most of Körös and Tisza counties and the southern part of Máramaros; Czechoslovakia was ceded 63,000 square km. with 3.5 million inhabitants; and the new kingdom of Serbs, Croats and Slovenes received the Bácska, the Baranya and the western Bánát, amounting to 21,000 square km. and 1.5 million inhabitants. Austria, itself dismembered, was promised today's Burgenland with 4,000 square km. and almost 300,000 inhabitants. A plebiscite, considered by Austrians somewhat dubious because of its prehistory and implementation, was held only about Sopron and its surroundings, where two-thirds of the voters elected to stay with Hungary.

Since the partition of Poland, no other country was treated by the Great Powers so mercilessly and so unjustly as historical Hungary. Thereafter 3,227,000 Magyars, according to the census figures, lived under foreign rule, although half of them inhabited homogenous communities on the borders of the three successor-states.

Almost every Hungarian family was directly hit by the tragedy of Trianon. The coronation city of Pozsony (Pressburg in German), the symbolic embodiment of Hungarian history, was suddenly called Bratislava; Kolozsvár, Kassa and Temesvár were re-named Cluj, Košice and Timisoara; and overnight relatives and friends living there became foreigners. Between 1918 and 1920 between 350,000 and 400,000 people fled or left the separated territories, mainly civil servants, officers and members of the middle class. Tens of thousands had to find shelter for months in railway waggons at stations or in improvised barracks. These politically conscious people, demoted from the ruling classes to homeless beggars, constituted an ideal "reservoir" for various extremists, populist rabble-rousers and the death squads of radical nationalist and anti-semitic officers.

Trianon was a trauma from which Hungary—regardless of the prevailing political attitude—has never completely recovered. In kindergartens and schools, during church services and in the press, the notion that the territories lost to the despised neighbours might one day be re-annexed was kept alive. The slogans repeated day by day—"No, no, never!" and "Rump Hungary is not a country; Greater Hungary is God's country"—moulded daily life in the schools even twenty years after Trianon. Classes began and ended with the Hungarian Credo, in which the resurrection of old Hungary was instilled into students' consciousness as "God's eternal truth":

> I believe in God,
> I believe in a Fatherland
> I believe in eternal divine justice
> I believe in Hungary's resurrection!
> Amen.

After Trianon, and probably also in view of the defeated rump state's encirclement by the Little Entente (the French-sponsored alliance of Czechoslovakia, Romania and Yugoslavia), Arthur Koestler, the Budapest-born writer, wrote: "The peculiar intensity of their existence can perhaps be explained by this exceptional loneliness. To be a Hungarian is a collective neurosis."

At any rate, rump Hungary became a homogeneous state. According to the 1920 census, only 10.4 per cent of the population, including 552,000 Germans (6.9 per cent) and 142,000 Slovaks (1.8 per cent), did not speak Hungarian as their mother tongue. The political scientist Ernest Gellner's conception of Central Europe applies as well if not better to post-Trianon Hungary: before Trianon, Hungary resembled a painting by Kokoshka—different colours, a pattern of great diversity, plurality and complexity, whereas the ethnographic map of rump-Hungary is more like a Modigliani— little shading and clear surfaces, each clearly demarcated from the others, ambiguities and overlaps having all but disappeared.[1]

In 1920 rump Hungary was teetering on the edge of bankruptcy. Although it retained 56 per cent of the total industrial capacity, even 82 per cent of heavy industry, and 70 per cent of the banks of Greater Hungary, its heavy industry, mostly concentrated in and around Budapest was cut off from its sources of raw materials and its natural markets. With eighty-two inhabitants per square kilometre Trianon-Hungary had the densest population in the Carpathian basin, with one-sixth living in the overpopulated capital. Budapest, like Vienna, was top-heavy in a dramatically shrunken country.[2]

Where domestic development was concerned, Trianon proved "a disastrous obstacle to democratization" (Thomas von Bogyay). After the failure of the bourgeois revolution and the bitter experience of the disastrous experiment of Communism, political instability, an economic downturn, social demoralization, increasing criminality and other symptoms of crisis provided an almost perfect breeding-ground for the historically well-known transformation of nationalism from an ideology of liberation to one of distraction. Humiliation and harassment of a formerly feared or envied group shaped the relationship between minority and majority in a fatal dialectical cycle. About 3.5 million Hungarians had to undergo this role-change three times after the First and Second World Wars in

Romania, Czechoslovakia and Yugoslavia. The sudden metamorphosis from rulers to outcasts was followed after the Vienna Awards by the Axis (1938 and 1940) by repossession of parts of the lost territories, and finally, after 1945, relapse into the role of a particularly suspect, potentially irredentist minority without effective protection.

No quick solutions to the general chaos reigning in the country occupied by the enemy after 1918 presented themselves. The Romanian occupation troops were able to ransack Budapest virtually unhindered between August and November 1919. They stole, among other things, 4,000 telephones—even from private homes. The value of goods plundered by the Romanian bands, mainly locomotives, railway carriages, machinery and draught animals, amounted to close on 3 billion gold crowns, twelve times more than the loan by which Hungary was put back on its feet financially four years later.[3] The hated treaty also caused a constant humiliation. Although Hungary was surrounded by countries much larger in area—Romania more than three times, Yugoslavia almost three times and Czechoslovakia one-and-a-half times larger—Hungary was only permitted a professional army of no more than 35,000 men without heavy artillery, tanks or aircraft. It had to agree to pay reparations, and an Allied Control Commission was set up to ensure compliance with the various conditions. Without the agreement of the League of Nations Hungary could not give up its independence, i.e. reunite with Austria.[4]

The only question on the minds of the overwhelming majority of Hungarians on both sides of the new borders during the subsequent years and decades was whether revision of the treaty could be attained by peaceful means or only by a victorious war. During the Paris peace conference in 1919/20 the British Prime Minister Lloyd George twice warned of a possible future threat to the peace of Central Europe posed by a Hungary bent on revenge: "There will never be peace in southeastern Europe if all these newly-established small states have a considerable Hungarian minority." One year later he again warned against forcing a third of Hungary's total population to live under foreign domination: "Peace will not rule if it turns out retrospectively that Hungary's claims are justified and that entire Hungarian ethnic groups have been transferred to Czechoslovakia and Transylvania [meaning Romania], merely because the conference had rejected dealing with the Hungarian question."[5]

There is no doubt even after publication of the relevant documents and records that the politicians of the three successor-states, led by Eduard Beneš, then Czechoslovak Foreign Minister (and subsequently President), were determined to make the largest possible territorial gains by whatever means. It is just as clear that they were supported in this primarily by France, and during the entire conference also by the British Foreign Office which, over the Hungarian question, had taken a position against its own Prime Minister. The radical domestic changes inside Hungary no longer had a decisive impact; all that the Great Powers in Paris had to do in the end was accept the *fait accompli* (the occupation of Hungary).

Why did Hungary receive no support at this fateful moment in its history either from the victors or from Western public opinion? Was it the old social élite of magnates, gentry, high clergy and the new-born upper middle class whose chauvinist approach destroyed first the mutual trust with the nationalities and then the world's respect and admiration after the suppression of the 1848/9 War of Independence? Or was Hungary blamed for having blindly followed the Austrian and German generals and diplomats into the war? Did Hungary thus have to pay the penalty for its totally unsuccessful nationalities and foreign policy of the previous fifty years?

The answer to such questions by Hungarian public opinion at the time was a resounding negative. Those responsible were the traitors of the old order, first and foremost Mihály Károlyi, an early agent of the Entente (in particular the French); his Jewish henchmen, such as the liberal Jászi and left-socialist Zsigmond Kunfi, were made the scapegoats. The Jewish Bolshevists, led by Béla Kun, figured as the main offenders; "the Jewish agents of world bolshevism", the Jewish intellectuals who subverted all national and Christian values, and the Jewish black market millionaires profiting from the nation's misery and from the soldiers serving in the field—it was they who had consigned Hungary to its fate. In short, the Jews and they alone were responsible for Trianon and the Hungarian tragedy.

The prominent role played by revolutionaries of Jewish origin (who regarded themselves as atheists and never acted on behalf of Jewry) in the workers' movements of Central and Eastern Europe was in no way a specifically Hungarian phenomenon. Names such as Rosa Luxemburg, Leon Trotsky, Victor Adler, Otto Bauer, Eduard Bernstein and Karl Radek are self-explanatory. Much has been written seeking to explain why Jews and members of minorities in general were represented far beyond their numerical proportion in revolutionary movements, and about the contradictory attitude of Socialists and Communists on the Jewish question. Jewish Messianism, conscious or unconscious renunciation of Jewish roots, conscious assimilation, the dissolution of nationalism into alienation by internationalism, Jewish self-hatred, the callous persecution of the Jewish class enemy and, last but not least, the redemption of humankind by the imminent World Revolution—all these applied to the leading actors in Hungary. Any attempt at a wide-ranging analysis of the motives and later careers of the individual protagonists would be beyond the scope of these reflections, but the politically significant question was not the "Why" but the obvious fact that the majority of Communist commissars (the estimates varying between 60 and 75 per cent) were Jews either by religion or by birth. Many Jewish intellectuals and scientists were to be found in the so-called "second reform generation" after the turn of the century, and among the guiding spirits of excellent journals such as *Nyugat* (The West) and *Huszadik Század* (Twentieth Century). The same was true of the "Galileo Circle" and the "Association of Freethinkers". However, these publications and groupings were élitist initiatives of a bourgeois-radical character, undertaken far from the seats of political power and unknown to the broad masses.

However, during the 133 days of the "Commune", as the Hungarians called the Soviet Republic, Jews appeared for the first time as rulers, bearers of an internationalist, atheist and Bolshevik (meaning also pro-Russian) regime. The brutal actions of the Red Guards and the revolutionary tribunals, especially after the suppression of increasing attempts at insurrection and strikes—in other words, the "Red Terror"—were blamed primarily on Tibor Szamuely and Otto Korvin, the functionaries responsible for domestic order. The former committed suicide, the latter was executed; both were Jews. The number of politically-motivated executions amounted to 300–400 (the highest estimate was 580).[6]

In vain did the representatives of the Jewish community and moderate conservative politicians, as well as independent writers, try to prove that most Jews not only did not ally themselves with Bolshevism but that, on the contrary, many industrialists, landowners and merchants were stripped of their assets, arrested or held as hostages. Jewry, Communism and "Red Terror" were nonetheless irrevocably lumped together over the next quarter of a century. "The experiences of 1918–19 have made the work of the reaction and restoration all too easy, greatly contributing to the failure of the gradual and general democratization that was characteristic of Western Europe to materialize in Hungary."[7]

The Revolution and Trianon thus destroyed the historic pact between the ruling political class and Hungarian Jewry. Of course, it was not only the part played by Jews in the radical revolutionary changes which led to this transformation. In his great work *The Dissolution of the Habsburg Monarchy* Jászi revealed the true reasons: namely, that Magyarization was no longer either needed or wanted, and nor was Jewish help in the fight against the nationalities— hence the radical change in public opinion. All of a sudden there was no longer a large body of national minorities but a competing Jewish middle class; as Jászi wrote, the ethnic bogeyman had been replaced by the Jewish bogeyman. "We were ruined not by outside enemies but by internal enemies," wrote one of the Christian-Socialist newspapers a few days after publication of the peace terms for Hungary at the beginning of 1920.[8] This Hungarian myth of a stab in the back had enormous significance for the dynamic of Hungarian anti-Semitism in the inter-war years. According to the argument habitually advanced, only the early anti-Semites recognized in time the disastrous consequences of the underlying evil, namely the promotion of emancipation and assimilation of Jews by the liberals. Thus the "Jewish Republic" of March 1919 marked only the climax of this development, and events had shown that assimilation had been only an outward manifestation. The Jew was now no longer merely the usurer, the profiteer condemned by God, but also the mortal enemy of the Hungarian nation as such.

The horrors perpetrated mainly after (but some also before) the German occupation on 19 March 1944 were the attendant circumstances of the organized mass murder of over half a million people, but these have tended to disguise their root-cause. For this one has to recall what is often forgotten: the chaotic birth of the era, lasting a quarter of a century, identified with the name of Miklós Horthy, who was elected the third (after János Hunyadi and Lajos Kossuth) Regent of the kingdom of Hungary on 1 March 1920.

After the withdrawal of Romanian troops, the newly-organized "National Army" marched into the capital during a heavy downpour of rain on 16 November 1919. At its head, on a white horse,* rode the commander-in-chief. Miklós Horthy de Nagybánya— temporarily Minister of War of the transitional government formed in Szeged—wearing the uniform of an admiral. After the trail of blood left behind by the officer detachments under his command, especially in the south and south-east, many people waited with baited breath, and the large Jewish community with undisguised alarm, to hear the first words of the counter-revolution's strongman.

The central theme of Horthy's reply to the speech with which he was welcomed was an accusation which became a precept of the "Christian-national" line. The Admiral, who spoke German better than Hungarian, called Budapest "*a bünös város*", the "guilty" or "sinful" city; "*bünös*" signified both adjectives. The capital had "denied its thousand-year history… flung its crown, its national colours into the mud, and wrapped itself in red rags".[9]

The fifty-one-year-old Vice-Admiral, who had been the last commander of the Austro-Hungarian navy, was politically an unknown quantity. In his *Memoirs* he described the period he spent as one of four aides-de-camp to Franz Joseph as the "five best years of my life". The old Emperor was his ideal: "the noblest, most chivalrous and most decent personage" he had ever encountered, and his guide in every difficult situation.[10] However, despite his firmly declared unshakeable loyalty to the House of Habsburg, Horthy behaved in a contradictory way when King Charles appeared unexpectedly and unannounced in Budapest on Easter Sunday, 27 March 1921, to reclaim his throne. Encouraged by Hungarian legitimists, he had already arrived from his Swiss exile the day before at Szombathely, travelling on to the capital accompanied by Count Antal Sigray, the government commissioner for western

---

* Note the role played by the white stallion in the earlier history of the Magyars. Horthy was thereafter often described as the "new Árpád".

Hungary. The last ruler of the House of Habsburg was honest and upright but politically inexperienced and twenty years younger than the Admiral—who, at their last meeting in the Palace of Schönbrunn, had declared his eternal loyalty in a tear-choked voice. After a two-hour confidential conversation between them, about the content of which contradictory versions exist, Charles returned to Switzerland. His claim that the Entente, in the person of the French Prime Minister Aristide Briand, had approved his démarche was at once officially denied by the French government. At any rate, Horthy made clear that, in face of a threatened military intervention by the Little Entente and the Great Powers, he had no intention, despite his loyalty to the King, of giving up the post of Regent, for which he had meanwhile acquired a taste.

Charles had misread the political conditions and possibilities in Hungary and Central Europe, and had taken Horthy's erstwhile oath of loyalty at face value. That is why he reappeared barely seven months later, on 20 October 1921. After the troops stationed in western Hungary swore a personal oath of allegiance to him with the encouragement of their regional commander Colonel Anton Lehár, a comrade-in-arms of Horthy from the days of the "White Terror", he announced the formation of a new government. Charles's march on Budapest with his loyalist soldiers resembled more an operetta in the style of the Colonel's famous brother Franz Lehár than a serious military operation. Thus the journey in an armoured special train from Sopron to Györ, a distance of 80 km., took ten hours because of the celebrations and welcomes in this traditionally Habsburg-friendly region. Horthy and his Prime Minister since April 1921, Count István Bethlen, had ample time meanwhile to comply with protests from the Great Powers and the Little Entente and mobilize loyal troops and paramilitary units. After a clash in the vicinity of Budapest with only a few casualties, Horthy had the King taken prisoner and handed him over to representatives of the Entente. The British exiled him to the Portuguese island of Madeira, where he died, aged only thirty-four, on 1 April 1922.[11]

The National Assembly, elected freely and by secret ballot (though boycotted by the Social Democrats because of the "White Terror"), resolved on 6 November 1921 to depose the House of Habsburg. Horthy's conduct *vis-à-vis* Charles's restoration attempts had allayed the suspicions of the successor-states and the Great Powers; he was now undisputed master in the castle of Buda, more than a Western-style constitutional monarch, but by no means a dictator.

Nothing in Horthy's professional career gave any indication of his later important, sometimes decisive role in Hungarian, even Central European history. His heroic reputation as the victor in the naval battle of Otranto in the Adriatic and as commander of the Austro-Hungarian navy were probably the crucial elements in the unanimous appointment of this professional officer from the Calvinist middle nobility as commander-in-chief of the Szeged National Army by the diverse counter-revolutionary groups even before the collapse of the Communist regime. Despite his participation in the various counter-revolutionary shadow governments, he cleverly managed always to go his own way. Thus, by linking up with the Transdanubian units commanded by Colonel Lehár he attained command of an army that had grown to 50,000 men—and, with it, power.

The Regent's surprising late career was due not only to luck but undoubtedly also to his personal qualities. Almost all foreign diplomats and visitors who met him praised his fine manners, sincerity, friendliness, rectitude and natural authority. As a young naval officer he had travelled the world, winning international military tournaments in fencing and tennis: he was a good horseman, hunter and bridge player. His talent for languages was also a great help to him. No less a man than James Joyce was his English teacher at Pula, which raises the question whether he was the source of the various Hungarian obscenities in *Ulysses*. Horthy also spoke French, Italian, Croatian and a little Slovak. The young officer brought home from his wide travels a lifelong admiration for England—and a large tattoo covering his left arm and part of his torso. When he was a young man, one of his diversions was singing, frequently accompanied in Pula by his friend Franz Lehár, at the time a naval bandmaster.[12]

However, the memoirs of Colonel Anton Lehár and the diary of one of the most notorious death-squad commanders, Pál Prónay, as well as reports by Horthy's diplomatic contacts and other documents that have become available over the years, throw light on darker chapters of his career. Recreating details about the numerous contradictions and inconsistencies in his life show a Janus-faced character, prey to inner conflicts which manifested themselves in his fluctuations between extreme right-radicalism and conservatism of the old school, between feeling and reason.[13] The outcome of such inner struggles often depended on the prevailing political situation, and on whomever then happened to have the greatest influence on him. This is evident from the ups and downs in the political triangle between Horthy and his two most important prime ministers, Count István Bethlen (1921–31) and Gyula Gömbös (1932–6). Horthy's inner conflict was also evident in his fatal oscillation between a moderate and a radical attitude to Jewish questions in the 1940s.[14]

Early fears about Horthy and a military dictatorship were by no means groundless. They were based on the "White Terror", which the German historian of Hungary Jörg Hoensch characterized as "the outrages perpetrated by right-wing extremist groups who enjoyed Horthy's protection and were never brought to justice, whose excesses greatly surpassed the 'Red Terror' in cruelty and numbers of victims". The victims were mainly Jews, real or supposed Communists, and many peasants who had dared to rise against the great landowners. No exact data exist, but estimated totals for the early 1920s vary between 626 and 2,000, others between 2,000 and 5,000. About 70,000 people were interned or arrested for shorter or longer periods.[15]

It is known from numerous domestic and foreign reports, eye-witness accounts and documents that, without the least semblance of legality, totally innocent men and women were beaten up and arrested, tortured and hanged. Two editors of the Social Democrat daily *Népszava* (People's Voice), Béla Somogyi and Béla Bacsó, were murdered barely a fortnight before Horthy's election as Regent, and their mutilated corpses thrown into the Danube. The murderers were among the officers of the special squads led by Prónay and Ostenburg, who on the day of the election formed a guard of honour at the entrance to Parliament. The commanders and some other officers proceeded into the Chamber with revolver holsters open and hand-grenades stuck into their belts. Horthy was elected by 131 votes out of 141.[16]

Throughout 1919 and 1920 he was under the direct influence of those right-radical young officers, who openly strove for a fascist military dictatorship. There were at the same time dozens of right-wing secret organizations—their number in 1920 was 101. Among the more significant were Ébredő Magyarok (Awakening Hungarians) and the Hungarian National Defence Association (called MOVE after its Hungarian initials); but the most important were the "Union of Etelköz", named after an early Magyar settlement at the mouth of the river Don, and the "Double Cross Blood Union". Their ideological leader was the former captain and secretary of state in Horthy's short-lived Ministry of War at Szeged, Gyula Gömbös.[17]

It is therefore not surprising that Horthy's relationship with the representatives of the gentry, such as Gömbös and his cronies, and the middle class moulded by them was far more relaxed than with the socially and often intellectually superior aristocrats. In any case he protected the murderous officer squads to the last and even succeeded, with the connivance of his current Minister of the Interior, in sabotaging the investigation into the double-murder of Somogyi and Bacsó initiated by the then Minister of the Interior, Ödön Beniczky, in response to international agitation. This minister, by then out of office, revealed the truth in 1925 in a sensational series of articles asserting that Horthy had been privy to the cover-up. The ex-minister was condemned to three years in prison, but released after three months. The newspaper was suppressed.[18]

A few months after Horthy's election his Prime Minister Count Pál Teleki, a convinced but "moderate" anti-Semite, introduced in Parliament the first anti-Jewish law in Europe since the Great War. This Numerus Clausus Law, passed on 22 September 1920, limited the proportion of Jewish university students to 6 per cent. The almost simultaneous reintroduction of corporal punishment added to the decline of the Teleki government's standing. The so-called "idea of Szeged" (*a szegedi gondolat*) was a nationalist-racist programme for a drastic "changing of the guard", whose leading principle, stressed by Gömbös, was the "Christian idea which we describe in short as race protection". This was the beginning of an unmistakable official Christian-nationalist, right-wing conservative counter-revolution, giving expression to an anti-Semitism of a kind which had been alien to the liberal élite of multinational Hungary.[19]

At the time the illusory vision of Hungary as a Christian bulwark against Bolshevism, Jewry and liberalism probably engrossed the rather weak intellect of the Regent as well. In 1922 he enthusiastically greeted the visiting Secretary-General of the American YMCA with the words: "I am delighted to meet the head of such an important anti-semitic organization." When the Hungarian currency lost value that same year, the Head of State declared in a conversation with the Austrian ambassador that this was the work of the "Elders of Zion"; because they had not succeeded in establishing Bolshevism, they were now trying to undermine the Hungarian economy. He did not have a great opinion of the neighbouring countries, with the exception of the Poles and possibly the Bulgarians. At the time of the British General Strike in 1926, Horthy, ever indignant about strikes and workers' protests, explained to the British military attaché that the world would have been eternally grateful to his government for an unsurpassable service if they had shot A.J. Cook, the miners' leader.[20]

A bizarre product of the racial-defence movement was the idea of "Turanism". This idea, directed against the West, strove for a union of the third, the "Turanian" world with Eastern Europe. Its programme proclaimed the unity of the Turanian peoples, who included the Turks, Tatars, Bulgarians, Finns, Uzbeks and Lapps, the Magyars being their western representatives. "Nordic morals" and "Turanian elemental force" were to serve as the basis for a new Hungary.[21]

The Horthy regime's romantic-nationalistic, populist, racist, anti-liberal, anti-intellectual and anti-cultural disposition, coupled with the purges and denunciations of professors and teachers (by no means only Jewish ones), led in the 1920s to an unprecedented brain-drain from the scientific-cultural milieu. In *Budapest 1900*[22] John Lukacs, the Hungarian-born historian, illustrates the astonishing international careers of so many gifted representatives of the Budapest generation of that period (see Chapter 35, below). Many of those who had opted to stay in the country, such as the composer Zoltán Kodály, the poet Mihály Babits and writer Zsigmond Móricz, and the scientists Gyula Pikler, Zsigmond Simonyi and Lajos Fülep, suffered harassment. The great poet Endre Ady was spared the fate of his friends by his untimely death, but even then incitement against this passionately anti-feudal and revolutionary voice continued: at a Roman Catholic convention in 1920[23] Bishop

Ottokár Prohászka claimed that Ady's soul had been "innoculated with Jewish blood".

It would be wrong to disregard the achievements of the Horthy era, above all the consolidation during the ten-year term of Count István Bethlen's government. Observers have often wondered how Horthy succeeded in remaining at the helm in a region where putsches and coups d'état were the norm and political stability was the exception. Though neither very cultured nor very intelligent, the Regent was shrewd and clever enough, at least at times, to listen to his advisers and to seek a middle course in difficult times.[24] That in spite of several crises Horthy left Bethlen, undoubtedly the most talented Hungarian politician of the inter-war years, free to formulate policy, and opted to reign rather than rule during that decade was proof that despite a few absurd ideas he was willing to curb his extremist friends, neutralise the hardliner Gömbös, and let Bethlen's liberal-conservative policy take its course.

By repressing right-wing radicalism, disarming the terrorist groups, reaching a compromise with the "tame" Social Democrats and depriving the divided Smallholders' Party of power, the Prime Minister prepared the ground for a restrictive electoral reform. The new electoral system entitled only 27.3 per cent (instead of 39.2 in 1920) to vote, and the reintroduction of the open ballot (except in large urban constituencies) guaranteed a comfortable majority for the Christian-Socialist grouping, renamed the "Unity Party". Domestic consolidation and Bethlen's open and pointed statements in his first two parliamentary speeches against any form of anti-Semitism and religious persecution won the confidence of the international world of finance. In 1923 the League of Nations accepted Hungary as a member, granting it a loan of 250 million gold crowns. Fiscal stability was restored, a currency reform was introduced in 1927, and after a modest upswing the value of industrial production stood 12 per cent higher in 1929 than in the pre-war years.

The sophisticated and highly educated Transylvanian aristocrat operated with great tactical skill and political perceptiveness in domestic and foreign policy, and proved outstandingly adept at parliamentary power play. Every party, from the Socialists to the Fascists, was represented in parliament, only the Communist Party being still banned. Yet during the entire Horthy regime far fewer of its leading figures were arrested, let alone executed, than in the "Fatherland of the Proletariat" during Stalin's purges. The press enjoyed almost total freedom (although almost a million adults were illiterate), the judiciary was independent and there were no restrictions on freedom of movement or travel. Despite anti-Semitic agitation by the extreme Right, even the provisions of the infamous Numerus Clausus Act of 1920 were tacitly watered down, and the proportion of Jewish university students rose in 1929–30 from 5.9 to 10.5 per cent. Foreign degrees were recognized without any difficulty.[25]

However, Bethlen left property and social conditions untouched. As before, 2,400 great magnates owned more than 36 per cent of the land; by contrast, 72.7 per cent of the peasantry owned only 10 per cent of it. The modest land reform had barely altered the miserable conditions of the totally or virtually landless mass who still made up 46 per cent of the 4.5 million peasants, a proportion five to six times higher than in neighbouring Romania, Yugoslavia and Czechoslovakia. The workers' real wages reached only 80–90 per cent of their pre-war level. At the same time the social division between the "top 52,000" and the rest was more marked than ever. In 1930/1 the élite 0.6 per cent of the population received over 20 per cent of unearned income, a much higher proportion than the comparable percentages for Germany or the United States. Despite prevailing anti-Semitism, the Jewish financial and industrial bourgeoisie could claim supremacy just as much as the "1,000-*hold* landowners".[26]

The global economic crisis and Hitler's seizure of power spelt the sudden end of this comparatively peaceful period, which saw a slow consolidation of the economy. Bethlen resigned in 1931, and a year later Gömbös, spokesman for the extreme Right, took over the government with a radical programme. However, in spite of his close relationship with Mussolini and later Hitler, his bark was worse than his bite. He carried out no drastic domestic changes before his unexpected death in 1936, but already during a meeting with the two dictators he set the agenda for Hungary's future foreign policy.

As a result of the revisionist course towards the successor-states and the strengthening of the right-wing camp, Hungary came increasingly under the political and economic influence of the Third Reich. With the help of the Axis powers (the term is said to have been coined by Gömbös) Hungary was now on the way to regaining parts of the old kingdom. This policy led, as we shall see, to considerable territorial changes in Hungary's favour but also to its entry into the war against the Soviet Union, entailing a heavy loss of Hungarian lives. At the beginning of 1941 even Horthy's beloved England (Churchill: "We have so many friends among the Hungarians!"[27]) followed an ultimatum with a declaration of war, whereupon the Hungarian government headed by László Bárdossy (executed as a war criminal in 1946) declared war on the United States. That gave birth to the best-known Hungarian joke of the war, which may have been invented in a BBC broadcast to Hungary. It consists of a conversation between President Franklin D. Roosevelt and Secretary of State Cordell Hull (in other versions with the Hungarian ambassador to Washington):

Hull: Mr President, I am sorry to announce that Hungary has declared war on us.
Roosevelt: Hungary? What kind of a country is it?
Hull: It is a kingdom.
Roosevelt: Who is the king?
Hull: They have no king.
Roosevelt: A kingdom without a king? Who is the head of state?
Hull: Admiral Horthy.
Roosevelt: Admiral? Now after Pearl Harbor we have another navy on our neck?
Hull: No, Mr President. Hungary has no navy, not even a seacoast.
Roosevelt: Strange. What do they want from us? Territorial claims, perhaps?
Hull: No, sir. They want territory from Romania.
Roosevelt: Did they declare war also on Romania?
Hull: No, Mr President, Romania is their ally.[28]

32. Adventurers, Counterfeiters, Claimants to the Throne: Hungary as Troublemaker in the Danube Basin

After the failed Kapp putsch in Berlin (12–17 March 1919) and in the midst of civil war in Russia, Horthy's Hungary, land of the victorious counter-revolution, was the last hope of the extreme Right. The participants in the Kapp putsch had received help from Hungary, and it was no accident that General Walter von Lüttwitz decamped to Hungary after the farcical episode. The murderers of the German Foreign Minister Walther Rathenau and Finance Minister Matthias Erzberger found temporary refuge in Hungary. General Erich Ludendorff gambled on the support of the newly-elected Regent Horthy, and after secret and confidential negotiations with Right-radical officers and politicians in Stephanskirchen (near Rosenheim) the die was cast. Ludendorff's concept of a "White International" was to be presented to Horthy by two special envoys.[1]

The Regent received the delegation on 17 May 1920, and was enthusiastic about the idea of annulling the so-called peace treaties in cooperation with the Bavarian, Austrian and Hungarian free corps, and subsequently liquidating the revolutionary and Socialist elements in Austria as well as in Prussia. Czechoslovakia would then be destroyed by a joint Hungarian-Austrian-Bavarian military operation. Hungary was to provide financial support and training facilities, and recover its pre-war borders as a reward for playing a key role in the affair. All this, of course, was to be the prelude to a massive military crusade against Bolshevism in Russia. The army of the (Russian) White Guards was to be supported in the mean time by counterfeit "Duma roubles". The conspirators wanted to forge 2 million of these "white" banknotes in Hungary; Horthy asked for further details, and instructed his closest cronies, Gömbös and

Prónay, commanders of the death squads, to continue the negotiations with Ludendorff's emissaries. Already on 1 June, three days
before the signing of the Treaty of Trianon, Gömbös informed the
German visitors, staying in one of Budapest's luxury hotels, that
Horthy was in complete agreement "so that now we can do something concrete about the matter".

A central committee was to be set up between the autumn of
1920 and spring of 1921 to procure weapons and raise a volunteer
corps in the three countries, as well as a central press office to coor-
dinate propaganda. Meanwhile the spokesman for the Russian
monarchists, General Vladimir Biskupski, contacted the Hungarian-German group. Horthy received Biskupski and the German
conspirators in separate audiences, even inviting Ludendorff's confidant Colonel Max Bauer and an emissary of the Bavarian Prime
Minister Gustav von Kahr to lunch at the royal summer palace of
Gödöllö. Bauer and Prónay also planned to send a band of Hungarian and Bavarian irregulars to Slovakia and the Sudetenland at
Christmas 1920 to provoke a rebellion and cause the collapse of
Czechoslovakia. Horthy promised his visitors further support for
the "White International", to include providing them with grain
deliveries and money for the acquisition of weapons from Germany.
However, the Hungarian Foreign Ministry and in particular Count
Pál Teleki, the Foreign Minister and later Premier, flatly rejected the
plan to print counterfeit roubles in Hungary. They refused even to
support Ludendorff indirectly through the "Awakening Hungarians" and MOVE.

Meanwhile rumours were spreading in Vienna, Berlin, Paris and
London, and above all in Prague, about seemingly fantastic but
nonetheless alarming conspiracy plans. Eventually the President of
Czechoslovakia, Tomáš Masaryk, personally took charge of the
matter, letting loose a Europe-wide thunderbolt. He leaked copies
of about fifty original documents—of concepts, the exchange of
letters between Ludendorff and Horthy, and minutes of the Hungarian-German secret meetings—to the London *Times* through his
old friend, the British East European expert R.W. Seton-Watson.
On 28 December 1920 the paper began printing a three-part series
entitled "European Conspiracy Exposed". The Czechoslovak Foreign Minister Eduard Beneš was so worried that he had already
ordered precautionary military measures.

The *Times* articles and the international media comments also revealed the key role played by a certain Ignác Trebitsch-Lincoln, who had been present at all the important meetings between Ludendorff, Horthy and Biskupski, and had evidently been one of the mentors of the "White International's" bizarre schemes. That was not the end of the grotesquerie: it was this very man, the closest collaborator of Max Bauer, who had sold the whole bundle of documents to the Czechoslovak authorities for 500,000 crowns (*ca.* \$40,000 at today's value).

Who was Trebitsch-Lincoln? And why did he betray his co-conspirators? Born in 1879 in the small provincial town of Paks in southern Hungary, this man called himself in his memoirs (published in 1931 in Vienna, afterwards in New York in English) "the greatest adventurer of the twentieth century". He had gained international "fame" as early as 1916 when, in the middle of the Great War, he published in English a similar mixture of fact and fiction entitled *Inventions of an International Spy*. This way why, despite all the indignation, people were gloating from Prague to London over Prussian officers having been taken in by such a notorious confidence trickster.

Although Trebitsch-Lincoln's reputation as a first-class scoundrel was well justified, he was far more than merely a rapacious swindler. No other Hungarian has ever been written about so copiously, in books and reports from Budapest to Shanghai, as this man. Yet only now, after the secret files of the British Foreign Office have been opened, and a Trebitsch biography by the British historian Bernard Wasserstein has been published that draws on them, has a better grasp of the fascinating life of this in many ways talented psychopath become possible.[2] The son of a respectable Jewish grain merchant, Trebitsch was successively a petty thief specializing in Budapest and Trieste in men's gold watches, a short-term student at the Royal Academy of Dramatic Art in Budapest, a journalist, a missionary—after his baptism on Christmas Day 1898—in a Presbyterian mission house in Hamburg, an Anglican clergyman in Montreal where in sermons delivered in Yiddish, Hungarian and English he exhorted Jewish immigrants to convert, and curate in the village of Appledore in Kent, England. A year later, having in the mean time adopted the additional surname Lincoln because of his admiration

for the American President, he miserably failed his ordination exam-
ination and abandoned his clerical ambitions.

The turning-point in his life came in 1906, when the British
chocolate magnate and philanthropist B.S. Rowntree engaged the
linguistically talented Hungarian as his private secretary and head of
a team of research workers who were conducting a large project of
surveying land tenure and taxation on the continent. At the end of
this research assignment Rowntree gave his assistant as a parting gift
an unsecured loan, which today would amount to about half a million dollars. The Rowntree connection also opened his way into
politics. In April 1909 Trebitsch secured nomination as prospective
Liberal parliamentary candidate for the North Yorkshire constituency of Darlington—his naturalization was rushed through a month
later. He then proceeded to Budapest and thence to Belgrade. On
the strength of letters of recommendation from the Foreign Office,
the British legations in those capitals had to organize meetings for
him with members of the respective governments and other high-
ranking personages. Trebitsch, who by then showed signs of megalomania, proposed various grandiose schemes for establishing an
English-Hungarian and English-Serb bank with assurances that
investments of several millions would be forthcoming, but it was
later discovered that the bankers whose names he submitted as
investors had never heard of him.

When Trebitsch-Lincoln was elected on 15 January 1910 as
Member of Parliament for Darlington, albeit with a majority of
only 29 votes, it was a sensation for several reasons. For one, the Liberals had lost ground in the entire country, and it was thus all the
more surprising that a young foreigner without means and with a
strong accent, who had never before participated in a British election and lacked any political experience, should have got into Parliament at his first attempt. The young MP left immediately for
Budapest to meet his widowed mother, and in an interview with
the *Pester Lloyd* he announced large-scale Anglo-Hungarian economic co-operation which of course came to nothing like all his
other fantastic projects. Meanwhile, although parliamentarians did
not then receive any remuneration, he was living the high life,
employing two private secretaries and looking after three relations
whom he had invited to England (they left soon after, sorely

disappointed). Trebitsch's political career was short-lived because when a premature general election was called for December 1910, the Liberals did not nominate him. The Austro-Hungarian ambassador to London had in the mean time informed the Foreign Secretary of the MP's youthful misdeeds; moreover he was bankrupt, but for political reasons his creditors did not take him to court.

As always this phony with uncanny persuasive powers managed to land on his feet. He rented a fourteen-room house in Watford (a town about 20 miles north of London), employed a staff of six, and also occupied a palatial mansion in Bucharest. In 1911/12 he founded two private firms and two joint-stock companies for the exploitation of oil deposits in Romania and Galicia and the importing of oil-drilling equipment. His contacts and self-confident manner helped him to win over such persons as a Prince Radziwill and a Prince Lobkowitz to act as board members for the project in Galicia. Only a dribble of oil was found, and during the Balkan War Trebitsch, in Bucharest, was once again insolvent. The spring of 1914 found him back in London, committing fraudulent acts against his erstwhile patron, Rowntree.

At the outbreak of the Great War the former journalist, failed missionary, discredited politician and bankrupt businessman, threatened with impending arrest as a confidence trickster, turned to the career in which he was to achieve worldwide notoriety—international espionage. In December 1914 he offered to work for the British intelligence services as a double agent, presenting the following fantastic scheme to a distrustful officer: he, Trebitsch, would go to the then neutral Netherlands, offer his services as a spy to the Germans operating there and, having gained their confidence, lure the Kaiser's fleet into the North Sea where the British Navy could then easily ambush and destroy it. Undaunted by a chilly reception, Trebitsch crossed on his own initiative to Rotterdam, where he offered his services to the German consul-general, having prepared a long memorandum in German on methods of communication. After his return he offered the British authorities what he alleged were German secret codes, but they wanted nothing to do with him. The Germans' reaction is unrecorded.

His biographer Wasserstein proves convincingly that, despite his bragging Trebitsch had never before been involved in spying. Be that as it may, in January 1915 he took passage on a liner for New York, where several new women friends and his three brothers living in the United States helped him along, and in May 1915 managed to place two sensational articles in the week-end supplement of the New York tabloid *World* about his espionage activities on behalf of the Germans. An ex-Member of the British Parliament as Berlin's agent! Inspite of being an amalgam of mostly ridiculous inventions, the well-publicized revelations were a first-class propaganda coup for the German side. The incensed British now went into action, and Trebitsch was arrested. However, the extradition process was long-drawn-out, and he could live comfortably even during his confinement in return for decoding intercepted German messages, of which he actually had no idea. Five days before the publication of his *Revelations of an International Spy* in January 1916, he escaped from jail.

After thirty-five days on the run Trebitsch was recaptured and returned to England, where he was sentenced for fraud to three years' imprisonment on the Isle of Wight. His naturalization had already been revoked. He was supposed to be released in June 1919, but at the last moment he was retained in custody. At the time the Soviet Republic was still in existence in Hungary, and the head of MI5 warned that Trebitsch was extremely dangerous, and could become "a kind of Central European Lenin". On being released nine days after the fall of Kun's regime, he proceeded not to Hungary but to Germany.

Within a few weeks, however, he managed once again to draw international attention to himself with his articles in the Right-radical *Deutsche Zeitung*, and through contacts with the entourage of the Kaiser and Crown Prince living in exile in the Netherlands (although he never had a chance of meeting, let alone interviewing either of them). However, he was able to worm his way into the confidence of Colonel Bauer and through him into the circle of conspirators, and on the first day of the Kapp putsch Trebitsch appeared before the astonished international press as the Foreign Ministry's head of publicity and chief censor, in which role he delighted in blue-pencilling or simply discarding the reports of British journalists. When all the fuss was over, the correspondent of the London *Daily Telegraph* wrote that there was something

Olympian about this scoundrel, the Hungarian Jew who made common cause with the most virulent anti-Semites. Rumours were abroad that he was a Russian, British and German spy—possibly all three versions were correct.

This was the background to the key role Trebitsch played in the launching of the "White International". However, he had enemies within the German radical Right, who feared that he was "an English spy disguised as a German nationalist", which of course was nonsense, but as a Jew he was still a red rag to some of them. Anyway he got wind of a letter in which Major Franz von Stephani, a co-conspirator who later became a Right-radical deputy in the Reichstag, suggested that Trebitsch should be done away with on his visit to Budapest. In spite of Bauer's protestations that he would be safe, Trebitsch disappeared soon after in Vienna—with a suitcase full of explosive documents. When the expected repercussions did not occur, the Czechs refused to pay the promised second instalment of his agreed fee (300,000 crowns), whereupon he sued the Prague authorities and threatened them with exposure; the Czechs then asserted that he had sold them forged papers. Although this was not true, the man who had first tried to hawk the documents about the "White International" to the French, British and Americans was kept in detention for four months in an Austrian jail and deported on his release in June 1921. According to a report by the British consul in Trieste, he was seen there, allegedly in possession of six different passports (three of them Hungarian).

Meanwhile he decamped to China, and on the ship succeeded in wheedling $15,000 from a gullible American millionaire for a highly imaginative project. He later served as adviser to several Chinese warlords, even accompanying them on arms-buying missions to Europe. In China Trebitsch had a chance to indulge his genuine inclination for the supernatural and mysticism. Having converted to Buddhism, he was initiated as a monk in May 1931 with the name Chao Kung, and for several years he had a following of twelve European novices of both sexes who lived with him under Spartan conditions in Shanghai or joined him on travels to Europe to meet co-religionists. In December 1937 Chao Kung sent a letter to Horthy by the hand of a Lithuanian nun, "Tao Lo",[3] who also took as a gift an inscribed copy of Chao Kung's latest book *Dawn or*

Doom of Humanity. When the Budapest tabloid *Az Est* (The Evening) reported that the Japanese wanted to crown Chao Kung emperor of China, the monk dismissed it as a case of mistaken identity. He himself wanted to return to Hungary and spend the rest of his life there. Chao Kung concluded with the lines from Vörösmarty's *Appeal:*

> Oh, Magyar, keep immovably
> Your native country's trust.
> For it has borne you, and at death
> Will consecrate your dust!

Trebitsch-Chao Kung was probably a manic-depressive with a pathological overestimation of his own worth. His last biographer compared him to a "pseudo-Messiah". But even in this later incarnation Kung he remained picturesque and hyper-active: in 1941 he wanted to fly to Berlin to talk to Hitler about Tibet, India and China, which caused discord in Nazi circles from Shanghai to Berlin— even at the Heydrich-Ribbentrop level. He was denied entry to both Berlin and Hungary, but the book dedicated by Chao Kung to Horthy survived the siege and fire at the palace, and with its edges singed and linen binding mildewed, is today housed with the rest of Horthy's books in the library of Parliament on the Danube embankment.

The story of the "White International", along with the machinations of Trebitsch-Lincoln, were long forgotten when a news flash from the Hague on 14 December 1925 struck Hungarian politics like a thunder: the retired Colonel Aristid Jankovich had been arrested while trying to change a forged 1,000-franc note at a bank. During his interrogation the Hungarian officer confessed that he had come to the Netherlands not as a private person but as the representative of the Hungarian Foreign Ministry, carrying in his diplomatic pouch French notes to the nominal value of 10 million francs. The Dutch authorities immediately informed their colleagues in Paris, and that same month the Paris police chief Beniot, accompanied by several high officials and detectives, arrived in Budapest. The French government asked the Hungarian authorities to initiate an investigation at once.[4]

The scandal spread to ever-widening circles. Police inquiries and investigations by a parliamentary committee, set up after much wrangling, revealed an explosive international and domestic background. The trail once again led to the Right-radical German officers' group around General Ludendorff. Their original idea had been to flood France with forged banknotes, but after Hitler's failed putsch attempt in Munich in November 1923 the Ludendorff people were willing to hand over the printing presses to their Hungarian friends via their old contacts with the Gömbös group. Hungarian government circles had, incidentally, already tried in 1920–1 to forge Russian, Yugoslav and Czechoslovak banknotes, always with the same aim: to cause as much damage as possible to the targeted countries and finance irredentist propaganda there.

Prince Lajos Windischgrätz, who played the key role, was an enigmatic and notorious figure. During his turbulent career he had flirted with the whole gamut of political groupings, from the Left to the extreme Right. In the autumn of 1918, shortly before the bourgeois revolution, he was Minister for Food Supply, and was sent by King Charles to Switzerland with the task of organizing transport for potatoes to alleviate the famine in Budapest. It is said that he misappropriated the large sum of money at his disposal, partly for his private gain and partly to finance counter-revolutionary propaganda. He was popularly nicknamed "the Potato prince". The Károlyi government took legal action against him, but this was later hushed up by the counter-revolutionary regime. Windischgrätz got his own back by becoming the wire-puller and prosecution witness in the witch-hunt against Károlyi, claiming that he had been a French spy.

The plan was worked out in the summer of 1923 with Bethlen's knowledge. Windischgrätz negotiated with Ludendorff and Hitler, who subsequently sent the German engineer Arthur Schultze to Budapest; he assisted in the purchase of the printing machines in Leipzig. Dezsö Rába, Windischgrätz's secretary, looked after procuring the necessary paper, also with German help. The counterfeiting workshop was set up in the cellar of the army's Cartographic Institute, with the full knowledge and consent of its head, the former Prime Minister Count Pál Teleki. It was there that the German expert, together with the professionals of the Institute, manufactured the plates. Printing began in 1924 after careful preparation, and between 30,000 and 35,000 thousand-franc notes were produced by the autumn of 1925.

The bundles of counterfeit notes were blessed by the Catholic bishop István Zadravetz, and the Chief of Police and Security of Budapest, Imre Nádossy, took personal charge of transporting the delicate consignment in a delivery van first to the Foreign Ministry and thence via diplomatic pouch to the West. (Both Nádossy and Zadravetz were members of the racist secret "Etelköz Association".) "What's in the parcels?" asked one official. "Counterfeit money, of course", replied Nádossy. The officials had the time of their lives enjoying "good old Uncle Imre's" sense of humour, and the consignment was dispatched forthwith.

The principal aim of the ringleaders was to support irredentist propaganda activity, especially in Czechoslovakia; organize free corps units; and, last but not least, harm the hated French, the chief culprits at Trianon. The Opposition and the political émigrés hoped that the scandal would precipitate the Bethlen government's fall, but in vain. Windischgrätz and Nádossy were sentenced on 26 May 1926 to four years' imprisonment each, while the other accused got away with sentences of between four months and a year. The two principal accused were pardoned as early as the beginning of 1928.

Against all expectations Bethlen survived the crisis. Since neither the Western Powers nor the liberal Opposition wished to risk a change to an extreme right-wing government. Bethlen offered his resignation, but Horthy would not accept it, and Britain and France pronounced themselves in favour of a continuation of Bethlen's policies. No harm befell Count Teleki either. In the mean time Windischgrätz's secretary, one of the chief witnesses, withdrew his testimony at the court of appeal, which meant that the legitimists, who had consistently worked for Bethlen's fall, lost their most important prosecution witness—who died of poisoning after an invitation to tea by Gömbös. Secret documents from the Bethlen archives, published in 1972, suggest that numerous high-ranking personages had been embroiled in the affair from the first. Windischgrätz and Gömbös, as well as Right-radical circles, exploited the matter subtly to blackmail Bethlen.

Barely a year and a half after this murky affair, Hungarian efforts at mobilizing world opinion in favour of a revision of the Treaty of Trianon and the restoration of lost territories achieved a significant success. On 21 June 1927 a full-page article appeared in the London

Daily Mail, entitled "Hungary's Place under the Sun". Its author, Lord Rothermere, was the owner of that newspaper and of others with circulations totalling millions. Rothermere, then aged fifty-nine, and in particular his elder brother Lord Northcliffe (born Alfred Harmsworth, 1865–1922), had revolutionized the British press scene. The essay, with a detailed map, proposed that the unfair provisions of the dictated treaty be revised; otherwise there was no prospect of maintaining long-term accord in Central Europe. The economically pointless and ethnically unjust borders, which could lead to another war, should be altered by plebiscites watched over by international observers. Rothermere suggested that the successor-states should voluntarily give up those border-territories whose population comprised at least 2 million Hungarians. The map, with some exaggeration, showed a million Hungarians in southern Slovakia, 600,000 in Transylvania and 400,000 in Voivodina.

The explicitly pro-Hungarian article hit the Continent like a bombshell, above all Hungary and the countries of the Little Entente. As expected, the attack from such a well-known British newspaper triggered off counter-reactions and a media war that lasted till 1929. The British Foreign Office was irritated and embarrassed, and even the Bethlen government was bewildered since the official line, with the slogan "Return everything!" (*Mindent vissza!*), implied the full restoration of the lands of St Stephen.[5] Yet Rothermere's article, followed soon after by a second one with the sensational title "Europe's Powder Keg", was incomparably more important for Hungary's fight against injustice than the not always professional propaganda activities of the Budapest Foreign Ministry.

While the mouthpiece of the British official viewpoint, *The Times*, turned up its nose at the amateurish efforts of the parvenu *Mail*, warning in an editorial of 27 July against the enormous damage which new frontier changes would cause to all involved, the Hungarian public fell into ecstasy. Every newspaper sent special correspondents to London. The old, passionately nationalist journalist Jenö Rákosi, who had already dreamed at the turn of the century of a Hungary with 30 million people (cf. Chapter 26), fully embraced the cause of the Rothermere campaign in his influential paper *Pesti Hirlap*.

"Rothermere will have a full chapter in Hungarian history to himself," wrote Rákosi in his paper. The conservative novelist Ferenc Herczeg, later president of the newly-formed "League for Revision" with a membership that soon approached 2 million in 900 branches, went even further in praise of Rothermere's pro-Hungarian journalistic activities: "Ever since Gutenberg invented printing, no other writing has had such an effect on human hearts as Rothermere's articles on Hungary!" Every word expressed by the distant press magnate was reverently repeated in the Hungarian press, likewise his Christmas message: "The day of liberation will come," his Lordship informed the Hungarians from Palm Beach, Florida: "My meeting here with representatives of public opinion has convinced me that the sympathy of the world would be on Hungary's side, if Hungary were to make a demand for the revision of the Treaty of Trianon."[6]

The Hungarians' enthusiasm for Rothermere knew no bounds. He himself admitted later that he had received 200,000 letters, postcards and telegrams from Hungary and from Hungarians all over the world, and at the height of the campaign he had to engage two Hungarian secretaries to cope with the correspondence. Artistic embroideries and simple wood-carvings, a golden fountain-pen from the city fathers of Budapest, an old Kossuth flag and the valuable sword of General Hadik, who had once raised Frederick the Great's hackles with his exploits in Berlin, were only some of the innumerable gifts with which he was inundated. Over 1.2 million Hungarians signed the vote of thanks, which a high-ranking delegation handed to him in twenty-five lavish leather-bound volumes. Horthy later wrote in his Memoirs: "Had there not been a deadline for the presentation, the entire nation would probably have added their signatures."

What persuaded Rothermere, both as a journalist and as a private person, to take up the cudgels for the Hungarians' case? What or who gave the impetus to the campaign? In his book *My Campaign for Hungary*, published in 1939, he recounted that he had stayed in Hungary with some friends at Whitsuntide in 1927, and been deeply impressed by the annual protest meeting against Trianon, which happened to be held at that time. He also found the Hungarian nation congenial....

It was not till fifty years later, when a letter from Lord Rothermere dated 30 April 1928 to Princess Stephanie Hohenlohe became known, that the riddle was finally solved:

As I have already told you on several occasions, my interest in Hungary was aroused principally by you. I had no idea that the enumeration of Hungary's woes and her unfair treatment would trigger off such worldwide sympathy.[7]

Rothermere's commitment to Hungary's case began early in 1927 at the roulette tables in the Monte Carlo casino, where he got to know the attractive, vivacious and highly intelligent "Steph", as she was known to her friends. At this first meeting he complained that there had been no interesting stories in his *Daily Mail* of late, whereupon the Princess told him about Hungary's shocking fate, which touched so many private lives: families separated, farms divided, and areas overwhelmingly populated by Hungarians granted to the greediest neighbouring countries by the Treaty of Trianon. During a subsequent lunch at the Rothermere villa, Steph—lacking a map—was only able to show the curious peer where Hungary was actually situated with the help of a small picture in the *Encyclopaedia Britannica*. It was on this occasion that Rothermere, whose press secretary was also present, made the memorable statement: "You know, my dear, until today I had no idea that Budapest and Bucharest are two different cities…"

But what were the Princess's motives? Certainly not, as she later asserted, her "patriotic sentiments for the Hungarian nation"; she did not speak a word of Hungarian and had never lived in the country although, strangely, she travelled all her life on a Hungarian passport. She was born some years before the turn of the century in Vienna as Stephanie Richter, of Jewish origin (according to her own information, only on her mother's side). The bright and physically precocious young girl was introduced through her father, a well-known lawyer, and with the help of a Princess Metternich into aristocratic circles, and after a purported affair with Archduke Franz Salvator, the Emperor's son-in-law, the pregnant Steph was quickly married off to Prince Franz Hohenlohe, the military attaché in the Austro-Hungarian Embassy in St Petersburg, who was up to his ears in debt. They were married in London in 1914, but hardly saw each other during the war (she worked as an Austrian Red Cross nurse) and were divorced in 1920; after the collapse of the Monarchy Hohenlohe, who had been born in Hungary, opted for Hungarian citizenship for family reasons. That was how Steph came to have a Hungarian passport and a title. When she met Rothermere she was living in Paris, and was alleged to own a villa in Biarritz; at any rate, she had excellent connections from Paris to London and from Vienna to Budapest, and lived—on what resources is unknown— the life of a high-flyer. For a decade she was his adviser and mistress, and was undoubtedly the inducement for his commitment to Hungary. Above all, she was his direct link with Hitler, to whom he regularly sent letters of congratulation on each anniversary of his seizure of power. She organized Rothermere's meeting with Hitler and carried on a liaison with, among others, Hitler's personal aide, Captain Fritz Wiedemann, for whom she arranged a meeting with Lord Halifax, the British Foreign Secretary. The then Czech Minister (later Foreign Minister) Jan Masaryk bitterly portrayed the role of this *éminence grise*:

If there is any decency left in this world? A great scandal will erupt one day when the role which Steffi Hohenlohe, née Richter, played during the visit of Wiedemann is revealed. This world-famous secret agent, spy and swindler, who is a full Jewess, constitutes today the centre of Hitler's propaganda in London. Wiedemann stayed at her place. She keeps Hitler's photograph on her desk, inscribed "To my dear Princess Hohenlohe—Adolf Hitler", and next to it a photograph of Horthy, dedicated to the "great stateswoman".[8]

The Hungarian connection of her friend and temporary employer had an important place in the turbulent life of this adventuress. During 1927–8 a plan was also afoot to have Lord Rothermere's young son, Esmond Harmsworth, crowned king of Hungary. The idea, mooted mainly by Rákosi and anti-Habsburg circles, may sound ridiculous today, but in the context of the Rothermere hysteria then prevailing in Hungary it was not confined to rumour. Rothermere himself wrote in his memoirs that military and economic circles, and in particular editor-in-chief Rákosi whom he had met several times in London, Paris and Venice, stated their willingness to put up Rothermere or his son as candidates. He appeared flattered, of course, that himself the idea of a Harmsworth dynasty should even be considered; he was "deeply touched by the honour that my Hungarian friends have shown me by suggesting my name for one of the oldest and most historical thrones of Europe".

In an undated personal note to Steph, Rothermere intimated the direction of his ambitions more openly than in his long-winded articles or interviews with Hungarian papers: "If they want to save the monarchy in Hungary, then there is only one man who is able to do so—Esmond Harmsworth. No Habsburg or royal prince from somewhere else can accomplish it." Since Hungary had signed a treaty of friendship with Mussolini's Italy, thereby breaking out of its international isolation, the question of a Hungarian kingdom played a significant role. Rákosi in particular wanted to involve Mussolini in it, and Rothermere too had met the dictator previously.

Esmond Harmsworth's trip to Hungary was actually a trial run— all he was supposed to do was accept an honorary doctorate from the University of Szeged on behalf of his father—but in fact the young man was received like a king or an heir to the throne.[9] On his arrival in Budapest he was greeted by the mayor, several former prime ministers and other dignitaries, and a crowd of about 100,000 appeared in front of his hotel. Thousands of Boy Scouts, postmen and railway employees in uniform, regional associations and peasant delegations from nearby villages in national costumes gave him a march-past. The young man was wined and dined and received by the Regent, the Prime Minister and the Cardinal-Archbishop. Organizations ranging from the right-wing "Awakening Hungarians" to the Jewish Ladies' Auxiliaries were represented at the various festivities. A firework display from the citadel of Buda and a grant map of the old and the amputated Hungary, symbolically depicted in a football stadium by girls wearing national costume, completed the program of events in Budapest. Harmsworth next travelled with his escort by special train to Debrecen and to Szeged where a street was renamed "Rothermere". An array of other streets, parks, gardens and settlements throughout the country and even a tennis trophy were named in his honour, and articles, songs and odes were dedicated to him.

After this journey by Rothermere's son, well-publicised internationally, Rákosi tried during a lengthy visit to England and later in an interview with Mussolini to get the Rothermeres to contend for the vacant throne of Hungary. Rothermere told the story that when he had objected that Hungary had no need for a king unfamiliar with the Hungarian language, the old journalist cited the example of Bulgaria: Prince Alexander of Battenberg, son of Prince Alexander of Hesse and nephew of the Russian Tsar Alexander II, had been elected in 1879 as the first ruler of the independent principality of Bulgaria. Rákosi's attempt to win Mussolini over to his idea was a resounding failure: the dictator informed him that, although he was set against the accession of one of the three Habsburg archdukes closest to the Imperial throne, Otto, Albrecht and Joseph, he considered it out of the question that the proud Hungarian nation would accept a journalist, and a foreign one at that, as its king.[10]

Horthy, Bethlen and Gömbös were from the very first against a Habsburg restoration, and totally against Rothermere's diverse monarchist ideas. The Hungarian ambassador in London reported to Bethlen as early as the summer of 1929 that the noble lord had put aside his royal aspirations, at least for the time being. In 1932 Princess Hohenlohe tried unavailingly to procure for herself an annuity from the Hungarian government as a reward for her "selfless work for Hungary". However, the same year Rothermere granted her a generous annual allowance, which he discontinued at the beginning of 1939. She sued him, but the case lapsed as soon as the war started.

Although during the 1930s Rothermere concentrated his interest on Hitler's Germany, he sponsored, with a Hungarian factory owner, a well-publicized non-stop flight from Newfoundland to Budapest by a plane named "Justice for Hungary". He congratulated Hitler on the occasion of the Vienna Awards in favour of Hungary, and was present on 11 November 1938 when Horthy rode into Kassa on a white horse.

It was probably an amalgam of personal motives—not least vanity but also his sympathy with Hitler and Mussolini, the fascination of the princess, an unexpected international echo and the exuberant reaction of the Hungarian public—which moulded Rothermere's attitude from beginning to end in the question of Trianon. Material interests played no part in the matter. He described in his memoirs the unbelievable enthusiasm with which the Hungarians had honoured him at the border, in Budapest and at Kassa as late as November 1938. With the outbreak of war soon after its publication,

Rothermere had to withdraw the book—which was not sparing in its acclaim for Hitler. Thus Steph's complaint that Rothermere had suppressed her role in Hungary had soon ceased to be relevant. Although in his role as Pretender Lord Rothermere may have been exposed to the ridicule of insiders in Britain, he was and remained a legend in Hungary. All the events that he and his son occasioned in 1927–8 and even in 1938 were manifestations of a characteristic that the Magyars call "*délibáb*"—literally *Fata Morgana* or illusion. This tendency that the psychoanalyst Sándor Ferenczi described as "magic thinking", this talent for daydreaming, shaped the attitude of both the élite and the populace in historic crisis situations, such as 1848–9, 1918–19 and most of all the Second World War. William M. Johnston's *The Austrian Mind* contained the following comment on the *délibáb* phenomenon:

Readiness to see the world through rose-coloured glasses induced Magyars to exaggerate their grandeur, while they ignored the misery of subject peoples. [...] Capacity for dreaming has made Magyars superlative advocates, ever ready to defend Hungary as an exception among nations.[11]

33. Marching in Step with Hitler: Triumph and Fall. From the Persecution of Jews to Mob Rule

On 3 April 1941 at 0915 the Hungarian news agency MTI issued a brief news flash: "The Royal Hungarian Privy Councillor and Prime Minister Count Pál Teleki has died suddenly under tragic circumstances during the night." A little later a short teleprinter report described how his valet had found the head of government dead in his bed around 0645. Both messages concealed the most important fact, namely that the respected sixty-one-year-old statesman had not died of natural causes. Teleki had ended his life with a bullet in his right temple—a protest by the desperate Prime Minister, forsaken by his commander-in-chief and friend the Regent, against the already decided and looming German-Hungarian attack on their southern neighbour, Yugoslavia.[1]

At 9 o'clock a cabinet meeting was convened with the Foreign Minister presiding. Its decision was to keep the suicide secret since "it could make a bad impression on the Germans. That would be dangerous now; German public opinion could turn against us." The tacit worry underlying this was the question of what would become of the territorial gains in the south promised in return for military cooperation. For fear of "misunderstandings" in the German-Hungarian relationship, at first not even the German ambassador Otto von Erdmansdorff was informed. His telegram with the suggestion that Hitler and Ribbentrop should send the Regent, the Foreign Minister and the widow telegrams of condolence arrived in Berlin at 2 o'clock in the afternoon; only during his visit of condolence to the Foreign Ministry was he told in "strictest confidence" about the suicide. The reason given by Teleki's deputy was over-exertion and anxiety over the deteriorating economic situation and his wife's serious heart condition.

Meanwhile news of the circumstances surrounding the death spread like wildfire through the capital. The government realized that further silence would be more suspicious and vexing than making the truth public. Eight-and-a-half hours after the body was discovered, a second communiqué was issued, with a medical certificate. A solemn state funeral was held on 7 April. The very next day the Germans attacked Yugoslavia and on 11 April, Good Friday, Hungarian units crossed the southern border. Hitler kept his word. Hungary received the Bácska (today part of Voivodina), the Baranya triangle and the Muraköz: altogether 11,475 square km. containing 1,030,000 inhabitants. However, the proportion of Hungarians was only 39 per cent (according to the Yugoslav census it was 30 per cent); Germans and Serbs made up 19 and 16 per cent of the population respectively (according to the Yugoslav census there were 47 per cent South Slavs).

Teleki had already been Prime Minister under Horthy and was the actual architect of the so-called revisionist policy. Formerly a loyal Habsburg legitimist but also the creator of the first "*Numerus Clausus*" legislation and co-creator of the "Jewish Laws" of 1938 and 1939, the Transylvanian aristocrat conducted at the same time an ever more difficult moderate "pendulum policy" between his deep-rooted fondness for England and the reality of increasing German influence.

In the framework of this diplomacy of small steps, Hungary had concluded in December 1940 a treaty of "eternal friendship" with Yugoslavia. After the Yugoslav government had joined and signed the German-Italian-Japanese triple pact on 25 March 1941, patriotic officers in Belgrade toppled the government and the regency, and given the under-age King Peter full powers. Hitler was furious, and resolved to launch an immediate attack on Yugoslavia. The Italians, Hungarians and Bulgarians were to assist in dismembering the country, which was already weakened by tensions between the Serbs and Croats. Teleki had previously succeeded in keeping Hungary out of the war as a "non-combatant" state, and summed up the principal aim of his foreign policy in secret letters to his ambassadors in London and Washington:

We have to stay out of the conflict at any price. The outcome of the war is doubtful. At any rate, the most important thing for Hungary is to remain unscathed when the European conflict ends. At all times we must only put our country, our youth and our army at risk on our own behalf and not on anybody else's.[2]

Teleki faced a terrible personal dilemma. In a letter to a relation written shortly before his death he openly revealed his apprehension: "We shall lose our honour before the world if we attack Yugoslavia. But my position is very difficult because the Regent, half of the government and the parliamentary majority are against me." Naturally he too was in favour of recovering the territories lost to Yugoslavia, but not as Nazi Germany's accomplice and not at the cost of an irrevocable break with Britain and the United States. He saw his life's work as being to win over world opinion for the just cause of the Trianon Treaty's revision. Now, however, the concept represented by the fanatically pro-German chief of the general staff Henrik Werth (an ethnic German) carried the day. Horthy was keen to be able to continue his work of restoring lost Hungarian land now in the south.

Teleki left letters addressed to Horthy—one a suicide note and the other a letter of resignation in case he should fail and remain alive:

Your Serene Highness!

We have become breakers of our word—out of cowardice—in defiance of the Treaty of Eternal Friendship. The nation feels this, and we have thrown away its honour. We have placed ourselves on the side of scoundrels—for there is not a word of truth in the stories of atrocities—against the Hungarians and/or the Germans! We shall become the despoilers of corpses, the most abominable of nations! I did not restrain you. I am guilty.

3 April 1941   Pál Teleki[3]

However, neither Teleki's dramatic warnings nor his final gesture of committing suicide could any longer influence events. Nor did the unusually forceful words of the British Minister Sir Owen O'Malley on the occasion of his condolence visit to the Regent on 7 April have any effect. Horthy stressed the "sacred duty of restoring the frontiers of Hungary". No assistance could be expected from Britain, and Hungary had to be extremely careful not to antagonize Berlin and invite later reprisals by Germany. O'Malley was very disappointed and warned the Regent that if he "entered into such a corrupt bargain with Germany or in any way acted as a Hungarian jackal to the German lion against a state with which he had just signed a treaty of eternal friendship, his country could expect no indulgence, no sympathy, and no mercy from a victorious Britain and United States of America and that he personally ... would be covered with well-deserved contempt and dishonour." Horthy remained unimpressed. "It's no use talking to me," he said, "I have made up my mind."[4]

Barely two months later the Hungarian military, convinced of a final German victory, succeeded in their efforts to enter the war against the Soviet Union. Teleki's successor, the former Foreign Minister László Bárdossy, was given a welcome pretext for declaring war by an incident unexplained to this day: the bombing of Kassa by Soviet aircraft (probably German ones with Soviet markings).

The growing dependence on the Third Reich, which was to lead eventually to the fateful military alliance with Germany, was connected with the recognition that only with Hitler's help could the pre-1920 borders, desired by the entire populace, be restored. The recovery of 40 per cent of the territories lost at Trianon was carried out between November 1938 and April 1941 within the framework of a continuous process, which had been decided before Hungary's entry into the war. The Vienna Award granted on 2 November 1938 by the Foreign Ministers of the Axis powers, Ribbentrop and Ciano, meant a territorial gain of 11,927 square km. of land with 1,060,000 inhabitants of whom, according to the Hungarian census of 1941, 84 per cent were Magyars. Despite the disappointment of the Hungarian public, Bratislava (Pressburg/Pozsony) remained in the hands of the new state of Slovakia created by Hitler. At the time of Czechoslovakia's dismemberment Horthy and the Teleki government grasped the opportunity this offered and seized that part of Carpatho-Ukraine which had belonged to the Hungary of St Stephen's crown: it encompassed 12,061 square km. and had almost 700,000 inhabitants. Even according to Hungarian estimates, only 10 per cent (1941) were Hungarian—according to Czechoslovak figures (1930) they made up a mere 5 per cent—while 70–75 per cent considered themselves Ruthenes (Ukrainians). The strip of land secured a Polish-Hungarian common border, and was thus strategically important to Hungary.

These considerations became irrelevant in September 1939 with the Germans' onslaught on Poland. At this point the Teleki government made a small show of defiance by refusing transit to German troop trains through Hungary on the grounds of its traditional friendship with Poland and out of consideration for Britain. After the defeat of Poland Hungary threw its frontiers wide open to over 100,000 Polish refugees, many of whom proceeded via Yugoslavia to join the British–French forces, although a considerable number remained in Hungary until the end of the war.

Still, entry into the Anti-Comintern Pact and quitting the League of Nations were clear signals that Hungary was being increasingly sucked into Germany's slipstream. Hitler understood how to play off the smaller states of Eastern and Central Europe against each other, while they fell over themselves in their race for his favour. He had formulated his policy towards Hungary and Romania as early as the beginning of 1938: to "keep both irons in the fire and act in the German interest according to prevailing developments".[5]

The Soviet ultimatum to Romania in June 1940 demanding the return of Bessarabia and northern Bukovina set things in motion in the whole of south-eastern Europe. Because Romania was an important supplier of oil to Germany, Hungary's ever-increasing pressure on it—which, incidentally, had terminated its Mutual Assistance Pact with Britain and France—threatened German interests. The danger of Soviet intervention if armed conflict arose between Romania and Hungary gave the final impetus for the Second Vienna Award.

After unsuccessful bilateral negotiations. Ribbentrop and Ciano decided on 30 August 1940 that Romania had to cede to Hungary northern Transylvania with its mainly Magyar and Székely-inhabited districts, a total of 43,103 square km. with 2,577,000 inhabitants, of whom at least two-fifths (according to Romanian data, almost half) were Romanian. At the same time over 400,000 Magyars remained in southern Transylvania. The Romanians regarded the Second Vienna Award as a national catastrophe, and staked everything on being able to reclaim the territories in the course of the war through exemplary devotion to Hitler. (The Führer met General Antonescu, the Romanian head of state, twenty times during the war. He had only four meetings with Horthy.)

The Hungarians' jubilation knew no bounds. The seventy-two-year-old Regent entered Kolozsvár (Cluj) at the head of the

Hungarian army on 15 September 1940, once again riding a white stallion. However, Hungarian opinion was far from satisfied; it wished to see southern Transylvania regained as well, but Hitler prevented any military action by Hungary. He observed to Count Ciano on the morning of 28 August 1940 at the Berghof that Hungary should acquiesce in any compromise, since its revisionary successes were entirely due to Fascism and National Socialism.[6]

Hungarian soldiers were cheered wherever they went by the populace, who had had to live for two decades separated from their nation and homeland and who had mostly been exposed to open discrimination. It should not be forgotten that it was only after the Second Vienna Award that Britain and the United States registered their protests, or rather questioned the award's validity. Diplomatic relations were severed after the attack on Yugoslavia. The political and cultural élite of the country regarded the series of territorial gains achieved without a war with an undiluted "sense of achievement".[7] The public did not take into account international repercussions, let alone the high price that Hitler would demand in return. This high price included recognition of the Berlin-controlled German Volksbund in Hungary and the extended rights of the German minority, laid down in a special agreement with the German Reich. Of the 720,000 German-speaking inhabitants 533,000 declared themselves as German nationals in the census of 1941. The Waffen-SS was given the right to recruit German volunteers in Hungary.

Dependence on Germany was becoming increasingly stifling in the economic sphere too. Half of Hungary's foreign trade had already been conducted with Germany as early as 1938, and 90 per cent of bauxite and oil production and a similarly high proportion of farm products were being exported to Germany by 1942. The German deficit in bilateral foreign trade amounted by the end of 1941 to 140 million marks, one billion in 1943, and in the following year 1.5 billion. The Reich's inability any longer to pay its debts led to growing paper money issue and, of course, inflation.[8]

At any rate, in the wake of the Second Vienna Award the domestic popularity of Horthy, who was now landed as the "*országgyarapító*" ("augmenter of the nation"), reached its pinnacle. This was not surprising, since within the short span of two-and-a-half years

Hungary—with German support—had increased its territory from 93,073 to 171,753 square km., and its population had increased by 5 million (2 million of them Magyars) to 14,683,000. This significant territorial and population expansion abruptly changed the homogeneous post-Trianon nation-state once again into a multi-ethnic state. The proportion of nationalities in the population increased between 1938 and 1941 from 7.9 to 22.5 per cent. Less well known was the politically significant fact that even after the census of 1941, 49.5 per cent of the population of the returned territories were not Hungarian. However, a certain cosmetic correction was attained by differentiating between mother-tongue and nationality, since 520,000 whose mother-tongue was other than Hungarian professed themselves Hungarian nationals (above all, Croats and Slovenes).[9]

A second and, for those affected, tragic consequence was that the number of Jews had risen by 80 per cent to 725,000. Being of Jewish religion as such was made redundant by the terms of the third Jewish Law (August 1941). Not only were quota regulations tightened but, in a serious defeat for the Christian churches, the Nazi race ideology was introduced as the basis for discrimination and later persecution. As Raoul Hilberg, the historian of the Holocaust, stresses in the Hungarian chapter of his seminal work, the Hungarian legislation surpassed even the Nuremberg laws in severity. All persons who had at least two Jewish grandparents were regarded as Jewish. In Germany—as against Hungary—a half-Jew who did not profess the Jewish religion and was married to a quarter-Jew was not classified Jewish. Likewise, regulations prohibiting marriage and extramarital sexual relations between Jews and non-Jews—regarded as "racial disgrace"—were rigorously applied. When the census questionnaires were appraised in 1944 from this viewpoint, the number of Christians designated as Jews was raised from 34,500 to 100,000. Loss of professional livelihood and later the "final solution" threatened a total of 825,000 people.[10]

In addition to the common line of territorial revisionism and economic dependence, there was also a pronounced politico-ideological proximity between Nazism and the Right-radical section of the Hungarian élite, particularly in the officer corps. The Prime Minister Gömbös had already congratulated Hitler on his appointment as Chancellor, commenting that they were both "old race-protectors, representing a common ideology".[11] At the same time it was Gömbös, derisively nicknamed "Gömbölini" because of his friendship with Mussolini, who gave a splendid example of how to deal with genealogical data in an arbitrary manner. He himself came from a Swabian family, and the last name of his father, an honest primary school teacher, was Knöpfle. The son, an ambitious social climber, is said to have fabricated the *"jákfai"* prefix of nobility to his name as well as some of his wartime medals. When the Jewish Laws came into force, millions of people had to procure birth certificates, baptism certificates and suchlike. The literary historian István Nemeskürty gave an account of the atmosphere prevailing in the summer of 1938:

This regulation has churned up the entire population, creating a general crisis of identity. It has turned out that almost everybody has Austrian, German, Slav, Romanian or Dalmatian ancestors; why and how can someone become Hungarian? The bewilderment was only augmented by the fact that the legislators had not found a clear definition of who was *not* a Jew. Everyone who could prove that none of his forebears, including his grandparents, was of the Jewish religion (or race) was described as "Christian", even including those who were, for instance, Muslims or had no religious denomination at all. Thus the word "Christian" came to describe not only believers of a certain religion but everyone who was not Jewish. In this way it became an erroneous, false *racist definition...* On top of this the aggressive propaganda of the German Reich began to spread at this time and citizens who had ancestors with German names were encouraged to profess their Germanness. These were then promptly mustered into the German army or the SS with the consent of the Hungarian authorities! At the same time the Arrow Cross movement was gathering strength: its followers felt that it would make them *bona fide* "Hungarians" and enjoy the support of the German Reich as well. Some re-Germanized their names, and others argued that their Slav-sounding names were in fact "old" Hungarian ones. Many of them sought ancestors, patents of nobility and heraldic confirmation with the help of "experts" who manufactured and forged these on a huge scale...[12]

After the Communists seized power this nightmare was to be repeated, though under different circumstances. People could then be fired, persecuted and even disfranchized according to their social origins, and in the early 1950s even "resettled" from the cities to the Puszta.

During those times of hectic genealogical research the democratic, anti-fascist circles could chalk up a small win on points against a particularly sinister political figure, Béla Imrédy. This highly gifted and ambitious financial expert, a former Finance Minister and President of the National Bank, had, in the words of his predecessor Bethlen,[13] carried out an unprecedented *volte face*. He not only switched over unconditionally to the German side after his appointment as Prime Minister in May 1938, but became head of the New Right, a radical fascist group in the government party, which subsequently split away from him. In Bethlen's opinion no other politician ever unleashed so much evil as Imrédy. He had presented the blueprint of the second Jewish Law at Christmas 1938 with graphic cruelty, declaring that "a single drop of Jewish blood" sufficed to spoil the character and patriotism of a person.[14]

Shortly thereafter Bethlen informed the Regent that a Budapest newspaper was preparing to publish documents from Czechoslovakia which showed that more than "a single drop of Jewish blood" did in fact flow in Imrédy's veins; one of his great-grandmothers was German-Jewish from Bohemia. As Horthy wrote in his memoirs, to avert a scandal he sent for the Prime Minister and showed him the documents; Imrédy was so overcome when he saw the papers that he fainted, and then offered his resignation. The story about the Jewish great-grandparent even amused readers and radio-listeners abroad. However, although this episode gave a little breathing space, Imrédy soon returned to the political arena as leader of a Nazi grouping. Although he could by then prove his Aryan "innocence" with the help of new documents, he was henceforth openly attacked by his Arrow Cross rivals because of his "Jewish blood".[15]

Incidentally, the most rabid Hungarian Right-radicals are the best proof that Ármin Vámbéry's dictum that Hungarians were the most interbred people in Europe was by no means unfounded. In 1941, according to the American historian Andrew Janos, twenty-one of the twenty-seven two- and three-star generals were of German or Slovak origin, as were no less than nine Hungarian arch-bishops and bishops including Cardinal Jusztinián Serédi (Sapoucek), the chaplain-in-chief of the army Bishop Zadravetz, and the ideo-logue of the extreme Right, Prohászka.[16]

In the typical Hungarian conditions of ethnic interbreeding, and according to criteria similar to those of the Jewish Laws, a third of government members between 1932 and 1944 were not Magyar.

The puppet regime installed after the German occupation on 19 March 1944 was headed by the former Hungarian ambassador to Berlin, Döme Sztójay, a man of Croat stock whose original name was Stojaković. While Gömbös and Imrédy had relied on radicalized civil servants and officers, the Arrow Cross built up a mass party with the help of social and political fringe groups and numerous urban workers. When it was given power by the German occupiers in the autumn of 1944, only one in five ministers in their government could have furnished "proof of Magyarness". The original name of the former Major Ferenc Szálasi, head of the Arrow Cross and "leader of the nation" (*nemzetvezetö*), was Salosjan. Born in Kassa the son of an officer, this man, who saw himself as a "messianic saviour-figure" (Margit Szöllösi-Janze), had—according to Horthy—Armenian, Slovak and German forebears and was at most only "a quarter Hungarian". In 1938 a Hungarian deputy claimed in Parliament that not only did Szálasi have no Hungarian blood but that he was not even a Hungarian citizen.[17]

Be that as it may, Hungarians lived between 1938 and 1944 in a topsy-turvy world in which people with German and Slav family names were agitating in the name of the Magyar race against people who, more often than not, had as little Magyar background as the agitators themselves. In a further twist, even Magyar surnames meant nothing, since "Magyarization" of family names had been practised for decades. The irrelevance of Magyar names as such was shown later during the death marches organized on the orders of Eichmann and his Hungarian accomplices, when the great lyric poet Miklós Radnóti and the outstanding writers Antal Szerb, Gábor Halász and György Sárközi among many others, all of them Hungarian patriots and faithful Christians from converted Jewish families, were killed.

However, it was not the Germans alone who forced the Hungarians to enter the war against the Soviet Union or to legislate against the Jews. In his essay published in 1948, but not widely read till forty years later, the great and scrupulously honest István Bibó put his finger on the still festering wound by saying that the Jewish Laws marked the "moral decline of Hungarian society":

These laws gave a large section of the middle and petty bourgeoisie the possibility of making profitable headway in life without any personal effort, thanks to the state and at the expense of the livelihoods of others. Large sections of Hungarian society got to like the idea that one could make a living not only by work and enterprise, but also by seeking out someone else's position, denouncing him, researching his ancestry, having him dismissed and claiming his business, *ergo* by the total usurpation of that person's existence.

Bibó assessed "an alarming image of greed, unscrupulous mendacity and, at best, calculating pushiness by a considerable section of this society. This was an unforgettable blow not only for the Jews affected by it but also for all decent Hungarians."[18]

The "Aryanization" of economic life and gradual elimination of Jews from it thus helped the rise of a new "Christian middle class". But there were other factors as well which caused the landslide in favour of the New Right and the Arrow Cross in May 1939 during the first secret (if not free) elections since 1920. The Arrow Cross gained 18 per cent of the seats in Parliament, but as much as 25 per cent of the votes; 30 per cent in Budapest; and in the so-called "red belt" around it a staggering 41.7 per cent as against only 17 per cent for the Social Democrats. That the ruling Unity Party, by now also strongly Right-oriented, was still able to win 70 per cent of the seats was due to the prevailing majority electoral system and to various manipulations, but in reality its share of the vote was only 50 per cent. The former Prime Minister István Bethlen ascribed this momentous swing in his 40-page memorandum—which saw the light only forty years later in English and four years after that in Hungarian—to the activities of Imrédy (deposed in the mean time), the mistakes of Teleki and steadily growing German pressure.

The Arrow Cross was a Fascist- and Nazi-influenced movement with a specific Hungarian element. Its followers wore brown shirts, and used the swastika and the Hitler salute. After being banned in 1933, it switched to green shirts and the arrow-cross, the emblem of St László (1077–95); their party salute was "*Kitartás!*" (Endurance). They embodied the grievances, even the hatreds, of broad heterogeneous sections of society, the whole spectrum of officials threatened by becoming *déclassé*, radicalized, often out-of-work and frustrated intellectuals, poorly-paid army officers, students hindered in their prospects of promotion and, last but not least, urban workers and the *Lumpenproletariat*. To the countless poor the Arrow

Cross promised deliverance from Jewish capitalists and the great aristocratic landowners; in short, it formed a protest movement against the power cartel of the feudal élite, high finance and the top bureaucracy. In 1938–9, it had 250,000–300,00 members but nonetheless had no prospect of wresting power from the ruling class and its symbol and guarantor, the Regent.[19]

The recovery of the considerable territories of Upper Hungary, Transylvania and southern Hungary offered the possibility of expanding the state bureaucracy and filling the positions with new men. Teleki and his young colleagues tried to give the predominantly non-Hungarian Carpatho-Ukraine a great measure of regional autonomy and a legal guarantee for the protection of the nationalities, but in vain because the newly-appointed officers and officials, indoctrinated over many years with the chauvinist-nationalist spirit and propaganda, had learned nothing from the past. Their coercive Magyarization measures and expropriation of non-Magyar property soon provoked opposition and resistance.[20]

The number of civil servants doubled between 1937 and 1943 to 93,800. In 1914 there was one civil servant per 377 inhabitants; in 1921 the ratio was 1 to 134, and in 1942, 1 to 100. This facilitated the allocation of positions to officials who had fled after 1919–20, and to landowners who had lost all or part of their properties in the successor-states due to land reform. In addition, successive governments made a policy of offering employment to the out-of-work, self-employed and graduates.

Old and new officials, out-of-work students and the manifold effects of a "graduate inflation" formed the mass-base of the extreme Right groupings. The constant and ever-more stridently repeated accusations, supported by statistics, that the proportion of Jews in the professions, in industry and banking, was intolerably high did not fall on deaf ears. Gyula Juhász, an expert on questions of ideology and nationality, and an authority on Hungarian foreign affairs in the inter-war years, verified that for the majority of the Hungarian intelligentsia racist ideology was above all a vehicle for occupying positions which the "assimilated" consequently had to give up.[21]

In this context it should not be overlooked that Hungary profited temporarily from the wartime boom. Industrial production increased by 20 per cent in 1939 alone, a larger increase than in the whole of the previous two decades. At the same time real wages rose by almost 10 per cent. The influence of the Arrow Cross decreased considerably between 1942 and 1944, but even at the time when the centre of gravity in the Horthy regime swung over from the radicals to the moderates, the pro-German attitude of the army command and officers presented potential danger. A British observer (and friend of Teleki) reported to the Foreign Office already in October 1938 that 80 to 90 per cent of the army were Nazis and that the young officers were intoxicated by Germany's success. About half of the military élite came from regions separated by Trianon, which possibly played an even greater role than being of German origin.

Under strong pressure from the German high command, Hungary soon had to give up all hope of being able to conduct a parallel war from the sidelines, and by mid-1942 had been forced to send a whole army to the Russian front. In the mean time Horthy had his elder son István—who, like his brother the younger Miklós, was pro-British and anti-Nazi—elected Deputy Regent by Parliament. Joseph Goebbels described the young Horthy's appointment in his diary as a "great misfortune because the son is even more philo-Semitic than the father". In his memoirs Horthy intimates that his son's fatal crash at the Eastern Front in August might have been due to German sabotage.[22] More important politically was the replacement of Prime Minister Bárdossy, who was far too obsequious and willing to make concessions to the Germans, by the anti-Nazi politician Miklós Kállay.

The destruction of the poorly equipped 207,000-strong Second Hungarian Army at Voronezh in January 1943 was the political and psychological turning-point in Hungary's participation in the Second World War. Over 40,000 soldiers died, 35,000 were wounded, many disappeared, and 60,000 were taken prisoner by the Soviets. Although the whole tragedy was officially glossed over, and information about it could only be gleaned from the Hungarian broadcasts of the London and Moscow radio stations, almost every family was affected directly or indirectly. Particularly heavy losses were suffered by members of the unarmed auxiliary labour battalions, wearing yellow armbands, inadequately equipped, poorly nourished and frequently tortured to death by sadistic NCOs; this was the fate of

Attila Petschauer,* who had won an Olympic gold medal in fencing for Hungary. Only 6,000–7,000 of the 25,000 labour servicemen assigned to the second Army ever returned. Their converted comrades had to wear a white armband; but their treatment later on was not much better than that of "full Jews".

While the Kállay government—with Horthy's knowledge—put out feelers in neutral capitals, and made contact with the Allies through special emissaries, the conservative-liberal anti-fascist groups, the Social Democrats and the Smallholders' Party, as well as the few hundred Communists, also began to organize. After a massive wave of arrests the latter founded a new illegal group named the "Peace Party" under the leadership of a young metalworker János Csermanek, who later called himself "Barna" and finally Kádár. Although there were sporadic protest actions by courageous intellectuals, no massive opposition or, up to the last days of the war, armed resistance worthy of mention was recorded.

An ominous portent of future atrocities was the bloodbath perpetrated in the Voivodina town of Ujvidék (Novi Sad) and environs at the beginning of 1942 against unarmed Serb and Jewish civilians: over 4,000 were killed, 1,250 of them Jews. Although the guilty generals and officers were later court-martialled and convicted, most of them managed to flee to Germany. Danilo Kiš left a distressing testimony of this event in his trilogy. It is less well known that in the autumn of 1944 not only many Germans but also Hungarians became innocent victims of reprisals by the victorious Tito Partisans.

At any rate, Kállay, the moderate and pro-Western head of government, conducted a clever see-saw policy between the threatening Third Reich and the sceptical Allies—this policy was called in contemporary political parlance the "*Kállai kettős*" (Kállay two-step).† Yet the majority of the Hungarian upper classes and officers still gambled on a German victory. Gratitude felt by a considerable part of public opinion to Germany, and in particular to Hitler, for the recovery of territories lost through the Treaty of Trianon played a role in this, added to fear of the Soviets and the obvious weakness

---

* Thinly veiled protagonist of the successful film *Sunshine*.
† A metaphor borrowed from a national dance, in which two steps to the right are followed by two steps to the left.

of liberal and democratic circles.[23] At the same time, increasing war-weariness could no longer be ignored, as well as the ill-concealed activities of those conservative-liberal forces who were deluded into hoping for a separate peace with the West and the arrival of British-American forces. Traitors and spies in the highest government circles kept Hitler and his cohorts up-to-date with the amateurish enterprises of the Hungarians.

At the same the "Jewish question" became an increasingly decisive factor in the German-Hungarian relationship. At the first Klessheim conference on 17 and 18 April 1943, to Horthy's question "what should he do with the Jews... he couldn't after all kill them", Ribbentrop bluntly replied that "they should be exterminated or at least put in concentration camps". At the beginning of May Goebbels noted in his diary that Hitler had commented to his Reichsleiters and Gauleiters that the "Jewish question" was being "solved least satisfactorily by the Hungarians"; Horthy, who "together with his family was extraordinarily badly tangled up with the Jews", would continue to resist every effort to tackle the Jewish problem aggressively. German calculations are clear from the various reports: SS-Standartenführer Veesenmayer, Hitler's later "plenipotentiary" in Hungary, indicated in a preliminary report that by handing over its Jews Hungary would for better or worse be tied to the "Reich's struggle for security and survival".[24]

"Plan Margarethe" for the occupation of Hungary by the Wehrmacht had been prepared long before.[25] Today we know almost everything about the pre-history of this occupation—about Hitler's ultimatum to the seventy-six-year-old Horthy, who had been lured into the trap during talks at Schloss Klessheim on 18 March, and the scenario worked out in Berlin by the SS and Gestapo, especially the Eichmann-Sonderkommando, for "resolving the Jewish question". Germany's tried and tested far-right friends now came into their own. About 3,000 patriotic and pro-Western politicians, officials, aristocrats and intellectuals were arrested and deported to concentration camps in Germany by the Gestapo and the collaborating Hungarian police and gendarmerie. Bethlen found shelter with friends in the country, and the deposed Prime Minister Kállay was given asylum in the Turkish embassy.

There was no military or civil resistance. Only one man, the parliamentary deputy Endre Bajcsy-Zsilinszky, drew a revolver when

Gestapo thugs tried to arrest him on the first day, 19 March, in his apartment on Attila boulevard in Buda. Shots rang out, and he was dragged wounded, to a waiting car. All he could do was call to the silent crowd in the street "Long live independent Hungary!"[26]

Bajcsy-Zsilinszky, born in 1886, was perhaps the most impressive and certainly the most courageous of wartime Hungarian politicians. From 1919 on he belonged to the circle around Gömbös, and was known as a radical "race-protector", who sharply criticized the Bethlen government orally and in writing. However, in glaring contrast to most of his comrades he later found his way in the direction of humanity and patriotism. He became a relentless critic of increasing German influence under Hitler, openly standing out against the Jewish Laws and condemning the massacre at Ujvidék. He challenged Horthy, whom he knew well, to change course. He fought untiringly to save Jewish journalists and intellectuals who had been called up to labour service at the front, and once wrote to Teleki that under these circumstances no decent man could any longer be an anti-Semite.

Bajcsy-Zsilinsky did not become a Leftist even in 1944, but remained a humanistic romantic, a patriot who still believed—like almost all Hungarians—that the best part of the regained territories could somehow be kept by Hungary. Released in October, he became President of the National Committee of Liberation in the underground movement in November. Two weeks later he was arrested, together with several officers, by the Arrow Cross and on 23 December 1944 sentenced to death and executed in the prison of Sopronkőhida. In 1945 a wide boulevard on the Pest side was named after him. His unfortunately isolated example indicates the opportunities, slender though they were, which evil types cast in the mould of an Imrédy impeded and destroyed. This prepared the ground for the subsequent reign of mob terror and mass-murder.

In an appendix to his seminal work on the destruction of Hungarian Jewry, Randolph Braham enumerates 107 regulations decreed after the German invasion.[27] Veesenmayer could report with satisfaction to Berlin that the anti-Jewish legislation was passed "with alacrity unusual for local conditions". But Jews were not the only victims. Up to the bitter end in the spring of 1945 tens of thousands of senselessly sacrificed soldiers were killed, as were resistance fighters and deserters, Catholic anti-Nazis and Social Democrats, members of the nobility and Communists. Tens of thousands of Hungarians, both soldiers and civilians, died in Soviet captivity, and 20,000 people died in the aerial bombing which began in April 1944. However, there is no doubting the validity of the comment made by Elie Wiesel, the Nobel Peace Price winner from the formerly Hungarian, now Romanian township of Sighet in Transylvania: "Not all victims were Jews—but all Jews were victims." Nowhere else in Central and Eastern Europe were more than 800,000 Jews (including converts) able to live for so long in relative safety as in Hungary. But nowhere else in Central and Eastern Europe were Jews sent to their death so quickly and so brutally. Under the supervision of Adolf Eichmann and his thugs, Hungarian gendarmes and detectives from Carpatho-Ukraine to northern Transylvania and the Hungarian Plains assembled Jews and those Christians who were defined as such by the racial laws into improvised ghettoes, mainly brickworks, where they were subjected to brutal interrogation and torture. Had they buried valuables or hidden them at Christian friends' houses? After they had been "dealt with", they had to march to the railway station, where cattle-trucks were waiting. After seventy people had been crammed into each truck, the gendarmes would seal the waggons, chalking the number of people on the outside. Inside was one pail with water and another for excrement. The Hungarians in charge proudly reported to their German masters that between 15 May and 7 July they had expedited 147 trains to Auschwitz, containing 437,402 Jews.

German Nazi propagandists were especially perfidious when in the summer of 1944 they showed in Switzerland a film demonstrating how brutally the Hungarian gendarmes had treated the deportees during their removal. News spread internationally about the persecution of Jews, putting an abrupt end to Hungary's special role during the first years of the war. For many till then the country had been an island of relative security; opposition newspapers could appear despite censorship, and critical Social Democratic and Liberal deputies could take the floor in Parliament. The Hungarian historian György Ránki pointed out that nowhere else in Eastern Europe had the Jews identified with the state as in Hungary, and that the tragedy of the Jews was therefore also a tragedy for Hungary. On 15 June, following in the footsteps of the Nazis, the Hungarian government's Commissioner of the Press pronounced the "death sentence" for all "Jewish books". He began the shredding of 447,627 volumes during a press conference. In a memorandum Count Bethlen, the former Prime Minister, quoted Bebel as saying that anti-Semitism was the Socialism of the stupid; in the case of Hungary it should read "of the very stupid".

What did Horthy do during this period of deportations and mass murder? The seed of the primitive and extensive hate-campaign of twenty-five years earlier had now borne fruit. István Deák wrote:

> Horthy remarked in his Memoirs that he was completely powerless at the time, and could not have stopped the deportations carried out not by Hungarians but by Eichmann and company, and that he had known nothing about the destination of the Jews. As far as his lack of power was concerned, that was probably true, but everything else was a lie. He had found out in good time what Auschwitz signified, but preferred to ignore it. That did not, however, hold for the Jews of Budapest! When it was their turn in June/July 1944, he ordered military action against the gendarmes, who, as he feared, were also planning a coup against him. In the event more than 40 per cent of Hungarian Jews survived. Horthy was not a monster, but he was not a humanitarian either. He was no democrat but never tried to be a dictator. He claimed to have been a lifelong anti-Semite. Still, under his reign and despite the deportations, more Jews survived the Nazi terror than in any other country in Hitler's Europe.[28]

In contrast to Romania, Hungary did not manage to change sides in 1944; Horthy was hindered from acting like King Michael for the simple reason that the supreme command and most of the officers were more pro-German than the Romanians. Moreover, Horthy's attempted "defection" on 15 October 1944 after the conclusion of an armistice through a delegation in Moscow, was amateurish, if not downright comic opera. He genuinely believed that he could cause a turn-around to take place merely by means of a proclamation over the radio and without appropriate military and political preparation. The Germans, of course, knew about everything beforehand, and kidnapped the old Regent's son Miklós on the day of the attempted capitulation. In order to achieve his son's release he was forced to withdraw his proclamation and legalize the takeover of government by the leader of the Arrow Cross, Szálasi.

The Arrow Cross reign of terror claimed the lives of tens of thousands during the final months of the war. While the "National Leader", dressed in mufti with a green shirt and green tie, was taking the oath on the crown in the white marble hall of the royal palace, in the presence of only fifty-five deputies and not many more members of the Upper House, the latter clad in their traditional Hungarian dress uniforms with embellished sabres and egret-feathered hats, his murderers were wreaking havoc in the streets of the capital. They rounded up thousands of Jews, shooting them at the Danube embankment, or handcuffing them together and throwing them by twos and threes into the icy Danube. Only one in each group had to be shot; as they plunged into the river, he would pull the others down with him. It has been estimated that the Szálasi regime claimed the lives of some 50,000 Jewish victims in Budapest. Added to these were the victims of the notorious death marches to Austria organized by Eichmann.

The attitude of the great majority of Hungarians was not active collaboration so much as "see nothing, hear nothing". Nowhere were there protests of any significance against the deportations and death marches. However, despite the weakness of the Hungarian resistance, at least 25,000 Jews survived in the capital, either with false papers or through being hidden by friends and non-Jewish relatives.

The capital had to pay a high price for the Arrow Cross regime and Hitler's order to defend the "fortress Budapest house by house". It was as late as 13 February 1945 that fighting at last ceased in the Castle district. On the night of 13 January the Germans had already blown up all the bridges across the Danube, and more than 30,000 houses were destroyed. As a result of the "scorched earth" policy, tens of thousands more civilians as well as Hungarian, German and Soviet soldiers had to die.

Szálasi and his staff left the country, taking the crown of St Stephen with them, on 29 March. An astounding footnote to this history was the flight of the entire military and civilian administration to the West in compliance with the evacuation orders of the Germans and the Arrow Cross; fear of the Soviet Army acted as the spur. Approximately a million civilians fled, most of them members of the middle class. Many later returned, but about 100,000 remained permanently in the West. The eight months of fighting on Hungarian soil, the removal of movable goods by the Germans and the Arrow Cross, as well as the seizures by Soviet and Romanian troops caused losses amounting to five times the national income for 1938 and about 40 per cent of the nation's total wealth. These included half of all industrial machinery, 40 per cent of the rail network, two-thirds of all locomotives and between 44 and 80 per cent of the total stock of cattle, horses, pigs and sheep. It has been estimated that some 900,000 people, or 6.2 per cent of Hungary's 14.5 million inhabitants (1941), died.[29] The estimate of Jewish victims amounted to 564,000 in the Greater Hungary of 1941 and 297,000 from Trianon Hungary (over 100,000 in Budapest).[30] About 600,000 Hungarians, including 100,000–120,000 civilians, were captured by the Soviets and 300,000 soldiers capitulated to British and US troops. It is significant that about 100,000 soldiers took the oath to Szálasi, and twelve Hungarian divisions fought to the bitter end on the German side.[31]

Because of the legacy of Trianon and the nationalities question, Hungary was in a far more difficult situation than the neighbouring countries. "In our case", wrote Gyula Juhász, "the most difficult task was to combine national objectives with the fight against Fascism. In the neighbouring countries it sufficed at the time if someone regarded himself as a Pole, a Czech or a Yugoslav. The national feeling was sufficient for the fight against Hitler. In our case the national feeling was not enough to make one anti-Fascist; for that one had at least to be a democrat." Horthy's regime drifted into a blind alley, with no protection against German imperialism, and it could not retain permanently the regained territories (later Hungary even lost an additional three villages to Czechoslovakia). One could quote Deák's verdict as consolation: it is unlikely that a different regime would have acted better, and others in Hitler's Europe fared even worse.[32]

And what of Horthy? Placed in German "protective custody" in October 1944, the mortified head of state left his country, never to return alive; the Americans freed him from captivity in the spring of 1945. In his Memoirs Horthy describes how in the various camps he had to learn to make his bed and scrub his mess-tin. A Yugoslav request for his extradition (because of the massacre in Voivodina) was rejected by the Americans; the Hungarians and the Soviets were not interested in initiating proceedings against him; after all, he had tried to change sides and hindered deportation of the Buda-pest Jews. Horthy settled with his family in Estoril in Portugal. He had no private fortune because, unlike many of the kings and republican heads of state of the inter-war years in Central and East-ern Europe, he was personally incorruptible. The Regent may have been a life-long anti-Semite, yet he and his wife were able for many years to live a comfortable life in exile thanks to the generous support of two Jewish families. He died on 9 February 1957, a few months after the Hungarian Revolution of October 1956.

Horthy and his regime remain a part of Hungary's past with which it has yet to come to terms. The repatriation of his mortal remains to Hungary—exclusively for family reasons—and the sol-emn burial service on 4 September 1993 with its emotional and political overtones, showed that the "Admiral on the white horse" is still a highly controversial figure in Hungarian history.

34. Victory in Defeat: 1945–1990

The scene on that Saturday afternoon was impressive. On 28 September 1946 close on a quarter of a million people packed the huge tradition-filled Heroes' Square in front of the Millenium Monument in Budapest. Many waved flags—Hungarian or red ones. Banners demanded "Removal of the People's Enemies from the Coalition" and "Forward to the People's Democracy!" It was the triumphant prelude to the first public congress of the Hungarian Communist Party (MKP), founded on 24 November 1919.[1] At exactly 14.30 a blond young man named János Kádár, the deputy General Secretary, gave the opening address; behind him on the tribune sat the leading functionaries of the Party and local and foreign guests.

Two-and-a-half hours later a festive meeting took place in the Opera House, where the heads of foreign delegations and representatives of the other Hungarian parties read out messages of greeting. On Sunday the 386 delegates, representing 4,800 local party organizations with 650,000 members, assembled for their three-day caucus in the Congress Hall of the Parliament.

During their party conference at Whitsun 1945 the Communists already claimed 150,000 members, but at the first free (also secret) general elections in November 1945 they came off only as the third—strongest element with barely 17 per cent, behind the bourgeois-peasant Smallholders' Party (57 per cent) and the Social Democrats (17.4). Nonetheless they demonstrated strength, and the self-confident, at times aggressive tone of their reports left no doubt that they were going all-out to be the determining factor in Hungarian politics.

Bourgeois politicians and many Social Democrats viewed with misgivings the dizzying rise of the Communists, whose proudly proclaimed membership figures were perplexing. And in fact they resembled a political and statistical miracle. Kádár himself admitted many years later that during the war there were only a few hundred (never more than 1,000) members, and after a wave of arrests in 1942–3 no more than 70–80, of whom he was in constant contact with only about ten activists.[2] In spite of this, the number of CP members had reached 30,000 in February 1945, rising by the end of the year to half a million. It was an open secret that the Communist Party, led largely by Jewish Muscovites, relied principally on the "minor Arrow Cross" followers (*kisnyilasok*), i.e. on people from the margins of society—unskilled labourers, members of the lower middle class and frightened civil servants—who felt threatened by the radical change and the generally unexpected return of Jewish owners of "Aryanized" shops, factories and apartments. In the early summer an editorial in the party newspaper *Szabad Nép* (A Free People) affirmed a certain "understanding" for the misguided "*kisnyilas*", and the crypto-Communist author József Darvas, officially a member of the National Peasants' Party, chimed in with alacrity.[3]

The membership statistics of the other parties also gave the impression of an astounding increase. As early as the summer of 1945 the Social Democrats proudly claimed half a million members, but what could one make of the fact that in a city, where a carnival of death and hell had still been raging between October 1944 and February 1945, the very people who for twenty-five years had been subjected to nationalistic, revisionist propaganda turned overnight into democrats, Socialists and even Communists? None of this was of any interest to the principal speakers at the Communist Party congress in 1946. Their task was to don the camouflage of grand-coalition and peoples' democracy and, in contrast to the leftist Social Democrats, strictly refrain from using Socialist slogans and not even to utter the word "Socialism". At the time the top leadership still counted on a lengthy period of transition pending the full collectivization of the economy and their complete seizure of power.

However, it turned out quite differently. Within less than two years the die was cast, and the Communists seized total power in Hungary—as in the other countries in the Soviet sphere of interest. At the beginning of 1949 Stalin let out the great secret: Peoples' Democracy would assume the function of the Dictatorship of the

Proletariat. But already, before this unmasking, the iron fist of the "Working Class", in other words the State Security Service and the military Counter Intelligence, had done away with every genuine, potential and concocted opposition, at first outside the CP and, soon after May 1949, within it too.

The conduct of the "liberators"—as in all Soviet-occupied territories—was not conducive to arousing friendly feelings towards the Soviet Union. Rape, plunder and brutal interference in domestic policy led to the hatred of the Soviets becoming even stronger than before the defeat. The uncertain fate of more than half a million prisoners of war, the abduction of tens of thousands of civilians to forced labour, the Soviet-supported Communist offensive to undermine and finally destroy the young Hungarian democracy, contributed in the ensuing months and years to a feeling among of the large and later overwhelming majority of Hungarians that with the new era under the red star a new bondage had begun.

The four men who gave the principal speeches in the venerable hall of Parliament in that Indian summer of 1946 knew better than most other delegates, and the 123 guests (not entitled to vote) from the state and Party apparatus, the army, the police, the press, the labour unions and large enterprises, that for historical and mass-psychological reasons Hungary was an extremely unfavourable breeding-ground for the Communists. This was also true, if to different degrees, of the other "Peoples' Democracies", except for Czechoslovakia, where a strong legitimate CP had already existed during the inter-war years. Despite complete control by Moscow and more or less similar developments throughout the Soviet sphere of power, the personalities of the four top functionaries in Hungary and their relationship to one another and to the masters in the Kremlin gave the country's post-war era a particularly dramatic, often surprising and occasionally gruesome character. The political turbulences and startling turns in the positions of the men at the summit of the Party and the state confirm the warning by Isaiah Berlin not to view history "as a motorway without exits":

At crucial moments... every accident, individuals with their decisions and actions, not necessarily foreseen even by themselves, and which are rarely foreseeable, are able to change the course of history... Our decision-making leeway is not wide. Let us say: one per cent. But that one per cent is what matters.[4]

It is possible, even probable, that without the distinctive personality of Mátyás Rákosi, Hungary would still have gone through the crucial junctions on the way to dictatorship and the status of Soviet colony (liquidation of the other parties, nationalization of the economy, pushing heavy industry especially armaments at the expense of consumers, expulsion of ethnic Germans, the arrest of real or alleged opponents, and so on.) Yet all historians of the post-war era agree that Rákosi was the driving force behind the bloody purges and the political coordination before and after Stalin's death. We should recall the words of the Swiss historian Herbert Lüthy: "History is not anonymous. It is known to us as a real happening only to the extent that we rip away the anonymity of the protagonists, individualizing and identifying them... Dates and facts do not really mean anything if we cannot get a picture of the consciousness of the personalities in action."[5]

As Secretary-General of the Party, Rákosi gave the first address about the "country's domestic and foreign-political situation and the tasks of the Party". Politburo member Imre Nagy (a former Agriculture and Interior Minister) spoke next about a "thriving agriculture for a prosperous peasantry". The third speaker, Rákosi's deputy in the Party apparatus, János Kádár, spoke of the "Party's organizational tasks", and finally Interior Minister László Rajk, as chairman of the nomination commission, presented the list of candidates for the new Central Committee.

Who was this First Man of the Party, who from 1945 to 18 July 1956 held steadily increasing personal sway as "Stalin's best pupil", who parcelled out authority and responsibility among covert rivals, and who directed the setting up of constantly changing power centres within the Party machinery?[6] Born in 1892, the first child of the grocer József Rosenfeld (Magyarized to Rákosi in 1904), he grew up in the small village of Ada, near Szabadka (today's Subotica). In spite of his humble background he was able to study at the Oriental Academy at Budapest after passing his high school exams with distinction.

In 1912 he went on a scholarship to Hamburg and in 1913 to London, where he worked as a clerk, returning to Hungary on the outbreak of war. As a sergeant on the Eastern Front he was captured in 1915, and during his three years as a prisoner-of-war learned

Russian and Italian. As one of the founding members of the Hungarian Communist Party, he became the youngest commissar in the top leadership of the short-lived Soviet Republic. After a brief spell of internment in Austria with other Communist leaders Rákosi re-emerged in the summer of 1920 in Moscow as an employee and later one of the secretaries to the executive committee of the Comintern. Thanks to his linguistic abilities—he also spoke French and Turkish—he helped during the early 1920s to launch Communist parties from Prague to Livorno and from Paris to Berlin, and in some cases was requested by the Comintern to arbitrate their internal faction fights. After criss-crossing Europe with six forged passports, he returned to Budapest, only to be arrested with forty activists a year later and, after a lengthy court case, sentenced to eight-and-a-half years' imprisonment. Rákosi became known world-wide in 1935 when, instead of being set free at the end of his term, he was sentenced to life imprisonment, this time for his activities in 1919, in the face of protests from all over the world. The Supreme Court eventually combined the two sentences, so that in 1940 the Communist leader was allowed to leave for the Soviet Union in exchange for the Hungarian flags seized by Tsarist Russian troops in 1849. After fifteen years and thirty-seven days the legendary comrade was received and honoured as a hero in the Fatherland of the Proletariat. He was even permitted to stand close to Stalin on the dais in Red Square for the anniversary celebrations of the Revolution on 7 November 1940.

In reality Rákosi owed his survival to the Horthy regime. Had he been released in 1935, he would almost certainly have become a victim of the purges. He would even have provided a sound reason—from a Soviet Communist viewpoint—for his liquidation because under interrogation in 1925 he had started much too soon to talk about Comintern matters. All he got now was a reprimand for the old sin, for which Stalin allegedly remarked that he had already atoned. Be that as it may, Rákosi only returned to Hungary on 30 January 1945 with his eleven-years-younger wife Fenya Fiodorovna Kornyilova, a prosecutor from Yakutsk in Northern Siberia, whom he had met at a rest home and married in 1942. However, in Hungary a quite different story was in circulation. In its "Personalities" column the Hamburg news magazine *Der Spiegel* printed in

June 1948 a brief report that Rákosi was "taking an aristocratic line. He has applied for a divorce from his Mongol wife, and wishes to marry Princess Odescalchi. He is following in the footsteps of many Russian Communist leaders, who married aristocrats after the victory of the Revolution." This would indeed have caused a sensation if it had been true, but in fact "Matyi" and Fenya lived happily together until his death on 5 February 1971.

During his twelve years in office Rákosi proved to be one of the best-educated, most eloquent and at the same time most morally evil politicians in Hungarian history. Without doubt, according to the playwright Gyula Háy, who had met him in his Soviet exile, he was the ugliest:

A short, squat body, as if the creator had been unable to finish his work for abhorrence: the head disproportionately large, topped by an enormous bald dome and fronted by a pallid, bloated face with a sweet-and-sour smile frozen on to it. Virtually no neck between the high shoulders, so that it was left more or less to the observer whether he called him a hunchback or not. Clumsy in movement, with a tendency to flatfootedness; short, stubby fingers...[7]

His biographers claim he had no passions: he neither drank nor smoked, nor—unlike "the number four", the good-looking chief ideologue József Révai—did he have affairs. Human emotions such as love and hate played no part in his life. Rákosi lived only for his power, but the tactics and strategy of handling power, the intensity with which even a number one exerted that power, depended on the distant despot Jossip Vissarionovich Stalin. The relationship of his vassal chieftains to the "Red Tsar" in the Kremlin remained for ever uncertain, unsteady, fluctuating.[8] Rákosi spent all his holidays on the Black Sea, and not even his inner circle knew whether and when he had met Stalin. Between 1945 and 1947 a reliable party comrade installed a direct radio communication with Stalin's office in the attic of Rákosi's villa. Its operator, a veteran of the Spanish Civil War, did not reveal even to his wife the nature of his job at the Party chief's house, and even in his memoirs published thirty-five years later did not waste any words about his undoubtedly exciting work.

The fact remains that Rákosi discussed every politically significant decision with the "Soviet friends" on the spot (the "advisers" were for ever present in all important institutions), or sought consent by telephone or by a letter sent by special courier to Stalin's personal secretary Alexander Poskryobyshev. The decisive move, which dealt the death-blow to the young democracy, was the arrest in February 1947 by Soviet security police of the Secretary-General of the Smallholders' Party, the deputy Béla Kovács. The second-ranking figure in by far the strongest coalition party, whose immunity had been explicitly confirmed by the parliamentary majority, was abducted to the Soviet Union on the pretext of "setting up armed terrorist groups and spying for a Western intelligence service against the Soviet Union", and only released in 1956.

The punishments, approved by all democratic parties, of extreme-Right politicians of the Horthy regime and, above all, of Arrow Cross members, meted out by specially established courts with the participation of party and trade union delegates, had already opened the way to the Communists' later arbitrariness. Between the end of the war and March 1948 the People's Courts sentenced 16,273 persons, albeit half of those to less than one year's imprisonment. Of the 322 death sentences 146 were carried out. Among those executed were Szálasi, the former Prime Ministers Bárdossy, Imrédy and Sztójay, and those officials of the Ministry of the Interior and the gendarmerie directly responsible for the deportation of Jews. Every party also endorsed the unjust and unacceptable forcible resettlement of a quarter of a million of Hungary's ethnic Germans.

Gatherings of rightist opposition deputies and their friends ("Hungarian Community"), blown up into a gigantic anti-state conspiracy, were used as a pretext for seven court cases with 260 sentences and the liquidation of the Smallholders' Party. In a famous speech delivered after the "Year of Change", Rákosi invented a term which was to become well-known—"salami tactics"—to describe the slice-by-slice destruction of political rivals.

Having proscribed and eliminated the bourgeois politicians as conspirators, Rákosi turned to the church. Within a few weeks 225 Catholic priests were arrested, and the show trials of Cardinal József Mindszenty and, two years later, Archbishop Grösz of Sopron were organized, resulting in sentences of life imprisonment and fifteen years respectively. Cases against the large Maort and Standard industrial enterprises led to the conviction of top executives and experts. Numerous other repressive measures became important building-blocks in the totalitarian system's intensifying reign of terror. In the end they all had their turn: the real opponents of the Communists, right and left Social Democrats in the coalition, and many others who did not fit in with Rákosi's concepts.

The open declaration of war against the heretic "Titoists" and the excommunication of the Yugoslav Communists from the Cominform (the Communist information bureau founded in the autumn of 1947) denoted the actual turning-point *within* the ruling Party, the overture to the great bloody purges. The search for enemies of the Party and agents of foreign powers within the ranks of the "victors" inaugurated in 1949 that chain of mysterious causes and unpredictable effects, national and international, which could only be grasped, to some extent at least, decades later. Rákosi, Nagy, Kádár and Rajk played different roles at different times in a bizarre drama which could be described as mixture of theatre of the absurd (Ionesco or Beckett), passages from Shakespeare, and a cheap thriller. In the first part Rákosi acted as producer and leading man, and in the final act it was János Kádár. Over the course of time all four key figures became transformed from hunter to hunted, from jailer to victim; Kádár was the only one who made a double role-change, culminating in insanity.

It is impossible to determine whether Rákosi's cruel, even sadistic conduct should be attributed to his long imprisonment—he was in jail between the ages of thirty-three and forty-nine; or to his inferiority complex and consequent dislike of his luckier or better-looking comrades, or to his slavish devotion to Stalin mixed with fear. It is well-known that Stalin declared at this time that all he had to do was lift his little finger and Tito would be finished—a fatal fallacy as far as Yugoslavia was concerned, leading inexorably to the events of 1956. In the case of the vassals, it was precisely Tito's resistance to the Soviet claim to absolutist leadership, on the principle that one could be a Communist without following the orders of the Kremlin, which exacerbated the ageing Stalin's paranoid suspicions.

Stalin did not like Rákosi for several reasons: first, he was a Jew, and secondly he could possibly have been an American spy. This last reservation was due to a famous photo showing Rákosi as a member of a delegation of the Hungarian coalition government, on the lawn of the White House with President Truman. While the other

Hungarian politicians stand stiffly behind or at the side of Truman, displaying embarrassed smiles, Rákosi stands on the American President's left and the two are chatting genially and laughing together. Of all people the Communist, embodiment of evil, seemed to have been an especially welcome guest. The solution to the puzzle is simple: Rákosi, alone among the Hungarian politicians, had earlier visited France and Britain for the consolidation of Hungary's position at the peace negotiations, and spoke fluent English. Stalin looked upon the scene as more than inappropriate, and was so enraged that even in July 1953—seven years later—his heirs still quoted the photo as evidence against the Party chief, then fighting for his political survival.[9]

Rákosi's fear of Stalin was understandable in view of the purges that had taken place within the Soviet apparatus. Yet Stalin appreciated slaves who not only showed boundless devotion to him, but were also clever and efficient. Even for the highest functionaries, access to Stalin was controlled for fifteen years by his personal secretary Alexander Poskryobyshev; this stocky man with a shaven head and a triple roll of fat at the back of his neck was also Rákosi's most important contact in the Kremlin—who knows, perhaps their shared ugliness formed an additional bond between them. At any rate, Rákosi sent the decisive correspondence about preparations for the greatest show-trial ever conducted in the satellite states directly to Poskryobyshev, with the request that his report be forwarded to "Comrade Filippov" (Stalin's code name for correspondence purposes).[10]

The Rajk trial was the starting signal in the entire Soviet Bloc for the witch-hunt for "Titoists" and agents of imperialism disguised as Communists: "enemies with party cards". We know today that the whole of the indictment against the former Hungarian Minister of the Interior and later Foreign Minister, including the death sentences, was authorized by Stalin. The arrests and interrogations by forty Soviet "specialists" under the direct supervision of General Fyodor Bielkin, chief of Soviet State Security in Eastern Europe, then named MGB, were prepared and carried out with his knowledge.

Why had Rajk been chosen as chief defendant? László Rajk as Minister of the Interior was just as convinced a Stalinist as his successors, a merciless destroyer of the bourgeois parties and chief architect of the repellent show-trial of Cardinal Mindszenty. His participation in the Spanish Civil War, his subsequent internment in a French camp, his role in the Communist underground in Hungary, his arrest and survival due to the intervention of his brother, the Secretary of State in the Arrow Cross government, provided the requisite "connection" with his erstwhile Yugoslav brothers-in-arms, as well as the "Fascist Horthy regime" and the "American secret service". Moreover he was young, slim, tall—and good-looking. As one of the few non-Jewish top functionaries he was doubtless the most dangerous potential rival of the ill-favoured Rákosi whose inferiority complex made him time and again quote from Shakespeare, and from Plato, during Politburo meeting about the danger of "lean and hungry" men.

As "Stalin's best pupil" Rákosi too went all the way in his extreme inhumanity, giving each arrest a particularly odious note. The world found out only from the memoirs and interviews of survivors and the later publication of secret documents why the accused had confessed, and through what sadistic methods of torture they had been transformed into their own accusers and informers on their comrades. Every political act in the underground or abroad was rigged into a crime, with the victims—completely cut off from the outside world—unable to defend themselves.[11]

On 29 May 1948 Rajk and his wife were invited by Rákosi for lunch. When they were saying their good-byes, the smiling Party chief promised that he would drop in on them within the next few days to see their new-born son. Rajk's closest friend and successor in the Ministry of the Interior, János Kádár, who had been involved in the preparations for the past few months, suggested to the Party leader that he would meet Rajk the following day for a game of chess in order to divert his attention; Kádár was a practised player. After a good hour Kádár said to his friend "Checkmate". Rajk drove home, and fifteen minutes later was arrested by a group of high-ranking security officers led by General Gábor Péter, Chief of State Security (ÁVH). When Rajk remained unyielding even after the most brutal torture with rubber truncheons, one evening Kádár and Mihály Farkas, Defence Minister and at the same time Party supervisor of the Secret Police, came and tried to persuade him to make a comprehensive confession. Rákosi had the whole conversation taped (the transcript was later used as a weighty means of pressure against Kádár). When the persuasive powers of these two failed, Rajk was tortured so severely that he made a short confession that same night.[12] The secret correspondence, appeals and records published since show the hatred and eagerness with which old accounts were being settled during the following years among the torturers as they fought for their own survival. In the event it was Rákosi himself who, despite his cunning, admitted in his notorious speech after the trial to a howling crowd of activists in the Budapest Sports Stadium: "I had to spend many sleepless nights before the execution of the plan was finalized." All his later attempts to shift responsibility to others were thus condemned to failure from the outset.

In the Rajk trial Stalin's classic method was used—the so-called "amalgam" or the linking of quite disparate elements. Hungarian Communists who had been living abroad for long periods, especially veterans of the Spanish Civil War, right and left ("Trotsky-ists"), Social Democrats, "Fascists" (e.g. wartime officers who had joined the resistance) and "Zionists" (Jewish Communists) were potential targets of the vigilance campaigns. Of the ninety-three who were condemned directly in connection with the Rajk trial and its sequels, fifteen were executed and eleven others did not survive their jail sentences. But that was only the beginning of the ever-faster-gyrating, fiendish merry-go-round of purges.

On 24 April 1950 the Head of State Árpád Szakasits—former Secretary General of the Social Democrats, now merged with the Communists—was invited with his wife to dine with the Party chief. Afterwards Rákosi had his guest arrested on the evidence of forged records, apparently proving that he had been an informer for the Horthy police. He was arrested there and then by General Gábor Péter who had been waiting next-door, and locked into the cellar of the Rákosi villa for a few days before being taken to prison. The verdict on the stonemason-turned journalist was a life sentence, and according to the usual practice his entire family were exposed to continual harassment.[13] Szakasits was freed six years later in 1956—incidentally at the same time as Zoltán Tildy, his predecessor as Head of State and erstwhile leader of the Smallholders' Party. He had been forced by the Communists to resign in July

1948, and his son-in-law, a diplomat, was executed for alleged corruption. Tildy and his wife were placed under house arrest for eight years. In a total of twenty political trials 180 leading Social Democrat politicians were sentenced to long prison terms, not to mention the many internees. Right- and left-wing Social Democrats, who fought bitter battles among themselves, suffered the same fate almost without exception.

Incidentally, of the two successors as State President one was a crypto-Communist in the guise of a Social Democrat, the other an alcoholic crypto-Communist masquerading under the name of a Smallholder (he remained in office for fifteen years). Under normal circumstances this would have remained completely irrelevant, except that the latter of these two helped Kádár in 1956, by way of a back-dated certificate of appointment of the so-called "Hungarian Government of Revolutionary Workers and Peasants", to lend an appearance of legality that was fragile even by Communist standards.

Almost simultaneously with the persecution of the Social Democrats, Rákosi and his closest accomplices, Defence Minister Mihály Farkas and General Gábor Péter, pursued a bloody purge of the top military. In the spring of 1950 twelve generals, among them the Chief of the General Staff and high-ranking officers were executed, and thirteen were sentenced to life imprisonment. (The changing of the guard was so successful that in 1954 only 15 per cent of the officer corps had higher than primary school education—however, two-thirds were Party members.)[14]

The basic method was always the same: false accusation, intimidation of witnesses, torture by deprivation of food, water, light and sleep, and if necessary by electric shocks and use of the traditional rubber truncheons. The role-change of perpetrator-victim was often dramatic: eight months before his own execution General Kálmán Révay, head of the Military Academy, had commanded a firing squad which shot his friend and comrade, former chief of Military Counter-Intelligence and a courageous resistance fighter, György Pálffy, in the courtyard of the military police headquarters.

Meanwhile propagandists fantasized about Hungary as the "land of iron and steel", promising a doubling of industrial production as well as a 50 per cent rise in real wages within only four years. In fact real wages and salaries fell between 1949 and 1952 by 20 per cent.

Small enterprises were in effect liquidated, and as a counter-move temporary rationing was introduced during the 1950s.

Diehard Communists were loyal to the Soviet Union, not to their own country. At issue were not only reparation payments, but also the notorious Soviet-Hungarian airline, shipping on the Danube, oil drilling and pumping, bauxite and aluminium mining joint companies. By 1954 the Soviets were able to pocket more than $1 billion in "profits" from Hungary. An administrator or manager only had to utter "suspicious" views about these unequal relationships, be rumoured to nurture anti-Soviet "nationalistic" resentments, be denounced, usually anonymously or at the whim of a functionary, to be put "on record"; and once a Secret Police file existed it was almost impossible to remain unscathed over the years. Between 1951 and May 1953 alone, around 850,000 police convictions were recorded; between 1950 and the first quarter of 1953, 650,000 people were arraigned, of whom 387,000 received sentences (most were fined). In addition 44,000 were interned and in the spring of 1951, 15,000 "bourgeois" and "unreliable elements" were deported, mainly from the capital to remote settlements where they were made to do agricultural work under harsh conditions. The black humour of the time divided the population into two groups: those who were already under arrest, and those who would be arrested next. The ubiquitous ÁVH could count on the services of more than 40,000 informers at any given time, and supposedly held records on over a million individuals, i.e. 10 per cent of the population.[15]

What many Hungarians believed at first, and many foreign observers said about the purges later—that the hated Communists were settling accounts with each other—was outstripped by the dynamics and dimensions of the permanent purges. Although between 1948 and 1951 a total of 400,000 members, largely former Social Democrats but also "minor Arrow Crossites" and "passive petit bourgeois", were purged from the Party, the "vanguard of the working class", now calling itself the MDP (short for Hungarian Workers' Party), still counted 828,000 comrades. Already at the beginning of the 1950s the Party employed 30–40,000 full-time functionaries and officials in its various committees and organizations. According to an informed estimate, between 1945 and 1985

2 million Hungarians, i.e. one in three adults, belonged for a shorter or longer time to the Communist Party (operating under various names).[16]

The initial enthusiasm of many Hungarians for the establishment of a supposedly equitable society which would give independence and prosperity to peasants through land reform, in which tens of thousands would find employment and upward mobility in the central and local administration, in which the youth would have access to secondary and tertiary education and with it the chance to level out the former huge differences of income—as the years passed, this abated more and more. The accelerated rearmament ordered by Stalin at a meeting of the satellites in the Kremlin in January 1951, which Rákosi translated into action with enthusiasm, led to a severe economic crisis in this agrarian country without resources. The armed forces, inflated to 200,000 men (with border patrols and the militia almost 300,000), together with armaments, swallowed up 25 per cent of the annual budget between 1950 and 1952. Just the wages and salaries of army personnel in one year were five times greater than the total expenditure on education.[17]

Even Stalin warned Rákosi against unbridled collectivization. In those years 9 per cent of arable land lay fallow, and the former granary of Central Europe had to import foodstuffs repeatedly to cover domestic needs. The peasants were harassed (also under Imre Nagy when he was Minister of Agriculture) with impossible delivery demands and threatened with fines. The so-called kulaks (71,000 families), peasants with more than 12 hectares of land, were brutally persecuted; even more peasants were forced into cooperatives, and the workers were outrageously exploited by the hated norm system whereby they had to fulfill artificially high or repeatedly increased production targets.

Within a short time even those who had kept this system going with initial enthusiasm from above, or those in the top echelons who had accepted (or rather had to accept) the reports of the Rajk and Szakasits trials with loud or tacit approval, themselves became victims in the cycles of repression. At the end of 1950 and beginning of 1951 Rákosi singled out as the main targets of his purges the so-called home-based Communists—those who had not been in Soviet exile. With Stalin's consent he ordered a veritable witch-hunt against these young functionaries. One of them was Kádár's successor in the Interior Ministry, Sándor Zöld, who had been elected to the Politburo with Kádár at the March 1951 party congress. At a meeting of this body in April Zöld was sharply criticized for his personnel selection; he then drove home without a word and with his service revolver shot his wife, mother, two small children and then himself. Zöld knew what awaited him in the torture chambers of the Secret Police. Thereupon the Party chief ordered the arrest of the other home-based Communists, chief among whom was the best-known top functionary, Kádár—"in order to impede their flight", as reported in a radio message to Stalin.[18]

A couple of days before 1 May the 13,750 Party organizations received the directive not to carry any pictures of Kádár during their march-past. Everybody took the hint. Kádár was charged with having been an informer for the Horthy police in 1943, dissolving the illegal CP on their orders, and establishing in its place a "Peace Party". Szakasits was said to have passed on the instruction to him.

In the eyes of the true Bolsheviks the "liquidators", as they were called from the times of Lenin's fight against the Mensheviks, were evil deviants and "objective" tools of the class enemy. What might seem to later generations a ridiculous splitting of hairs was a matter of life and death at the time. The charge of "deviationism" could easily be used as a pretext against one's potential opponents. Kádár was still at large and even acted as a member of the leadership, yet he had to write increasingly self-incriminatory weekly reports for Rákosi about his earlier conduct. It was a variation of the technique described by Arthur Koestler in his novel *Darkness at Noon*, and also known from the great Moscow show trials.[19]

In contrast to most Muscovite and home-based Communists, Kádár, born out of wedlock in 1912 in the port city of Fiume (today's Rijeka) to a half or wholly Slovak washerwoman and household-help, actually came from the class in whose name he later acted, namely the working class. He met his natural father and three half-brothers for the first time only in 1960 when he was already head of the Party. Kádár—he changed his name officially from Czermanik (later Csermanek) in 1945—grew up among the poorest in the country and later in the capital. It was an exceptional achievement in those days for anyone from such a background even to complete four classes of the higher elementary school. The trained typewriter mechanic (who never actually worked in that capacity) soon found his way to the Communists. The fact that Kádár had formally belonged for five full years to a Budapest district organization of the Social Democrats, and there met artists and intellectuals, may well have shaped his later attitude. In all he spent a total of seven years in various prisons, by far the worst being three-and-a-half in solitary confinement between 1951 and 1954. However, in contrast to what is asserted in most reference works, he was never tortured; unnerved, humiliated and psychologically at the end of his tether, he signed the requisite confessions without any need for physical force. In a secret trial shortly before Christmas 1951 he was given a life sentence.[20] Kádár was spared the fate of his friend Rajk, whom, as Interior Minister, he had persuaded to confess eighteen months earlier first by false promises and then by torture; he personally attended Rajk's execution by hanging, an experience that must have been remained with him for the rest of his life. At the beginning of the 1950s the motto was "survival".

When, contrary to all expectations, he was released in 1954, Rákosi—the very man who had had him arrested—now received him solicitously, expressed pleasure at seeing him again, and inquired after "Comrade Kádár's" health. Kádár, as he would later tell his biographer, was also pleased, above all because he was still alive, and did not reproach the "Chief". The two men agreed that after taking a holiday Kádár would be appointed Party secretary of the capital's Thirteenth District—something that would strike any ordinary mortal as unbelievable. Kádár's words spoken at a banquet held in May 1972 for his sixtieth birthday could perhaps serve as at least a partial explanation for this odd situation: "Only certain things can be credited to an individual as a service. Let us say—and I for one would regard this as a kind of service—when someone recognized at the right time that he is neither a leopard nor a tiger, but also not a mouse." It would perhaps be truer to compare the longest-serving successful politician of the Communist world to a fox, and a particularly cunning one at that.[21]

In any case, while Kádár languished in solitary confinement under incomparably worse conditions than under Horthy, the entire nation had to celebrate in March 1952 the sixtieth birthday of "Stalin's best pupil". Almost forty years later one of the chief manipulators described in a pamphlet the racy details of the preparations. These might have been planned by the general staff.[22] The highlight of the festivities was a gala performance in honour of Rákosi in the Opera House. There he sat under his own giant likeness, flanked on the right by a similarly huge image of Stalin and on the left by one of Lenin, "modestly" accepting the innumerable tributes paid to him and the singing of a song specially composed for the occasion.

During that late autumn and winter the persecution mania of Stalin reached a new zenith. The notorious Slánsky trial in Prague (eleven out of the fourteen accused were Jews) and the Moscow conspiracy of the "murderers in white aprons" (nine top doctors, six of them Jews, were said to have tried to murder Stalin on the orders of the American-Zionist espionage services) were a warning for everyone, but especially for functionaries of Jewish origin.

In this tense situation a personal emissary from Stalin turned up in Rákosi's office at the beginning of January 1953, and reported that General Fyodor Bielkin from the Soviet Ministry of the Interior had been unmasked as a British spy, and revealed under interrogation that Gábor Péter, with whom he had staged the whole Rajk trial, was also a British spy and traitor. In the tried and tested manner Rákosi invited in the Police Chief—and his wife, who ran his secretariat—to dinner the following evening. On their arrival the commander of the host's bodyguard handcuffed both of them, and they were locked for safety's sake in the icy cellar of the villa while eighteen high-ranking security officers were dismissed from the ÁVH. Only after the purge was over were Péter and his wife transferred to the special jail.

Gábor Péter (alias Benö Eisenberger) had already been an NKVD agent before the war and was regarded as most trusted tool of the Soviets', even by Stalin personally.[23] That a man such as the Communist General Secretary Slánsky, who had spent the war years in the Soviet Union, or a top agent like Péter, with whom at a reception in the Kremlin in 1948 Stalin clinked glasses as a special sign of esteem, could now be sacrificed to the anti-Semitic persecution mania of the ageing dictator showed that all party chiefs of Jewish origin were now under threat, including Rákosi.

Elias Canetti's reflections on power are applicable also to Rákosi (and naturally to his master in the Kremlin): "... the actual intention of the true dictator is as grotesque as it is unbelievable: he wants to be the *only one*, he wants to survive all others, so that no one else should survive *him*."[24] To prove his reliability and indispensability to Moscow, Rákosi lost no time and ordered the arrest of prominent Jewish Communists, doctors and members of the Jewish community. He too now wanted to prepare a "Zionist trial" with Zoltán Vas, one of the few popular Muscovites—a man who had spent fifteen years in jail with Rákosi, as the chief defendant. It has only recently become known from Swedish sources of plans to prosecute in a special trial some of the doctors and functionaries of the Jewish community arrested at the time for having allegedly murdered Raoul Wallenberg in January 1945 (the date and circumstances of Wallenberg's death have never been discovered).[25]

Then on 5 March 1953, in the midst of the totally unpredictable last great wave of purges from Moscow to Prague and Budapest, Stalin died. At first there was no political reaction. The Hungarian dictatorship even celebrated an overwhelming victory of the unity ticket in the so-called parliamentary elections: 98 per cent of the electorate voted, and 98.2 of the votes cast were in favour of the MDP. The "Wise Leader and Teacher of our People and our Party", since the summer of 1952 both Party Chief and Prime Minister, appeared to be at the height of his power, but appearances were deceptive. Much was happening, not only in Budapest but in Moscow. As early as June the collective leadership struck its first fateful blow. We know today that Stalin's heirs fought each other like scorpions in a glass bottle, but they were united on one point: that Hungary was potentially the most dangerous trouble-spot, and Mátyás Rákosi, the man responsible for the highly disquieting situation, should immediately resign as Prime Minister. A large Hungarian party and government delegation—its members "chosen" by their "hosts"—was summoned to visit Moscow on 13–16 June. The members of the collective leadership, first and foremost Secret Police Chief Beria and Prime Minister Malenkov, but also Party Secretary Khrushchev and Foreign Minister Molotov, attacked their devoted Hungarian disciple with unprecedented sharpness and irony in Stalin's study in the presence of his astonished attendants. The collective leadership decided unanimously that the fifty-seven year old Imre Nagy, deputy Prime Minister and Politburo member, should become Rákosi's successor.

If it were asked today why a popular uprising broke out in October 1956 in Hungary and only there, then two factors have to be taken into consideration against the background of general developments in the Eastern bloc from de-Stalinization to partial reconciliation with the heretic in Belgrade. First, Hungary was the only Bloc member where—already four months after Stalin's death, on the initiative of a worried Soviet leadership—Stalinism was openly condemned and a new reform course was proclaimed; and secondly, only there did two factions with two diametrically opposed concepts in the Party battle on for over three years over the future direction to be taken. The popular uprising could only happen when the Party, notably its top echelon, became so divided on the question of de-Stalinization that it could no longer assert its power.

The optimistic new beginning and all that happened later can only be viewed in conjunction with the personality, career and inner transformation of the new Prime Minister Imre Nagy. He was, and remains, a key figure in those events, and one of the principal questions is: why was the Soviet leadership united in choosing him as the head of government? A purist could demur that it was incomprehensible for the head of government in a sovereign state to be unseated and another appointed as the result of decisions taken in a foreign capital. However, this was the political reality, and in this one case it was a boon: without Soviet authority Nagy could not have been appointed, nor could "the baldhead" (as Rákosi was known in Opposition circles) have been banished.

Be that as it may, from Moscow's viewpoint Imre Nagy represented the ideal solution. He was one of the very few non-Jewish Muscovites; he had spent a total of twenty years in Soviet emigration, was an agrarian expert, and as Minister for Agriculture after 1945 had carried out the popular land reform. He was afterwards Minister of the Interior for a short time, and subsequently President of Parliament until September 1949, when he was ousted from the Politburo after lengthy conflicts with Rákosi and his loyal followers due to "right-opportunistic deviation" over the agrarian question. Because of his opposition to the over-hasty collectivization of agriculture, Nagy had temporarily to step back into the second rank, but after his self-criticism he was re-instated into the top leadership, both in the government and in the Politburo, evidently with Moscow's backing. Now the Soviet leadership explicitly confirmed the correctness of his former opposition over the agrarian question and condemned his expulsion from the Politburo.

This man, who gave the impression of a jovial professor and—in contrast to Rákosi—spoke to the people in lucid, pleasant-sounding Hungarian, was willing to launch a "new line", based on the trust of his Soviet patrons. At a closed meeting of the Party's Central Committee, the new Prime Minister-designate made an epoch-making speech—which, however, did not become public knowledge any more than the significant party resolution that followed. A wall of silence surrounded the affair. Some details only became known after thirty-three years, and the speech was published as late as 1989. Nagy held Rákosi primarily responsible for the deplorable state of affairs and not only him but also the other three members of the notorious "quartet"—Mihály Farkas for breaking the law, Ernö Gerö for his adventurous economic policy and József Révai for the poor state of education and culture. He spoke of "intolerable conditions characteristic of a police state". The resolution was a sweeping indictment of the Rákosi clique: "It was improper that Comrade Rákosi gave the ÁVH direct instructions on how to conduct their investigations and whom to arrest, and it was improper for him to order physical mistreatment of those arrested, which is against the law."

Despite Imre Nagy's good intentions and changes of personnel, power over the political apparatus still remained in the hands of Rákosi and his followers. The fact that another Muscovite. Ernö Gerö, was appointed Minister of the Interior (on Soviet orders) was not likely to encourage faith in "Socialist legality". Yet the speech given in Parliament by Imre Nagy as the new head of government on 4 July 1953 came as a bombshell. The promise to end police despotism, disband the internment camps, decree an amnesty and revoke deportations immediately enabled tens of thousands, including the author of this book, to return to normal life. Work norms were also lowered and the forced collectivization of agriculture was stopped. The standard of living rose and important reforms considerably improved the atmosphere. But that was only the beginning. Rákosi promptly launched a counter-attack, which from the outset restricted the room for manoeuvre of Nagy and his comrades-in-arms.

The main issues in the struggle between Nagy and Rákosi were the scrutiny of the secret trials and purges, the priorities of economic policy (light versus heavy industry), and the revival of the People's Front—not as a "transmission belt" for the Party's instructions but as a means of winning the confidence of the people. In no other Eastern bloc country was there such a fierce political battle. It was not about ideological hair-splitting but about the freedom, wellbeing and personal future of hundreds of thousands of oppressed, disfranchised and, in part even up to the autumn of 1956, imprisoned people. In Hungary the surviving victims of the trials—writers, journalists and artists, especially the former standard-bearers of the Rákosi era—were those who, betrayed by the ruling clique and plunged into conflicts of conscience, gathered around Imre Nagy, who was still isolated at the top. They dictated the tempo of the reform movement.

Rákosi meanwhile cleverly exploited the power struggles in Moscow, especially the fall of Beria in June 1953 and of Malenkov in the spring of 1955; both had promoted Nagy. At that time and more than thirty years later, the rumour was deliberately spread that Nagy was "Beria's man", later even that he was an NKVD agent. His biographer, János M. Rainer, concludes in the hitherto most thorough study that at the time of the great purges Nagy, like so many others, acted as a temporary informer, rendering "modest services" to the "organs", but definitely not as an "agent".[26] Even so, neither genuine nor forged documents can alter or detract from the position of Imre Nagy in Hungarian history between 1953 and 1958.

The ups and downs of the power struggles in Moscow and in the relationship with Yugoslavia were closely connected with the murderous jockeyings for position and feelings of bitter resentment and paranoia of the leading cadres in Hungary. Their conclusions, warnings and above all mutual denunciations fill countless pages in the reports of the Soviet ambassador and later Party chief Yuri Andropov and of his press attaché, the future Secret Service chief, Vladimir Kriushkov, both of whom spoke and understood Hungarian after their long stay in Budapest.

All his life, especially in crises, Imre Nagy tended to adopt an often passive wait-and-see policy, in which his later heart condition probably also played a role. Still, following his defeat by Rákosi, he refused the usual self-criticism. In the spring of 1955 he was expelled with the Kremlin's consent from all Party bodies and toppled from the post of prime minister, which then went to András Hegedüs, a thirty-three-year-old functionary from peasant stock and a Rákosi and Gerö favourite.

After Nikita Khrushchev's historic squaring of accounts with Stalin and his policies during the Twentieth Congress of the Communist Party of the USSR and under pressure from Tito, the campaign for the rehabilitation of Rajk and the other victims of Rákosi's reign caused disarray in the Party machinery. The turmoil in Poland, especially the bloody conflicts in Poznan, encouraged the beleaguered Party chief to use this tragedy as a "coup" against the Opposition, which was becoming increasingly strong and defiant. The Soviets realized too late that Rákosi had become a political liability. Anastas Mikoyan, Khrushchev's trouble-shooter, was sent to Budapest, where for weeks he carefully prepared Rákosi's removal and took part in the decisive meeting of the Central Committee on 18 July 1956.

The news of Rákosi's stripping of power came as a political earthquake. The public was delirious that, straight after the Central Committee session, the dictator should disappear in the direction of Moscow "for health reasons". The rehabilitated Kádár's re-entry into the Politburo was also received with enthusiasm. Yet a bitter pill had to be swallowed straight after this, when Rákosi's place was taken by another old Kremlin hand, Ernö Gerö. Even more disappointing was the non-appearance on the scene of Imre Nagy, who in the mean time had been expelled from the Party, and from his professorship at the Economics University. But the clamour for him became increasingly strident. Knowledgeable observers claim with hindsight that the last chance to avert an explosion of bottled-up fury at the unbearable and cynical offences against the people and their nation would have been a genuine changing of the guard—in other words, the re-appointment of Imre Nagy as head of government and the selection of Kádár instead of the discredited Gerö as First Secretary of the Party. Without that, the situation could only become more dangerous.

As so many times before in Hungarian history, a funeral set the masses in motion. In this case it was the public burial of the

rehabilitated victims of the first great show-trial, Rajk and his companions; what is more, it took place on a profoundly symbolic date:
6 October, the day of mourning for the thirteen martyred generals
of the revolutionary army executed by the Habsburgs in 1849. A
crowd estimated at 200,000 waited in the cold, drenching rain and
howling winds to pay their last respects to the dead. As well as the
mourning, there was also a palpable sense of threatening determination. Although the man who now carried the hopes not only of
the intellectuals but also of a large section of the people—Imre
Nagy—was allowed to rejoin the Party, that was all; nothing more
happened on the political scene. Half of the Politburo, including
Gerö, Kádár and Hegedüs, went on a state visit to Yugoslavia for a
full week. In the event it was the disturbances in Poland and the
Soviets' threatening gestures against Gomulka's return to the top
leadership which provided the detonator for the explosive accumulated tensions in Hungary. On 23 October students demonstrated their solidarity with Hungary's traditional friends, the Poles.

As in 1848, so in 1956, intellectuals and students were the harbingers of the "unexpected revolution", of which Hannah Arendt
rightly wrote "that never before had a revolution attained its goals
so rapidly, so thoroughly and with so little bloodshed".[27] Since then
thousands of works by Hungarians and foreigners—books, pamphlets, studies, essays by participants and eyewitnesses—have been
published on the course and consequences of these events. All serious presentations agree that the numerous propaganda writings of
the Kádár regime between 1957 and 1988 told little of the truth
about the fundamental questions.

October 1956 was a natural political phenomenon without a
focus, without a concept and without coordinated leadership. That
the almost 900,000-strong Party was a colossus with feet of clay
that, apart from a few functionaries, evaporated from one day to the
next was proved by the events that took place between 23 October
and 4 November. The key players in the armed clashes were mainly
young workers, students and soldiers, but also members of the so-
called "*lumpenproletariat*". It was the people from the "streets of
Pest" (*Pesti utcán*)* who fought with weapons in their hands from

---

* This was the title of a moving collection of portraits of young men and women
sentenced to long prison terms after the defeat of the uprising.

the beginning to the bitter end against superior forces, and who can be hailed as the real heroes of those tempestuous days. This time too, as so often in Hungarian history, hero and traitor—Imre Nagy and János Kádár—played contrasting symbolic roles which were also politically decisive.

We know today from original sources that after the outbreak of the spontaneous uprising the situation in the centres of power in Moscow and Budapest changed not merely from day to day but often from hour to hour. Politburo members, even the chief protagonist Khrushchev, wavered in their opinions, which changed during a single meeting as they strove not to endanger their own positions.[28] In Budapest the reformers, led by Imre Nagy who strictly adhered to Party discipline, wanted a correction of the system, not its abolition. Hardly anyone within his closer circle and among his thousands of convinced followers suspected that in the Hungary of the autumn of 1956 a correction was tantamount to the end of the system.

Yet during the evening of 23 October Nagy's first meeting in front of the Parliament with a vast crowd of people estimated at 200,000 showed that something hitherto unheard-of in a Communist country was in the offing. His opening word "Comrades!" was answered by whistles, and his mollifying, pedestrian explanations by obvious disappointment. Hours before shots were aimed at the demonstrating people in front of the radio building, and before the appearance of Soviet tanks summoned by the panic-stricken Gerö, a popular rising had begun. This elemental outburst of rage by the Hungarian people against the symbols of dictatorship and foreign rule, combined with the panicky and provocative reaction of Party leaders blinded by their monopoly of power, caused events in the capital and later all over the country to run out of control. Particularly intolerable were the lies put out over the radio about a "counter-revolution"; these focused the young people's unbridled rage on the mendacious political puppet-show by Rákosi's heirs, further increasing their resolve. Alexander Solzhenitsyn expressed this aptly in his acceptance speech when presented with the Nobel Peace Prize for Literature in 1970: "Force can only shroud itself by lies, and lies can only be upheld by force." To most Hungarians Imre Nagy was a symbol of new departures. Those who demanded among other things his appointment as Prime Minister on that radiantly beautiful, memorable autumn day hoped to gain from a Nagy government free elections, a free press, the reintroduction of Hungarian national holidays and national symbols, and, after the early evening hours, negotiations for the withdrawal of Soviet troops.

As it turned out, the sixty-year-old bearer of the people's hope was installed as Prime Minister during the night of 23 October, but he remained at first a prisoner of his past and his surroundings in Party headquarters. Isolated from the "Pest streets", from the young people who had taken up arms, he too appeared to represent the Soviet-dictated hard line; he too spoke in his radio address about counter-revolution. On 25 October Kádár replaced Gerö as First Secretary on the initiative of Mikoyan and Suslov, who were staying in Budapest from 24 to 31 October, yet the fighting continued, and what occurred in the fantasy world of the Party committees in their headquarters in Academy Street, encircled by Soviet tanks, became increasingly irrelevant.

Nagy, the vacillator, was in trouble. Exhausted, suffering from heart trouble, he was being crushed between the grindstones of his loyalty to the Party and the Soviets, his deep-rooted patriotism, the pressure from the streets and the personal urgings of his closest advisers. His popularity began to wane.

The change, linked to the name of Nagy, became apparent only on 27 October with the reshuffling of the government and the beginning of negotiations with the freedom fighters, who were no longer being labelled as counter-revolutionaries. Several thousand young people compelled this change of course because they were determined to fight till the very end, and because they enjoyed the moral and frequently also the practical support of the population. The Soviet leadership and their dogsbodies—now at the helm of a disintegrating party—had to acknowledge with a gnashing of teeth that in the midst of the Soviet bloc's greatest crisis, the lifelong Communist and Muscovite Imre Nagy was choosing the side of the people. The three core points that Nagy decided on for himself and the country were: first, the events were not a counter-revolution but a national, democratic revolt encompassing the entire populace (28 October); secondly, this urgently necessitated re-introduction of the multi-party system, dissolution of the CP and establishment of the Hungarian Socialist Workers' Party; and thirdly it necessitated too a proclamation of neutrality and withdrawal from the Warsaw Pact (1 November). An armistice came into force on 28 October, and for 150 hours Hungarians lived in a virtually surreal overall mood of expectancy. But after initial to-ing and fro-ing the die was cast already on 31 October in Moscow in favour of a massive intervention, i.e. before Hungary's withdrawal from the Warsaw Pact and proclamation of neutrality could come into effect.

When on 29 October Nagy moved from Party headquarters to the Parliament building a few hundred metres away, he gave a signal to the Party and perhaps to the world: that the political centre should henceforth no longer be the Party but the government residing in the tradition-hallowed Parliament. But the free world, which had waited so many years for such an event that would weaken the Soviet sphere of influence, was at that moment focused on something quite different: the closure of the Suez Canal by the Egyptians and the anachronistic reaction to this from Britain and France. The Hungarians, as so often in their history, had to rely on themselves and were left to the mercy of an oppressive hostile power.

In his efforts to unite the reformist élite and the people in this terribly difficult, nerve-racking and deadly-dangerous tightrope walk, Nagy believed that he could rely on the active support of the First Secretary, János Kádár—or so it seemed at the beginning of November. On the evening of the 1st, the Nagy government's Minister of State*—Kadar—extolled the Communist intellectuals and youths as "the driving impulse behind the glorious rebellion" against "Rákosi's despotism and political gangsterism".[29] At the time when this recorded speech was broadcast, Kádár and the man who had set up the defection—Minister of the Interior, old Communist, Spanish Civil War veteran and Soviet agent, Ferenc Münnich—were probably already on their way to Moscow. They had decamped from Parliament in the early afternoon to the Soviet embassy.

Preparations for the crushing of the freedom fight by the Soviets were entering their last phase. Britain and France, the Western

---

* The Minister of State was a minister without portfolio but in an elevated position. This designation was used both before and after 1945.

powers engrossed in the Suez adventure, as well as the United States as "onlooker without direct interests" (Henry Kissinger), gave the split Soviet leadership virtual *carte blanche* in Hungary. Tito condemned the first Soviet intervention but endorsed the second one. The leaders of the satellite parties, even including Gomulka in Poland, supported the Soviet measures.

On a foggy, damp and chilly Sunday, 4 November, at 4 a.m. Soviet tanks began their general attack on Budapest. The freedom fighters, although they numbered about 10,000, had no chance against the overwhelmingly superior forces. The Hungarian army remained in barracks. Many young Hungarians put up a desperate resistance.

Most of the 2,700 officially registered dead and 19,000 wounded had originally taken up arms in the naive expectation of Western aid. Encouraged by Radio Free Europe's ambiguous commentaries with the general drift that the West and the United Nations would not leave Hungary in the lurch, phantom hopes were being aroused. Only gradually did the Hungarians appreciate the moral bankruptcy of the "Western liberation concept" as represented by President Eisenhower and Secretary of State Dulles. Details of the Tito regime's two-faced attitude did not come to light till many years later.

Prime Minister Imre Nagy, who had accepted the "sanctuary" offered by Yugoslavia on the morning of 4 November 1956 and fled with his forty-three closest associates to its embassy, did not know that it was nothing but a put-up job. From the memoirs of the former Yugoslav ambassador to Moscow, Veljko Mičunović, it is clear that all the details of the intervention, including who would be the next party and government chief, had been discussed between Khrushchev and Tito on the island of Brioni forty-eight hours before the attack. Accordingly, Nagy was supposed to be persuaded directly or indirectly from Belgrade during his stay in the embassy— from 4 to 22 November—to resign officially and to acknowledge the "workers' and peasants' government" under Prime Minister Kádár, set up on 4 November simultaneously with the Soviet attack.

The Hungarian people's tragedy of 1956–7 is in some ways reminiscent of the War of Independence in 1848–9. On this occasion as on the previous one, it was the Russians who brutally crushed a war of independence.

After 4 November 1956 János Kádár was the man of the moment. The playwright Háy once wrote of him: "His personality had a certain fascination, a fascination of weary compromise."[30] This observation might have been appropriate for the Kádár of the 1960s and '70s, but in the early days after his arrival in the shadow of Russian tanks, he was a traitor by definition, the stooge of a hated regime in the service of a foreign power. By contrast Imre Nagy became a tragic hero of Hungarian history. He, better than anybody, knew how tens of thousands had been consumed in the accelerating purge-machinery in Moscow and later in Budapest, and how the prosecutors and Communist journalists who built castles of falsehood, as was required of them, remained steadfast to the end. Perhaps he could still have saved himself by resigning by self-criticism, but in that historic moment he wanted to remain true to himself and to the idea of *his* October.

Now it was the turn of the Russians and especially Kádár. He repeatedly promised Imre Nagy and his friends safe-conduct, and immunity from punishment to the participants in the rising. The breach of these promises, the abduction of the entire Nagy group by the Soviets, their deportation to Snagov in Romania followed by their transportation back to Hungary in April 1957, and finally the secret trial and execution in June 1958 of Nagy, General Maléter, the journalist Miklós Gimes and others, remained for three decades an ineradicable moral burden of guilt on the Kádár regime. The fact that during a year and a half no communiqué appeared about their whereabouts and fate, and that even their closest relatives, interned in Romania, had no news of them until their trial, add the final touch to this picture of barbaric retribution.

Of course, this was not confined only to the main characters. After the smashing of the workers' councils, which had resisted for weeks, and after the protest actions of intellectuals and students, 22,000 individuals were condemned, of whom 229 were executed, for their part in the Revolution: far more than after 1848–9, more than after the fall of the Soviet Republic in 1919, and even more than after 1945.[31]

However, there was a double standard in operation. The supremo of the torturers Gábor Péter, the Party representative in the Secret Service, ex-Minister of Defence Mihály Farkas, and his son Vladimir

Farkas, who as a lieutenant-colonel had been responsible for the torture of many innocent people, were released already as early as 1959–60. According to the memoirs of the son, the two Farkas lived in a prison that resembled a two-star hotel.

Imre Nagy became transformed in the view of history from a servant of evil into the martyr of the nation and of the fight for freedom. In his closing words at the trial, before being executed on 16 June 1958, he did not ask for mercy but defended his actions which, he said, would ultimately be judged by the Hungarian nation and the international workers' movement.

The events of 1956 were a spontaneous uprising which rapidly expanded into a revolution aimed at overturning a system forced on the population from outside, and which in two phases finally led to an unwinnable war of independence. It was, in the full meaning of the word, a clean revolution. No looting took place, there were no anti-Semitic actions to speak of, although the "leading quartet" and most of the high-ranking officers of the Secret Police in the worst times were of Jewish origin, and there were only sporadic acts of revenge against officers and soldiers of the State Security and police, claiming some innocent victims as well. The government and the freedom fighters categorically condemned lynch law. It was precisely because the aim of this "anti-totalitarian" Revolution was not to restore the pre-war feudal-capitalistic system, and because the Communist regime was swept away by those who had professed to represent it, that the Hungarian autumn had such enormous historical significance.

As in the case of the great freedom fights of the past—the Rákóczi uprising of 1704–11 and the War of Independence of 1848—victory on the battlefield (which this time happened to be the streets of Budapest) was denied, in spite of such a great national show of strength. But the fame of this courageous small nation reverberated all over the world. Of the 210,000 Hungarians who fled—many of the leaders escaped to Austria and some to Yugoslavia—only 40,000 returned to Hungary.

The trauma of Russian repression belongs just as much to the self-image of Hungarians as the memory of how in 1849 and after 1945 the West had left the small country to its fate. The defeat of 1956 opened up old wounds. It has also to be remembered that for many the anti-Russian propaganda of the Horthy regime had been retrospectively confirmed by the inconceivable behaviour of the Red Army towards the civilian population, and that even the leading Communists despaired of this in 1945. Already on the first evening of the Revolution the crowd burned books about Marx, Lenin and Stalin and pictures of them, and loathing of the cult of Stalin, the Soviet Union and foreign rule generally—which, if simply bearing them were not enough, had to be constantly praised—erupted again and again everywhere. Resentment against the Russian superpower, now the Soviet Union, was nowhere as strong in the "fraternal countries" (apart from Poland) as in Hungary. This is hard to understand unless one also understands the psychosis of a defeated nation.

Coming, as it did, after the 1953 workers' uprising in Berlin, the Hungarian Revolution intensified the push for national and personal liberty into an enormous explosive force, inflicting immense loss of prestige on the Soviet Union and the cause of world Communism. Although Tito had betrayed the originally Yugoslav-supported reformers around Nagy, placing himself squarely on the side of the Kádár-Münnich group, he also gave vent to the bitter truth in a public speech made at the time in Pula: "Socialism has been compromised." A long and winding road, mostly concealed and covert, led from Budapest 1956 to the Prague Spring in 1968 and the Polish Solidarity movement in 1980, which in turn gave an unmistakable impetus to the intellectual and subsequent political ferment in Kádár's Hungary, by then "the merriest barrack of the Socialist camp".

During the time of the revenge campaign, of course, especially after the shock of the totally unexpected secret trial of Nagy, the generally gloomy situation recalled the bitter cry by the great poet Mihály Vörösmarty in 1849: "No more hope! No more hope!" Just as it had been a century earlier, all that the oppressed and gagged country received was rhetorical comfort, particularly from the hypocritical political theatre of the United Nations. It took six years before international pressure achieved at least a comprehensive amnesty for political prisoners in Hungary. The politically inflated price, exploited for propaganda, was the cancellation of the annual debate on Hungary from the UN agenda.

In a strange transformation the hated "Gauleiter from Moscow" became over the years and decades the "father of the nation", respected even by some of his erstwhile victims, and the universally despised stooge of a superpower became an internationally respected statesman. And as early as the 1960s, Hungary changed from the "Sick Man of the Eastern Bloc" to its figurehead. A well-known Polish writer described his impressions in the '60s after his first visit to Hungary since 1956:

I do not understand why my Hungarian colleagues are so dissatisfied. Look at the lavish shop-windows, the price tags, inquire who has travelled abroad and how often, listen to the tone and the openness of the press! Almost everything is incomparably better than it is with us, let alone the astonishing popularity enjoyed by Kádár as opposed to Gomulka. We won in October 1956, but in the long run we have lost. The Hungarians lost at the time, but in the end they have won.[32]

The question that was already being asked at the time and was frequently repeated later was: although the popular rising had been defeated by force of arms, had it in fact gained a victory after all? In hindsight, and on the basis of documents available today, this question can definitely be answered in the negative. Given the realities in the Eastern bloc, Kádár was not able to achieve what Imre Nagy had stood and died for—a democratic multi-party system and genuine independence—but he had not striven for that. In spite of progress on all fronts, the fundamental fact remained that his "Revolutionary Workers' and Peasants' Government" was born on 4 November 1956 and became viable only by way of a constitutional fiction. Despite all concessions, the regime had to maintain that fiction for almost thirty-three years because it was what it lived by. The events of 1956, Kádár's repeated treachery *vis-à-vis* Imre Nagy and his real role behind the scenes in the Rajk case remained taboo topics until the end of his regime. Nonetheless, despite the past, it has to be admitted that this professional functionary became—next to István Bethlen, and possibly even more so—the most successful and certainly the longest-serving Hungarian politician of the twentieth century.

In November 1957 the then forty-four-year-old János Kádár had to start from scratch, and without illusions rebuild the state party. The profound distrust of the workers and intellectuals was clear from the extremely small membership of the newly-established "Hungarian Socialist Workers' Party"; by December 1956 it had attracted only 103,000 members. Less than 300,000 old members rejoined by the deadline of 1 May 1957. A Deputy Minister of the Interior of the time estimated the number of actual "class enemies" (former landowners, kulaks, merchants, priests, officers and public servants) at 700,000. Therefore, according to the official admission, "active enemies" still far outnumbered convinced supporters of the Party.

That policy of constant improvisation, of cautious reforms within the framework of monopolistic power, satisfying the people's need for more affluence and a little more freedom, the policy of "who ever is not against us is with us"—all that was later to be called "Kadarism"—began only in 1962–3. However, it bore relatively plentiful fruit within a relatively short time. With the aid of a $600 million long-term loan from the Soviets and other Eastern bloc countries and the boosting of small private enterprises by tax concessions and other measures, the real wages of workers and of other strata rose considerably. By 1960 *per capita* income was already 20–25 per cent higher than in 1956. Privatization and de-politicization proved for a long time to be the most important pillars of the system.

The lack of help from the West in October and November 1956 and the probability that its Suez adventure had contributed to the decisive victory of the interventionists in the divided Moscow leadership caused deep disappointment both to the élite and to the man in the street. Thus political resignation engendered by salutary disillusionment may well have contributed just as much to the consolidation of the Party's regained power as the crushing of the opposition. The interaction of various factors—a change in the foreign policy climate, unlimited Soviet support (after March 1957) combined with Khrushchev's victory over his Stalinist rivals in June 1957 and, last but not least, the widespread apathy of the people—provided the Hungarian Communists with time, opportunity and the necessary elbow-room for a complete "overhaul" of the Party and the state. The thaw and the marginal concessions (professional advancement without Party membership, greater tolerance in cultural life and the abatement of day-to-day harassment) led to a process of consolidation and normalization, which no one would have dared to anticipate in 1956. The peculiar truce reached its seeming peak as early as 18 October 1964 when Kádár paid warm tribute his "paternal friend and elder brother" Khrushchev after the latter's unexpected fall from power. He stated in this famous speech that the Hungarian CP's moderate political line would not change by an iota—a statement that caused a sensation at the time and strengthened his popularity. Nothing could have illustrated the process of change better than the fact that the two most hated men of 1956 were regarded as the guarantors of relaxation eight years later.

The freedom to travel to the West, which was of immense psychological importance, contributed greatly to the acceptance and growing popularity of the regime. In 1954, 3,040 Hungarians (functionaries, officials, sportsmen and, believe it or not, ninety-five private individuals) were permitted to travel to the West. In 1958 the number had grown to 15,500, in 1962 to 65,000 and in 1963 to more than 120,000. Hungarians in exile in Vienna, Munich and Zurich called it "Kádár's revenge" when more and more of their friends and relatives appeared on their doorsteps. By 1986 the number of travellers to the West had risen to 708,000.[33] Hungary was far ahead of the other Eastern bloc countries in regard to access to further education, priority of specialized knowledge over the red Party book for various positions in industry and administration, and a tolerable climate for small businesses.

One should not underestimate with hindsight the enormous significance of Kádár's style of leadership and government. A point in favour of his achievement as a politician was that, without ever questioning the basis of a one-party dictatorship or absolute loyalty to the Soviet power structure, he was able to obtain in part active cooperation and in part benevolent toleration of the regime by wide sections of society. He became popular because he could get the Party to accept the principle that one should not promise the people a bed of roses but tell the truth, even when it was unpalatable. His style as an orator was also a welcome respite from the tone of Stalinist times. In place of overpowering political jargon he used normal, everyday expressions, often mentioning the break with the past; he would chat, exhort, mock and tell anecdotes. Never a "covert" democrat, he was a cautious reformer, a tactician with an uncanny political instinct, a gifted technician of power who understood that, despite its monopoly of power and Soviet backing, the Party could not in the long term operate in a political vacuum. Kádár's almost puritanical lifestyle, personal modesty and sense of humour even gained him the temporary favour of the great poet Gyula Illyés and the national populist writer László Németh. At the same time he was publicity-shy and disliked talking about himself—and being flattered by others. In contrast to the other leaders in the Eastern bloc, Kádár was strongly averse to any form of personality cult. No pictures of him hung in public offices, nor were his photos carried during parades.

Little was and is known about this man who governed the country for thirty-two years. Even the biography planned as an introduction to an English-language collection of his speeches was published only after a formal resolution of the Politburo in spite of Kádár's categorical refusal even to consider the project. In the end the author of the biography was permitted only three days to talk to him without using a tape-recorder or taking notes. The book of course ignored most of the compromising material about the past.[34] Maybe the time is not yet ripe for a balanced judgement, in the form of a biography, about the illusions and lies, promises and traps, tragedies and treason, successes and finally failure of this unusual man, who for longer than anyone else helped to shape Hungary's history. That is also valid for the ups and downs of his relationship with Leonid Brezhnev during the eighteen years of "immobilism" in Moscow. It is unclear to this day to what extent Kádár encouraged and supported, or criticized and (according to the latest Russian publications) betrayed, the "Prague Spring" and specifically Alexander Dubček, whom he had met on nine occasions between January and August 1968.

The encouraging economic reforms were gradually watered down after the invasion of Czechoslovakia on 21 August 1968, in which Hungary participated with two divisions. And Kádár himself became the target of a campaign orchestrated by the Soviets with local "blockheads"—some of it, of course, conducted surreptitiously. New sources indicate that between 1972 and 1974 he was able to save himself only by agreeing to Soviet demands to remove the most important reformers from key positions. Nonetheless he succeeded between 1978 and 1980 in booting out the Kremlin's moles, the "guardians of workers' interests", and pensioning off his longstanding number two Béla Biszku, nine years his junior, without giving any reasons for it. At the same time he was able to "save" his probably most important and personally most loyal adviser, the Politburo member György Aczél. Being the only Jew in the highest echelon, this old Communist, who had spent 1,868 days in prison under the Rákosi régime, had always been regarded by the Soviet leadership as unreliable. The subtle, often cynical and for a long time successful tactic of neutralizing and later winning over non-Communist or critical intellectuals was linked with his name. He helped many who were willing to compromise, and harmed the very few who would not do so within the framework of a complex triangle of support, toleration and prohibition (called in Hungarian the "Three Ts"). Although demonized by rightist-populists after the collapse of Communism as the true villain of the Kádár era, Aczél had contributed greatly to the creation of an island of measured and relative freedom in cultural life, in glaring contrast to the other Eastern bloc countries. In spite of this, Kádár and Aczél, as well as the entire top leadership with very few exceptions (namely Imre Pozsgay and Mátyás Szürös in the late 1980s), never regarded nationalism as a means of winning over the people, but rather as a factor of subversion against Communism.

What were the reasons for the peaceful collapse of the system, which only a few years previously Western publications had extolled as the "Communist wonderland"? Several factors transformed the political climate during 1987–8 to an extent which was nothing less than dramatic, spelling the abrupt end of "Kadarism". First, an economic crisis (inflation, investments on credit, a lowering of living standards, and increased poverty and social differences) eroded the confidence which had been the basis of the compromise between the regime and the people. Second, the Gorbachev-line and Moscow's new options in foreign and domestic politics, as well as the general bloc-wide decay of "real Socialism", especially in Poland, affected the Hungarian Party's claim to leadership. Third, the crystallization of a new alternative political élite into groups and parties such as the Hungarian Democratic Forum (MDF), the Free

Democrats (SzDSz), the Young Democrats (FIDESZ) and subsequently the reborn Smallholders, created the basis for a multi-party system. And finally the decline of the ageing Party leader's authority and the impact of a new political dynamics from Moscow opened the way to an intra-Party conflict, which was only resolved by a putsch against Kádár. His tragedy was that he had gambled away the chance of a dignified exit at a time and in a form of his own choosing.

The name of the man who contrived behind the scenes the removal of the afflicted Party chief's power, and of "his" Politburo before and during an extraordinary Party Conference on 22 May 1988, was Károly Grósz. This professional functionary, whom Kádár had appointed as Prime Minister a year earlier, was concerned not with the future of reforms but, like most other "apparatchiks", only with power. However, Grósz lost power barely a year later, and retired completely from politics after the liquidation of the Party.

Imre Pozsgay, Politburo member and the minister best known in the West, was the first publicly to come to terms with the events of 1956 by labelling them a "popular rising" and no longer "counter-revolutionary", thus anticipating the final report of a Central Committee team. However, Pozsgay subsequently proved a bad tactician, who probably lacked the nerve to split the party at the decisive moment. Now it was the radical reformers who set the pace towards a multi-party system and free elections. Miklós Németh (the Party's forty-year-old economic expert, elected Prime Minister in November 1988), Rezsö Nyers (the sixty-year-old creator of the "New Economic Mechanism", later demoted by Moscow at Kádár's request), and Foreign Minister Gyula Horn were the ones who, in the year of transition to Western-style democracy, set the agenda for two events which had worldwide political ramifications: the dismantling of the "Iron Curtain" along the border with Austria in May and, in face of furious protests from East Berlin, promulgating a government resolution on 11 September 1989 which allowed all East German citizens who had fled to Hungary free passage to West Germany. It was a courageous and farsighted decision, which at the same time marked the beginning of the end of the East German state, the GDR.

Precisely because the radical reformers accomplished an irreversible break with the Stalinist past on their own, the change of system that followed did not take the form of a collapse but was achieved (as in Poland) by means of a "round table discussion" with the Opposition which opened the way to free, equal and secret elections. A Centre-Right coalition presided over by the historian József Antall won the elections and, backed by a parliamentary resolution reached by an overwhelming majority, terminated Hungary's membership of the Warsaw Pact and finalized arrangements for the withdrawal of Soviet troops. Ten years later the new Hungary became a member of NATO and applied for admission to the European Union, but that is another story.

The events of 1956 provide an inexhaustible source of spiritual, political and moral strength for the post-revolutionary generation as well. Only since 1989 has it been possible to speak of a "victory in defeat". 23 October was proclaimed a national holiday. The funeral of Imre Nagy and his four companions in misfortune on 16 June 1989, the thirty-first anniversary of their execution, in Heroes' Square, attended by hundreds of thousands of people, and their reinterment in heroes' graves in Plot 301 of the very cemetery where they had been unceremoniously dumped into unmarked mass graves, marked a watershed in Hungary's modern history.

And what of János Kádár? On 12 April 1989, now seriously ill, he made a rambling, totally confused speech of apology before the Central Committee. His allusions to his role in the Rajk trial, frequently interspersed with digressions and stereotyped phrases, and especially to his responsibility for the *volte face* in November 1956 and the execution of Imre Nagy could serve as a case for psychoanalytical study or as the subject of a stage-play. He described the "tragedy of Imre Nagy" as his "own personal tragedy". We do not know whether Kádár had watched the funeral ceremony for Nagy, which was broadcast nationally on television and radio, or whether by then he was already on his own deathbed. By an irony of fate he died on 6 July, the very day on which Imre Nagy was rehabilitated by the Supreme Court.

However, more than 100,000 people paid their last respects to Kádár by filing past his coffin, which lay in state in the entrance hall of the then Party building. All surveys conducted since the change of system show that people remember him as a jovial "father figure" and his times as a "Golden Age", ranking him, despite majority

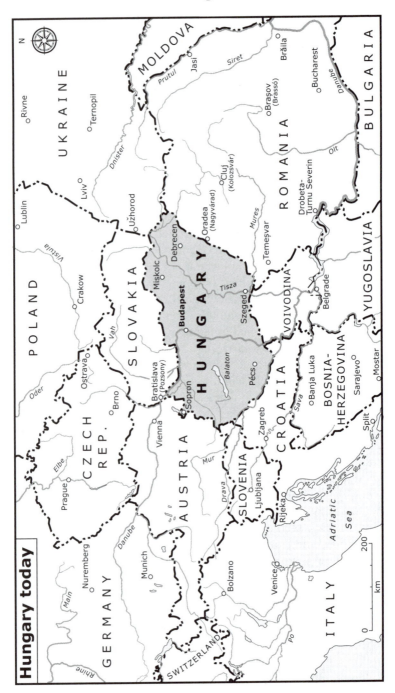

Hungary today

disapproval, above Franz Joseph or Horthy as the most significant historical personage of the twentieth century.[35] The retrospective glorification of the Kádár régime, especially by the younger generation, this flight into collective amnesia, could be partly a reaction to the enormous problems of today—as everywhere in the former Communist world.

And Rákosi? A slender volume entitled *In Exile* appeared in June 1994 with a cover showing him as an elderly man sometime in the 1960s, as he goes with a bucket in each hand to the well in the Kyrghyz village of Tokmak, near the Chinese border. The author Eugenia Biró, sister-in-law of the dictator who died in 1971, protests in it against the "slandering" of Rákosi and calls for the "historical truth" about him to be told—but she doubted whether she would live to see that. In that prediction she was wrong: in contrast to Rajk, Nagy and Kádár, Rákosi has his place today fixed as one of the greatest political criminals, who appallingly betrayed the dreams of the tens of thousands on Heroes' Square of whom we wrote at the beginning of this chapter.

During the memorable funeral ceremony for Nagy in the same square on 16 June 1989 an unknown twenty-five-year-old bearded man spoke in the name of the younger generation. His name was Viktor Orbán. In an extraordinarily pointed speech considering the conditions of the time, he demanded an escape from the "Asiatic dead-end" Hungary had got into, negotiations for the immediate withdrawal of Russian troops, national independence, and political liberty. Nine years later, at the age of thirty-five, Orbán (now without a beard) became Prime Minister at the head of a Centre-Right coalition. He was narrowly defeated by a Socialist-Liberal coalition in the parliamentary elections of April 2002. However, this young and charismatic politician, who moved from a left-of-centre position at the start of his career to an increasingly nationalistic, neo-conservative one as Prime Minister, is certain to play a significant role in future Hungarian politics as well.

35. "Everyone is a Hungarian": Geniuses and Artists

Coming home one day during the early 1950s in a state of excitement, the British-Hungarian humorist George (György) Mikes announced a surprising piece of news to his wife: "Imagine, the mother of Leo Amery [member of Churchill's war cabinet and proud representative of the imperial idea] was a Hungarian! It says so in her obituary." His wife looked up and said dryly: "What of it?" "What do you mean, what of it?" Mikes was obviously irritated that his sensational news had not produced the desired effect. "Why shouldn't she have been? Everyone is a Hungarian," she said and continued reading. The topic was no longer of interest to her, Mikes wrote later. As a man used to seeing the crux of any matter, he perceived his wife's reply as an axiom, and told the story in an anthology published for American Hungarians, enriched by a few good examples from Britain.

The American historian William O. McCagg Jr quoted a similar story in his 1972 book about Jewish nobles and geniuses in Hungary: a well-known physicist, on returning from a congress in Buenos Aires where he had exchanged information with colleagues from all over the world, was asked how so many people from so many different countries were able to communicate with each other. He answered in astonishment: "Why, naturally we all spoke Hungarian." The author added that this anecdote contained at least a kernel of truth. During the last decades Hungarians have played an outstanding role in the international community of scientists:

Many people know the names of Leo Szilárd and Edward Teller, who cooperated on the development of the atom and hydrogen bombs, or of Albert Szentgyörgyi, the biologist. Every expert has heard of Theodor von Kármán and John von Neumann, of Georg Pólya, Georg von Hevesi and

Jenö [Eugene] Wigner, eminent figures in modern mathematics, chemistry and physics. A great number of Hungarians can be found in the last fifty years in other branches of the international intelligentsia and the sciences as well. Just to mention a few: Karl Mannheim and Oszkár Jászi in the field of sociology, Sándor Ferenczi and Franz Alexander in psychology, Georg Lukács in Marxist philosophy, Karl Polányi in political economy and his brother Michael, who with phenomenal brilliance combined the natural and social sciences.[1]

At any rate, it is no exaggeration that the Hungarian scientists who migrated to the United States played a decisive role in the development of the atom bomb and partly in that of the hydrogen bomb as well. In a study of intellectuals who went to America between 1930 and 1941 Laura Fermi, widow of the great Italian atom physicist, emphasized that Hungary with its population of 10 million had about the same influence on scientific developments there as the Federal Republic of Germany with its (before re-unification) 60 million inhabitants.[2]

The atom physicist Leo Szilárd, born in Budapest in 1898, played the key role in the story of the atom bomb, both technically and in the political decision-making.[3] Like so many other eminent scientists of Jewish origin he completed his studies in theoretical physics in Germany, which he left after Hitler's seizure of power. In 1938 he travelled to the United States from London where, with his exceptional powers of persuasion, he belonged to those nuclear physicists who at an early stage recognized the tremendous significance of the "chain reaction" for atomic energy and at the same time were alarmed by news of a successful splitting of the atom in Germany. Szilárd borrowed $2,000 from a friend for a gram of radium, and in March 1939 repeated the Berlin experiment. On the seventh floor of his laboratory at Columbia University in New York, he eagerly watched with his Canadian colleague Walter Zinn to see whether neutrons would result from splitting the uranium. "We pressed the button—we saw signs of light," wrote Szilárd later. "During that night I came to realize that the world had entered a road full of worries." That evening Teller was at home, and to relax played Mozart; he was an excellent pianist. Suddenly the telephone rang. "*Megtaláltam a neutronokat!* [I have found the neutrons]", cried Szilárd, speaking Hungarian for security reasons.

The Italian Nobel Prizewinner Enrico Fermi and Szilárd's compatriot Jenö Wigner, Professor of Chemistry at Princeton, were impressed by Szilárd's experiments and arguments, but Fermi, an immigrant from an enemy country, at first got no support from the American military. Wigner and Szilárd therefore wanted to suggest to Albert Einstein that he use his influence with Queen Elisabeth of Belgium, whom he knew well, to prevent the Germans acquiring any more uranium from the (Belgian) Congo. On a humid day in July 1939 the two of them drove to Long Island for a meeting, and drove around for half an hour in a small village until they finally located his summer house. Wigner related that although it was the first time Einstein had ever heard of the possibility of a chain reaction, he understood the whole nuclear concept within fourteen minutes. He dictated a letter to Belgium in German—Wigner made notes, translated the text into English, gave it to Szilárd, and travelled to California for his holidays.

In the mean time, however, Szilárd had reconsidered the entire matter: foreign countries should not find out anything about a possible chain reaction. So instead he contacted a banker, a former associate of President Roosevelt who was willing to pass on a letter by Einstein to the President. Szilárd then wrote to Einstein, asking him to check his draft letter, and sign it. There was now just one problem: Szilárd could not drive. He therefore persuaded Teller, a Budapest-born graduate of Göttingen University also working at Columbia, to drive him to Long Island.

The two of them set out on 2 August 1939. But Szilárd had once again forgotten the location of Einstein's summer quarters. They asked around, but nobody knew exactly. Szilárd finally asked a little girl of about eight, whether she knew where Einstein lived. She had no idea. Szilárd then said: "You know, the old man with the long white hair..." "He lives two houses up the street," the child replied. Einstein was friendly, offered them tea, and also asked Teller to sit down. The two-page letter written by Szilárd referred to Fermi's and his own work, soliciting quick and concerted action by the government in order to promote nuclear research, acquire uranium and, if possible, develop a bomb. Einstein read through the letter slowly and signed it. By 3 October it was in the hands of the President.

Teller recalled later: "It was the most auspicious time, straight after the occupation of Poland by Nazi Germany and the Soviet Union. Roosevelt grasped the great danger in an instant. He immediately dictated instructions to the chief of the Bureau of Standards to convene a meeting to discuss the measures suggested in Einstein's letter." The road to the development and completion of the atom bomb was long and obstructed by problems. At the time Fermi, Szilárd and Teller were not even American citizens. The three Hungarians Szilárd, Wigner and Teller—known in Chicago as the "Hungarian Mafia"—were appointed members of a six-man advisory body established by Roosevelt for matters relating to uranium. By February 1940 they managed with great difficulty to obtain $6,000 from the Pentagon to purchase materials for the experiments. Not till 2 December 1942 did a reactor in Chicago provide the means to perform a controlled chain reaction.

Fermi led the experiments, and Wigner was responsible for the theoretical research. On that historic day, 2 December, forty-two people were present in the big laboratory: an Italian (Fermi), two Hungarians (Wigner and Szilárd), a Canadian and thirty-eight Americans. Wigner had brought a bottle of Chianti from Princeton. They all clinked glasses, and drank to the prospect that this first controlled chain reaction would benefit mankind and make people less prejudiced. Fermi signed the Chianti label, followed by the others, and because the names of the witnesses to this historic event were nowhere recorded, the label was later to serve as an attendance list. Washington was advised by a coded telegram: "The Italian navigator has just landed in the New World. The natives are friendly."

The famous Manhattan project, the construction of the atom bomb in Los Alamos. New Mexico, was successful. Within a few days of the summer of 1945 three atom bombs were exploded—the first as a test, the two others over Hiroshima and Nagasaki. Wigner received the Nobel Prize in 1963 for his pioneering research in nuclear physics, and Teller became known throughout the world as the "father of the hydrogen bomb". Since its power of destruction far exceeded that of the A-bomb, Teller was soon exposed to harsh criticism, which became even louder when he advised President Reagan in connection with his "Strategic Defense Initiative" (SDI): "Star Wars" could no longer be regarded as a fantasy.

The role of the "Hungarian mafia" and the many other prominent scientists from Hungary—such as John von Neumann, inventor of the computer; Theodore von Kármán, head of research of the
US Air Force; Georg de Hevesy, winner of the Nobel Prize for
chemistry for his research into isotopes; and John G. Kemény, mathematician and President of Dartmouth College—earned them the
nickname "The Martians". Dozens of anecdotes circulated about
them in Chicago and Los Alamos. The *Yankee Magazine* published
the following:

Kemény, von Neumann, Szilárd, Teller and Wigner were born in the same
quarter of Budapest. No wonder the scientists in Los Alamos accepted the
idea that well over one hundred years ago a Martian spaceship crashlanded
somewhere in the centre of Europe. There are three firm proofs of the
extraterrestrial origins of the Hungarians. They like to wander about (like
gypsies radiating out from the same region). They speak an exceptionally
simple and logical language which has not the slightest connection with
the language of their neighbours. And they are so much smarter than the
terrestrials. In a slight Martian accent John G. Kemény added an explanation, namely that it is so much easier to learn reading and writing in Hungarian than in English or French that Hungarian pupils have much more
time left to study mathematics.[4]

The myth of the Hungarians' E.T. (extraterrestrial) origins could
already have been born earlier. Thus in *The Making of the Atomic
Bomb*, Richard Rhodes (New York, 1996) reports that "at Princeton a saying gained currency that Neumann, the youngest member
of the new Institute for Advanced Studies, twenty-nine in 1933,
was indeed a demigod but that he had made a thorough, detailed
study of human beings and could imitate them perfectly."

Once, when the Nobel Prizewinner Wigner was asked how
Hungary had produced so many geniuses in that generation, he
retorted that Hungary had produced only one genius in that time,
Johnny von Neumann. The well-known economist and adviser to
the British Labour government in the 1960s, Nicholas (Lord)
Káldor, wrote in 1985 in his last essay (he died in 1986): "Johnny
was without question the only person who came near to being a
genius."[5]

The Hungarians called him "Jancsi". His father was a banker who,
like so many other successful Jewish entrepreneurs, was ennobled

before the First World War by Emperor Franz Joseph; he opposed his son's mathematical studies, despite his obvious talent, arguing that "one can't earn any money by mathematics". Father and son eventually reached a compromise: Johnny studied chemistry in Berlin but also attended Einstein's physics seminar. At the same time he gained a doctorate in chemical engineering in Zurich, and graduated from his mathematics studies at the University of Budapest *summa cum laude*. Neumann was possibly the greatest mathematician of the twentieth century, but there was no Nobel Prize for mathematics—according to Kármán, this was because Nobel lost his girlfriend to a mathematician and never forgave her. Although Neumann played an important role in the development of the atomic bomb, he only became Washington's most influential scientist during the Eisenhower era. The development of the nuclear deterrent theory as well as the invention (together with the Austrian economist Oscar Morgenstern) of the "game-theory" are associated with his name.

When an émigré Russian colleague remarked to him in 1946 "I hear, Johnny, that you don't think of anything else but the Bomb", he replied: "That is totally wrong. I am thinking about something far more important than the Bomb. I am thinking about computers." Actually Neumann had summarized his thoughts in 1945 in a 101-page "First Outline" about the improvement of the current adding machines; it has been called the "most important document ever written about the computer and its functions". When he decided to build the "Von Neumann computer" at Princeton, the US Army and Navy carried two-thirds of the costs and the Institute one-third. An American colleague on the project declared four decades later: "Neumann was without any doubt a genius. That meant among other things that he could grasp a totally new field unbelievably fast. Before he designed the computer he took two weeks off to study electronics, in order to be able to supervise the construction of the plant."

But even a genius has no protection against cancer. He battled against his illness from the summer of 1955, and was in a wheelchair when at the beginning of 1956 he received the highest American decoration, the Medal of Freedom, from President Eisenhower personally. While in hospital he wrote his last book, *The Computer and the Brain*. Politicians, generals and admirals sought his advice up till the very last. He was guarded even at night lest he should divulge military secrets while asleep, but when he actually began to hallucinate, he did so in Hungarian. He died soon after his fifty-third birthday. During that time he converted to Catholicism: "There is probably a God. Many things are easier to explain if there is a God than if there isn't."

In addition to the genius János Neumann, the history of Hungarian science contains many other outstandingly gifted people and Nobel Prizewinners—no wonder it has repeatedly been asked how such a small country has been able to produce so much talent. However, with the exception of Albert von Szent-Györgyi, the first Hungarian to receive the Nobel Prize for Medicine and Physiology (in 1937), none was actually a Hungarian citizen. Of the first three Prizewinners on the "Hungarian list" one is regarded (rightly) as German, and the two others are recorded as Austrians. Of the other "real Hungarians" four had American, one Swedish and one British citizenship. The 1986 Nobel Prizewinner for Chemistry, John C. Polányi, is the son of the Hungarian polymath Professor Michael Polányi and his Hungarian wife, was born in Berlin, studied in Manchester (where his father was a professor at the University), and since 1962 has occupied the chair of Chemistry at the University of Toronto. The case of Elie Wiesel is even more complicated. His place of birth (in today's Romania) belonged for only three years to Hungary after 1941; he was deported to Auschwitz and was the only member of his family to survive; studied in Paris, and has for many years held US citizenship.

Leaving aside such ledger-keeping efforts as trying to compile a complete list of Nobel laureates, it remains true that the Hungarians in America have had a lasting influence. One reason why most of the internationally known Hungarian scientists (by no means only natural scientists) have gained fame abroad is the great turmoil after the First World War: the swing of the pendulum between the "red" and "white" terror, and between the short-lived Soviet Republic, dominated by Jewish commissars, and the anti-Semitic tendencies, especially in education, of the twenty-five-year Horthy régime. Historians and other writers interested in the "secret of Hungarian talent", such as Laura Fermi and William O. McCagg Jr, have

stressed that most of this scientific diaspora were either Jews or converted Jews who felt threatened and left their country as early as
1919–20. Since many of them not only studied abroad but remained there, they had a head-start over Germans who sought
refuge in the United States and elsewhere only after Hitler came to
power.

But a Jewish background alone does not explain it. Geniuses
such as Béla Bartók or Zoltán Kodály were no more Jewish than,
for instance, the Nobel Prizewinner George de Békésy or such
notable writers and poets as Gyula Krudy, Zsigmond Móricz, Endre
Ady and Attila József. Also, one must not overlook the extraordinarily high standard of Hungarian secondary schools, especially
those élite high schools attended by most of the "Martians". Also
the quality of intellectual life in the exuberant, fast-growing capital,
which had been bubbling over with vitality ever since the nineteenth century, formed a natural background for remarkable achievements. A further influence, the waves of emigration for political and
not exclusively ethnic reasons, must also be taken into account.

The year 1994 impressively exemplified the continuity of the
Hungarian "secret" when two men of Hungarian birth were among
the American citizens who received the Nobel Prize. János Harsányi,
who left Hungary in 1950, was a pharmacist, a philosopher and
eventually an economist at the University of California at Berkeley,
and received the award for his achievements in game theory (in the
footsteps of Johnny von Neumann). György Oláh was already a
respected chemist before leaving Budapest for Canada in 1956;
from there he went on to the United States, where he was appointed
Professor of Chemistry at the University of Southern California. A
small country was thus represented at Stockholm by two top scientists, even though they carried American passports. The Nobel laureate Békésy perhaps helps us to understand the "Martians" better:

If a person travelling outside Hungary is recognized as a Hungarian due to
his accent (something which—beyond a certain age—is impossible to
drop), the question is asked in almost every case: "How is it possible that a
country as small as Hungary has given the world so many internationally
renowned scientists?" There are Hungarians who have tried to give an
answer. For my part: I cannot find an answer, but I would mention one
thing. When I lived in Switzerland, everything was peaceful, quiet and

secure. In Hungary life was different. We were all involved in an ongoing struggle for almost everything we wanted. Sometimes we won; sometimes we lost; but we always survived. It did not bring things to an end, not in my case anyway. People need such challenges, and these have existed throughout Hungary's history.[6]

Edward Teller once remarked that it was virtually incumbent upon a Hungarian abroad to be much better than others. When the mathematician John G. Kemény (1926–92) fled from Hitler to New York with his parents aged fourteen, he did not speak a word of English, and attended the same school as Henry Kissinger. During his successful entrance exam at Princeton the professor noted his foreign accent and asked where he came from. On hearing Kemény's reply the examiner exclaimed "God, not another Hungarian!" Kemény later became President of Dartmouth College, one of the oldest American schools, and at the peak of his career was appointed by President Carter in April 1979 to chair a twelve-man special commission to investigate breakdowns in the vicinity of the atomic power plant at Three Mile Island. Another Hungarian scientist, Bálint Telegdi, who had won the prestigious Wolf Prize for Mathematics, recalling his youth in a talk in Budapest, remarked that a young Hungarian abroad might do well to hide his nationality since too much will be expected of him if it is made known.

However, there was another profession in the United States besides science which was probably even more crowded by Hungarian talent. A sign on the wall of a director's office in a great Hollywood film studio warned "It is not enough to be Hungarian", to which someone is said to have added "but it may help". Although no eyewitness can be located who actually saw the sign, the story may be instructive even as an urban myth. It was one of the familiar gibes against the Magyars, others being "If you enter a revolving door ahead of a Hungarian, he comes out first" and "What is the difference between a Romanian and a Hungarian? Each is willing to sell his mother, but only the Hungarian delivers." These of course are said by non-Hungarians, and mostly stem from Hollywood.

The combination of admiration and malice in these quips is easy to explain. Hollywood was indeed partly a Hungarian creation, and at certain stages in its existence Hungarian producers, directors, cameramen, composers and actors put their stamp on the American film industry. Non-Hungarians claim to this day that the Hungarians somehow clung together, forming a "Magyar clique". The reason for this undeniable sense of a common bond was and is the peculiar mixture of language and accent. Apart from foreign young lovers, zealous spies and linguists there would hardly be a normal person on earth who would voluntarily undertake to learn the language of a people whose closest linguistic ties are with the 30,000 Ostiaks and Voguls from the Finno-Ugrian ethnic family to the west of the Urals. The most important distinctive feature, however, is the accent, that loud or soft "singsong", which derives from the mother-tongue. Even the famous playwright Ferenc Molnár is said to have given the "very refined, slightly old-fashioned" German that he habitually spoke a Hungarian inflection. The accent was and is the trademark of the Hungarians.

The most famous Hungarian mathematician of the past decades, Pál Erdös (1913–96), who published 1,475 significant scientific essays, and constantly travelled with a small suitcase, "the man who loved numbers" (the title of his biography),[7] lectured in such gibberish-sounding English in America and Britain that subtitles had to be used in an American documentary about his life. When the future Nobel laureate George de Békésy had to pass Immigration Control, the official asked him whether he was healthy. Békésy promptly replied "No!" to general bewilderment, until someone realised that he had thought he was being asked whether he was wealthy.

It was therefore especially difficult for Hungarians trying their luck in the film industry without any knowledge of English. Yet two of the legendary figures of Hollywood, Adolph Zukor and William Fox, were Hungarian immigrants—among over 400,000 who went to the United States before 1914. Of these one in four returned home,[8] but Zukor and Fox stayed on and soon made film history. The two came from the same neighbourhood, near the Tokaj wine-growing region, Zukor from Ricse and Fox from Tolcsva.[9] Admittedly Fox arrived in American as a baby; Zukor came aged fifteen, and worked first as an upholsterer and later, successfully, as a furrier. But his dominant interest was a very different, new "industry". He quickly understood the potential of the so-called "nickelodeon" automats, in which moving pictures could be viewed for 5 cents—even in railway carriages. Zukor raised the admission price to 10 cents, and so began making real money, which enabled him to become a film producer. He funded, together with English and French investors, the first full one-hour film about the life of Queen Elizabeth I of England with Sarah Bernhardt in the title role, and acquired the rights for the United States for the then large sum of $18,000. He achieved the great breakthrough with his first silent film, which was shown in the New York Lyceum Theatre. Thus encouraged, Zukor engaged the first film stars, such as Mary Pickford and John Barrymore, and established his own firm called "Famous Players in Famous Plays", which became Paramount Pictures and soon had 1,000 movie houses all over the United States. The preconditions of Paramount's dizzying rise to world-wide recognition were the founding of his own studios, putting films into theatres and eventually into cinemas, but first and foremost a new form of advertising which created stars out of actors. Zukor never quite cut his contacts with the old country, and visited his parents' grave in the Jewish cemetery of Ricse several times. He died at the age of 104.

William Fox was already fascinated by the prospects for development of the new medium as a young man. He was six years younger than Zukor, and started his career as a manufacturer's agent. He founded a company for purchasing and lending films with a starting capital of $1,600. When he became dissatisfied with the quality of the productions on offer, he took matters into his own hands; he also acquired fifteen "movie palaces" in Brooklyn. Within the span of fourteen years his Fox Film Corporation increased its market value by twenty-five times, but in 1930 the banks and his rivals hit out; Upton Sinclair described the shady deal in a book on the subject. Fox had to sell his share—for $20 million.[10]

Hollywood now demanded the best directors, production designers, cameramen and actors. While the influence of Hungarian directors and artists continues to this day to be exaggerated in official and semi-official PR publications, the reality is impressive enough as it is. The directors George Cukor (not to be confused with Zukor) who shot the international hit *My Fair Lady*, Joe Pasternak and Charles Vidor were of Hungarian origin—as, naturally, was Michael Curtiz (formerly Mihály Kertész), who became the most successful

Hungarian director after Alexander Korda. Mihály Kertész, originally an actor himself, shot "the first Hungarian dramatic artfilm in 1912 with Hungarian actors, Hungarian scenery and a Hungarian topic".[11] By 1918—there were already fifteen professional film directors, then a considerable figure by international standards—he made a further thirty-eight films. Kertész, like Korda, left Hungary at that time to escape persecution by the various officer gangs, and went to Hollywood via Vienna. He called himself Michael Curtiz after 1919, and during his thirty American years shot as many films as he had in Hungary, among them the cult film *Casablanca*.

Despite, or perhaps because of his successes, Michael Curtiz was constantly ridiculed behind his back by extras and stagehands for his fractured English. The actor David Niven even adopted Curtiz's slip of the tongue as the title of his best-selling memoirs *Bring on the Empty Horses*. This came about during the filming of one of his typical American films. Several hundred extras on horseback thundered past the camera in the midst of a battle. After the crowd scenes had been shot Curtiz wanted to show the defeat as well, with the horses galloping bareback in the opposite direction without their dead or wounded riders. At that instant he let slip the oft-cited Hollywood chestnut: "Bring on the empty horses!" It was of course not this linguistic innovation that went down in the annals of the film industry but the coveted Oscar which Curtiz received from the Film Academy in 1943.[12]

But by far the most notable and famous of all the Hungarians in the history of films was László Sándor Kellner—known to the world as Sir Alexander Korda—born in 1893 in the village of Pusztatúrpásztó in the heart of the region once inhabited by Cumans and Jazygs. This exceptional man was originally a journalist, film critic and publisher of movie magazines. His career began at Kolozsvár in Transylvania, and he soon founded his own firm, which he called Corvin. Korda was not only a great director and scriptwriter but also a first-rate organizer, the first producer who ever worked with writers, dramaturges and literary editors, who served as the connecting link between the studio and the important writers. Korda shot nineteen films before 1918, all based on highbrow literary pieces transformed into scripts by excellent men of letters. The largest Hungarian film studio today is still located in Korda's one-time workshop.

As a participant and head of the largest film studio Korda, together with almost all directors and dramaturges, played active roles during both the Károlyi regime and the Communist Soviet Republic. After the triumph of the counter-revolution Korda, Curtiz and most of the other film people fled to Vienna, where for a time no fewer than thirty-eight film-makers found a temporary home. The cultural historian István Nemeskürty summed up the situation in his popular history of Hungarian film:

The 1920s brought about the bankruptcy of Hungarian film production and art… The systematic persecution by the Horthy-Fascists resulted in the loss of Hungary's best directors. The white terror was raging. Soldiers with egret-feathered caps—the symbol of the counter-revolutionary army—were given cinemas as rewards; war-widows, left-oriented citizens and Jews were booted out from their cinemas… Korda's departure left behind a tangible gap.[13]

Korda's gifted brothers Zoltán (also a director) and Vince (production designer) also left the country during the 1920s and joined their internationally famous brother.

Korda commuted between Hollywood, Berlin, Vienna, Paris and London, where he eventually accomplished his great breakthrough by establishing his own company, London Film Productions. Between 1931 and 1956 he produced and/or directed hundreds of films: to mention only the highlights in the long list of successful productions, which in fact created the British film industry, *The Private Life of Henry VIII, Rembrandt, Anna Karenina, The Four Feathers* and one particularly good example of Korda's style, *The Scarlet Pimpernel*. The story of this highly intelligent but pretending to be simple-minded "typically British" hero from the time of Napoleon had been written by the Hungarian Baroness Emma Orczy, and was turned into a script by Korda's favourite scriptwriter Lajos Biró. The star of this cult film was the archetypal dashing Englishman Leslie Howard, who died in an air crash during the Second World War. Originally named László Steiner, he was born in Budapest, and emigrated as a child with his parents to London, where he worked as a bank clerk before going into films. Incidentally, in *The Scarlet Pimpernel* the cameraman, stage designer and, of course, the three Korda brothers were all Hungarians. The music was composed by Miklós Rózsa, who subsequently gained international renown in

Hollywood. This Hungarian, who died aged eighty-eight in 1995, and who also worked for Hitchcock, Zukor and other directors, won three Oscars (1946, 1948 and 1959). Another Hungarian film composer, Joseph Kosma, wrote the *chanson* about "fallen leaves" which, interpreted by popular singers, became known all over the world.

Yet another Hungarian, John Halas, made a career for himself in London as a maker of animated cartoons, among them one of Orwell's *Animal Farm*. Alexander Korda, knighted by Queen Elizabeth II, was not only a giant of movie history but, according to the unanimous recollections and reports of many Hungarians, also outstandingly generous; he is said to have supported numerous people in the old country with money and other gifts.

This almost endless list of Hungarians who gained success in films and the theatre is still led by Zsazsa Gábor, who came across as the best-known Hungarian from a list of forty personalities in a survey conducted in 1995 among 400 young business people in twenty-two countries,[14] but unfortunately her fame is due rather to escapades with rich men than to her film roles. Close on her heels followed none other than the porno-queen and temporary Italian parliamentary deputy Cicciolina (Ilona Staller). When the Hungarian movie actress Eva Bartok died in a London hotel in 1998, German, Austrian and British newspapers published long obituaries of the sixty-nine-year-old ex-wife of Curt Jürgens and one-time girlfriend of Frank Sinatra and the Marquis of Milford Haven (Prince Philip's cousin and best man). Although the Budapest-born Éva Szöke played in forty films she was, according to the London *Times*, "famous for her famousness". Although she spoke five languages and acted with Burt Lancaster and Bernhard Wicki, she never lost her Hungarian accent either in English or German.[15]

Other notable actors and actresses from Hungary, some long forgotten, include the silent movie star Vilma Bánky, Ilona Massey, Béla Lugosi the first and most frightening movie Dracula, and Pál Lukács, who as Paul Lukas was successful in Hollywood with his suave good looks and "slight Hungarian accent"; he won an Oscar in 1943 for his part in *Watch on the Rhine*.

The currently best-known American Hungarian, Tony Curtis (originally Bernie Schwartz), though New York-born, had to fight against his broad Hungarian accent. His father, a poor Jewish tailor, came to New York in 1921 with his family: "My first words were Hungarian. At home I hardly ever heard any English, not even Yiddish; we spoke only Hungarian... I wasn't conscious of living in America until I went to primary school at the age of six or seven. I believed that Mátészalka was somewhere around the corner, and was convinced that Budapest was at the end of our street." Fifty years later and after close on 100 films, the world-famous actor and his eldest daughter visited his father's birthplace in the small town of Mátészalka, 30 km. from the Ukrainian border. Tony Curtis (meanwhile married for the umpteenth time, this time to a model thirty-five years his junior), accepted the honorary chairmanship of an association set up to collect money for the restoration of synagogues in Hungary, and named, in honour of his father Emanuel Schwartz, the "Emanuel foundation for Hungarian culture".[16]

Not all Hungarians had success-stories in the film industry. The greatest Hungarian comedian of all times, Gyula Kabos, had to leave the film studio in Budapest because of the anti-semitic decrees when already aged fifty and start a new career in America. He died of a broken heart in 1941.

In the German-speaking film world it was above all singers and dancers such as Martha Eggerth (wife of Jan Kiepura), the operetta diva Gitta Alpár (wife of Gustav Fröhlich) and (for longest of all) Marika Rökk who spread Hungary's reputation and, unwittingly, the cliché "Puszta, Paprika, Piroska*". Of the "three Géza von" team of directors—Bolváry, Cziffra and Radványi—the last-named made film history in Hungary and Europe with his 1947 *Irgendwo in Europa* (Somewhere in Europe). Today István Szabó is perhaps the internationally best-known director; he received an Oscar in 1981 for his *Mephisto* (with Klaus Maria Brandauer in the lead), as did the cartoonist Ferenc Rófusz for *The Fly.*

The best-known Hungarian writer and above all playwright to this day is Ferenc Molnár (1878–1952), the son of a Budapest doctor, who is thought by many to have been an Austrian. He had, in fact, lived for many years in Vienna, and perhaps his plays are nowhere else as regularly on the playbills as there, yet he wrote his

---

* Piroska is a typical Hungarian girl's name.

forty-one plays, eleven novels, eight volumes of stories and reports (including the interesting war correspondent's report from the First World War) exclusively in Hungarian. He was profoundly modern with his charming novel about the world of schoolboys, *The Boys from Pál Street*, and his superb tragicomedy of toughs and barkers from the Budapest amusement park, *Liliom*. He captured, like no other, the psychological and spiritual atmosphere of the multicultural capital bursting at its seams, including the milieu of the Pest workers and petit bourgeoisie.

The "legend from the wrong side of the tracks" with the servant girl Julie, Liliom and the underworld characters was a flop at its première in Budapest in 1919, but it was filmed in many variations, and as the musical *Carousel* (composer Richard Rodgers, librettist Oscar Hammerstein) performed countless times after 1945. Between 1913 and 1948 more than a dozen of his plays (*The Swan, The Play's the Thing, The Guardsman* etc.) were performed on Broadway in various adaptations. Molnár's plays, with brilliant ideas and dialogue, sparkling with that typical Pest banter, were staged in twenty-eight languages, and twenty-five were made into films. He was the only non-English writer whose works appeared in an English-language anthology. At his peak Molnár worked exceptionally fast: he wrote *Liliom* in twenty-one days, sitting in the still extant Budapest literary and journalistic coffeehouse, the New York.[17]

Molnár was also a master of the anecdote. The following are some oft-cited prime examples recorded by Friedrich Torberg, who for five years from 1945 shared Molnár's New York emigration:

Once, when he had to appear at court as a witness at what was for him an unearthly hour (before noon), and when his friends eventually managed with great difficulty to drag the famous night-owl into the street in the morning—he pointed in utter astonishment at the people hurrying to and fro and asked "Are they all witnesses?" Returning from a visit to Budapest, he drew up the following really instructive formula about the economic situation prevailing there: "There are only 2,000 pengös* in all of Budapest, and someone different spends them each night."[18]

Molnár lived from 1940 till his death in 1952 in room no. 835 on the eighth floor of the famous Plaza Hotel in New York ("Always

---

* The *pengö* was the Hungarian currency before the Second World War.

take the cheapest room in the best hotel!'"). The essayist and Molnár translator Alfred Polgar referred to this axiom when he wrote in the obituary of his friend: "I think he has a right to such a place up there too, in the section for those who have written good plays: a small room but in the house where the great ones live."[19]

Like Korda, one of the most successful dramatists and librettists of the twentieth century, Menyhért (Melchior) Lengyel, born in 1880, came from a typical little town on the edge of the Hungarian *puszta* of the Hortobágy, Balmazujváros. His play *The Typhoon* was performed in Vienna, Berlin. Paris and New York, and he wrote the libretto for Béla Bartók's *The Magic Mandarin*, as well as the script for the cult films *Ninotchka* (with Greta Garbo) and *The Blue Angel* (with Marlene Dietrich).

The most renowned and successful Hungarian dramatist of today is George (György) Tábori, who has become an important figure especially in the German-speaking countries. Born in Budapest, the son of a journalist killed at Auschwitz, he began to write in English in London, and as the correspondent and press officer of the BBC during the Second World War worked in the Balkans and the Near East. He published several novels which attracted little response at the time. His older brother Paul, also living in London, wrote numerous popular scientific books and was for a while president of International PEN. George subsequently spent almost a quarter of a century in the United States, mostly in California and New York. Although working as a scriptwriter and assistant director with such notable figures as Alfred Hitchcock, Anatole Litvak and Joseph Losey, and on friendly terms with Chaplin and Brecht (his first Broadway play *Flight into Egypt* was directed by Elia Kazan), Tábori made his real breakthrough relatively late in life in Germany and Austria. His black humour, acrid wit and deeply humane though often shocking poetry always revolve around love, hatred and death. In what is perhaps his most successful play hitherto, *Mein Kampf* (first performance May 1987 in the Wiener Akademietheater), he presents a shockingly grotesque pair: the Jewish hawker Schlomo Herzl and Adolf Hitler as inmates of a Viennese flophouse. In Tábori's plays hatred and laughter, love and humour in the post-Auschwitz Jewish-Hungarian tradition link his personal history and Jewish history in general with that of Germany (and Austria). When Tábori received the Georg Büchner Prize in 1992, Wolf Biermann spoke of "stories which timid children would rather not listen to yet still cannot get enough of".[20] One of these is *Horrorfarce*[21] (Peter von Becker), a play about Auschwitz. Some of these are what a German critic Peter von Becker called "Horrorfarce" 21—examples are *The Cannibals*, about Auschwitz, and *My Mother's* Courage, dedicated to the survival of his mother.

The fact that George Tábori fits into the tradition of those Hungarian Jews living working and writing in several languages like Arthur Koestler, the sociologist Karl Mannheim, the superb artist and photographer László Moholy-Nagy, the photo-journalist Stephan Lorant and the "Martians" of the natural sciences does not surprise those familiar with Hungarian history. However, he is unique in the German theatre in not only having written plays but having also directed and sometimes even acted in them—and he still unites these roles within his person. He is perhaps the last living link between Hungarian history and British-American exile. Central European cultural tradition and postmodernism. Although Tábori—even if somewhat hesitantly at first—still speaks flawless Hungarian in company, and although his childhood and early youth belong to the old country, his international standing is not linked to Hungary, and *vice versa*: probably because of the trauma of 1944–5 his plays are less well-known in Budapest than in Germany and Austria.

Another writer of world renown was Arthur Koestler, whose life encompassed Budapest, Vienna, Berlin, Moscow, Madrid and London. Born in Budapest in 1905, he studied in Vienna and grew up bilingual. As a journalist he worked for the newspapers of the Ullstein press in Berlin, and joined the German Communist Party (KPD) in 1931. Although he never forgot his Hungarian and repeatedly paid brief visits to his native city, where he had been a close friend of Attila József, he was basically moulded by the intellectual and political atmosphere of the Weimar Republic. He first became known internationally as the correspondent of the London *News Chronicle* in the Spanish Civil War, when he bravely and nonchalantly travelled to Franco-occupied territory to gather material about the German and Italian intervention. The most dangerous of these journeys ended in his being arrested and sentenced to death: an international press campaign resulted in his release after four months in jail.

During the spring of 1938 Koestler left the KPD and after 1940—despite being often attacked, slandered and at first hardly believed—he became the first writer to analyse to a logical conclusion his disastrous experiment with Communism. After his *Spanish Testament (Dialogue with Death)* he wrote *Darkness at Noon*, his classic *roman à clef* about the Moscow show trials, and a collection of essays entitled *The Yogi and the Commissar,* which not only went through numerous editions but was dynamite in countries such as France with a strong Communist Party. Koestler acquired a permanent place in the history of "mythoclasts" long before Solzhenytsin, but far fewer people listened to his message.

In London, having adopted British citizenship, he never once wavered from his rejection and exposure of totalitarianism. His two volumes of autobiography present an unparallelled, thrilling introduction to the Europe of the 1930s and '40s, threatened by both brown and red expansionism. Later he wrote around a dozen books on various scientific and quasi-scientific subjects, including the phenomenon of coincidence. He identified with Hungary during the 1956 crisis, and in his first indignation wanted to storm the Hungarian Legation with other like-minded intellectuals. After his friends managed to hold him back from this venture, he vented his anger by at least throwing stones and breaking a few windows. At least that is the version which his friend George Mikes spread by word of mouth and in writing, and which was taken up in David Cesarini's biography of Koestler, published in 1994 .[22] He organized international protest meetings after the defeat of the Revolution. Before the British Labour leader, Hugh Gaitskell, made a trip to a Moscow for a meeting with Khrushchev, Koestler rang him at midnight, imploring him to ask for the release of Tibor Déry and other arrested writers.

Koestler spoke accent-free German because of his mother and his schooling in Vienna, but by his own admission he dreamed in Hungarian and suffered on account of his strong and indelible Hungarian-German accent when he spoke English. Yet it was in English that he wrote all his books during his life in London. He was an extraordinarily stimulating, often obnoxious intellectual who sometimes drank to excess and was adored by women. In 1983, when terminally ill, he committed suicide together with his much younger wife Cynthia.

And what about the great figures of Hungarian literature who remain unknown to this day? Some ex-Communist writers such as Tibor Déry and Gyula Háy became internationally known after their arrest in 1956, although Háy's plays had already been performed in the German-speaking world. Déry's short stories exposing the inhumanity of the Stalin era could also be found in various foreign publications. The bitter truth is that far fewer Hungarian writers were known abroad after 1945 than during the inter-war years. Yet the various associations during the time of "late Kadarism" still had 3,000 artists, 600 writers and seventy film directors on their membership lists. Compared to the Czechs and Poles, the Hungarians were at a hopeless disadvantage internationally in the 1970s and '80s. The only exception was the humorist Ephraim Kishon. His real name was Hoffmann, but as a young journalist on the staff of *Ludas Matyi*, the regime's comic magazine, he called himself Ferenc Kishont. In 1949 he migrated to Israel, where he again acquired a new name, and mastered modern Hebrew to the extent that he could write humorous sketches for newspapers and later in book form in that language, which is extremely difficult for a Hungarian to learn. As he admitted in his *Recollections*, it was primarily thanks to his gifted translator from English, Friedrich Torberg, that he became a bestselling writer in German-speaking countries.

In the last years of the twentieth century some Hungarian writers attained *succès d'estime*. This is no doubt due to the greater attention paid by publishers, which can be attributed to the existence of so many excellent translators. The chronicler of the Holocaust, Imre Kertész, achieved great success with the new edition of his shattering Auschwitz Report, not only because its publication coincided with the new wave of reassessing the past, but also because this time the German version had a talented translator. György Konrád, Péter Esterházy, Péter Nádas, György Dalos, István Eörsi, László Krasznahorkai and some other Hungarian writers also have a loyal following, but sadly some of the country's most significant twentieth-century novelists such as Gyula Krúdy, Zsigmond Móricz and Dezső Kosztolányi have been translated only sporadically and decades after their work first appeared or not at all. The same is true of its poets, including even the greatest of them, such as Endre Ady, Attila József and Gyula Illyés. It is a tragedy because probably in no other country are there so many good poets in proportion to the population. The uniqueness of the language, political turbulence and the lack of literary lobbies are probably responsible for the dearth of interest in Hungarian literature.

In contrast to literature, the Hungarians were and are truly a great power in music. The two undoubted Hungarian musical geniuses, Béla Bartók (1881–1945) and Zoltán Kodály (1882–1967), had begun to collect folksongs with the aid of a phonograph in remote Slovak- and Romanian-inhabited country areas around the beginning of the twentieth century, and became convinced that the popular songs played by the beloved Gypsy orchestras had little or nothing to do with old Hungarian folk music. They were saviours of the national musical heritage, but at the same time resolute opponents of the unbridled nationalism of the inter-war years. In contrast to Kodály, Bartók was an excellent pianist. From his *Improvisations on Hungarian Peasant Songs* and the sonatas for violin and piano to the avant-garde opera *Bluebeard's Castle* (1911, with libretto by the future film theoretician Béla Balázs) and the expressionist one-act pantomime *The Miraculous Mandarin* (1924), from the string quartets to the *Cantata Profana*, he was a pioneer of modern music and admired throughout the world.

Bartók was also, like Kodály, a human being in a time of inhumanity. A British musical encyclopaedia laconically writes of him: "Hungarian composer; lived in the United States since 1940, died there as a poor man." That is true enough, but the reason for his emigration in 1940 when nearly sixty is not stated. As he wrote to friends after the Austrian *Anschluss*, "There is a danger that Hungary will capitulate before this murderous and predatory regime. It is unimaginable to continue living and working in such a country." And later: "Unfortunately almost all educated Christians pay homage to the Nazi system. I am truly ashamed to belong to that class." In a testament written shortly before his departure he laid down that after his death no streets should be named for him or memorial plaques set up in his honour as long as streets and squares bore the names of "those two men" (meaning Hitler and Mussolini).[23]

Bartók left of his own free will, and his emigration was a gesture which conveyed a moral message in the clearest terms. Kodály stayed in Hungary till his death, but he used his position as "an international institution" to help people under both dictatorships. His *Psalmus Hungaricus*, the opera *Háry János, Dances from Galánta* and the *Marosszék Dances* conjure up lost traditions from Hungary and Transylvania. Bartók honoured him as the master of Hungarian classical music: "If I am asked who is the one whose works absolutely embody the Hungarian spirit, I always have to answer: Kodály."[24] The third renowned composer of this generation but less a national and modern one was Ernö Dohnányi* (1877–1960), who moved to the United States in 1948 and whose orchestral pieces, piano concertos and operas were composed more in the German musical tradition.

The two composers who hold similarly outstanding positions in the musical world of our time are György Ligeti (born 1923) and György Kurtág (born 1926). Ligeti, born in a small Transylvanian township, spent his school years in Cluj/Kolozsvár, and after the end of the Second World War studied at the Academy of Music in Budapest, where he later lectured on musical theory. Bartók became his compositional model. His first works were banned during the Communist era as formalistic-decadent, and he found out only after his flight in 1956 that Kodály as president of the Academy had personally intervened on his behalf when he was to be dismissed from his position. He fled to Vienna, from where he moved to Cologne settling finally in Hamburg and remaining a professor at the College of Music there until 1989. His compositions were at first the subject of vehement controversy, but the enthusiastic reception of his *Atmosphères*, which had its première at the Donaueschingen music festival in 1961, confirmed his final acceptance; and when Stanley Kubrick used extracts from it and from the choral pieces *Lux aeterna* and *Requiem* for his film *2001: A Space Odyssey.* Ligeti—a rarity for a young contemporary composer—they became known to a worldwide audience. That the film music was used without his consent and that he was paid only after bringing in lawyers is mentioned only in parentheses. One of his greatest successes was the opera of the absurd, *Le Grand Macabre*, composed in the 1970s, a hymn to the victory of Love over Death, a rejection of the populist gurus' pretentious ideologies and slogans.

---

* Grandfather of the conductor Christoph von Dohnányi and the German politician Klaus von Dohnányi.

Critics acclaim Ligeti's originality in all of his creative phases. The Swiss musicologist Thomas Schacher summarised his significance as follows:

> For the past forty years Ligeti has personified the contemporary musical world, first as a shrill exponent of New Music and bogey of the middle classes, then increasingly as a much-wooed composer, and lately even as an advertisement of conservative concert organizers. He is mentioned today in the same breath with Stockhausen, Boulez, Nono or Berio, the other great names of his generation. He enjoys worldwide recognition, and has been awarded the highest honours the Western world has to offer.[25]

But is it possible to say that his music is Hungarian? The Budapest newspaper *HVG* asked this on the occasion of Ligeti's seventy-fifth birthday, to which the composer replied: "I am an Austrian citizen living in Hamburg and Vienna; as a child I held Romanian, as a young man Hungarian citizenship. Wherever I live I am a Hungarian Jew from Transylvania. I have learnt most of what I know about composition from Ferenc Farkas. My ideal was Bartók. The rhythm of my music stems from the rhythm of the Hungarian language; since I think in that language, it also indirectly determines my musical thinking."[26]

Ligeti is a close friend of the other great Hungarian composer György Kurtág, who received for his lifework Germany's highest cultural award, the DM 250,000 Ernst von Siemens Prize for Music, in June 1998. The media-shy composer emphasized once that Ligeti has been not only his friend but also his mentor, and that all his life Bartók had been his model.[27] Kurtág is regarded by many as an "unwieldy" composer of the New Music. The jury's introduction to his subtle *Játékok* (Games)—improvised short pieces (some very short), which have since been collected into a collection of several volumes—explains that his sounds and rhythms are never lost in a system. He has drawn not only on old and new Hungarian, but also on Russian, German, English and French texts for his polyglot and many-voiced song cycles. Born in Lugos (Lugoj) in the Serbian Banat, he was familiar from childhood with the languages of the Romanian, Serbian, German and other ethnic groups living there, in addition to his Hungarian mother-tongue. This diversity, especially the distinctive position of Russian, demonstrates the unusual range of this great musician, who has also set to music poems by

Hölderlin and Paul Celan, prose by Samuel Beckett and *Kafka Fragmente*.

However, it is Hungary's great conductors and soloists whose repute has spread and been preserved all over the world. Sir Georg Solti (originally György Stern), who as musical director of Covent Garden Opera House in London, then chief conductor of the Chicago Symphony Orchestra (where he succeeded another Hungarian, Fritz Reiner) and a celebrated star at the Salzburg Festival, made musical history. On his death aged eighty-six he was buried in Hungary in accordance with his express instructions. His obituaries began on the front pages of every major newspaper and filled entire pages. At the end of his *Memoirs*, which he finished on the very eve of his death in 1997, Solti described a visit to his father's village at Lake Balaton and the old Jewish cemetery where his ancestors are buried: surrounded by the graves and standing on a hillock with a view of the lake, he felt a sense of belonging for the first time in sixty years.[28] Thus the road of this great conductor, hounded out of his country, led through Munich, Frankfurt, London, Chicago, Vienna and Salzburg back to his native country.

Space does not permit tributes to other outstanding conductors: George Szell in Cleveland, Antal Doráti in Dallas and Eugene Ormandy (Jenö Blau) in Philadelphia, who all enlarged the fame of these great orchestras. How could one forget the erstwhile world-renowned violinists Jenö Hubay, Joseph Szigeti or Sándor Végh, who became an institution at the Salzburg Festivals? The tradition of the internationally celebrated pianists Ilonka Kabos, Annie Fischer, Lajos Kentner (known in the West as Louis Kentner), Andor Földes and Géza Anda is being continued by the highly gifted András Schiff and Zoltán Kocsis.

Although the Golden Years of the Budapest operetta, which—because of the multiple cultural loyalty of its Jewish virtuosos—cannot be separated from the Viennese culture of the time, are long past, Franz Lehár and Imre Kálmán still enjoy great popularity. Other talented composers, such as Paul Ábrahám, Viktor Jakoby and Albert Szirmay, could not hold their own on Broadway after their arrival in America. Incidentally, the operetta by Kálmán, *Countess Maritza* (1924), which is set in Transylvania, was used by the Hungarian revisionism of the inter-war years; in the famous duet

the town of Varasdin, whose beauty is extolled in the German version, was changed in the Hungarian one to Kolozsvár, the capital of
Transylvania lost to Romania.[29] This shift of the focus of attention
provided a welcome opportunity for a quasi-political demonstration, and the duet sometimes had to be encored almost twenty
times in each performance. Viennese modern culture was influenced in other spheres as well by Hungarians of multiple cultural
loyalty, such as Ludwig Hevesi, standard-bearer of the Viennese
Sezession,* the film theoretician Béla Balázs, the economist Karl
Polányi and the philosopher Georg (György) Lukács.

It belongs to one of the peculiar traits of Hungarian cultural history that the best-known and most controversial Marxist philosopher of the twentieth century, Georg Lukács (1885–1971), son of
an ennobled Jewish banker, had a far greater influence in Germany,
and in American, British, French and Italian intellectual circles of
the Left, than in his native country. This had less to do with his
enigmatic past in the Communist movement than with his unpalatable written Hungarian.[30] After his studies in Florence, Berlin and
Heidelberg, and the publication of his early works *Soul and Form*
(1910) and *The Theory of the Novel* (1920), both highly praised by
Max Weber and Thomas Mann, Lukács would under normal circumstances have become, as he put it, "an interesting, eccentric
senior lecturer". Instead he joined the Hungarian Communist Party
in 1918, and acted as commissar for cultural affairs from 21 March
1919 during the Kun regime. When war broke out against Czechoslovakia and Romania he became a political commissar of the 5th
Division. Shortly before his death the valiant warrior told the story
that "for the sake of man's incarnation as part of the historical process" he had had eight deserters from the Red Army summarily
courtmartialled and shot.

After the defeat of the short-lived Soviet Republic, Lukács lived
in Vienna for almost ten years, then between 1931 and 1933 in
Berlin, and subsequently in Moscow. He had to recant abjectly and
repeatedly in public because of his unconventional philosophical
and political views (his *History and Class Consciousness*, published in
1923, influenced generations of deviants), which were criticized by

* Various groups of Austrian artists who in 1897 "seceded" from official art institutions to establish more modern schools.

Lenin and later by the Rákosi clique; otherwise, Lukács remarked in 1962, "I would have been rehabilitated by now and buried under a special memorial." He contributed to the process of soul-searching within the CP in the revolutionary year 1956, and took part in Imre Nagy's government and the newly-formed Party leadership. He was arrested and taken to Romania with Nagy but not put on trial, and was even re-admitted to the Party in 1967. He constantly fought against modern directions in literature and art, reproaching Kafka and Joyce for their "late-bourgeois decadence". In his last years he affronted many Hungarians with his absurd statement: "In my opinion even the worst socialism is better than the best capitalism."

Although of only minor effect in Hungary, Lukács directly and indirectly influenced quite a number of outstanding Hungarian intellectuals, who during the First World War gathered in the so-called "Sunday Circle", a philosophical and cultural discussion group. Eminent scholars such as the sociologist Karl Mannheim, the famous Polányi brothers, the art historian Arnold Hauser (author of *A Social History of Art and Literature*), well-known artists, writers and psychoanalysts all started their careers in that circle.

It has fallen mainly to Americans to study the long-ignored influence of Hungarian émigrés on modern art in Vienna, and especially on the Germany of the Weimar period. The pioneering role of the Hungarian avant-garde in Vienna and the activities of the artists gathered around the journal *MA* ("Today")* with their manifold links to the Bauhaus have only lately been opened to the interested German-speaking public by way of exhibitions and studies.[31] According to the American art historian Lee Congdon, Hungarian expatriate intellectuals and artists played a decisive role in moulding Weimar culture.[32]

Space does not allow us to dwell here on more than two great figures from this group: László Moholy-Nagy (a second cousin of Solti's mother) and Marcel Breuer, whose works are exhibited, esteemed, even admired to this very day. After the collapse of the Soviet Republic Moholy-Nagy (1895–1946) emigrated first to Vienna and then to Berlin. In 1923 he joined the Bauhaus under

---

* Published by the former metalworker and autodidact Lajos Kassák (1887–1967).

Walter Gropius, where he ran the metal workshop. He became co-publisher and typographical designer of the Bauhaus books in Dessau, worked as a typographer and graphic artist in Berlin and Amsterdam, and created stage designs for Otto Klemperer's avant-garde Kroll Opera in Berlin and for Erwin Piscator, the expressionist theatre director. In 1937 he was invited to head the "New Bauhaus" school in Chicago, later the "Institute of Design". In addition to his activities as an educator from Weimar to Chicago, he conducted radical experiments with painting, photography, plastics, graphics, film-making, advertising and industrial design, stage design and film. Art historians are convinced that the multifarious nature of this unusual artist's interests and talents explain his lack of deserved renown.

He used materials unusual for his time, such as aluminium and celluloid panels. His greatest interest was the analysis of light and motion. His photographs are so rare today that in a Sotheby auction in 1995 his "View from the Berlin TV-tower" reached $44,500, the reserve price being $25,000. After he knew that he had leukaemia, he told one of his closest collaborators at the institute in Chicago: "I don't know yet about my paintings, but I'm proud of my life."[33]

The great architect and designer Marcel Breuer (1902–81) was also active at the Bauhaus in Dessau, where he took charge of the furniture workshop. He designed the first tubular steel chairs and worked as a self-employed architect in Berlin. When the Hungarian chamber of architects refused him membership in the 1930s, he went first to England and then to the United States, where he established an architectural practice with Gropius, became a professor at Harvard, and opened architectural offices in New York and Paris. His buildings in New York, one of them with a mural by Jackson Pollock, are cherished today as monuments to the modern architecture of his time.

From Moholy-Nagy we must turn to the work of the internationally admired and exhibited Hungarian photographer[34] André Kertész (1894–1985), who emigrated to Paris in 1925 and then to New York in 1936. His sensitive and at the same time unconventional manner of photographing people and the human condition in rural Hungary, but also in Paris and New York, soon catapulted this autodidact into an unchallenged primacy in international photography. Medals, prizes and great retrospective exhibitions all over the world demonstrated that above and beyond his commercial work for various glossy magazines he was recognized as an artist.

The other eminent photographer who worked at this time in Paris bore the name Gyula Halász, but called himself Brassaï professionally after his home town, Brassó, in Transylvania. He started work as a journalist and used his pseudonym for his photos. Brassaï (1899–1984), who went to Paris in 1924, was inspired to take up photography by Kertész, but unlike him was interested in scenes from Paris nightlife, graffiti on walls and the works of the surrealist writers and artists. He made his living from worldwide orders for *Harper's Bazaar*, but demonstrated his true expertise in photographic books such as *Conversations with Picasso, On the Tracks of Proust* and *The World of Henry Miller*. Exhibitions and books about "Paris at night" made him internationally known, and he received the gold medal for photography at the Venice Biennale. His credo was "The mobility of a face is accidental. What I am looking for... is permanence."[35]

Our third photographer is Robert Capa, whose photo reports from the Spanish Civil War made him known overnight. It is little known that he was born Endre Friedmann in Budapest in 1913, and left there because he was arrested and beaten up for taking part in a leftist demonstration. He started using his professional name only in Spain. He covered four wars as a photo journalist: his pictures of the siege of Madrid and the well-known one of the mortally wounded republican soldier, and his last photos from the Indochina war made this Hungarian a legend in his field. He was killed by a landmine in Indochina aged only forty, but produced 70,000 negatives and gained world fame.[36]

When Stephan Lorant, another photo-pioneer from Budapest (born in 1901), died at the age of ninety-six, obituaries of the "founder of modern photojournalism" (*The Times*) appeared in leading newspapers all over the world.[37] As an émigré he worked first as a photographer and cameraman, but began his career in journalism in Munich, where he made the *Münchner Illustrierte* the first photojournalistic paper in Europe, rapidly increasing its circulation to 700,000. Pictures, he observed, were like notes of music which he gathered into a symphony. He invented a new montage technique, which enabled photos to extended parallel to the text across several double-page spreads. After Hitler took power, Lorant was taken into "protective custody" for six months but released after protests by the Hungarian government, and went via Budapest to London, where he published his first bestseller, *I Was Hitler's Prisoner*—he had learned some English in prison with the aid of a dictionary. The pocket edition of this book sold half a million copies.

Lorant founded the satirical magazine *Lilliput*, and close on its heels the first modern illustrated paper, *Picture Post*. One of Lorant's numerous books contains a picture of himself walking with Winston Churchill, a contributor to *Picture Post*, in the garden of Chartwell in 1941. Its ingenious layout secured the magazine a weekly circulation of 1.5 million. Indignant about his "enemy alien" status in England, Lorant moved to the United States, and started a third successful career by developing a new literary genre: the illustrated book on contemporary historical themes. Books on Lincoln and Roosevelt, his famous *Story of an American City* about Pittsburgh, and photo-stories about America and Germany brought him money, fame and numerous prizes. Whether Kafka really found a job for him playing the violin in a movie house during his early stay in Czechoslovakia, whether he really seduced Greta Garbo after a screen test in Berlin, whether these and other stories recorded in his "Recollections" are really authentic is no longer known by anyone. It is perhaps enough that the London *Times* listed him among the 1,000 prominent people who have "made their indelible mark on the twentieth century".

Ever since 1917 the coveted Pulitzer Prize has been awarded annually in the United States for outstanding journalistic and literary achievement, It is accepted as the ultimate recognition of responsible and original journalism, and the names of the recipients—writers and newspapers—are regularly reported in the world media. The founder of this most respected of journalistic awards, a certain József Pulitzer, came from the small southern Hungarian township of Makó, where his father was a bankrupt grain merchant, and migrated to the United States aged seventeen. Pulitzer joined the First New York Cavalry Regiment as a volunteer. He had always wanted to be a soldier, but was not robust and had poor eyesight, and was rejected by the Austrians, the French and finally the

English.[38] In 1865, after the end of the American Civil War, friends suggested that he start a new life in the Mid-Western town of St Louis, which had a large German-speaking population—Pulitzer was bilingual in Hungarian and German—and after working at odd jobs he landed an apprenticeship with the local German paper *Westliche Post*.

The young man who had started his journalistic career with a rather inadequate education and command of English became part-owner of the paper within a few years. He was a passionate fighter against crime and corruption, and in spite of his innate shyness and fractured English, he won a seat in the lower house of the Missouri state legislature when barely twenty-two. However, his destiny was journalism, not politics. After acquiring the controlling interest in the German newspaper, Pulitzer sold it for the round figure of $30,000. He then bought the bankrupt *St Louis Dispatch*, merged it with the *Post*, and with tremendous energy and remarkable journalistic and organizational talent transformed the daily *St Louis Post-Dispatch* into one of the great independent newspapers of America. "Accuracy, brevity, accuracy" was his motto, written on the walls of every one of his newsrooms. He also introduced the meaningful headline so that the reader would grasp the essence of an article in the first paragraph. Of course the popular newspaper had its enemies. The turning point came in 1883 when Pulitzer acquired the great daily paper the *New York World*, eventually establishing an evening edition as well. His first step was to reduce the price to 2 cents, while other papers sold for 3–4 cents; the result was a leap in circulation. The paper demanded a federal income tax on high earnings, as well as measures against monopolies and high tariffs. This owner, publisher and supreme editor-in-chief made journalistic history with his crusades for principles and ideas—never for the prejudices and interests of individual groups. He was also a munificent benefactor, particularly where the future of journalism was concerned. Thus he bequeathed $2 million in his will for the establishment of a School of Journalism at Columbia University and to endow the Pulitzer Prize. The end of the Pulitzer saga was tragic: around the age of forty he lost his sight, and then sailed restlessly around the world in his yacht the *Liberty*, dying on board in 1911 in the port of Charleston, South Carolina.

Pulitzer's physical and psychological problems—his shattered
nerves and bouts of depression brought on by overwork, and the
rapid deterioration of his eyesight—could of course have been
treated effectively a few years later by some of his former countrymen. In fact, Hungarian psychiatrists have in the mean time gained
worldwide recognition; many went abroad during the Horthy
regime, and others followed in the last phase of the Second World
War and the ensuing Communist dictatorship. One who did not
emigrate was the founder of the "Hungarian school", Sándor
Ferenczi, Freud's closest collaborator.[39] The Hungarian doctor and
neuropsychiatrist deeply admired the founder of psychiatry, and the
affection between them is apparent in more than 1,000 letters they
exchanged up till Ferenczi's death in 1933. Ferenczi's fame attracted
many foreigners to Budapest. An outstanding representative of
Hungarian psychoanalysis was Lipót (Leopold) Szondi (1893–
1986), whose theory and therapy of fate-analysis (anankology), and
his "Szondi test", which is still used in clinical practice, attained
international recognition. Lucky circumstances brought him to
Switzerland via the concentration camp of Bergen-Belsen, and he
was active in the Szondi Institute for Anankology in Zurich until
his death. Mihály Bálint (1896–1970), a Ferenczi disciple who
migrated to England in 1939, became known in emigration for his
psychoanalysis of "thrill", the anxiety-pleasure sensations in extreme situations. His name lives on in the so-called Bálint groups, a
form of psychoanalytical and psychotherapeutic medical training,
which he introduced.

   One of the numerous Hungarians working in the United States
who should not be omitted from this list is the anthropologist Géza
Róheim, who employed psychoanalytical methods and concepts in
anthropological fieldwork in Somalia and Central Australia *inter
alia*. Between 1911 and 1928 he devoted his attention to Hungarian
ethnology, and later to the subject generally. One of his main interests at the time was Hungarian mythology, especially the shamans
("*táltos*") and the use of magic. He pointed out that Hungarian
folklore had been exposed to innumerable Croat, Serb, Czech,
Romanian and German influences. He was accused by some of
"lacking patritotism", but when he died in America in 1953 he
was buried, as he had requested, wrapped in a Hungarian flag.

The eulogy was given by the Hebrew scholar Raphael Patai in Hungarian. The best-known Hungarian scholar in the United States today is Thomas C. Szasz, Professor of Psychiatry at the State University of New York Health Science Center in Syracuse— author of several scientific works on psychiatry and at the same time a radical critic of psychiatry and psychoanalysis. Paul Harmat writes in his work on Hungarian psychology that Szasz has both admirers and enemies in great numbers. That psychoanalysis has a different status in Hungary and in the United States was illustrated when the American novelist Bernard Malamud was asked on a visit to Budapest what he considered the difference between living there and in New York. He replied that if two intellectuals first meet in New York, one would ask the other: how much time have you spent in analysis? In Budapest, the question would be: how much time have you spent in prison or in a camp?

The so-called Hungarian hegemony in Los Alamos and Hollywood was parallelled by the Hungarian "boom" in Britain. Never before did Hungarians exert so much influence on a country's national economy as the two economists Thomas (Tamás) Balogh and Nicholas (Miklós) Káldor did during the Labour governments of the 1960s in Britain. Both came to England in the 1930s: Káldor did research and taught at Cambridge, while Balogh did the same at Oxford. Both were left of centre. Balogh was one of Harold Wilson's closest advisers, and for a while even Minister for Energy. (The two were nicknamed "Buda" and "Pest".) As the first Hungarian member of the House of Lords, Balogh began his maiden speech with the remark: "My Lords, this chamber has listened to many voices over the centuries, but I presume to none as yet which spoke with a genuine Hungarian accent." He schemed, connived and mistrusted his colleagues, but remained one of the Prime Minister's closest confidants.[40]

The situation was different with Káldor, a witty and open-hearted man, who was also made a life peer a couple of years after Balogh. He was the Wilson government's tax expert, and introduced a top marginal rate of 98 per cent on incomes from capital investments; the controversial and long forgotten Selective Employment Tax (SET) for the restructuring of the workforce from service industries to the production sector is also connected with his name. He wanted to convince the former colonial governments that economic planning and the principle of equality led to prosperity. His intentions were good but his advice caused great difficulties. He was one of two Hungarian advisers at different times to Kwame Nkrumah, the first President of independent Ghana, the other being the professor of economics József Bognár, and the two unwittingly contributed greatly to the trends which led to Nkrumah's fall.

The most famous and controversial Hungarian of our times is not a scientist, an artist, a politician or an inventor, but the world's most successful speculator and at the same time one of its most notable philanthropists. This is George (György) Soros,[41] whose private wealth is estimated at $5 billion. Funds established by him for private investors are said to be worth $17–18 billion. An example may suffice to prove his phenomenal success as the "king of speculators": had an investor put $1,000 at the disposal of the Soros Quantum Fund in 1969, and re-invested the dividends, he would now have over $2 million! Despite occasional blunders with yen and DM exchange rates, his fund has shown unbelievably high growth since its inception: 35 per cent annually.

Born in 1930, the son of a Jewish lawyer, he survived the German occupation and the Nazi terror in 1944 with false papers under the name of Sándor Kiss, Soros was known only to international investors until 1992. He attained unfavourable publicity, especially in Britain, as "the man who broke the Bank of England" when on one monumental day in 1992 he made "a billion dollars" (more precisely 958 million) by correctly assessing that the British government would eventually devalue the pound. The fact that when Soros came to Britain in 1947 he was desperately poor and financed his studies at the London School of Economics by working on the railways and later as a costume jewellery salesman lent his raid on the pound a special piquancy in the eyes of British commentators and taxpayers. He migrated to New York in 1956 and became a share dealer on Wall Street. With a $4 million loan from rich investors he established the Quantum Fund in 1969 in a Caribbean tax haven outside the supervisory orbit of the US finance authorities, and amassed a huge fortune by daring tax-free and unregulated speculations. As manager of the fund Soros personally earned 15 per cent of the profits.

Since his triumph over the pound, the image of George Soros has changed dramatically. He is constantly quoted not only in the international media but also by heads of state and government of countries whose currencies succumbed to a devaluation spin, such as Thailand's in 1996. A year later President Mahathir bin Mohamed of Malaysia called him a "robber and bandit".

Yet the world's best-known investor, who has meanwhile taken US citizenship, is far more than the "king of speculators". After the great turning-point in 1989 Soros retired from day-to-day business matters, leaving the administration of the Fund to a close collaborator, and since then has become the world's greatest philanthropist. He established his "Open Society" foundation in 1979 in the spirit of his former teacher at the London School of Economics, the philosopher Sir Karl Popper, and launched it with a pioneering initiative in his home country, Hungary. There a Soros Foundation was established in cooperation with the Academy of Sciences (the Kádár regime was still in power), and under the supervision of his personal representative—the last surviving defendant in the Nagy trial, the journalist and later liberal parliamentarian Miklós Vásárhelyi— annual grants of $3 million, subsequently $10 million, were made for language courses, support of journals and literature, and scholarships for students and researchers travelling abroad (proper tenders always had to be produced). The later Prime Minister Viktor Orbán was among those who were enabled to spend a year at Oxford with the help of a Soros scholarship.

Soros Foundations were created even before the collapse of Communism in the Soviet Union and Poland, and after the change in almost all the Central and East European countries, including the Ukraine and the Baltic states. Hundreds of millions of dollars (according to official statistics $300 million in 1994, $350 m. in 1995, $362 m. in 1996 and $428 m. in 1997) are pouring into thirty-one countries in Europe, Asia, Southern Africa and Latin America, as well as several social institutions in the United States fighting drug abuse and juvenile delinquency. Soros has donated more money to promote an "open society" than the American government and major official bodies.

His influence has by no means exclusively won him friends. He was denounced in Romania as an "agent of revanchist Hungary" and in Hungary as the "agent of international Jewish capital", a "Judeo-Communist plutocrat" who was morally undermining the Hungarian character with his benefactions. To the governments of Serbia, Croatia, Belarus and sometimes the Czech Republic Soros was like a red rag to a bull since they could not treat the self-confident, anti-authoritarian billionaire just as they wanted. Macedonia owes its economic survival, or at least the stabilization of its position, to support from the Soros Foundation. His opponents claim that his investments in Eastern Europe are made to give his image a shine and for personal aggrandizement. It is true that Soros is not averse to honours and world-wide publicity; the *New Yorker* has described him as a "billionaire with a Messiah complex".

In his lectures and books he has expressed his inner conflicts, much to the derision of his many critics, for example: "As a participant in the market. I am trying to be on the winning side, as a citizen and human being I am trying to serve the common good." At any rate, Soros is at the centre of contention not least because he frequently offers advice publicly to politicians about their policies towards Russia and the Balkans, or about liberalizing drug and immigration policies. In short, he acts like a "statesman without a state", but with a vast fortune and the personal power of distributing millions of dollars according to his whims, and only for positive purposes.

Time magazine chose as its 1997 "Man of the Year" another American of Hungarian origin, Andy Grove, thus giving him instant fame, especially in his home country.[42] We have here again an American-dream rags-to-riches career, Grove has changed the world with the computer chips produced by his firm Intel, which delivers 90 per cent of micro processors for PCs, and has an annual turnover of $25 billion, with profits amounting to $6.8 billion in 1997. András Gróf came to New York aged twenty without any knowledge of English, and as early as 1960 the *New York Times* trumpeted the success of a young Hungarian who on his arrival could not tell the difference between the words "horizontal" and "vertical", yet graduated in chemical engineering from City College of New York as best in his class. With enormous ambition, diligence and ability he achieved a dizzying career even in American terms. What is more, he had to overcome partial deafness; only after twenty years and five operations did he regain his hearing. Grove retired from the presidency of Intel in 1998, but remained on the board; in 1997, according to the report in *Time*, he collected over $100 million in income and bonus payments. In contrast to the peripatetic Soros, he has not re-visited Budapest.

No depiction of Hungarians in the world of finance would be complete without a mention of André Kosztolany, the best-known stock market commentator in the German-speaking world, and Alexandre de Lamfalussy (Sándor Lámfalussy), the most respected banker of Hungarian origin in Europe. The incorruptible maverick Kosztolany, born in 1906 in Budapest (he died in Paris in 1999) but holder of a US passport, was a bestselling writer in Germany and the epitome of a Hungarian cosmopolitan. Although he spent more time in Munich and Paris than in Budapest, and considered himself, as he said, at home in ten cities, the finance writer "was still a committed Hungarian patriot".

For a quarter of a century Kosztolany wrote a regular column for *Capital*, and his books about money and the stock market have sold more than a million copies in eight languages. At a meeting of expatriate Hungarians on his ninetieth birthday, the present writer personally witnessed his mastery of Hungarian, although the "wise speculator" had lived outside his homeland for over seventy years. Incidentally, one of the speakers at this function, Otto von Habsburg, spoke in beautiful, polished Hungarian although he has never lived in the country. But the private tutor of the last King and Emperor's eldest son had been a Hungarian Benedictine, who taught him complete mastery of the language.

The banker Lamfalussy was also beholden to the Benedictines for their assistance to him in Belgium after his flight from Hungary in 1949. Having graduated from the Benedictine high school at Sopron, he studied briefly at the University of Budapest before escaping to the West with two friends in the Scout movement. While studying at the Catholic University of Louvain in Belgium, he earned his living as a tourist guide and even as a street-sweeper. After subsequent studies at Oxford, the Hungarian refugee, by now a Belgian citizen, began his successful career at the Banque de Bruxelles, followed in 1976 by a leading position in the BIS (Bank for International Settlements) in Basel, where from 1985 (now ennobled by the Belgian king as Baron Lamfalussy) he served as general manager. In 1994 he assumed the presidency of the European Monetary Institute in Berlin, forerunner of the European Central Bank. He owns a house on Lake Balaton, and was a member of an informal international economic advisory body consulted from time to time by the former Prime Minister Orbán.

Space does not permit us to do more than merely mention other well-known Hungarians, such as Victor Vasarely (Vásárhelyi), "inventor of Op Art" (1908–97); the historian of Central Europe, François (Ferenc) Fejtö from France; the authority on myth and religion Karl (Károly) Kerényi (1897–1973) from Switzerland; or Mihály Csikszentmihályi, the psychologist and writer from Chicago; or Peter (Lord) Bauer (1915–2002), Professor of Economics at the London School of Economics; André Deutsch (1917–2000), creator of one of the most distinguished publishing houses in post-Second World War London; the famous media manager Josef von Ferenczy in Germany; and the inventor of the "Rubic Cube", Ernö Rubik, in Hungary itself.

To enumerate the outstanding Hungarian successes in sport (sixteen gold medals at the 1948 Olympic Games in London and almost as many at Helsinki in 1952 and Melbourne in 1956) would occupy several pages. Or the "golden era" of Hungarian soccer with the wonder team of Puskas, Kocsis, Bozsik and Hidegkuti beating England in 1953 for the first time ever on home ground at Wembley by 6-3 and somewhat later by 7-1 in Budapest. The tradition of the champions in fencing, water-polo, swimming and many other sports played an important role in preserving and strengthening national identity in times of political repression and foreign domination. And who could overlook the triumphs of the Hungarian chessplayers, headed by the world champion Judith Polgar?

After the German edition of this book was published, quite a number of Hungarian émigrés wrote to the author admonishing him for ignoring other outstanding Hungarians in the fields of natural and human sciences, music (the pianist György Cziffra), ballet, architecture, medicine, finance, and industry (Sir Peter Abeles in Australia, C. Munk in Canada, and others).

Among the important politicians of Hungarian descent one should mention first of all the Democratic Congressman Tom Lantos of

California, one of the many Jews saved by Raoul Wallenberg in Budapest. The Governor of New York Sate, George Pataki, is partly of Hungarian origin, and he visited the birthplace of his paternal grandfather in a small village in eastern Hungary. The father of the French Minister of Interior, Nicolas Sarkozy, came as a Hungarian refugee after the crushing of the 1956 Revolution to France. Neither Pataki nor Sarkozy (Sarközi) can speak Hungarian. For several years, the Hungarians were proud of the fact that the wife of the then French Prime Minister, Raymond Barre, née Eva Hegedüs, was not only Hungarian-born but also regularly attended Hungarian cultural events and accompanied her husband on a state visit to her native country.

One could indeed fill the telephone diretory of a small town with the names of all these talents from Hungary. Yet even this probably would not satisfy all Hungarians at home and abroad. The insatiable appetite for recognition abroad is a reflection of the deep-rooted uncertainty and fear concerning the nation's slow death ever since Johann Gottfried von Herder's oft-quoted and never forgotten prophesy.

Summing-up

Eleven hundred years of separate development are irrevocably drawing to a close—under the twin forces of economic globalisation and the dynamic of European unification. Regardless of setbacks and the influence of groups marching backwards into the future, the political, economic, cultural and communication pressures from outside Hungary will—I believe—prove in the long run to be irresistible.

Yet it would be unwise to deny that the contradictions between the pro-European outward-looking feelings and the profoundly nationalistic sense of mission, harking back even to the concept of the crown of St Stephen as symbol of the "political nation", have also shaped developments in the years since the collapse of the Communist system and the Soviet empire. In this sense history and its changing interpretation have influenced the tortuous process of transition—from dictatorship to democracy, from central planning to market economy, from Russian domination to NATO membership—more than anyone could have predicted at the outset.

It is a matter for intense dispute among historians and political writers how far one can explain the codes of behaviour and the psychological attitudes of the élite and the people at large through the knowledge of history, particularly as far as recent history is concerned. The notion of "a 1,000-year-old Hungarian Christianity" and Hungary as "the country of Maria or St Stephen" combined with the frequent references to the "Christian Hungarian middle class" has resurrected a cult of history which observers compare to the atmosphere prevailing at the time of the celebrations, in 1938, of the 900th anniversary of St Stephen's death.

Post-Communist Hungarian economic history has to be regarded as a remarkable success for most of its citizens. Rising productivity and the massive influx of Western capital have been the main sources of the Hungarian economic success story. Though the four free elections since 1990 resulted in four changes of government, the Hungarian workers appear to have accepted the stagnation of real wages and widening inequalities in income and wealth with surprising equanimity. According to a comprehensive statistical account, compiled by the Central Office of Statistics for the 1990–2001 period, the purchasing power of the average real incomes in 2001 still fell short by 10 to 11 per cent of the level recorded in 1989. Nevertheless, there is no reason to doubt the fact, stressed in the publication, that the overall financial situation of the households has considerably improved. Nor should one forget the role of the black economy, estimated to account for about one third of economic activity. At the time of this writing Hungary's per capita gross domestic product was just about half of the European Union's average.

The upheavals in the turbulent national history, as I tried to illustrate in the preceding pages, created a curious ambivalence about foreigners, inspiring either awe or disdain. The durability of the myth about Hungarian racial purity coupled with frequent open anti-Semitic outbursts on the extreme Right, tacitly tolerated by centre-right politicians and publications, has become a sensitive issue in the public debate about Hungary's future perspectives. The projection of a small, nobly embattled people engaged in a struggle against the "Tel Aviv–New York axis" recalls the obnoxious anti-Semitic propaganda of the 1920s and '30s in a country which is still haunted by the memory of the Hungarian Holocaust and the responsibility, shared with the Third Reich, for the extermination of almost 600,000 Hungarian Jews.

Any sensible reading of Hungarian history since the time of St Stephen can confirm that there is scarcely a family, particularly among the élites, which has no "foreign" blood in it, to say nothing of the great military, political, literary and scientific figures of Slav, Romanian, German and Jewish descent who contributed so much to the survival of the Hungarian nation-state. The deep-rooted fear of the nation's slow death provides the sombre background to the old dispute over whether being Hungarian is a matter of choice. According to demographic research, in the year 2001 the population practically slumped to its 1960 level. It was only due to the migration to Hungary that at the time of the last census it reached

10.2 million. Figures about the neighbouring countries show a steady decline in the actual number and percentage share of the Hungarian ethnic minorities. During the 1990s the number of Hungarians in Romania fell by almost 12 per cent to under 1.5 million. Similar tendencies have been registered in Slovakia, Ukraine, Croatia and Serbia. The reasons are threefold: low birth-rate, migration and assimilation to the majority nations. In view of these facts and of the loosening bond with the mother tongue in the second and third generations of Hungarians living in other countries, the oft-quoted figure of 15 million Hungarians in the world has to be revised.

Stability in Central and Eastern Europe depends in the first place on the treatment of minorities. The war in Yugoslavia must remain a permanent reminder of the dangers of ethnic nationalism. The presence of over 2.5 million Hungarians in the neighbouring countries is a consequence of the 1920 Treaty of Trianon. Their fate has always been a reflection of the degree of democracy enjoyed and the tolerance shown by the political élite of the majority nations. This in turn has also been affected by their relationship with Hungary and its government of the day. Even since the collapse of Communalism there have been ups and downs, depending on the extent of the nationalistic backlash in the countries concerned.

Under the conditions of an enlarged European Union (certain to materialise in 2004–6) the minorities question can only be diffused through a European approach, monitored by corresponding watchdog institutions in Brussels. The road towards an acceptable solution—maximum equality within guaranteed borders—is long and fraught with difficulties, particularly when the national issue is exploited as a vote-catching ploy at the time of national or regional elections. One has to start with the school- and history books in all the countries in order to combat effectively the hostile images and stereotypes disseminated for centuries on all sides.

In Hungary itself the crucial problem for the future is not merely economic reform, as is often presumed in the West, but also the unsolved question of the conjunction of patriotism and liberalism, of the national idea and social progress. The country's greatest poets from Sándor Petőfi and Endre Ady to Attila József were at the same time convinced patriots *and* Europeans. Bridging this yawning gap between the two tendencies in the country's political culture is the fateful question for the future of the "victors in defeat" and for Hungary's place in a changing Europe.

Notes

Chapter 1 "Heathen Barbarians" overrun Europe: Evidence from St Gallen

1. Johannes Duft, *Die Ungarn in Sankt Gallen*, Zurich 1957; J. Duft, A. Gössi and W. Vogler, *Die Geschichte des Klosters St Gallen*, 1986; Werner Vogler (ed.), *Die Kultur der Abtei Sankt Gallen*, Zurich 1993.
2. Bálint Hóman and Gyula Szekfü, *Magyar Történet* (Hungarian History—hereafter *Hung. Hist.*), 5 vols, Budapest 1936: vol. 1, p. 92; Karl Szabó in *Die Öster-reichisch-Ungarische Monarchie in Wort und Bild*, 24 vols, vol. 1: *Geschichte Ungarns*, pp. 43–55.
3. Cf. V. Heuberger, A. Suppan and E. Vyslonzil (eds), *Das Bild vom Anderen*, Frankfurt/Main 1998, pp. 18, 28ff.
4. Fernand Braudel (ed.), *Europa—Bausteine seiner Geschichte*, Frankfurt-Main 1989, p. 51.
5. Georges Duby, *Europa im Mittelalter*, Stuttgart 1986, pp. 9, 23.

Chapter 2 Land Acquisition or Conquest? The Question of Hungarian Identity

1. Cf. Hóman and Szekfü, *Hung. Hist.*, op. cit., vol. 1, pp. 1–131; György Györffy, *István király és müye* (King Stephen and his work), Budapest 1977, pp. 15–54; György Székely and Antal Bartha, *Magyarország története* 10 vols, vol. 1: pp. 265–575; Péter Hanák (ed.), *Die Geschichte Ungarns*, Essen 1988, pp. 1–29; C.A. Macartney, *Hungary: A Short History*, Edinburgh, 1971, p. 7; Pál Engel, *Magyarok Európában. A kezdettöl 1440-ig* (Hungary in Europe. From the Beginnings to 1440), Budapest 1990.
2. Egon Friedell, *Kulturgeschichte der Neuzeit*, Munich 1996, p. 13.
3. Cf. György Dalos, *Mythen der Nationen*, Berlin 1998, p. 531.
4. Herwig Wolfram, *Die Geburt Mitteleuropas. Geschichte Österreichs vor seiner Enstehung, 378–907*, Berlin 1987. esp. pp. 311–75.
5. Cf. György Györffy, *A magyarok elödeiröl és a honfoglalásról. Kortársak és krónikások hiradásai* (About the Ancestors of the Hungarians and the Conquest—Accounts by Contemporaries and Chroniclers), Budapest 1986; Thomas von Bogyay, *Grundzüge der ungarischen Geschichte*, Darmstadt 1990, pp. 3–13; see also the discussion in *Historia*, special issue about the Conquest (in Hung.), 1966/2.
6. Georg Stadtmüller, *Geschichtliche Ostkunde*, vol. 2, Vienna-Munich-Zurich 1963, p. 31.

7. Quoted in "Die ungarische Landnahme in der ausländischen Geschichts-schreibung" in *Magyar Tudomány*, Budapest 95/12, p. 1407f.
8. Hóman and Szekfü, op. cit., vol. 1, p. 123; Bogyay, *Grundzüge*, 33–6; Béla Köpeczi (ed.), *Kurze Geschichte Siebenbürgens*, Budapest 1990, esp. pp. 107–240.
9. Cf. among others R.W. Seton-Watson, *A History of the Roumanians*, London 1934, repr. 1963, pp. 1–16.
10. Die Székler in Ferenc Glatz (ed.), *Magyarok a Kárpátmedencében* (Hungarians in the Carpathian Basin), Budapest 1988; *Öst.-Ung. Monarchie; Ungarn. Kurze Geschichte*, pp. 241–67. Cf. Jókai, vol. 1, Vienna, 1888, pp. 318–26.
11. Sándor Eckhardt, "Das Ungarnbild in Europa" in *Ungarische Jahrbücher* 1942. The German translation of the essay from the collection *Mi a Magyar?* (What is a Hungarian?), Budapest 1938, is purged of critical remarks not in line with Nazi doctrine.
12. Ibid.

Chapter 3 From Magyar Mayhem to the Christian Kingdom of the Árpáds

1. Jenö Szücs, "König Stephan in der Sicht der modernen ungarischen Geschichts-forschung" in *Sudostforschungen*, Munich, vol. XXXI, 1972, pp. 17–35.
2. Macartney, *Hungary*, p. 13.
3. In *Népszabadság*, Budapest, 19 Aug. 1997.
4. Kálmán Benda—Erik Fügedi, *Tausend Jahre Stephanskrone*, Budapest 1989.
5. Bogyay, *Grundzüge*, op. cit., p. 22.
6. Quoted in Julius von Farkas (ed.), *Ungarns Geschichte und Kultur in Dokumenten*, Wiesbaden 1955, pp. 11–12.
7. Katalin Sinko, "Árpád versus Saint Stephen: Competing heroes and competing interests in the figurative representation of Hungarian history", *Ethnologia Europaea* XIX, 1989, pp. 67–83.

Chapter 4 The Struggle for Continuity and Freedom

1. See Ekkehard Völkl (ed.), *Bayern und Ungarn. Tausend Jahre enge Beziehungen*, Regensburg, 1988, pp. 9–21.
2. Gyula Pauler, *Geschichte der ungarischen Nation unter den Königen aus dem Hause Árpáds*, vol. 1, Budapest 1899, pp. 9–21.
3. Julius von Farkas, "Das Ungarnbild in Deutschland", *Ungarn-Jahrbuch*, Berlin 1942, pp. 402–4.
4. Farteas, *Ungarns Geschichte und Kultur*, op. cit., pp. 15–17.
5. Paul Hunfalvy, linguist, quoted and expanded by Béla von Pukánszky in *Geschichte des deutschen Schrifttums in Ungarn*, Münster 1931, vol. 1, p. 27.
6. The concepts originate from the writer and essayist László Németh from his influential anti-Semitic (partly also anti-German and anti-"assimilationist") work *A minőség forradalma* (The revolution of quality). For the "thin" Magyars see esp. vol. 2, reprint Budapest 1992, pp. 849–52, 934–5.
7. Denis Silagi, *Ungarn*, Hanover 1972, second expanded edn, p. 12.

8. Mihály Babits in "Mi a magyar?" (What is the Hungarian?), Budapest 1939, p. 37.
9. See György M. Vajda, *Wien und die Literaturen in der Donaumonarchie*, Vienna-Cologne-Weimar 1994, pp. 15–17. E.J. Görlich, "Grillparzer und Katona" in *Ungarn-Jahrbuch*, 1973, vol. 3, pp. 123–34.
10. Eckhardt, "Das Ungarnbild", op. cit.
11. Quoted in Hanák (ed.), *Die Geschichte Ungarns*, op. cit., p. 29.
12. Eckhardt, "Das Ungarnbild".

Chapter 5   The Mongol Invasion of 1241 and its Consequences

1. Thomas von Bogyay (ed.), *Der Mongolensturm. Berichte von Augenzeugen und Zeitgenossen 1235/1250*, Graz 1985.
2. Ibid., pp. 43–8; Hanák (ed.), *Die Geschichte Ungarns*, op. cit., pp. 31–4: see also Jenö Szücs, *Nemzet és Történelem* (Nation and History), Budapest 1984.
3. Bogyay, *Der Mongolensturm*, p. 42; Ferenc Glatz, *A Magyarok krónikája* (The Chronicle of the Hungarians), Budapest 1996, p. 98f, states the losses at no more than 300–400,000.
4. Bogyay, *Der Mongolensturm*, pp. 168–70.
5. Gunther Stökl, *Osteuropa und die Deutschen*, Oldenburg/Hamburg 1967, p. 86. For Hóman, see vol. 1, p. 147f; for Hantsch. *Die Geschichte Österreichs*, vol. 1, p. 90.
6. Szücs, "König Stephan".
7. Ladislaus Rosdy, *Sieben Versuche über Ungarn*, Vienna-Munich 1966, p. 31.
8. Quoted in ibid., p. 28.

Chapter 6   Hungary's Rise to Great Power Status under Foreign Kings

1. Duby, *Europa in Mittelalter*, op. cit., p. 87.
2. Macartney, *Hungary*, op. cit., p. 42.
3. Ibid., p. 50.

Chapter 7   The Heroic Age of the Hunyadis and the Turkish Danger

1. Quoted in Eckhardt, "Das Ungarnbild in Europa", op. cit. Here too is the quotation from Hebbel which follows.
2. Macartney, *Hungary*, pp. 54 ff.
3. Quoted in Farkas (ed.), *Ungarns Geschichte und Kultur*, op. cit., pp. 35–40.
4. Quoted in Hanák (ed.), *Die Geschichte Ungarns*, p. 43.

Chapter 8   The Long Road to the Catastrophe of Mohács

1. Jenö Szücs, *Die drei historischen Regionen Europas*. Frankfurt 1990, p. 53.

2. Pukánsky, *Geschichte des deutschen Schrifttums,* op. cit., pp. 38–9.
3. Rosdy, *Sieben Versuche,* op. cit., p. 46; Hóman and Szekfü, *Magyar Történet,* vol. 1. pp. 12–13.
4. Géza Ottlik, *Iskola a határon* (School at the Border), Budapest 1959.

Chapter 9   The Disaster of Ottoman Rule

1. Cf. Hóman and Szekfü, *Hung. Hist.,* Szekfü, *Der Staat Ungarn,* vol. 3, pp. 48–59; Gábor Barta, *Az erdélyi fejedelemség születése* (The birth of the Transylvanian principality), Budapest 1984; *Short History,* vol. ?, pp. 243–55.
2. Bogyay, *Grundzüge,* op. cit., p. 89f. Cf. also Hóman and Szekfü, op. cit.; I. Szabó, *Ungarisches Volk—Geschichte und Wandlungen,* Budapest-Leipzig 1944, quoted in Bogyay, pp. 84 and 90.
3. Quoted in Rosdy, *Sieben Vessuche,* p. 11.
4. Hóman and Szekfü, *Hung. Hist.,* op. cit., pp. 497–9.
5. Cf. Franz Pesendorfer, *Ungarn und Österreich. Tausend Jahre Partner oder Gegner,* Vienna 1998, p. 99.
6. For quotations see Eckhardt, "Das Ungarnbild", op. cit.

Chapter 10   Transylvania the Stronghold of Hungarian Sovereignty

1. Cf. *Kurze Geschichte, Siebenbürgens,* op. cit.
2. Cf. Szücs, *Die drei historischen…*; Bogyay, *Grundzüge.*
3. Hóman and Szekfü, *Hung. Hist.,* p. 3.
4. Cf. *Kurze Geschichte,* op. cit., pp. 310–27, 329–41.
5. Ibid., pp. 186–9, 292–8; Hóman and Szekfü, *Magyar Történet,* pp. 329–33.
6. Text in Farkas (ed.), *Ungarns Geschichte und Kultur,* pp. 72–5.
7. Quoted in Eduard Winter, *Barock, Absolutismus und Aufklärung in der Donaumonarchie,* Vienna 1971, p. 57.

Chapter 11   Gábor Bethlen—Vassal, Patriot and European

1. Golo Mann, *Wallenstein,* Frankfurt 1971, pp. 150–3, 170, 195, 225f.
2. Ágnes Hankiss, 'Gábor Bethlen' in *Kötéltánc* (Tight-rope Walk), pp. 328–65; C.V. Wedgwood, *The Thirty Years War,* London 1938, pp. 94 and 98.
3. Hankiss, ibid.
4. Quoted in Gyula Szekfü, *Bethlen Gábor,* Budapest 1929, p. 219.
5. See *Gábor Bethlen Emlékezete* (In Memory of Gábor Bethlen): *Letters* (in Hung.), Budapest 1980.
6. Text in Farkas (ed.), *Ungarns Geschichte und Kultur,* pp. 75–9.
7. Cf. Interview about Nation and History in *Europai utas* (European Traveller), Budapest 98/1; about "Heresies too are historical facts", *Magyar Hirlap,* Budapest, 31 May 1997. See also his book *Reconstruction and Embourgeoisement 1711– 1867,* Budapest 1990, and *The Dangers of History,* Budapest 1987 (both in Hung.).

Chapter 12 Zrinyi or Zrinski? One Hero for Two Nations

1. Cf. Antal Szerb. *Magyar Irodalomtörténet* (History of Hungarian Literature—hereafter *Hung. Lit.*), Budapest 1934, 1978, p. 163.
2. Bogyay, *Grundzüge*, pp. 84ff.
3. V.-L. Tapié, *Die Völker unter dem Doppeladler,* Graz-Vienna-Cologne 1975, p. 154.
4. Text in Farkas (ed.), *Ungarns Geschichte und Kultur,* pp. 60–9.
5. *Krones Handbuch der österreichischen Geschichte,* p. 591.

Chapter 13 The Rebel Leader Thököly: Adventurer or Traitor?

1. Jenö Szücs, *Die drei historischen...,* p. 85.
2. Macartney, *Hungary,* p. 87.
3. Tapié, *Die Völker...,* p. 145.
4. Richard F. Kreutel (ed.), *Kara Mustafa vor Wien* (Kara Mustafa before Vienna), Graz-Vienna-Cologne 1955, pp. 83ff.
5. Béla Köpeczi, *Magyarország a kereszténység ellensége—A Thököly felkelés az európai közvéleményben* (Hungary the Enemy of Christendom—The Thököly Insurrection in the Public Opinion of Europe), Budapest 1976.

Chapter 14 Ferenc Rákóczi's Fight for Freedom from the Habsburgs

1. E. Zöllner, *Geschichte Österreichs* (History of Austria), p. 256.
2. Bogyay, *Grundzüge,* p. 87.
3. Macartney, *Hungary.*
4. Hóman and Szekfü, *Hung. Hist.,* vol. 4; Szekfü, *Der Staat Ungarn,* p. 263.
5. Jacob Burckhardt, *Reflections on History,* trans. M.D.H., London 1950.
6. Text in Farkas (ed.), *Ungarns Geschichte und Kultur,* pp. 78–84.
7. Ibid.; see also *II. Rákóczi Ferenc Emlékiratai* (The Memoirs of Ferenc Rákóczi II), Budapest 1979.

Chapter 15 Myth and Historiography: an Idol through the Ages

1. Domokos Kosáry, *Ujjáépitées és polgárosodás 1711–1867* (Reconstruction and Embourgeoisement 1711–1867—hereafter *1711–1867*),Budapest, 1990,pp. 29f.
2. Ibid.
3. Saint-Simon, *Memoires* (ed. Alfred de Boislisle), vol. 23. Paris 1971, pp. 259–61.
4. Kelemen Mikes, *Briefe aus der Türkei* (Letters from Turkey), Graz-Vienna-Cologne 1978, pp. 265–7.
5. Cf. Introduction and biography by Ferenc Glatz in the new edition of Szekfü's controversial work *Három nemzedék* (Three Generations), Budapest (1920)

1989, pp. i–xxxviii. See also Introduction and bibliography by Ferenc Glatz to the reprint (Budapest 1983) of Szekfü's *Forradalom után* (After the Revolution), first published in 1947.

6. Szekfü, *Forradalom után*, p. 156.

Chapter 16 Hungary in the Habsburg Shadow

1. Kosáry, *1711–1867*.
2. Moritz Csáky, *Von der Aufklärung zum Liberalismus* (From the Enlightenment to Liberalism). Vienna 1981, p. 13.
3. Macartney, *Hungary*, p. 99. Cf. also Kosáry, *1711–1867*.
4. John Paget, *Hungary and Transylvania with remarks on their condition, social, political and economical*, 2 vols, London (John Murray), 1839, pp. 41, 42–3, 45–6.
5. Homan and Szekfü, vol. 4, pp. 432, 460, 477.
6. Kálmán Benda on the "traitor" Sándor Károlyi in *História* (Hung.). Cf. also Kosáry, *1711–1867*.
7. Kosáry, *1711–1867*.
8. Robert A. Kann, *Geschichte des Habsburgerreiches* (A History of the Habsburg Empire 1526–1918), Vienna-Cologne-Graz 1977, pp. 80 and 217–19.
9. Miss (Julia) Pardoe, *City of the Magyar...*, 3 vols, London 1840, vol. 2, pp. 287–9.
10. Paget, op. cit., p. 60.
11. Stephan Vajda, *Felix Austria*, Vienna 1988, p. 48.
12. Henry Vallotton, *Maria Theresia*, Munich 1978, p. 48.
13. Quoted in Edward Crankshaw, *Maria Theresa*, London 1971, p. 94.
14. Vajda, *Felix Austria*, p. 378; Macartney, *Hungary*, p. 97. Cf. also Béla Grünwald, *A régi Magyarország* (Old Hungary), Budapest 1910.
15. Szekfü, *Hung. Hist.*, vol. 4, p. 494.
16. Julius Miskolczy, *Ungarn in der Habsburg Monarchie* (Hungary in the Habsburg Monarchy), Vienna 1959, p. 9.
17. Vallotton, *Maria Theresia*, p. 300.
18. Adam Wandruszka, *Das Haus Habsburg* (The House of Habsburg), Vienna-Freiburg 1978, p. 159.
19. Vallotton, *Maria Theresia*, p. 305.
20. Cf. Sinkó, "Arpad versus Saint Stephen", op. cit., pp. 70f.; Bogyay, *Grundzüge*, p. 95; Szekfü, vol. 4, pp. 573ff.
21. Cf. Grünwald, *A régi Magyarország*, op. cit.
22. The concept by Paul Ignotus, *Hungary*, London 1972, p. 44.
23. Szerb, *Hung. Lit.*, p. 206.
24. Paget, *Hungary and Transylvania*, op. cit., p. 177.
25. Gyula Farkas, *A magyar irodalom története* (History of Hungarian Literature), Budapest 1936, p. 104.
26. Cf. Kosáry, *1711–1867*; Bogyay, *Grundzüge*, pp. 98–100; Stöckl, *Osteuropa und die Deutschen*, p. 77.
27. Cf. Kosáry, *1711–1867*; Macartney, *Hungary*, p. 98.
28. Quoted in Grünwald, op. cit.
29. Kosáry, *1711–1867*.

514   *Notes*   [pp. 177–195]

Chapter 17   The Fight against the "Hatted King"

1. Tapié, *Die Völker under dem Doppeladler,* op. cit., p. 214.
2. Wandruszka, *Das Haus Habsburg,* pp. 172ff. Cf. François Fejtö, *Joseph II, Kaiser und Revolutionär* (Emperor and Revolutionary), Stuttgart 1956.
3. Quoted after Ludwig Némedi, "Deutsche aus ungarischer Sicht [Germans viewed by Hungarians]", *Ungarische Jahrbücher,* Berlin 1940, p. 46.
4. Benda and Fügedi, *Tausend Jahre Stephanskrone,* pp. 166–73.
5. Kosáry, *1711–1867;* Macartney, *Hungary,* p. 105.
6. Kosáry, *1711–1867,* pp. 155–6.
7. Grünwald, *A régi Magyarország,* op. cit.
8. Miskolczy, *Ungarn in der Habsburg Monarchie,* op. cit., p. 14.
9. Farkas (ed.), *Ungarns Geschichte und Kultur,* p. 407.
10. Quoted in Eckhardt, "Das Ungarnbild in Europa", op. cit.
11. Némedi, "Deutsche…", op. cit., p. 58.
12. Farkas, op. cit., p. 104.
13. *Ideen zur Philosophie der Geschichte der Menschheit* (Ideas on the philosophy of human history), book 16, Suphan edition, vol. XIV, Berlin 1909, p. 269.
14. Wandruszka, op. cit., p. 174.

Chapter 18   Abbot Martinovics and the Jacobin Plot: a Secret Agent as Revolutionary Martyr

1. Cf. Ágnes Hankiss, "Gábor Bethlen", op. cit., pp. 253–85; Szekfü, *Der Stadt Ungarn,* op. cit., pp. 90–4; Kálmán Benda, *A magyar Jakobinusok* (The Hungarian Jacobins), Budapest 1957.
2. Cf. Szekfü, *Der Staat Ungarn,* Benda, *A magyar Jakobinusok,* op. cit.
3. Szekfü, op. cit., pp. 94–7; Bogyay, pp. 101f.; Denis Silagi, *Ungarn und der geheime Mitarbeiterkreis Kaiser Leopolds II* (Hungary and Emperor Leopold II's secret circle of collaborators), Munich 1961.
4. Cf. Szekfü, op. cit., and Vilmos Fraknói, *Martinovics élete* (The Life of Martinovics), Budapest 1921.
5. Hankiss, "Gabor Bethlen", op. cit., esp. pp. 274–82.

Chapter 19   Count István Széchenyi and the "Reform Era": Rise and Fall of the "Greatest Hungarian"

1. Burckhardt, *Reflections on History,* pp. 218, 392f.
2. Szekfü, *Der Staat Ungarn,* p. 150.
3. Denis Sinor, *Hungary,* London 1959, p. 251.
4. György M. Vajda, *Wien und die Literaturen,* op. cit., p. 31.
5. Harold Steinacker, *Austro-Hungarica,* Munich 1963, pp. 27 and 277–80.
6. Kosáry, *1711–1867.*
7. Szerb, *Magyar Irodalomtörtenet,* pp. 259f.
8. Grünwald, ibid., p. 45.
9. Pardoe, ibid., pp. q74f.

10. George Barany, *Steven Széchenyi and the Awakening of Hungarian Nationalism 1791–1841*, Princeton, NJ 1968; Denis Silagi, *Der grösste Ungar. Graf Stephan Széchenyi* (Count Stephen Széchenyi, the Greatest Hungarian), Vienna-Munich 1967. Cf. Kosáry's essay in *A történelem veszedelmei* (The Dangers of History), Budapest 1987, and Széchenyi's diary (in Hung.), Budapest 1978.
11. See his *Diaries*, e.g. pp. 315–20.
12. Silagi, op. cit., p. 10.
13. Szekfü, *Der Staat Ungarn*, p. 151.
14. Quoted in Rosdy, *Sieben Versuchen...*, op. cit., pp. 78ff.
15. Silagi, op. cit., p. 24.
16. Ibid., p. 8.
17. Franz Grillparzer, *Werke*, vol. 5, p. 404.
18. 27 Aug. 1943, quoted in Rosdy, ibid.
19. Quoted according to Friedrich Kaintz, *Grillparzer als Dichter* (Grillparzer as poet), Vienna 1975, p. 614.
20. Ernst Joseph Görlich, "Grillparzer und Katona", *Ungarn-Jahrbuch*, 1971, vol. 3, pp. 123–34. For the case of Pyrker see also Szerb, *Hung. Lit.*, pp. 308–10.
21. Szerb, *Hung. Lit.*
22. Steinacker, *Austro-Hungarica*, pp. 277–80.
23. Quoted in Silagi, *Der grösste Ungar*, p. 40.
24. Cf. Rosdy, *Sieben Versuchen*.
25. Silagi, *Der grösste Ungar*, p. 45.
26. Quoted in György M. Vajda, *Wien und die Literaturen*, p. 125.
27. István Deák, *The Lawful Revolution: Louis Kossuth and the Hungarians, 1848–1849*, New York 1979.
28. Széchenyi's Diaries (Hung.), Appendix, pp. 1407–8.

Chapter 20 Lajos Kossuth and Sándor Petőfi: Symbols of 1848

1. *Népszabadság*, Budapest, 21.4.1992.
2. Deák, *Lawful Revolution*, p. 100.
3. Golo Mann, *Deutsche Geschichte im 19. und 20. Jahrhundert* (German History in the 19th and 20th Centuries), Frankfurt/Main 1958, p. 214.
4. A.J.P. Taylor, *The Habsburg Monarchy*, London 1947, p. 52.
5. Edward Crankshaw, *The Fall of the House of Habsburg*, London 1963, p. 31.
6. Franz Herre, *Franz Joseph von Osterreich*, Cologne 1978.
7. See esp. Domokos Kosáry, *Kossuth Lajos a reformkorban* (Lajos Kossuth in the age of reform), Budapest 1946, and Deák (ed.), *Kossuth Hagyaték* (Kossuth's legacy), esp. Robert Hermann on Kossuth's career, Budapest 1994, pp. 7–154 (Hung.). See also commemorative book for the 150th anniversary of Kossuth's birth, 2 vols, 1952.
8. See Andrew Janos, *The Politics of Backwardness in Hungary, 1825–1945*, Princeton, NJ, 1982.
9. See Miklós Szabolcsi (ed.), *A magyar sajtó története* (The history of the Hungarian press), 3 vols, Budapest 1970, esp. for this period Domokos Kosáry in vol. 1, pp. 665–714.

10. Quoted in Deák, *The Lawful Revolution*, p. 50.
11. Stephan Vajda, *Felix Austria*, p. 484.
12. Kosáry, *Kossuth Lajos*, p. 755.
13. Kosáry, *Kossuth in der Reformzeit* (Kossuth in the reform era).
14. Deák, op. cit., p. 61.
15. *Grillparzers Werke* vol. 1, pp. 13, 178ff. For the Revolution see Kann, ibid., pp. 275–91: Tapié, ibid., pp. 267–71. In his book published on the 150th anniversary of the 1848 Revolution a German historian even transforms Kossuth into a "Bohemian"!
16. See György Spira's summary in *Magyar Történelem* (Hungarian history) *1848–1890*, Budapest, vol. 1, pp. 59–435.
17. See Crankshaw, *The Fall*.
18. For details see Kosáry, *1711–1867*, ibid.; Deak, op. cit.; Spira, ibid.
19. Trans. in István Lázár, *Hungary: A Brief History*, chap. 10.
20. Spira (see n. 16); Deák, op. cit., Kosáry, *1711–1867*.
21. Translations from Gyula Illyes, *Petőfi*, by G.F. Cushing, Budapest 1973; pp. 284, 471.
22. For the chauvinist insinuations during the election campaign see a good compilation in *HVG*. Budapest, 30 May 1998. It should be noted that G.F. Cushing is an outstanding connoisseur of Hungarian literature in Britain.
23. See György Dalos' essay in *Lajos Kossuth*, Frankfurt 1998. On Petőfi *Mythos*, pp. 86f.

Chapter 21   Victories, Defeat and Collapse: The Lost War of Independence, 1849

1. Quoted in György M. Vajda, *Wien und die Literaturen...*, p. 124. Cf. also Deák, *Kossuth Hagyaték*, for the arrival, p. 73.
2. Quoted in Kosáry, *1711–1867*, p. 339.
3. Cf. Kosáry, *1711–1867*, and Deák, op. cit.
4. Kosáry, *1711–1867*, p. 344.
5. Cf. Bogyay, *Grundzüge*, op. cit., pp. 197–208.
6. Kann, *Geschichte*, p. 289. Almost verbatim also in Macartney.
7. See an excellent description in both of István Deák's books: *The Lawful Revolution* and *Beyond Nationalism: a Social and Political History of the Habsburg Officer Corps, 1848–1918*. London 1990.
8. Deák, *Beyond Nationalism*, pp. 34–5; see also *The Lawful Revolution*, pp. xvii–xviii and 141.
9. For details see, apart from Deák, also Tapié, Bogyay, Kosáry, Herre.
10. For the full text see Dalos (ref. in Ch. 20, n. 23).
11. Deák, *Beyond Nationalism*, p. 34.
12. Quoted by Dalos, op. cit., p. 62.
13. Cf. Kosáry, *1711–1867*; Deák, *The Lawful Revolution*; Robert Hermann, ibid.
14. Kann, *Geschichte*, pp. 275–82.
15. Ibid., p. 282.
16. "Der Magyarische Kampf" (The Magyar struggle), *Neue Rheinische Zeitung*, 13 Jan. 1849, in *MEW*, vol. 6, p. 165.

17. For an assessment see Kosáry, pp. 369–79; Bogyay, pp. 108f.; Kann, p. 287; Deák, op. cit.
18. Quoted in Deák, p. 38.
19. Ernst Hanisch, *Der kranke Mann an der Donau. Marx und Engels über Österreich* (The Sick Man on the Danube: Marx and Engels on Austria). Vienna–Munich–Zurich 1978, pp. 170–2.
20. Ibid.
21. Herre, *Franz Joseph*, op. cit., p. 88.
22. Alan Sked, *The Decline and Fall of the Habsburg Empire, 1815–1918*, London 1989, p. 101.
23. Zöllner, *Geschichte Österreichs*, op. cit., p. 398.
24. Deák, *Beyond Nationalism*, p. 329.
25. Text in *Ungarns Geschichte und Kultur*, ibid., pp. 119f.
26. Kosáry, *1711–1867*; Deák, *Beyond Nationalism*, p. 298.
27. For the role of the Jews see Béla Bernstein, *A negyvennyolcas szabadságharc és a zsidók* (The 1848 War of Independence and the Jews), with introduction by Mór Jókai, 1896, 2nd edn published 1939 (at the time of the "Jewish Laws") and 3rd after the collapse of Communism. Cf. Raphael Patai. *The Jews of Hungary: History, Culture, Psychology*, Detroit 1996, pp. 277–82.
28. Deák, *Beyond Nationalism*, p. 324.
29. Bogyay, op. cit., p. 111. Cf. also Kann, loc. cit., and Deák and Herre, loc. cit.
30. Kann, *Geschichte*, p. 315.

Chapter 22   Kossuth the Hero versus "Judas" Görgey: "Good" and "Bad" in sacrificial mythology

1. Domokos Kosáry, *A Görgey-kérdés története* (The history of the Görgey question—hereafter *Görgey*), Budapest 1994. If not otherwise indicated, most of the personal data about Görgey originate from this seminal work.
2. Cf. for the various disputes Deák, *The Lawful Revolution*, passim.
3. Ibid., p. 321.
4. Kann, *Geschichte*, p. 315.
5. Quote in Kosáry, *Görgey*.
6. For Szemere's attacks cf. Hanisch, *Der kranke Mann*, op. cit., pp. 211–18; Ambrus Miskolczy, "Kossuth, unser Zeitgenosse" (Kossuth, our contemporary), *Europäische Rundschau*, Vienna 99/4.
7. For details see Benda and Fügedi, ibid., pp. 188–97.
8. For the reprisal campaign see Deák, *Beyond Nationalism*, pp. 336–41.
9. Lajos Hatvany in his introduction to the publication *Agg Kossuth levelei egy fiatal leányhoz* (The aged Kossuth's letters to a young girl), Budapest 1919, p. 8.
10. See Robert Hermann, ref. in Ch. 20, n. 7; commemorative volume for the 150th anniversary of Kossuth birth, vols 1 and 2, 1952; Szekfü, *Az öreg Kossuth* (Kossuth in old age), *1867–1894*; Deák, *Beyond Nationalism*, pp. 342–6; Kosáry, *Görgey*.
11. Alexander Herzen, *My Past and Thoughts*, 4 vols, London 1968, vol. 3, p. 1038.
12. MEW, vol. 8, p. 392.
13. Ibid., p. 549.

14. Franz Pulszky, *Meine Zeit, mein Leben* (My times, my life), 3 vols, Pressburg-Leipzig 1882, p. 90, quoted in Hanisch, ibid., p. 404.
15. Tibor Frank, *Egy emigráns alakváltásai. Zerffi Gusztáv pályaképe* (The changing roles of an emigré: Gusztáv Zerffi's career), Budapest 1985; T. Frank, *Marx and Kossuth*, Budapest 1985 (in Hung.). All data from these two works and additional material from Hanisch, ibid., pp. 221ff.
16. See Szekfü and Kosáry in the Commemorative volume; Robert Hermann, op. cit.; Hóman and Szekfü, *Hung. Hist.*, vol. 5, pp. 452–6.
17. All quotes from Kossuth's original letters, see note 9.
18. Quoted by Tamás Katona in *Kossuth Lajos Irások és beszédek* (Lajos Kossuth's writings and speeches), Budapest 1994, p. 7.
19. John Lukacs, *Budapest 1900: a Historical Portrait of a City and its Culture*, London 1988, p. 120; Deák, ibid., p. 350; Ferenc Glatz, *A magyarok* (The Hungarians), ibid., Budapest 1996. p. 490.
20. Quoted from Robert Hermann, ref. in Ch. 20, n. 7.

Chapter 23 Who was Captain Gusev? Russian "Freedom Fighters" between Minsk and Budapest

1. Béla Fogarasi and Béla Illés, *Magyar-szovjet történelmi kapcsolatok* (Hungarian-Russian historical connections), Budapest 1945.
2. Ibid., pp. 31–4.
3. *Népszabadság*, 28 Jan. 1995.
4. Lehel Szeberényi, *The Poet and his Guardian Angel*, Budapest 1965 (in Hung.); Miklós Jovánovics, *Népszabadság*, 25 Mar. 1995.
5. Szeberényi, op. cit.
6. Gyula separate (Julius), *Born 1900: Memoirs*, London, 1974.
7. Tamás Aczél and Tibor Méray, *Tisztító Vihar* (Cleansing storm), London 1959, pp. 24–9 (in Hung.).

Chapter 24 Elisabeth, Andrássy and Bismarck: Austria and Hungary on the Road to Reconciliation

1. For the description of the festivities cf. Mór Jókai in *Österreichisch-ungarische Monarchie in Wort und Schrift: Ungarn* (Austro-Hungarian monarchy in words and writing: Hungary), vol. 3, pp. 163–8; Brigitte Hamann, *Elisabeth, Kaiserin wider Willen* (Elisabeth, the Reluctant Empress), Munich 1992, pp. 267–280, especially also for quotations from *Pester Lloyd* and eyewitnesses.
2. Heinrich Benedikt, "Die Casa d'Austria, das Reich und Europa" (The House of Austria, the German Reich and Europe) in Otto Schulmeister (ed.), *Spectrum Austriae*, Vienna 1980, p. 85.
3. Harold Steinacker, *Austro-Hungarica*, p. 281.
4. Tibor Simányi, *Julius Graf Andrássy*, Vienna, n.d.
5. Kann, *Geschichte*, p. 333.
6. Hamann, *Elisabeth*, pp. 267–72.

7. Ibid., pp. 274f.
8. István Lázár, *Kleine Geschichte Ungarns* (Hungary—a Brief History), Vienna 1990, p. 152.
9. Hamann, *Elisabeth*, pp. 241 and 248.
10. For his journalistic achievements see *A magyar sajtó története* (History of the Hungarian press), vol. II, 1–2.
11. On the renaming of Falk Street see *Helyek* (Places), Budapest 1998, pp. 95–8.
12. Katalin Sinkó, 'Zur Entstehung der staatlichen und nationalen Feiertage in Ungarn (1850–1991)' (On the origins of national holidays in Hungary) in Brix and Stekl, *Der Kampf um das Gedächtnis* (The fight for remembrance), Vienna-Cologne-Weimar 1997, pp. 251–71.
13. *HVG*, 25 July 1998. For Gödöllö cf. Brigitte Hamann and Elisabeth Hassmann, *Elisabeth—Stationen ihres Lebens* (Elisabeth—stages of her life), Vienna-Munich 1998, pp. 104–9.
14. Hamann, *Elisabeth*, p. 274.
15. Hamann, *Rudolf, Kronprinz und Rebell*, Vienna-Munich 1987, p. 303.
16. Simányi, *Andrássy*, p. 103.
17. Elisabeth von Österreich, *Tagebuchblätter von Consantin Christomanos* (Pages from C.C.'s diary), pp. 196, 205–7.

Chapter 25   Victory in Defeat: The Compromise and the Consequences of Dualism

1. Bela Király, *Ferenc Deák*, Budapest 1993, pp. 16f. (in Hung.)
2. Stadtmüller, ibid., p. 140.
3. Herre, *Franz Joseph*, pp. 228–36.
4. Hamann, *Elisabeth*, p. 261.
5. Robert Musil, *The Man without Qualities*, trans. Sophie Wilkins and Burton Pike, London: Picador, 1995, pp. 180 and 490–1.
6. Kann in *Spectrum Austriae*, op. cit., p. 123.
7. Tapié, *Die Völker...*, p. 301.
8. Friedrich Engel-Janosi and Helmut Rumpler (eds), *Probleme der franzisko-josephinischen Zeit 1848–1916*, Munich 1967. See also Péter Hanák, *Die Stellung Ungarns in der Monarchie* (Hungary's position in the monarchy), p. 84.
9. Quoted in B. Sutter, *Die Ausgleichsverhandlungen zwischen Osterreich und Ungarn 1867–1918* (Compromise negotiations between Austria and Hungary 1867–1918), 1968, pp. 71–111.
10. Adam Wandruszka and Peter Urbanitsch (eds), *Die Habsburgermonarchie*, vol. III, parts 1–2: *Die Völker des Reiches* (The people of the empire), Vienna 1980. For the quoted figures see Laszló Katus, *Die Magyaren*, pp. 410–88.
11. Macartney, *Hungary*, p. 173.
12. Quoted in Sked (see ref. in Ch. 21, n. 22), p. 234.
13. Hamann, *Elisabeth*, p. 227.
14. Engel-Janosi and Rumpler, *Probleme der franzisko-josephinischen Zeit*, op. cit., p. 76.
15. Hanák, *Die Stellung...*, op. cit.

16. Deák, *Beyond Nationalism*, p. 179. For the figure of ministerial personnel see Katus, p. 477.

17. Ignác Romsics, *Magyarország története a XX. Században* (Hungary's history in the twentieth century), Budapest 1999, p. 20.

18. Quoted in Simányi, *Andrássy*, p. 261.

19. Musil, *The Man without Qualities*, pp. 30–1.

20. Quoted in Jörg Hoensch, *Geschichte Ungarns 1867–1983* (A History of Hungary 1867–1983), Stuttgart 1984, p. 28.

21. Kann in *Spectrum Austriae*, op. cit., p. 126.

22. Johann Weber, *Eötvös und die ungarische Nationalitätenfrage* (Eötvös and the Hungarian nationalities question), Munich 1966, p. 101.

23. Ibid., pp. 141f. Cf also Katus, ibid., p. 410.

24. Quoted in Lajos Gogolák, "Ungarns Nationalitätengesetze und das Problem des magyarischen National- und Zentralstaates" (Hungary's nationalities laws and the problem of the Magyar national and central state) in *Die Habsburgermonarchie*, pp. 1263f.

25. Gusztáv Gratz, *A dualizmus kora* (The era of dualism), Budapest 1934, reprint 1992, 2 vols, vol. 2, p. 65.

Chapter 26   Total Blindness: The Hungarian Sense of Mission and the Nationalities

1. Quoted in John Lukács, *Budapest um 1900*, p. 126.

2. Gogolák, "Ungarns Nationalitätengesetze…", pp. 1263f.

3. Ibid., pp. 1288–9.

4. Lukács, op. cit., pp. 128–9.

5. Katus, *Die Magyaren*, pp. 483f. Cf. also Oszkár Jászi, *The Dissolution of the Habsburg Monarchy*, Chicago, 1929, pp. 279–81.

6. Gogolák, op. cit., pp. 1292f.

7. Quoted in Hamann, *Rudolf*, pp. 277f.

8. Ibid., p. 403.

9. Géza Jeszenszky, *Az elveszett presztízs* (The Lost Prestige), Budapest 1986, pp. 196 and 221.

10. Gogolák, op. cit.

11. Cf. Lajos Gogolák, *Mocsáry Lajos és a nemzetiségi kérdés* (Lajos Mocsáry and the nationalities question), Budapest 1943, quoted in Gogolák, *Monarchy*, ibid., pp. 1283f. For Mocsáry's abortive fight see also Gusztáv Gratz, *A dualizmus kora*, and Jászi, ibid.

12. Szerb, *Hung. Lit.*, p. 353.

13. Quoted in György M. Vajda, *Wien und die Literaturen…*, op. cit., pp. 95f.

14. Szerb, *Hung. Lit.*, pp. 313–15; Weber, *Eötvös*, op. cit., pp. 15 and 75.

15. Paul Valéry, *Works*, vol. 7a, Frankfurt 1995, p. 173.

16. Steinacker, *Austro-Hungarica*, p. 2.

17. Quoted in János M. Bak and Anna Gara-Bak, "The Ideology of a 'Millennial Constitution in Hungary'", *East Europe Quarterly*, XV/3, Sept. 1981.

18. Steinacker, op. cit., pp. 2f., 95.

19. Gratz, op. cit., vol. 2, pp. 370–2.
20. Szerb, *Hung. Lit.*, pp. 473–7.
21. Gratz, op. cit.

Chapter 27   The "Golden Age" of the Millennium: Modernization with Drawbacks

1. For details cf. László Tarr (ed.), *Az ezredév* (The Millennium), Budapest 1979; Ilona Sármány-Parson, "Ungarns Millenniumsjahr" in Brix and Stekl, *Der Kampf um das Gedächtnis* (The fight for the memory), pp. 273–91.
2. Ezredév, "Sie war nur eine Lehrerin" (She was only a school teacher), pp. 231–4.
3. Ibid., pp. 93f.
4. Iván Berend and György Ránki, *Hungary: A Century of Economic Development*, New York 1974, Berend and Ránki. *The Development of Manufacturing Industry in Hungary (1900–1944)*, Budapest 1960; Katus, *Die Magyaren*, Péter Hanák, ibid.
5. Berend and Ránki, *Hungary* Katus, op. cit.
6. Jászi, *The Dissolution of the Habsburg Monarchy.*
7. Mihály Károlyi, *Memoirs: Faith without Illusions*, London 1956.
8. Ibid.; Katus, op. cit. Cf. also article about the Esterházy exhibition by H.C. Kosler, "Immer treu zu Habsburg" (Always loyal to the Habsburgs), *Frankfurter Allgemeine Zeitung* (FAZ), 22 July 1995.
9. Károlyi, *Memoirs.*
10. Political archives of the Foreign Ministry, Bonn: Austria no. 92, vol. 1, Below-Hohenlohe of 20 June 1900, quoted by Péter Hanák in *Der Garten und die Werkstatt. Ein Kulturgeschichtlicher Vergleich Wien und Budapest um 1900* (The garden and the workshop: a historic-cultural comparison of Vienna and Budapest around 1900), Vienna-Cologne-Weimar 1992, p. 86.
11. Ibid.
12. Ibid.
13. Katus, op. cit.
14. Cf. Gyözö Concha, "A gentry" in *Budapesti Szemle*, 1910, vols 400–401, pp. 1–34, 173–99, from Katus, op. cit., Cf. also John Lukács, *Budapest um 1900*, and Andrew János, ebd.
15. Cf. Concha, op. cit., Lukács, op. cit., p. 89, and Ignotus, *Hungary*, pp. 80–8.
16. See Jókai in *Öst.-Ung. Monarchie*, and John Lukács, ibid., p. 99.
17. Lukács, ibid., p. 184n; Patai, ibid., pp. 379f. Ignotus, op. cit., Romsics, *Magyarország története…* (for ref. see Ch. 25, n. 17).
18. See the pioneering study by William O. McCagg Jr, *Jewish Nobles and Geniuses in Modern Hungary*, 2nd edn, Boulder, CO, and New York 1986. In the introduction to the 2nd edn the author stresses that he is neither a Hungarian nor a Jew; he was the first to use this question as a central theme after research visits to Hungary in 1966–7 and 1969. All historians of this period in general and of the relationship between Jews and Hungarians in particular, rely on his work.
19. Quoted in György M. Vajda, *Wien und die Literaturen…*, pp. 212–16.

20. Otto Friedländer, *Letzter Glanz der Märchenstadt* (The last sparkle of the fairytale city), Vienna 1977, pp. 130–5.
21. Cf. Katus, op. cit.; Lukács, ibid., p. 193.
22. Katus, op. cit.
23. Gyula Illyés, *Puszták Népe* (People of the Puszta), quoted from the German edn, Nördlingen, 1985, pp. 6f.
24. Iván T. Berend, "Budapest anno, metropolis in the East", *Népszabadság*, Budapest, 4 June 1997. Cf. also Katus, op. cit.; Lukács, ibid.
25. From the Parliamentary Bulletin, quoted in Ezredév, op. cit., pp. 206–8.
26. Katus, op. cit., p. 432. Cf. also Hanák, *Ungarn in der Donaumonarchie* (Hungary in the Danube monarchy), Vienna-Munich-Budapest 1984, pp. 284–91.
27. Hanák, ibid.
28. Sebastian Haffner, *Anmerkungen zu Hitler* (Comments on Hitler), Munich 1978, p. 128.

Chapter 28   "Magyar Jew or Jewish Magyar?" A Unique Symbiosis

1. Robert A. Kann, *Jewish Social Studies 1945*, quoted in George Barany, "Magyar Jew or Jewish Magyar?", *Canadian-American Slavic Studies*, spring 1974.
2. Quoted in Wolfgang Fleischer, *Das verleugnete Leben. Die Biographie des Heimito von Doderer* (The disowned life: the biography of Heimito von Doderer), Vienna 1996, p. 37.
3. Rolf Fischer, *Entwicklungsstufen des Antisemitismus in Ungarn 1867–1939* (Developmental stages of anti-Semitism in Hungary 1867–1939), Munich 1988, p. 9.
4. Katus, op. cit., Péter Hanák, *Zsidókérdés, asszimiláció, antiszemitizmus* (The Jewish question, assimilation, anti-Semitism), Budapest 1984, pp. 355–7.
5. Rolf Fischer, op. cit., pp. 32–5; Hamann, *Rudolf*, pp. 266f.
6. Viktor Karády, "Assimilation and social crisis" (in Hung.), *Világosság*, Budapest 1993/3.
7. Fischer, op. cit., pp. 36–8; Laszló Gonda. *A zsidóság Magyarországon* (The Jews in Hungary) *1526–1956*, Budapest 1992, pp. 162–9; Hanak, *Ungarn in der Donaumonarchie*, pp. 297–304; Tibor Erényi, *A zsidók története Magyarországon* (The history of the Jews in Hungary), Budapest 1996, pp. 49–55.
8. Andrew Janos, *The Politics of Backwardness* (for ref. see Ch. 20, n. 8), pp. 114–18.
9. Hoensch, *Geschichte Ungarns 1867–1983* (for ref. see Ch. 25, n. 20), pp. 40–1.
10. Fischer, *Entwicklungsstufen*, op. cit., p. 40.
11. Cf. the original text of Eckhardt's "Mi a magyar?" (Who is a Hungarian?) with the German-censored version in *Ungarische Jahrbücher*, Berlin 1942. See also the anti-Semitic outbursts of Farkas in *Das Ungarnbild des Deutschtums* (The Hungarian image in Germany). For Komlós see his essay (in Hung.) in *Magyar-zsidó szellemtörténet a reformkortól a Holocaustig* (Hungarian-Jewish intellectual history from the reform era to the Holocaust), 2 vols, vol. 2, pp. 291–311.
12. Cf. Paul Lendvai, *Antisemitismus ohne Juden* (Anti-Semitism without Jews), Vienna 1972, pp. 270–2; for personal experiences cf. the same author's *Blacklisted: a journalist's life in Central Europe*, London/New York, pp. 8–34.

13. Janos, op. cit., pp. 117 and 170–80.
14. Cf. Deák, *Beyond Nationalism*, p. 177.
15. Ibid., p. 236.
16. Komlós, op. cit. (n. 11 above).
17. Quoted in Janos, op. cit., p. 115n.
18. Patai, *The Jews of Hungary*, op. cit., pp. 344f.
19. Hanák, *The Garden*, op. cit.
20. See McCagg, *Jewish Nobles*, op. cit.; Janos, op. cit., pp. 112–14, 178; Patai, op. cit., pp. 368, 371.
21. McCagg and Patai, opp. cit.
22. McCagg, p. 32, points out that all data originate from the works of the National Socialist Klaus Schickert, *Die Judenfrage in Ungarn* (The Jewish question in Hungary), Essen 1937, and the anti-Semitic statistician Alajos Kovách, *A zsidóság térfoglalása Magyarországon* (The encroachment of Jews in Hungary), Budapest 1922.
23. Randolph Braham, *The Politics of Genocide: The Holocaust in Hungary*, rev. and enlarged edn, 2 vols, New York 1994, vol. 1, pp. 556–71; for the Kasztner case, vol. 2, pp. 1104–13. Cf. also *HVG*. Budapest, 10 Feb. 1996, pp. 67–69.
24. For Vámbéry cf. his memoirs *The Story of my Struggles*. See also Patai, op. cit., pp. 392–8, for Vámbéry, Goldziher and Munkácsi. Cf. also Goldziher's *Diary* (Hung.), Budapest 1984 (ed. Sándor Schreiber).
25. For hair-raising and abstruse ideas still being disseminated, see his pamphlet *Questions about our prehistory: False linguistic comparisons* (Hung.), Budapest 1998.

Chapter 29 "Will Hungary be German or Magyar?"
The Germans' Peculiar Role

1. Franz von Löher, *Die Magyaren und andere Ungarn* (The Magyars and other Hungarians), Leipzig 1874. For quotations see pp. 32, 170, 179, 188.
2. Ibid., p. 328.
3. Cf. Farkas, *Das Ungarnbild des Deutschtums*, op. cit., pp. 408f. See also the censored version of Eckhardt in *Ungarische Jahrbücher*, ibid.
4. Walter Weiss, Nikolaus Lenau in *Tausend Jahre Österreich* (ed. Walter Pollak), Vienna 1973, vol. 1, pp. 63–6.
5. Antal Mádl, *Auf Lenaus Spuren* (On the tracks of Lenau), Budapest-Vienna 1982.
6. Farkas and Eckhardt, opp. cit.
7. Miss Pardoe, *City of the Magyars*, 3 vols, London 1840, vol. 3, ch. XXL, pp. 340ff.
8. Details from Edouard Ritter von Liszt, *Franz Liszt. Abstammung, Familie, Begebenheiten* (Origins, family, events), Vienna-Leipzig 1937, pp. 6–9.
9. For a comprehensive essay see Friedrich Gottas, "Die Deutschen in Ungarn" (The Germans in Hungary) in *Die Habsburgermonarchie*, pp. 340–410.
10. Ibid., p. 382.
11. Ibid., p. 394.

12. Zöllner, *Geschichte Österreichs*, p. 420. For Bismarck's and Germany's policy on Hungary in the second half of the 19th century see István Diószegi, *Bismarck and Andrássy* (Hung.).
13. Rudolf Kiszling, *Erzherzog Franz Ferdinand von Österreich-Este*, Graz-Cologne 1953. Quotations on pp. 148f.
14. Hanák, *Der Garten*, op. cit., p. 85.
15. Janos, *Politics of Backwardness*, op. cit., p. 112.
16. List from Károly Manherz, *Die Ungarndeutschen*, Budapest 1998.

Chapter 30 From the Great War to the "Dictatorship of Despair": The Red Count and Lenin's Agent

1. Joseph Roth, *The Radetzky March*, trans. Joachim Neugroschel, London (Penguin), 1995, pp. 296–7.
2. Hugo von Hofmannstahl, *Ottavia Gräfin Degenfeld. Briefwechsel* (Correspondence with Countess Ottavia Degenfeld), Frankfurt, p. 304.
3. Mária Ormos, *Magyarország a két világháboru között, 1914–1945* (Hungary between the two world wars, 1914–1945), Budapest 1998, pp. 8–12; Romsics, ibid., p. 102: Manfried Rauchensteiner. *Der Tod des Doppeladlers. Österreich-Ungarn und der erste Weltkrieg* (Death of the Double Eagle: Austria-Hungary and the Great War), Graz-Vienna-Cologne 1993, pp. 68–74.
4. *Geschichte des Habsburgerreiches*, p. 381.
5. Ibid., p. 443. Other sources claim that Tisza struck the table with his fist. Cf. Ignotus, *Hungary*, p. 142. See also Jászi, *Magyariens Schuld*, op. cit.
6. Romsics, (for ref. see Ch. 25, n. 17), pp. 104f.
7. See Sked for "positive evaluations", ibid., pp. 308–30.
8. "Austria-Hungary" in *Cambridge Modern History* (1910), vol. 12: *The Latest Age*, pp. 174–212.
9. Romsics, op. cit., p. 101.
10. Kann, op. cit., p. 464.
11. Károlyi, *Memoirs* (Hung.), p. 136.
12. Paul Valéry, *Oeuvres* II: "Notre Destin et les Lettres" Paris 1957–60, pp. 1056–76.
13. Quote from Tibor Hajdu, biography of Károlyi (Hung.), Budapest 1982.
14. Quoted in Rauchensteiner, op. cit., p. 471.
15. Quoted in Lukacs, ibid., p. 112n.
16. Péter Hanák, "On Hungarian society at the beginning of the century" (Hung.), in *Történelmi Szemle*. Budapest 1962, pp. 210–45.
17. See Hajdu, Károlyi biography. See also Világosság special issue 1995/5; Jászi in *Magyarens Schuld—Ungarns Sühne, Revolution und Gegenrevolution in Ungarn* (The Magyars' guilt—Hungary's atonement, revolution and counter-revolution in Hungary). Munich 1923; for Károlyi's portrait see pp. 107–15.
18. Jászi, op. cit., pp. 56–9.
19. Hoensch, ibid., pp. 91f.
20. Cf. Rudolf L. Tökés, *Béla Kun and the Hungarian Soviet Republic*, Washington, DC 1967, p. 49; György Borsányi, *Béla Kun, Politikai Életrajz* (Political biography), Budapest 1974.

21. Jászi, op. cit., p. 59.
22. Quotation in Dan Diner, *Das Jahrhundert verstehen* (To understand the century), Munich 1999, p. 98.
23. Cf. Jászi, op. cit., pp. 107–15.
24. Ibid.
25. Cf. Thomas Sakmyster. *Hungary's Admiral on Horseback: Miklós Horthy 1918–1944.* Boulder, CO/New York 1994. See also Károlyi's Memoirs.
26. Cf. Diner, op. cit.
27. Romsics, op. cit., pp. 128f.; Bogyay, ibid., pp. 127f.
28. Romsics, op. cit., Tökés, *Bela Kun,* op. cit.
29. Tökés, ibid. For the reprisals against the family see the recollections of his wife, published in Budapest in 1966, pp. 418–20. She had spent nine years in a camp. In June 1937 Stalin rang Kun in his apartment and asked him (he had by then been removed from all his functions) to receive a French journalist, as the foreign press had reported his arrest. A few days later Kun was arrested.
30. For the loss of documents see Borsányi, *Bela Kun* (see n. 20 above).

Chapter 31   The Admiral on a White Horse: Trianon, Death Knell of St Stephen's Realm

1. See Ernest Gellner, *Nationalismus und Moderne,* Berlin 1991.
2. Romsics, Magyarország története (for ref. see Ch. 25, n. 17), pp. 152–5. On the economy after Trianon see *HVG*, Budapest, 7, 15, 22 July 1989.
3. Gusztáv Gratz, *A forradalmak kora* [The era of revolutions] *1918–1920,* Budapest 1935, pp. 238f.; Bogyay, ibid., p. 131.
4. Gratz, ibid.; Romsics, p. 145.
5. Romsics, ibid., pp. 139–41. See also Special issue *História,* "What happened at Trianon?", Budapest 1995., pp. 5f.
6. For estimates see Janos, ibid., p. 202n., Tökés, *Belakun,* op. cit., and Hajdu, biography of Károlyi, pp. 2128–34, and in *Népszabadság,* 20 Mar. 1999.
7. Bogyay, *Grundzüge,* p. 129: Hoensch, pp. 87–106; Borsányi and Erényi on the role of the Jews in the workers' movement in: Világosság, Budapest 92/2. The best work for the reform generation: Zoltán Horváth, *Die Jahrhundertwende in Ungarn* (The turn of the century in Hungary), Neuwied 1966. For the lynch-law of the "White Terror" see Jászi, *Magyariens Schuld,* ibid., pp. 167–79.
8. *Neue Post,* Budapest, 22 Jan. 1920, quoted in Rolf Fischer, *Antisemitismus,* p. 14.
9. *Pester Lloyd,* 17 Nov. 1919. Budapest, quoted in Rolf Fischer, ibid., p. 131. Cf. also Peter Gosztony, *Miklós von Horthy,* Göttingen 1973, p. 27.
10. Miklós Horthy, *Memoirs* (in Hung.), Budapest, p. 80.
11. The most balanced version is in Sakmyster, *Hungary's Admiral,* pp. 91–122. For Horthy's rose-tinted description see his *Memoirs,* pp. 147–62. For a spiteful, diametrically opposite version see Erich Feigl, ed., *Kaiserin Zita. Legende und Wahrheit* (Empress Zita, legend and reality), Vienna 1978, pp. 456–96.
12. Sakmyster, ibid., pp. 1–29; Horthy, *Memoirs,* pp. 9–114.
13. Cf. Anton Lehár, *Gegenrevolution und Restaurationsversuche in Ungarn, 1918–1921* (Counter-revolution and restoration attempts in Hungary), Munich

1973, and Pál Prónay, extracts (in Hung.) from his posthumously published diaries, Budapest 1963.

14. Ignotus, ibid., pp. 149–60; István Deák, 'Nikolaus von Horthy, Admiral und Reichsverweser' in *Europäische Rundschau*, Vienna 94/2, pp. 71–85. See also Sakmyster, op. cit.

15. Rolf Fischer, op. cit., p. 134; Hoensch, pp. 99–111. Romsics mentions more than 1,000 ("possibly" 2,000) victims, ibid., p. 132. See also Janos, *Politics of Backwardness*, p. 202n.

16. Sakmyster, op. cit., pp. 52–6.

17. Rolf Fischer, op. cit., pp. 134, 146f. See also Janos, *Politics of Backwardness*.

18. Sakmyster, op. cit., pp. 136f.

19. For a comprehensive analysis see Braham, *Politics of Genocide* (for ref. see Ch. 28, n. 23), vol. 1, pp. 16–32, works by Rolf Fischer, Ignotus, Hoensch, and Romsics, ibid., pp. 194f. See also Gyula Juhász, *Uralkodó eszmék Magyarországon* (Ruling ideas in Hungary), Budapest 1983.

20. Quotations in Sakmyster, in sequence: pp. 147f., 152, 422.

21. Fischer, ibid., p. 146. See also Kosáry's interview in *Europai utas*, Budapest (January 1998) on "Turanist" ideas: "We must not become insane—such visions are sure signs of wounds caused by historical trauma."

22. Lukács, ibid., pp. 139–41.

23. *Nemzeti Ujság*, 26 Oct. 1920, Public Speech, quoted in Fischer, ibid., p. 111.

24. Deák (Rundschau), ibid., Cf. also his review of Sakmyster's book in *New York Review of Books*, 8 April 1999.

25. For an assessment of the Bethlen Era see Sakmyster, op. cit., pp. 123–66: Ignotus, *Hungary*, pp. 157–63; Hoensch, ibid., pp. 106–122. For a comprehensive analysis see Romsics, *Bethlen István*, Budapest 1999 (Hung.).

26. Romsics, *Magyarország története* (Hungary's history), pp. 190–200.

27. Quoted in Gosztonyi, ibid., p. 96.

28. Quoted in Sakmyster, op. cit., pp. 320f. There are numerous versions in Hungary herself, embellished according to demand.

Chapter 32 Adventurers, Counterfeiters, Claimants to the Throne: Hungary as Trouble maker in the Danube Basin

1. For the "White International" see Sakmyster, ibid., pp. 64–8: Bernard Wasserstein. *The Secret Lives of Trebitsch Lincoln*, London 1988, pp. 159–74: Endre Gömöri. *Die Wahrheit über Trebitsch* (The truth about Trebitsch), Berlin 1985, pp. 146–63. For the German background see Hagen Schulze, *Weimar, Deutschland, 1917–1933*, Berlin, pp. 212–20.

2. Bernard Wasserstein, op. cit. The following details were taken from this, by far the best biography of Trebitsch.

3. Cf. for Hungarian details Gömöri, op. cit., pp. 5f., 218–20.

4. For the background and details cf. *Bethlen István titkos papirjai* (István Bethlen's secret papers), ed. Miklós Szinai—László Szücs, Budapest 1972, pp. 34f., 60f.,

222–33, 237f.; Gyula Juhász, *Magyarország külpolitikája* [Hungary's foreign policy] *1919–1945*. Budapest 1988, pp. 102f.; L. Nagy Zsuzsa, *Bethlen liberális ellenzéke* (Bethlen's liberal opposition). Budapest 1980, pp. 155–65: Romsics, *Bethlen*, pp. 194–8; Ignotus, *Hungary*, pp. 161f.

5. Viscount Rothermere, *My Campaign for Hungary*, London 1939: Pál Nádori, "Lord Rothermere akció" (Hung.) in *ELTE Aktái* 1968/10, pp. 91–118: Miklós Zeidler. *A Magyar Reviziós Liga Trianontól Rothermereig* (The Hungarian League for Revision from Trianon to Rothermere), Századok, Budapest 1990, p. 5f.

6. For all articles and explanations of and by Rothermere 1927/8 see the book by Lajos Léderer, correspondent of the *Pesti Hirlap* (Hung.), Budapest 1928.

7. Quoted in Franz Hohenlohe, *Stephanie. Das Leben meiner Mutter* (Stephanie: the life of my mother), Vienna 1991, p. 50, and Rudolf Stoiber and Boris Celovsky, *Stephanie von Hohenlohe. Sie liebte die Mächtigen der Welt* (Stephanie von Hohenlohe: She loved the powerful of this world), Munich–Berlin 1988, p. 76. See the two books, esp. the second one, also for the Princess's life and her relationship with Rothermere.

8. Quoted in Stoiber and Celovsky, *Stephanie*, p. 173. For copies of Rothermere's letters, congratulatory telegrams and messages to Hitler and his replies, see Hohenlohe, ibid., pp. 156f., 164–70, 172–4.

9. For Harmsworth's visit to Hungary see Stoiber and Celovsky, p. 75: Miklós Vásárhelyi. *A lord és a korona* (The lord and the crown), Budapest, no date; András D. Bán, "King Radomir" (Hung.), in *2000*, Budapest, October 1990.

10. For the machinations around the crown, cf. Rothermere, ibid., pp. 93–7, 133–45; Stoiber—Celovsky, ibid., pp. 78f. For the reports of the Hungarian ambassadors from London and Rome Nádori, ibid., pp. 106–9; Bethlen's secret files, ibid., pp. 314f., 335–49. For Rothermere's contacts see his book, pp. 175–90. Cf. also Magda Ádám. *Richtung Selbstvernichtung. Die Kleine Entente, 1920–1938* (Direction self-destruction: The Little Entente 1920–1938), Budapest-Vienna 1988, pp. 76–9; Zeidler, ibid., pp. 110–15; L. Zsuzsa Nagy, ibid., pp. 182–7. See also *HVG*, 6 Sept. 1997, pp. 89–91.

11. William M. Johnston, *The Austrian Mind: an Intellectual and Social History 1948–1938*, Berkeley and Los Angeles 1983, p. 347.

Chapter 33 Marching in Step with Hitler: Triumph and Fall. From the Persecution of Jews to Mob Rule

1. Cf. Loránt Tilkovszky, *Teleki Pál titkos halála* (Pál Teleki's mysterious death), Budapest 1989. For Teleki's personality and politics see Anton Czettler, *Pál Graf Teleki und die Aussenpolitik Ungarns, 1939–1941* (Count Pál Teleki and Hungary's foreign policy, 1939–1941), Munich 1996.

2. Dated 3 March 1941, in Lajos Kerekes (ed.), *Allianz Hitler—Horthy—Mussolini. Dokumente zur ungarischen Aussenpolitik (1933–1944)* (The Hitler-Horthy-Mussolini alliance, documents on Hungarian foreign policy), Budapest, p. 289.

3. Quoted in Czettler, op. cit., p. 33, and Tilkovszky, op. cit., pp. 106f.

4. Sakmyster, *Hungary's Admiral*, p. 261.
5. Quoted in Manfred Nebelin, *Deutsche Ungarnpolitik, 1939–1941*, Opladen 1989, p. 149.
6. Ibid., p. 142.
7. Cf. Gyula Juhász in *História*, Budapest 92/1, pp. 8–10, and Romsics, pp. 246f.
8. Romsics, p. 256; also Hoensch, p. 148. See also Iván T. Berend and György Ránki, *Magyarország a fasiszta Németország életterében* (Hungary in the economic sphere of fascist Germany), Budapest 1960, p. 189.
9. Juhász, op. cit.; Romsics, pp. 249f.
10. See Raoul Hilberg, *Die Vernichtung des europäischen Judentums* (The destruction of European Jewry), Frankfurt 1994, vol. 2, pp. 859–927; cf. Randolph Braham, *Politics of Genocide*, op. cit. Also Christian Gerlach and Götz Aly, *Das letzte Kapitel. Der Mord an den ungarischen Juden* (The last chapter: the murder of the Hungarian Jews), Stuttgart, 2002.
11. Quoted in György Ránki. *A harmadik birodalom árnyékában* (In the shadow of the Third Reich), Budapest 1988, p. 211.
12. In *Tiszatáj*, December 1998, pp. 78f., cf. also his book *Mi magyarok* (We Hungarians), Budapest 1989, pp. 16–19 and 465–7.
13. István Bethlen's memoirs (Hung.), ed. Ignác Romsics, Budapest 1988, pp. 132–6.
14. Quoted in Ignotus, ibid., p. 186.
15. Horthy, *Memoirs*, p. 231.
16. Janos, *Politics of Backwardness*, p. 232n.
17. Horthy, *Memoirs*, and Margit Szöllösi-Janze, *Die Pfeilkreuzlerbewegung in Ungarn* (The Arrow Cross movement in Hungary), Munich 1989, p. 103. The name of the deputy was Dezsö Sulyok, cf. his memoirs *Zwei Nächte ohne Tag* (Two nights without a day), Zurich 1948.
18. Cf. István Bibó, *Zur Judenfrage* (On the Jewish question), Frankfurt 1990, pp. 32f. This long essay, published in 1948, is probably still the best contribution to this topic, not least because it was written not by a Jew, a Communist or a Socialist, but by a progressive bourgeois thinker.
19. Cf. Szöllösi-Janze, op. cit., p. 133.
20. Hoensch, p. 147; see also Juhász, op. cit. (see n. 7 above).
21. Cf. Juhász, ibid., p. 10.
22. Horthy, *Memoirs*, pp. 262–4.
23. Romsics, p. 263.
24. *Goebbels Tagebücher* (Diaries), 8 May 1943; Braham, ibid., pp. 240f.; Horthy, op. cit., pp. 373–86. See Peter Longerich, "Ungarn—Das letzte Kapitel" in *Eine Gesamtdarstellung der nationalsozialistischen Judenverfolgung* (Hungary—the last chapter, in: An overall picture of the National Socialist persecution of the Jews), Munich-Zurich 1998, pp. 565–70.
25. Cf. György Ránki, *1944 Marcius 19. Magyarország német megszállása* (19 March 1944. Hungary's occupation by Germany), Budapest 1978.
26. Ránki, ibid.; see also Lorant Tilkovszky, *Bajcsy-Zsilinszky*, Budapest 1986 (Hung.).
27. Braham, op. cit., vol. II, pp. 1189–1201.
28. Deák, *Rundschau* (for ref. see Ch. 31, n. 14), pp. 82, 85.
29. Romsics, pp. 267f.

30. *Braham*, vol. II, pp. 1143–7; László Varga, "Ungarn" in Wolfgang Benz (ed.), *Dimensionen des Völkermordes* (Dimensions of the genocide), Munich 1991, pp. 331–43.
31. Romsics, p. 265.
32. Deák, ibid., pp. 84f.

Chapter 34   Victory in Defeat: 1945–1990

1. Sándor Vida (ed.), *Pártkongresszusok és pártkonferenciák* (Party congresses and party conferences) *1918–1980*, Budapest 1985, pp. 41–8.
2. László Gyurkó, *Arcképvázlat történelmi háttérrel* (Portrait sketch with historical background), Budapest 1992, pp. 68–70 and 118f. Miklós Molnár, *De Béla Kun à János Kádár*, Paris 1987, pp. 105, 115.
3. *Szabad Nép* (A Free People), "Open word on the Jewish question", 25 Mar. 1945, Budapest. For the political machinations of anti-Semitism cf. János Pelle, *Az utolsó vérvádak* (The last ritual murder accusations), Budapest 1995.
4. *Recollections of an Historian of Ideas: Conversations with Isaiah Berlin*, Scribner's, New York. Cited from pp. 52 and 184 of German edn, *Den Ideen die Stimme zurückgeben*, Frankfurt, 1994.
5. "Wozu Geschichte?" (Why history?) in *Der Monat*, December 1967.
6. Unless otherwise noted, all details from the two Rákosi biographies by Árpád Pünkösti, Budapest 1992 and 1996.
7. Julius Hay, *Geboren 1900* (Born 1900), Hamburg 1971, p. 249.
8. Cf. Pünkösti, see n. 6 above.
9. Cf. János Nemes, *Rákosi Mátyás születésnapja* (Mátyás Rákosi's birthday), Budapest 1988, pp. 109–10.
10. Cf. Arkadi Waksberg, *Gnadenlos, Andrei Wischinski—der Handlanger Stalins* (Andrey Vishinsky—Stalin's henchman), Bergisch Gladbach 1991, pp. 231f., 388f. See János M. Rainer in the 1998 *Yearbook* of the 1956 Institute: Telegram to Comrade "Filippov" and Rákosi's messages to Stalin's secretariat, pp. 103, 119 (Hung.).
11. Cf. Georg Hermann Hodos, *Schauprozesse, Stalinistische Säuberungen in Osteuropa* (Show trials, Stalinist purges) *1948–1954*, Frankfurt 1988; Paul Lendvai, *Blacklisted: A Journalist's Life in Central Europe*, London and New York, 1998, esp. pp. 98–122.
12. Vladimir Farkas, *Nincs mentség, az ÁVH alezredese voltam* (No excuse: I was a lieutenant colonel in the ÁVH), Budapest 1990.
13. Cf. Klára Szakasits, *Fent és lent, 1945–1950* (Up and down, 1945–1950), Budapest, 1985.
14. Romsics, ibid., op. cit. p. 344.
15. Ibid., p. 341.
16. Molnár, ibid., p. 290.
17. Romsics, ibid., p. 344. Cf. János M. Rainer, "Stalin and Rákosi" in *Yearbook 1998*, 1949–1953, pp. 98–100 (in Hung.).
18. Cf. Farkas, *No excuse*, Yearbook, pp. 116f.
19. About the dilemmas of a book on Kádár, cf. A. Pünkösti's talk with Tibor Huszár about his work on a Kádár biography, in *Mozgó Világ*, 97/11, Budapest (in Hung.).

20. Ibid. Cf. Farkas, *No excuse.*
21. Quoted in Paul Lendvai, *Das eigenwillige Ungarn* (Independent Hungary), 2nd edn, Zurich-Osnabrück 1988, p. 61.
22. Nemes, *Rakosi,* op. cit.
23. Farkas, *No excuse*: Pünkösti, ibid. Cf. C. Andrew and Oleg Gordievski, *KGB,* London 1990, pp. 292f., 338f., 346. Háy claims in his memoirs that Péter was also involved in recruiting in Vienna Kim Philby, the infamous British spy, for the KGB.
24. Elias Canetti, *Das Gewissen der Worte* (The conscience of words), Frankfurt/ Main 1981, p. 35.
25. Cf. Mária Ember. "The Swedish ambassador reports from Vienna to Stockholm" in *Yearbook 1998,* pp. 193–213 (in Hung.).
26. János M. Rainer, *Imre Nagy,* political biography (in Hung.), vol. I: *1896–1953,* Budapest 1996, see esp. pp. 199–213.
27. V. Szereda and J.M. Rainer, *Döntés a Kremlben 1956* (Decision in the Kremlin 1956: the discussions of the Soviet presidium about Hungary), Budapest 1996; V. Szereda and A. Sztikalin, *Hiányzó lapok 1956 történelméböl* (Missing pages from the history of 1956 [documents from the archives of the former Central Committee of the Communist Party of the USSR]), Budapest 1993.
28. László Gyurkó, 1956, *Budapest 1996,* pp. 388–97 (in Hung.). Cf. Géza Alföldy, *Ungarn 1956,* Heidelberg 1997, pp. 113–15.
29. Háy, *Geboren 1900,* p. 316.
30. Ibid., p. 320.
31. Cf. Paul Lendvai, "Zehn Jahre danach" (Ten years after) in *Der Monat,* October 1966, also in Paul Lendvai, *Grenzen des Wandels* (The limits of change), Vienna 1977, p. 63.
32. Ibid., p. 69.
33. Lendvai, *Blacklisted,* pp. 251f. Cf. Romsics, ibid., for travels to so-called Socialist countries (1960: 300,000, 1980 5.2 million!), p. 422.
34. Cf. Gyurkó, *Arcképvázlat* (Portrait sketch), ibid.
35. Christoph Reinprecht, *Nostalgie und Amnesie,* Vienna 1996, pp. 126f., 184f. Cf. *Népszabadság,* 26 June 1999, p. 24.

Chapter 35 "Everyone is a Hungarian": Geniuses and Artists

1. McCagg, *Jewish Nobles,* op. cit. (for ref. see Ch. 27, n. 10), pp. 15f.
2. Laura Fermi, *Illustrious Immigrants,* Chicago-London 1968, p. 57.
3. György Marx, *The Voice of the Martians,* Budapest 1994, pp. 17–42, 79–95.
4. Ibid., p. 58.
5. Norman Macrae, *John von Neumann,* New York 1992, p. 250; Marx, ibid., pp. 120–8.
6. György Marx, "The tracks of Hungarian scientists in the 20th century" (Hung.) in *História,* Budapest 99/4. For Hungarian Nobel laureates see Mihály Beck, ibid., 97/2.
7. Cf. Paul Hoffmann, *Der Mann, der die Zahlen liebte* (The man who loved numbers), Berlin 1999.
8. Katus in *The Habsburg Monarchy,* vol. III, p. 423.

9. Emil Lengyel, *Americans from Hungary*, New York 1948. For details see also Georg Köváry, *Ein Ungar kommt selten allein* (A Hungarian seldom arrives on his own), Vienna 1984. p. 162.

10. Lengyel, ibid., p. 214.

11. István Nemeskürty, *Wort und Bild, Die Geschichte des ungarischen Films* (Word and picture: history of the Hungarian film), Budapest-Frankfurt 1980, pp. 33–46.

12. Köváry, op. cit., p. 164.

13. Nemeskürty, *Wort und Bild*, p. 65. For Korda see esp. pp. 34f.

14. *Népszabadság*, Budapest, 20 Dec. 1995.

15. *The Times*, London, 4 Aug. 1998; *FAZ*, 5 Aug. 1998; *Süddeutsche Zeitung*, 5 Aug. 1998.

16. For details on the family cf. *Tony Curtis: The Autobiography*, New York 1993.

17. Georg Köváry, *Der Dramatiker Franz Molnár*, Innsbruck 1984, pp. 42f.; cf. also Emil Lengyel, *Americans from Hungary*; Ladislas Farago, *Strictly from Hungary*, New York 1962, pp. 11–37; Friedrich Torberg, *Tante Jolesch*, Munich 1977, pp. 168–83.

18. Torberg, ibid.

19. Quoted by Köváry, ibid., pp. 129f.

20. Quoted in George Tábori, *Theaterstücke I*, Frankfurt 1994.

21. Cf. Peter von Becker, *Diese Stücke—ein Leben. Über George Tábori* (These plays—a life: about George Tábori), ibid., pp. vii–xxi.

22. David Cesarini, *Arthur Koestler*, London 1994, p. 446.

23. Letters quoted from Vilmos Juhász, in *Magyar Album*, ed. Sándor Incze, American Hungarian Studies Foundation, Elmshurst College, Elmshurst, IL, 1956, pp. 8–21.

24. Quoted by Ferenc Bónis in *Neue Zürcher Zeitung*, 3 Apr. 1998, international edn, p. 54.

25. Thomas Schacher in *Neue Zürcher Zeitung*, 18 Oct. 1997, int. edn, p. 53.

26. *HVG*, Budapest, 16 May 1998, pp. 101f.

27. Interview in *Neue Zürcher Zeitung*, 13 June 1998, int. edn, pp. 49f., and *Süddeutsche Zeitung*, 20 June 1998.

28. See *Solti on Solti: A Memoir*, London 1998, pp. 241–2.

29. Quoted in the stimulating book by the cultural historian Moritz Csáky, *Ideologie der Operette und Wiener Moderne. Ein kulturhistorischer Essay* (The ideology of operetta and the Viennese Modern, a cultural-historical essay), Vienna-Cologne-Weimar 1998, pp. 215f. For the "Varasdin forgery" see ibid., pp. 293f.

30. Numerous books have been written on and by Lukács. On the man himself cf. Éva Fekete and Éva Karádi, *Georg Lukács. Sein Leben in Bildern, Selbstzeugnissen und Dokumenten* (His life in pictures, personal testimonies and documents), Stuttgart 1981.

31. Cf. Peter Weibel (ed.), *Jenseits von Kunst* (Beyond art), Vienna 1997, pp. 12–15, 67–81; Eva Bajkay, *Die Ungarn am Bauhaus*, pp. 82–6.

32. Lee Congdon, *Exile and Social Thought: Hungarian Intellectuals in Germany and Austria*, Princeton, NJ 1991. See also Mary Gluck, *Georg Lukács and his Generation, 1900–1918*, Cambridge, MA, 1985.

33. Quoted by Catherine David, *Moholy-Nagys experimenteller Einsatz* (Moholy Nagy's experimental commitment) in Weibel, ibid., pp. 87–92. See also the anthology *László Moholy-Nagy. 100 Foto*, Budapest 1995 (Hung.).

34. Cf. *Ungarische Avantgarde in 20. Jahrhundert. Ausstellungskatalog* (exhibition catalogue), Linz 1998, pp. 186–231.

35. *Le Monde des Livres*, Paris, 21 Nov. 1987, Jean-François Chévrier, "Brassaï à l'écrit".

36. *HVG*, Budapest, 6 June 1998, pp. 95–7, *FAZ*, 4 Jan. 1997.

37. *The Times*, London, 18 Nov. 1997; *FAZ*, 20 Jan. 1997; *Süddeutsche Zeitung*, 22 Feb. 1996; *Der Spiegel*, 48/1997.

38. Emil Lengyel, *Americans from Hungary*, pp. 84–92; *Népszabadság*, 12 Apr. 1997, 22 Apr. 1997, 2 May 1997; *Die Furche*, Vienna, 14 May 1998; *Illustrierte Neue Welt*, Vienna, April 1997, p. 19.

39. Cf. Paul Harmat, *Freud, Ferenczi und die ungarische Psychoanalyse*, Tübingen 1988; *Neue Zürcher Zeitung*, int. edn, 15–16 Mar. 1997; ibid., 3 Dec. 1996, pp. 33–52. Ferenc Erös, "Über die Geschichte der Psychoanalyse in Ungarn" in Weibel, *Jenseits von Kunst*, pp. 627–30. Cf. also Patrizia Giamperi-Deutsch about the Freud-Ferenczi correspondence, ibid., pp. 621–6. The Malamud quotation in *História*, Budapest, p. 29.

40. Richard Crossman, *The Diaries of a Cabinet Minister*, vol. 1, London 1975; Roy Jenkins, *A Life at the Centre*, London 1991, p. 41; George Weidenfeld, *Remembering My Good Friends*, London 1994, p. 331.

41. *Cf. George Soros im Gespräch mit Krisztina Koenen*, Frankfurt 1994; Connie Bruck, "The World According to Soros", *New Yorker*, February 1995, pp. 54–78; *Time*, 10 July 1995; George Soros, *The Crisis of Global Capitalism*, New York 1998; interview with *Der Spiegel*, 51/1998; Robert Slater, *The Life, Times, and Trading Secrets of the World's Greatest Investor*, New York 1995; *Time*, 28 Apr. 1997; *The Economist*, London, 25 Oct. 1997; *News*, Vienna, 21/1999. For his activities in Hungary cf. *Népszabadság*, 3 Apr. 1996, p. 29.

42. Cf. *Time*, 29 Dec. 1997–5 Jan. 1998; Interview with *Die Zeit*, 15 Aug. 1997; Andy Grove, *Only the Paranoid Survive*, New York 1996.

Significant Dates in Hungarian History

ca. 3000–2000 BCE
Dissolution of the Finno-Ugrian-speaking group of peoples.

ca. 1550 BCE
Dissolution of the Ugrian-speaking community.

1000–500 BCE
Period of the first Hungarians.

500–900 CE
Development of a Hungarian tribe within the domain of the West Turkic and Khazar peoples.

ca. 830
Establishment of the first Hungarian principality between the Don and Lower Danube. Separation from the Khazar empire.

892
Magyars link up with the Frankish king Arnulf in a punitive campaign against Prince Svatopluk of Moravia (the Legend of the White Horse).

894
Simeon the Great of Bulgaria attacks Byzantium, which asks for Magyar assistance, while the Bulgarians link up with the Pechenegs.

895–6
Defeated by the Pechenegs in Transylvania, the Magyars under the leadership of Árpád settle the Great Plain and Pannonia.

899–968
Plunder forays into Central and Western Europe as far as Spain and Italy.

906

Magyars destroy Moravia, creating room for their own state.

924

Magyars invade Saxony, and retreat only against payment of tribute.

933

Defeated by Henry I at Merseburg; end of tribute payments.

943

Magyar plunder raid as far as the walls of Constantinople.

955

Magyars decisively defeated by Otto the Great at the Lechfeld near Augsburg. Settling down process under Árpád's grandson Taksony (955–72) who puts an end to raids and initiates first contacts with Rome. The Pope sends first missionaries. Organised conversions to Christianity, however, only....

975

...during the reign of Prince Géza (972–7), who invites Bavarian monks into the country. Bruno of St Gallen becomes first Bishop of Hungary.

995

Géza's son Vajk, baptised Stephan (István), marries Gisela, daughter of Henry the Quarrelsome, Duke of Bavaria. Increasing German influence.

1000

Coronation of St Stephen I (997–1038). Opting for Roman Catholicism (and the West). Archbishopric of Györ established. County system introduced.

1025

Emperor Conrad II cedes region between the rivers Fischa and Leitha to Hungary.

From 1038

End of central power under Stephen's nephew Peter I Orseolo (1038–41, 1044–6). Vassalage to Holy Roman Empire. Cuman and Pecheneg incursions.

1058

Andrew I (András) (1046–60) declares independence from the Holy Roman Empire. Reassertion of royal power under Béla I (1060–3) and Géza I (1074–7) in the aftermath of pagan revolts and throne upheavals.

1091

Part of Slavonia and Croatia annexed by Hungary during the reign of St Ladislas (László) (1077–95). Reforms of church and state ordered by Pope Gregory VII.

1102

Dalmatian coast (threatened by Venice) and part of Croatia freely submit to Hungarian "protection". Coloman I (Kálmán) (1095–1116) first King of both countries. Byzantium attempts to gain influence in Hungary and force its withdrawal from the Adriatic. Hungary turns towards Bohemia and Austria and Western culture. Settlement of "Saxons" in Transylvania (Hermannstadt) and the Zips. Formation of lower service nobility.

1162

Following the death of Géza II (1141–62) renewed struggles between pretenders to the throne. Byzantine support for Béla III (1172–96), son-in-law of Emperor Manuel I Comnenos, creates basis for later feudalism.

1182

Reconquest of southern provinces. Byzantine interests in Balkans protected by Hungary. Expansion of towns and foreign trade. Cultural orientation towards Italy and France, troubadours at the Hungarian royal court. Flourishing architecture. Béla's son Andrew II (1205–35), father of St Elizabeth of Thuringia, under pressure (following a hopeless war against Galicia) enacts....

1222

...the Golden Bull, giving nobles the right of armed resistance if rulers are in breach of treaty, exemption from taxation, and release from taking part in wars beyond the borders.

1224

Right of self-administration *(Andreaneum)* for Transylvania's Saxons.

1225

Expulsion of Teutonic Knights as they attempt to establish a state within a state. Henceforth Premonstratensian and Cistercian orders in the country bring French influence assisted by the Crusades.

1241

Béla IV (1235–70) defeated by Mongol horsemen. Hungary depopulated and devastated. Central authority weaker but townships on the rise, becoming the protectors of the throne. New settlement of foreigners from French, Walloon and Rhineland regions.

1246

The last Babenberg ruler Frederick II the Quarrelsome dies in battle against Hungarians. Austria becomes vassal state of the Holy Roman Empire.

1251

Styria temporarily occupied by Hungary.

1270

Stephen V (1270–2) lacks control, especially over absorbing the Cuman horsemen. On Stephen's death....

1272

...his widow the Cuman-born Princess Elisabeth becomes Regent until coming of age of their psychopathic son (Ladislas IV) (1272–90), known as 'the Kun'. Hungary descends into chaos.

1278

Rudolph victorious on the Marchfeld with support of Hungarian troops: King Ottokar of Bohemia dies in battle.

1301

Extinction of the male line of the House of Árpád with the death of Andrew III (1290–1301). Succession conflicts between Bohemia, the Wittelsbachs and France (Angevins).

1308

Under pressure from the Vatican, Charles Robert of the Angevins is crowned King of Hungary. As Charles I (Károly Róbert) (1308–42) he restores calm and reasserts royal power. Promotes townships and trade. Start of conflicts with Venice. Charles marries Elisabeth, daughter of the Polish king Vladislav I Lokietek, securing a claim to the Polish throne for their son.

from 1350

Louis the Great (Nagy Lajos) (1342–82) consolidates hold on Dalmatia, but Turkish threat increases. Flowering of culture and sciences; universities founded in Pécs and Buda. Backing up the lesser nobles *vis-à-vis* the magnates. Non-Magyar regions become principalities (Moldavia, Wallachia) paying tribute. Several campaigns for the throne of Naples. Black Death in Europe (in Hungary till 1360 and in 1380–1).

1370

Louis elected King of Poland; his daughter Hedvig becomes Queen of Poland. His daughter Maria becomes Queen of Hungary and reigns—interrupted an interlude by Charles II of Durazzo in 1385–6—until her consort Sigismund of Luxemburg (1387–1437; Holy Roman Emperor 1433–7) ascends the throne.

1396

Magnates responsible for defeat by Turks at Nicopolis, and wrest additional prerogatives. Bulgaria becomes Turkish province. Athens occupied.

1403

The Vatican attempts to set up Charles of Durazzo (King of Naples since 1396) in Hungary. The resulting disorder prevents any benefit from the defeat of the Turks (by Timur Lenk) at Angara (Ankara).

1410

After Sigismund's election as German King his second wife Barbara Cillei becomes Regent. Hussite mission.

1421
Sigismund's daughter Elizabeth marries Prince Albrecht of Austria; Habsburgs to inherit Hungarian Crown.

1430
Dalmatia lost to Venice.

1433, 1436
Hussite uprising in Hungary. Ottomans advance.

1437
Unsuccessful peasant revolt in Transylvania. Anti-German riots, civil war. Albrecht of Austria (Albrecht II King of Germany from 1438) demands Hungarian throne for the Habsburgs, but dies soon after.

1439
His son Ladislas Postumus or László V (1440/4–57) removed by Polish king Vladislav.

1444
On Vladislav's death in the battle against the Turks at Varna, János Hunyadi becomes Governor of Hungary.

1453
Turks take Constantinople and press forward in the Balkans (Serbia 1457, Bosnia 1463, Herzegovina 1483).

1456
Victory over Mehmed II at Belgrade. Apart from Turkish wars, continuous fighting with Emperor Frederick III who occupied Western Hungary.

1463
Mathias I Corvinus (1458–90), son of Hunyadi, victorious over Turks. Expansion of rule to Bohemia (crowning). Moravia, Silesia and Lusatia: confronting Poles and Habsburgs. Administration reformed, standing army, blossoming cultural life.

1485
In the course of the succession fight with Emperor Frederick III over Bohemia and Hungary, Vienna is taken. For a short time Hungary is the strongest power in Central Europe.

1490

Following Mathias's death, war with the house of Jagiello for the Hungarian Crown. The Assembly elects and crowns the Bohemian Vladislav II (1490–1516) King of Hungary.

1491

Treaty of Pressburg, a compromise with Bohemia, Poland and the Habsburgs (Maximilian I German King from 1493, Emperor 1508–19) over the right of succession on the extinction of the male line.

1514

Hostilities between magnate families and towns; peasant uprisings under leadership of György Dózsa (crushed by János Zápolyai). Codification of customary law *(Opus Tripartitum)* by István Werböczy produces a lasting split in society: only nobles acknowledged as constituting the crown of St Stephen, peasants and burghers disregarded. Although never signed by the King, the "Three-Part Lawbook" remained the basis of legal practice until 1848.

1515

King Vladislav and Emperor Maximilian reconfirm Treaty of Pressburg. Louis II (1516–26), in a personal union King of Bohemia, marries Maria of Habsburg. Archduke Ferdinand marries Anna of Bohemia-Hungary.

1517

The Theses of Martin Luther launch the Reformation; promoted by regional reigning princes, in Hungary mainly by immigrants.

1526

King Louis II loses life and country at the Battle of Mohács. The Turks capture Buda and Pest, and with Buda as capital set up a "National Kingdom" under János Zápolyai (1526–40) against Ferdinand of Austria, thereby splitting Hungary into three parts: Royal Hungary in the West, the Turkish vassal state in the Centre, and Transylvania, which considered itself the bearer of "true Magyardom" and the seed of a new state.

1529

Turks besiege Vienna and keep carrying out further attempts after 1532.

1538

Dispute over the crown of St Stephen between János Zápolyai and King Ferdinand I (1526–64), who had ruled the German states since 1521 on behalf of his brother Charles V, whom he succeeded as Emperor in 1556. The dispute ends with Treaty of Nagyvárad (Oradea) securing the Habsburg succession. Nonetheless....

1540

... Zápolyai's newborn son János Zsigmond is acclaimed King and immediately crowned. The Regent is Isabella of Jagiello.

1541

Following Zápolyai's death and five campaigns in the region Suleiman incorporates Central Hungary into the Ottoman Empire.

1559

János Zsigmond (1540/59–71) takes over government as Prince of Transylvania. Relinquishes the crown to the King of Hungary, Maximilian I (1563–76; Emperor Maximilian II 1564–76) by the Treaty of Speyer. Lutheran, Calvinist and Unitarian religions treated as equals. Tribute paid to Porte.

1571

István Báthory (1571–76) elected Prince of Transylvania; from 1576 also King of Poland. His brother Kristóf (1576–81) becomes his deputy in Transylvania. Strengthens the army (serving Székelys exempted from "eternal serfdom"). Kristóf's son and successor Zsigmond Báthory (1581–98, 1601–2 and 1607–8) wants repeatedly to resign and conspires alternately with the Habsburgs, Wallachia and the Turks. Reintroduces serfdom.

1598

Zsigmond Báthory hands over Transylvania to Emperor Rudolph I, but resumes reign as Prince in 1601–2. Beginning of religious discord. Feuding magnates.

from 1591

Renewed fighting between the Habsburgs and the Turks, the so-called Long War (till 1606) bringing devastation to all regions. For Hungary both national and religious freedom at stake. Tactical manoeuvrings, frequent changing of loyalties.

1604

Hajdu insurrection. Leader István Bocskai elected Prince of Hungary and Transylvania. Forces peace treaty with Vienna.

1606

Bocskai mediates peace between Vienna and the Porte (his death soon afterwards most likely murder). Since Rudolph I (1576–1608, Emperor Rudolph II till 1612) does not recognize the "rebels",....

1608

... he has his brother Archduke Mathias proclaimed King Mathias II (1608–19; Emperor from 1612). On the other hand Gábor Báthory (1608–13), Prince of Transylvania, promotes (with Turkish help) Hungarian interests and the Reformation.

1618

Ferdinand II (Habsburg) becomes King of Hungary (Emperor 1619–37). Clash over closure of a Lutheran church in Bohemia leads to demonstrations and the "defenestration" of two Prague councillors. Start of the Thirty Years' War.

1619

Gábor Bethlen (1613–29) supports Bohemia and starts a war of liberation against the Habsburgs. Captures Royal Hungary and....

1620

...is elected King but not crowned. Secures Estate-based self-administration and religious freedom. Pacts are made with Protestant states in Central and Northern Europe. New prosperity and international recognition.

1625

Ferdinand III (1625–57) elected King of Hungary (Emperor from 1637). Concerned only with war in the Empire.

1630

György Rákóczi I (1630–48) chosen, with the support of *hajdus*, as Prince of Transylvania in succession to Bethlen. Unrest in Upper Hungary. Renewed fighting with the Turks.

1644

Alliance with Sweden. Territorial gains for Hungary but peace (with freedom of worship among others) under pressure from Turks. Peace negotiations to end the European war start in Münster and Osnabrück.

1647

Ferdinand IV (died 1654) crowned King of Hungary.

1648

After signing the Peace Treaty of Westphalia, Vienna again turns its attention to Hungary: period of freedom-fighters Pál Pálffy and Miklós Zrinyi. Their plan, to make Prince György Rákóczi II (1648–60) King of Hungary fails. Rákóczi conquers part of Wallachia and aims to become….

1657

…King of Poland. However, the Turks drop him; the Tartars capture his army, and Rákóczi dies in battle against the Turks. Principality of Transylvania under Turkish control administered by Mihály Apafi I.

1664

Zrinyi dies.

1666

Ferenc Wesselényi conspires against King Leopold I (1655/7– 1705; Emperor from 1658), elected with support from the Vatican, but despite French financial assistance and participation of the high nobility, fails.

1671

Péter Zrinyi, Ferenc Frangepán and others decapitated, only Ferenc Rákóczi pardoned.

1673

Vienna invalidates the Hungarian constitution and appoints an Imperial governor. Brutal persecution of Protestants.

1678

Kuruc uprising, Imre Thököly (married to the widow of Ferenc Rákoczi I) drives the Imperial forces out of Upper Hungary; schemes even with Ottoman Empire to create an independent national state.

1683

After defeat of the Turks before the walls of Vienna (battle of Kahlenberg) the Kuruc fighters defect to the Imperial side. Thököly flees with the Turks.

1684

Start of the reconquest. Viennese, Polish and Venetian alliance against the Ottoman Empire. Financial assistance from the Vatican.

1686

Buda liberated.

1687

Transylvania re-united with Hungary. Habsburg hereditary kingdom proclaimed; Joseph I (1687–1711; from 1690 King of Germany, from 1705 Emperor) crowned King of Hungary.

1697

Imperial general Prince Eugen of Savoy victorious at Zenta.

1699

Peace of Karloca (Karlowitz): Hungary, Transylvania, most of Slavonia and Croatia now under Austrian control. The Habsburgs focus on the Southeast and East. While their forces are tied down in the War of the Spanish Succession,....

1703

...a new rebellion of the Kuruc (with help from France) breaks out under the leadership of Ferenc Rákóczi II, Prince of Transylvania and reigning Prince of Hungary; the Habsburgs "deposed"

1711

Peace of Szatmár: re-establishment of the old hereditary right of succession, restitution of the privileges of the nobility. Charles III (1711–40; Emperor Charles VI).

1716

Victories of Prince Eugen at Pétervárad (Petrovaradin) and Belgrade. Austria the dominant power in Southeastern Europe.

1722

Passing of the Pragmatic Sanction, the new Habsburg law of hereditary succession admitting women. Constitutional autonomy for Hungary pledged.

1723

Gubernatorial council set up.

1731

Carolina Resolutio: only Catholics admitted to state employment.

1735

Ferenc Rákóczi II dies in Turkey.

1740

Maria Theresa and Frederick II of Prussia begin their reigns almost simultaneously. Prussia invades Silesia. Austrian Wars of Succession (till 1748).

1741

Coronation of Maria Theresa (1740–80) as "King" of Hungary, September 11: her address to the Diet in Pressburg, 60,000 volunteers rush to her aid and rescue the Austrian empire. Rebuilding of the country. New settlers (mainly from Germany). Reforms (but failure of efforts towards religious freedom; rabid Counter-Reformation). After the return of regions (i.e. Zipser townships, port of Fiume, Temes Bánát) Hungary makes up more than half of the Habsburg lands. Military successes of Hungarian regiments, e.g. the battle of Kolin and advance to Berlin.

1761

"Military Frontier" established in Transylvania.

1765

Grand Principality of Transylvania.

1767

Enactment of Urbarial Patent, increasing centralism particularly under Joseph II (1780–90; Emperor from 1765). Patent of

Toleration: administrative reform with German declared official language, and abolition of serfdom—all resisted by the nobility who force cancellation of crucial reforms.

1790

Joseph's brother King Leopold II (1790–2) returns the crown of St Stephen, assures the Diet's sovereignty, and plans a constitutional monarchy. This does not pass owing to the untimely death of this enlightened ruler.

1794/5

Francis I (1792–1835; Emperor Francis II) crushes alleged "Jacobin conspiracy" (Ignác Martinovics among others). High taxation for wars against Napoleon. Resistance of the counties.

from 1799

Although Hungary not a war zone, creeping devaluation of the banknotes causes serious financial losses.

1805

Third War of the Coalition (England, Austria, Russia) on the Hungarian frontier. The French occupy Vienna.

1806

End of the Holy Roman Empire.

from 1807

Blockade of the Continent.

1809

Napoleon offers Hungary separation from Austria, without success (nobles fear for their privileges).

1812

Nobles dispute the ruler's right to issue banknotes without approval by the Diet, which is no longer convoked.

1814/15

Congress of Vienna, new order in Europe, Metternich's system.

1822/3

Vienna uses military force to tackle counties.

from 1825
   "Era of reform": in the newly convoked Diet István Széchenyi
   delivers his maiden speech in Hungarian.

from 1830
   Economic reforms: Széchenyi fights *aviticitas*. Start of mechani-
   zation and modernization.

1831
   "Long Estates' Assembly" (till 1836). Upper House refuses to go
   along with further reforms.

1835
   Ferdinand V (1835–48: Emperor Ferdinand I) has no influence
   on events, leaves government to his Crown Council.

1836
   Miklós Wesselényi, Lajos Kossuth and others arrested.

1840
   They are released. Kossuth founds the opposition daily *Pesti
   Hirlap*.

1844
   Hungarian declared the official language (replacing Latin). Liberal aristocrats (Lajos Batthány, István Széchenyi, the Károlyis and
   Andrássys) support growing national consciousness and strengthen
   the national movement.

1848
   Revolution. February: in France (Louis Napoleon President, from
   1852 Emperor). March: in Germany (National Assembly in the
   Paulskirche), Vienna (Metternich flees to England) and Hungary (15 March). June: in Prague (Slav Congress). Count Lajos
   Batthyány becomes Prime Minister. Resistance of Croats, Serbs
   and Slovaks. Franz Joseph I (1848–1916) replaces his uncle on
   the throne.

1849
   Following Vienna's imposed constitution, independence is declared (Kossuth becomes Governor). Russian armed intervention, brutal Austrian suppression (theory of forfeiture), execution

of Batthyány and thirteen generals (at Arad). German centralised bureaucracy.

1853

Crimean War (till 1856), partly caused by Russian efforts to assist the Balkan nations to free themselves from the Sublime Porte. Intervention of Western powers.

1859

Italian War of Unification (till 1861). Austria loses Lombardy.

1860

István Széchenyi commits suicide in Vienna.

1866

Prussia at war against the Habsburgs. Defeat at battle of Sadowa (Königgrätz, today Hradec Králové in Czech Republic) and loss of Venice permanently weaken Austria. Consequence:....

1867

...Austro-Hungarian Compromise, the Dual Monarchy. Partial autonomy to Transleithania (= realm of the crown of St Stephen). German–Austrian region: Cisleithania.

Count Gyula Andrássy Prime Minister. Franz Joseph crowned. Liberal nationalities law but increasing tensions with minorities (Hungarians outnumbered in the Kingdom which included Transylvania, Croatia and Slavonia). Internal political conflicts with Slavs affect foreign policy problems with Russia. Significant emigration to America.

1873

Stock Exchange crash. League of Three Emperors: Austria-Hungary, Russia, German Reich.

1875

Kálmán Tisza becomes Prime Minister. Initiates policy of Magyarization. Merger of liberals.

1878

Subsequent to another Russo-Turkish (1877) war Bismarck initiates Congress of Berlin; Montenegro, Serbia and Rumania independent; among others Russia gets Bessarabia; Austria-

Hungary occupy Bosnia-Herzegovina. (Serbia proclaimed kingdom in 1882.)

1894
Death of Kossuth in Turin, Italy.

1896
Millennium of the Conquest; great celebration.

from 1900
Tensions with the crown weaken cohesion of the two partners of the Dual Monarchy. Government crises, reforms stalled.

1905
Moravian Compromise: language and nationality questions resolved. After Russia's defeat by Japan, uprising in St Petersburg, bloodily suppressed. Disturbances in Budapest, government crisis. Threat of military intervention using loyal troops. Consent to widen franchise. Plans for social reforms.

1906
Trade war against Serbia.

1908
Revolution of Young Turks. Austria-Hungary annexes Bosnia-Herzegovina. Bulgaria becomes a kingdom. Albania becomes an independent state. Tensions with Russia.

1910
Industrial workers demonstrate for universal suffrage.

1912
General strike.

1912/13
Balkan Wars. Serb territorial gains.

1914
28 June: heir to the Habsburg throne and his wife assassinated in Sarajevo on the orders of a secret society for greater Serbia (the Black Hand). Franz Ferdinand advocated trialism (with Slavs). At first Hungary rejects war with Serbia, fearing internal instability, but finally yields to the Crown Council and declares war.

1916

King Charles IV (1916–18; Austrian Emperor Charles I) succeeds to the throne on the death of Franz Joseph.

1917

Charles's peace initiatives (Sixtus Letters) fail. United States enters the war. Russian revolution: Tsar Nicholas II resigns (March). Bolshevik putsch (October). US President Wilson's Fourteen Points welcomed by nationalities.

1918

4 Oct.: Austria-Hungary joins German quest for ceasefire. 17 Oct.: Emperor Charles proclaims "Federal State" resulting in the Hungarian declaration of independence. After a naval mutiny and general uprising, Kaiser Wilhelm II renounces the German throne. Charles "relinquishes all participation in affairs of government". 16 Nov.: following his abdication the National Assembly declares the Republic.

1919

Hungarian Soviet Republic led by Béla Kun. Entry of White Army under Admiral Miklós Horthy.

1920

Horthy elected Regent and proclaims Kingdom of Hungary with vacant throne. Peace Treaty of Trianon reduces Hungary to one-third of the lands of the crown of St Stephen; loss of Croatia, Transylvania and Slovakia.

1921

Royal restoration attempt by King Charles IV fails, and the House of Habsburg-Lorraine deposed. Count István Bethlen Prime Minister. Era of consolidation.

1922

King Charles dies in Madeira. Hungary admitted to League of Nations, but nonetheless feels empathy for "March on Rome" and Mussolini's seizure of power in Italy.

1926

Establishment of an Upper House.

1929

Worldwide economic crisis. Black Friday. Mass unemployment.

1931

Banks collapse in Hungary. Count Gyula Károlyi head of government.

1932

Prime Minister Gyula Gömbös seeks close relations with Italy and Germany. Aggressive foreign policy intensifies after....

1933

...Adolf Hitler becomes Chancellor of the German Reich. Franklin D. Roosevelt US President.

1934

In spite of civil war and assassination of the Austrian Federal Chancellor Dollfuss by the Nazis, solid economic cooperation with Austria.

1938

German troops march into Austria. Béla Imrédy Prime Minister, leader of an extreme right-wing group. Sudeten crisis and Munich agreement. Under the "Vienna Award" by the Axis Foreign Ministers re-annexation of southern Slovakia and southern Carpatho-Ukraine. Anti-Jewish laws (co-author Count Pál Teleki).

1939

After Imrédy's resignation Teleki forms new government. Signing of the Anti-Comintern Pact with Germany, Italy and Japan. Hungarian troops march into the rest of Carpatho-Ukraine. Quitting the League of Nations. Electoral gains for the Arrowcross. Harsher anti-Jewish laws. Hungary neutral at the outbreak of war: refuses passage for German military convoys, opens borders to 100,000 Polish refugees after Poland's defeat.

1940

Denmark, Norway, the Netherlands and Belgium over-run by German troops. Italy enters war. France capitulates (Vichy regime). Soviet ultimatum to Romania over Bessarabia. Concerned about threatening hostilities, "Second Vienna Award":

re-annexation of Northern Transylvania and the Székely region by Hungary (30 August). Horthy's triumphal entry to Kolozsvár (Cluj), in return for special privileges for Germans in Hungary. Hungary joins Three-Power Pact (Germany, Italy, Japan). Friendship treaty with Yugoslavia; when its government too joins the Three-Power Pact a military putsch follows in Belgrade. King Peter II, a minor, assumes full powers.

1941

As a personal protest against the looming war with Yugoslavia Prime Minister Pál Teleki commits suicide (April), and is succeeded by the Foreign Minister László Bárdossy. 8 Apr.: Germans invade Yugoslavia; beginning 11 Apr. Hungarian troops occupy the previous Magyar regions in Yugoslavia. 27 June: Hungary declares war on Soviet Union. August: Third Anti-Jewish Law. Britain declares war on Hungary, Hungary on the United States, 12 Dec.

1942

Bárdossy replaced by Miklós Kállay as Prime Minister. At the behest of Horthy contact sought with Britain and the United States. Increased losses on the Eastern front.

1943

January: 2nd Army destroyed at the river Don. Secret negotiations with the Western Allies about changing course. (Battle of Stalingrad; German surrender in North Africa; Allies land in Italy.)

1944

19 Mar.: German troops occupy Hungary (operation "Margarete"). During a meeting with Hitler, Horthy is bullied into naming Döme Sztójay (puppet) Prime Minister. German ambassador superseded by a "Plenipotentiary of the Greater German Reich". 437,000 Jews deported to Auschwitz. (Allies land in Normandy.) When Romania renounces German alliance (23 Aug.), General Géza Lakatos forms new government and attempts similar step. Horthy declares in a radio address that he had asked the Soviet Union for a ceasefire (15 Oct.); retraction under German pressure (16 Oct.) and "protective custody". Ferenc Szálasi

"Führer of the Nation", terror regime of the Arrowcross. A Provisional National Assembly and a Provisional Government under Colonel-General Béla Dálnoki Miklós formed (22 Dec.) in Russian-occupied Debrecen.

1945

Red Army takes Budapest (13 Feb.) End of hostilities in Hungary on 4 Apr. Twelve Hungarian divisions fight to the end on the German side. "Land reform". Smallholders' Party wins parliamentary majority.

1946

Hitherto a kingdom in name, Hungary becomes a republic.

1947

Peace treaty signed in Paris: borders redrawn according to Trianon (1920). Rejection of the Marshall Plan.

1948

"Year of Change", Communist takeover (salami tactics), liquidation of the Social Democrats. Treaty of Friendship with the Soviet Union.

1949

Mátyás Rákosi, the Communist leader, head of the MDP (Hungarian Workers' Party), virtual dictator. Cardinal Mindszenty put on trial. Hungary becomes a Peoples' Republic. Foreign Minister László Rajk accused of "Titoism" and executed.

1952

Rákosi also becomes Prime Minister (till July 1953).

1953

Death of Stalin. Popular uprising in Berlin. After elections, Imre Nagy as Prime Minister (till April 1955) proclaims a "New Course". Concentration camps closed, amnesty, economic reforms.

1955

Nagy branded deviationist and purged from the Party. András Hegedüs is new Prime Minister. Warsaw Pact founded. Austria regains sovereignty. Short period of "thaw". Hungary admitted to United Nations.

1956

XX Congress of the Communist Party of the Soviet Union. Stalinism condemned. Following Khrushchev's speech, Rajk rehabilitated. Upheaval in Poland: Gomulka once again party Secretary (as till 1948). Rákosi relieved of his post as First Secretary of the Central Committee, replaced by Ernö Gerö.
23 Oct.: Popular insurrection. Nagy once again PM, János Kádár First Secretary of the MDP.
24–29 Oct.: Intervention and withdrawal of Soviet troops.
1–11 Nov.: Nagy declares withdrawal from Warsaw Pact and neutrality. Appeals for UN help. (Concurrent Suez crisis.) Hungarian Socialist Workers' Party (HSWP) formed. Mindszenty in US embassy.
4–11 Nov.: Red Army crushes so-called Counter-Revolution.

1957

Agreement over Soviet troops stationed in Hungary.

1958

Nagy and closest collaborators executed after secret trial (June). Nikita S. Khrushchev General Secretary of the Communist Party of the Soviet Union (CPSU) and Chairman of the Council of Ministers.

1960

"Socialist transformation" of agriculture (collectivization). Kádár consolidates his rule.

1963

Amnesty for political detainees. Trade agreements with the Federal Republic of Germany.

1964

Accord with the Vatican. Khrushchev falls and Leonid I. Brezhnev takes over as General Secretary of the CPSU.

1965

Brezhnev in Budapest. HSWP opts for policy of economic reform.

1966

New election system; individual candidates instead of party list.

1968

Liberalization of the market and prices ("Goulash communism"). Participation in the military intervention in Czechoslovakia to end the "Prague Spring".

1971

Amnesty and exile for imprisoned Cardinal Mindszenty.

1972

Adoption of a new constitution: upgrading of Parliament, passive franchise for all.

1973

Hungary full member of GATT. Diplomatic relations with Federal Republic of Germany.

1974

Pope Paul VI relieves Cardinal Mindszenty of his duties.

1975

Opponents of reforms take action with Soviet backing; several top reformers removed. Signing of Helsinki Agreement (CSSE).

1976

Cardinal L. Lékai named Archbishop of Esztergom and Primate of the Catholic Church of Hungary.

1977

Kádár received in the Vatican.

1978

The United States returns the crown of St Stephen and insignia. Minority languages permitted in official use. Karol Wojtyla elected Pope as John Paul II.

1979

Soviet troops invade Afghanistan (December).

1979-80

Rising prices generate heated discussions about fiscal policy and role of trade unions.

1980

Banishment of the scientist and critic of the Soviet system Andrei Sakharov, who is also denounced in Hungary. Strikes in Gdansk. The "Solidarity" trade union forces Gierek out of office.

1981

Wojciech Jaruzelski declares Martial Law in Poland.

1982

Hungary admitted to IMF. Further liberalization. Travel to the West fully liberalized. After death of Brezhnev, Yuri Andropov becomes CPSU General Secretary.

1984

Konstantin Chernenko CPSU General Secretary.

1985

Mikhail Gorbachev General Secretary, Gromyko head of state, Eduard Sheverdnadze Foreign Minister. Kádár General Secretary of HSWP. Parliamentary and local elections.

1987

Károly Grósz becomes Prime Minister.

1988-9

Renunciation of the Soviet claim of hegemony leads to signs of disintegration on the peripheries. The Baltic states achieve independence; conflicts of minorities (Armenia/Azerbaijan 1988, Moldavia 1989) become more violent. Retreat from Afghanistan. Re-emergence of "Solidarity" in Poland. "Round Table" ends with dissolution of the Polish Communist Party. During an extraordinary national conference of the Party, Kádár and the politburo are removed. Grósz takes on the post of General Secretary as well. Demonstrations against the handling of minorities in Romania. Nov. 25: Miklós Németh becomes Prime Minister.

1989

Introduction of community service. The HSWP relinquishes its leadership role. Imre Nagy is rehabilitated and ceremonially reburied. Freedom of assembly and press and to demonstrate. Border opening for citizens of the German Democratic Republic (East Germany). Elimination of the Iron Curtain. 7 Oct.: Mikhail Gorbachev's address ("Those who come late ...") signals the collapse of the GDR. 9 Nov.: The Berlin Wall opened. Amendment of the constitution: multi-party system, separation of powers, the office of President becomes non-party; election of Bruno Straub. Miklós Németh Prime Minister and Gyula Horn Foreign Minister. "Peoples' Republic" changed to "Republic" of Hungary.

1990

Agreement on withdrawal of Soviet troops. Hunagarian Democratic Forum emerges as the strongest party after first free elections (J. Antall Prime Minister). Member of Council of Europe.

1991

Agreement on association with the European Community (EC).

1994

Entry application to EC. Agreement with NATO ("Partnership for Peace"). Absolute majority for socialists, Gyula Horn Prime Minister.

1996

Demands for autonomy for Hungarian minorities in neighbouring countries.

1997

Hungarian-Romanian basic agreement on the rights of Hungarians in Romania. Pact of Cooperation with Italy and Slovenia. Referendum on joining NATO.

1998

Negotiations for European Union (EU) membership begin. Electoral victory of Alliance of Young Democrats (FIDES). Viktor Orbán Prime Minister.

1999

Hungary NATO member.

2002

The Orbán government coalition is narrowly defeated by a Socialist-Liberal alliance; Peter Medgyessy takes over as Prime Minister.

Index

* After the abolition of the Holy Roman Empire in 1806, numbering of subsequent Austrian (Habsburg) Emperors was started again from I.